AMERICAN PARTY POLITICS *essays and readings*

AMERICAN PARTY

POLITICS *essays and readings*

DONALD G. HERZBERG
Eagleton Institute of Politics
Rutgers—The State University

GERALD M. POMPER
College of Arts and Sciences
Rutgers—The State University

HOLT, RINEHART AND WINSTON, INC.
New York • Chicago • San Francisco

March, 1967

Copyright © 1966 by Holt, Rinehart and Winston, Inc.

All Rights Reserved

Library of Congress Catalog Card Number: 66–13287

2552354

Printed in the United States of America

To the Memory

of Max J. Herzberg and Moe J. Pomper

PREFACE

Party politics has been described as America's leading team sport. Increasingly it is also the most important serious activity of the nation. The power of government is now crucial to all our lives, and politics is the means of controlling that power. In writing this book we hope to aid students of all ages to understand the American party system.

In the academic world most books on general subjects tend to be either traditional textbooks or collections of readings. We believe each is inadequate, and we seek here to provide another alternative. Textbooks tend to be of a low level of conceptualization, as the necessity to present basic information forces a restriction of original speculation. Since none of them are written by more than a handful of individuals, they also tend to reflect a severely limited view of the subject matter. Given the diversity of approaches to any discipline today and the availability of materials, we find it educationally unsound to restrict students in this way.

Collections of readings suffer from rather different defects, in our opinion. While they include a wide variety of materials, there is likely to be little apparent relationship among the different selections. Interpretation and correlation of the articles is left to the reader alone or requires the use of valuable class time. The lack of any integrative material in the volume itself is apt to bewilder the reader.

In this book we have tried to avoid these pitfalls. We introduce each of the six major sections with an extended original essay on the particular topic. These essays are not meant to be used as substitutes for chapters in a textbook, as presentations of factual information, or simply as preliminary notes to the selected readings. They are, rather, attempts to conceptualize, generalize, and interpret in regard to a specialized subject. Admittedly we present speculative and tentative ideas, in the hope that they will stimulate thought and discussion and aid in the integration of the following articles. Having deliberately avoided the established and the obvious, we trust that no reader will regard our ideas as unchallengeable.

The readings that follow the essays are narrower in scope; each deals with a particular aspect of the topics under discussion. Our stress has been on more modern approaches to the study of party politics and on analytical and theoretical works. Where useful, we have also included readings with a historical, personal, or reformist emphasis. Aside from references to leading works of political science, we have eliminated most of the footnotes in the original articles. We hope that students will be encouraged by the selections to read further, both in these sources and in the rest of the literature. We have added headnotes to each selection to indicate its significance and summarize the contents.

The authors share one basic and common conviction: American parties are a functional part of a functional political system. We believe in the merits of the American party system and hold that, for the most part, it has served the nation well. There are differences between us in the ways we view the system, as well as differences in our experience, training, and methods. Rather than attempt some definitive reconciliation of these divergences, we have come to regard them as an asset. In the tradition of American parties themselves, we have accepted diversity and present both our points of view to the reader. The result, we believe, is a more comprehensive and provocative book.

As a practical method of operation, we have divided major responsibility for the topics and the accompanying essays. Herzberg has been concerned with the sections on *The Practice of Politics, Party Organization,* and *Results and Prospects.* Pomper has handled the sections on *The American Party Systems, The Electoral Process* and *Voting and Elections.* The opinions expressed in the essays are those of the individual author, but there is little in them on which we disagree. As a result of this method of operation, there may be some overlap in content. We have considered this permissible in order to offer the reader a series of distinct and coherent essays. We have each read and collaborated on the entire work, and accept mutual responsibility for any errors.

Our efforts have been improved by the help of many persons. We have benefited from the advice, insight, and criticism of our associates at Rutgers—The State University. In particular, we would like to thank David Cayer, Mark Ferber, Herbert Kagi, Eugene Meehan, Donald Riddle, William Steele, and Paul Tillett. We also acknowledge our obligation to the authors and publishers who have given us permission to reprint their original works.

Our greatest debt is to Lisa Fairman, who unselfishly devoted her able efforts to the tiresome, detailed work of collecting articles and permissions, preparing the manuscript, and correcting proofs. In the process, she has gained, if not knowledge, at least our admiration and gratitude. Her work was ably assisted by Bette Misdom.

Our families, of course, have provided the necessary psychic and physical support. As we come to the end of this project, we are grateful to Marc and David Pomper, and John and Joan Herzberg, for "shushing" when "shushed at"; and to Marlene Herzberg and Marlene Pomper for telling us, too, when we have said enough.

NEW BRUNSWICK, NEW JERSEY   G.M.P.
JANUARY 1966   D.G.H.

CONTENTS

Party Reform and the Future 497

I. THE AMERICAN PARTY SYSTEMS

Gerald M. Pomper

American parties are competitive organizations that seek political power through mass support. As defined by this sentence, parties are organizations with relatively narrow aims, patterned relationships between leaders and followers, and an established body of commitments and incentives for the members. A party can be distinguished from other organizations—corporations or interest groups, for example—by two properties: it concentrates on political power as a goal and it relies on popular support as the means to that goal.

We reject Edmund Burke's much-quoted definition of a political party as "a body of men united on some particular principle." Principles and policies may be important to some members of a party, and often are employed to win popular support, but they alone do not define a party. Furthermore, a political party must be distinguished from the voters who endorse it in an election. The voters are the object of the parties' attention, rather than an intrinsic element; they are a resource parties seek to develop in the quest for power. It is this quest that clearly identifies the party.

Like any group of human beings, parties do not always pursue their stated objectives. Power through popular election is the primary goal, but parties can be diverted to secondary ends, such as ideological purity or material satisfactions. Our analysis will proceed more easily, however, if we concentrate on the essential character of the parties. The search for power has defined the parties and conditioned their response to the American environment.

THE ENVIRONMENT OF POLITICS

American parties have been shaped by their environment and have also acted to control that environment. Many observers have noted the significance of the legal structure of the Constitution, the electoral system, and the underlying social character of the nation. Less noted, but also important, have been the independent and deliberate choices of the parties.

The Constitution has been an obvious influence on the party system. By establishing a federal system, with power divided between national and state governments, the Constitution required parties to disperse their efforts to gain power among the various authorities. Federalism has therefore encouraged decentralization of the parties. The emphasis of the parties has not been placed on the more prominent national government but, if anywhere, on government at the state level. The reasons for this relate to the parties being self-interested organizations. Most of the "prizes" that parties seek are more available at the state level. There

1

are about 10,000 elected state officials and some half a million elected local officials, compared to a paltry 537 at the national level. About three times as many appointive positions are available in state and local government as in the federal bureaucracy. Moreover, patronage—as contrasted to the merit system—is more common as a means of appointment at these levels. The Governor of Pennsylvania can make some 40,000 patronage appointments, ten times the number available to the President.

For the most part, state governments handle the functions that are most related to the self-interest of the parties, for example, construction, purchasing, law enforcement, the regulation of morality, and social welfare. In fact, aside from national defense, the spending of state and local governments is well above that of the federal government. The states also control the function of government most crucial to the parties, the regulation of the electoral process, a further cause for the parties to concentrate their efforts at this level.

The constitutional framework of the national government has also significantly shaped the parties. With executive power held by a single elected official, the President, there has been an incentive for a two-party system. Unlike a cabinet form of government, there is no way in which a coalition of parties can share in the control of the administration. To win the great prize of the presidency, the competing factions and local interest have been required to unite, however loosely, under the labels of no more than two major parties.

The separation of the executive branch from the legislative branch of government has also had the effect of de-emphasizing the ideological content of the parties. Given this division of institutions, with its concomitant restrictions on power, it is difficult for any party to present and enact a comprehensive policy program. Encouragement is given, rather, to parties without a policy emphasis. This has been the effect of other institutional checks as well, for example, federalism, judicial review, and a written Constitution.

The electoral system has further defined the parties, as Schattschneider (2)[*] points out. Given the single-member, single-ballot plurality method of election, power is most efficiently sought through two major parties.[1] This method encourages a loose system, however. Party candidates at the local level are not controlled by any national leadership. Nominated by direct local primaries, they are not required to espouse a particular policy or to appeal to designated voting groups. The national party, as a result, contains many diverse personalities and groups and lacks a common ideology. A similar effect follows from the workings of the Electoral College. With the election of the President requiring a majority of all electoral votes, incentives are provided for national parties able to make appeals to states of varying interest and character. The electoral system, while encouraging unity, does not require agreement on policy. The common party label can cover a multitude of differences.

The influences of the Constitution and the electoral system, while important, can be exaggerated. Legal arrangements are derived from, and sustained by,

[*] Numbers in parentheses refer to the number of a specific article.

[1] The significance of the single-member district system is disputed on empirical grounds by Maurice Klain, "A New Look at the Constituencies: The Need for a Recount and a Reappraisal," *American Political Science Review*, vol. 49 (December 1955), pp. 1105–1119, and on theoretical grounds by Colin Leys, "Models, Theories, and the Theory of Political Parties," *Political Studies*, vol. 7 (June 1959), pp. 127–146.

underlying social realities. The character and diversity of American society has probably been the most important conditioning factor affecting the American parties. The United States has been a heterogeneous society, a nation of continental dimensions with wide variations in topography, climate, and economic resources. The area of Texas alone is larger than that of any country in Europe except the Soviet Union. Americans follow some 1000 major occupations, adhere to over 250 religious denominations, and trace their ancestry to every area and ethnic group of the world. Multiple loyalties result from this social diversity, and politics comes to reflect a number of social divisions rather than a single two-sided conflict. The identification with social class, for example, has been balanced, and often displaced, by countervailing loyalties to region, religion, ethnic group—and even party itself.

In their search for power, the parties have adapted to this diversity. In order to appeal to the various groups of people in the nation, parties have been cross-sectional. To allow for regional variations in social problems, attitudes, and policies, they have been decentralized. To accommodate the differences and conflicts in values, they have been nonideological. Such parties have not been well suited to strong leadership or consistency in their policies. However, historically prosperous and secure from foreign attack, the United States could afford the luxury of parties that de-emphasized public affairs and concentrated on their own narrower concerns and on mediation between conflicting groups.

It is apparent that American parties have been heavily influenced by their environment. We would also argue, however, that they have not been entirely passive groups, but have acted to affect their conditions. The two major parties dominate the political system, but this duopoly is not only the result of legal and historical factors. Republicans and Democrats have united to curtail or destroy other parties. Electoral laws, enacted by bipartisan coalitions, often make it extremely difficult for a new party to win a place on the ballot. If a third party does arise, one of the major parties will make further efforts to destroy it by absorbing the most popular parts of its program. In this way, the Democrats of 1896 destroyed the Populists by adopting their call for unrestricted coinage of silver.

Similarly, the parties have contributed to their own decentralization. Thus, they have gone beyond the constitutional mandate that a senator or representative be an inhabitant of the state from which he is elected. In addition, the parties have established informal locality rules, requiring members of Congress to be natives or long-term residents of the areas they represent. These rules stemmed from the design of the parties themselves and not from the parochialism of the voters. This was demonstrated by the 1964 election of Robert Kennedy as Senator from New York, only two months after he had moved to the state. Generally, while the formal barriers between state and local governments have waned in recent years, the parties have maintained severely decentralized organizations. Presently, the lack of cohesion which characterizes the parties is the bulwark of American federalism, rather than the reverse.[2]

[2] This same basic conclusion is reached by Morton Grodzins, "American Political Parties and the American System," *Western Political Quarterly*, vol. 13 (December 1960), pp. 974–998, and William H. Riker, *Federalism: Origin, Operation, Significance* (Boston: Little, Brown, 1964), esp. Chap. 4.

The absence of ideology in American politics can also be attributed partially to the decision of the parties themselves. This choice may derive from a recollection of the Civil War, "the time when America had such parties, when to the astonishment of each side, North and South found themselves at war."[3] Whether or not one postulates an "historical memory" of this kind, American parties have made efforts to suppress ideological differences rather than to bring them out. Many opinion studies, for example, have shown considerable lack of agreement in the United States on such questions as the protection of civil liberties, equal treatment of Negroes, and the maintenance of democratic "rules of the game."[4] By not bringing these issues into public debate, the parties have promoted an ideological consensus in America instead of simply reflecting one that already existed.

THE CHARACTER OF THE PARTIES

We can now examine the character of the parties more closely, concentrating on four particular attributes. The parties are commonly described as (1) two in number; (2) decentralized in organization; (3) cross-sectional in membership; and (4) nonideological and flexible in their policies.[5] In a general sense, these are accurate statements about the past and present character of the parties. On further analysis, however, we find that there are many qualifications and limitations that must be stated.

Superficially, the most obvious characteristic is the two-party dominance of American politics. All contemporary congressmen, senators, and state governors, as well as all but a handful of state legislators and city councilmen elected on a partisan ballot, are self-styled Republicans or Democrats. Minor parties have been excluded from the presidency and restricted to transient control of scattered states. Present support for third parties is restricted to disparate fringe groups such as bitter-end segregationists, slightly comical factions such as vegetarians, or propagandistic groups such as the Socialists.

The two-party pattern is apparent on the surface, but it may not extend much below the surface. American parties are also said to be decentralized, so much so that some people argue that there are not two, but one hundred parties in the nation, two for each state. This is an overstatement, but it is certainly true that there are not two unified parties facing each other in equal competition in every constituency. More accurately, there are two parties lacking cohesion that compete with one another on relatively equal terms in the nation as a whole, but this national competition is not duplicated in every area. The parties evidence uneven and distinct geographical distributions of their strength, so that a presidential election may be resolved, for example, into a balance between Democratic strength in the urban Northeast and Republican dominance in the rural Plains.

---

[3] Dennis Brogan, *Politics in America* (New York: Doubleday, Anchor, 1960), p. 47.

[4] See Herbert McClosky, "Consensus and Ideology in American Politics," *American Political Science Review,* vol. 58 (June 1964), pp. 361–382, and James W. Prothro and Charles M. Grigg, "Fundamental Principles of Democracy," *Journal of Politics,* vol. 22 (May 1960), pp. 276–294.

[5] A typical description is that of Clinton Rossiter, *Parties and Politics in America* (Ithaca, N.Y.: Cornell University Press, 1960), p. 37, who describes them as "loose, supple, interest-directed, principle-shunning, coalition-forming."

Equal two-party competition is even less frequent at lower levels. State elections are commonly contests between the Democratic cities and the Republican farms and suburbs, or between the Democratic metropolitan vote and the Republican "upstate" (New York), "downstate" (Illinois), or "outstate" (Michigan) vote. On the county and city level equal party competition is extremely rare.

There is not a single two-party system throughout the nation, but rather a series of systems, each consisting of a different number of parties or fractions of parties. There are two-party systems in some areas, one-party dominance in others, and some intermediate forms.[6] Three-way competition may take a place among two factions of the majority party and a weaker minority party, the typical situation in the Border states.[7] In a few areas, such as New York, there is the equivalent of a multi-party system. The kaleidoscope of parties and factions becomes resolved, nationally, into the two camps of Republicans and Democrats. These are meaningful entities, for the members of each camp act together in the search for power, particularly to win the presidency, and in govermental bodies at all levels. Each remains, at the same time, a collection of disparate groups.

Parties are also characterized as decentralized. We shall consider party organization in more detail in Chapter III. Here we would note only that decentralization is not the same as complete independence. Local and state parties possess considerable autonomy, but they do recognize a common allegiance to national symbols, candidates, and purposes. Despite great differences in policy and ambitions, the disparate groups, searching for power, have recognized the value and the necessity of national party identification. Limited attempts at independent action—such as the Dixiecrat movement of 1948—have been conspicuous failures.

A third apparent feature of the parties is their cross-sectional composition. Each party attempts to appeal to all groups in the society. The degree of diversity is indicated by the leadership of each group, Democrats including both Lyndon Johnson and Alabama Governor George Wallace, and Republicans comprehending such diverse personalities as Senator Jacob Javits and Barry Goldwater.

The degree of intraparty differences can be exaggerated, however, if we focus on individuals. There is greater unity within the parties than such examples suggest. Congressional voting shows a considerable degree of party cohesion, at least in regard to basic social and economic issues. The combined vote of both houses on the antipoverty program in 1964 is illustrative. Of the Democrats, 256 were in favor, and 51 were opposed, with all but two of the latter group from the South. Of the Republicans, 32 were in favor, but 166 were opposed. In summary, five-sixths of each party took opposing stands.[8] Similarly, the voters do not divide equally between the parties. There are distinct class, religious, ethnic, and residential differences among the electoral supporters of each party. While they do not deliberately spurn any group, the parties are not simply mirror images of one another.

---

[6] The most widely used classification schemes are Austin Ranney and Willmoore Kendal, "The American Party Systems," *American Political Science Review*, vol. 48 (June 1954), pp. 477–485, and Joseph A. Schlesinger, "A Two-dimensional Scheme for Classifying the States according to Degree of Interparty Competition," *American Political Science Review*, vol. 49 (December 1955), pp. 1120–1128.

[7] See John Fenton, *Politics in the Border States* (New Orleans: Hauser Press, 1957) .

[8] New York *Times*, July 24, 1964, and August 9, 1964.

Finally, American parties are characterized as nonideological, advocating and adopting policies not from a commitment to social goals but simply as a means of winning office. "It is sometimes necessary to rise above principle," according to a political maxim. Even our most noted leaders have taken a pragmatic attitude toward vital social issues. In response to a plea for emancipation of the slaves, Lincoln wrote:

> My paramount object is to save the Union, and not either to save or destroy slavery. If I could save the Union without freeing any slaves, I would do it—and if I could save it by freeing all of the slaves, I would do it—and if I could save it by freeing some, and leaving others alone, I would also do that.[9]

A neglect of ideology would be likely in an organization devoted to the pursuit of power, but the parties have not been totally devoid of such goals. Lincoln made it clear that his noncommittal attitude on slavery did not modify his "oft-expressed personal wish that all men, everywhere, could be free." Among modern leaders, McClosky (4) finds distinct partisan differences on many vital social issues. These spokesmen are not simply passive weather vanes, changing their policy direction with every passing wind of public opinion. That parties give policy questions serious consideration is further indicated by the frequency of platform disputes at national conventions. Ultimately, such conflicts can even result in a party split, as in the Democratic party in 1948 or in the Republican in 1964.

In fact, parties cannot avoid policy commitments. Parties must take a stand on issues in order to attract and hold many members of the organization. Similarly, some proportion of the voters will cast their ballots on the basis of these positions. In an effort to win these votes, the party takes a position and becomes identified as representing at least a general attitude toward issues. If successful, the officials elected on the party label must make policy decisions. By their actions, they further define the party's positions.

While parties are not devoid of ideology, they have generally subordinated it to other goals. The lack of ideology has not been inherent; it has been a strategy the parties have often adopted. Victory in elections has usually been accorded the highest priority. If this objective has necessitated the abandonment of some policy goals, American parties have customarily made the sacrifice. The revision of party policies is not done lightly or even painlessly, but power seeking is commonly emphasized. The preference for ideology shown by the 1964 Republican nomination of Barry Goldwater was a startling exception to the usual party practice.

PARTY DYNAMICS

As an over-all generalization, subject to qualification and amendment, it remains true that United States politics is conducted by two decentralized, cross-sectional, and nonideological parties. We may now turn to the relationships between these groups and the resulting party systems. American politics evidences four characteristic features: stability, dualism, consensus, and competitiveness.

[9] Letter to Horace Greeley, August 22, 1862, in Richard Hofstadter, ed., *Great Issues in American History* (New York: Random House, Vintage, 1959), vol. 1, p. 411.

The parties exist in a stable political environment. There has been little serious challenge to the legal framework, the economic system, or the territorial integrity of the United States. The parties have reinforced stability by their own decided preference for compromise and moderation. Social equilibrium has been further promoted by the persistence of voter loyalties, discussed at greater length in Chapter V. Parties do not need to seek support anew at each election, but begin with a large, assured fraction of the electorate. They are, in effect, guaranteed survival and substantial strength.

Persistent voter loyalty, however, has diverse and occasionally conflicting sources. The variety of party support is seen in the politics of many states. California Democrats are illustrative. The party is supported by Deep South emigrants who follow an inherited tradition, as well as by newly enfranchised Mexican-Americans; by San Francisco residents seeking to avert domination in state politics by the more populous southern countries, as well as by ideological liberals of Los Angeles concerned only with national issues; by upwardly mobile white ethnic groups concerned about "forced integration," as well as by Negroes endorsing open-housing laws.

These circumstances affect party strategy and generally discourage social innovation by the parties. The stable political environment is accepted as a fact of life. The security that the parties enjoy furthers their satisfaction with the system by which they have prospered. The diversity of their support makes victory unlikely by the single-minded championing of one set of interests or policies. Instead, the emphasis is placed on building a coalition from diverse groups. The parties do not attempt to convert supporters of the opposition, a largely fruitless task. Instead, they concentrate on retaining their own past support while winning the relatively small increment of votes necessary to victory. Attention to the specialized goals of diverse groups and to retaining loyalties of the past, however, restricts bold, broad, and novel social action.

Party efforts are also conditioned by dualism, a second major feature of American politics. The loyalties of the voters, as well as other causes we have examined, confine partisanship and interparty competition to the two-party mold. Each party faces only a single opponent. This further assures each of survival and, even by chance alone, of the occasional enjoyment of power. The burdens of office, in turn, tend to make a party moderate and responsible.

Competition between the parties centers on the uncommitted or wavering voters. Such electors, if concerned with issues at all, probably find attractive elements in the proposals of each faction. To gain such voters, the parties will tend to imitate one another's most appealing policies, becoming similar in their positions. They will be moderate groups, with limited policy differences, appealing to the undecided voters.

In most cases, uncommitted voters are not concerned with issues and lack interest in politics generally. The parties will seek their votes in other ways, such as presenting personable candidates or stirring resentment of the opposition by blaming it for current ills. Emphasis also comes to be placed on the efficiency of party operations. Victory comes not from the espousal of policy to an ideological electorate, or the social consciousness of a cohesive group, but from conducting a clever campaign and getting out the vote.

Dualism also limits the electoral influence of nonparty groups. A social movement cannot win votes in its own name, but must work through the two major parties if it is to succeed. As confirmed by the frustrating experience of many causes, from abolition to segregation, the voters are too convinced of the virtues of the two-party system to be attracted to new parties. The major parties lack cohesion and are imperfectly competitive, but they are the only available vehicles for mass politics.

As a result, the parties gain autonomy from the interest groups they include. A party is assured of voter support, but the interests are not. A party, of course, wants group support, but it bargains for it in a very restricted market, where the real choice is between only two competitors. Ultimately, the groups must make their decision, even if only on the grudging basis of "the lesser of two evils."[10] Those at the extremes of the political spectrum are particularly restricted in their choice, with only one party likely to be even remotely acceptable. Dualism sustains the parties while denying fringe groups an effective independent outlet. Schattschneider's analysis (2) is particularly relevant here.

Consensus is a third characteristic of the party system. It results partially from the electoral limits on the parties, and partially from the deliberate choice of the parties. Neither party has favored fundamental changes. Both accept the formal structure of the government, such as the Constitution, as well as the equally important but unwritten rules, such as the two-party system itself.

Each party accepts the other's existence. With rare exceptions, for example, the passage of the Alien and Sedition Acts of 1798, an American party has not tried to destroy its opposition.[11] Each has tacitly accepted the inevitability of its own defeat and the consequent loss of cherished offices. The peaceful transfer of power has been exceptional and difficult in most nations. In the United States, it is hardly noticed. A President of one party not only accepts his replacement by the leader of the opposition but he also provides the refreshments, transportation, and pageantry for the inauguration into office.

The parties also accept each other's policies. The transfer of power does not mean a reversal or abolition of past programs, except in marginal cases. Policies that are controversial when first enacted tend to become permanent institutions. Democrats after the Civil War accepted the Reconstruction amendments, and Republicans have extended the welfare programs of the New Deal. The transfer of power can be peaceful and relatively ungrudging because the change in public office does not endanger the dearest interests and beliefs of the defeated faction.[12] This principle further reinforces the stability of the total political system.

Competitiveness is the final feature of American politics. The party systems can be analyzed in terms of both the degree and the source of the competition between them. The degree of competition is measured by the relative division of the vote between contending groups and the frequency with which power is transferred between them. A perfectly competitive two-party system would be one in which each party tended toward 50 percent of the vote and each election

[10] See E. E. Schattschneider, *The Semi-sovereign People* (New York: Holt, Rinehart and Winston, 1960), esp. Chaps. 2 and 3.

[11] An exception was the brief attempt of the Mississippi Democratic party to make it all but impossible for the Republicans to organize—see the New York *Times*, April 12, 1964.

[12] V. O. Key, Jr., called this process "moving consensus". See *Politics, Parties and Pressure Groups,* 5th ed. (New York: Crowell, 1964), pp. 222–227.

resulted in a transfer of power. Such perfect competition does not exist anywhere, in the United States or abroad. For many reasons, it is highly doubtful that it could exist for any length of time. Incumbency provides advantages for the party in office; social trends usually favor one party over another; and organizational and campaigning skills are rarely distributed evenly between the parties. As a result, one party eventually becomes more dominant in any jurisdiction, with the minority opposition acting as critic, benefiting from the majority's errors, and hoping that events, social trends, and its own efforts will reverse the order of the parties.

Competitiveness also varies in regard to its source. The most notable form in the United States is two-party competition, but there are many instances in which internal party contests are also significant. Even on the national level, there are divisions between "presidential" and "congressional" wings of each party, between Southern and Northern Democrats, and between moderate and conservative Republicans. The smaller the geographical area, the less competition is likely to be restricted to contests between the parties.

In most states, interparty competition is supplemented and complicated by disputes among party factions, especially in the majority party. In general, these two forms of competition tend to be substitutes for one another. As competition between the parties increases, disputes within each party tend to be moderated. Conversely, a party free of meaningful challenge from its nominal opposition is more likely to evidence factional competition. Thus, the one-party states of the South are not truly under monolithic party control. The common Democratic label contains a variety of contending personality cliques, social interests, and ideological groups.[13] On the local level, competition is still more restricted and is commonly confined to nonpartisan contests or to the primary elections of the dominant party, according to Gilbert and Clague (8).

Competition also affects party behavior. Interested in winning office, parties react to the threat to their power posed by a meaningful opponent. Parties are likely to be open to new members as a means of attracting workers, moderate in their policies in order to avoid alienating support, and active in campaigning in order to maximize their voter support. In general, competitive parties tend to be more responsive to public demands, even when the demands are voiced only by a minority group. Unsure of success, parties must work to gain the crucial margin of support between victory and defeat.

By contrast, a party assured of majority status or resigned to a permanent minority position need not exert itself. It is more likely to be closed in its membership, extreme in its policies, inactive in campaigning, and unresponsive to public demands. Competition is likely to be restricted to cabals among leaders disputing for the rewards of power. Thus, the traditional urban machine, assured of victory, could disregard most broad public needs and restrict its efforts to individual favors and patronage. Similarly, extreme conservatives in the Republican party, or doctrinaire Marxists, assured of defeat, can restrict their membership and impose tests of ideological purity. A party faced with the realistic possibility of either victory or defeat is necessarily more adaptable.

[13] See the classic descriptions of these systems in V. O. Key, Jr., *Southern Politics* (New York: Knopf, 1949), Chaps. 2–12, as well as his later and more general work, *American State Politics: An Introduction* (New York: Knopf, 1956).

These four characteristics—stability, dualism, consensus, and competitiveness—define the American party system. Changes now evident in American politics, as described by David (58), are particularly related to the last characteristic. In almost every state there is now functioning two-party competition. Nationally, as a result, the parties evidence increasing centralization, internal homogeneity, and sharper interparty policy differences. The other characteristics are more resistant to change. Some voters will change their party identification, but most will retain their existing loyalty. The bases of party support may be revised, but the dualistic pattern is well established as an American habit and value. Few groups challenge the party consensus. Indicative of the continuing quality of the party systems is the reluctance of voters to support any third party. It is estimated, for example, that only 4 percent of the electorate would follow Barry Goldwater into a new conservative movement.[14] The radical left in the United States is small, disorganized, and without influence.

Given these characteristics, American politics is one of limited heat. Elections do not represent a dire threat to any group or to either party. By their consensus on fundamentals, and by their channelling of group interests, the parties serve to satisfy social needs and to reconcile competing demands. The parties are not inherently concerned with policy questions, but they provide an effective mechanism by which the voters can impose responsibility and achieve their goals.

In order to win the political power they seek for their own purposes, the parties must satisfy others. To win the mass support they need, they must champion mass demands. Party politics is particularly crucial in this matter with regard to low-status groups. The major resource of such groups is their numbers, which are obviously crucial in popular elections. The have-nots of society can, and do, use their power of numbers to overcome the advantages of wealth, prestige, education, and social power held by higher-status groups. There is, consequently, a drift in modern democracies toward greater concern for social welfare and the distribution of benefits among the more numerous but less privileged groups. Such changes, however, are only gradual and incremental. They are most likely when a competitive party mechanism is available, forcing the parties to search for votes. In their pursuit of power, then, the parties serve not only their own interests but, under the proper conditions, the interest of popular, representative democracy and the needs of democracy's citizens.

[14] The *Harris Survey,* April 12, 1965.

THE NATIONAL PARTY SYSTEM

1. In Defense of the American Party System

Edward C. Banfield

Both foreign and domestic authorities have severely criticized American parties for their lack of principle and their fondness for patronage and other material satisfactions. Edward Banfield, Professor of Government at Harvard University, argues that such parties are the necessary price we pay for the political stability and the peaceful adjustment of social conflicts in the United States. He sternly warns against precipitate changes in these parties.

* * *

The American party system has been criticized on four main grounds: (1) The parties do not offer the electorate a choice in terms of fundamental principles; their platforms are very similar and mean next to nothing; (2) they cannot discipline those whom they elect, and therefore they cannot carry their platforms into effect; (3) they are held together and motivated less by political principle than by desire for personal, often material, gain, and by sectional and ethnic loyalties; consequently party politics is personal and parochial; and (4) their structure is such that they cannot correctly represent the opinion of the electorate; in much of the country there is in effect only one party, and everywhere large contributors and special interests exercise undue influence within the party.[1]

[1] These criticisms are made, for example, by the French political scientist, Maurice Duverger, in *Political Parties* (New York: Wiley, 1954). For simi-

These criticisms may be summarized by saying that the structure and operation of the parties do not accord with the theory of democracy or, more precisely, with that theory of it which says that everyone should have a vote, that every vote should be given exactly the same weight, and that the majority should rule.

"It is a serious matter," says Maurice Duverger, a French political scientist who considers American party organization "archaic" and "undemocratic," "that the greatest nation in the world, which is assuming responsibilities on a world-wide scale, should be based on a party system entirely directed towards very narrow local horizons." He and other critics of the American party system do not, however, base their criticisms on the performance of the American government. They are concerned about procedures, not results. They ask whether the structure and operation of the parties is consistent with the logic of democracy, not whether the party system produces —and maintains—a good society, meaning,

lar criticisms by Americans, see especially Committee on Political Parties of the American Political Science Association, *Toward a More Responsible Two-party System* (New York: Holt, Rinehart and Winston, 1950), and E. E. Schattschneider, *Party Government* (New York: Holt, Rinehart and Winston, 1942). Criticisms of American parties are summarized and analyzed in Austin Ranney, *The Doctrine of Responsible Party Government* (Urbana: University of Illinois Press, 1954). Defenses of the American party system include A. Lawrence Lowell, *Essays on Government* (Boston: Houghton Mifflin, 1889), Chaps. I, II; Arthur N. Holcombe, *The Political Parties of Today* (New York: Harper, 1925); and *Our More Perfect Union* (Cambridge: Harvard University Press, 1950); Pendleton Herring, *The Politics of Democracy* (New York: Norton, 1940); and Herbert Agar, *The Price of Union* (Boston: Houghton Mifflin, 1950).

Reprinted from *Political Parties, U.S.A.*, ed. Robert A. Goldwin (Chicago: Rand McNally, 1964), pp. 21–23, 26–31, 33–37. Copyright © 1961 by the Public Affairs Conference Center, The University of Chicago. All rights reserved.

among other things, one in which desirable human types flourish, the rights of individuals are respected, and matters affecting the common good are decided, as nearly as possible, by reasonable discussion.

If they were to evaluate the party system on the basis of results, they would have to conclude that on the whole it is a good one. It has played an important part (no one can say how important, of course, for innumerable causal forces have been at work along with it) in the production of a society which, despite all its faults, is as near to being a good one as any and nearer by far than most; it has provided governments which, by the standards appropriate to apply to governments, have been humane and, in some crises, bold and enterprising; it has done relatively little to impede economic growth and in some ways has facilitated it; except for the Civil War, when it was, as Henry Jones Ford said, "the last bond of union to give way," it has tended to check violence, moderate conflict, and narrow the cleavages within the society; it has never produced, or very seriously threatened to produce, either mob rule or tyranny, and it has shown a marvelous ability to adapt to changing circumstances.

Not only has the American party system produced good results, it has produced better ones than have been produced almost anywhere else by other systems. Anyone who reflects on recent history must be struck by the following paradox: those party systems that have been most democratic in structure and procedure have proved least able to maintain democracy; those that have been most undemocratic in structure and procedure—conspicuously those of the United States and Britain—have proved to be the bulwarks of democracy and of civilization. . . .

A MODEL PARTY SYSTEM

Let us imagine a system free of the alleged defects of ours. In this model system, every citizen is motivated—highly so—by political principles, not subsidiary ones, but ones having to do with the very basis of the society. (In France and Italy, Duverger says approvingly, political warfare "is not concerned with subsidiary principles but with the very foundations of the state and the nature of the regime.") The electoral system, moreover, is such as to give every side on every issue exactly the weight that its numbers in the population warrant; no group or interest is over- or under-represented ("One's thoughts turn," Duverger says, "to the possibility of a truly scientific democracy, in which parliament would be made up of a true sample of the citizens reproducing on a reduced scale the exact composition of the nation, made up, that is, according to the very methods that are used as a basis for public opinion surveys like the Gallup polls.")

Assuming that the society is divided by the usual number of cleavages (e.g., haves versus have-nots, segregationists versus anti-segregationists, isolationists versus internationalists, etc.), the following would result:

1. There would be a great many parties, for no citizen would support a party with which he did not agree fully.
2. The parties would tend to be single-issue ones. If logically unrelated issues (for instance, segregation and isolationism) were linked together in a party program, only those voters would support the party who chanced to be on the same side of all the linked issues. The number of these voters would decrease as the number of issues so linked increased.
3. Parties would be short-lived. They would come into and pass out of existence with the single issues they were organized to fight.
4. In their election campaigns and propaganda, parties would emphasize their single defining principles. This would tend to widen the cleavages along which the parties were formed.

5. Ideological issues, not practical problems, would constitute the substance of politics.

6. The number of such issues pressing for settlement at any one time (but being incapable of settlement because of their ideological character) would always be more than the system could accommodate.

7. Coalitions of parties would seldom form, and such as did form would be highly unstable. Party leaders would find compromise almost impossible because it would lead to loss of highly principled supporters.

8. Coalitions of parties being unstable, governments would also be unstable and therefore lacking in power and decision.

9. Those selected for positions of political leadership would tend to be ideologues skilled in party dialectics and symbolizing the party and its positions. Practical men, especially those with a talent for compromise and those symbolizing qualities common to the whole society, would be excluded from politics.

10. Matters having no ideological significance (a category that includes most local issues) would either be endowed with a spurious one or else would be left outside the sphere of politics altogether. . . .

Now let us introduce into the model system one of the alleged defects which the critics find most objectionable in the American party system. Let us suppose that at least half of the electorate is prevailed upon to exchange its vote in matters of fundamental principle for advantages that have nothing to do with principle, especially private profit, sectional gain, and nationality "recognition."

One effect of this would be to reduce greatly the intensity of ideological conflict and to make political life more stable and conservative. This, in fact, seems to be what happened when American parties first came into being. John Adams tells in his diary how in 1794 "ten thousand people in the streets of Philadelphia, day after day, threatened to drag Washington out of his house and effect a revolution in the government, or compel it to declare war in favor of the French Revolution and against England." After parties had been organized, however, patronage took the place of ideological fervor. "The clubs of the social revolutionists which had sprung up in the cities, blazing with incendiary ideas caught from the French Revolution," Henry Jones Ford says, "were converted into party workers, and their behavior was moderated by considerations of party interest."

Another effect would be to encourage the formation of a few (probably two) stable parties. These might begin as alliances among the profit-minded, the sectional-minded, and the nationality-minded, but to attract support from principled voters the parties would have to seem to stand for something—indeed, for anything and everything. Since no faction of them could hope to win an election by itself, principled voters would attach themselves to those parties that they found least objectionable. The parties would develop corporate identities and mystiques; principled voters would then subordinate their differences out of "loyalty" to the party and in response to its demands for "regularity." Competition for middle-of-the-road support would cause the parties to offer very similar programs. This competition might lead to there being only two parties, but this result would probably be insured by introducing another supposed defect into the system: a principle of representation (single-member districts and plurality voting) which, by letting the winner take all, would force small parties to join large ones in order to have some chance of winning.

In one way or another, the "defects" of the system would tend to produce these consequences—consequences which have in fact been produced in the United States:

1. A strong and stable government would be possible. The country would be governed by the party that won the election, or (given the particular complexities of the American system) by two closely similar parties engaged in give-and-take and, therefore, in a sense constituting one party under two names.

2. There would be a high degree of continuity between administrations elected from different parties. Elections would not shake the nation to its foundations because the competing parties would be fundamentally in agreement. Agreement would be so built in by countless compromises within the parties (each of which would be under the necessity of attracting middle-of-the-road support) that a change of party would seldom entail complete reversal of policy in an important matter.

3. There would exist many substructures of power that would be largely or wholly impervious to the influence of political principle or ideology. "Machines"—party organizations of the profit-minded, the sectional-minded, and the nationality-minded—would not be inclined to offer pie in the sky or to stir the emotions of the masses because they could count upon getting their votes in other ways. These essentially apolitical centers of power would therefore exert a stabilizing and conservative influence throughout the political system. By making business-like deals with the leaders of the "machines," the President could sometimes buy freedom to do as he thought best in matters of principle.

4. The diversity of the principles and the multiplicity of the interests within the party would be another source of strength to the leader elected from it. He could afford to offend some elements of the party on any particular question because there would be enough other elements unaffected (or even gratified) to assure his position. The more fragmented his party, the less attention he would have to pay to any one fragment of it.

5. The assertion of interests (as distinguished from principles) would be encouraged. The profit-minded, the sectional-minded, and the nationality-minded would in effect give up representation on matters of principle in order to get it on matters involving their interests. Thus two different systems of representation would work simultaneously. The party leader would act as a trustee, disregarding interests in favor of principles ("Congress represents locality, the President represents the nation," Ford wrote in 1898.) Meanwhile legislators dependent on machines and, in general, on profit-minded, sectional-minded, and nationality-minded voters would act as agents of interests. The trustee of principles (the President) and the agents of interests (Congressmen) would of necessity bargain with each other; by allowing the agents of interests some successes—but only in this way—the trustee of principles could win their support in the matters he considered most important. Thus, there would be achieved that balancing of interests and of interests against principles (the most important principles usually being vindicated) that a good party system should produce.

6. The formation of deep cleavages would nevertheless be discouraged. The competition of the parties for the middle-of-the-road vote; their tendency to select practical men of wide popular appeal, rather than ideologues, for positions of leadership; and the definition of the politicians' task as being that of finding the terms on which people who disagree will work together, rather than that of sharpening ideological points—these would all be unifying tendencies.

Some critics of the American party system have attributed its alleged defects to the absence of class consciousness in our society. No doubt there is some truth in this. But causality may run the other way also. We may be lacking in class consciousness because our politicians are prevented by the nature of the party system from popularizing the rhetoric of the class struggle; the party system actually induces the voter to forgo the allurements of principle and ideology by offering him things he values more: e.g., personal profit, sectional advantage, and nationality "recognition."

In those countries where the voter expresses at the polls his ideology rather than his interests, he may do so not from choice but because the party system leaves him no alternative. In such countries, class warfare may be the principal subject-matter of politics simply because matters of greater importance to the voters are not at stake. . . .

The hope that the two-party system might be made to offer a choice between distinct alternatives is illusory for at least two reasons. One is that a party which does not move to the middle of the road to compete for votes condemns itself to defeat and eventually, if it does not change its ways, to destruction. But even if this were not the case, the parties could not present the electorate with what reformers think of as "a valid choice." The reason is that the issues in our national life are such that there does not exist any one grand principle by which the electorate could be divided into two camps such that every voter in each camp would be on the "same" side of all issues. The idea of "left" and "right" is as close as we come to having such a grand principle, and it has little or no application to many issues. The logic of "left" and "right" does not, for example, imply opposite or even different positions on (for example) foreign policy, civil liberties, or farm subsidies. Without a grand principle which will make unities—opposed unities—of the party programs, the electorate cannot be offered "a valid choice." A choice between two market baskets, each of which contains an assortment of unrelated items, some of which are liked and some of which are disliked, is not a "valid" choice in the same sense that a choice between two market baskets, each of which contains items that "belong together" is a "valid" one. In the American party system, most items are logically unrelated. This being so, "valid" choice would become possible only if the number of parties was increased to allow each party to stand for items that *were* logically related, if one issue became important to the exclusion of all of the others, or if, by the elaboration of myth and ideology, pseudo-logical relations were established among items.

The hope that the parties might commit themselves to carry out their programs is also illusory. A party could do this only if its leaders were able to tell the President and the party members in Congress what to do, and could discipline them if they failed to do it. Therefore, unless, like the Russians, we were to have two sets of national leaders, one in governmental office and another much more important one in party office, it would be necessary for our elected leaders—in effect, the President, since only he and the Vice President are elected by the whole nation—to control the Congressmen and Senators of their party. This would be possible only if the President could deny re-election to members of Congress who did not support the party program. Thus, instead of merely bringing forward and electing candidates, as they do now, "responsible" parties would have to govern the country. We would have a parliamentary system with the President in a position somewhat like that of the British Prime Minister, except (a very important difference) that, not being a part of the legislature, he could not use it as a vehicle through which to exert his leadership. The legislature would in fact have no function at all.

This great shift of power to the President would remedy another "defect" in the party system: its receptivity to the demands of interest groups. With the President in full control of Congress, logrolling would cease or virtually cease. It would do so because no one could any longer make the President pay a price for assistance in getting legislation passed; the traders who now sell their bits and pieces of power to the highest bidders would have to lower their prices and would probably go out of business. With their opportunities for exercising influence vastly reduced, interest groups would be less enterprising both in their efforts to anticipate the effects of governmental action and in bringing their views to the attention of the policy makers.

The making of policy would thus pass largely into the hands of technical experts within the majority party, the White House, and the executive departments. These would be mindful of principles and impatient of interests. They would endeavor to make "coherent" policies, meaning, presumably, policies not based on compromise. In all important matters, however, "the public interest" would prove an insufficient guide; the experts, when confronted with the necessity of choosing between alternatives that were equally in the public interest —that is, when no authoritative, ultimate criterion of choice existed for them to apply —would by the very necessities of the case have to balance the competing values as best they could, which means that they would have to fall back upon their personal tastes or professional biases.[2] Thus they would do badly (but in the name of "impartial administration") what is now done reasonably well by the political process.

The destruction of political traders and of local centers of power would mean also that the President's power would derive from somewhat different sources than at present. Instead of relying upon logrolling and patronage to get the votes he would need in Congress, he would have to rely

upon direct appeals to the electorate. To some extent he might manipulate the electorate by charm and personality; TV and the arts of Madison Avenue would become more important in politics. But in order to get elected he would have to depend also, and to a greater extent, upon appeals to political principle or ideology. Whereas the political trader maintains his control by giving and withholding favors to individuals (a circumstance which makes his control both dependable in its operation and cheap), the President would have to maintain *his* by the uncertain and costly expedient of offering to whole classes of people—the farmer, the aged, the home owner, and so on—advantages that they would have only at each other's expense. If charm and the promise of "something for everybody" did not yield the amount of power he required to govern the country, the President might find it necessary to exploit whatever antagonisms within the society might be made to yield more power. Class and ethnic differences might in this event serve somewhat the same function as logrolling and patronage do now. Mayor LaGuardia, for example, depended for power upon direct, personal appeal to the voters rather than upon organization. His charm and his support of "liberal" programs are well remembered. But it should not be forgotten that he depended also upon exploitation of ethnic loyalties and antipathies. According to Robert Moses,

It must be admitted that in exploiting racial and religious prejudices LaGuardia could run circles around the bosses he despised and derided. When it came to raking ashes of Old World hates, warming ancient grudges, waving the bloody shirt, tuning the ear to ancestral voices, he could easily out-demagogue the demagogues. And for what purpose? To redress old wrongs abroad? To combat foreign levy or malice domestic? To produce peace on the Danube, the Nile, the Jordan? Not on your tintype. Fiorello LaGuardia knew better. He knew that the aim of the rabble rousers is simply to shoo into office for entirely extraneous, illogical

[2] This argument is developed in E. C. Banfield, *Political Influence* (New York: Free Press of Glencoe, 1961), Chap. 12.

and even silly reasons the municipal officials who clean city streets, teach in schools, protect, house and keep healthy, strong and happy millions of people crowded together here.[3]

That a President might rely more upon appeals to political principle does not at all mean that better judgments or results would follow. For the discussion of principles would probably not be *serious;* it would be for the purpose of securing popular interest and consent, not of finding a wise or right course of action. As long ago as 1886, Sir Henry Sumner Maine observed that democracy was tending toward government by salesmanship. Party and corruption had in the past always been relied upon to bring men under civil discipline, he said, but now a third expedient had been discovered:

> This is generalization, the trick of rapidly framing, and confidently uttering, general propositions on political subjects. . . . General formulas, which can be seen on examination to have been arrived at by attending only to particulars few, trivial or irrelevant, are turned out in as much profusion as if they dropped from an intellectual machine; and debates in the House of Commons may be constantly read, which consisted wholly in the exchange of weak generalities and strong personalities. On a pure Democracy this class of general formulas has a prodigious effect. Crowds of men can be got to assent to general statements, clothed in striking language, but unverified and perhaps incapable of verification; and thus there is formed a sort of sham and pretence of concurrent opinion. There has been a loose acquiescence in a vague proposition, and then the People, whose voice is the voice of God, is assumed to have spoken.[4]

Efforts to create "levity of assent," as Maine called it, will become more impor-

tant in our politics to the extent that other means of bringing men under civil discipline are given up or lost.

2. The Two-party System

E. E. Schattschneider

The monopoly of American politics by the two major parties is one of the most obvious and most important features of our political system. In this classic analysis E. E. Schattschneider, Professor Emeritus of Government at Wesleyan University, explains the influence of the electoral system on the number and character of the parties. He praises the two-party system for providing both a majority party with the power and responsibility to govern and a minority that can securely offer an alternative to the voters.

* * *

The two-party system is the most conspicuous feature of American political organization. How does it happen that party politics in the United States has been organized on this pattern? In spite of the fact that the two-party system has been explained by saying that it is a mark of the "political maturity" of Anglo-American peoples (while the multiparty systems of prewar France expressed the "national character" of Frenchmen), we are reasonably certain that definite circumstances, easily identified, make this system inevitable in the United States regardless of the personal preferences of individual critics. We could not discard the two-party system and adopt a multiparty system in the United States, exactly as a lady might change her hat, even

[3] Robert Moses, *LaGuardia: A Salute and a Memoir* (New York: Simon & Schuster, 1957), pp. 37–38.

[4] Sir Henry Sumner Maine, *Popular Government* (New York: Henry Holt, 1886), pp. 106–108.

if we wanted to do so. What we wish for has very little bearing on what we get in the style of parties.

What do we mean by the expression "the two-party system"? Certainly not that there have been only two parties. We have in fact usually had about as *many* parties as the French had in the palmiest days of the Third Republic, though few people have ever heard of most of them. Attempts to break up the two-party system by organizing third party and minor party movements have been made in substantially every presidential election in the last century. What we have in mind when we say that we have a two-party system is an organization of politics in which there are two major parties and a number of minor parties. The major parties monopolize power, while the minor parties use the elections as an occasion for a subsidiary political agitation that does not lead to power. The major parties maintain their position in the face of a continuing effort to undermine it. In view of the assaults made on the major parties by the minor parties, it must be said that the two-party system (the monopoly of votes and power maintained by the major parties) is one of the most firmly established American institutions. The strength of the two-party system is important because the politics of the major parties in a two-party system is fundamentally unlike the politics of a multiparty system. If this is true, the system deserves examination and analysis.

The relation between the major and minor parties is the crucial point in the two-party system. In the United States the minor parties are excluded from power. This is done so effectively that these parties cease to be genuine parties at all and should probably be spoken of simply as educational movements. In a multiparty system the distinction between major and minor parties is not clearly marked, if it exists at all, and all parties may hope to get a fraction of the power to govern, though none hopes to get the whole of the power to govern. In practice the two-party system means that there are only two major parties, one or the other of which usually has the power to govern, though they may share power sometimes, and that no minor party is able to become a third major party permanently. The gap between the second major party and the greatest minor party is enormous and insurmountable; no minor party in American history has ever become a major party, and no major party has ever become a minor party.

The monopoly of power by the major parties is real. It means that ordinarily they will poll not less than 95 per cent of the total popular vote cast in a presidential election. They will usually win every one of the places in the electoral college, all but a handful of the seats in the House and Senate, and all but one or two of the governorships of the states; and, with the exception of two or three states, they will win all or very nearly all of the seats in both houses of the legislatures. Only in municipal elections, where nonpartisan ballots are used more extensively, is the monopoly of the major parties relaxed appreciably, and even this concession is slightly unreal. Attacks on the monopoly of the major parties have produced only the most negligible results. The two-party system is therefore the Rock of Gibraltar of American politics. How does it happen that the two-party system is one of the fixed points of the political universe? There is in fact nothing mysterious about the causes of this condition. The demonstration is mathematical and conclusive.

Causes of the two-party system

The American two-party system is the direct consequence of the American election system, or system of representation, which is only another way of saying the same thing. The elective process is used more extensively in the United States than it has ever been used anywhere else in the world. About 800,000 officials in the national, state, and local governments are elected by the people. This is a colossal performance, and *since parties are built around elections* it would be amazing if the form of the party system were not influenced profoundly by the nature of these elections. The bulk of the elective places in the government are of two principal kinds: (1) members of legislative bodies, and (2) executives. It is probably most instructive to examine first the process of electing representatives to legislative bodies, more particularly the election of members of the United States House of Representatives, as a type.

With certain exceptions that need not be considered here, members of the United States House of Representatives are elected from single-member districts, one district for each representative. Consequently, to elect 435 members, separate elections are held in approximately 435 districts, and in each case the candidate receiving the greatest number of votes wins, even if he does not receive a majority of the votes cast. Though this arrangement seems simple, the results from the standpoint of the parties are amazing. As far as the parties are concerned, the *geographical distribution of their electoral strength* becomes, as a consequence of this system, one of the decisive factors in determining the outcome of the election. That is, the result of the election is determined by *two* factors: (1) the size of the vote, and (2) the geographical distribution of the vote; the total vote cast for the candidates of the two parties does not alone decide the issue. The single-member district system complicates all calculations governing the outcome of elections by injecting into them the second factor. Even a very slight change in the geographical distribution of the party vote in an election held under the single-member district system may produce an effect that seems incredible when first observed. If, for example, one were told merely that a given party received a total of 10,000,000 votes in all of the 435 districts taken together, out of a vote of

40,000,000, it would be impossible to guess even approximately the number of seats won by the party until something were known of the distribution of the vote. In an extreme case the party in question might win all of the seats, or it might win none at all merely by virtue of the fact that it received 25 per cent of the total vote. The accident of the geographical distribution of the popular support of a party has therefore been made a factor of great consequence by the special kind of election system used in the United States.

A precisely proportionate representation of the parties in the House, i.e., propor-

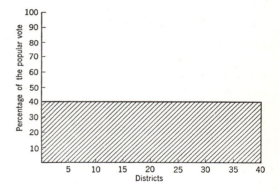

Fig. 1 An imaginary election.

A party receiving 40% of the total popular vote *distributed uniformly* throughout the electorate (i.e., the party candidates receive 40% of the vote in each district) would win no seats at all.

tionate to the popular vote, would result in the single-member district system if all of the electoral strength of all of the parties were concentrated perfectly by congressional districts in each case. That is, if party A received 100 per cent of the vote in some districts and no votes whatever in the others, and party B likewise received all of the votes cast in a number of the districts and none whatever in any other districts, and so on, each would be represented in the House in exact proportion to its popular strength. On the other hand, if the vote of all parties were distributed uniformly

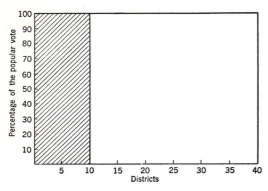

Fig. 2 An imaginary election.

A party receiving 25% of the vote perfectly concentrated in 10 districts out of 40 (i.e., the party in question receives 100% of the vote in 10 districts and no votes whatever in the remaining 30 districts) would win 25% of the seats. In this kind of election representation would be exactly proportional to the popular vote.

throughout the country (so that a party receiving 33 per cent of the total vote would receive 33 per cent of the vote in each of the 435 districts) it follows that the

strongest party would win all of the seats and the other parties would win none whatever.

Since it is unlikely, however, that party strength will be concentrated perfectly or will be distributed with perfect uniformity throughout the country, the number of seats likely to be won in an election is highly unpredictable even when the total party vote is known. This is so true that relatively slight adjustments of the system of representation affecting the factor of distribution may produce great consequences. A major change in the system, such as a provision that all representatives be elected at large on a single national ticket, would give the strongest party all of the seats, while the other parties would be reduced to zero, as has been demonstrated in the dictatorships where this device has been used to destroy the opposition parties. Again, an arrangement whereby congressmen are elected on a state-wide basis (i.e., from 48 districts, each state being one district—as

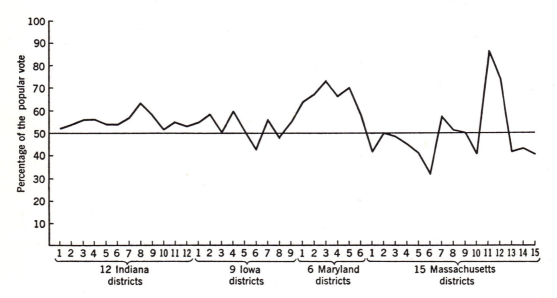

Fig. 3 A real election.

Percentage of popular vote cast for Democratic candidates for Congress in 42 districts in Indiana, Iowa, Maryland, and Massachusetts in 1932. They received 54% of the popular vote but won 29 seats, while the Republicans with 46% won only 13 seats.

presidential electors are now elected) would exaggerate the victory of the winning party even more than the present system does. This can be demonstrated by comparing the vote in the electoral college with the results of the congressional election. On the other hand, a system of proportional representation or vocational representation by abolishing the geographical factor, would almost certainly destroy the two-party system altogether.

DISTORTION OF RESULTS BY THE SINGLE-MEMBER DISTRICT SYSTEM

We are now in a position to observe the effects on the parties of the single-member-district-system-plus-plurality-elections. First, this system tends to exaggerate the representation of the winning party. Second, the greater the victory the more will it be exaggerated proportionately. Thus a party getting 55 per cent of the vote is likely to win 60 per cent of the seats, let us say. If, however, it gets 65 per cent of the vote it is likely to win 85 per cent of the seats, and so on, though it is not asserted that these proportions are accurate, or that they can be expressed in a precise mathematical formula. The corollary of this proposition is that the smaller the percentage of the popular vote reecived by a given party, the more likely it is to receive less than its proportionate share of the seats. Without pretending to state an accurate formula, we can say that the tendency is about as follows: if a party receives 45 per cent of the popular vote, it is apt to get only about 40 per cent of the seats. If it gets 35 per cent of the popular vote it may get only 15 per cent of the seats, depending, of course, on the vagaries of the geographical distribution of its popular vote. If a party gets less than 25 per cent of the popular vote it is apt to get very few seats, if any at all. Restated, the general proposition is that, other things being equal, the higher the percentage of the total popular vote cast for a party, the more cheaply (in terms of votes) will the party win seats in Congress. On the other hand, the smaller the percentage of the total popular vote cast for a party, the more expensively (in terms of votes) will seats in Congress be acquired. Obviously, the individual voter can make his own vote weigh more heavily by voting for major party candidates than by voting for minor party candidates.

Although the tendency of the single-member district system described in the preceding paragraph is not stated with the precision of a mathematical formula, it is clear that the operation of the system is to exaggerate the victory of the strongest party and to discriminate radically against lesser parties. The system discriminates *moderately* against the second party but against the third, fourth, and fifth parties the force of this tendency is multiplied to the point of extinguishing their chances of winning seats altogether. The odds against a minor party are especially great because it is certain to be no more than the third party, *unless it has strongly concentrated its strength in one section*. . . .

SIGNIFICANCE OF THE TWO-PARTY SYSTEM

Does the fact that we have a two-party system make any difference? Most emphatically, it does! The distinctive characteristics of the major party in a two-party system are strongly marked; the parties in a multi-party system belong to another species entirely. What are the special qualities of American politics that result from the fact that we have a well-established two-party system?

First, *the two-party system produces majorities automatically*. Since there are only two major parties actually in the competition for power and these parties monopolize the vote, it is almost certain that one of them will get a majority. The voters have *no other place to go*. When the alternatives are simplified to this extent, there must be more of one than of the other, i.e., there must be a majority of one or the other. The difficulty of assembling a majority is thus reduced very greatly. Party politicians work hard to assemble a majority, but they do not perform miracles by piecing together a great diversity of groups having an infinity of free choices. On the other hand, because they have only two alternatives, the groups, segments, classes, and occupations have less bargaining power than might be supposed. If this were not the case the difficulties of assembling a majority would be so great that no majorities would ever be produced at all. Party managers perform great labors of negotiation in order that their party, and not the other major party, may get a majority, but one or the other is certain to get it; the value of this fact to the party managers is difficult to exaggerate.

THE MODERATING EFFECT
OF THE ATTEMPT
TO CREATE A MAJORITY

The second effect of the two-party system is the fact that it produces moderate parties. The basis of the moderating effect of the process of creating a majority has already been described in an earlier chapter dealing with the multiplicity of interests. These influences affect both major parties equally. A large party must be supported by a great variety of interests sufficiently tolerant of each other to collaborate, held together by compromise and concession, and the discovery of certain common interest, and so on, and bearing in mind the fact that a major party has only one competitor and that party managers *need not meet every demand made by every interest*. To make extreme concessions to one interest at the expense of the others is likely to be fatal to the alignment of interests that make up the constituency of a major party. The process moderates the course of party action, though the language of politics is usually immoderate. A homogeneous party might be oppressive, but the tentative aggregates of miscellaneous elements collected within the loose framework of a major party are unthinkable as instruments of tyranny. The major party cannot afford to take an extreme stand, but neither is it condemned to futility. When one stops to consider the amount of thought and energy that has been devoted to the effort to protect people against oppression, it is difficult to imagine anything more important than the tendency of the parties to avoid extreme policies.

A generation ago President Lowell, writing about English major parties, said that the Liberal and Conservative parties tended to move toward the political center of gravity, i.e., they tended to be alike. Indeed, the most common criticism made of the American parties is not that they have been tyrannical but that they have been indistinguishable. A closer view of the process of accumulating a majority will illustrate how strong is the tendency of the parties to move toward the middle of the road.

Assume that the community is composed of 1,000 interest groups of uniformly equal weight. Assume, furthermore, that the worst is true, that each of these groups can be appealed to only on the basis of its special interests. Since these groups are equal, it would be necessary for a party to attach to itself 501 of these groups in order to win. The amount of bargaining, compromise, and concession required to create a loose confederation of these interest groups is stupendous, even if we concede that all must sooner or later join one or the other of two rival camps. In the course of these negotiations the groups participating in the bargain must give as well as get. They must recognize other interests; if they cannot cooperate they are certain to be defeated. On the one hand, *isolation is the extreme peril to be avoided by any interest* at all costs; on the other hand, neither of the parties can afford to be identified exclusively with one interest or with a few interests. While it is true that the parties compete for the support of the interests, it is also true that the interests compete for the support of the parties. Moreover there are 1,000 interests and only two parties. For this reason it is extravagant for a major party to offer too much for the support of any one special interest; as purchasers of political support the parties have a buyers' market.

The foregoing paragraph understates the complexities of the process, however. It assumes that it is possible to get the support of 501 whole groups, each group joining the party as a solid block. As a matter of fact, it is very rarely possible to mobilize 100 per cent of any social group. Usually even under favorable circumstances 60 per cent or 70 per cent of any group is the maximum response that can be elicited in a political agitation. All political organization is subject to a law of imperfect mobilization of social interests, the consequence of the fact that each individual person has many interests and belongs to many groups. This fact forces us to revise our calculations entirely. The party must get varying degrees of support from more than 501 interest groups in every 1,000 in order to win the election. If it is able to get 70 per cent of every group to which it appeals, it must win the support of 715 groups, i.e., it must get 70 per cent of the support of 715 groups in order to get a majority. If the party is able to get only 60 per cent of the support of every group to which it appeals, it must win 834 out of the 1,000 groups in this theoretical community. These calculations assume, however, that the party will get *no* support from any group not solicited, an assumption that is certainly inaccurate.

The corollary of the proposition that no party can win the unanimous support of any social group courted by its managers is that the party may hope to get *some* support from all groups whether they have been solicited or not; this is the unearned increment of politics to which reference was made in Chapter III. If the party gets support elsewhere on *general grounds* it needs proportionately less intensive support

from the special interest groups to whom it has made special appeals. It may be more profitable therefore to make general appeals to a very wide public in order to attract these remainders, than it is to exploit the special interests by special, but exclusive, appeals. This is a matter of extreme importance in the theory of party politics. Party politics is not a matter of mobilizing one great homogeneous group against another homogeneous group. Even more important, it is not a matter of mobilizing one aggregate of solid blocks against another aggregate of equally solid blocks of voters. The collision of parties is cushioned by the fact that there are no solid blocks, not even in the world of interest groups. The Democratic and Republican parties have always drawn some support from all sections of the country and from all strata of society. Both parties appeal generally to the whole country in addition to their special appeals to special interests. Striking confirmation of the importance of these general appeals to the great public may be found in the tendency of the party vote to rise or decline uniformly throughout the country from one election to the next. While there are important differences in the geographical and social distribution of the support of these parties, there is a strong tendency of all interest groups to maintain diplomatic relations with both parties just as there is a tendency on the side of the parties to keep contact with all interests. The appeal of a major party tends to become universal. The hospitality of the parties to all interests is one of their most pronounced characteristics.

Measured on a scale of radicalism and conservatism from Left to Right, both parties try more or less successfully to spread over the whole political rainbow from one extreme to the other. Specimens of nearly all shades of opinion are found in both parties; for strategic reasons the parties need to be strong on both wings. A party so equipped can move in either direction with the trend of public opinion, whereas a party exclusively radical or conservative is bound sooner or later to find itself dependent on an isolated minority interest and to discover that it has lost its freedom to adapt itself to the movements of opinion in the nation. The more intensive the appeal to a special interest becomes, the more exclusive it will be also, but isolation is precisely the condition most likely to destroy the influence of any minority. As a consequence of the catholicity of the major parties it is impossible for the party in power to oppress any element of the opposition party without oppressing a corresponding element within its own ranks. Every interest within the constituency of one major party has an opposite number in the competing major party; it is always closer to *some* elements of the opposition party than it is to most elements in its own party. Some of the limitations of pure interest politics are made evident by this discussion; the appeal to special interests is not enough. Finally, the fact that the two-party system is strongly established (that the choices are limited) makes the bargaining position of the parties vis-à-vis the interests strong; the parties need not yield to extreme demands from any interest.

3. Federalism and the Party System

David B. Truman

Federalism, the division of power between the national and state governments, has been a basic influence on American politics. It has contributed greatly to the decentralized organization of the parties by promoting independent centers of power. David B. Truman, Dean of Columbia College, finds other reasons equally important in explaining the lack of cohesion within the parties, particularly the character of political interests and issues. These latter factors must change before party centralization is likely.

* * *

I

To speak loosely of "the party system," especially when dealing with federalism in the United States, is to run the risk of begging the central question in this inquiry, for the nature of the party enterprise rests on the extent to which the elements collectively designated by the term actually constitute a system. Differentiating factors of structure and function bisect the "system" from various directions and in bewildering fashion, creating patterns of autonomy and subordination, some stable and some fluid, which seriously embarrass generalization.

The structural elements of party can be classified in the conventional fashion—following the formal, frequently statutory provisions for the diversity of committees, conventions, and individual functionaries—by national, state, and local levels. Such classification, while formally appropriate, is likely to take insufficient account of the extent to which the persistent and effective relationships among men and groups of men active in party affairs are clustered around one or a number of individual offices located on one or two or all three levels of the formal hierarchy.

It is a commonplace to point out that the party on the national level in the United States is, and throughout the country's history has been, focused on the presidency. Such national or interstate machinery as exists is primarily, though not exclusively, concerned with the nomination and election, perhaps especially the renomi-

From Arthur W. MacMahon, ed., *Federalism: Mature and Emergent* (New York: Doubleday & Company, 1955), pp. 116–124, 132–134, with footnotes deleted by permission of the Trustees of Columbia University in the City of New York.

nation and relection, of a President. So much is this the case that, despite the practice by both parties since 1928 of maintaining at least a nuclear national headquarters in continuous operation and despite the normal efforts of the defeated presidential candidate to give substance to his titular leadership, the party which has failed to win the White House presents a somewhat truncated, if not fractionated, appearance, which it is likely to retain until after the next nominating convention. Moreover, when the presidency is not at stake both parties show strong symptoms of "mid-term atomization."

The essential supportive structures for members of the Congress typically are not national or interstate. The chairmen and staffs of the national committees provide some services and assistance for duly nominated candidates for the Congress. The organizationally separate and often jealously independent campaign committees maintained by the "parliamentary" parties in the Senate and the House of Representatives seem to perform much the same sort of function, although their activities have never been closely studied.

The party in the Senate and the House of Representatives is not without significance as a means of allocating positions of power and influence in the legislative branch or even as a vehicle for the formulation of public policy, and the "record" of the congressional parties is not irrelevant to the fortunes of aspirants for election or reelection to the Congress. But the risks and sanctions to which most members of Congress are particularly sensitive have their focus within the states and localities. The relationships which the legislator has established and maintained within the constituency are primary and crucial; others are secondary and incidental. This seems to be the case despite the evidence that, especially in the case of the House of Representatives, the bulk of the voters in general elections, cast their ballots on the basis of party pref-

erence rather than attachment to the personal qualities of individual candidates for the national legislature; that is, party percentages in most districts tend to shift in the same direction. This is the case in presidential years, when the party is in a sense symbolized in the person of the chief candidate, but is equally apparent in the midterm elections. This paradox seems to point to the underlying significance of the nominating as against the electoral function of party structure, of which more will be said below.

At the state and local levels the structural patterns are varied and complicated, but not essentially different in kind. The significant organizations in the states may be centered upon the governorship, with control reaching down effectively into the counties and municipalities, or upon the United States Senators or upon both in some form of combination. Specialization in the localities may be built individually or in combination around the positions of mayors, sheriffs, or other prime sources of patronage and power such as the office of surrogate in the counties of New York State. Such specialized structures may include a variety of other elective offices, such as seats in the state legislature, in the United States House of Representatives, and even in the Senate. As often as not, however, congressional candidates will operate through more or less independent organizations of their own creation, even in the general election campaign. In the case of Representatives, this is often a reflection of the relative indifference of the more inclusive state and local organizations toward the congressional ticket, as compared with more lucrative sources of patronage. Senators may function independently for quite different reasons. Not only are they more conspicuous in the political affairs of their constituencies and secure in their positions for a longer period of time, but also they are likely to command other means of political power in greater abundance, including federal patronage.

The structural scheme of parties in the American federalism thus displays a confusing complexity, both in its formal aspects and in its informal operation. The system, to the extent that it can be given the name, is composed of a tremendous variety of elements imperfectly and rather unpredictably articulated, capable of showing a remarkable degree of separatism and autonomy. Moreover, the degree of articulation which exists to make the system is of a peculiar sort. The relationships between the more obscure and the more prominent elements in the system show a defensive, unilateral quality. In areas where general elections mean anything, it is a rare local or state party unit which, personal and factional feuds aside, is indifferent to the vote-pulling power of those occupying the principal positions on the ticket. But the concern is in a sense parasitic, to derive support from the leading figure on the ticket rather than to supply it. Given the tendency of voters, even when the form of the ballot does not help, to simplify their tasks by voting a "straight ticket," state and local elements are understandably interested in a nominee at the top of the list who may carry the whole slate into office with him. But these segments of the system are able, in marked degree, to cut themselves off from the head of the ticket when the latter is regarded as a handicap and succeed with remarkable frequency in checking the effects upon them of a swing of voting sentiment adverse to the occupant of the top place. Similarly, there are significant relationships between the presidential party and the "constituency parties," illustrated by the common appeal by a member of the Congress for executive adoption of a particular policy or for a favorable presidential announcement in order to improve the prospects of hard-pressed candidates in special areas, but these carry no guarantee of reciprocal support either on the floor of the Congress or in subsequent election campaigns.

II

Although the system—made up of the presidential parties, the "parliamentary" parties, the constituency parties, and the various other state and local aggregations—is structurally unstable and disjointed, the distribution of power within it is not even or merely haphazard. Here again, however, the danger of hasty generalization is great. It is customary to refer to the distribution of power within the American party system as decentralized. This is the generally accepted view, yet its implications in the context of federalism and for possible future trends are not clear unless some account is taken of the relative significance of the various functions of the party and of the degree of decentralization of power in connection with the most important of them. Parties, in any representative system, perform a compromise of functions, including nominating candidates for public office, mobilizing an electorate for their support, distributing patronage and other perquisites of public position, developing and protecting those formulas for social adjustment and accommodation which we collectively refer to as public policies, and a host of less obvious and self-conscious services. In different places and at different times one or another of these may be more conspicuous than the rest, which vastly complicates the tasks of historians and comparative analysts of the political process. Except perhaps in those political situations where a basic consensus is lacking or is being challenged, however, the nominating function seems to be the most fundamental or at least the most persistently focal. This has been strikingly the case in the United States since at least as far back as the caucuses and juntos of the later colonial years and, especially on the national level, conspicuously so since the great changes in the period associated with the name of Andrew Jackson, when the presidential party assumed most of the characteristics it displays today. It is around the nominating function that the states in recent decades have constructed the most elaborate and complicated systems of statutory regulation, and the intensity of feeling associated with the spread of the direct primary in the first decade of the present century reflected in part a recognition of the fundamental importance of the nomination process. James Bryce made no more acute observation concerning the American scene than he did when he noted that the nomination of candidates for public office was not only the most important but the most distinctively American function of party organization.

It is in connection with the nominating of candidates that the decentralization of power in the American party system is most apparent. Looking at the presidency it is clear that the changes in practice which developed in the eighteen-twenties—changes largely of degree, perhaps, but of such measure that their significance can scarcely be exaggerated—involved an increase in the importance of localism in the selecting process. The congressional caucus had been the instrument of a limited and comparatively homogeneous national elite, disposing of an office which had little of the quality of popular symbolism that it possesses today. Its members were not, of course, lacking in attachment to states and sections, but theirs was a national and central power reflecting the effects of close association in the institutional frame of the national legislature. The shift of initiative to the state legislatures and later to the national delegate conventions was a response to demands from more heterogeneous elements in the population and eventuated in a shifting of the power of decision, if not of initiative, from the national to the state or local level.

In Jackson's day, and for decades thereafter, the utility of the national convention lay not only in the announcement of a defensible nomination, but also in the sharpening of an effective electoral mechanism. In fact, the first national convention of the Democratic party was apparently more a rally to spur Jackson's state and local cohorts into vigorous activity than a device for selecting the candidate, as, in fact, conventions in which incumbent Presidents have sought renomination have usually been ever since. In later years the leaders of state and factional delegations had not only convention votes to market among the managers of aspiring candidates but also a canvassing and electoral organization as well. Both were needed, even though the former were of more immediate importance.

Perhaps the most significant, if largely undocumented, change in recent years, a change which may account for some of the recent criticism of the national convention, is that the electioneering functions of the presidential party have become increasingly centralized while the power over nominations remains decentralized. Although those voters who alter their choices late in the campaign may be strongly influenced, as the survey studies indicate, by personal solicitation, the presence of the presidential candidates in every living room, by way of radio and television, reduces the need for an army of canvassers in presidential campaigns as the development of the metropolitan press alone never did. In recent presidential elections both the behavior and the informal testimony of many urban functionaries support this interpretation; the circulars and posters are still distributed to the local clubs and headquarters, but the effort necessary to put them in the hands of individual voters is recognized as being of little or no value. State and local leaders are not powerless or completely unnecessary in the electioneering efforts of the presidential party, but both central direction and central execution of a presidential campaign have become in recent years not only a possibility but in large measure an actuality.

Yet the nomination function, excepting the renomination of an incumbent President, remains essentially decentralized. Despite such devices as the presidential primary and the centrally directed pre-convention efforts of the leading aspirants, local and frequently extraneous considerations not only enter into but even dominate the selection of delegates and the horse-trading decisions behind the scenes at the convention. In fact, the evidence clearly suggests that in areas where one-party dominance, as in the South, operates to avoid disturbance to distinctive local practices, the only significant function of a state party may be to select reliable delegates to inter-state party councils. The leaders of the presidential party may no longer need to rely heavily upon a decentralized machinery for conducting an election campaign, but they are still dependent on forging a cohesive coalition of state and local leaders for the opportunity to conduct one.

Decentralization of the nominating function is more striking and more significant as it affects Senators and Representatives. Regardless of the method of selection, by one or another form of the predominant direct primary or by convention, the influences which are chiefly responsible for the selection of candidates are local rather than national. The importance of this fact is merely underscored by the evidence that, under normal conditions, in about half the congressional constituencies, success in the primary is tantamount to election. This is typically due to the "one-party" complexion of many such areas, but it may result as well from the individual candidate's effectiveness in creating or associating himself with an organization within the constituency which can assure his selection or redesignation. The implications for the party system are much the same in either case.

Even a casual glance at the career lines of Senators and Representatives, as well as of state and local officials from whose ranks they are normally recruited, will indicate that most of them have had long and intimate association with the areas which they represent, more than is required by the symptomatically significant custom demanding residence in the district from which the legislator is chosen. No precise data on this point exist in the literature, but the impression is that a member of Congress is more likely than the average of the population to have been born, raised, educated, and trained in the area from which he is chosen. A constituency, perhaps especially an urban one, may take up a comparative newcomer who has achieved sudden prominence, but his survival is likely to depend ultimately upon his knowing his constituency, not in abstract, intellectual terms, but through supportive associations with individuals and groups. He must have satisfactory "connections," either with the leadership of a dominant party organization or with influential individuals primarily concerned with assuring his continuance in office or a combination of the two.

These connections may not be able to assure his election; the fortunes of the national party may be ebbing so rapidly that nothing can assure his individual survival or the nominee of the opposing party may more successfully exploit local dissatisfactions. But the aspirant will have no chance even to face these risks, except as he chooses to attempt a normally unsuccessful "independent" candidacy, unless he has the support necessary for nomination.

The structure responsible for nominating the legislative candidate need not be parochial or anti-national in its attitudes. This is not its principal significance but rather the fact that it is the locus of discretion in the nominating process. In its operations it need display no dependence upon, no functional association or identification with, the leadership of the presidential or the "parliamentary" party. Bryce made the point effectively in a brief comparison of local party organizations in Britain and the United States:

An organization which exists, like the political associations of England, solely or mainly for the sake of canvassing, conducting registration, diffusing literature, getting up courses of lectures, holding meetings and passing resolutions, has little or no power. . . . But when an organization which the party is in the habit of obeying, chooses a party candidate, it exerts power, power often of the highest import. . . .[1]

Decentralization of the functions of nominating and promoting the election of members of the Congress is reflected in a lack of cohesion on important policy matters within the "parliamentary" parties—within the party in either House and between the party in one chamber and "the same" party in the other—and in fairly frequent rejection of the legislative leadership of "the party's" President when it "controls" the White House. It is too easy to underestimate the influence of party affiliation upon legislative voting and to ignore the evidence that it is more reliably predictive of such behavior than any other factors so far identified. But on controverted issues of prime significance the leaders of the "parliamentary" parties not infrequently find themselves in the minority among their nominal following or split into two opposing wings, and the Administration may have to count on appreciable support from a segment of the "opposition" in Congress for the enactment of a basic portion of its legislative program, often despite extraordinary efforts by a popular President through public appeals and pronouncements, efforts which depend for effectiveness upon their infrequent use.

This state of affairs leads to criticism of the party system and demands for party "responsibility" by those who desire a central place among the functions of party for the formation of a more coherent and enforceable program. Of such criticisms the recent report of the American Political

Science Association's Committee on Political Parties may be taken as representative. A common shortcoming of such appeals, illustrated in the committee's proposals, is that in their enthusiasm for programmatic elegance they tend to underestimate the significance of the decentralized nominating function. It seems unlikely that any amount of policy talk in local meetings or of platform writing by interstate bodies will increase discipline within the congressional parties or cohesion within the Administration as a whole, unless they are preceded by a centralization of the risks and sanctions associated with the selection of candidates for seats in the legislature. It may be doubted, in fact, whether in any party system dominated by two major aggregations, even in a country less extensive and socially less complex than the United States, cohesion is provided primarily by the programmatical element rather than by a central leadership whose policy tendencies are but vaguely known and whose displeasure with a parliamentary follower is enforceable at the nominating stage. If the legislator's risks are localized, he will look in that direction when making difficult choices on matters of public policy.

III

The American party system thus tends to be characterized by decentralization of power with respect to its most crucial function, by structural confederation, and by a lack of coherence in matters of major policy. What have the facts of federalism to do with this? To what extent is this an inescapable consequence of the federal system itself? Federalism, by the constitutional protection of constituent governments, creates at least the possibility, as Herbert Wechsler has argued, that the states will control the composition and influence materially the legislative processes of the national entity. If, as Arthur Holcombe suggests, the national political party is the principal agent

[1] James Bryce, *The American Commonwealth*, 2d edition, (New York: The Macmillan Company, 1891), vol. 2, p. 76.

for restricting these tendencies, its effectiveness in the United States has been something less than complete. Is the molding force of the federal system itself such that a party system operating within it must inevitably show the characteristics of political organizations in the United States?

This is a question of considerable importance for an understanding of the American experience and for an estimate of its potentialities in the future. It is a question which the Committee on Political Parties tends to avoid by treating party organization as a matter dissociated from that of governmental structure. Thus it asserts that: "In the case of the American party system, the real issue is not over the federal form of organization but over the right balance of forces within this type of organization."

The basic political fact of federalism is that it creates separate, self-sustaining centers of power, privilege, and profit which may be sought and defended as desirable in themselves, as means of leverage upon elements in the political structure above and below, and as bases from which individuals may move to places of greater influence and prestige in and out of government. This does not mean simply that a socio-economic interest group, dominant within a state or, more typically perhaps, a group of contiguous states, will utilize state powers to protect itself from assault both from within the area and from the national center. This is true enough; it merely restates the facts underlying the original choice of a federal rather than a unitary structure for the second American constitution, and it points to the familiar fact of sectional politics present through most of our history and recurrent with each wave of state creation.

The separate political existence of the states in the days of the nation's industrial and political maturity, on the other hand, provides effective access to the whole governmental structure for interest groups whose tactics may be local or sectional but whose scope is national. Separatism, whether within the federal system or in the form of a specious demand for making a governmental activity "independent of politics" at whatever level of the structure, has frequently been a refuge for interests bent on defensive or evasive action, and the "states' rights" argument has often had about it an air more of expediency than of principle. This is not new. But it is the fact of federalism which permits an interest group or other enterprise of national scope, in alliance with lesser interests which may be primarily local or sectional, to prevent or negate action on the national level and to insure inaction or indulgence in the states. It was not merely Yankee stubbornness and dedication to local self-government which in the thirties prevented federal action to foster integrated development of the Connecticut River Valley. Such sentiments may have been more than mere expedient romanticism, and they might alone have affected the outcome of the proposal and the fortunes of elected state officials and members of Congress, but they received significant support and direction from private utility interests whose reach was nationwide. Nor were the interests exclusively local or sectional, though such were allied at least peripherally, which induced the Congress to alter in favor of state action a Supreme Court decision asserting or permitting national control of insurance. These illustrations are not cited by way of indictment but merely of illustration. In the maturity of the federal system the existence of the states as self-contained centers of power permits the use of them and associated party units by interests which are state or local only in a tactical sense. This is not equivalent to the separatism of a geographically defined interest, though it appears in the same garb and owes its significance as a technique to the continued existence of the states as power centers. Its effects on the party system are conducive to neither centralization nor cohesion at the national level.

In viewing the states as channels of access for interest groups, however, it is easy to forget that elective positions within the states, especially the governorships, are prizes in themselves and that the political "game" may be merely a means from the viewpoint of the interest group leader but is likely to be an end in itself for many of the more active partisans. It is perhaps a commentary on the instrumental, almost a-political attitudes of many academic observers of politics that they lay such stress upon the American parties as alliances of socio-economic interest groups. They are, of course, alliances of groups, but parties are not distinguishable exclusively or even primarily in terms of their socio-economic policy content. In varying but important measure they are purely political, focused upon securing and holding power for their leading elements as an end in itself. The grand patterns of sectional and perhaps class alliances which have successively dominated our presidential politics for periods lasting up to several decades can in the large view perhaps be explained most meaningfully in terms of socio-economic interest. But at shorter range the detailed patterns take on a more exclusively political appearance. There is here no intended implication of petty place-seeking but rather a suggestion that to aspire to be among those who govern and to associate for that objective as an end in itself is both normal and honorable. The evidence which indicates that enduring attachment to a party is for many voters a loyalty independent of, though not dissociated from, socio-economic interest supports the assumption that similar attachments to party, clique, and faction exist among the more active elements in political organizations.

The significance of this point in the present context is that, given the multitude of elective positions in the system (only partially a consequence of federalism) and given the absence of a clearly defined and recognized path from one position to another in the loose hierarchy of political careers (a consequence more of a decentralized party system than directly of federalism itself), conflicting but interdependent clusters of loyalty and aspiration build up around various positions in the governmental structure. Thus, within a given "party," the career aspirations and prospects of a state governor, a United States Senator, and a member of the House of Representatives are likely to be ambiguous to one another or to others in the political structure with whom they must deal. Each may want one of the other offices; the governor and Senator may both have presidential ambitions which are mutually exclusive; the Senator or the Representative, though occupying a "national" office, may hope to move to the governorship and is likely to be far more closely dependent upon the state governor, from considerations either of preference or of expediency, than upon the leaders of the "parliamentary" party or upon a President bearing the same party designation. This is a simplified and hypothetical example, but it illustrates the role played by the offices established in the federal structure, and especially the state governor, in fractionating and decentralizing the party system, in encouraging the development of largely independent, hostile, and internally cohesive factional groupings. . . .

In this connection it is worth while to point out that a considerable element of localism has inevitably been injected into American politics, regardless of constitutional structure, by such factors as the patterns of immigration from Europe. Immigration itself has rarely provided a controversy of national scope, and nativist movements have been conspicuous on occasion but of no lasting significance. Ethnic issues as such, perhaps excluding the Negro question, have not had the impact on national politics that they have had, for example, in Canada. But with the tendency for individual nationality groupings to concentrate in particular areas, especially in the cities, and to find in their common rootlessness and frequently in the experience of discrimination and exploitation a basis in addition to national origin for cohesion and interdependence, they have constituted a means to power and influence for locally oriented political organizations outside and inside their own ranks.

It is these geographically defined factors, accentuated by a low-temperature, domestic politics, which give major force and relevance to the possibility of state control over the composition of the national governing bodies, through the electoral college and related means, which Herbert Wechsler points out in his chapter. Structural elements in the system—some, it is argued here, inherent in federalism—alone encourage an irreducible minimum of decentralization and disruption in the party system. But it is as these reflect the underlying pace of the political process and as they are harnessed to regionally differentiated issues and clusters of organization that they find their most impelling dynamic.

As in other national systems, moreover, there are additional governmental arrangements which support and in some instances reflect the decentralizing tendencies apparent in the process as a whole. Not the least important of these is the practice of frequent elections specified by the calendar and the related constitutional provision for unequal terms of office. Decentralizing in intent, they have operated to accentuate localized concerns, especially in the midterm primaries and elections at the national level. But in a system in which any election may be relevant to all others in an area, whether they are held simultaneously or not, the very frequency of elections and campaigns can accentuate and exploit local

and transitory animosities and consolidate localized patterns of control. This point has never been more dramatically illustrated than it was in the tragic years leading up to the Civil War. During the decade of the eighteen-fifties "the baneful influence of elections almost continuously in progress, of campaigns never over," accentuated local and sectional hostilities. Aided by the fact that at that time elections to the Congress were not held at a uniform date throughout the nation, the upthrust of localism further crippled already imperfect efforts to forestall a fatal break. In Nichols' words, "The incessant procession of artificially ordered election conflicts frequently meant nothing more than the routine return of pleasurable electioneering excitement; but in the 1850's it had become dangerous." "It was," he points out, "harder for the statesman at the capital city to calm the emotions stirred in these countless local contests when their representatives brought them to Washington."

The difference between this fateful decade and the more normal course of our politics is one of degree, the more so as a multiplicity of local elections may support a professional corps of politicians whose organized relationships within the area can be utilized to resist an effort at centralization.

A representative and significant response to such an effort is provided by the Hatch Act of 1939. Stimulated by Franklin Roosevelt's awkward and ill-fated attempt at a "purge" of rebellious Representatives and Senators in the Democratic primaries of 1938, a bipartisan combination in the Congress took steps to forestall the possibility that a centralized party leadership could be built upon presidential patronage, through the device of a statutory prohibition against political campaign activity by federal employees below the policy-forming level whether they are in the classified civil service or not. This was an effort at insurance against an extremely remote contingency, since the requirement of senatorial confirmation and the practice of senatorial courtesy have made patronage a comparatively feeble instrument of centralized leadership except in the opening months of an Administration or for purposes of securing renomination for an incumbent President. It is impossible to estimate precisely the effects of this restriction or of the comparable provision in the 1940 legislation restricting the annual expenditures of national committees, but at minimum their enactment testifies to the strength of the decentralizing tendencies. . . .

VI

In a federal system decentralization and lack of cohesion in the party system are based on the structural fact of federalism, but, it has been argued here, the degree to which these become the dominant characteristics of the distribution of power within the political parties is a function of a variety of other governmental and social factors which are independent of the federal structure or are merely supportive of its tendencies. Within the American structure there clearly are limits beyond which centralization and coherence in the parties may not go. Nevertheless, accepting the argument that the national political party is the most responsive instrument of restraint upon federalism's centrifugal tendencies, it may be appropriate briefly to inquire into the circumstances which might produce a gradual shift in the locus of power within the American parties.

It seems clear that the prospects for such a shift must rest fundamentally upon the emergence or intensification of a dominant and persistent set of interests and issues which will tend to cut through rather than to unify constituencies, especially the states, and which demand standardized national solutions. These would imply a more intense and urgent, perhaps a more explosive, politics; that would seem to be the price of

change. Here is not the place to attempt a detailed examination of any such issues, but it seems entirely possible that their most likely source would lie in the problems of an increasingly urbanized and industrialized society, as Arthur Holcombe suggested more than twenty years ago in his anticipation of the replacement of sectional by class politics. Another complex of such issues may emerge or may be in process of emerging out of the problems besetting the new American leadership on the international scene.

Neither of these complexes of issues appears to hold much promise of startling immediate developments within the party realm. In the unlikely event of an increasingly even industrialization of all the states, it is by no means certain that an expanding economy will not so check the importance of intersecting issues of full employment, social security, and the like, that the demands of commodity and of section will still be dominant. Nor in such circumstances is it at all sure that leadership forces will not prefer the occasional inconveniences of a decentralized politics to the less manageable potentialities of an opposite trend. And in the realm of foreign policy it is by no means clear that an emerging consensus on direction and general posture will not leave the center of the stage free for geographically defined issues of pace and of precise application.

These obstacles aside, the dominance of issues capable of dividing major constituencies internally presupposes their emergence or evocation in sections now monopolized by a single party and the development of a vigorous and genuine bipartisan pattern. This result is not likely to be the work of a single day and not only because of the stubborn disinclination of voters to alter partisan attachments once they have been formed, though this is a factor of no inconsiderable importance. Rather, as V. O. Key has amply demonstrated in his study of the South, a single-party monopoly based on the assertion or defense of a dominant sectional interest tends to inhibit the identification and expression of intersecting national issues. It induces a fluid factionalism along personal and clique lines incapable of the organization necessary to sustained expression of such issues from within and to effective response to their assertion from without. Moreover, the purely political advantages of a one-party monopoly are considerable and not to be surrendered without resistance. Only the most intense conflict over persistent issues is likely to prevail over efforts by an invigorated majority party to capture the leadership of an emerging opposition and to hamstring its efforts with all the statutory and polemic resources at the command of an entrenched group.

The federal structure itself imposes no insuperable obstacles to a shift in the locus of power within the party system, but it seems improbable that the country will soon dispense with the talents of the politician skilled in the manipulation and reconciliation of decentralized and recalcitrant power blocs.

4. Issue Conflict and Consensus among Party Leaders and Followers

Herbert McClosky,
Paul J. Hoffman,
and Rosemary O'Hara

In this path-breaking study, the authors illuminate the place of issues in American politics. Contrary to the common belief, they find that there are distinct policy differences among party leaders, but that the differences are much less among the voters of each party. They also find that Republican activists are significantly different from all other groups, thus raising questions about the future course and prospects of the G. O. P. Herbert McClosky, the senior author, is Professor of Political Science at the University of California, Berkeley.

* * *

American political parties are often regarded as "brokerage" organizations, weak in principle, devoid of ideology, and inclined to differ chiefly over unimportant questions. In contrast to the "ideological" parties of Europe—which supposedly appeal to their followers through sharply defined, coherent, and logically related doctrines—the American parties are thought to fit their convictions to the changing demands of the political contest. According to this view, each set of American party leaders is satisfied to play Tweedledee to the other's Tweedledum.

I. PRESSURES TOWARD UNIFORMITY AND CLEAVAGE

Although these "conclusions" are mainly derived from *a priori* analysis or from casual observations of "anecdotal" data (little systematic effort having been made so far to verify or refute them), they are often taken as confirmed—largely, one imagines, because they are compatible with certain conspicuous features of American politics. Among these features is the entrenchment of a two-party system which, by affording both parties a genuine opportunity to win elections, tempts them to appeal to as many diverse elements in the electorate as are needed to put together a majority. Since both parties want to attract support from the centrist and moderate segments of the electorate, their views on basic issues will, it is thought, tend to converge. Like giant

From the *American Political Science Review,* vol. 54, no. 2 (June 1960), pp. 406–427, with footnote omissions.

business enterprises competing for the same market, they will be led to offer commodities that are in many respects identical. It is one thing for a small party in a multi-party system to preserve its ideological purity, quite another for a mass party in a two-party system to do so. The one has little hope of becoming a majority, and can most easily survive by remaining identified with the narrow audience from which it draws its chief supporters; the other can succeed only by accommodating the conflicting claims of many diverse groups—only, in short, by blunting ideological distinctions.

Constraints against enlarging intellectual differences also spring from the loosely confederated nature of the American party system, and from each national party's need to adjust its policies to the competing interests of the locality, the state, and the nation. Many party units are more concerned with local than with national elections, and prefer not to be handicapped by clear-cut national programs. Every ambitious politician, moreover, hopes to achieve a *modus vivendi* tailored to the particular and often idiosyncratic complex of forces prevailing in his constituency, an objective rarely compatible with doctrinal purity. Often, too, local politics are largely nonpartisan in ways that scarcely affect the great national issues around which ideologies might be expected to form. The development and enforcement of a sharply delineated ideology is also hindered by the absence in either party of a firmly established, authoritative, and continuing organizational center empowered to decide questions of doctrine and discipline. Party affiliation is loosely defined, responsibility is weak or non-existent, and organs for indoctrinating or communicating with party members are at best rudimentary.

Cultural and historical differences may also contribute to the weaker ideological emphasis among American, as compared with European, parties. Many of the great historical cleavages that have divided European nations for centuries—monarchism *vs.* republicanism; clericalism *vs.* anti-clericalism; democracy *vs.* autocracy, etc. —have never taken root in this country. Apart from the slavery (and subsequently the race) issue, the United States has not experienced the intense class or caste conflict often found abroad, and contests of the capitalism *vs.* socialism variety have never achieved an important role in American politics. In addition, never having known a titled nobility, we have largely been freed from the conflicts found elsewhere between the classes of inherited and acquired privilege.

Consider, too, the progress made in the United States toward neutralizing the forces which ordinarily lead to sharp social, and hence intellectual and political, differentiation. The class and status structure of American society has attained a rate of mobility equalling or exceeding that of any other long established society. Popular education, and other facilities for the creation of common attitudes, have been developed on a scale unequalled elsewhere. Improvements in transportation and communication, and rapid shifts in population and industry have weakened even sectionalism as a source of political cleavage. Rural-urban differences continue to exist, of course, but they too have been diminishing in force and have become less salient for American politics than the differences prevailing, for example, between a French peasant proprietor and a Parisian *boulevardier.* In short, a great many Americans have been subjected in their public lives to identical stimuli—a condition unlikely to generate strong, competing ideologies.

The research reported here was designed not to refute these observations but to test the accuracy of the claim that they are sufficient to prevent differences in outlook from taking root in the American party system. We believed that the homogenizing tendencies referred to are strongly offset by contrary influences, and that voters are preponderantly led to support the party whose opinions they share. We further thought that the competition for office, though giving rise to similarities between the parties, also impels them to diverge from each other in order to sharpen their respective appeals. For this and other reasons, we expected to find that the leaders of the two parties, instead of ignoring differences alleged to exist within the electorate, would differ on issues more sharply than their followers would. We believed further that even in a brokerage system the parties would serve as independent reference groups, developing norms, values, and self-images to which their supporters could readily respond. Their influence, we felt, would frequently exceed that of ethnic, occupational, residential and other reference groups. In sum, we proceeded on the belief that the parties are not simply spokesmen for other interest groups, but are in their own right agencies for formulating, transmitting, and anchoring political opinions, that they attract adherents who in general share those opinions, and that through a feedback process of mutual reinforcement between the organization and its typical supporters, the parties develop integrated and stable political tendencies. Other hypotheses will be specified as we present and analyze our findings.

II. PROCEDURES

The questions considered in this paper were part of a large field study made in 1957–1958 on the nature, sources, and correlates of political affiliation, activity, and belief in the American party system (hereafter referred to as the PAB study). Pilot studies on Minnesota samples had led us to suspect that many "settled" notions about party affiliation and belief in America would not stand up under careful empirical scrutiny; further, we felt that little progress would be made in the exploration of this subject until a comprehensive por-

trait of party membership in America had been drawn. Accordingly, a nationwide study was launched to acquire a detailed description of party leaders and supporters, gathering data on their backgrounds, political experiences, personality characteristics, values, motivations, social and political attitudes, outlooks on key issues, and related matters.

For our samples of party "leaders" we turned to the Democratic and Republican national conventions, largely because they are the leading and most representative of the party organs, their delegates coming from every part of the United States and from every level of party and government activity. Our samples ranged from governors, senators, and national committeemen at the one end to precinct workers and local officials at the other. In the absence of comprehensive information about the characteristics of the party élites in America, no one can say how closely the convention delegates mirror the total party leadership. We felt it fair to assume, nevertheless, that the delegates represented as faithful a cross section of American party leadership as could be had without an extraordinary expenditure of money and labor. Using convention delegates as our universe of leaders also held some obvious advantages for research, since the composition of this universe (by name, address, party, state, sex, place of residence, and party or public office) can usually be ascertained from the convention calls. Of the 6,848 delegates and alternates available to be sampled, 3,193 actually participated; 3,020 (1,788 Democrats and 1,232 Republicans) completed and returned questionnaires that were usable in all respects. The proportion of returns was roughly equivalent for both sets of party leaders.

The rank and file sample, which we wanted both for its intrinsic value and for its utility as a control group, was obtained by special arrangement with the American Institute of Public Opinion. In January

1958, Gallup interviewers personally distributed our questionnaire to 2,917 adult voters in two successive national cross-section surveys. Some 1,610 questionnaires were filled out and returned, of which 1,484 were completely usable. This sample closely matched the national population on such characteristics as sex, age, region, size of city, and party affiliation, and though it somewhat oversampled the upper educational levels, we considered it sufficiently large and representative for most of our purposes. Of the 1,484 respondents, 821 were Democratic supporters (629 "pure" Democrats, plus 192 whom we classified as "independent" Democrats) and 623 were Republican supporters (479 "pure" Republicans, plus 144 "independent" Republicans). Forty respondents could not be identified as adherents of either party.

The lengthy questionnaire developed for the study was designed to be self-administered. It contained, in addition to questions on the respondents' personal backgrounds, a number of queries on their political history and experience, their attitudes toward the party system and toward such related matters as party organization, discipline and responsibility, their self-images with regard to social class and liberalism-conservatism, their reference group identifications, and their views on party leadership and ideology. The largest part of the questionnaire consisted of 390 scale items, randomly arranged, which when sorted and scored fell into 47 scales for measuring the personality, attitude, and value characteristics of each of the respondents. We had validated and used all but three of these scales in earlier studies.

The questions most relevant for the present article were those which asked each respondent to express his attitudes toward twenty-four important national issues, and to state whether he believed support for each issue should be "increased," "decreased," or "remain as is." The list of issues and the responses of each sample will be found in Tables II-A through II-E, where for convenience of analysis, the issues have been grouped under five broad headings: Public Ownership, Government Regulation of the Economy, Equalitarianism and Human Welfare, Tax Policy and Foreign Policy.

In tabulating the results, we first scored each individual on each issue and then computed aggregate scores for all the members of a given sample. To begin with, percentages were used to show the proportion who favored increasing, decreasing, or retaining the existing level of support on each issue. But as it was clumsy to handle three figures for each issue, we constructed a single index or "ratio of support" which would simultaneously take account of all three scores. The index was built by assigning a weight of 1.0 to each "increase" response in the sample, of 0 to each "decrease" response, and of .50 to each "remain as is" (or "same") response. Thus the ratio-of-support score shown for any given sample is in effect a mean score with a possible range of 0 to 1.0, in which support for an issue increases as the scores approach 1.0 and decreases as they approach 0. In general, the scores can be taken to approximate the following over-all positions: .0 to .25—strongly wish to reduce support; .26 to .45—wish to reduce support; .46 to .55—satisfied with the *status quo;* .56 to .75—wish to increase support; and .76 to 1.00—strongly wish to increase support. Note that the differences in degree suggested by these categories refer not to the *strength of feeling* exhibited by individuals toward an issue but rather to the *numbers of people* in a sample who hold points of view favoring or opposing that issue.

Because they include "same" and "no code" as well as "increase" and "decrease" responses, our ratios of support sometimes flatten the differences between groups. Had we employed only the percentage scores for the "increase" or "decrease" responses, the differences between samples would in many instances have seemed larger. Nevertheless, the ratio of support offers so many advantages that we have employed it as our principal measure. For one thing, as the equivalent of a mean score, it takes into account all scores, omitting no respondent from the tabulation. For the same reason it enables us to assess the amount of dispersion or homogeneity exhibited by any sample and makes it easy to calculate significances of difference. Reliance upon a single, uniform statistic also allows us to make ready comparisons not only *between* but *within* samples, and to determine quickly how large the differences actually are. By observing whether a ratio of support is above or below .50 we can see at once whether a particular group predominantly favors or opposes the issue in question, and how strongly it does so. The use of ratio scores also makes it possible to compare issues as well as groups, *e.g.*, to see whether one issue is more preferred than another.

For further information on the meaning of the issue responses, we also compared samples on a number of related scales and items. Tabulating and statistical operations were carried out to control for demographic influences like education, occupation, age, and sectionalism; to ascertain homogeneity of opinion within the several samples; to rank the issues according to the magnitude of the differences between samples; to compare members' positions on issues against official platform statements; and to determine whether leaders and followers are able to name the issues which actually divide the parties. Some of the findings yielded by these operations will be considered here, while others, for reasons of space, will have to be reserved for future publications.

A word of caution before we turn to the findings. The respondents were offered only the twenty-four issues that impressed us in February, 1957, as most significant and enduring. However, they may not all be as salient today as they seemed at that time. Nor, within the limitations of a single questionnaire, could we explore every issue that informed observers might have considered important. Some presumably vital issues such as states rights, political centralization, and expansion of government functions could not be stated explicitly enough within our format to be tested properly. These are issues that are so generalized as to encompass many other specific issues, and so highly charged as to awaken a profusion of symbolic and emotive associations.

The *form* of our issue questions may also be open to criticism, for space limitations prevented our subjects from indicating how strongly they felt and how much they knew about each of the issues. This deficiency, however, may be less important than it appears, since for the groups we most wanted to compare (*e.g.*, Democratic *vs.* Republican leaders), the degree of political knowledge and intensity is likely to be rather similar. The difficulty is greater when comparing leaders with followers, but is somewhat offset by controlling for education and socio-economic status. Although some subtleties of interpretation are bound to be lost because these variables have been omitted, we are satisfied that our issue questions in their present form furnish a useful measure for assessing *group* (as distinguished from *individual*) opinion.

Finally, one may wonder about the value of opinions stated on a questionnaire compared with the worth of views formally expressed by an organization or implicit in the actions of its leaders. Advantages can be cited on both sides. The beliefs expressed in official party statements or in legislative roll calls, it might be claimed, represent the *operating* beliefs of the organization by virtue of having been tested in the marketplace or in the competition of legislative struggle. Positions taken on issues on which a party stakes its future may be more valid evidence of what the party truly believes than are the opinions expressed by individual members under conditions of maximum safety. On the other hand, the responses to the issue and attitude questions

TABLE I   Average Differences in the Ratio-of-Support Scores
among Party Leaders and Followers
for Five Categories of Issues

Category of Issues	Democratic Leaders vs. Republican Leaders	Democratic Followers vs. Republican Followers	Democratic Leaders vs. Democratic Followers	Republican Leaders vs. Republican Followers	Democratic Leaders vs. Republican Followers	Republican Leaders vs. Democratic Followers
A. Public ownership of resources	.28	.04	.06	.18	.10	.22
B. Government regulation of the economy	.22	.06	.08	.10	.12	.16
C. Equalitarianism, human welfare	.22	.05	.08	.21	.06	.25
D. Tax policy	.20	.06	.06	.20	.04	.26
E. Foreign Policy	.15	.02	.05	.08	.07	.10
Average differences in ratio scores for all categories	.21	.04	.07	.15	.08	.20

Sample Sizes: Democratic Leaders, 1,788; Republican Leaders, 1,232; Democratic Followers, 821; Republican Followers, 623.

in the PAB study represent the anonymous, private opinions of party leaders and followers, uncomplicated by any need to make political capital, to proselytize, to conciliate critics, or to find grounds for embarrassing the opposition at the next election. Hence they may for some purposes represent the most accurate possible reflection of the "actual" state of party opinion. The controversy over the value of the two approaches is to some extent spurious, however, for they offer different perspectives on the same thing. In addition, considerable correspondence exists between the party positions evident in congressional roll calls and the privately expressed opinions of the party leaders in our study.[1]

III. FINDINGS: COMPARISONS BETWEEN LEADERS

No more conclusive findings emerge from our study of party issues than those growing out of the comparisons between the two

[1] The complexities affecting the determination of party votes in Congress are thoroughly explored in David B. Truman, *The Congressional Party: A Case Study* (New York, 1959).

sets of party leaders. Despite the brokerage tendency of the American parties, their active members are obviously separated by large and important differences. The differences, moreover, conform with the popular image in which the Democratic party is seen as the more "progressive" or "radical," the Republicans as the more "moderate" or "conservative" of the two. In addition, the disagreements are remarkably consistent, a function not of chance but of systematic points of view, whereby the responses to any one of the issues could reasonably have been predicted from knowledge of the responses to the other issues.

Examination of Tables II-A-E and III shows that the leaders differ significantly on 23 of the 24 issues listed and they are separated on 15 of these issues by .18 or more ratio points—in short, by differences that are in absolute magnitude very large. The two samples are furthest apart in their attitudes toward public ownership and are especially divided on the question of government ownership of natural resources, the Democrats strongly favoring it, the Republicans just as strongly wanting it cut back. The difference of .39 in the ratio scores is

**TABLE II-A   Comparison of Party Leaders and Followers
on "Public Ownership" Issues,
by Percentages and Ratios of Support**

Issues	Leaders		Followers	
	Dem. N = 1,788	*Repub.* N = 1,232	*Dem.* N = 821	*Repub.* N = 623
	(%s down)			
Public ownership of natural resources				
% favoring: increase	57.5	12.9	35.3	31.1
decrease	18.6	51.9	15.0	19.9
same, n.c.*	23.8	35.2	49.7	49.0
Support ratio	.69	.30	.60	.56
Public control of atomic energy				
% favoring: increase	73.2	45.0	64.2	59.4
decrease	7.2	15.3	7.1	10.0
same, n.c.	19.6	39.7	28.7	30.6
Support ratio				
Mean support ratios for the public ownership	.83	.65	.79	.75
category	.76	.48	.70	.66

* n.c. = no code.

the largest for any of the issues tested. In percentages, the differences are 58 percent (D) vs. 13 percent (R) in favor of increasing support, and 19 percent (D) vs. 52 percent (R) in favor of decreasing support. Both parties preponderantly support public control and development of atomic energy, but the Democrats do so more uniformly.

V. O. Key, among others, has observed that the Republican party is especially responsive to the "financial and manufacturing community," reflecting the view that government should intervene as little as possible to burden or restrain prevailing business interests. The validity of this observation is evident throughout all our data, and is most clearly seen in the responses to the issues listed under Government Regulation of the Economy, Equalitarianism and Human Welfare, Tax Policy. Democratic leaders are far more eager than Republican leaders to strengthen enforcement of anti-monopoly laws and to increase regulation

of public utilities and business. Indeed, the solidarity of Republican opposition to the regulation of business is rather overwhelming: 84 percent want to decrease such regulation and fewer than .01 percent say they want to increase it. Although the Democrats, on balance, also feel that government controls on business should not be expanded further, the differences between the two samples on this issue are nevertheless substantial.

The two sets of leaders are also far apart on the farm issue, the Democrats preferring slightly to increase farm supports, the Republicans wanting strongly to reduce them. The Republican ratio score of .20 on this issue is among the lowest in the entire set of scores. The magnitude of these scores somewhat surprised us, for while opposition to agricultural subsidies is consistent with Republican dislike for state intervention, we had expected the leaders to conform more closely to the familiar image of the

**TABLE II-B Comparison of Party Leaders and Followers
on "Government Regulation of the Economy" Issues,
by Percentages and Ratios of Support**

	Leaders		Followers	
Issues	*Dem.* *N = 1,788*	*Repub.* *N = 1,232*	*Dem.* *N = 821*	*Repub.* *N = 623*
		(%s down)		
Level of farm price supports				
% favoring: increase	43.4	6.7	39.0	23.0
decrease	28.1	67.4	27.6	40.3
same, n.c.	28.5	25.8	33.4	36.7
Support ratio	.58	.20	.56	.41
Government regulation of business				
% favoring: increase	20.2	0.6	18.6	7.4
decrease	38.5	84.1	33.4	46.2
same, n.c.	41.3	15.3	48.0	46.4
Support ratio	.41	.08	.43	.31
Regulation of public utilities				
% favoring: increase	59.0	17.9	39.3	26.0
decrease	6.4	17.6	11.1	12.0
same, n.c.	34.6	64.5	49.6	62.0
Support ratio	.76	.50	.64	.57
Enforcement of anti-monopoly laws				
% favoring: increase	78.0	44.9	53.2	51.0
decrease	2.9	9.0	7.9	6.6
same, n.c.	19.1	46.1	38.9	42.4
Support ratio	.88	.68	.73	.72
Regulation of trade unions				
% favoring: increase	59.3	86.4	46.6	57.8
decrease	12.4	4.5	8.9	10.6
same, n.c.	28.3	9.2	44.5	31.6
Support ratio	.73	.91	.69	.74
Level of tariffs				
% favoring: increase	13.0	19.2	16.6	15.2
decrease	43.0	26.3	25.3	21.3
same, n.c.	43.9	54.5	58.1	63.4
Support ratio	.35	.46	.46	.47
Restrictions on credit				
% favoring: increase	24.8	20.6	26.1	25.7
decrease	39.3	20.6	22.2	23.8
same, n.c.	35.9	58.8	51.8	50.5
Support ratio	.43	.50	.52	.51
Mean support ratios for "government regulations of the economy" category	.59	.48	.58	.53

**TABLE II-C Comparison of Party Leaders and Followers
on "Equalitarian and Human Welfare" Issues,
by Percentages and Ratios of Support**

Issues	Leaders		Followers	
	Dem. *N = 1,788*	*Repub.* *N = 1,232*	*Dem.* *N = 821*	*Repub.* *N = 623*
		(%s down)		
Federal aid to education				
% favoring: increase	66.2	22.3	74.9	64.8
decrease	13.4	43.2	5.6	8.3
same, n.c.	20.4	34.5	19.5	26.8
Support ratio	.76	.40	.85	.78
Slum clearance and public housing				
% favoring: increase	78.4	40.1	79.5	72.5
decrease	5.6	21.6	5.8	7.9
same, n.c.	16.0	38.3	14.6	19.6
Support ratio	.86	.59	.87	.82
Social security benefits				
% favoring: increase	60.0	22.5	69.4	57.0
decrease	3.9	13.1	3.0	3.8
same, n.c.	36.1	64.4	27.5	39.2
Support ratio	.78	.55	.83	.77
Minimum wages				
% favoring: increase	50.0	15.5	59.0	43.5
decrease	4.7	12.5	2.9	5.0
same, n.c.	45.2	72.0	38.1	51.5
Support ratio	.73	.52	.78	.69
Enforcement of integration				
% favoring: increase	43.8	25.5	41.9	40.8
decrease	26.6	31.7	27.4	23.6
same, n.c.	29.5	42.8	30.7	35.6
Support ratio	.59	.47	.57	.59
Immigration into United States				
% favoring: increase	36.1	18.4	10.4	8.0
decrease	27.0	29.9	52.0	44.6
same, n.c.	36.9	51.7	37.6	47.4
Support ratio	.54	.44	.29	.32
Mean support ratios for "equalitarian and human welfare" category	.71	.50	.70	.66

Republican as the more "rural" of the two parties. It appears, however, that the party's connection with business is far more compelling than its association with agriculture.

The Republican desire to reduce government expenditures and to promote independence from "government handouts" prevails on the farm question as it does on

**TABLE II-D   Comparison of Party Leaders and Followers
on "Tax Policy" Issues,
by Percentages and Ratios of Support**

Issues	Leaders		Followers	
	Dem. *N = 1,788*	*Repub.* *N = 1,232*	*Dem.* *N = 821*	*Repub.* *N = 623*
		(%s down)		
Corporate income tax				
% favoring: increase	32.3	4.0	32.0	23.3
decrease	23.3	61.5	20.5	25.7
same, n.c.	44.4	34.5	47.5	51.0
Support ratio	.54	.21	.56	.49
Tax on large incomes				
% favoring: increase	27.0	5.4	46.6	34.7
decrease	23.1	56.9	13.8	21.7
same, n.c.	49.9	37.7	39.6	43.6
Support ratio	.52	.24	.66	.56
Tax on business				
% favoring: increase	12.6	1.0	24.6	15.9
decrease	38.3	71.1	24.1	32.6
same, n.c.	49.1	27.8	51.3	51.5
Support ratio	.37	.15	.50	.42
Tax on middle incomes				
% favoring: increase	2.7	0.8	4.5	3.0
decrease	50.2	63.9	49.3	44.3
same, n.c.	47.1	35.3	46.2	52.6
Support ratio	.26	.18	.28	.29
Tax on small incomes				
% favoring: increase	1.4	2.9	1.6	2.1
decrease	79.2	65.0	77.5	69.6
same, n.c.	19.4	32.1	20.9	28.3
Support ratio	.11	.19	.12	.16
Mean support ratios for "tax policy" category	.36	.19	.42	.38

other issues, while the Democratic preference for a more regulated economy in which government intervenes to reduce economic risk and to stabilize prosperity is equally evident on the other side. Party attitudes on this issue appear to be determined as much by ideological tendencies as by deliberate calculation of the political advantages to be gained by favoring or opposing subsidies to farmers. Comparison of our findings with Turner's earlier data on farm votes in Congress suggests, in addition, that the sharp party difference on the farm issue is neither a recent development nor a mere product of the personal philosophy of the present Secretary of Agriculture.

Having implied that agricultural policies partly result from principle, we must note

TABLE II-E   Comparison of Party Leaders and Followers
on "Foreign Policy" Issues,
by Percentages and Ratios of Support

Issues	Leaders		Followers	
	Dem. N = 1,788	Repub. N = 1,232	Dem. N = 821	Repub. N = 623
		(%s down)		
Reliance on the United Nations				
% favoring: increase	48.9	24.4	34.7	33.4
decrease	17.6	34.8	17.3	19.3
same, n.c.	35.5	40.7	48.0	47.3
Support ratio	.66	.45	.59	.57
American participation in military alliances				
% favoring: increase	41.5	22.7	39.1	32.3
decrease	17.6	25.7	14.0	15.4
same, n.c.	40.9	51.6	46.9	52.3
Support ratio	.62	.48	.62	.58
Foreign aid				
% favoring: increase	17.8	7.6	10.1	10.1
decrease	51.0	61.7	58.6	57.3
same, n.c.	31.1	30.7	31.3	32.6
Support Ratio	.33	.23	.26	.26
Defense spending*				
% favoring: increase	20.7	13.6	50.5	45.7
decrease	34.4	33.6	16.4	15.4
same, n.c.	44.8	52.8	33.0	38.8
Support ratio	.43	.40	.67	.65
Mean support ratios for "foreign policy" category (excl. defense spending)	.54	.39	.49	.47

* Issues of defense spending were separated from other foreign policy issues because the scores for some of the leaders and all of the followers were distorted by the launching of Sputnik I in November 1957, making leader and follower samples noncomparable. However, comparisons between leaders and followers of the two parties can be made since they were roughly affected in the same way.

that on three other issues in this category (trade unions, credit, and tariffs), principle seems to be overweighed by old-fashioned economic considerations. In spite of their distaste for government interference in economic affairs, the Republicans almost unanimously favor greater regulation of trade unions and they are more strongly disposed than the Democrats toward government intervention to restrict credit and to raise tariffs. Of course, party cleavages over the credit and tariff issues have a long history, which may by now have endowed them with ideological force beyond immediate economic considerations. The preponderant Democratic preference for greater regulation of trade unions is doubtless a response to recent "exposures" of corrupt labor practices, though it may also signify that the party's perspective toward the trade unions is shifting somewhat.

The closer Republican identification with business, free enterprise, and economic conservatism in general, and the friendlier

Democratic attitude toward labor and toward government regulation of the economy, are easily observed in the data from other parts of our questionnaire. Republican leaders score very much higher than Democratic leaders on, for example, such scales as economic conservatism, independence of government, and business attitudes. On a question asking respondents to indicate the groups from which they would be most and least likely to take advice, 41 percent of the Democratic leaders but only 3.8 percent of the Republican leaders list trade unions as groups from which they would seek advice. Trade unions are scored in the "least likely" category by 25 percent of the Democrats and 63 percent of the Republicans. Similarly, more than 94 percent of the Republican leaders, but 56 percent of the Democratic leaders, name trade unions as groups that have "too much power." These differences, it should be noted, cannot be accounted for by reference to the greater number of trade union members among the Democratic party leadership, for in the 1956 conventions only 14 percent of the Democrats belonged to trade unions, and while an even smaller percentage (4 percent) of the Republicans were trade unionists, this disparity is hardly great enough to explain the large differences in outlook. The key to the explanation has to be sought in the symbolic and reference group identification of the two parties, and in their underlying values.

Nowhere do we see this more clearly than in the responses to the Equalitarian and Human Welfare issues. The mean difference in the ratio scores for the category as a whole is .22, a very large difference and one that results from differences in the expected direction on all six issues that make up the category. On four of these issues—federal aid to education, slum clearance and public housing, social security, and minimum wages—the leaders of the two parties are widely separated, the differences in their ratio scores ranging from .36 to .21. The

percentages showing the proportions who favor increased support for these issues are even more striking. In every instance the Democratic percentages are considerably higher: 66 *vs.* 22 percent (education); 78 *vs.* 40 percent (slum clearance and housing); 60 *vs.* 23 percent (social security); and 50 *vs.* 16 percent (minimum wages). The Democratic leaders also are better disposed than the Republican leaders toward immigration: twice as many of them (36 percent *vs.* 18 percent) favor a change in policy to permit more immigrants to enter. The over-all inclination of both party élites, however, is to accept the present levels of immigration, the Democratic ratio score falling slightly above, and the Republican slightly below, the midpoint.

More surprising are the differences on the segregation issue, for, despite strong Southern influence, the Democratic leaders express significantly more support for enforcing integration than the Republicans do. Moreover, the difference between the two parties rises from .12 for the national samples as a whole to a difference of .18 when the southern leaders are excluded. In his study of Congress, Turner found that the Republicans gave more support to Negro rights than the Democrats did. The reversal of this finding in our data does not necessarily mean that a change has occurred since Turner made his study, but only that the votes of the congressional parties do not always reflect the private feelings of the national party leadership. Then, too, Southern influence is disproportionately stronger in the Democratic congressional party than in the national Democratic organization as a whole, and disproportionately weaker in the Republican congressional party than in the Republican organization as a whole.

Examination of the actual magnitude of the ratio scores in this category reveals that the Republicans want not so much to abrogate existing social welfare or equalitarian measures as to keep them from being broadened. The Democrats, by comparison, are shown to be the party of social equality and reform, more willing than their opponents to employ legislation for the benefit of the underprivileged. Support for these inferences and for the greater liberalism of the Democrats can be found elsewhere in our data as well. Analysis of the scale results show Republican leaders scoring higher than Democratic leaders on such measures as chauvinism, élitism, conservatism, and right-wing values, and lower on tolerance, procedural rights, and faith in democracy. No differences worth noting, however, were found for ethnocentrism, faith in freedom, or the California F scale. The Democrats had a slightly higher average score on the left-wing scale, but the number of leaders in either party who scored high on this measure was fairly small.

The self-images and reference group identifications of the two parties also should be noted in this connection. For example, many more Democratic than Republican leaders call themselves liberal and state that they would be most likely to take advice from liberal reform organizations, the Farmers' Union, and (as we have seen) from the trade unions; only a small number consider themselves conservative or would seek advice from conservative reform organizations, the National Association of Manufacturers, or the Farm Bureau Federation. The Republicans have in almost all instances the reverse identifications: only a handful regard themselves as liberal or would seek counsel from liberal organizations, while more than 42 percent call themselves conservative and would look to the NAM or to conservative reform organizations for advice. Almost two-thirds of the Republicans (compared with 29 percent of the Democrats) regard the Chamber of Commerce as an important source of advice. Businessmen are listed as having "too much power" by 42 percent of the Democrats but by only 9 percent of the Republicans. The Democrats are also significantly more inclined than the Republicans to consider Catholics, Jews, and the foreign born as having "too little power." While self-descriptions and reference group identifications often correspond poorly with actual beliefs—among the general population they scarcely correspond at all, in fact—we are dealing, in the case of the leaders, with a politically informed and highly articulate set of people who have little difficulty connecting the beliefs they hold and the groups that promote or obstruct those beliefs.

Our fourth category, Tax Policy, divides the parties almost as severely as do the other categories. The mean difference for the category as a whole is .20, and it would doubtless have been larger but for the universal unpopularity of proposals to increase taxes on small and middle income groups. Table II-D shows that the differences between the parties on the tax issues follow the patterns previously observed and that tax policy is for the Democrats a device for redistributing income and promoting social equality. Neither party, however, is keen about raising taxes for *any* group: even the Democrats have little enthusiasm for new taxes on upper income groups or on business and corporate enterprises. The Republican leaders are overwhelmingly opposed to increased taxes for *any* group, rich *or* poor. This can be seen in their low ratio scores on the tax issues, which range from only .15 to .24. But while they are far more eager than the Democratic leaders to cut taxes on corporate and private wealth, they are less willing to reduce taxes on the lower income groups. These differences, it should be remarked, are not primarily a function of differences in the income of the two samples. Although there are more people with high incomes among the Republican leaders, the disproportion between the two samples is not nearly great enough to account for the dissimilarities in their tax views.

Of the five categories considered, Foreign Policy shows the smallest average difference, but even on these issues the divergence between Democratic and Republican leader attitudes is significant. Except for defense spending the Democrats turn out to be more internationalist than the Republicans, as evidenced in their greater commitment to the United Nations and to American participation in international military alliances like NATO. Twice as many Democrats as Republicans want the United States to rely more heavily upon such organizations, while many more Republicans want to reduce our international involvements. Both parties are predominantly in favor of cutting back foreign aid —a somewhat surprising finding in light of Democratic public pronouncements on this subject—but more Republicans feel strongly on the subject. Our data thus furnish little support for the claim that the parties hold the same views on foreign policy or that their seeming differences are merely a response to the demands of political competition.

Nevertheless, it would be incorrect to conclude that one party believes in internationalism and the other in isolationism. The differences are far too small to warrant any such inference. Traces of isolationism, to be sure, remain stronger in the Republican party than in the Democratic party—an observation buttressed by the finding that twice as many Republicans as Democrats score high on the isolationism scale. The pattern of Republican responses on both the issue and scale items signifies, however, that the leaders of that party generally accept the degree of "internationalism" now in effect, but shrink from extending it further. Consider too, the similarities in the leaders' scores on defense spending, for despite their greater leaning toward isolationism, the Republicans are no more inclined than the Democrats to leave the country defenseless.

In treating issues in the Elmira election study of 1948, Berelson, Lazarsfeld, and McPhee found it helpful to distinguish between "style" and "position" issues. "Style" issues principally yield symbolic, psychological, or subjective gratifications, and

have relatively intangible consequences; "position" issues reflect direct, personal and material interests, and have more objective consequences. According to the Elmira report, "position" issues (or what politicians might call "bread and butter" issues) divide voters more sharply than style issues. Most of the issues tested in the present study would have to be classified as "position" issues, but five of them—United Nations, international alliances, foreign aid, immigration, and segregation—could be classified as style issues. Four others— natural resources, atomic energy, education, and slum clearance—contain both symbolic and material elements and can best be described as "mixed."

Although the classification is crude, the findings it yields are generally consistent with the claims of the Elmira study. On the fourteen position issues—taxes, trade unions, tariffs, minimum wages, farm prices, social security, credit restrictions, and the regulation of business, public utilities and monopolies—Democratic and Republican leaders show an average ratio score difference of .21. On the style issues the two parties differ by .13—a significantly smaller difference. Largest of all, however, are the differences for the "mixed" issues, which average more than .30. This result should occasion little surprise, for when ideology and interest are *both* at work, partisanship is likely to be intensified. Several considerations could account for the superiority of position over style issues as causes of political cleavage: they are "bread and butter" issues, and are thus more often subject to pressure by organized interest groups; they have immediate and tangible consequences, which may lead politicians to pay greater attention to them than they do to issues whose payoff is more uncertain; and, finally, they are not so likely to be part of the common core of values upon which the community structure rests.

Comparison of the magnitude of the differences between groups can be seen in Table III, where we have ranked the issues,

TABLE III   Rank Order of Differences in the Support-Ratio Scores of Party Leaders and Followers*

Democratic vs. Republican Leaders	Diff. between Ratio Scores**	Democratic vs. Republican Followers	Diff. between Ratio Scores	Democratic Leaders vs. Followers	Diff. between Ratio Scores	Republican Leaders vs. Followers	Diff. between Ratio Scores
Issues		*Issues*		*Issues*		*Issues*	
1. Natural resources	+.39	Farm supports	+.14	Immigration	+.25	Fed. aid to edu.	−.39
2. Farm supports	+.38	Gov't reg. of business	+.12	Anti-monopoly	+.15	Taxes-large income	−.32
3. Fed. aid to edu.	+.37	Taxes-large income	+.10	Taxes-large income	−.15	Taxes-corp.	−.28
4. Taxes-corp.	+.33	Minimum wages	+.09	Taxes-business	−.13	Taxes-business	−.27
5. Reg.-business	+.33	Taxes-business	+.09	Reg. pub. util.	+.12	Natural resources	−.25
6. Taxes-large inc.	+.28	Reg. pub. util.	+.07	Tariffs	−.11	Pub. housing	−.23
7. Pub. housing	+.27	Taxes-corp.	+.07	Restrict. credit	−.09	Reg. business	−.22
8. Reg. pub. util.	+.26	Social security	+.07	Natural resources	+.09	Social security	−.22
9. Social security	+.23	Fed. aid to edu.	+.06	Fed. aid to edu.	−.08	Farm supports	−.22
10. Taxes-business	+.22	Reg. trade unions	−.05	Foreign aid	+.08	Minimum wages	−.18
11. Minimum wages	+.21	Natural resources	+.05	Reliance on U.N.	+.07	Reg. trade unions	+.17
12. Reliance on U.N.	+.21	Public housing	+.05	Minimum wages	−.05	Immigration	+.13
13. Anti-monopoly	+.20	Taxes-small income	−.04	Social security	−.05	Reliance on U.N.	−.12
14. Atomic energy control	+.18	American participation, NATO	+.04	Reg. trade unions	+.05	Enforce integration	−.12
15. Reg. trade unions	−.18	Atomic energy control	+.04	Atomic energy control	+.04	Taxes-middle income	−.11
16. American participation, NATO	+.13	Immigration	−.03	Farm supports	+.02	Atomic energy control	−.10
17. Enforce integration	+.12	Defense spending	+.02	Reg. business	−.02	American participation, NATO	−.10
18. Tariffs	−.11	Taxes-middle income	−.02	Enforce integration	+.01	Reg. public utilities	−.07
19. Foreign aid	+.10	Reliance on U.N.	+.02	Taxes-middle income	−.01	Anti-monopoly	−.04
20. Increase immigration	+.10	Tariffs	−.01	Taxes-corporation	−.01	Foreign aid	−.03
21. Taxes-small income	−.08	Enforce integration	−.01	Taxes-small income	−.01	Taxes-small income	+.03
22. Taxes-middle income	+.08	Restriction credit	+.01	American participation, NATO	−.01	Restriction credit	−.01
23. Restriction credit	−.07	Foreign aid	−.01	Public housing	.00	Tariffs	−.01
24. Defense spending	+.03	Anti-monopoly	.00	Defense spending	***	Defense spending	***

N's. Democratic Leaders: 1,788; Republican Leaders: 1,232; Democratic Followers: 821; Republican Followers: 623.

* The plus sign means that the first group listed in the heading is more favorable to the issue named than the second group; the minus sign means that the second group is the more favorable.

** Size of difference required for differences to be significant at .01 level: Democratic Leaders vs. Republican—.048; Democratic Followers vs. Republican Followers—.068; Democratic Leaders vs. Democratic Followers—.054; Republican Leaders vs. Republican Followers—.063.

*** Leaders and Followers cannot be compared on defense spending, for reasons given in footnote to Table II-E.

high to low, according to the size of the difference between the groups being compared. By presenting a rank-order of differences for the two leader groups, for the two follower groups, and for the leaders and followers of each party, this table makes it possible to observe not only which issues most and least divide the several party groups, but whether they divide the leaders and followers in the same way.

Notice that the issues commonly thought to be most divisive do not always evoke the greatest cleavage between the parties. Immigration, tariffs, civil rights, monopoly control, and credit regulation fall toward the lower end of the rank order, while farm supports, federal aid to education, slum clearance, social security, minimum wages, public housing, and issues dealing with the regulation and taxation of business fall toward the upper end. Though by no means uniformly, the older, more traditional issues appear to have been superseded as sources of controversy by issues that have come into prominence chiefly during the New Deal and Fair Deal.

IV. COMPARISONS BETWEEN FOLLOWERS

So far we have addressed ourselves to the differences between Democratic and Republican *leaders*. In each of the tables presented, however, data are included from which the two sets of party *followers* may also be compared.

The observation most clearly warranted from these data is that the rank and file members of the two parties are far less divided than their leaders. Not only do they diverge significantly on fewer issues—seven as compared with 23 for the leader samples —but the magnitudes of the differences in their ratio scores are substantially smaller for every one of the 24 issues. No difference is larger than .14, and on the majority of the issues the disparity is smaller than .05. Insofar as they differ at all, however, the followers tend to divide in a pattern similar to that shown by the leaders, the correlation between their rank orders being .72. All the issues on which the followers significantly disagree are of the "bread and butter" variety, the more symbolic issues being so remotely experienced and so vaguely grasped that rank and file voters are often unable to identify them with either party. Policies affecting farm prices, business regulation, taxes, or minimum wages, by contrast, are quickly felt by the groups to whom they are addressed and are therefore more capable of arousing partisan identifications. It should also be noted that while the average differences are small for all five categories, they are smallest of all for foreign policy—the most removed and least well understood group of issues in the entire array.[2]

Democratic and Republican followers were also compared on a number of scales and reference group questions. The results, while generally consistent with the differences between the leaders, show the followers to be far more united than their leaders on these measures as well. Even on business attitudes, independence of government, and economic conservatism, the differences are small and barely significant. No differences were found on such scales as tolerance, faith in democracy, procedural rights, conservatism-liberalism (classical), the California F scale and isolationism. The

[2] For comparative data on party affiliation and issue outlooks among rank and file voters, see Angus Campbell, Phillip E. Converse, Warren E. Miller, and Donald E. Stokes, *The American Voter* (New York: Wiley, 1960), esp. Chaps. 8 and 9 dealing with issues and ideology.

average Democrat is slightly more willing than the average Republican to label himself a liberal or to seek advice from liberal organizations; the contrary is true when it comes to adopting conservative identifications. Only in the differential trust they express toward business and labor are the two sets of followers widely separated.

These findings give little support to the claim that the "natural divisions" of the electorate are being smothered by party leaders. Not only do the leaders disagree more sharply than their respective followers, but the level of consensus among the electorate (with or without regard to party) is fairly high. Inspection of the "increase" and "decrease" percentage scores (Tables II-A-E) shows that substantial differences of opinion exist among the electorate on only five of the 24 issues (credit restrictions, farm supports, segregation, and corporate and business taxes). Of course, voters may divide more sharply on issues at election time, since campaigns intensify party feeling and may also intensify opinions on issues. Available data from election studies allow no unequivocal conclusion on this point, but even the party-linked differences found among voters during elections may largely be echoes of the opinions announced by the candidates—transient sentiments developed for the occasion and quickly forgotten.

V. LEADER CONFLICT AND FOLLOWER CONSENSUS: EXPLANATIONS

Considering the nature of the differences between the leader and follower samples, the interesting question is not why the parties fail to represent the "natural division" in the electorate (for that question rests on an unwarranted assumption) but why the party élites disagree at all, and why they divide so much more sharply than their followers?

Despite the great pressures toward uniformity we have noted in American society, many forces also divide the population culturally, economically, and politically. The United States is, after all, a miscellany of ethnic and religious strains set down in a geographically large and diverse country. Many of these groups brought old conflicts and ideologies with them, and some have tried to act out in the new world the hopes and frustrations nurtured in the old. Then, too, despite rapid social mobility, social classes have by no means been eliminated. No special political insight is needed to perceive that the two parties characteristically draw from different strata of the society, the Republicans from the managerial, proprietary, and to some extent professional classes, the Democrats from labor, minorities, low income groups, and a large proportion of the intellectuals. Partly because the leaders of the two parties tend to overrespond to the modal values of the groups with which they are principally identified, they gradually grow further apart on the key questions which separate their respective supporters. The Republican emphasis on business ideology is both a cause and a consequence of its managerial and proprietary support; the greater Democratic emphasis on social justice, and on economic and social levelling, is both the occasion and the product of the support the party enjoys among intellectuals and the lower strata. These interrelationships are strengthened, moreover, by the tendency for a party's dominant supporters to gain a disproportionate number of positions in its leadership ranks.

The differences which typically separate Democratic from Republican leaders seem also to reflect a deep-seated ideological cleavage often found among Western parties. One side of this cleavage is marked by a strong belief in the power of collective action to promote social justice, equality, humanitarianism, and economic planning, while preserving freedom; the other is distinguished by faith in the wisdom of the natural competitive process and in the supreme virtue of individualism, "char-

acter," self-reliance, frugality, and independence from government. To this cleavage is added another frequent source of political division, namely, a difference in attitude toward change between "radicals" and "moderates," between those who prefer to move quickly or slowly, to reform or to conserve. These differences in social philosophy and posture do not always coincide with the divisions in the social structure, and their elements do not, in all contexts, combine in the same way. But, however crudely, the American parties do tend to embody these competing points of view and to serve as reference groups for those who hold them.

Party cleavage in America was no doubt intensified by the advent of the New Deal, and by its immense electoral and intellectual success. Not only did it weld into a firm alliance the diverse forces that were to be crucial to all subsequent Democratic majorities, but it also made explicit the doctrines of the "welfare state" with which the party was henceforth to be inseparably identified. Because of the novelty of its program and its apparently radical threat to the familiar patterns of American political and economic life, it probably deepened the fervor of its Republican adversaries and drove into the opposition the staunchest defenders of business ideology. The conflict was further sharpened by the decline of left-wing politics after the war, and by the transfer of loyalties of former and potential radicals to the Democratic party. Once launched, the cleavage has been sustained by the tendency for each party to attract into its active ranks a disproportionate number of voters who recognize and share its point of view.

Why, however, are the leaders so much more sharply divided than their followers? The reasons are not hard to understand and are consistent with several of the hypotheses that underlay the present study.

1. Consider, to begin with, that the leaders come from the more articulate segments

of society and, on the average, are politically more aware than their followers and far better informed about issues. For them, political issues and opinions are the everyday currency of party competition, not esoteric matters that surpass understanding. With their greater awareness and responsibility, and their greater need to defend their party's stands, they have more interest in developing a consistent set of attitudes—perhaps even an ideology. The followers of each party, often ignorant of the issues and their consequences, find it difficult to distinguish their beliefs from those of the opposition and have little reason to be concerned with the consistency of their attitudes. Furthermore, the American parties make only a feeble effort to educate the rank and file politically, and since no central source exists for the authoritative pronouncement of party policy, the followers often do not know what their leaders believe or on what issues the parties chiefly divide. In short, if we mean by ideology a coherent body of informed social doctrine, it is possessed mainly by the articulate leadership, rarely by the masses.

2. Differences in the degree of partisan involvement parallel the differences in knowledge and have similar consequences. The leaders, of course, have more party spirit than the followers and, as the election studies make plain, the stronger the partisanship, the larger the differences on issues. The leaders are more highly motivated not only to belong to a party appropriate to their beliefs, but to accept its doctrines and to learn how it differs from the opposition party. Since politics is more salient for leaders than for followers, they develop a greater stake in the outcome of the political contest and are more eager to discover the intellectual grounds by which they hope to make victory possible. Through a process of circular re-

inforcement, those for whom politics is most important are likely to become the most zealous participants, succeeding to the posts that deal in the formation of opinion. Ideology serves the instrumental purpose, in addition, of justifying the heavy investment that party leaders make in political activity. While politics offers many rewards, it also makes great demands on the time, money, and energies of its practitioners—sacrifices which they can more easily justify if they believe they are serving worthwhile social goals. The followers, in contrast, are intellectually far less involved, have less personal stake in the outcome of the competition, have little need to be concerned with the "correctness" of their views on public questions, and have even less reason to learn in precisely what ways their opinions differ from their opponents'. Hence, the party élites recruit members from a population stratified in some measure by ideology, while the rank and file renews itself by more random recruitment and is thus more likely to mirror the opinions of a cross section of the population.

3. Part of the explanation for the greater consensus among followers than leaders resides in the nature and size of the two types of groups. Whereas the leader groups are comparatively small and selective, each of the follower groups number in the millions and, by their very size and unwieldiness, are predisposed to duplicate the characteristics of the population as a whole. Even if the Republicans draw disproportionately from the business-managerial classes and the Democrats from the trade union movement, neither interest group has enough influence to shape distinctively the aggregate opinions of so large a mass of supporters. Size also affects the nature and frequency of interaction within the two types of groups. Because they comprise a smaller, more selectively chosen, organized, and articulate élite, the leaders

are apt to associate with people of their own political persuasion more frequently and consistently than the followers do. They are not only less cross-pressured than the rank and file but they are also subjected to strong party group efforts to induce them to conform. Because their political values are continually renewed through frequent communication with people of like opinions, and because they acquire intense reference group identifications, they develop an extraordinary ability to resist the force of the opposition's arguments. While the followers, too, are thrown together and shielded to some extent, they are likely to mingle more freely with people of hostile political persuasions, to receive fewer partisan communications, and to hold views that are only intermittently and inconsistently reinforced. Since, by comparison with the leaders, they possess little interest in or information about politics, they can more easily embrace "deviant" attitudes without discomfort and without challenge from their associates. Nor are they likely to be strongly rewarded for troubling to have "correct" opinions. The followers, in short, are less often and less effectively indoctrinated than their leaders. The group processes described here would function even more powerfully in small, sectarian, tightly organized parties of the European type, but they are also present in the American party system, where they yield similar though less potent consequences.

4. Political competition itself operates to divide the leaders more than the followers. If the parties are impelled to present a common face to the electorate, they are also strongly influenced to distinguish themselves from each other. For one thing, they have a more heightened sense of the "national interest" than the followers do, even if they do not all conceive it in the same way. For another, they hope to improve their chances at the polls by offering the electorate a

recognizable and attractive commodity. In addition, they seek emotional gratification in the heightened sense of brotherhood brought on by the struggle against an "out-group" whose claim to office seems always, somehow, to border upon usurpation. As with many ingroup-outgroup distinctions, the participants search for moral grounds to justify their antagonisms toward each other, and ideologies help to furnish such grounds. Among the followers, on the other hand, these needs exist, if at all, in much weaker form.

VI. LEADERS VERSUS FOLLOWERS

In comparing each party élite with its own followers we were mainly interested in seeing how closely each body of supporters shared the point of view of its leaders, in order to test the hypothesis that party affiliation, even for the rank and file, is a function of ideological agreement. In predicting that the parties would tend to attract supporters who share their beliefs, we expected, of course, to find exceptions. We knew that many voters pay little attention to the ideological aspects of politics and that, in Gabriel Almond's phrase, a party's more "esoteric doctrines" are not always known to its followers. Nevertheless we were not prepared for the findings turned up by this phase of the inquiry, for the differences between leaders and followers—among the Republicans at least—are beyond anything we had expected. Indeed, the conclusion is inescapable that the views of the Republican rank and file are, on the whole, much closer to those of the Democratic leaders than to those of the Republican leaders. Although conflicts in outlook also exist between Democratic leaders and followers, they are less frequent or severe.

If we turn once again to the table of rank order differences, we see that the Democratic followers differ significantly from their leaders on twelve of the 23 issues, and that the average difference in the ratio scores of the two samples is .07. Democratic leaders and Republican followers differ significantly on only eleven of the 23 issues, with an average difference between them of only .08. Notice, by contrast, that Republican leaders and followers diverge significantly on 18 of the 23 issues, and show an average difference of .16. To complete the comparison, the Republican leaders and Democratic followers were in disagreement on 19 of the 23 issues, their average difference being .20. As these comparisons make plain, there is substantial consensus on national issues between Democratic leaders and Democratic and Republican followers, while the Republican leaders are separated not only from the Democrats but from their own rank and file members as well.

Examination of the Democratic scores shows the leaders to be slightly more "progressive" than their followers on most of the issues on which differences appear. The leaders are, for example, more favorable to public ownership of natural resources, to regulation of monopolies and public utilities, to a reduction of tariffs, and to a liberalized credit policy. They are more internationalist on the foreign aid and United Nations issues and substantially more sympathetic to the maintenance and expansion of immigration. The results showing the relative radicalism of the two samples are not unequivocal, however, for on several issues—federal aid to education, minimum wages, and taxes on business enterprise and large incomes—the followers take the more radical view. Nor are the differences significant on such issues as atomic energy, slum clearance, segregation, farm price supports, government control of business and trade unions, and taxes on middle and small income groups. In general, the followers turn out more radical chiefly on a few of the bread and butter issues—a reflection, no doubt, of their lower socio-economic status. When we control for occupation, the differences between Democratic leaders and followers on these issues largely disappear.

Consideration of the scores of Republican leaders and followers shows not only that they are widely separated in their outlooks but also that the leaders are uniformly more conservative than their followers. Only on the immigration issue is this trend reversed. The followers hold the more "radical" ideas on the two public ownership issues, on five of the six equalitarian and human welfare issues, on four of the seven regulation-of-the-economy issues, and on four of the five tax policy issues. They are also more willing to place greater reliance upon the U.N. and upon international military alliances. Observe that the largest differences occur on those issues which have most sharply separated New Deal-Fair Deal spokesmen from the hard core of the Republican opposition—federal aid to education, redistribution of wealth through taxes on business, corporations and the wealthy, public ownership of natural resources, public housing, regulation of business, social security, farm price supports, minimum wages, and trade union regulations.

In short, whereas Republican leaders hold to the tenets of business ideology and remain faithful to the spirit and intellectual mood of leaders like Robert A. Taft, the rank and file Republican supporters have embraced, along with their Democratic brethren, the regulatory and social reform measures of the Roosevelt and Truman administrations. This inference receives further support from the scores on our Party Ideology scale where, on a variety of attitudes and values which characteristically distinguish the leaders of the two parties, the Republican followers fall closer to the Democratic than to the Republican side of the continuum. Thus, in addition to being the preferred party of the more numerous classes, the Democrats also enjoy the advantages over their opponents of holding views that are more widely shared throughout the country.

Assuming the findings are valid, we were obviously wrong to expect that party differentiation among followers would depend heavily upon ideological considerations. Evidently, party attachment is so much a function of other factors (*e.g.* class and primary group memberships, religious affiliation, place of residence, mass media, etc.) that many voters can maintain their party loyalties comfortably even while holding views that contradict the beliefs of their own leaders.

Still, we are not entitled to conclude that issue outlook has no effect on the party affiliation of ordinary members. It is conceivable, for example, that the Republican party has come to be the minority party partly because the opinions of its spokesmen are uncongenial to a majority of the voters. We have no way of knowing from our data —collected at only a single point in time— how many "normally" Republican voters, if any, have defected to the Democrats or fled into independency because they disapprove of Republican beliefs. At the present stage of the analysis, we have no grounds for going beyond the proposition that political affiliation without conformity on issues is possible on a wide scale. In future analyses we shall attempt to learn more about the nature of the relationship between belief and party affiliation by stratifying voters according to the frequency with which they conform to the beliefs of their party leaders. We hope, in this way, to discover whether those who conform least are also less firm in their party loyalties.

VII. THE HOMOGENEITY
OF SUPPORT
FOR LEADERS AND FOLLOWERS

So far we have only considered conflict and agreement *between* groups. We should now turn to the question of consensus *within* groups. To what extent is each of our samples united on fundamental issues?

In order to assess homogeneity of opinion within party groups, standard deviation scores were computed on each issue for each of the four samples. The higher the standard deviation, of course, the greater the disagreement. The range of possible sigma scores is from 0 (signifying that every member of the sample has selected the same response) to .500 (signifying that all responses are equally divided between the "increase" and "decrease" alternatives). If we assume that the three alternative responses had been randomly (and therefore equally) selected, the standard deviations for the four samples would fall by chance alone around .410. Scores at or above this level may be taken to denote extreme dispersion among the members of a sample while scores in the neighborhood of .300 or below suggest that unanimity within the sample is fairly high. By these somewhat arbitrary criteria we can observe immediately (Table IV) that consensus within groups is greater on most issues than we would expect by chance alone, but that it is extremely high in only a few instances. Although the Republican leaders appear on the average to be the most united and the Democratic leaders the least united of the four groups, the difference between their homogeneity scores (.340 vs. .310) is too small to be taken as conclusive. The grounds are somewhat better for rejecting the belief that leaders are more homogeneous in their outlooks than their followers, since the hypothesis holds only for one party and not for the other.

While generalizations about the relative unity of the four samples seem risky, we can speak more confidently about the rank order of agreement *within* samples. In Table IV we have ranked the issues according to the degree of consensus exhibited toward them by the members of each of the four party groups. There we see that the leaders of the Republican party are most united on the issues that stem from its connections with business—government regulation of business, taxes (especially on business), regulation of trade unions, and minimum wages. The Democratic leaders are most united on those issues which bear

**TABLE IV   Consensus within Party Groups: Rank Order
of Homogeneity of Support on Twenty-four Issues**

Average Rank Order*	Issue	Democratic Leaders		Republican Leaders		Democratic Followers		Republican Followers	
		Rank Order	Sigma	Rank Order	Sigma	Rank Order	Sigma	Rank Order	Sigma
1	Tax on small incomes	1	.220	6	.270	1	.224	1	.250
2	Tax on middle incomes	3	.276	4	.248	6	.292	2	.278
3	Social security benefits	5	.282	8	.296	2	.266	3	.286
4	Minimum wages	6	.292	5	.268	4	.276	4	.294
5	Enforcement of anti-monopoly	2	.246	13	.321	8	.324	7	.314
6	Regulation of public utilities	8	.307	10	.300	10	.336	5.5	.310
7	Slum clearance	4	.276	23	.386	3	.274	5.5	.310
8	Regulation of trade unions	12	.356	3	.240	9	.331	15	.345
9	Government regulation of business	17	.376	1	.192	20	.363	8	.315
10	Tax on business	9	.338	2	.236	19	.362	16	.348
11	Level of tariffs	10	.350	16	.344	11	.338	9	.316
12	Public control of atomic energy	7	.302	20	.362	7	.312	13	.340
13	Federal aid to education	13	.360	24	.394	5	.283	11	.322
14	Foreign aid	19	.383	12	.317	12.5	.340	12	.340
15	Tax on large incomes	11	.356	9	.298	17	.358	22	.379
16	American participation in military alliances, NATO	14	.370	18	.351	14	.350	14	.344
17	Immigration into U.S.	21	.399	17	.345	12.5	.340	10	.318
18	Corporate income tax	16	.375	7	.284	21	.371	17	.361
19	Restrictions on credit	22	.400	14	.324	16	.358	18	.362
20	Defense spending	15	.371	15	.334	22	.380	21	.366
21	Public ownership of natural resources	20	.393	19	.354	15	.352	19	.362
22	Reliance on U.N.	18	.380	22	.384	18	.359	20	.365
23	Level of farm supports	24	.421	11	.306	23	.414	23	.397
24	Enforce integration	23	.416	21	.382	24	.418	24	.399

* The range of sigma scores is from .192 to .421, out of a possible range of .000 (most united) to .500 (least united). Hence, the lower the rank order the greater the unity on the issue named.

upon the support the party receives from the lower and middle income groups— taxes on small and middle incomes, anti-monopoly, slum clearance, social security, and minimum wages. The Republican leaders divide most severely on federal aid to education, slum clearance, U.N. support, segregation, and public control of atomic energy and natural resources; the Democratic leaders are most divided on farm prices, segregation, credit restrictions, immigration, and the natural resources issue.

Among the followers the patterns of unity and division are very similar, as attested by the high correlation of .83 between the rank orders of their homogeneity scores. Both Republican and Democratic followers exhibit great cohesion, for example, on taxes on small and middle incomes, social security, slum clearance, and minimum wages. Both divide rather sharply on segregation, farm price supports, defense spending, U.N. support, and taxes on large incomes. The two sets of followers, in short, are alike not only in their opinions on issues but in the degree of unanimity they exhibit toward them.

Inspection of the homogeneity data furnishes additional evidence on the between-group comparisons made earlier. Whereas Democratic and Republican followers divide on issues in approximately the same way, the two sets of leaders differ from each other in this respect also (the correlation between their rank orders on homogeneity is only .28). Democratic leaders and followers tend to unite or divide on the same issues for the most part (r equals .77), but Republican leaders and followers are not parallel in this respect either (r equals .30). The pattern of homogeneity and dispersion among Republican followers is, in fact, much closer to that of the Democratic leaders (r equals .75).

In computing scores for homogeneity we were in part concerned to test the belief that political parties develop greatest internal solidarity on those questions which most separate them from their opponents. According to this hypothesis, external controversy has the effect of uniting the members further by confronting them with a common danger. Whether or not this hypothesis would be borne out in a study of small, sectarian parties we cannot say, but it receives no support from the present study of the American mass parties. Comparisons of the rank order data in Tables III and IV show that there is no consistent connection between inter-party conflict and intra-party cohesion. The correlations between the rank orders of difference and the rank orders of homogeneity are in every case insignificant.

SUMMARY AND CONCLUSIONS

The research described in this paper—an out-growth of a nationwide inquiry into the nature and sources of political affiliation, activity, and belief—was principally designed to test a number of hypotheses about the relation of ideology to party membership. Responses from large samples of Democratic and Republican leaders and followers were compared on twenty-four key issues and on a number of attitude questions and scales. Statistical operations were carried out to assess conflict and consensus among party groups and to estimate the size and significance of differences. From the data yielded by this inquiry, the following inferences seem most warranted:

1. Although it has received wide currency, especially among Europeans, the belief that the two American parties are identical in principle and doctrine has little foundation in fact. Examination of the opinions of Democratic and Republican leaders shows them to be distinct communities of co-believers who diverge sharply on many important issues. Their disagreements, furthermore, conform to an image familiar to many observers and are generally consistent with differences turned up by studies of Congressional roll calls. The unpopularity of many of the positions held by Republican leaders suggests also that the parties submit to the demands of their constituents less slavishly than is commonly supposed.

2. Republican and Democratic leaders stand furthest apart on the issues that grow out of their group identification and support—out of the managerial, proprietary, and high-status connections of the one, and the labor, minority, low-status, and intellectual connections of the other. The opinions of each party élite are linked less by chance than by membership in a common ideological domain. Democratic leaders typically display the stronger urge to elevate the low-born, the uneducated, the deprived minorities, and the poor in general; they are also more disposed to employ the nation's collective power to advance humanitarian and social welfare goals (*e.g.*, social security, immigration, racial

integration, a higher minimum wage, and public education). They are more critical of wealth and big business and more eager to bring them under regulation. Theirs is the greater faith in the wisdom of using legislation for redistributing the national product and for furnishing social services on a wide scale. Of the two groups of leaders, the Democrats are the more "progressively" oriented toward social reform and experimentation. The Republican leaders, while not uniformly differentiated from their opponents, subscribe in greater measure to the symbols and practices of individualism, *laissez-faire,* and national independence. They prefer to overcome humanity's misfortunes by relying upon personal effort, private incentives, frugality, hard work, responsibility, self-denial (for both men and government), and the strengthening rather than the diminution of the economic and status distinctions that are the "natural" rewards of the differences in human character and fortunes. Were it not for the hackneyed nature of the designation and the danger of forcing traits into a mold they fit only imperfectly, we might be tempted to describe the Republicans as the chief upholders of what Max Weber has called the "Protestant Ethic."[3] Not that the Democrats are insensible to the "virtues" of the Protestant-capitalistic ethos, but they embrace them less firmly or uniformly. The differences between the two élites have probably been intensified by the rise of the New Deal and by the shift of former radicals into the Democratic party following the decline of socialist and other left-wing movements during and after the war.

3. Whereas the leaders of the two parties diverge strongly, their followers differ only moderately in their attitudes toward issues. The hypothesis that party beliefs

[3] Max Weber, *Protestant Ethic and the Spirit of Capitalism* (London, 1948), Chap. V.

unite adherents and bring them into the party ranks may hold for the more active members of a mass party but not for its rank and file supporters. Republican followers, in fact, disagree far more with their own leaders than with the leaders of the Democratic party. Little support was found for the belief that deep cleavages exist among the electorate but are ignored by the leaders. One might, indeed more accurately, assert the contrary, to wit: that the natural cleavages between the leaders are largely ignored by the voters. However, we cannot presently conclude that ideology exerts no influence over the habits of party support, for the followers do differ significantly and in the predicted directions on some issues. Furthermore, we do not know how many followers may previously have been led by doctrinal considerations to shift their party allegiances.

4. Except for their desire to ingratiate themselves with as many voters as possible, the leaders of the two parties have more reason than their followers to hold sharply opposing views on the important political questions of the day. Compared with the great mass of supporters, they are articulate, informed, highly partisan, and involved; they comprise a smaller and more tightly knit group which is closer to the well-springs of party opinion, more accessible for indoctrination, more easily rewarded or punished for conformity or deviation, and far more affected, politically and psychologically, by engagement in the party struggle for office. If the leaders of the two parties are not always candid about their disagreements, the reason may well be that they sense the great measure of consensus to be found among the electorate.

5. Finding that party leaders hold contrary beliefs does not prove that they *act* upon those beliefs or that the two parties are, in practice, governed by different outlooks. In a subsequent paper we shall

consider these questions more directly by comparing platform and other official party pronouncements with the private opinions revealed in this study. Until further inquiries are conducted, however, it seems reasonable to assume that the views held privately by party leaders can never be entirely suppressed but are bound to crop out in hundreds of large and small ways—in campaign speeches, discussions at party meetings, private communications to friends and sympathizers, statements to the press by party officials and candidates, legislative debates, and public discussions on innumerable national, state, and local questions. If, in other words, the opinions of party leaders are as we described them, there is every chance that they are expressed and acted upon to some extent. Whether this makes our parties "ideological" depends, of course, on how narrowly we define that term. Some may prefer to reserve that designation for parties that are more obviously preoccupied with doctrine, more intent upon the achievement of a systematic political program, and more willing to enforce a common set of beliefs upon their members and spokesmen.

6. The parties are internally united on some issues, divided on others. In general, Republican leaders achieve greatest homogeneity on issues that grow out of their party's identification with business, Democratic leaders on issues that reflect their connection with liberal and lower-income groups. We find no support for the hypothesis that the parties achieve greatest internal consensus on the issues which principally divide them from their opponents. . . .

Thus, the parties must be considered not merely as spokesmen for other interest groups but as reference groups in their own right, helping to formulate, to sustain, and to speak for a recognizable point of view.

STATE AND LOCAL PARTY SYSTEMS

5.   Interparty Competition, Economic Variables, and Welfare Policies in the American States

Richard E. Dawson and James A. Robinson

The American states differ in their politics. Competition ranges from the apparently monolithic one-party systems of the South to the intensely competitive states of the West. The states also vary in the services and welfare benefits they provide for their citizens. In this article, Richard Dawson of Washington University and James Robinson of The Ohio State University analyze various measures of party competition. They question the hypothesis that welfare benefits are greater in areas of greater partisan conflict and suggest that "external conditions" such as wealth, urbanization, and industrialization are more significant factors in determining welfare programs.

* * *

I. INTRODUCTION

The object of this paper is to discover the relationship among the extent of interparty competition, the presence of certain economic factors, and the extent of nine public welfare policies, using the American

From the *Journal of Politics*, vol. 25, no. 2 (May 1963), pp. 265–287, by permission of the Southern Political Science Association.

states as the units for investigation. The fifty states share similar institutions and a similar cultural history, but they differ with respect to economic and social conditions, political activity, and public policy. Therefore, they provide a large number of political and social units in which some important variables can be held constant while others are varied.

Our primary concern is the relation between political processes and the policies adopted by political systems. In this study, public policies, or more particularly, social welfare policies of the various state political systems, are the dependent variables. Public policy, its formulation, implementation and effects, is one of the major interests of students of politics. Political science is concerned with ways in which formal and informal institutions, and economic, social, philosophical and geographic conditions influence the adoption and implementation of policy.[1] For purposes of clarity it seems useful to place the problem of the relationship between party competition and welfare policies within a larger context of political studies.[2]

We begin with the assumption that public policy is the major dependent variable that political science seeks to explain. The task of political science, then, is to find and explain the independent and intervening variables that account for policy differences. The major categories of political theory might be portrayed in this manner:

Moving from left to right, this diagram assumes that a variety of external conditions (external, that is, to boundaries of the political system) influence the development of different types of political systems. Process, as activity and interaction between the variables and parts of that system, in turn gives rise to the formulation and implementation of public policies. Policy, in this context, is the outcome of activity or interaction among external conditions, political system, and political process. As the outer solid arrows indicate, external variables and system variables might also affect policy directly, without being mediated by process variables. Likewise external variables may directly influence process without being specifically influenced by system variables. We assume that the most likely mechanism of development is that in which external conditions and system are mediated by process, and that external conditions are mediated by both system and process, and that external conditions are mediated by both system and process as they influence policy outcomes. As the broken-lines suggest, policy outcomes also may influence the

[1] For discussions of the use of the concept policy as a focus for research in political science, see: David Easton, *The Political System* (New York: Alfred A. Knopf, 1953), esp. pp. 125–148; Charles S. Hyneman, *The Study of Politics* (Urbana: University of Illinois Press, 1959), esp. pp. 101–108 and 165–173; Harold D. Lasswell, "The Policy Orientation," in *The Policy Sciences* (eds.) Daniel Lerner and Harold Lasswell, (Stanford, California: Stanford University Press, 1951), pp. 3–15; and James A. Robinson, "The Major Problems of Political Science," in *Politics and Public Affairs*, (ed.) L. K. Caldwell. (Bloomington, Indiana: Institute of Training for Public Service, Indiana University, 1962), pp. 161–188.

[2] Robinson, *loc. cit.*

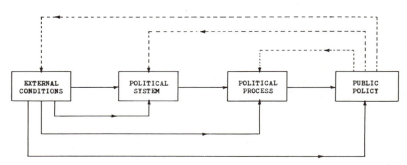

other variables. One would expect policy outcomes to affect the external conditions of one point in time, which would then act on future policy outcomes.[3]

Because the terms political system, political process, and public policy have been used in different ways, it might be useful to designate more specifically what we mean by them in this context, although this is obviously not the occasion for resolving the argument about what uses are universally appropriate. The term system refers to an integrated group of interacting elements designated jointly to perform a given function.[4] *Political system* refers to that group of related variables whose task is the authoritative allocation of values for a given society; the search for typologies of political systems is a continuing occupation of political science.[5] *Process* refers to the activity within the system, the inter-action of the system's sub-variables and sub-components, throughout a period of time; types of policy processes include bargaining, hierarchy, polyarchy, and the price system.[6] *Policy* consists of the *goals* (objectives of or commitments made by the political system), the *means* by which they may be implemented and the *consequences* of those means.[7] As such, public policies are the chief output of the political system and constitute the allocation of values for the society.

When our study is put in this context it will be clear that we are primarily concerned with whether differences in policy are related to differences in process, holding system variables constant. More specifically, we want to discover whether differences in

social welfare policies are related to a particular political process within these systems, namely, the degree of inter-party competition.

By using the American states we are able to hold many of the most important system characteristics constant. It would obviously be erroneous to say that the states are exactly alike in all respects, but in fundamental formal structure the forty-six states that we consider are very similar.[8] They have written constitutions, with authority divided among legislative and judicial branches. They have bicameral legislatures, and except in North Carolina, the governor participates in the legislative process through the potential use of the veto. The state constitutions contain a bill of rights similar to the first ten amendments to the United States Constitution, and the highest court has the right of judicial review. Although other details of political organization, structure and process within the systems vary from state to state, the basic institutions are remarkably similar. Thus, by using the American states as units of analysis we can hold the basic system variables constant, concentrating attention on the relations between process and policy.

However, the external socio-economic conditions within which these state systems operate vary markedly. Wealth, the per cent of population living in urban areas, and the per cent of residents engaged in industrial, professional and commercial occupations, as well as the complex of social, economic and ideological factors that surround these conditions, are not the same in all of the states. For example, the per capita income of Connecticut ($2,817) is nearly three times that of Mississippi ($1,053). To further illustrate, the per cent of residents living in urban areas ranges from 86.6 in

[3] Harry Eckstein, *Pressure Group Politics: The Case of the British Medical Association* (London: Allen and Unwin, 1960), p. 8.

[4] Easton, *op. cit.*, p. 129.

[5] See James S. Coleman, "The Political Systems of the Developing Areas," in Gabriel Almond and James S. Coleman, *The Politics of the Developing Areas* (Princeton: Princeton University Press, 1960), pp. 532–576.

[6] Robert A. Dahl and Charles E. Lindblom, *Politics, Economics and Welfare* (New York: Harper & Brothers, 1953).

[7] Robinson, *loc. cit.*, p. 169.

[8] Forty-six of the fifty states are used. Alaska and Hawaii are omitted because they were states for only part of the twenty year period considered. Nebraska is left out for two reasons: it does not have a bicameral legislature, and its legislature is elected on a non-partisan basis. Minnesota is also excluded because its legislature is non-partisan.

New Jersey to 26.6 in North Dakota.[9] The relations between socio-economic conditions and political systems, process and public policy has long been of concern to the student of politics.[10] Golembiewski, in a recent study of the relations between a group of "sociological factors" and state political party strength, reports significant statistical relationships between variables such as per cent of population urban, population density, per cent of Negroes in the population, median income and industrialization on the one hand and classifications of party competition on the other.[11]

Although the concept process has long been widely used in the study of politics, little research on the relation between process variables and types of public policy has been undertaken. In recent years interest has increased in how processes within organizations affect policy.[12] Two studies formulated hypotheses regarding the influence of process upon policy in the relations between inter- or intra-party competition and the adoption of welfare policies. Key offered several hypotheses concerning the differences in public welfare policies in states with loose multifactional one-party systems and in states with two cohesive factions competing in a one-party system.[13] He found that southern states with loose multifactional systems, in which the coherence and continuity of competition is less, tend to pursue more conservative policies, *i.e.*, policies favorable to the interest of the upper socio-economic groups or the "haves." In states with competition between two cohesive and enduring factions, more liberal policies are adopted, *i.e.*, policies more responsive to the interests, needs and/or desires of the "have nots." Lockard expanded on the work of Key and asked: "How much difference does it make in the long run whether a state has a set of competitive parties or whether one-party dominance prevails?"[14] He divided the six New England states into one-party (Maine, New Hampshire and Vermont) and two-party states (Massachusetts, Rhode Island and Connecticut) and found that the two-party states receive a larger portion of their revenue from business and death taxes; spend more money for services such as aid to the blind, old-age assistance, and aid to dependent children; and are less likely to have legislative apportionment schemes that favor small minorities, especially certain economic interest groups.[15]

Our study expands the hypotheses of Key and Lockard concerning party competition and welfare policies, testing them with a larger number of states and policies, and applying slightly more rigorous statistical techniques. Our initial hypothesis can be briefly stated: *The greater the degree of inter-party competition within a political system, the more liberal the social welfare measures that system will adopt.* After testing this hypothesis, we shall consider whether a state's economic condition is more closely related to its liberalism than is inter-party competition.

---

[9] United States Department of Commerce, Bureau of the Census, *Statistical Abstract of the United States: 1960* (Washington: U.S. Government Printing Office, 1960), p. 312. United States Department of Commerce, Bureau of the Census, *Census of Population: 1950, Vol. I*, (Washington: U.S. Government Printing Office, 1952), Part I, pp. 18–23.

[10] See, for instance: Aristotle, *Politics*, translated by Benjamin Jowett, (New York: Random House, Inc. 1943), esp. Books IV and V; Dahl and Lindblom, *op. cit.*, and Seymour Martin Lipset, *Political Man* (Garden City, New York: Doubleday & Company, 1960), esp. Chapter II, "Economic Development and Democracy."

[11] Robert T. Golembiewski, "A Taxonomic Approach to State Political Party Strength," *The Western Political Quarterly*, XI (1958), pp. 494–513.

[12] *E.g.*, James A. Robinson, *Congress and Foreign Policy-making* (Homewood, Illinois: The Dorsey Press, 1962), pp. 168–190; Robinson, *The House Rules Committee* (Indianapolis: Bobbs-Merrill Co., 1963), pp. 57–109.

[13] V. O. Key, Jr., *Southern Politics in State and*

Nation (New York: Alfred A. Knopf, 1951), esp. pp. 298–314.

[14] Duane Lockard, *New England State Politics* (Princeton, New Jersey: The Princeton University Press, 1959), pp. 320–340.

[15] *Ibid.*, pp. 326–337.

II. INTER-PARTY COMPETITION

The familiar classification of party systems into one-, two-, and multi-party types is inadequate for American state parties.[16] As Ranney and Kendall point out, this simple three-category scheme classifies Mississippi and the Soviet Union as one-party systems. But the party systems of these two political units differ in certain vital respects. "Opposition candidates can (and sometimes do) oppose candidates of the dominant party in Mississippi. They can not (and do not) in the Soviet Union. So the question arises whether any useful purpose can be served by continuing to call them both 'one-party systems.' "[17] Even if totalitarian one-party systems were excluded, difficulties would remain in using this classification scheme. Because of Republican dominance in Vermont and New Hampshire and Democratic dominance in Mississippi and South Carolina, all four of these political party systems are often lumped together as one-party systems. This classification, however, overlooks significant differences be-

tween the inter-party competition found in South Carolina and that in New Hampshire. Although the Republicans nearly always win the major offices in New Hampshire, the opposition almost always runs a candidate who polls from 30 to 49 per cent of the vote. In South Carolina, on the contrary, the minority party seldom runs a candidate, and when it does, he ordinarily polls a mere 5 to 20 per cent of the vote. Lumping the states together encourages a disregard for certain important differences between these states.

To meet these problems, Ranney and Kendall, Key, and Golembiewski devised other classifications. Ranney and Kendall divide American systems into the multi-party, two-party, and modified one-party, the one-party and the totalitarian one-party types.[18] Key classifies the states as Strong Republican, Less-Strong Republican, Competitive, Leaning Democratic, and Strong Democratic.[19] Golembiewski revives a threefold scheme, but one more applicable to the American state parties: one-party states, weak minority-party states, and two-party states.[20]

The basis for dividing the state party systems in each of these schemes is the level of competitiveness between the two major political parties within each state.[21] At least three factors must be considered in designing a tool for measuring inter-party competition: (1) time period; (2) offices; and (3) which of several ways of looking at competitiveness, within the context of the two preceding factors, most accurately measures competition?

Competition must be measured for a period of time, but how long a period should be considered in formulating an adequate measure? . . . It seemed most use-

[16] V. O. Key, op. cit.; Duncan MacRae, Jr., "The Relation between Roll Call Votes and Constituencies in the Massachusetts House of Representatives," American Political Science Review, XLVI (1952), pp. 1046–1055; Julius Turner, "Primary Elections as the Alternative to Party Competition in 'Safe Districts'," Journal of Politics, XX (1953), pp. 197–210; William J. Keefe, "Parties, Partisanship and Public Policy in the Pennsylvania Legislature," American Political Science Review, XLVII (1953), pp. 450–464; V. O. Key, Jr., American State Politics (New York: Alfred A. Knopf, 1956), Chapter 8; Austin Ranney and Wilmoore Kendall, "The American Party System," American Political Science Review, XLVIII (1954), pp. 477–485; Joseph A. Schlesinger, "A Two-Dimensional Scheme for Classifying the States According to Degree of Interparty Competition," American Political Science Review, LIX (1955), pp. 1120–1128; Robert Golembiewski, loc. cit., pp. 494–513; Lockard, op. cit., Chapter 12; Joseph A. Schlesinger, "The Structure of Competition for Office in the American States," Behavioral Science, V (1960), pp. 197–210; William H. Standing and James A. Robinson, "Inter-Party Competition and Primary Contesting: The Case of Indiana," American Political Science Review, LII (1958), pp. 1066–1077.

[17] Ranney and Kendall, loc. cit., p. 478.

[18] Ibid., pp. 480–481.
[19] Key (1956), op. cit., p. 99.
[20] Golembiewski, loc. cit., p. 501.
[21] We also consider competition only between the two major national political parties. Thus, the measure of competition does not account either for intra-party competition or the impact of minor third parties.

ful to adopt the twenty-one period from 1938 to 1958 as a base. This period appears long enough to lessen the influence of short-term deviating factors and short enough to avoid the impact of basic shifts in party identification such as occurred in the 1860–1864 and the 1932–1936 elections.[22] Likewise it eliminates the extremely one-sided election results of the early New Deal when many states deviated from previous and subsequent patterns of voting.

The next step in designing a measure of inter-party competition is the selection of offices. The units adopted by other researchers vary. Key used only the office of governor.[23] Ranney and Kendall included electoral results for president, governor, and United States senator.[24] Golembiewski used only state offices, the governor and the legislature.[25] In his 1955 study, Schlesinger used the offices of governor and president.[26] In his 1960 study he considered the governor, senators, congressmen, and six state-wide elective offices.[27]

The decision about which offices to consider is partly arbitrary and partly dependent upon the problem. . . . For this study the office of governor and each branch of the state legislature are used. These are the state institutions most directly involved in identifying problems of public policy, and recommending and selecting alternatives to meet them.

After the base time period has been selected and the choice of offices has been made, it is necessary to decide how to measure the degree of competition for the selected offices for the chosen time period. The degree of inter-party competition refers primarily to the extent to which both parties possess the opportunity of gaining control of the various offices around which the competition takes place. In a competitive situation the "out-party" must have the possibility to become the "in-party," and the position of the in-party must be threatened by the possibility that the out-party could gain control. The assumption is that the possibility of gaining control of the decision-making machinery influences the behavior of the out-party and the constant threat of being put out of office influences the behavior of the in-party.[28]

At least three dimensions of inter-party competition form the competitive process: (1) the margin of comparative popular support, including the relative strength of the two parties in the electorate and/or the relative number of seats they hold in the legislature;[29] (2) the relative percentage of time that the parties have controlled the offices or institutions under consideration;[30] and (3) the percentage of time that control of the offices has been divided between the parties, one party controlling one office and the other party the other offices at the same time.[31] Although these three dimensions are related, it is possible to obtain different results from them. For example, New Hampshire, when measured according to the percentage of times the governorship and both houses of the state legislature have been controlled by the predominant party, would be ranked with Georgia, Mississippi, and other Southern states. However, when

[22] For a discussion of the stability and changes in American party identification see Angus Campbell, *et al.*, *The American Voter* (New York: John Wiley & Sons, Inc., 1960), esp. pp. 149–167. Also see V. O. Key, Jr., "A Theory of Critical Elections," *Journal of Politics*, XVII (1955), pp. 3–18, and Duncan MacRae, Jr., and James A. Meldrum, "Critical Elections in Illinois: 1885–1958," *American Political Science Review*, LIV (1960), pp. 669–683.

[23] Key (1956), *op. cit.*, p. 99.

[24] Ranney and Kendall, *op. cit.*, pp. 482–484.

[25] Golembiewski, *loc. cit.*, p. 499–500.

[26] Schlesinger (1955), *loc. cit.*, pp. 1120–1128.

[27] Schlesinger (1960), *loc. cit.*, p. 199.

[28] These assumptions are based primarily on two-party systems. The mechanisms would be somewhat different for the various parties in a multi-party system.

[29] The closeness of the vote was used in the measures of competition employed by Ranney and Kendall and Key. The percentage of the seats of the state legislature controlled by the minority party was used by Golembiewski.

[30] Golembiewski and Schlesinger consider this dimension as part of their measurement devices.

[31] Golembiewski and Schlesinger also consider this dimension.

competition is measured according to the percentage of popular vote the predominant party has received in the race for governor and the percentage of seats it has held in the legislature over the twenty-one years period, New Hampshire appears much more competitive than any of the Southern states. Although the Republicans controlled the governorship in New Hampshire and the Democrats in Mississippi during the entire twenty-one year period, the Republican party in New Hampshire received 55.5 per cent of the two-party vote for governor, while the Democrats received 100 per cent of the popular vote for the same office in Mississippi.

We measured each of these dimensions of inter-party competition. In measuring the first dimension we ranked each state according to the total percentage of the two-party popular vote the predominant party received in the elections for governor from 1938 to 1958; according to the percentage of seats the predominant party has held in the state senate over the same period of time; and according to the percentage of seats held by the predominant party in the "lower" house of the state legislature. This was done by averaging the per cent of major party vote the parties received in each gubernatorial election and the per cent of seats the parties have held in each house during each term of the state legislature of the twenty-one year period. The states were ranked on a continuum from those closest to fifty per cent to those most distant from fifty per cent. Competition along this dimension was first considered separately for each of the three institutions, then the three measurements were combined into one by averaging the three percentages. According to these measurements the states are ranked as follows:

State:	Rank: Per Cent of Popular Vote for Governor	Rank: Per Cent of Seats in Senate Held by Major Party	Rank: Per Cent of Seats in House Held by Major Party	Rank: Average of the Three Percentages
1. Ala.	41	43.5	41.5	41
2. Ariz.	30	36	32	33
3. Ark.	40	43.5	40	40
4. Calif.	34	9	5	11
5. Colo.	1	4.5	11	15
6. Conn.	7.5	2	22.5	9.5
7. Del.	2.5	1	3	1
8. Fla.	39	40	39	39
9. Ga.	45	39	41.5	43
10. Idaho	15	4.5	9	6
11. Ill.	4.5	10	4	4
12. Ind.	9	16	15	13.5
13. Iowa	23	31	31	29
14. Kans.	20.5	32	27.5	23
15. Ky.	25	25.5	26	24
16. La.	43	43.5	45	44
17. Me.	28	33	29	30
18. Md.	16	19	27.5	25
19. Mass.	10	7	2	3
20. Mich.	4.5	22	18	17
21. Miss.	45	43.5	45	46
22. Mo.	17	11.5	6	22
23. Mont.	11	3	1	2
24. Nev.	24	15	16.5	16

State:	Rank: Per Cent of Popular Vote for Governor	Rank: Per Cent of Seats in Senate Held by Major Party	Rank: Per Cent of Seats in House Held by Major Party	Rank: Average of the Three Percentages
25. N. H.	26	23	16.5	19
26. N. J.	6	24	19	20
27. N. Mex.	12	28	25	26
28. N. Y.	18.5	11.5	14	12
29. N. C.	36	38	37	37
30. N. Dak.	27	34	36	35
31. Ohio	2.5	18	20	17
32. Okla.	32.5	35	34	34
33. Ore.	32.5	25.5	24	27
34. Pa.	14	14	7	7
35. R. I.	20.5	6	13	8
36. S. C.	45	43.5	45	45
37. S. Dak.	31	29	33	31
38. Tenn.	38	21	30	32
39. Tex.	42	43.5	43	42
40. Utah	7.5	8	8	5
41. Vt.	35	30	35	36
42. Va.	37	37	38	38
43. Wash.	18.5	13	10	9.5
44. W. Va.	22	20	21	21
45. Wis.	29	27	22.5	28
46. Wyo.	13	17	12	13.5

In some instances, *e.g.,* California and Connecticut, great differences occur in the rankings of a state for the different political units. In spite of several cases like this, however, the correlations between these rankings are quite high, as indicated in Table I. Because each of these three institutions— the governorship, the senate and the house of representatives—plays a key role in the determination of state policy, the average of the percentages of popular vote for governor, the per cent of seats held in the senate, and the per cent of seats held in the house is the best over-all measure of inter-party competition along this dimension.

In measuring the second dimension, the relative per cent of time during the twenty-one year period that the major party has controlled the offices under consideration, the rank order of the states is determined

TABLE I Rank Order Correlations between Four Measures of Inter-Party Competition

	Popular Vote for Governor	Membership in Senate	Membership in House	Average
Per cent popular vote for governor		.80	.80	.85
Per cent members of major party in senate	.80		.93	.95
Per cent members of major party in house	.80	.93		.95
Average of above three percentages	.85	.95	.95	

by taking the number of terms of the senate, the number of terms of the house of representatives, and the number of terms for governor and finding the per cent of terms that the major party has been in control. Thus, if there were eleven terms of the state senate, eleven terms of the house of representatives, and five terms of governor, and the major party controlled five terms of the senate, seven terms of the house of representatives, and three terms as governor, the major party would have controlled the offices about 56 per cent of the time. The states are then ranked on a continuum with the states closest to 50 percent considered the most competitive and those most distant from 50 per cent the least competitive. Separate rankings can be made for each office by considering the percent of time the major party has controlled that particular institution. Again, because policies are made by the three institutions and because the parties compete for control of each of them, the measure considering the three jointly is appropriate to measure the competitiveness between the parties for control of the formal policy-making machinery of government. It must be pointed out that there were no changes in control of any of these offices in 14 of the 46 states. Thus, there are fourteen ties in the ranking of the states on this dimension.

The final dimension of competition is the percentage of times that control of the government, in this case the governorship, the senate, and the house, has been divided between the two parties during the twenty-one year period. This measure is computed by counting the number of times, at two year intervals, that one party has held one of three institutions and the other party has controlled the other two and then computing what percentage this is of the total number of two year periods. The states are then ranked according to these percentages, 100 percent being the most competitive and 0 percent being the least competitive. Once more there are a substantial number of ties, fifteen.

These three operations are our measures of inter-party competition. We have said that these three dimensions are related but that there can be significant differences between them in particular states. None the less, the high coefficients obtained from correlating the ranks of the states along these dimensions suggest that they are measuring either the same phenomena or at least very closely related phenomena. The correlations between these measures are given in Table II.

III. WELFARE POLICIES

Welfare policies are those programs that directly or indirectly redistribute wealth, *i.e.,* whose purpose is to benefit the lower socio-economic groups at the expense of the upper income groups. The extent of welfare policies is assumed to be related in part to the ability of the lower-bracket groups to find political channels for the expression of their viewpoints and to exert influence upon the decision-makers.[32] Welfare mea-

32 See Key (1951), *op. cit.,* p. 309 and Lockard, *op. cit.,* pp. 326–327.

TABLE II   Rank Order Correlations between Three Dimensions of Inter-Party Competition

	Margin of Control	*Extent of Control*	*Divided Control*
Margin of control		.86	.84
Extent of control	.86		.90
Divided control	.84	.90	

sures include a wide range of public policies, some of which, like gift and death taxes, are specifically designed to redistribute wealth, and others, like educational expenditures, which are designed for other purposes but whose latent effect is redistribution of wealth and other values by providing equal educational opportunities for all in spite of wide discrepancies in private income.

The basic means by which governments affect the distribution of values include the collection of money through tax or revenue policies and the expenditure of money through a variety of programs. We use nine state policies or programs as indices of welfare measures. Four of these are revenue policies and five are expenditure policies. The selection of policies has been arbitrary, based to a great extent on the ready availability and comparability of data, as well as on an attempt to cover a wide range of substantive policies, and to include policies not affected by federal programs as well as those that are encouraged by federal action. As with the previous variables, the states are comparatively ranked. In all of the policies except the per cent of revenue coming from the federal government, the higher the tax rate or the higher the expenditures, the more extensive are the state's welfare programs. In regard to the per cent of revenue coming from the federal government, the higher the percentage, the lower the willingness of the state to support its own social welfare programs. To compare their welfare policies, we ranked forty-six states according to:

1. The per cent of the state's revenue derived from death and gift taxes.
2. The per cent of the state's revenue from the federal government.
3. The per capita amount of all general revenue.
4. State and local tax revenue according to personal income.
5. The average per pupil expenditure for education.

6. The average payment per recipient of aid to the blind.
7. The average payment per family for aid to dependent children.
8. The average payment per recipient in old-age assistance.
9. The average weekly benefit for total unemployment compensation in the state's unemployment insurance program.[33]

IV. EXTERNAL CONDITIONS

Theories of political science contain a great deal of both speculative and empirically-founded suggestions on the influence of external socio-economic-physical and psychological factors on the development of political systems, the processes that take place within them, and the policies that systems and processes produce. A large number of external conditions can be hypothetically related to these political variables. The factors most commonly related to political systems and processes have been economic ones. Aristotle, DeTocqueville, Hegel, Marx, Beard, Dahl and Lindblom, Golembiewski, and Lipset discuss, with varying degrees of empirical verification, the relations between economic factors and processes within the political systems. Lipset, in his study of the relations between economic development and stable democratic governments in Western Europe, the English speaking democracies and Latin America, uses four major indices of economic development: (1) wealth, (2) industrialization, (3) urbanization, and (4) education.[34]

As indicators of external conditions, the forty-six states will be ranked according to per capita income; the percentage of inhabitants engaged in occupations other than

[33] The data upon which these rankings are based are taken from the Council of State Governments, *The Book of the States, 1960–1961*, Vol. XIII (1960), (Chicago: The Council of State Governments).
[34] Lipset, *op. cit.*, pp. 54–60.

agriculture, forestry, and fishing; and the percentage of the state's population residing in urban areas.[35] Inasmuch as different levels of wealth, urbanization, and industrialization represent modes of life, values, or attitudes, each of these indices probably measures a complex of factors. For instance, living in urban areas usually means greater interdependence, greater access to cultural and educational facilities, and greater exposure to a wider range of religious and ideological positions, than does living in rural areas. Thus, when one measures the

V. REPORT
AND ANALYSIS OF RESULTS

To investigate the hypothesis that the greater the degree of inter-party competition in a political system, the more extensive or "liberal" the social welfare policies a political system will adopt, rank order correlations were tabulated between the three major indices of competition and the nine social welfare policies. The rank order correlation coefficients between these two sets of variables are in Table IV.

TABLE III   Rank Order Correlations between Three Measures of External Conditions

	Per Capita Income	Industrialization	Urbanization
Per capita income		.74	.82
Industrialization	.74		.81
Urbanization	.82	.81	

degree of urbanization, he measures much more than the fact of living in an urban area. He also measures the complex of patterns that accompany urban life. The same can be said for wealth and industrialization. Because it is presumed that these indices are measuring economic factors, one would expect to find a fairly close relationship between these three factors, especially between industrialization and urbanization. The rank order correlations between these three variables among forty-six states are reported in Table III.

We shall now investigate the relation between these three external factors and both the process and policy variables. We shall then look at the relation between process and policy variables, controlling for the influence of these external conditions.

The correlation coefficients between the competitive measures and the per cent of revenue from death/gift taxes and the per cent of revenue from the federal government are somewhat lower than those for other policies. The correlations between the tax revenue based on personal income and the competitive measures are slightly negative. With these exceptions, the data confirm a relationship between the degree of inter-party competition and the extent to which the states have adopted social welfare measures. If the indices are measuring what we presume they are, the hypothesis that more liberal social welfare measures are adopted by more competitive party systems holds for forty-six states. This is consistent with the reports made by Key and Lockard.[36]

[35] Data for these socio-economic measures were taken from Bureau of the Census, *Statistical Abstract of the United States: 1960* (Washington: U.S. Government Printing Office, 1960) and Bureau of

the Census, *Census of Population: 1950, Vol. I* (Washington: U.S. Government Printing Office, 1952).

[36] Key (1951), *op. cit.*, pp. 298–314, and Lockard, *op. cit.*, esp. pp. 320–340.

**TABLE IV   Rank Order Correlations between Public Policies
and Inter-Party Competition**

Policies	Party Competition Measures		
	Average Per Cent of Popular Support for Governor, Senate, and House	*Per Cent of Time the Predominant Party Has Controlled Units of Government*	*Per Cent of Times Control Has Been Divided between Parties*
Per cent of revenue from death/gift taxes	.44	.37	.25
Per cent of revenue from federal government	.32	.27	.41
Per capita amount of state revenue	.55	.50	.47
Tax revenue in relation to personal income	—.23	—.08	—.21
Per pupil expenditure	.64	.65	.71
Aid to blind	.58	.57	.55
Aid to dependent children	.63	.59	.52
Unemployment insurance	.63	.69	.63
Old age assistance	.53	.55	.53

If these findings are valid, the more competitive a party system, the more responsive it is to the interests and desires of the lower economic groups or the "have nots." Conversely, the less competitive a party system, the less responsive it is to the lower bracket economic groups and the more responsive it is to the interests of the "haves" and to powerful special economic interests. Lockard offers the following propositions to explain this relationship:

Proposition 1. "In the two-party states the anxiety over the next election pushes political leaders into serving the interests of the have-less elements of society, thereby putting the party into the counter-vailing power operation."[37]

Proposition 2. ". . . in the one-party states it is easier for a few powerful interests to manage the government of the state without party interference since the parties are not representative of the particular elements that might pose opposition to the dominant interest groups."[38]

Similarly, writing about southern politics, Key suggests that

Proposition 3. ". . . over the long run the have-nots lose in a disorganized politics. They have no mechanism through which to act and their wishes find expression in fitful rebellions led by transient demagogues who gain their confidence but often have neither the technical competence nor the necessary stable base of political power to affectuate a program."[39]

Proposition 4. "A loose factional system lacks the power to carry out sustained programs of action, which almost always are thought by the better elements to be contrary to its immediate interests. This negative weakness thus resounds to the benefit of the upper brackets."[40]

[37] *Ibid.*, p. 337.

[38] *Ibid.*
[39] Key, *op. cit.*, p. 307.
[40] *Ibid.*, p. 308.

These hypotheses suggest that the process of competition between two organized and enduring political parties, or as is the case in the South, two stable factions within a one-party arrangement, lead to more liberal social welfare policies because competition forces the candidates and/or parties to appeal to the have-not groups for support. At the same time, the competitive process inhibits the influence of special economic interests by its development of countervailing forces. In regard to the relationship between party competition and the importance of pressure politics, Golembiewski offers and tests the following proposition:

> Proposition 5. "Weak party cohesion is generally associated with strong pressure politics, and strong party cohesion with weak pressure politics. And party cohesion is a direct function of the degree of competition between political parties, that is, the more marked is interparty competition the more pronounced is party cohesion."[41]

Using his own classification of party systems and Zeller's measures of pressure politics and party cohesion, Golembiewski confirmed this proposition.

A correlational analysis suggests that there is a common variance between two or more variables. A correlation indicates the extent to which one variable changes when another is changed; it alone cannot prove causal relations between variables. The high correlations between competition and policy suggest only that the welfare policies

vary in direction and extent as variations occur in inter-party competition. They do not reveal whether the adoption of welfare measures is an effect of party competition or vice-versa. This co-variance may result from the fact that one of the two variables influences the other or from the fact that both are related to a third variable or set of variables.

There has been a competing hypothesis throughout this investigation that both inter-party competition and welfare policies might be related to various external socio-economic factors. In regard to the relationship between external conditions and the level of inter-party competition, Lockard suggests that:

> Proposition 6. "The diversity or lack of diversity of economic interests in a state tends to be reflected in the prevailing party system and the mode of its operation."[42]

> Proposition 7. "In the first place, of course, it is the diversity in part that creates the atmosphere for two-party competition and the absence of diversity facilitates one-partyism."[43]

We now report our findings on the relation of economic factors to inter-party competition and welfare policies. The rank order correlations between the three socio-economic variables and the three major measures of inter-party competition are summarized in Table V.

[41] Golembiewski, *loc. cit.*, pp. 510–512.

[42] Lockard, *op. cit.*, p. 337.
[43] *Ibid.*, p. 9.

TABLE V   Rank Order Correlations between External Conditions and Inter-Party Competition

External Conditions	Party Competition Measures		
	Average Per Cent of Popular Support for Governor, Senate and House	Per Cent of Times the Predominant Party Has Controlled Units of Government	Per Cent of Times Control Has Been Divided between Parties
Per capita income	.71	.65	.73
Urbanization	.58	.54	.56
Industrialization	.59	.48	.57

These correlations confirm a relationship between these external conditions and the level of inter-party competition. Note that the relationship between per capita income and the competitive measures is consistently higher than that with the other socio-economic measures. Golembiewski found statistically significant relations between a group of "sociological" factors and categories of party competition. His findings support the following propositions:[44]

Proposition 8. Where the per cent of urban population is high the political party system is likely to be competitive or two-party.

Proposition 9. Where the population density is high the party system is likely to be competitive or two-party.

Proposition 10. Where the Negro percentage of the population is low the system is likely to be competitive or two-party.

Proposition 11. Where the total median income is high the party system is likely to be competitive or two-party.

Finally, the relation between the external socio-economic conditions and public welfare policies must be considered. One might hypothesize important relations between socio-economic conditions and public policies for at least two reasons. First, the wealth of a state might condition the ability of a state to pay for welfare policies.

Proposition 12. The wealthier the state, the greater its ability to afford extensive social welfare policies.

Second, different types of societies presumably desire and/or require varying degrees of policies or programs that might fall under the heading of welfare legislation. In a more industrialized and urbanized state more social welfare legislation, such as unemployment insurance and aid to dependent children, presumably would be needed or desired than in a less urbanized or industrialized state.

[44] Golembiewski, *loc. cit.*, p. 511.

Proposition 13. The more urbanized and industrialized a state, the greater the desire and/or need of its inhabitants for social welfare legislation.

Proposition 14. The more urbanized and industrialized a state, the greater the degree of interdependence between its population; and the greater the level of interdependence, the greater the tendency of the people to look toward the government or the political system to handle basic socio-economic problems, or to adopt social welfare policies.

The rank order correlation coefficients tabulated between the socio-economic variables and the policy variables are presented in Table VI.

These correlations signify rather strong relations between the three socio-economic factors and public welfare policies. As with the party competition variables, the socio-economic variables are negatively correlated with the amount of tax revenue in relation to the level of personal income variable. The highest correlations are between per capita income and policy. As was found in the correlations between the socio-economic factors and party competition, the per capita income coefficients are consistently higher than those with the other two socio-economic variables. Note also that the correlations between per capita income and policy are higher than any of those found between measures of inter-party competition and the welfare policies.

Thus far we have found that the policy variables are related to competition variables, competition variables are related to socio-economic factors, and the policies are also correlated with the socio-economic factors. These findings conform to hypothesized relations. With system variables held constant, the socio-economic factors influence the political process, both directly and through their influence on system, and process variables influence the adoption of public policies and socio-economic factors also affect policy outcomes, hypothetically mediated by process.

**TABLE VI   Rank Order Correlations between Public Policies
and External Conditions**

Policies	Socio-Economic Variables		
	Per Capita Income	Urbanization	Industrialization
Per cent of revenue from death/gift taxes	.54	.46	.41
Per cent of revenue from federal government	.62	.65	.69
Per capita amount of state revenue	.55	.33	.24
Tax revenue in relation to personal income	—.03	—.41	—.44
Per pupil expenditures	.88	.67	.63
Aid to blind	.74	.63	.47
Aid to dependent children	.64	.56	.47
Unemployment insurance	.73	.64	.56
Old age assistance	.69	.61	.47

The policy variables correlated highly with both inter-party competition (process) and the socio-economic factors; and process variables, in turn, are associated with socio-economic conditions. The finding of associations among these variables still leaves unanswered the question of the effect inter-party competition has upon the adoption of public social welfare measures. It is not known from these statistics whether inter-party competition has any independent influence upon the level of social welfare or whether the high positive correlations between policies and competition stem from the dual relationship between socio-economic factors and policy and between socio-economic factors and competition. Conversely, the meaning of the relationship between socio-economic factors and policy is unclear because both are so highly correlated with competition. To what extent, for example, are the high correlations found between inter-party competition and policies independent of the relation between both of these variables and per capita income? The correlations computed thus far suggest that the wealthier states have more competitive party processes *and* more "liberal" social welfare measures. Do they have the more liberal welfare measures because they are wealthier, or does the process of competition between the parties intervene to influence the extent of welfare policies?

In order to sift out the relative influence of these factors, it is necessary to measure the relation between party competition and public policies while holding wealth constant. This has been done by dividing the states into three groups according to their per capita income. Because there are forty-six states, the first fifteen on the per capita income continuum were placed in one group, the wealthiest one-third; the next sixteen into a second group, the middle one-third; and the remaining fifteen into a third group, the poorest one-third. Then rank order correlations were computed between inter-party competition and policies within each of the three groups. The rank order correlations are shown in Table VII. They suggest that the correlations not controlling for wealth were more a reflection of per capita income and its relationship with inter-party competition than they were of inter-party competition.

TABLE VII   Rank Order Correlations between Inter-Party Competition (Average Popular Support Measure) and Three Welfare Policies, Holding Wealth (Per Capita Income) Constant

Policies	Average Popular Support for Governor, Senate, and House			
	Upper ⅓	*Middle* ⅓	*Lower* ⅓	*46 States*
Per pupil expenditures	.13	.34	.37	.64
Unemployment insurance	−.13	−.22	.41	.63
Old age assistance	.07	.24	.21	.53

In order to further isolate the influence of inter-party competition and wealth upon welfare policies, correlations were computed between per capita income and the same three policy measures, controlling for inter-party competition. The states were divided into three groups according to competition as measured by the average per cent of popular support for governor, the senate and the house of representatives. The results are displayed in Table VIII.

With inter-party competition controlled for, a somewhat different situation is found than that resulting from controlling wealth and correlating competition and policies. Although most of the correlations are lower for the three controlled groups than they were for the forty-six states, they are not as low as those between competition and policies when wealth was controlled. In fact, one of the correlations is even slightly higher in the controlled group, and each is higher than all but one of the correlations when wealth is controlled.

These last two sets of correlations indicate that wealth influences or at least is related to the extent of welfare policies, independent of the influence of party competition. On the other hand, inter-party competition is related to the extent of public social welfare policies through their joint relationship with per capita income. If the data reported and operations used have measured what we have presumed them to measure, inter-party competition does not play as influential a role in determining the scope of welfare policies as earlier studies suggested. The level of public social welfare programs in the American states is more an effect of socio-economic factors, especially per capita income. High levels of inter-party competition are highly related both to socio-economic factors and to social welfare legislation, but the degree of inter-party competition does not possess the important intervening influence between socio-economic factors and liberal welfare programs that our original hypoth-

TABLE VIII   Rank Order Correlations between Per Capita Income and Three Welfare Policies, Holding Inter-Party Competition Constant

Policies	Per Capita Income			
	Upper ⅓	*Middle* ⅓	*Lower* ⅓	*46 States*
Per pupil expenditures	.75	.70	.81	.88
Unemployment compensation	.37	.60	.41	.73
Old age assistance	.47	.46	.70	.69

esis predicted. In short, evidence points to the relatively greater influence of certain external conditions over one aspect of the political process in the formulation of welfare policies.[45]

6. Continuity and Change in Ohio Politics

Thomas A. Flinn

The bases of party loyalty vary from state to state. Oberlin Professor Thomas Flinn analyzes party strengths in Ohio, showing the diversity of party support in an important state that has often been called the "most typically American." Each party is found to have strength based on sectional, ethnic, and class factors as well as on that related to patterns of migration to the state and responses to specific political issues.

* * *

The size and composition of major party followings in Ohio were remarkably stable for about a century. Variations from the established pattern did occur while continuity was the dominant characteristic, and finally there was a major break. This study attempts to describe these elements of continuity and change in the followings of the major parties in Ohio.

The principal purpose of the study is to make clearer the evolution of the party system in Ohio and incidentally in the nation in so far as a clearer view of Ohio politics may provide it. Another purpose of the study is to show the force of tradition and habit in determining voting preferences

and also the conditions associated with the disruption of long established loyalties. Finally, it is also an objective of this study to demonstrate some techniques for measuring continuity and change in voting behavior. These techniques are, I hope, sensitive and precise, easily comprehended, economical in terms of the time and resources of the researcher, and, therefore, potentially useful to others interested in similar studies and problems.

METHOD

The county is obviously the unit with which one works in seeking to identify party followings over any considerable period of time across an entire state, especially one the size of Ohio. Use of smaller units involves very severe difficulties: the returns are not readily available; the number of units becomes so large as to make analysis very difficult or, at least, very expensive; demographic data are unavailable or else difficult to manipulate.

The elections with which one works are obviously the important statewide elections. I have taken presidential and gubernatorial elections. Others might have been added, and their addition would have been helpful particularly in consideration of the period since World War I. During that time presidential elections seem often to have been unusual or somehow unrepresentative, and the picture of party strength and followings gained from gubernatorial elections is somewhat distorted by the personal popularity of two Democrats, Donahey and Lausche, which was often more than the popularity of their party. Consideration of other elections, however, would have extended considerably the necessary statistical series[1] and

[45] For further comment on this article, see Elliott James, "A Comment on Inter-Party Competition, Economic Variables, and Welfare Policies in the American States," *Journal of Politics*, vol. 27, no. 1 (Feb. 1965), pp. 185–191.—Editor's note.

[1] I was greatly assisted in preparing the statistical series for this study by funds from a Ford Foundation grant to Oberlin College for research in public affairs.

From the *Journal of Politics*, vol. 24, no. 3 (August 1964), pp. 521–544 by permission of the Southern Political Science Association.

other dimensions of the study too. Hence, they are omitted with regret.

Nor is every presidential and gubernatorial election included. In general, an election or group of elections was considered if there was reason to think the number and identity of major party supporters might have changed since the last election which had been analyzed. That judgment was made if any one of the following had occurred: a decline in the relative strength of one of the major parties as determined by inspection of statewide returns; disappearance of one major party and its replacement by another; a substantial shift in position on public policy by one or both of the major parties; an event or events generally recognized as important in national politics. Not every election which met the test was actually considered. Choice from the eligibles was somewhat arbitrary, but many were chosen if the promise of change was great or the need to demonstrate continuity strong.

Most of the analysis is in terms of the two-party vote for the reason that it is easier and quicker to compute major party shares of the two-party vote than major party shares of the total vote. There are two exceptions. The statewide strength of the major parties is defined partly in terms of the total vote. This is informative, and computation is no great problem. The other exception occurs when there was a third-party vote which was large and/or geographically concentrated. Use of the two-party vote in such cases can be seriously misleading. For example, the Democratic share of the two-party vote increased astonishingly in several pre-Civil War elections in some Ohio counties where it had been small in previous elections. In fact what happened is that the vote of the anti-slavery parties was concentrated in these counties and was drawn almost entirely from the following of the Whigs. The confusion is avoided if in three-party contests the major party vote is described as a share of the

total vote. One other point in regard to the data: it is the Democratic percentage of the two-party or total vote which is used unless otherwise specified.

Given an election for analysis and the necessary data the immediate objective was an answer to the questions: one, was there any general tendency for the various counties to increase or decrease support for either of the major parties relative to some reference point in the past; two, did any county or group of counties depart from the general tendency and thereby change relative position? Given an answer to these questions and knowledge of the demographic character of the various counties, then a description of the composition of major party followings may be offered.

More than one method would yield answers to the two questions above, but regression analysis seemed most suitable.[2] The regression equation ($Y_p = a + bX$) carries in a compact and easily comprehended form an answer to the question involving general tendency. For example, the average percentage of the vote received by the Democratic Party in two-party contests with the Whigs was computed at one point in the study for every county reporting in the relevant elections,[3] and these may be called the X-values. The percentage of the total vote received in each county by the Democratic candidate in 1848 when faced by both Whigs and Free Soilers was computed for the sake of this illustration, and these may be called Y-values. The regression equation expressing the relationship between the average Democratic vote in straight fights with the Whigs and the Democratic vote in a three-cornered fight with Whigs and

[2] A description may be found in any introductory statistics text. V. O. Key, Jr., in his *A Primer of Statistics for Political Scientists* (New York: Thomas Y. Crowell, 1954), pp. 74–81, provides a simple, clear discussion of scatter diagrams and regression. A clear but somewhat more elaborate description may be found in Hubert M. Blalock, Jr., *Social Statistics* (New York: McGraw-Hill, 1960), pp. 279–285.

[3] The manner in which the average was computed is described later.

Free Soilers was: $Y_p = .98 + .95X$. To see the significance of the equation, substitute for the X in the equation some of the actual values of X. Take a county in which the Democrats had averaged 50% of the vote in two-party contests with the Whigs. The predicted value of Y (Y_p) or the predicted Democratic share of the total in 1848 is 48.5%. In a county where the value of X was 20 the predicted value of Y is 19, and in a county where the value of X was 70 the predicted value of Y is 67.5. Since the value of X was not less than 20 in any country, it can be said simply that the Democratic vote declined a little bit in every county and slightly more in counties where the Democrats were strongest. The change is rather small, and not nearly enough to account for the Free Soil vote (11% in the state) which must have been drawn from the Whigs barring some highly improbable movements of voters.

The regression equation expresses a general tendency. If the coefficient of correlation is high (between .8 and 1.0), then it can be said that most counties followed the general tendency closely; that is, Y values (actual values) and Y_p values (predicted values) would be similar or nearly similar in most although not all cases unless the correlation is extraordinarily good.[4] If the coefficient of correlation is lower, then it is apparent that more counties deviated from the general tendency or that the magnitude of the deviation in most cases was great or that these things both happened. The counties which are deviant in behavior can be discovered by comparing Y and Y_p values. Some deviation, perhaps as much as 3 or 4 percentage points, might easily be caused by such things as the relative intensity of the campaign effort in the county and the impact of local personalities and local politics. Deviations of greater magnitude suggest the presence of more underlying factors and

[4] In the foregoing illustration the coefficient of correlation was plus .93.

indicate that the county or counties showing the deviation are changing their position relative to other counties.

WHIGS AND DEMOCRATS

The first contest in Ohio between Whigs and Democrats was the gubernatorial election of 1832 and the last was the gubernatorial election of 1853. Of the 17 presidential and gubernatorial contests between Whigs and Democrats, the Whigs won 8 and the Democrats 9. The average Democratic percentage of the total vote in these 17 elections was 48.9 and the Whig 47.3, a figure which underestimates the strength of the Whigs since they suffered most from the efforts of third-party candidates. In a series of two-party contests[5] the Whigs had an average vote of more than 55% in 29 counties and an average varying from a bare majority to 55% in another 15 counties. The Democrats for their part had an average vote of more than 55% in 21 counties and an average vote varying from a mere majority to 55% in another 14. The geographical distribution of the vote is given in the facing map, which shows as nearly as possible the one-half of the counties relatively most Democratic and the half most Whig.

An explanation for the pattern that can be seen in the following map is to be found in the pattern of settlement, which can be described generally although precision seems unattainable. The northeastern part of the state is the Western Reserve of Connecticut, which had claimed the area but then had relinquished the claim while

[5] Eight of the 17 presidential and gubernatorial elections fought by Whigs and Democrats were two-party contests if a very small third-party vote in the presidential election of 1840 is ignored. Six of these 8 elections for which returns were immediately available were used for computing county averages. The 2 elections omitted were the gubernatorial elections of 1832 and 1836. There is no reason to think their inclusion would alter the averages appreciably.

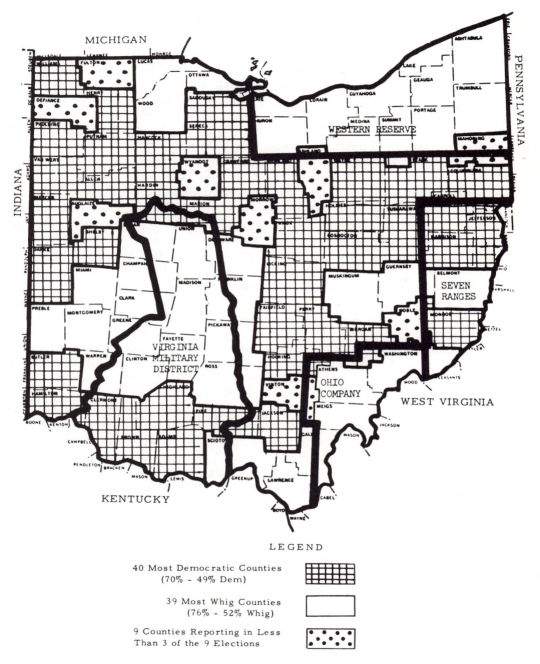

LEGEND

40 Most Democratic Counties (70% - 49% Dem)	▦
39 Most Whig Counties (76% - 52% Whig)	▢
9 Counties Reporting in Less Than 3 of the 9 Elections	▨

Map 1 Relative strength of party preference expressed by the average vote in six two-party elections, 1832–1853.

retaining the right to dispose of the land through grants. The settlers were drawn overwhelmingly from New England, and had the same political loyalties as did their relatives and neighbors who remained behind. The southeastern corner of the state was purchased by the Ohio Company, a New England association; and like the Western Reserve was settled heavily by New Englanders who retained the political preferences of the section from which they had come.

The area known as the Seven Ranges (seven ranges of townships) was the first surveyed and first settled section of Ohio. The population seems to have been drawn to a considerable extent from western Pennsylvania although settlers from other areas could be found there too. Whig and Democratic voters were closely matched in terms of numbers. The more Democratic counties just to the west and to the north also included many Pennsylvanians among their early settlers, but they can be distinguished in part from the Seven Ranges by the large number of Pennsylvania Germans who settled in Stark, Wayne, Ashland, and Richland counties.[6] Tuscarawas, although evenly divided in this period, resembled the counties just to the north in that it had a substantial Pennsylvania German element.

The large area bounded for the most part by the Scioto River on the east and north and by the Little Miami River on the west is the Virginia Military district. Its history is in some ways similar to that of the Western Reserve. The area was claimed by Virginia which surrendered its claim while retaining the right to make land grants in the area to its revolutionary veterans. Settlers in the area seem to have been somewhat mixed in terms of origin, but accounts of early settlement in the Military District contain numerous references to persons from Kentucky and Virginia. For whatever

reason, most of the counties in the District were Whig to greater or less degree. The exceptions are Clermont, Brown, and Adams on the Ohio River, Pike and Highland just to the northeast of them, and Hardin at the far northern end of the district.

The tier of counties running north and south just to the east of the Virginia Military District including Licking on the north and Jackson on the south was Democratic during the era of competition between the Whig and Democratic parties. This group of counties was settled by Pennsylvanians, Virginians, and sundry others in proportions which will apparently never be known. Counties in northwestern Ohio[7] seem to have been even more mixed in terms of the origin of their settlers. Pennsylvanians seem almost ubiquitous, but they were joined by immigrants whose immediate or remote origin was in states both to the north and south of Pennsylvania.[8] Beginning in the thirties and continuing for many years German immigrants spread over northwestern Ohio, and more will be said about them later.

To summarize: the areas in the northeast and southeast settled predominantly by New Englanders were faithfully Whig. The other large concentration of Whig voters was in the Virginia Military District. The settlers seem to have been largely southern, but it was the party of Clay they followed

[7] The area I refer to as northwest Ohio includes Crawford, the counties north and west of it to the boundaries of the state, and south along the Indiana border including Darke and Shelby counties. Auglaize is counted as a part of the area although a very small corner of it falls within the Virginia Military District. This leaves a residual category south of Darke and Shelby and west of the Military District, and it can be called southwest if a label is needed. These definitions are rather arbitrary. Some justification could be offered, but it would probably be more complex than persuasive.

[8] Most of the foregoing observations concerning the origin of the settlers of Ohio are based on Henry Howe's *Historical Collections of Ohio* (Columbus: Henry Howe & Son, 1890), and I am indebted to Professor Wilfrid Binkley who drew my attention to it.

[6] Called "backbone counties" since they are on the divide between the Lake Erie and Ohio River watersheds.

and not the party of Jackson. Where Pennsylvanians were numerous, Whig majorities hardly ever were large; and in some areas settled heavily by Pennsylvanians, the Democrats did very well indeed. There were also indications that the German element in Ohio was strongly Democratic whether Pennsylvania German, German Swiss, or simply German.

REPUBLICANS AND DEMOCRATS

In 1855 the Republican Party appeared on the ballot in the place of the Whig and anti-slavery parties of earlier years. Salmon Chase, its candidate for governor, won an impressive victory. The new party carried the state for its presidential candidate in the next year, and held the governorship in 1857 and 1859. In these four elections between the formation of the Republican Party and the splintering of the Democratic Party in 1860 the Republicans averaged 49.4% of the total vote and the Democrats 46.0.[9] The Democratic average was only about three percentage points less than it had been in the previous period when its leading competitor was the Whig Party, but the change was sufficient to put the Democrats into a clear minority position. In this period the Republicans had an average vote of more than 55% of the total in 36 counties. They had an average vote ranging from a bare majority to 55% in another 21 counties. The Democrats had an average of more than 55% in only 11 counties and an average ranging from a mere majority to 55% in another 20 counties.

The general trend shows Democratic losses in counties where the party had received an average vote of more than 40% in competition with the Whigs with the heaviest losses coming in counties where the Democrats had done best.[10] At the 50% level the predicted vote is 46%, and at the 60% level the predicted vote is 53%. The Democrats made some compensating gains in counties which had been heavily Whig. These gains were, of course, not enough to prevent a decline in the total Democratic vote.

This is, of course, a statement of general tendency; and not every county conformed to it.[11] A majority of the counties in the Western Reserve (7 of the then existing 11) gave to the Democrats a share of the vote significantly smaller than would be expected by reference to the general trend.[12] The Democratic vote not only failed to show the anticipated increases in this area which had been strongly Whig but declined absolutely. Four of the 6 counties entirely within the original seven ranges of townships in eastern Ohio showed decreases in Democratic strength greater than would be expected.

A majority of the Whiggish counties (4 of 6) in or immediately adjacent to the Ohio Company area departed from the trend by giving significantly more than predicted support to the Democrats. The general trend called for some increases in these 4 deviant counties, but more than the called for increase appeared. This is somewhat surprising when it is recalled that the population of the Ohio Company area was similar to that of the Western Reserve in terms of origin. Six of the 17 then organized counties in northwest Ohio also gave the Democrats more support than the trend would suggest. Typically this meant that antici-

[9] The elections of 1855, 1856, and 1857 were three-party contests with the American or Know-Nothing Party providing the alternative to the major parties. The usual judgment is that American Party voters were actually or potentially Republicans, and there is no reason to doubt that judgment.

[10] Democratic county averages in the period 1832–1853 were X-values in the regression analysis, and Democratic averages in the four specified elections from 1855 through 1859 were the Y-values. The regression equation is: $Y_p = 11.85 + .69X$.

[11] The coefficient of correlation is plus .74.

[12] Y values in these 7 counties were 4 or more percentage points less than Y_p values. In this discussion and in similar ones which follow a difference of 4 or more percentage points between Y and Y_p values is designated significant.

pated decreases did not occur. Some other counties also departed from the trend by giving the Democrats more or less than anticipated support, but they are scattered with the exception of a cluster in the center of the state (Franklin, Pickaway, and Fairfield counties) where the Democrats held their vote or actually gained against the trend.

In general, the Whig vote passed into the Republican Party with some small increments. Exceptions occurred but they are not sufficient to destroy the essential accuracy of the statement. To put the matter a little differently, the appearance of the Republican Party created relatively little disturbance in the followings of the major parties in Ohio. It is the element of continuity which is most impressive.

In the election of 1860 Douglas, the leading Democratic candidate, got just more than 43% of the total vote in Ohio and other Democratic candidates contributed approximately 5.5% to a Democratic total of 49%. The combined Democratic vote was somewhat better, measured as a share of the total vote, than any vote the Democrats had received since the organization of the Republican Party. In the war elections, however, the Republican majorities were very heavy; but this situation did not last long. There was a resurgence of Democratic strength as early as the gubernatorial election in 1865, and the Democrats very nearly won the governorship in 1867 and 1869. By 1870 no one could doubt that vigorous two-party competition was again the prevailing condition in Ohio.

In the period from 1870 through the presidential election of 1892 very close contests were the rule. The Republicans did win all 6 of the presidential elections, and 7 of the 11 gubernatorial elections. However, the average Republican share of the total vote was only 49.3%; and the average Democratic share was 47.4%. In a set of 6 elections in this period the Republicans achieved an average vote[13] of more than

55% in 29 counties and an average vote which varied from a bare majority to 55% in another 16 counties. The Democratic Party had an average vote of more than 55% in 26 counties and an average vote which varied from a mere majority to 55% in another 17 counties, which shows again the sharpness of the competition.

Relative to the period 1855–1859 the general trend shows a Democratic gain of 3 or 4 percentage points.[14] At the 30% level the predicted vote is 34%. At the 50% level the predicted vote is 54%, and at 70% the predicted vote is 73%.

Most counties followed the trend closely.[15] The Democrats, however, did significantly worse than expected in the eastern counties of Trumbull, Mahoning, and Jefferson, suffering slight losses instead of making small gains. The same thing happened in most of the Ohio Company counties. On the other hand, the Democrats did significantly better than expected in 8 of the 20 northwestern counties. Deviations from the trend occurred in some other counties, but show no pattern. The facts which stand forth clearly are: one, that the Democrats made a small but fairly general recovery from their setback in the fifties; and, two, that Republican and Democratic followings had survived disunion and civil war almost intact.

In the gubernatorial election of 1893 the Democrats took the worst beating they had suffered since the Vallandigham election of 1863. The defeat was apparently the conse-

---

13 The averages are based on major party shares

of the two-party vote in the presidential elections of 1872, 1884, and 1892 and in the gubernatorial elections of 1873, 1883, and 1889. These elections were chosen somewhat at random. They do span the period, and in none of these elections was third-party activity particularly effective. Inspection of the returns for the whole period indicates that variation from one election to another was so small that selection of any 6 elections would produce about the same averages.

14 Averages in the earlier period were X-values, and averages in the later period were Y-values in the regression analysis. The line of regression is expressed by the equation, $Y_p = 3.71 + .99X$.

15 The correlation coefficient is plus .90.

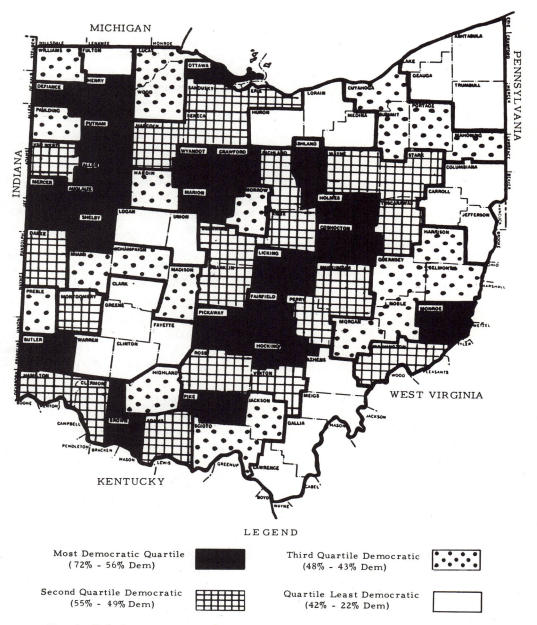

LEGEND

Most Democratic Quartile (72% - 56% Dem)

Second Quartile Democratic (55% - 49% Dem)

Third Quartile Democratic (48% - 43% Dem)

Quartile Least Democratic (42% - 22% Dem)

Map 2 Relative strength of party preference expressed by the average vote in six elections, 1870–1892.

quence of worsening economic conditions. Whatever the reason, the Democrats did worse in the period beginning in 1893 and running through 1904 than they had done in the preceding 20 or more years averaging only 43.6% of the total vote in 8 gubernatorial and presidential elections. Several of the best showings made by Democrats were those made by Bryan in 1896 and 1900. During this period some fierce battles were fought within the Republican Party with Hanna and Foraker as the leading protagonists.

In 1905 the tide changed sharply, and the Democrats elected a governor. They won the governorship again in 1908, and held it in 1910. The Democrats in these 3 elections averaged 50.4% of the total vote which compares with a Republican average of 44.7%. The third-party vote was socialist. In these elections the Democrats had an average vote of more than 55% of the two-party vote in 27 counties and an average vote which ranged between a bare majority and 55% in another 28 counties. The Republicans had an average vote in excess of 55% in 13 counties and an average vote ranging from a mere majority to 55% in another 20 counties.

Relative to the period 1870–1892, the Democratic vote increased in the areas where it had been low and remained steady or decreased slightly in areas where it had been high.[16] At the 30% level the predicted voted is 39%. At the 50% level the predicted vote is 53%, and at the 70% level the predicted vote is 66%.

Most counties followed the general trend closely.[17] The Democratic vote was significantly less than expected in some scattered counties. The Democratic vote was significantly more than expected in 7 of the 20 northwestern counties and in 10 of the 12 Western Reserve counties where deviation from predicted values meant an absolute increase greater than anticipated. It appears that the pattern evident in the period 1870–1892 persisted through the vicissitudes of the nineties and into the progressive era with the significant change that the Democrats gained substantially in areas where they had been weak, particularly in what had been the resolutely Republican Western Reserve.

The Democrats repeated their success in the presidential and gubernatorial elections of 1912, contests much confused by the progressives. The Republicans recovered the governorship in 1914 only to lose the state again in the presidential and gubernatorial elections of 1916.

FOREIGN WARS, DEPRESSION, AND CHANGE

In 1918 Democrat James M. Cox was re-elected governor with 50.6% of the vote in a two-party election. He carried only 7 counties with more than 55% of the vote and another 22 counties with 55% or less. Frank Willis, the Republican candidate, carried 59 counties and 31 of these with a vote of 55% or more. Victory under these conditions was itself a change from what had gone before.

The general trend shows a decline in the Democratic vote relative to the period 1905–1910 of 1 percentage point or more in every county where it had been more than 37% with the heaviest losses coming in the counties where the Democrats had been strongest.[18] It is the deviations from the trend which account for the Democratic victory[19] with sixteen counties giving Cox significantly more support than would be predicted by reference to the trend. Among

---

[16] The 1870–1892 averages are X-values, and the 1905–1910 averages are Y-values in the regression analysis. The line of regression is expressed by the equation, $Y_p = 19.26 + .67X$.

[17] The coefficient of correlation is plus .91.

[18] This is, of course, the general tendency. The averages for the 1905–1910 period were the X-values and the 1918 returns were the Y-values in the regression analysis. The line of regression is expressed by the equation $Y_p = 9.49 + .72X$.

[19] The coefficient of correlation is plus .76.

these counties are those which included the major cities of Cleveland, Akron, Columbus, Cincinnati, Hamilton-Middletown, Dayton, and Toledo. For the first time in this study the most urban areas in the state are found behaving in a distinctive manner. Previously they had seemed to blend into the countryside and to behave in ways consistent with the regional pattern. The other counties which gave Cox more than anticipated support were scattered in east central and south central Ohio. Twenty counties gave Cox significantly less than anticipated support. Some were scattered, but 11 were in northwest Ohio.

In 1920 Cox was again a Democratic candidate, this time for president. He lost the state to another Ohioan, Warren Harding, who got 58.5% of the total to Cox's 38.6%. In terms of the two-party vote Cox carried 8 counties, 3 with more than 55% of the vote, while Harding carried 80 counties, 60 with more than 55% of the vote.

Relative to the three pre-war gubernatorial elections in the period 1905–1910, the Democratic vote dropped everywhere; and the biggest losses were in the counties where they had done best.[20] At the 30% level the predicted vote was 25%, and at the 70% level the predicted vote was 53%.

Deviating from the trend[21] and giving Cox significantly more than anticipated support were 25 counties, but the difference between the predicted and actual vote although labelled significant was fairly small in most cases. Nearly all these counties were in what can generally be called east central and south central Ohio. Twenty counties gave Harding significantly more than anticipated support. This group included 9 of the 12 counties in the Western Reserve and 8 of the 20 counties in northwest Ohio. The movement of the Reserve counties represented a reassertion of old habits.

Northwest Ohio has been mentioned several times, usually for giving to the Democrats more votes than called for by the general trend. In 1918 and 1920, however, the area is distinguished by a move to the Republicans stronger than anticipated by reference to the state trend. Many of these counties (as indicated by Map 2) had become strongly Democratic. This fact taken in conjunction with the fact that the most Democratic counties showed the greatest decline in 1918 and 1920 and the fact that many northwestern counties ran ahead of the trend means obviously that very large shifts of voters took place in the area. For instance, the Democratic vote changed in Auglaize County from an average of 69% in the 1870–1892 period, to an average of 63% in the period 1905–1910, to 42% in 1920.[22] The sequence in some other counties in the area was this: Defiance—63, 58, 38; Fulton—38, 44, 25; Henry—62, 66, 33; Mercer—70, 68, 44; and Putnam—65, 68, 48.

A feature which distinguishes northwestern Ohio is its large German population, which is difficult to identify by county. The first census which gives foreign born by country of birth and by county of residence is the census of 1870, but Germans had been coming into Ohio since the thirties. The census of 1910 enumerates the foreign born and also identifies second generation Americans by county of descent if born in the United States of parents both born in the same foreign nation. Use of 1870 figures on the number of German born or use of 1910 figures combining German born and second generation Germans probably means a substantial underestimate of the German element in the population of most counties. Although this may be seriously disputed, it is possible a more accurate estimate may be obtained by adding together the 1870 figures and both the 1910 figures. The German element in any county would thus be defined as the per cent of the total 1870

---

[20] The averages for the 1905–1910 period were the X-values and the 1920 returns were the Y-values in the regression analysis. The line of regression is expressed by the equation, $Y_p = 4.05 + .70X$.

[21] The coefficient of correlation is plus .68.

[22] These averages are, of course, those defined and computed earlier in this study.

population born in Germany plus the per cent of the 1910 population born in Germany plus the per cent of the 1910 population enumerated as second generation Germans. By this measure, 11 counties in the northwest are 15% or more "German."

The relative size of the German element in these northwestern counties explains several things. In the first place, these counties are not all equally Democratic in the period before the first world war; in fact, all are not Democratic. These differences in party preference relate directly to the proportion of Germans in the population. Where Germans are relatively numerous, the Democrats do best; and where Germans are relatively few, the Democrats do worst.[23] In the second place, the relative size of the German population relates directly to the vote changes which appear when averages from the 1905–1910 period are compared with the 1920 presidential returns. Where Germans are relatively numerous, the decline in the Democratic vote is greatest; and where Germans are relatively few, the decline is least.[24]

Outside the northwest 10 counties had populations 15% or more German around the time of World War I according to the measure employed here. Seven of the 10 were large urban counties;[25] and, as noted before, many of them deviated from the statewide trend in 1918 by giving the Democrats significantly more than anticipated support. In 1920 most merely followed the trend. It seems the German element in these urban counties did not behave as did the German element in more rural counties or else it was offset by counter movements. The 3 more rural counties outside the northwest with significant German populations (Erie and Huron just to the east and Scioto in the southeast) followed the trend set by the northwestern counties fairly well.

In 1932 Roosevelt carried Ohio with 49.9% of the total vote which compared with Hoover's 47.0%. In FDR's column were 55 counties, 27 of which he carried by more than 55% of the two-party vote. Hoover carried 33 counties, 13 with more than 55% of the two-party vote.

The old pattern was largely restored. Relative to the 1905–1910 period, the Democratic share of the two-party vote increased everywhere except in the counties which had been most Democratic, and there the Democratic vote was stable or else declined but little.[26] At the 30% level the predicted vote was 34%. At the 50% level the predicted vote was 51%, and at the 70% level the predicted vote was 67%.

[23] The 20 counties in the region were ranked from 1 to 20 according to the per cent of the population classified as German, the most German county being ranked first and so on. The counties were also ranked according to their average Democratic vote in the 1905–1910 gubernatorial elections, the most Democratic being ranked first and the least Democratic being ranked last. The two rank orders were compared, and a rank order correlation of plus .60 was obtained. Lucas (Toledo), the most urban county in the region showed the least relationship between the two factors being considered; so it was dropped from consideration and a new rank order correlation of plus .68 was obtained. These rank order correlations are high enough to justify the judgment that differences in behavior relate to the relative size of the German population even though the presence of other factors must also be conceded. The coefficients are Spearman rank order coefficients.

[24] A regression analysis was made with the per cent German in each county being the X-value and the percentage point decline from the 1905–1910 average to the 1920 presidential vote being the Y-value for each county. Lucas was omitted since, as already stated, its behavior seems not typical of the area. The line of regression is expressed by the equation, $Y_p = 9.21 + .39X$. At the 10% German

level the predicted decline in the Democratic vote is 13 percentage points, and the predicted drop at the 20% level is 17 percentage points; at the 30% level 21 percentage points, and at the 50% level 29 percentage points. The coefficient of correlation is plus .69.

[25] Butler (Hamilton-Middletown) 28% German; Cuyahoga (Cleveland) 42%; Franklin (Columbus) 20%; Hamilton (Cincinnati) 55%; Loran (Elyria-Lorain) 24%; Montgomery (Dayton) 27%; Stark (Canton-Massalon) 18%.

[26] In the regression analysis the 1905–1910 averages were X-values and the 1932 returns were Y-values. The line of regression is expressed by the equation, $Y_p = 9.5 + .82X$.

Most counties followed the trend closely.[27] Among the exceptions were eight counties in the northwest which gave FDR significantly more than expected support as did some other scattered counties. On the other hand, 9 counties in east central Ohio[28] gave FDR significantly less than expected support as did the metropolitan counties of Hamilton (Cincinnati) and Franklin (Columbus) and a few scattered counties.

FDR carried Ohio again in 1936 getting 58% of the total vote compared to Landon's 37.4%. In terms of the two-party vote, FDR carried 44 counties with more than 55% of the vote and another 23 counties with smaller majorities. Landon carried 21 counties, only 4 with more than 55% of the vote.

The pattern in 1936 shows a sharp break with past habits. Relative to the 1905–1910 period, the Democratic vote increased very substantially where it had been low and declined where it had been 60% or higher.[29] At the 30% level the predicted vote was 46%. At the 50% level the predicted vote was 55%, and at the 70% level the predicted vote was 64%.

Deviations from the trend were numerous and sometimes strikingly large.[30] Thirteen of the 16 counties which could be classified as metropolitan in 1930[31] gave significantly more than anticipated support to FDR. In the industrial areas of the Western Reserve and eastern Ohio Democratic gains were very large. The general trend called for increases in those areas, and these counties ran ahead of the trend. Mahoning County (Youngstown) was most spectacular. It had given Roosevelt 45% of its two-party vote

in 1932, but gave him 72% of the two-party vote in 1936. Some other counties gave significantly more than expected support to the Democrats; however, differences between expected and actual votes were not so great, and the counties were scattered.

More counties gave the Democrats significantly less than predicted support than gave them more than predicted support. In most of these cases the deviation from the trend was enough to meet the test of significance that is used here but little more. Ten of the northwestern counties were in this group; the others were scattered but were mainly counties where the Democrats had been usually weak. In simplest terms, the 1936 election saw imposed on the old pattern very heavy Democratic gains in some of the industrial counties and some weakening of the Democratic sentiment among traditional supporters in the northwest.

In 1940 FDR got 52.2% of the Ohio vote in a two-party contest with Willkie. The distribution of the vote bears little resemblance to anything which has been described before.[32] The election did not, however, mark the creation of a lasting new pattern; so a thorough analysis seems not to be essential. But the election does offer an opportunity to consider again the behavior of the German element under the impact of a foreign war with Germany as the opponent. The analysis will be limited to the 19 counties in northwestern Ohio whose behavior at the time of the first world war related directly to the relative size of their German populations. There the decline in the Roosevelt vote from 1936 to 1940 varied from 29 to 9 percentage points. Inspection of the data shows that Ottawa County deviated widely from the apparent trend in the area; so it was eliminated. It was discovered once again that there was a direct

[27] The coefficient of correlation is plus .82.
[28] Counties south of the Western Reserve, west of the Seven Ranges, north of the Ohio Company grant, and east of the Virginia Military District.
[29] In the regression analysis the 1905–1910 averages were the X-values and the 1936 returns the Y-values. The line of regression is expressed by the equation, $Y_p = 31.8 + .46X$.
[30] The coefficient of correlation is only plus .47.
[31] Counties with a city of 50,000 or more population or adjacent thereto with 10,000 or more persons employed in mining and manufacturing.

[32] The relationship to the 1905–1910 period is expressed by the regression equation, $Y_p = 42.51 + .06X$, and by the correlation coefficient, plus .05. The relationship to the 1936 election is expressed by the regression equation, $Y_p = 29.14 + .30X$, and by the correlation coefficient, plus .25.

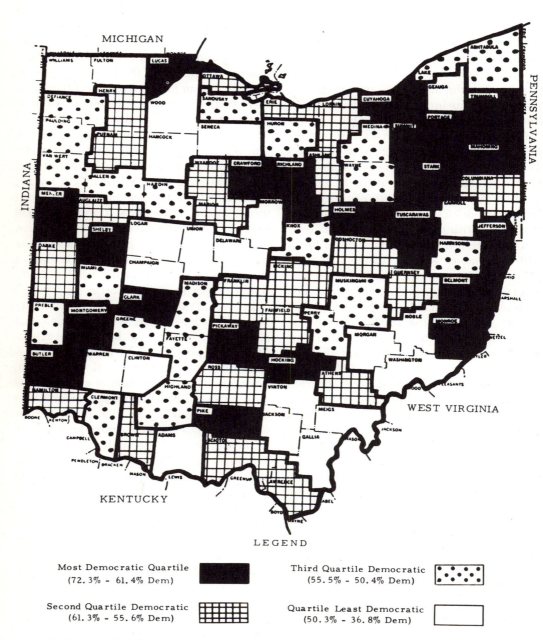

Map 3   Relative strength of party preferences expressed shares of the two-party vote for President, 1936.

relationship between the size of the German population and the vote change.[33] The larger the German element the greater the decline in the Democratic vote.

In the post World War II era (1946 to the present) the Republicans won 3 of the 4 presidential races but only 2 of the 7 gubernatorial elections. The average Republican share of the total state vote for president was 55.3% in contrast to a Democratic share of 44.7%. The average Republican share of the vote for governor was 47.6% in contrast to 52.4% for the Democrats.

The success of the Democrats in gubernatorial elections has been attributed to the personal popularity of Frank J. Lausche who was elected governor 4 times in the period under consideration.[34] Analysis of the 1952 elections indicates that and something more fundamental. In 1952 Eisenhower took 57% of the total vote for president while Lausche took 56% of the vote for governor. County by county comparison of the two-party vote for governor and for president indicates Stevenson typically ran about 15 percentage points behind Lausche,[35] a difference which must be attributed in part anyway to the popularity of the candidates relative to their opponents. But 10 of the 15 counties which gave Stevenson significantly less support than would be anticipated by reference to the general trend were counties with sizable German elements indicating this group could give expression to old loyalties in a gubernatorial but not a presidential election.

Results of a different and somewhat more extended analysis of gubernatorial and presidential returns are similar. In 1952 Lausche's share of the two-party vote exceeded Stevenson's in the various counties of the state by a median of 13.5 percentage points. Twelve counties gave Lausche a vote which exceeded Stevenson's by 20 percentage points or more; 8 were in the northwest. In 1956 when DiSalle was the Democratic candidate the Democratic vote for governor exceeded the Democratic vote for president by a median of 5.0 percentage points. Fifteen counties gave DiSalle a measure of support which exceeded Stevenson's by 7 or more percentage points. Twelve were in the northwest indicating that DiSalle as well as Lausche was the beneficiary of a traditional German Democratic vote which did not carry over to presidential candidate Stevenson.

In 1956 the Democratic vote for president on a county by county basis was about 60% of what it had been 20 years earlier[36] and in the gubernatorial election about two-thirds of what it had been in the presidential election of 1936.[37] In these two elections the Democratic candidates got less support than would be expected by reference to the trend in a number of northwestern and east central counties. As can be inferred from what has been said before, the decline of Democratic strength in the northwest was substantially more in the

[33] Percentages German were the X-values in the regression analysis and percentage point declines in the Democratic vote the Y-values. The line of regression is expressed by the equation, $Y_P = 9.69 + .42X$. At the 10% level (10% German) the predicted decline in the Democratic vote is 14 percentage points, and 18 percentage points at the 20% level. At the 30% level the predicted drop is 22 percentage points, and at the 50% level 31 percentage points. The coefficient of correlation is plus .62.

[34] He also served a term as governor in 1945–1946.

[35] Taking the gubernatorial returns as the X-values and the presidential returns as Y-values, the line of regression is expressed by the equation, $Y_P = 14.72 + 1.02X$. The coefficient of correlation is .81.

[36] In the regression analysis the Democratic share of the two-party vote in 1936 furnished the X-values and the Democratic share of the two-party vote in 1956 the Y-values. The line of regression is expressed by the equation, $Y_P = 1.38 + .59X$. The coefficient of correlation was plus .67.

[37] In the regression analysis the Democratic share of the two-party vote in 1936 furnished the X-values and the Democratic share of the two-party vote in 1956 the Y-values. The line of regression is expressed by the equation, $Y_P = 2.12 + .67X$. The coefficient of correlation was plus .74.

presidential than in the gubernatorial election. In the more support than expected category were some scattered counties plus a group in south central Ohio. In general, however, the pattern shown by the 1956 elections is similar to that of 1936 which leads to the conclusion that the 1936 pattern represents with some modifications a modern norm although it is much less well established than norms in earlier periods.[38]

Today the strongest Republican counties are in most cases counties which have always been strongly Republican. Relatively less strong but clearly Republican counties are a more mixed lot. Some are counties which have a long tradition of being Republican but others in northwest and in east central Ohio are counties which once had been counted by the Democrats as theirs. In the relatively Democratic counties are many in the south and in the northwest which were traditionally Democratic. The most Democratic counties since 1936 and at the present are the urbanized and highly industrialized counties.

SUMMARY AND COMMENT

From 1832 to the first world war the size of major party followings in Ohio were nearly equal and remarkably stable. Shocks occurred, and were followed by one or more uneven contests. Examples are the reorganization of the party system in 1853, the Civil War, and the depression of 1893. In each case, however, recovery follows; and each party reappears with close to its former strength. It would be tempting to say this constitutes support for the view that two-party systems have a built-in tendency toward equilibrium; but the fact is that the same areas and presumably the same people and their progeny support a given party before and after these shocks to the political system. There is no regrouping going on as the equilibrium model implies but instead the regeneration of old loyalties to their earlier vigor.

The groups on whose loyalty the party system rested in this period were sectional in two senses: (1) sectionally concentrated within the state; and (2) sectional in terms of origin. The location of party followings within the state can be summarized more quickly by a glance at maps 1 and 2 than by words. So far as origin is concerned and insofar as definite statements are possible, sectionalism in Ohio was not a projection of the north-south conflict. The Whig-Republican following was both Yankee and southern in origin. Democrats were sometimes southern in origin, but it seems that Pennsylvania and particularly the Pennsylvania Dutch furnished the broader base for the party.

There was also an ethnic-sectional basis for Ohio politics. The strongest Whig and Republican counties were Yankee, and many but not all the strongest Democratic counties had in them strong German elements.[39] It goes beyond the data reported here, but this finding plus scattered references in the literature suggest that one of the basic divisions in American politics for many years was this division between Yankee and German.[40]

---

[38] The 1958 gubernatorial election which saw DiSalle reverse the verdict of 1956 by beating O'Neill decisively does not resemble closely the 1936 election. The 1960 presidential election, however, brought out a vote which differed from the 1956 presidential election only in that Kennedy gained about 1 percentage point over Stevenson in the various counties for every 2 per cent of the population enumerated as Roman Catholic by the 1936 religious census. Results of this analysis of the 1960 election are reported more fully in my study which is to be published by the *Western Political Quarterly* under the title, "How Mr. Nixon Took Ohio: A Short Reply to Senator Kennedy's Question." There was no gubernatorial election in 1960, DiSalle having been elected to a four-year term in 1958.

[39] Examination of several counties in northern Ohio (Erie of "Erie County" fame, Sandusky, and Seneca) where there were both German and Yankee elements show that for many years and to some extent down to the present there is a very sharp difference in voting behavior between German and Yankee townships.

[40] For instance, Lee Benson, *The Concept of Jacksonian Democracy: New York as a Test Case*

The obvious importance of sectional and ethnic factors in Ohio demonstrates that there was, at least, no clear-cut class basis for statewide party followings from the time of Jackson to that of Wilson. With reference to the Jacksonian era this conclusion is in general agreement with that reached by Lee Benson from his examination of New York politics.[41] The inference should surely not be drawn from these statements, however, that party programs had no class character at any time through this whole long period. As a matter of fact, the contrary is easily granted; and given this concession one is faced with the conclusion that there was at different times in the past if not at all times an issue oriented politics with class implications on one level while on another level there was electoral response in terms of group loyalties and antipathies which had little direct connection with issue politics. Such a conclusion is, of course, consistent with the findings of modern voting and opinion studies. The point to be made here is that the breach between issue politics and electoral response is a long existing condition and that theory in its effort to digest this hard fact should appreciate that it is not dealing with a phenomenon which is only contemporary or perhaps a passing aberration.

Ohio politics after World War I is not all of one piece. The presidential vote fluctuates within wide margins; gubernatorial and presidential returns follow different courses. Consequently the period must be treated in pieces. In 1920 the Democrats were badly defeated in the presidential election, and one of the factors which contributed to the decisive defeat was the massive shift of German Democratic voters in northwest Ohio from their traditional mooring to the Republican candidate. In the next two presidential elections the Republicans repeated their triumph, but the Democrats held the governorship through most of the twenties. In 1932 FDR won by a small but clear margin an election which from the point of view of this study was striking because of the restoration of the pre-World War I pattern which, of course, reflected electoral divisions which existed in the time of Jackson.

The major break in Ohio politics comes between 1932 and 1936, and is registered in the presidential election of 1936. Urban industrial counties which before had found the Democratic Party moderately attractive at best, moved decisively into the Democratic camp. A partially off-setting movement of traditional Democratic voters to the Republican Party was going on also in the early thirties in east central and northwest Ohio. In the case of the former area the movement may have been the consequence of a secular trend, but in the case of the latter area the movement is apparently an expression of dissatisfaction with the New Deal. The 1940 presidential election was much confused, but one feature which stands out clearly is the shift of the "German counties" to the Republican Party, a shift similar to that which occurred in 1920. The sensitivity of German nationality groups in the midwest particularly to foreign policy issues has been commented upon before, but the findings here do add another illustration which corroborates the more general observation.

After the second world war the Republicans won 3 of 4 presidential contests, but did much less well in the gubernatorial elections. One of the reasons was the willingness of traditional German Democratic areas to give substantially greater support

(Princeton, N.J.: Princeton University Press, 1961), pp. 173–175, pp. 177–179, p. 185. Benson estimates that contrary to the traditional view voters of New England descent voted only about 55–45 Whig. Still this is in marked contrast with his estimate for both old and new German elements, and it is also true, according to Benson's estimates, that the Yankee element was the only large group to show a Whig majority. See also Leon Epstein's comments on the German vote in Wisconsin in his study, *The Politics of Wisconsin* (Madison, Wisc.: The University of Wisconsin Press, 1958), p. 36.

[41] Benson, *ibid.*, p. 146, p. 150, p. 184.

to Democratic candidates for governor than to Democratic candidates for president. Frank Lausche's success in Ohio has been treated sometimes as an almost inexplicable phenomenon, but it appears that his success was due in part to the response of an identifiable section of the electorate whose very old and deep partisan loyalties had been subjected to severe stresses in the area of foreign policy.

Today it is the 1936 pattern amended by some further weakening of Democratic strength in east central and northwest Ohio which is the norm for Ohio politics although it is not so well established as earlier norms. The pattern is clearly modern in that the major industrial centers deliver the big battalions to the Democratic Party while the small towns and more rural areas generally produce Republican majorities. Nevertheless, there are anomalies in the pattern and differences of behavior between counties which can be accounted for only by the lingering effect of loyalties which antedate the New Deal. It is fair to conclude by saying that party followings in Ohio cannot now be defined only by reference to class and status; the definition must include also traditional loyalties which have little to do with the usual economic and social variables.[42] As Key and Munger argue in their Indiana study, electoral behavior is not simply a function of social and economic status.[43]

[42] Observers of Ohio politics are sometimes impressed by the caution with which state politicians treat economic and social issues, a style which seems to contrast with that seen in other states which are similar to Ohio in some respects. An explanation for this fact, if it is a fact, may be that political style reflects the nature of party followings which in Ohio include not only the usual class and ideological elements but to a more than ordinary degree traditional elements.

[43] V. O. Key, Jr., and Frank Munger, "Social Determinism and Electoral Decision: the Case of Indiana," in *American Voting Behavior*, Burdick and Brodbeck, eds. (New York: The Free Press of Glencoe, 1959), pp. 281–299.

7.   State Legislators in Southern Politics

Malcolm E. Jewell

The South has always been a peculiar area of the nation, requiring specialized political analysis. The politics of the region is presently undergoing rapid change. Malcolm Jewell, Professor of Political Science at the University of Kentucky, focuses on representation in the legislatures of Southern states. His analysis considers the effect of four trends: urban growth, reapportionment, increased Negro voting, and additional Republican representation. The eventual outcome may be one-, two-, or even three-party government.

* * *

In a symposium on southern politics of the last decade appearing in the *Journal of Politics* in 1948, H. C. Nixon described the typical southern legislature as "chiefly a body of Democratic, small-town or rural white men, a majority of whom represent a minority of the white population of the state, not to mention the restricted suffrage by which the members were chosen in a party primary."[1] More than fifteen years later his description is still accurate: the legislature represents primarily rural, white Democrats. Despite variations from state to state, the legislative pattern has been one of strong conservative control, minimizing conflict within the legislature or between the legislature and governor. Below the surface the forces of change are already apparent, however. The Supreme Court decision in *Baker* v. *Carr* and the organizational effort of both Republicans and

[1] H. C. Nixon, "The Southern Legislature and Legislation," *Journal of Politics*, X (1948), 412.

From the *Journal of Politics*, vol. 26, no. 1 (February 1964), pp. 177–187, 195–196 by permission of the Southern Political Science Association.

Negroes suggest that by 1970 there will be major changes in the power structure of most southern legislatures, changes that will make them more representative and that will increase the degree of competition in legislative elections and the degree of conflict in legislative sessions. In some legislatures the beginnings of change are already apparent.

REAPPORTIONMENT
AND URBAN REPRESENTATION

In March of 1962, when the *Baker* v. *Carr* decision was announced, not a single southern state had reapportioned both houses fully on the basis of the 1960 census, but there was wide variation among the states in the degree of malapportionment. In Arkansas, Kentucky, and Virginia there were no major constitutional obstacles to apportionment by population, the apportionments were no more than ten or twenty years out of date, the smallest percentage of the population that could elect a legislative majority averaged almost 40 percent, and the vote in rural counties (under 25,000 population) was worth only about twice as much as the vote in the largest counties. In five other states the problem was somewhat more serious: Louisiana, Mississippi, North Carolina, South Carolina, and Texas had substantial constitutional obstacles to apportionment by population in one or both houses. The Mississippi apportionment was largely determined by the specific allotment of seats in the 1890 constitution. Each South Carolina county had a single state senator. Constitutional provisions discriminated against the larger counties in both houses in Texas and the lower houses in North Carolina and Louisiana. The smallest proportion of the population that could elect a legislative majority averaged about one-third, and the vote in rural counties was worth from two to five times as much as in the largest counties. (In South Carolina the apportionment was much better

than this in the House and much worse in the Senate.)

In five states there were vast distortions in apportionment. These were caused by constitutional provisions in Florida and Georgia and in the Oklahoma House and by the failure to reapportion for half a century in Alabama, Tennessee, and in the Oklahoma Senate. A majority in the legislatures could be elected by about one-fourth the population, and in Florida by one-eighth. The value of the vote in rural counties ranged from three to fifteen times as much as in the largest counties in four states, while in Florida the ratio was thirty-to-one. In several of these states the apportionment also disadvantaged one region of the state; in Tennessee it discriminated against Republican areas. In Florida, where the apportionment was most distorted, it virtually guaranteed conflict between the legislature and a governor elected by urban as well as rural votes. In Georgia, on the other hand, the county unit system guaranteed that the governor, as well as the legislature, would be responsive primarily to rural voters.

The trend of population to metropolitan areas in the fifties and the pattern of inadequate or nonexistent reapportionment following the 1960 census meant that in the decade prior to *Baker* v. *Carr* the degree of malapportionment increased throughout the South. A comparison between 1955 figures (compiled by Dauer and Kelsay) and 1961 figures shows that the minimum percentage of the population needed to elect a majority dropped in every southern legislative body except two (the Louisiana House and Mississippi Senate). The median drop was 3 percent. The sharpest drops were in some of the most urban states: Virginia, Texas, Florida, and Tennessee.[2]

[2] Manning J. Dauer and Robert G. Kelsay, "Unrepresentative States," *National Municipal Review*, XLIV (1955), pp. 571–575. National Municipal League, *Compendium on Legislative Apportionment* (New York, 2d ed., 1962), pp. iii, iv. The

In the first sixteen months after the *Baker* v. *Carr* decision eight southern legislatures enacted new apportionment laws covering one or both houses. In most cases they acted after prodding by state or federal courts. In Florida and Mississippi the voters (primarily urban voters) rejected the first apportionment plans enacted as constitutional amendments, and the legislators were forced to try again. The apportionment laws passed in Tennessee, Virginia, Alabama, and Oklahoma were rejected by the courts. The Tennessee legislature made a second effort to meet the judicial requirements; the Virginia case was appealed to the Supreme Court; the court in Alabama imposed an apportionment plan based on some parts of the legislative plan; and the court in Oklahoma rejected a legislative compromise and imposed its own plan based strictly on population standards. The Georgia legislature reapportioned only one house, meeting the requirements of the federal court. The Kentucky legislature reapportioned both houses effectively enough to meet any likely judicial tests. Legislative and judicial action was prompt enough so that new apportionments formed the basis for the 1962 elections in Tennessee, Alabama, and Georgia, special elections in Florida early in 1963, and regular elections in Kentucky in 1963.

In five states the *Baker* v. *Carr* decision had no direct impact during the first sixteen months. In Texas, North Carolina, South Carolina, Louisiana, and Arkansas one or both houses had been reapportioned by the legislature (or in Arkansas by a state court prior to *Baker* v. *Carr*) following the 1960 census, although in all of these states constitutional provisions prevented the apportionments from being based fully on population. In most of these states the issue of reapportionment was attracting increased attention and was the subject of legislative debate if not action, in the months following *Baker* v. *Carr*.[2a]

It is too early to judge how full the tides of reapportionment will be in southern states. It is already evident that southern legislatures will go no further than is required by the courts. The Supreme Court will have to settle the contradictions which have already begun to emerge from lower federal and state court decisions. Judicial standards of population equality have varied considerably in cases arising in southern states. A federal court required that the two largest counties in Oklahoma, with one-third of the population, have 34 percent of the Senate seats and 31 percent of the House seats. The federal court in Virginia invalidated an apportionment in which the maximum disparity was $2\frac{1}{2}$ to 1 in the Senate and 4 to 1 in the House. Similarly, the federal court in Tennessee said that the reapportionment there fell short of constitutional standards when it gave the four metropolitan counties, with 43 percent of the adult population, just under one-third of the seats in each house. On the other hand, a federal court unanimously approved an apportionment in Florida (later rejected by the voters) as "rational" and "free from invidious discrimination" even though eleven urban counties with 72 percent of the population would have had 49 percent of the House seats and only 24 percent of the Senate seats.

The pattern of reapportionment in the South will also be clearer when the courts decide whether or not substantial equality is necessary in *both* houses.* The federal court in Virginia asserted strongly that this

---

figures on the value of the vote are from: Paul T. David and Ralph Eisenberg, *Devaluation of the Urban and Suburban Vote* (Charlottesville: Bureau of Public Administration, University of Virginia, 1961).

2a A limited reapportionment of the Louisiana House withstood judicial challenge and took effect in the December primary. The North Carolina Senate was reapportioned in October.

* In the case of Reynolds v. Sims, 377 U.S. 533 (1964), the Supreme Court mandated equality of representation in both houses of state legislatures. (Eds.)

was necessary, and this was the principle followed by the court in Oklahoma. In the Alabama case the federal court said that population must be used to some extent as the standard for both houses. In Tennessee the federal court said that population must be the only standard in at least one house. In Georgia the federal court stated that one house must be apportioned according to population and deliberately avoided a decision concerning what standard should apply to the other house. The efforts by legislators in Alabama, Mississippi, and other states to abandon the population standard entirely for one house indicates the importance of this question. It will also affect the chances for reapportionment in North Carolina, South Carolina, and Texas, where constitutional provisions have undermined or eliminated the population principle in one house.

The gradual growth of urban representation in southern legislatures resulting from legislative and judicial action will have a number of consequences, some more clearly discernible than others. It should increase competition in the legislative primaries. A study of recent legislative primaries in five southern states showed that, with few exceptions, metropolitan districts had a larger proportion of contested primaries and a larger proportion won by narrow margins than rural districts had. In Alabama and Louisiana there was a distinctly lower level of competition in black belt counties than in other rural counties.[3] Reapportionment may affect the types of districts used in some states. In those southern states which use multi-member districts for metropolitan counties, reapportionment is creating some unusually large districts. In Alabama, the number of representatives in the single legislative district of Jefferson county rose

from 7 to 17, and those in Davidson county, Tennessee, increased from 6 to 9 under the new apportionment. Jefferson county has had from 23 to 36 candidates for 7 House seats in recent years, and Davidson county has had from 17 to 39 candidates running for 6 seats. The presence of so many candidates on the ballot is confusing to the voters and places a premium on well-known names.

Reapportionment may force changes in the rotation system common in some states. Rotation agreements occur in a state Senate or the House when there are several counties in a district. Party committees in each county formally agree to rotate the legislative seat every two or four years from county to county. Rotation agreements have been used by each party in some one-party House districts in Kentucky, and have been used in nearly all multi-county Senate districts in Alabama. In Tennessee and North Carolina, where there has been some use of rotation agreements, state law provides for primary voting only in the county from which the candidate is to be chosen if a rotation agreement is in effect. Until invalidated by a federal court following *Baker* v. *Carr,* Georgia law *required* rotation agreements in multi-county senatorial districts and permitted voting only in the county from which the candidate would come. The result was to discriminate against large counties joined in senatorial districts with small counties.

Unless a state increases the size of its legislature, a growth in urban seats is sure to increase the number of multi-county districts suitable for rotation agreements, although some districts may become so large as to make rotation impractical. If reapportionment is carried out regularly after each decennial census, it will become increasingly difficult to implement rotation agreements. (It may be no coincidence that two of the states with extensive and long-established rotation patterns, Alabama and Tennessee, had not reapportioned for half

[3] Malcolm E. Jewell, "Competition and Factionalism in Southern Legislative Primaries and Elections" (Paper presented at the 1962 meeting of the American Political Science Association, Washington, D.C., September, 1962), pp. 13–16.

a century prior to *Baker* v. *Carr*.) With the numerical growth of urban representatives, rural interests may decide that the principle of self-protection requires that legislative experience be given priority over rotation.

Perhaps the most important aspect of reapportionment, and certainly the most difficult to predict, concerns the effect of greater urban representation on voting patterns in the legislature. Are there significant differences between urban and rural representatives, and if so on which issues do these differences become sharpest? A study of past roll calls may be deceptive because a change in representation would affect the balance of power on committees and consequently the bills emerging from committee for a vote on the floor. Nevertheless, previous roll calls provide the most tangible alternative to sheer speculation about the effects of reapportionment on legislative voting.

The most detailed southern study of this question has been made in Alabama by Murray C. Havens. In a study of the 1955–1956 session of the Alabama House, he found statistically significant differences (at a level of significance of .05) in voting among urban, rural, and mixed representatives on only about one-fourth of the contested roll calls. The sharpest urban-rural differences were on the issue of reapportionment and racial questions. Urban-rural differences were sharply defined on only a few labor, health, education, and welfare issues. Nor were there many roll calls with significant urban-rural differences on other issues where they might be anticipated: taxation, municipal affairs, appropriations, and highways. Havens found, in a small sample of these roll calls, that factional differences (for and against the Folsom administration) were sometimes, but not consistently, more significant than urban-rural differences.[4]

One obvious shortcoming of roll call analyses is that they usually do not discriminate between major bills and trivial bills. Evidence from both North and South suggests that there are probably relatively few roll calls in most legislative sessions in which there are sharply defined urban-rural voting alignments. Yet these are likely to include some of the most important issues faced by the legislature. In addition to the Alabama study, evidence from Florida suggests that metropolitan or urban legislators are likely to have a more liberal attitude toward racial issues. Studies of both Florida and Alabama have cited "right to work" issues as another category on which urban-rural alignments appear, and this might be expected on other labor issues as well. Evidence from states throughout the country suggests that malapportionment leads to a distribution of tax revenue, for such purposes as highways and education in particular, that is heavily weighted in favor of rural counties. In Florida, for example, revenue from race tracks is distributed evenly among counties—even though the largest county has more than three hundred times as many people as the smallest.[5]

There is no certainty that greater urban representation will produce a more liberal attitude toward social and economic issues in general. On some issues there may be a conservative coalition between suburban and rural legislators. The nature of urban representatives depends to a considerable extent on the districting practices followed in the cities. Where a metropolitan county is divided into single-member districts, there are likely to be differences in the voting behavior of legislators from low-income and high-income districts. Where, as in many southern states, legislators from

[4] Murray C. Havens, *City Versus Farms?* (University, Ala.: Bureau of Public Administration, University of Alabama, 1957).

[5] William C. Havard and Loren P. Beth, *The Politics of Mis-Representation* (Baton Rouge: Louisiana State University Press, 1962), pp. 16–19, 79–82. Hugh Douglas Price, "Florida Politics and the Pork Choppers," in Malcolm E. Jewell, ed., *The Politics of Reapportionment* (New York: Atherton Press, 1962), p. 89.

the metropolitan districts are elected at large, greater uniformity in legislative voting during a session may be anticipated from those legislators.

In the North reapportionment is likely to have the greatest effect in those states where it leads to a change in the partisan balance of power and particularly where it reduces the incidence of divided government. Similarly, in the South reapportionment is likely to have the greatest effect in states where a small clique of rural legislators has been able to maintain tight control over one or both houses sometimes in conflict with the governor. Examples of this are found in the Georgia and Florida legislatures and in the South Carolina Senate. The implications of reapportionment for such state legislatures should be obvious from the description of their power structure in subsequent pages. Because the Negro vote and the Republican vote have been drawn primarily from metropolitan areas, reapportionment should also contribute to the growing importance of Negro and Republican representation in southern legislatures.

THE PROSPECTS
FOR NEGRO REPRESENTATION

Negro registration increased rapidly in the late 1940's, following the demise of the white primary; during the 1950's the growth was slower. In the eleven states of the confederate South, estimated Negro registration rose from 600,000 in 1947 to 1,300,000 in 1960. How rapidly Negro registration and voting will grow in the 1960's depends of course on the vigor of Negro organizations, the effectiveness of federal safeguards, and the strength of governmental resistance in some southern states. The obstacles to Negro voting have been greatest in the deep South and particularly in those counties, primarily rural, with a large proportion of Negro population. As a consequence, despite the existence of many rural legislative districts with a population of from 40 to 70

percent Negro, there are few in which the voting population is more than one-third Negro and almost none in which it is over half Negro. Moreover, population trends in most southern states are causing a decline in the number of southern districts that are over 40 percent Negro. Progress toward more equitable apportionment in southern states being made more rapidly than progress in removing the obstacles to Negro voting, obstacles which tend to be least in metropolitan counties. All of these factors support the prediction that Negro influence in the legislature will grow more rapidly in metropolitan than in rural constituencies. In several southern metropolitan counties the Negro registration is close to 20 percent of the total registered voters.[6]

The extent of Negro influence in legislative elections depends partly on the types of districts used in the metropolitan counties. Although Negro political organizations may influence the choice of white legislators through endorsements carrying great weight with Negro voters, the acid test of Negro representation is the election of Negro legislators. Since Negro population is usually concentrated in certain sections of southern cities, the single-member district system provides Negroes with the best chance of concentrating their vote and maximizing its effectiveness. The only metropolitan county in the deep South having single-member districts is that containing New Orleans, which assigns one, or occasionally two, members to each of 17 wards and has single-member Senate districts. All other counties in Louisiana having more than one House member elect them at large. Negro registration has been as high as one-third in two New Orleans House districts, but Negro influence on the Democratic primary has been reduced by the substantial proportion of Negroes registered as Republicans. Two other states that might be more

[6] Margaret Price, *The Negro and the Ballot* (Atlanta: Southern Regional Council, 1959). U.S. Commission on Civil Rights, *Voting* (1961), p. 22.

accurately classified as border states use single-member districts: Kentucky, which uses them exclusively, and Oklahoma, which uses them for some of the larger counties but has at-large elections in some two and three member House districts. Louisville has frequently had a Negro in the Kentucky legislature.

When the Georgia legislature reapportioned the Senate in October, 1962, the question of districting arose with regard to urban countries which, for the first time, were getting more than a single senator. Proponents of the at-large system warned that Negro legislators would probably be chosen from one or more districts if a district system were used, and this was one of the arguments that led the legislature to adopt an at-large system. (Districts were used as a basis of residence for candidates, and not for voting.) A constitutional amendment was also adopted to perpetuate the at-large system. After a hectic legal battle involving one federal court and two state courts, a state judge ruled that voting must be by districts in the 1962 election (and this permitted nomination of a Negro legislator without a runoff), but the constitutional amendment requiring at-large elections was approved. A brief filed in federal court charged that the at-large election "results in invidious dilution of a voter's vote due solely to his race." Although the federal court agreed that the at-large system "presents serious questions as to whether it is violative of the Fourteenth and Fifteenth Amendments," the court declined to rule on the point, leaving unanswered a constitutional question which could have far-reaching implications for Negro representation in state legislatures.

In all other southern states metropolitan counties electing more than one member to either house use at-large elections. In Arkansas, Georgia (in the House), North Carolina, South Carolina, Virginia, and (with one exception) Tennessee the metropolitan counties use a pure at-large system in which all candidates run against each other. In Alabama, Florida, Mississippi, and Texas the metropolitan counties use an at-large system with places, in which candidates run for a specific place or position but are voted on by all voters in the county. The pure at-large system gives Negro voters, or any other group, a better chance to elect one or two legislators by voting only for these. Fear of such "one-shot" voting by Negroes led Shelby County, Tennessee, where Negroes constitute nearly one-third of the registered voters, to shift to the place system in 1960.[7]

THE GROWTH OF REPUBLICAN REPRESENTATION

During the 1950's the southern legislatures could be divided into two categories: those that consistently had a small bloc of Republican members and those in which Republicans were rare or nonexistent. In the first category were only five of the thirteen states: Virginia, North Carolina, Kentucky, Tennessee, and Oklahoma. Most of the Republican legislators in these states were elected from traditional Republican counties, most of which were concentrated in the mountain areas of southwestern Virginia, western North Carolina, southeastern Kentucky and eastern Tennessee. In Oklahoma the traditional Republican counties are in the north-central part of the state. In almost one-fifth of the Kentucky House districts, for example, the Republicans won every election during this period, often without any Democratic opponent. In Tennessee there were ten House districts (out of one hundred) in which the Republicans won every election during the 1950–1960 period and in none of which the Democrats consistently ran candidates. In both

[7] For a study of the consequences of a similar change in voting mechanics for city offices in Memphis, see William E. Wright, *Memphis Politics: A Study in Racial Bloc Voting* (Eagleton Cases in Practical Politics) (New York: McGraw-Hill Co., 1962).

states most of these districts incorporate counties traditionally Republican in presidential races, and most of the Tennessee districts had been electing Republican legislators consistently as far back as 1920. During the 1950's there were no Republicans in the legislatures of Louisiana, Mississippi, and South Carolina, and an insignificant number in the legislatures of Alabama, Arkansas, Georgia, Texas, and Florida.

The opportunities for *increased* Republican representation lie not in the traditional Republican counties, primarily rural, but in the metropolitan centers, usually those gaining seats in the new apportionments. It is in the metropolitan counties of the South that the Republican party had its largest percentage of the presidential vote in 1952, 1956, and 1960 (outside of traditionally Republican counties), and it is here that the largest number of Republican candidates for Congress have been found. It is also in the metropolitan South that the Republicans have made the greatest progress recently in running legislative candidates and, in a few states, winning additional legislative seats. Since 1950 the Republicans have run legislative candidates consistently in Louisville and frequently in other Kentucky metropolitan counties. In Alabama and Louisiana Republican candidates have been found almost entirely in metropolitan counties (except for a handful of traditionally Republican Alabama counties).

The most significant Republican advances at the start of the 1960's, came in the two most urbanized southern states: Texas and Florida. The Republican party in Texas ran only 5 legislative candidates in 1956, 33 in 1958, 22 in 1960, and 101 candidates in 1962 out of a possible 181. Two-thirds of the candidates have been in the ten largest metropolitan counties, and in 1962 nearly complete Republican slates were run in several of the largest counties. The party won seven House seats in 1962,

including six in Dallas, and a number of its candidates in metropolitan counties ran strong races.

The Republican party began to gain legislative seats in Florida during the 1950's, increasing from three in 1951 to seven in 1955 and 1957. The next advance came in the special 1963 election following reapportionment when the Republicans elected a second senator and increased House membership from 5 to 16. In the four elections from 1955 through 1962, the Republicans ran candidates, on the average, for one-fifth of the House seats; about 60 percent of these candidates were in the seven largest metropolitan counties. The only county where the party consistently won was Pinellas (St. Petersburg). The potential impact of reapportionment on Republican legislative strength is more dramatically illustrated in Florida than anywhere else. Those seven counties, where Republican legislative strength is concentrated, increased their House representation from 18 to 46 seats in the 1963 apportionment. The Republicans ran candidates for 27 of those 28 new seats in the special 1963 election, and they won 11 of them. . . .

PATTERNS OF CHANGE

The stable legislative patterns in the South are undergoing change, change induced by four interrelated factors: population trends to urban areas, judicially induced reapportionment, the growth of Republican strength in national and state elections, and the rising tide of Negro votes. In the three most urban states of the South, Louisiana, Texas, and Florida, we find examples of the varied patterns that this change may take. As out-groups begin to become more fully represented in the legislature, there will be a structuring of the increasing conflicts among these groups. This is likely to take the form of factions within the Democratic legislative party, factions that are evident in primary elections as well as in roll-call voting. The experience of Louisiana, where legislative factions have been more meaningful than in other states, suggests, however, that this trend toward factions is likely to be uneven, incomplete, and inconsistent over a period of years. The mechanical (i.e. districting) as well as political obstacles to the election of Negro legislators and the unity displayed by legislators in some states in opposition to school desegregation suggest that it will be a long time before Negro legislators are integrated into legislative factions.

The growth of legislative factions and the increase in Republican legislators in states like Florida and Texas result in part from the same causes. The trends are likely to develop along parallel lines and both will be intensified by reapportionment. But there is an inherent contradiction between the two trends. In a county, such as Dallas, the election of Republican legislators may put pressure on Democrats to abandon the divisive tactics of slating; in a state, such as Florida, Democrats might eventually have to unite to prevent the Republicans from holding the balance of power. Some southern legislatures may move from a one-party system to a "three-party" system, at least during a transitional period. Republicans, representing predominantly the more conservative, suburban interests in metropolitan counties, might vote with southern, urban Democrats in Florida on racial issues but would vote with the conservative wing of the Texas Democratic party on economic issues.

The trend of the 1960's in some southern states is toward increased legislative factionalism, but legislative factions seldom have the cohesion, organizational strength, or continuity that is characteristic of legislative parties. In most southern states the obstacles to a strong two-party system at the gubernatorial and particularly the legislative level remain formidable, despite

reapportionment. In the 1970 legislature the various interests in southern states will be better—but not perfectly—represented. Conflicts among these groups will be structured more fully, but seldom neatly between two groups, whether called parties or factions. . . .

8. Electoral Competition and Electoral Systems in Large Cities

Charles Gilbert and Christopher Clague

The party organizations of large cities differ significantly from those in nation and state. Nonpartisan elections are common, intraparty contests often substitute for two-party competition, and interest groups and social interests may perform the functions traditionally attributed to the formal parties. In this selection, the authors—professors at Swarthmore College—classify the party systems of major cities into eight major categories.

* * *

There is great variation in the political structures of our major cities; but there are also some recurring broad patterns. Political "competition" thus occurs in differing forms as well as in different degree in our several cities; and *electoral* competition is influenced by the variant political structures. Here we essay an introductory outline of these broad types of political structure. Our purpose is twofold: to place the election data and electoral systems in context, and to try to identify the major factors determining context. Thus, the outline that follows is not derived from the

From the *Journal of Politics*, vol. 24, no. 2 (May 1962), pp. 324–331 by permission of the Southern Political Science Association.

electoral data themselves; it stems from a systematic perusal of newspapers and from the limited monographic and periodical literature.[1]

1. One type is that of the dominant (usually Democratic) organization which is relatively cohesive, strongly controlled, and secure. Examples are Chicago and Pittsburgh. Cohesion, control, and security are always relative, but these two cities certainly score high today. So does Philadelphia despite the distinguishing characteristic discussed just below.[2]

2. A second type differs from the first but marginally, so some say; others find the difference crucial. This type also "enjoys" Democratic party dominance, but with the difference that a "good government," anti-organization, and programmatic element holds some offices or at least substantial influence. The pattern is thus partly one of uneasy alliance between two now traditional sets or urban political forces: those underlying the "organization," and those based in the interests and ideologies of reform. Probably the position of the anti-organization element depends in large part on the "enlighten-

ment" and support of downtown businessmen. There is something of a political division of labor in which certain city-wide aspects of policy are left to the executive (for the division is typically a governmental division also), while local benefits and political patronage are primarily left to the political professionals and the council. The two groups sometimes contest primaries, but there are incentives to cooperation in general elections and in most phases of the conduct of government. In these several respects Philadelphia and St. Louis are similar, though St. Louis's Democratic organization is much weaker and less centralized.[3] Perhaps New York City (which is, on the whole, *sui generis*) can be said to be moving in this direction, and a number of cities conform to the pattern in a more fragmentary fashion.

3. A third type is the partisan (effectively one-party) city with two or more enduring factions (plus, perhaps, some more ephemeral and peripheral factions). Baltimore is the best example, and New Orleans could be placed in this class.[4] A more-or-less one party state politics, state political factions, the habit and state-wide incidence of primary competition, or such electoral requirements as run-off primaries or multi-member districts may help explain this structure; but this study can offer no evidence on these points.

---

[1] Besides the regularly published literature, the series of *City Politics Reports* now being compiled and mimeographed by the Joint Institute for Urban Studies of Harvard and M.I.T. under the editorship of Edward C. Banfield provide an excellent introduction to the diversity and possibilities for comparative study in the field of city politics. These Reports have been extremely useful to us in this study. They are hereafter cited as *City Politics Reports,* followed by the name of the city covered in the particular report.

[2] Chicago elections are formally nonpartisan for council but not for mayor. Of the large literature on Chicago politics, cf. M. Meyerson and E. Banfield, *Politics, Planning, and the Public Interest* (Glencoe, Ill., 1955); and W. R. Gable, *The Chicago City Council: A Study of Urban Politics and Legislation* (1953), and R. G. Geisler, *Chicago Democratic Voting, 1947–57* (1958), both unpublished Ph.D. dissertations, University of Chicago. For Pittsburgh, see F. Hawkins, "Lawrence of Pittsburgh: Boss of the Melon Patch," *Harpers,* July, 1956; and for Philadelphia, J. Reichley, *The Art of Government* (New York, The Fund for the Republic, 1959).

[3] On this pattern in St. Louis, see the St. Louis *Post Dispatch,* editorial of March 8, 1959, R. H. Salisbury, "St. Louis Politics . . . ," 13 *Western Political Quarterly* (1960), pp. 498–507; and *City Politics Reports: St. Louis.* For Philadelphia, see Reichley, *op. cit.*

[4] On Baltimore, see Edwin Rothman, *Factional Machine Politics: William Curran and the Baltimore City Democratic Organization,* 1929–46 (Unpublished Ph.D. dissertation, Johns Hopkins University, 1948). On New Orleans, see L. Reissman, K. H. Silvert, and C. W. Wing, Jr., *The New Orleans Voter* (New Orleans, Tulane Studies in Political Science, Vol. II, 1955), Chap. 1.

4. A fourth type differs significantly from the third. Here, the dominant (Democratic) party is weakened or divided, not by enduring factions, but by shifting coalitions based on ward organizations or by relatively weak control of city-wide primaries because ethnic blocs or other interest groups rival the influence of party organization. Democratic parties in Buffalo and Cleveland share the latter infirmity, which is probably augmented in Cleveland by nonpartisan primary elections.[5] Cities in this category may be more subject to occasional two-party competition than any of the preceding types.

5. Some cities are characterized by organized and enduring competition between a *local* party (or "association") and one of the two national parties. Cincinnati and Kansas City (both formally nonpartisan) are the two chief examples; though the 1957 defeat of "PR" in Cincinnati may have altered this pattern, and the 1959 "organization" victory in Kansas City has certainly changed the competitive balance. In Kansas City Republicans have been active in the Citizens' Association and in Cincinnati the Democrats were locally merged in the Charter "Party" until the defeat of PR. In each city the local party has been called a cover for opposing partisans by "regulars" of the dominant national party; but the charge is not wholly accurate in either city and seems least well-founded in Cincinnati. Up to 1957 this political structure gave rise to sharp and regular competition in Cincinnati, while in Kansas City party alternation in power has been secular rather than regular. One

reason for this may be the chronic factionalism in Kansas City's Democratic organization.[6]

6. A sixth type is that of the more-or-less party-competitive city. Interestingly enough, no city in our selection clearly falls into this category over the entire period although two cities belonged to it for several years. One—Buffalo—was closely contested over most of the period, but now seems dominantly Democratic due in part to demographic movements and the redrawing of council district lines by the Democratic majority. The other—Indianapolis—has been moving more slowly toward Democratic predominance; but its electoral system, together with the state political environment, probably help to keep it in the competitive category.[7] Neither city is subject to strong organization "control," as distinguished from electoral dominance; and party factionalism and nationality politics in Buffalo especially tend to undermine Democratic control.

7. A final partisan category comprises two cities in one-party regions which are formally partisan but informally nonpartisan. Houston and Memphis are the two cities.[8] These cities have in common their location in one-party areas and the repressive effects of race on political competition. There are no permanent factions today—at least not formally organized or publicly advertised; though personal factions form on occasion, and one or more "slates" appear in about half of Hous-

---

[5] St. Louis's relatively weak and decentralized political organization should perhaps place the city in this category rather than in (2); it has elements of both types. Cleveland elections are effectively partisan though formally nonpartisan; but the nonpartisan primary appears to afford more opportunity for opposition to either party organization, or even to both of them.

[6] See Ralph Straetz, *PR Politics in Cincinnati* (New York, 1958); A. Theodore Brown, *The Politics of Reform—Kansas City's Municipal Government, 1925–1950* (Kansas City, Community Studies, Inc. 1958); and the *City Politics Reports* on Cincinnati and Kansas City.

[7] Three of the city's nine councilmen must be from the minority party.

[8] On Houston, see *City Politics Reports: Houston.* Memphis is more difficult to locate since its emergence from the Crump period. It has commission government with four-year terms, which would seem to make electoral competition difficult to organize.

ton's elections.[9] Presumably the bifactionalism of Louisiana politics has helped to exempt New Orleans from this category.

These, then, are the principal partisan types. Inter-party competition appears to have declined in several cities during the post-war period and has not increased in any. Several cities that were closely contested in the 1930's—either regularly or occasionally—have become dominantly Democratic.[10] As Table 1 shows, all of the cities that have undergone changes in party control of government during the period have gone Democratic. In addition, two less regularly partisan cities underwent a basic shift in the balance of political power: New Orleans in 1946, and Kansas City in 1959. Finally the demise of PR in Cincinnati had at least the temporary effect of reactivating the Democratic party locally, diminishing the Charter vote, and thus enhancing the Republican control of council.

As the outline indicates, however, electoral "dominance" is not the same thing as organization "control," and control in the wards or districts does not always mean city-wide control. These differences show up in primary elections, which are in general more closely contested in cities of types 3 and 4 than of types 1 and 2. Moreover, many city councils exhibit frequent factionalism and/or personal independence, except for cities of types 1 and 2. Mayors and councils (or important factions in councils) are often at odds, except in cities of type 1 and

the (formally nonpartisan) cities of type 5.[11] City parties and factions often fail as solvents of the separation of powers or crystalizers of legislative purpose in both partisan and nonpartisan cities.

8. Thirteen of our cities employ nonpartisan elections. As some formally partisan cities are nonpartisan in fact, so some formally nonpartisan cities are *de facto* partisan in varying degrees. The starting points in any analysis of nonpartisanship must be the writings of Charles Adrian. His typology of nonpartisan elections covers most of our cities, and readers are referred to it for a more detailed treatment.[12] A number of our cities, as distinguished from those already mentioned, are quite effectively nonpartisan.

Readers may feel that a total of eight types of twenty-four cities is neither heroic nor heuristic; but we hope that the outline will meet the two-fold purpose set out above. It should indicate that the organization of electoral competition differs among our major cities, and that it varies in importance *vis a vis* primary elections and other intra-organization contests, intra-governmental rivalry, and nonpartisan competition among interests that is not always reflected in elections.

The outline should also suggest some factors influencing the role and degree of electoral competition in large cities. Four principal types of influence can be provisionally identified. One is that of electoral behavior relating to larger jurisdictions, principally state and national and especially national. A second conglomerate influence

[9] A 1955 change in Houston's election law made it possible to vote for city "slates" by simply pulling one lever on the voting machine.

[10] Baltimore, Chicago, and Pittsburgh have been dominantly Democratic and well organized—either centrally or factionally—since the early '30's or earlier; and Philadelphia was strongly Republican (though threatened in the mid-30's). Buffalo, Cleveland, Indianapolis, New York, and St. Louis have more complicated histories in which competition —at least for city-wide offices—in the 1930's was, for reasons peculiar to each city, either close or contingent; but each (with the exception of Buffalo and Indianapolis) has settled down to Democratic dominance in our period.

[11] In neither of the type 5 cities is the separation of powers a real problem. Both are manager cities, and Cincinnati's mayor is elected by council from among its membership.

[12] "A Typology of Non-partisan Elections," 12 *Western Political Quarterly* (1959), p. 449. See also, "Some General Characteristics of Non-partisan Elections," 46 *American Political Science Review* (1952), p. 766; and (with O. P. Williams), "The Insulation of Local Politics under the Non-partisan Ballot," *Ibid,* Vol. 53 (1959), p. 1052.

TABLE 1   Party Division of City Governments

City	Election Year	Council		Mayor	City	Election Year	Council		Mayor
Baltimore	1943	20–0	D	R	Kansas City[2]	1944	8–1	Reform	R
	1947	20–0	D	D		1946	7–2	R	R
	1951	20–0	D	D		1948	7–2	R	R
	1955	20–0	D	D		1951	7–1	R[2]	R
	1959	20–0	D	D		1955	8–1	R	R
						1959	5–3	R[2]	R
Buffalo	1945	11–4	R	R					
	1947	8–7	R		New Orleans[3]	1942	4–0	RDO	RDO
	1949	8–7	R	R		1946	3–1	CCDA	CCDA
	1951	8–7	R			1950	6–1	CCDA	CCDA
	1953	9–6	D	D		1954	5–2	CCDA	CCDA
	1955	9–6	D			1958	6–1	CCDA	CCDA
	1957	11–4	D	D					
	1959	13–2	D		Philadelphia	1943	20–2	R	R
						1947	22–0	R	R
Chicago	1943	39–9	D	D		1951	14–3	D	D
	1947	32–17	D	D		1955	14–3	D	D
	1951	33–16	D	D		1959	15–2	D	D
	1955	38–11	D	D					
	1959	46–3	D	D	Pittsburgh	1945	9–0	D	D
						1947	9–0	D	
Cincinnati[1]	1945	5–4	R			1949	9–0	D	D
	1947	5–4	R			1951	9–0	D	
	1949	5–4	R			1953	9–0	D	D
	1951	5–4	R			1955	9–0	D	
	1953	5–4	C			1957	9–0	D	D
	1955	5–4	C			1959	9–0	D	D
	1957	5–4	R						
	1959	5–2–2	R-C-D	D	St. Louis	1945	23–6	R	R
						1947	20–8	R	
Cleveland	1945	19–14	D	D		1949	15–14	D	D
	1947	10–12	D	D		1951	17–12	D	
	1949	22–10	D	D		1953	20–9	D	D
	1951	21–11	D	D		1955	25–4	D	
	1953	20–13	D	D		1957	25–4	D	D
	1955	22–11	D	D		1959	25–4	D	
	1957	22–11	D	D					
	1959	25–8	D	D					
Indianapolis	1947	6–3	D	D					
	1951	6–3	R	R					
	1955	6–3	D	D					
	1959	6–3	D	D					

[1] In Cincinnati, R is Republican Party; C is Charter Party; D is Democratic Party.
[2] In Kansas City, R is Reform (later called Citizens' Association) and D is the Democratic organization itself an alliance of factions. In 1951 one councilman was both R and D; and in 1959 three councilmen were both R and D (thus, these two years could be listed as 8–1, and 8–0).
[3] In New Orleans, RDO is "Regular Democratic Organization," and CCDA is "Crescent City Democratic Association" (the Morrison faction).

is that of the interests involved in city politics—demographic groupings, economic interests, and ideologies. Organizational traditions and allegiances affecting party cohesion make a third factor. A fourth is that of local government institutions and, in particular, electoral systems. While this characterization of influences (especially the second) is a broad one, it probably contains the more universal of the factors which, in the outline above, effects electoral competition and thus, with less tangible local traditions, interact within the cities and determine their "type."[13]

[13] Cf. J. L. Freeman, "Local Party Systems: Theoretical Considerations and a Case Analysis." 64 *American Journal of Sociology* (1958), p. 282, for a similar characterization, except that the third factor is omitted.

II. THE PRACTICE OF POLITICS

Donald G. Herzberg

The men who hold political office are the most essential components of government, whether they are called public servants or politicians. Distrust for the men who seek the power and responsibility of public office is a widespread American phenomenon, illogical and irrational as it may appear. Americans do not refer to "public servants" but to "politicians," and disdain for those who seek any kind of political or governmental power continues to run deep in our society. This is not a new phenomenon. History shows that the politician's lot has been an unhappy one for hundreds of years. William Shakespeare, in *King Lear,* characterized the politician in the following way: "Get thee glass eyes and like a scurvy politician seem to see things thou dost not." And John Gay in his *Fables* insisted, "that politician tops his part, who readily can lie with art; the man's proficient in his trade, his power strong, his fortune made."

Americans have joined the ranks of those writers who have spoken disparagingly of the politician. The distinguished Wendell Phillips said that "politicians are like the bones of a horse's foreshoulder—not a straight one in it." Artemus Ward's comment on the politician is the most well known and sums up the general attitude toward those in politics: "I am not a politician and my other habits are good." The poet Walt Whitman was also a newspaperman, and the following is his description of a pre-Civil War Democratic national convention as it originally appeared in the *Brooklyn Eagle:*

> The members who composed it were, seven-eighths of them, the meanest kind of bawling and blowing office-holders, office-seekers, pimps, malignants, conspirators, murderers, fancy-men, custom-house clerks, contractors, kept-editors, spaniels well-train'd to carry and fetch, jobbers, infidels, disunionists, terrorists, mail-riflers, slave-catchers, pushers of slavery, creatures of the President, creatures of would-be Presidents, spies, bribers, compromisers, lobbyers, sponges, ruin'd sports, expell'd gamblers, policy-backers, monte-dealers, duellists, carriers of conceal'd weapons, deaf men, pimpled men, scarr'd inside with vile disease, gaudy outside with gold chains made from the people's money and harlots' money twisted together; crawling, serpentine men, the lousy combinings and born freedom-sellers of the earth.

Since Whitman was a Democrat, one can only speculate what he might have said about a Republican gathering!

These strong feelings that there is something dishonest and distasteful about those who go into political life have remained as part of our heritage to this day. Public opinion surveys have found that parents are emphatic about not wanting their children to grow up to be politicians. The image of the city-style political "boss" hangs on and colors the view held today that political compromise is somehow dishonest. The reasons for the prevalence of the view of the politician as a fat and unattractive cigar-smoking self-seeker are to be found in the teaching of government and politics in our schools, particularly in the emphasis on great men—not politicians.

Our schools have failed to present properly and sympathetically the role of the men who must be politicians in order to make our national, state, and local governmental machinery function smoothly. Too often the organizational outline of government is neatly taught, with little attention given to the human requirements of staffing that system. There are references to senators and presidents and the other component offices such as governor, mayor and councilman, but little attention is paid to the processes by which men come to occupy these offices. The necessity for give and take, for compromise, is never associated with the selected examples of great men from history about whom our children are taught; Washington, Jefferson, and others are not usually thought of as politicians but as great statesmen of all time. The politician, rather, is that terrible creature about whom the Muckrakers made much ado and the reformers are always battling—the reformers, naturally, are always on the side of the people and are never presented as politicians. Our schools are failing to place in perspective all types of politicians, particularly the almost-vanished party hack, and at the same time, failing to present the very particular political characteristics of the reformers. For these men, too, are politicians, and surely their image is different from that of the hack politician. By failing to explore deeply all the aspects of "political man," our schools have failed to instill in students an understanding of the role of the politician in our society. American children are growing up as cynics, distrustful of all who come forward to serve. There is room for honest criticism, but we reach a danger point when the majority of people exhibit total distrust of those in public office.

In the long run there is no greater peril to the democratic system than this cynicism, because apathy and distrust lead to nonparticipation in the electoral and governmental process. Full participation in the decision-making process is a right that men have fought for throughout history. In the United States we have been fighting for these rights since the beginning of our history—and the battle is not yet won. There have been scores of civilizations in which the great majority of people has had no say in their ultimate fate. In the ancient city-state of Athens, which was one of man's earliest attempts at democratic government, most inhabitants of the city were not free citizens. Yet from this city we inherited the ideals of democracy. And now in the United States we are on the threshold of the truly free society—where every adult citizen who wishes may participate in his government. Our civilization represents a fundamental and momentous change from those that have gone before us; for the first time in history a society is asserting that it is possible for millions of men and women to govern themselves. In the light of human experience, our method is still regarded as an experiment. The fundamental question confronting us at this point in history is whether a nation conceived as ours and constituted of people of such diverse cultures and national origins can not only govern itself in order to survive but also create a better atmosphere and more desirable circumstances for living. This question does not apply just to our national government but to the endless numbers of local and state governments as well, all of which constitute our governmental system.

The dangers inherent in this cult of cynicism affect not only the aspect of self-government related to the election of officeholders but also the candidacy of the private citizen for public office. Countless numbers of citizens—who must give of their time for no monetary return—are required to staff the governments of our cities, counties, and states. So many men, when asked to serve, have pleaded how little time they have available or that involvement would hurt their business or that the imposition on their personal lives would be too troublesome. Much of this sort of begging off from the responsibility of public office is a direct outgrowth of the attitude that there is something "shady" about politics (hence the harm to business) or that one does not have a duty to participate in government (hence the ability to go conscience free in refusing). Men will respond eagerly to the trumpet of war, joining in large numbers to defend a threat to our government, but how sparse is the response to the request to partake of that government in peacetime! There is need for a better understanding of the role of the politician and for the realization that all citizens must maintain an interest in politics if we are to be successful in our experiment in government.

In our multiplistic society, it has been the role of the politician to serve as a mediator between the citizenry and the government, federal, state, and local, as well as between various nongovernmental groups. As our society grows more complex and government continues to expand its services, the necessity for the politician will grow. We will continue to need men with abilities in law, city planning, sewage disposal, road building, social and health services, and in all the various functions that governments perform all over the United States. The politician, then, is not the old-fashioned manipulator but the twentieth-century expert who is *also* a politician. The New Deal, with its vast social welfare program, and the continued expansion of this program under both Republican and Democratic administrations, in a sense destroyed the need for the old-style city bosses with the basket of food under their arms and the ton of coal in their trucks. Today the citizen needs the expert politician to help him in his relationship with the government. And the services performed by governments today demand specialized talents among those who are to staff it.

The complexities of twentieth-century living have altered the nature of the demands made on persons who seek public office. The political hack has nearly disappeared and is being replaced by a new breed of politician. He tends to be well educated, well trained, and in general has a strong desire for public service.

The politician in mid-twentieth-century America is many men and he tends to wear many hats. Part of the cynical attitude toward politicians stems from a confusion over the several varieties that exist. Some hold elective office, some appointive office, some hold no office but only influence, some operate in one way and others have entirely different modes of operation. Their beliefs, duties, motivations, ethics, and personal characteristics make them very different men. By and large, however, politicians tend to have one common quality—they have, at some point in their personal lives, made the decision to enter public service because they felt they had a contribution to make. Once launched, the course of their careers may differ entirely, some becoming full-time politicians, devoting a lifetime to public service, others serving only a short term of office and then retiring again to private life. The lure of politics—which is, after all, simply the art of persuading those who hold the power to do something that is deemed desirable for the community at large—can be very great both to the individual and the larger group. The League of Women Voters or the National Education Association or the American Medical Association are in politics—though they might deny it—because they are interested in persuading. Surely the image of these organizations is a good one; they are political forces and, in a sense, politicians, because they enter the political process. Each group is speaking for an interest of some kind, whether it is good government or better teacher's salaries or no medicare; each is fulfilling a role that is vital and necessary in order to make democracy survive.

One type of politician is the man who works full time at it. Others are the party officers or the other persons who do not actually hold office but who are involved in the political process. Many of these men are lawyers or are in the insurance or real estate business, and frequently a large measure of their business stems from their political activities. Many of them operate behind the scenes and usually exert a greater influence over the political process than those who hold the power. They may be the men who seek the candidates or advise others on the way in which an issue might be best handled. An example is the former Attorney General of New Jersey, David Wilentz, who for a long time held no formal political position, although he is now National Committeeman from New Jersey. Nevertheless, he has been the political mentor of Middlesex County, New Jersey, for the last thirty years. Knowledgeable people are aware that he is the man who controls the destiny of the party and its candidates. Dissident Democrats from time to time run their campaigns against the "boss"—but—rarely win.

Other politicians who devote full time to politics are those who hold political office. These full-time politicians are in jobs sufficiently demanding that they have little time to pursue private business interests. Some, however, are able to remain associated with private interests that do not conflict with their public trust. John Bailey, State Democratic Committee Chairman in Connecticut, (see 13) and now National Chairman exemplifies the man in party politics who devotes full time to his job. Ray Bliss of Ohio, now Republican National Chairman, also devotes full time to his new job. Jesse Unruh, the Speaker of the California Assembly, devotes full time to the job of politics, although most state legislative offices are considered part-time political positions. Unruh has had much influence on the California Assembly and he has brought the same kind of full-time devotion to politics to bear upon the office of Speaker, making it an important and powerful post.

These men have been called bosses. But their method of operation is not that of the old urban-style boss. They are men who believe that the practice of good government is good politics. They surround themselves with men and advisers who share this belief and who bring to the art of government a high degree of training and experience. All of these men put in long hours, and many of them devote more time to their political trade than do their counterparts in business and professions.

The part-time politician—the state legislators or the municipal officials who have run for office on a party ticket, and in some municipalities oftentimes on a party platform—differs in degree from the full-time politician. His political career and his ambitions may be very different. Such men are either starting a career or don't want a career. They are often citizens interested in good local government. There are some half million of these people holding office in the United States today. In addition to those who hold part-time elective offices, there are some two and a half million more persons who hold appointive offices in government. Adding the estimated million more persons who hold political party positions in the United States, and the five or ten million more citizens who perform some task for the political party of their choice, we find that the majority of people involved in politics do not devote full time to it, nor do they derive their source of income from politics. These are the citizen-politicians, and they are politicians by definition. Little attention is paid to these members of the political body when the characterization of the "politician" is proclaimed.

In the history of our country we have had a tradition of the citizen-soldier, the man or woman who puts aside his peacetime pursuits in time or war and then, when the danger has passed, returns to his peacetime job. This kind of devotion should be emphasized in relation to the citizen-politician—we need to develop the tradition in this country of encouraging more people to enter politics. We must develop large numbers of individuals who are willing to devote some portion of their time to government and politics. In New Jersey alone, for example, there are over 550 legal communities, and with the exception of six cities where the governing jobs are full time, these communities are governed by citizens for whom politics is an avocation. The mayors, councilmen, members of zoning, recreation, school, and library boards of these cities must all come from the ranks of the citizen-politician. What is true in New Jersey is true in the United States as a whole. In the coming decades governments and politics are going to need to triple the number of citizens willing to participate. In order to attract people to the field the image of the politician as a self-serving individual must be changed. In a sense this has already begun on a national scale with the emphasis that has been placed upon public service by both Presidents Kennedy and Johnson. Certainly the widespread publicity presently being given to politics is helping to focus attention on this area and to improve the calibre of those going into politics. People who believe strongly in good government must help to erase the unfavorable image of the politician, defend the profession, and hope that the time is past when a President can say "politics . . . I have no liking for that word . . ."

This chapter is also concerned with the tools that are available to the politician. Some are used primarily for campaigning purposes, while others are useful once a politician is in office. The majority of those covered here are concerned with public opinion.

The politician's most important tool is money. Political campaign expenses are increasing annually, and the private resources of most men who seek political office are not adequate to meet the requirements of modern campaigns. Will Rogers once observed that politics "has got so expensive that it takes a lot of money even to get beat with." The problem of raising funds is common to both parties and is compounded by the particular electoral status of the party seeking funds. Richard Schier (17) has written about a Democratic party fund-raising effort in a Republican area, whereas the White and Owens selection (16) deals with the finance organizations of both parties in the state of Michigan. Without money, few of the modern techniques of polling and advertising would be available to political candidates.

Polling is a modern technique which permits a candidate to determine the way in which his personality is being conveyed to the general public. Polling also permits a politician to take a reading on those issues that can be used most effectively in his constituency. In a sense, polling is simply an enlarged and modern pulse-taking, replacing the smaller and more personal contact with the voter. Hand in hand with the use of the polling firm is the use of the public relations and advertising firms. Some public relations firms have become so involved in the political process that they literally take over and run a campaign professionally. In the 1964 campaign an advertising agency in New York City was given responsibility for one aspect of the public relations activities in Robert Kennedy's Senate campaign: according to one writer, the job was to change the image of the former Attorney General from one of toughness and ruthlessness to that of a man whose only desire was to be a good senator.[1]

Television was recognized as a powerful force in politics following the appearance of vice presidential-nominee Richard Nixon in the 1952 fund crisis. The effectiveness of television was again confirmed in 1960 when the televised debates gave Kennedy the exposure that he had heretofore lacked and permitted him to overcome the image of a young and inexperienced man.

The press, though theoretically independent and free, nevertheless, is a potent source of influence in politics through its editorials and even more so through its news columns. The men who write the stories are human beings with their own viewpoints, and as Theodore White has said in *The Making of the President 1960*, the way in which the press is treated can make a tremendous difference in its reporting.[2]

These varied public opinion tools are all aspects of twentieth-century politics and they are, in large measure, also responsible for the decline in the power of the old-style city boss. As the mass media have made politicians more accessible to the general public, and as the public has become more informed about the country and world at large, the calibre of those entering politics has risen. The communications media are weapons in the battle of the ballot box that could be used in the future to change the image of the politician for the better, causing better men to enter politics, or they could be used to present superficially attractive candidates who have little in the way of ability. It is to be hoped that it will not be the latter course.

[1] See Terry Smith, "Bobby's Image," *Esquire*, vol. 63, no. 4 (April 1965), p. 65.
[2] See Theodore H. White, *The Making of the President 1960* (New York: Atheneum, 1961), pp. 333–338, for this journalist's view of the attitudes of the two candidates toward the press and the resulting coverage.

THE POLITICIAN

9.   The Profession of Politics

John F. Kennedy

This commencement address, delivered June 3, 1957, at Syracuse University by then Senator Kennedy, explores the avenues open to the student and scholar in public life. The speech discusses the mutual disdain and distrust with which politicians and scholars have traditionally regarded one another. Senator Kennedy also sounded a summons to students that was to become familiar after he became President—to enter public service and apply their talents toward solving the great public problems of their time.

* * *

Anyone who is interested in the history of the United States Senate always feels a great sense of privilege and responsibility in coming to this state and to this part of the state. For New York has had a long parade of unusually distinguished men who served their nation in the Chamber of the Senate—and one of these of whom I am particularly reminded today was a very distinguished member of the opposite party—Elihu Root. His father was the second principal in the history of the Syracuse Academy—and Root himself was always fond of upstate New York. Perhaps one of the most dramatic moments of his life came in Utica in 1906 when as Secretary of State he agreed to speak for his party in this state. The opposition had imported a gang of hecklers to make his speech impossible. Having secured copies of his address in advance, they had . instructions to start interruptions on particular lines—shouting, for example, on the first reference to the late President McKinley, "Let McKinley

rest in peace," with the others roaring their approval. Unfortunately for the hecklers, the meeting was packed with Root admirers and Hamilton College students; and the first one who started to interrupt was pushed in the face, and the rest were bodily threatened. Finally, when a great roar arose from the crowd to throw out one heckler, Root raised his right hand to quell the uproar, and in a powerful voice cried out: "No, let him stay—and learn!"

I trust that all of you will stay—I can only speculate as to how much you will learn—but I will welcome any heckling at the close of these ceremonies. I hope the example of Elihu Root will be an inspiration to all of those whom we honor on this solemn day of Commencement. For them, the pleasures, the values and the friendships of college days are coming to an end—the identical group sitting here this morning will probably never gather again—and the sands of time will gradually erase most of the memories which seem so important today.

But what concerns us most on these occasions is not what you graduates leave behind but what you take with you, what you will do with it, what contribution you can make. I am assuming, of course, that you are taking something with you, that you do not look upon this university as Dean Swift regarded Oxford. Oxford, he said, was truly a great seat of learning; for all freshmen who entered were required to bring some learning with them in order to meet the standards of admission—but no senior, when he left the university, ever took any learning away; and thus it steadily accumulated.

The high regard in which your education at Syracuse is held is evidenced by the intensive competition which rages between those hoping to benefit from it. Your campus is visited by prospective employers ranging from corporation vice-presidents to professional football coaches. Great newspaper advertisements offer inducements to chemists, engineers, and electronic specialists. High public officials plead for more college graduates to follow scientific pursuits. And many of you will be particularly persuaded by the urgent summons to duty and travel which comes from your local draft board.

But in the midst of all of these pleas, plans and pressures, few, I dare say, if any, will be urging upon you a career in the field of politics. Some will point out the advantages of civil service positions. Others will talk in high terms of public service, or statesmanship, or community leadership. But few, if any, will urge you to become politicians.

Mothers may still want their favorite sons to grow up to be President, but, according to a famous Gallup poll of some years ago, they do not want them to become politicians in the process. They may be statesmen, they may be leaders of their community, they may be distinguished lawmakers—but they must never be politicians. Successful politicians, according to Walter Lippmann, are "insecure and intimidated men," who "advance politically only as they placate, appease, bribe, seduce, bamboozle, or otherwise manage to manipulate" the views and votes of the people who elect them. It was considered a great joke years ago when the humorist Artemas Ward declared: "I am not a politician, and my other habits are good also." And, in more recent times, even the President of the United States, when asked at a news conference early in his first term how he liked "the game of politics," replied with a frown that his questioner was using a derogatory phrase. Being President, he said, is a "very fascinating experience . . . but the word 'politics' . . . I have no great liking for that."

Politics, in short, has become one of our most neglected, our most abused and our most ignored professions. It ranks low on the occupational list of a large share of the population; and its chief practitioners are rarely well or favorably known. No education, except finding your way around a smoke-filled room, is considered necessary for political success. "Don't teach my boy poetry," a mother recently wrote the headmaster of Eton; "Don't teach my boy poetry, he's going to stand for Parliament." The worlds of politics and scholarship have indeed drifted apart.

Unfortunately, this disdain for the political profession is not only shared but intensified in our academic institutions. To many universities and students we politicians represent nothing but censors, investigators and perpetrators of what has been called the "swinish cult of anti-intellectualism." To others, we are corrupt, selfish, unsavory individuals, manipulating votes and compromising principles for personal and partisan gain.

Teachers as well as students, moreover, find it difficult to accept the differences between the laboratory and the legislature. In the former, the goal is truth, pure and simple, without regard to changing currents of public opinion; in the latter, compromises and majorities and procedural customs and rights affect the ultimate decision as to what is right or just or good. And even when they realize the difference, most intellectuals consider their chief function to be that of the critic—and politicians are sensitive to critics (possibly because we have so many of them). "Many intellectuals," Sidney Hook has said, "would rather 'die' than agree with the majority, even on the rare occasions when the majority is right." Of course, the intellectual's attitude is partly defensive—for he has been regarded with so much suspicion and hostility by political figures and their constituents that a recent survey of American intellectuals by a national magazine elicited from one of our foremost literary figures the guarded response, "I ain't no intellectual."

But this mutual suspicion was not always the case—and I would ask those of you who look with disdain and disfavor upon the possibilities of a political career to remember that our nation's first great politicians were traditionally our ablest, most respected, most talented leaders, men who moved from one field to another with amazing versatility and vitality. A contemporary described Thomas Jefferson as "A gentleman of 32, who could calculate an eclipse, survey an estate, tie an artery, plan an edifice, try a cause, break a horse, dance a minuet, and play the violin."

Daniel Webster could throw thunderbolts at Hayne on the Senate Floor and then stroll a few steps down the corridor and dominate the Supreme Court as the foremost lawyer of his time. John Quincy Adams, after being summarily dismissed from the Senate for a notable display of independence, could become Boylston Professor of Rhetoric and Oratory at Harvard and then become a great Secretary of State. (Those were the happy days when Harvard professors had no difficulty getting Senate confirmation.)

This versatility also existed on the frontier. Missouri's first Senator, Thomas Hart Benton, the man whose tavern brawl with Jackson in Tennessee caused him to flee the state, was described with these words in his obituary: "With a readiness that was often surprising, he could quote from a Roman Law or a Greek philosopher, from Virgil's Georgics, The Arabian Nights, Herodotus or Sancho Panza, from the Sacred Carpets, the German reformers or Adam Smith; from Fenelon or Hudibras, from the financial reports of Necca or the doings of the Council of Trent, from the debates on the adoption of the Constitution or intrigues of the kitchen cabinet or from some forgotten speech of a deceased Member of Congress."

This link between American scholarship and the American politician remained for more than a century. A little more than one hundred years ago, in the Presidential campaign of 1856, the Republicans sent three brilliant orators around the campaign circuit: William Cullen Bryant, Henry Wadsworth Longfellow and Ralph Waldo Emerson. (Those were the carefree days when the "egg-heads" were all Republicans.)

I would urge therefore that each of you, regardless of your chosen occupation, consider entering the field of politics at some stage in your career. It is not necessary that you be famous, that you effect radical changes in the government or that you be acclaimed by the public for your efforts. It is not even necessary that you be successful. I ask only that you offer to the political arena, and to the critical problems of our society which are decided therein, the benefit of the talents which society has helped to develop in you. I ask you to decide, as Goethe put it, whether you will be an anvil —or a hammer. The formal phases of the "anvil" stage are now completed for many of you, though hopefully you will continue to absorb still more in the years ahead. The question now is whether you are to be a hammer—whether you are to give to the world in which you were reared and educated the broadest possible benefits of that education.

It is not enough to lend your talents merely to discussing the issues and deploring their solutions. Most scholars, I know, would prefer to confine their attention to the mysteries of pure scholarship or the delights of abstract discourse. But "Would you have counted him a friend of Ancient Greece," as George William Curtis asked a century ago during the Kansas-Nebraska Controversy, "who quietly discussed the theory of patriotism on that Greek summer day through whose hopeless and immortal hours Leonidas and his three hundred stood at Thermopylae for liberty? Was John Milton to conjugate Greek verbs in his library, or talk of the liberty of the ancient Shumanites, when the liberty of

Englishmen was imperilled?" No, the duty of the scholar—particularly in a republic such as ours—is to contribute his objective views and his sense of liberty to the affairs of his state and nation.

This is a great university, the University of Syracuse. Its establishment and continued functioning, like that of all great universities, has required considerable effort and expenditure. I cannot believe that all of this was undertaken merely to give the school's graduates an economic advantage in the life struggle. "A university," said Professor Woodrow Wilson, "should be an organ of memory for the state for the transmission of its best traditions. Every man sent out from a university should be a man of his nation, as well as a man of his time." And Prince Bismarck was even more specific—one-third of the students of German universities, he once stated, broke down from overwork; another third broke down from dissipation; and the other third ruled Germany. (I leave it to each of you to decide which category you fall in.)

But if you are to be among the rulers of our land, from precinct captain to President, if you are willing to enter the abused and neglected profession of politics, then let me tell you—as one who is familiar with the political world—that we stand in serious need of the fruits of your education. We do not need political scholars whose education has been so specialized as to exclude them from participation in current events—men like Lord John Russell, of whom Queen Victoria once remarked that he would be a better man if he knew a third subject—but he was interested in nothing but the Constitution of 1688 and himself. No, what we need are men who can ride easily over broad fields of knowledge and recognize the mutual dependence of our two worlds.

I do not say that our political and public life should be turned over to college-trained experts who ignore public opinion. Nor

would I adopt from the Belgian Constitution of 1893 the provision giving three votes instead of one to college graduates (at least not until more Democrats go to college). Nor would I give the University of Syracuse a seat in the Congress as William and Mary was once represented in the Virginia House of Burgesses.

But I do urge the application of your talents to the public solution of the great problems of our time—increasing farm foreclosures in the midst of national prosperity—record small business failures at a time of record profits—pockets of chronic unemployment and sweatshop wages amidst the wonders of automation—monopoly, mental illness, race relations, taxation, international trade, and, above all, the knotty complex problems of war and peace, of untangling the strife-ridden, hate-ridden Middle East, of preventing man's destruction by nuclear war or, even more awful to contemplate, by disabling through mutations generations yet unborn.

No, you do not lack problems or opportunities—you do not lack the ability or the energy; nor, I have tried to say, do you lack the responsibility to act, no matter what you have heard about the profession of politics. Bear in mind, as you leave this university and consider the road ahead, not the sneers of the cynics or the fears of the purists, for whom politics will never be an attraction—but bear in mind instead these words which are inscribed behind the Speaker's desk high on the Chamber Wall of the United States House of Representatives, inscribed for all to see and all to ponder, these words of the most famous statesman my state ever sent to the Halls of Congress, Daniel Webster: "Let us develop the resources of our land, call forth its power, build up its institutions, promote all its great interests and see whether we also in our day and generation may not perform something worthy to be remembered."

10.   Ethics and the Politician

Stephen K. Bailey

This essay was written for the Center for the Study of Democratic Institutions by the former Mayor of Middletown, Connecticut, and present Dean of the Maxwell School at Syracuse University. The subject is the question of ethics and the politician and covers the problems that confronted Mr. Bailey every day when he was mayor of a town of thirty thousand persons. Dean Bailey raises the major questions concerning the proper exercises of ethics and, relating to his own experience, says, "I had nothing in my system that told me what was right but I did have something in my system that told me to search for what was right." Bailey concludes with the reminder that power can ennoble as well as corrupt, and that the ethical problems that confront elective officers are the same as those that confront all human beings.

* * *

Any attempt to construct what John Buchan once called "an essay in recollection" is fraught with ethical puzzles. When it is addressed to the moral dilemmas of a political experience of some years ago, ethical issues are piled crazily one on top of the other. And they are nudged into further disarray by the tricks that rationalization and memory play upon all autobiographers. In view of the number of friends whose good names must be protected against my possibly accurate reporting of their (and my) occasional moral lapses; in view of the impossibility, six to eight years after events, of my recapturing the precise pattern of considerations which shaped the matrix within which decisions were made; and in view of the inscrutability of many of the ethical issues with which I, as mayor of a city of 30,000, had to deal, it is clear that this essay must be content with the perennially probable rather than the historically precise.

Insofar as I refer specifically to experiences in Middletown, Connecticut, during the years when I was mayor of that city, I hope that friends there will show me the same charity that Huckleberry Finn showed Mark Twain. Referring to *The Adventures of Tom Sawyer*, Huck commented, "That book was made by Mr. Mark Twain, and he told the truth, mainly. There was things which he stretched, but mainly he told the truth. That is nothing. I never seen anybody but lied one time or another, without it was Aunt Polly. . . ." And Huck Finn was perceptive in spotting the moral flaw in Aunt Polly and in her old maid sister, Miss Watson: a flaw of self-righteousness so hideous that when Huck learned that Miss Watson was living "so as to go to the good place," Huck could "see no advantage in going where she was going," so he made up his mind he wouldn't try for it.

I have worried far more about the ethical consequences of my decisions as mayor since leaving office than I ever did as an incumbent. And perhaps this is the first point to be made. Most elected executives find that there is an ethics of *action* which is normally far more compelling than the urge to balance with precision the ethical niceties of pressing public issues. There are times when the good of the community demands firmness and decision at the expense of marginal injustice. Those who would make justice the sole criterion of the good society are not only, in my judgment, myopic in their ethical vision, they establish an impossible operating norm for administrators. Justice, in the sense of "just deserts," presumes omnipotence and omniscience. An elected mayor in a "weak-mayor" form of government, alas, has

From Stephen K. Bailey, *Ethics and the Politician* (Santa Barbara: The Fund for the Republic, Inc., 1960), by permission of the Center for the Study of Democratic Institutions and the author.

neither. He may desire to be just, but occasions arise when justice is not the highest ethical priority. If a local hospital, which has run a countywide ambulance service for years, suddenly decides for budgetary reasons to disown this responsibility, it may be unjust to make the taxpayers of a single city in the county pick up the check for keeping the countywide ambulance service going on an emergency basis. But, here, what is necessary overrides what is just.

And emergency actions by an authorized executive have meaning and value quite apart from the justice or injustice of any decision taken by the executive under his emergency authority. The justification for the emergency powers of the public executive are, I believe, not only in the necessities of organization under stress; there is a most significant social therapy in the public's sense that "somebody is in charge." The sight of Winston Churchill making his way through the rubble of blitzed London and barking orders to subordinates had the effect of strengthening resolve and dissolving fear among the affected public. Even lowly political executives at times perform this valuable emergency role.

But even when an emergency does not exist, there are frequently statutory deadlines or political deadlines—budgets, elections, schedules of compliance established by a higher level of government—which precipitate executive decisions largely uncomplicated by labored ethical considerations. Deadlines are great strengtheners of the resolve to choose. Those who would build theories of decision-making removed from the context of the clock and the calendar know nothing of the inner life of a political executive. And, even then, no executive in public life is free from having his life arbitrarily and often whimsically scheduled by real or fancied immediacies which are superimposed upon the clock and calendar, no matter how carefully the latter have been anticipated.

In brief, although almost every issue with which an elected executive must deal is charged with ethical dilemmas, it is rare that the executive has either the time, the context, or the liver for constructing balanced ethical judgments. He does what he must. Ethically, elected executives tend, like successful fighter pilots, to "fly by the seat of their pants." Speed is the enemy of deliberation, and, in administration, speed—in the sense of dispatch—is often the condition of maintaining a tolerable if ineffable balance among those interests, obligations, and necessities which crowd the world of the elected executive.

All of this is not meant to suggest that ethical considerations are somehow peripheral to an elected executive's life. It is only to say that ethical issues are rarely trotted out for leisurely inspection and deliberate choice. This may be unfortunate, but my guess is that if ethical considerations were always carefully and honestly articulated in decision-making, the ensuing chaos—moral and administrative—would be impressive.

If we are talking about the real world, then, we are talking in large measure about the *inarticulate* moral premises of the office holder—the ethical signposts which a harried political executive catches out of the corner of his eye.

With this statement, of course, the essay could well end. Any attempt to list all of the precepts, proverbs, fables (and their rationalized versions) which conscience picks to guide or to justify actions would lead to an endless and formless recitation of the obvious and the inscrutable. And ultimately such a recitation would tell us nothing about conscience itself; that ego-tempered temperer of egos; that culture-bound transcender of culture; that ultimate sorter of ethical ambiguities. It gets us nowhere to suggest that all of the Philosophy 1–2 classroom stumpers are present in political life—as they are in all life. Should a cancer specialist be honest or kind? Ultimately, is it more honest to be kind or more kind to be honest? Is a half-truth a worse enemy of the truth than a falsehood? Should promises be kept if the situation changes (and when doesn't it change)? Should friends be reported if you know them to be mostly good and you know that they probably will not do it again? Should you subject someone to the consequences of wrongdoing if you are reasonably sure that the penalty is sufficiently harsh and inelastic as to be inequitable?

To pretend that there are clear religious, moral, or legal answers to such questions is to fly in the face of all sensitive moral inquiry.

How difficult the means-ends questions of living really are is known by every parent who ponders such matters. After a generation of permissiveness in raising children, we are finally returning to a belief that metes and bounds backed by sanctions are ultimately kinder to the growing child and the society than uninhibited license. But how many sanctions? How extensive the metes and bounds? Someone once commented that the Lord had left the two most difficult and important jobs in the world to amateurs: citizenship and parenthood. Elected political executives, at least most of them, are also amateurs, and their jobs may be no less difficult or important than the others mentioned. What is common to the life of all of these amateurs is that the value questions are extraordinarily complex, and the chances of adequate time for deliberation are slim.

But are there not peculiar ethical risks run by elected political executives? Surely, most people are not faced frequently with questions of bribery, spoils, corruption, favoritism. The difficulty is, neither are elected political executives, and even when venality raises its head it rarely looks to the responsible political executive as ugly as it appears in newspaper cartoons or Sunday sermons. Venality, like virtue, is rarely unambiguous. G. K. Chesterton wrote perceptively when he suggested that the error of Diogenes "lay in the fact that he omitted to notice that every man is both an honest and a dishonest man. Diogenes looked for his honest man inside every crypt and cavern. But he never thought of looking inside the thief. And that is where the Founder of Christianity found the honest man. He found him on a gibbet and promised him paradise."

When the nicest people have rationalized their selfishness with a tactical deference to the public interest, elected political executives are often grateful that they are too preoccupied to be ethically astute. Even where venality seems clearest, as in the rare case of an attempt at straight bribery ("Mayor, here's a thousand dollars in five-dollar bills if you get that easement through the council"—the political version of "payola"), the ethical issues may not be self-evident. Let us make some assumptions: suppose that the mayor knows that the easement will go through "on its merits" (begging what *that* slippery phrase means). Suppose further that the mayor knows that the party needs money not only to run the forthcoming election but to pay debts on a past election. Suppose the mayor knows further that the voting public has not responded favorably and positively to the appeal of the American Heritage Foundation for everyone to give to the party of his choice. Suppose finally that the mayor believes that a working two-party system is the nation's and the community's greatest safeguard of democracy and freedom. If it could be proved to the mayor's satisfaction that the lack of $1,000 at the moment could do irreparable damage to the two-party system in the area, would it be a higher principle in a naughty world for the mayor to accept the money on behalf of the party, or to refuse the money?

Stated this way, the issue is still not very complex for most people. "They've known what's right and wrong since they've been ten." You do not accept bribes, period; and you most certainly do not compound evil by cheating the briber. This is all very clear. But is it, really? There are ways of playing slight variations on this theme which would remove from the sternest Presbyterian moralist any burden of guilt. The briber has made a number of contributions to the party over the years. The latest thousand is simply another indication of his belief in the great principles of the party. On the easement question, every party member on the council, including the mayor, attempts to examine the issue on its merits. But a "will to believe" has set in—a subtle coloration of the problem. Good old Joe is a friend who provided all the favors for the party picnic. Isn't it fortunate that the merits of the easement case are on his side?

And bribery can take so many forms: money, favors, flattery, help in time of trouble, influence in building status. To pretend that bribery is a simple and easily spotted phenomenon is naive. To pretend it takes place only in politics is silly. I have seen the egos of older university professors successfully bribed by astute and ambitious instructors; I have seen great institutions bribe men into conformity with promises of promotions or demotions. I have seen them kill, spiritually, those who resisted. I have received threats that unless such-and-such happened, I'd be voted out of office at the next election. Is this not attempted bribery? Is money any more a thing of value than power or status or re-election? If there are clear moral distinctions here, they escape me, even though our cultural inheritance sanctions certain kinds of bribery and frowns on others.

I once asked a municipal judge in Middletown to tell me what pressures were most constant in trying to influence his impartial administration of justice. He thought a minute and then said, laughingly, "the university deans and the town clergy." But why should he have laughed? Certainly few would question the motives of deans and clergy in attempting to save the reputations of individuals known to them, and under their keep, who have been accused of wrong-doing. But what of the wrong-doer who has no "friend in court"? Anyone who has ever watched a municipal court in action over a period of time knows that "political influence" is frequently a corrective for the partial justice that results from the rich litigant's capacity to purchase superior legal talent. Middle-class justice is not always equitable to the poor. This is not to condone political influence in courts of law, it is to suggest that without political influence certain inequities might be greater than they are and that those inequities need as much attention as overt or covert political influence.

I was never asked to fix a traffic or parking ticket in Middletown; but I cannot swear that tickets were not occasionally fixed while I was mayor. And I am not sure that under certain circumstances (*e.g.*, a hectic woman delayed in buying her six children school clothes) I would not have paid the dollar fine myself rather than penalize her for something beyond her effective control. Nothing is more unjust than unexceptional law except law that is all exceptions. Surely, one of the most difficult ethical problems in all governance is the drawing of lines between rules and exceptions. That the lines, to be moral, must be drawn near the rules end of the spectrum I do not question. But that exceptions are never warranted seems to me the most callous of all moral judgments.

To the moralist, words like bribery, favoritism, spoils, patronage, graft, are as clear and as evil as though bottled and marked with skull and crossbones. To those with political responsibility, on the other hand, it occasionally seems clear that poison can be therapeutic. The fact that poison is labelled with a skull and crossbones and placed back on a high shelf of the medicine closet may not mean that it is never to be used; only that it is to be used with care and in small doses. It is possible that if an elected executive had infinite time he might be able to discern ways to achieve his goals without using morally uncomfortable means—although the question of where rationalizations begin and end with this sort of game plays hob with moral certainty. But if giving an unskilled job to a not-incompetent nationality-group representative might make the difference between winning or losing on an urban renewal referendum of vast benefit to the entire city for years to come, I know few elected executives who would boggle over making such an appointment even if the executive was convinced that someone else might do the unskilled job better.

George Bernard Shaw once wrote what many politicians must at times have felt. Shaw learned that a Labour candidate named Joseph Burgess had refused to compromise on some issue and had thereby lost his seat in Parliament. Shaw commented bitterly:

> When I think of my own unfortunate character, smirched with compromise, rotted with opportunism, mildewed by expediency—dragged through the mud of borough council and Battersea elections, stretched out of shape with wire-pulling, putrefied by permeation, worn out by twenty-five years pushing to gain an inch here, or straining to stem a backrush, I do think Joe might have put up with just a speck or two on those white robes of his for the sake of the millions of poor devils who cannot afford any character at all because they have no friend in parliament. Oh, these moral dandies, these spiritual toffs, these superior persons. Who is Joe, anyhow, that he should not risk his soul occasionally like the rest of us?

I was once confronted with a possible kickback on a fire truck purchase. The party representative reminded me that it cost money to run elections; that generosity from fire truck manufacturers to those who had the insight to see the need for public safety in their communities was rather standard; and that no one would really suffer. The gift would come as a preordained slice of the salesman's commission, who would give of his own income because "he believed in the principles of the Democratic Party." I drew myself up to my maximum height, stared at my good friend, and said in what I am sure must have been the most patronizing of tones, "If the party needs four or five hundred dollars, I shall be happy to try to raise the money personally; but I shall not do it that way." I then went a step further. I called the poor fire truck salesman into the office and made him add about $400 worth of extra equipment to the fire truck at the bid price he had quoted. In a swift double blow I had proved my moral worth and defended the taxpayers' interests. I had proved that at least in one American community "public office is a public trust."

I had also proved that it is easy to be moral when the pressure is not really on. Suppose the party coffers *had* been empty? Suppose my confident bluff to raise "four or five hundred dollars" for the party had been called? Suppose the alternative to a Democratic re-election was the election of a rather disreputable Republican gang who would have practiced "boodle" with more frequency and with infinitely less flair than the Democrats? What then? And why should we refuse to accept money for the imperative cause of political party machinery, almost regardless of source, when the so-called "good" people of the community would not be caught dead giving to their political party—to the system of options which does far more than the Constitution to guarantee freedom and democracy?

I could not be a partner to a kickback, not because I had carefully weighed the moral issues but because my moral viscera told me it was wrong. Unfortunately, my moral viscera are not always right. If they were right in this particular case, they were right for reasons removed from the issue at hand. They were right because, without sufficient time and eloquence, I could not have explained any contrary action—if forced to by the local newspaper or an official inquiry—to the satisfaction of the adult public whose moral viscera are quite as dogmatic as mine. I thereby would have undercut the public's faith in my honesty and would have damaged that most priceless of all public executive resources: the public's confidence. There would then have been an unhappy and unproductive feedback into everything else I did or tried to do as an elected official. The moral dilemma remains, however: for I am confident that if I had had the insight to have taken the kickback and the time and eloquence to have explained to the public why I had done it—describing to them the impossible position they put politicians into by their not assuming disinterested responsibility for financing party campaigns—they would have seen the point and respected me for my action. They even might have taken the lesson to heart and decided to give to their party as frequently and as richly as they give to other causes they value —such as community chests and churches.

The only serious ethical struggle I had with party leaders in Middletown dealt with a request for a zoning exception. Here I was firm, morally aroused, and dogmatic, and would be to this day. A contractor, who had contributed liberally to both political parties locally, hired a leading Democratic lawyer to plead for a commercial spot zone in a strictly residential area. The people of the area were almost solidly opposed to the change. Even if they had not been, nothing can ruin the orderly and esthetic development of a growing city like politically inspired spot zoning in contravention of a general plan. The members of the zoning committee, to their credit, said to me, "Mayor, there's a lot we'll do for the party, but we won't do this." The final showdown on this case took place in the

lawyer's office with all major party leaders present. I walked in swinging. I made it quite clear that if the plumbing broke down in city hall, I would hire a licensed Democratic plumber over a licensed Republican plumber any day of the week; that if the law did not force us to go to bid, I would buy insurance from a Democratic rather than a Republican insurance agent; but that when it came to what Edmund Burke once called "the permanent forces" in the community, I was ready to do battle. I suggested that although there was much in politics that one rendered to Caesar, almost without qualms, city planning was rendered only to God. A few party leaders were upset; but most of them were understanding; and the lawyer in question, who over the years has been one of the most brilliant as well as constructive forces in the community and state, had the grace to accept my position without rancor.

But I have already dwelt far too long on such matters. In my two years as mayor, these kinds of party issues would not have represented more than one-fiftieth of my working time.

Contrary to what many people seem to believe, the hard ethical issues of public life rarely concern party politics. Party decisions tend to roll according to pre-set patterns. Every elected executive works out a few obvious benchmarks for relationships with political leaders (for example, "consult party leaders on all appointments, but solicit their help in trading little appointments to the party for big appointments to you"). In any case, to suggest that most party officials are frequently ethical "problems" is to distort their normal role beyond recognition. For every occasion when a party leader asked me for a favor that disturbed my conscience, I can think of a dozen times when the same party leader helped me defend the public interest against the importunities of non-party pressure groups.

Upon reflection, it is my firm belief that insofar as party politics interferes with the pursuit of the public interest, it is largely a result of the necessities of campaign finance. Most venality in public life could be abolished or reduced to insignificance if the public would assume responsibility for broadly-based campaign financing and would insist upon the public auditing and disclosure of all campaign gifts and expenditures. This would not eliminate corruption entirely, for wherever power and money converge some venality will be found. But our present method of financing political campaigns is, in my estimation, the single most corrupting factor in our political life—local, national, and, especially, state.

If what have been discussed so far are not the major ethical issues of the elected executive, what are? To the man who is ethically sensitive, the hairturning issues are those which involve impossible choices among contending interpretations of the public interest. Again, the necessity of dispatch is psychologically therapeutic; but the drain on energy and conscience is substantial nonetheless. Take ten or a dozen problems which faced me as mayor, and which are typical of perhaps a hundred I faced in two years as an elected executive.

1. A peacock farm on the edge of town kept neighbors awake for a month or so a year during the peacock mating season. The city government was asked by the neighbors to see to it that the birds were quieted. Ethical question: is a temporary irritation—including loss of sleep—for ten families worth the destruction of a hobby and a partial livelihood for one person?
2. A leading department store on Main Street said it had to have a rear access service garage on Broad Street or it would be forced to leave town. Broad Street was zoned residential. Ethical question: would the loss of the department store be a greater loss than a break in the city's zoning pattern?
3. The best detective on the chronically underpaid police force is suspected of taking protection money from some local two-bit gamblers. The evidence is too vague and unsubstantial to stand in court. Ethical question: is the *possibility* of the evidence being correct important enough to warrant a substantial investigation, with a consequent probable loss in efficiency and morale in the police department during and long after the investigation, a certain loss in public confidence in the whole force, and the ever-present possibility that the rumor was planted by a crank? And out of the many pressing issues coming across the mayor's desk, how much time and effort does such an investigation warrant from the mayor himself?
4. The whole scheme of volunteer fire departments is looked upon by the chief of the city's only paid department as wasteful, inefficient, and dangerous to the public safety. The volunteers claim that their fire-fighting record is topnotch, that they save the taxpayers money. Ethical question: if neither side can be proved incorrect, how does one weigh the values of volunteer community endeavors against marginal inefficiencies in operation of a vital service?
5. Many years ago, one department store was far-sighted enough to have bought up some land for off-street parking. This off-street parking gave the store quite a competitive advantage. The city, in a new municipal parking program, needed a portion of the private parking lot assembled by the department store years before. When established, the municipal lot might destroy the store's competitive advantage. Ethical question: at what point does the

public interest demand that private far-sightedness be penalized?

6. Two mayors in four years happened to have lived on Wyllys Avenue. Wyllys Avenue desperately needed repaving. But so did some other streets in the city. Ethical question: should Wyllys Avenue be paved, granted a heavy presumption that many citizens would claim that the mayor had "taken care of himself"?

7. A federal grant-in-aid cut in half the city's welfare load, making a sinecure out of one of the two city welfare positions. The holder of the sinecure was a Negro appointed by the opposition party. Ethical question: should work somehow be "made" for the Negro, or should he be dropped? (For anyone who knows the problems of status, morale, and upward mobility among Negro appointed by the opposition the political questions posed by this case are easy compared to the long-range ethical questions.)

8. The virulent opposition of a local printer-publicist might be tamed on a few key issues with the proper placing of a few city printing contracts. Ethical question: obvious.

9. Buying of tires in wholesale lots would save the taxpayers $300 a year—about one cent per citizen per annum. A score of little Middletown tire merchants would lose ten dollars or more in income. Ethical question: how does one balance one cent each for 30,000 people *versus* ten dollars each for twenty merchants?

10. Parents concerned with the safety of their children on the way to and from school are constantly demanding increased police protection and more sidewalks. A more legitimate demand would be hard to imagine. But there are limits. Ethical question: granted that *total* safety never can be assured,

what grounds beyond obvious necessity and "the squeaky wheel gets the grease" can be found for awarding or denying protection?

11. A health officer is technically qualified and conscientious, but egregiously officious. Ethical question: is the damage done to the city government's relations with its citizens by the meticulous and unfeeling enforcement of ordinances likely to be sufficiently serious to warrant the health officer's dismissal?

12. There is a likelihood that one of the major industries in town will have to close down a sizable slice of its operations. This may mean 2,000 unemployed. A steel company is looking for a New England site for a steel mill. It finds an "ideal" location in Middletown. That "ideal" location is a stretch of the Connecticut River which is unspoiled and is deeply treasured by small-boat owners and by nature lovers. Ethical question: is the provision of employment for 2,000 people worth the destruction forever of natural beauty?

These are samples of the tough ones. And in most cases the ethical values are sufficiently balanced so that no matter which side the mayor takes, half the concerned citizens in the community will charge him—and with considerable justification in their own minds—with having sold out. This is one of the reasons for the low image of politicians in our society: the fact that the losing cause in public policy generally has substantial merit on its side, with the consequence that the loser can see nothing but venality or partiality in the elected official's decision. People get sore at politicians for the same reason they throw pop-bottles at umpires: the disagreements always come on the close ones. If only citizens could pause on occasion to realize that the issues really are complex; that most elected officials do the best they can to be fair; that the peaceful resolution of conflict is a vast service to humankind and a most difficult art; that Solomon himself was perplexed by some of the issues posed by communities of men!

If I should be asked today how I resolved, in my own mind, the ethical dilemmas posed in the previous paragraphs, I should not know how to answer. Most of the dilemmas were not mine to resolve alone. Other people shared official power with me, and many citizens without official power assumed substantial unofficial responsibility for community decisions. There is not the loneliness and, perhaps, terror in executive decision-making at the local level which I assume there must often be at higher executive levels in American government. Consequences of errors in judgment are far less apocalyptic.

But insofar as I had to make up my mind by myself, or felt that my judgment might be determining in the minds of others, I did repair to two or three very general propositions for ethical guidance. In practice, the propositions were never articulated, but in retrospect I know that they were there. All of them had been woven into my life by parental, religious, and academic influences—in most cases by all three. My father, although never a minister, was a Professor of Religion and a firm believer in the Social Gospel. My studies at Oxford had brought me close to Immanuel Kant and Jean Jacques Rousseau. Ideas like "the categorical imperative" and "the general will" were connected in my mind with such Biblical injunctions as "Let justice roll down as waters; and righteousness as a mighty stream." I had nothing in my system that told me what was right; but I did have something in my system that told me to search for what was right.

The most helpful single question I could ask myself seemed to be, "What do you want Middletown to be like ten years from now?" Against this, many things fell into place. I wanted more beauty, fewer slums,

less bigotry, more recreation, more community spirit, a more sustained sense of public responsibility, a more dynamic and prosperous economy, better education, a stronger and more truly competitive two-party system, and a heightened sense of personal dignity for all. These were some of the benchmarks against which specific ethical issues were measured or rationalized. They were not my marks. They were the marks of the civilization of which I was a miniscule and clouded reflection. As Carl Becker once wrote:

To have faith in the dignity and worth of the individual man as an end in himself; to believe that it is better to be governed by persuasion than by coercion; to believe that fraternal goodwill is more worthy than a selfish and contentious spirit; to believe that in the long run all values are inseparable from the love of truth and the disinterested search for it; to believe that knowledge and the power it confers should be used to promote the welfare and happiness of all men rather than to serve the interests of those individuals and classes whom fortune and intelligence endow with temporary advantage—these are the values which are affirmed by the traditional democratic ideology. . . . They are the values which since the time of Buddha and Confucius, Solomon and Zoroaster, Plato and Aristotle, Socrates and Jesus, men have commonly employed to measure the advance or decline of civilization, the values they have celebrated in the saints and sages whom they have agreed to canonize. They are the values which readily lend themselves to rational justification, yet need no justification.

There are, perhaps, two other matters which ought to be touched upon in an essay of this nature. The first has to do with the effect of power upon personality. Acton is quite explicit that "All power corrupts and absolute power corrupts absolutely." This I cannot gainsay. I remember one evening when I was returning with political friends from a television performance. For a half hour they told me what a brilliant performance mine had been. By the end of the half hour I was aware only that a new political star had been born on the horizon: namely, myself, and that I could not long deny the people of the State of Connecticut the chance to vote for me either for Governor or at the very least for United States Senator. It was not until I got home that my wife—with that wonderful sixth sense of a level-headed and thoughtful woman—reminded me that my performance had, in fact, been a little on the mediocre side—but that she was sure I had just had an off night. The most devastating traps of public office are the ones set to catch the ego. It is so easy to forget that the tribute is to the office, not to the person. Even a mayor stands out a little: fathers bring up their daughters to "shake the mayor's hand"; the mayor sits at head tables; he officiates; he is often the central figure in ceremony. All this inflates the sense of personal worth and waters the thirsty garden of vanity. The consequences are often pathetic, often silly, sometimes dangerous.

But Acton was wrong in suggesting that the only flowers in the garden of vanity are the weeds of corruption. Power may corrupt, but it also can ennoble. The sense that you, and the office you hold, are widely valued often creates a heightened sense of responsibility, a desire to live close to the public expectation, a wish to become a kind of community example. Too few people appreciate the ennobling effect of public office. I have seen men utterly transformed by a judgeship. A politician—an old pro in western Connecticut—once confided to me that he hated all judges. "What are they but some hack lawyers who happened to know a politician?" And he went on, "After you've made 'em, what do they do? They turn around and kick you in the teeth! They draw their robes around them as though they were Solon or something! You can't touch them! Who the hell do they think they are?" The fact is that they think they *are* Solon; they suddenly realize that instead of petty politicians they are

an essential part of the fabric of civilization—a fabric which can last only so long as there is a widespread public belief that judges in courts of law will try to be just. And what is true of judges is equally true of elected executives.

The ennobling effect of public office is one of its greatest psychic dividends. Those who believe that men seek to hold public office only because it gives them power and status do not appreciate the importance to many men of simply feeling that the job they hold makes them better members of the human race. The heightened capacity for doing good in the world is one of the key attractions of political power and, from my limited observations, is a far more fundamental factor in determining the direction of men's ambitions than the baubles and tinsel of temporary status and deference.

This brings me to my final point. All ethical questions ultimately revert to propositions about the nature of man. The underlying complexity of ethical questions stems from the fact that man is morally ambiguous and teleologically inscrutable. Perched precariously on a whirling planet, blind to his origins, blind to his reasons for being, beset by the terrors of nature and of his own creation, man wobbles drunkenly between a certainty that he is nothing and an occasional, blinding revelation that he has a transcendent dignity and perhaps destiny. When man feels alienated from his universe, he may huddle in fear with his fellow men; but he cannot reach them with that fullness of feeling, that intenseness of identity, which is suggested by the Christian concept of love, or by the civil concept of community. I am not a mystical person, but I sense strongly that my best moments as mayor came when I felt—in an almost religious way—that what we were attempting to do in Middletown had meaning beyond itself. I remember Fred Smith, the editor of the local paper, once writing me an intimate note when I was particularly discouraged about the public response to some issue. "Never," he wrote, "lose faith in your neighbors." And he went on to explain, not that they were perfect, but that he had known them for a long time, and that they would ultimately respond to the good if they could be shown the good.

Surely this is the ultimate ethical postulate in a democracy: not that man is good, but that he is capable of good; not that he is free from corruption, but that he is desperately sick of it; not that he has fashioned the good society, but that he has caught an unforgettable glimpse of it. Ultimately the ethical problems of the elected executive are what they are for all human beings: the struggle to discover ends and means which heighten man's sense of individual worth in an ever more extensive and inclusive community.

11.   What's He Like and How Will He Do?

James Reston

James Reston, the veteran New York Times *Washington correspondent, and now the Associate Editor, in this article depicts the character, personality, methods, ambitions, and hopes of President Johnson. Reston observes that Johnson "sees politics as an exercise in adapting oneself to all sorts of people and situations, of discussing and bargaining with legitimate groups in search of a consensus." In analyzing the differences between Presidents Kennedy and Johnson, Reston says, "Kennedy's purpose was to make men think; Johnson's is to make men act. Both were reformers but went about it in different ways. Kennedy demanded re-forms by challenging the conformists; Johnson got Kennedy's reforms by seeming to be a conformist."*

* * *

The inauguration of a President of the United States starts with a prayer and ends with a dance. This is not a bad combination. Most of the great occasions in life involve a little intermittent laughing and crying, and the installation of a new President is clearly a great occasion. It is a kind of birth or wedding in the nation's family life.

By some curious combination of intuition and caprice, it lifts one fallible mortal from among the millions and says: Go guide half the human race. No wonder the people pray. It asks the man in the Big White House to govern a vast, almost ungovernable continental nation, to "preserve, protect and defend" a Constitution which his fellow countrymen interpret in different ways, to lead a worldwide coalition of proud, independent and competitive nations, and to preserve the peace in a rebellious and revolutionary world. In the face of such a preposterous challenge, the people naturally look around for whatever heavenly help or earthly escape they can find. They kick up their heels and they pray—some for the President, some for the country, and many for both.

Who, then, are we praying and dancing for? Who is this Lyndon Baines Johnson of Texas who will be installed on Wednesday as the 36th President of the United States? What is the explanation of this extraordinary man?

Lyndon Baines Johnson is to the politics of America what his State of Texas is to the other states. He is a gargantuan figure; he is a whopper. Measuring him for history is like measuring an active volcano with an inch-tape. He barbecues people who try and eats them for breakfast.

From The New York *Times* Magazine (January 17, 1965), pp. 8–9+. © 1965 by The New York Times Company. Reprinted by permission.

When you interview him, he ends up with your life story. He does not want to be analyzed or classified; he wants to be loved. Anything you say he said, he can usually neutralize with something else he said on the other side. If you say he's liberal, he can prove he's conservative, or vice versa. If you suggest he's from the South, he will insist he's from the West, or the other way around. If you don't tell the precise truth about him, which is almost inevitable, he thinks you are dishonest, and if you do, he feels you are disloyal.

This, however, is the caricature of Mr. Johnson and, like all caricatures, it magnifies one feature and minimizes all the rest. It is amusing, but it is unfair. The big slouching Texas Ranger on the ranch, the master politician on the telephone, the restless, sleepless "arm-twister," trading favors for votes in the smoky back room —all so dear to the cartoonists—are all true, but misleading.

He is more than that—far more. It is too early to say that he is a leader of men in the classic sense of being "quick to know and to do the things that the hour and his nation need," particularly in the foreign field. He has not yet proved that he can get and keep and inspire the best men in the nation to serve him, or even that he has mastered the art of using his staff and his time effectively. But he is a shrewd and knowledgeable man, an elemental force of nature who commands respect and even a certain amount of fear.

"When you come into the presence of a leader of men," Woodrow Wilson observed, "you know you have come into the presence of fire—that it is best not incautiously to touch that man—that there is something that makes it dangerous to cross him."

Johnson conveys this feeling and it is both his strength and weakness. His technique works but it hurts. He can make men do what he wants them to do but he does not make them like it or him in the

process. There is a kind of intimidating shamelessness about him that makes men feel that if they don't go along there may be the most frightful and embarrassing row. But he is a highly intelligent man who is not to be dismissed as just another brilliant political operator.

He is far more complex than the boys in the back room. The master politician on Capitol Hill and in the White House is not the same as the "Last Hurrah" types out of Tammany, Boston or Chicago, though Johnson has been hurt by the popular confusion of the two. The political leader in the capital has to deal not only with the masses of men but with a highly intelligent Cabinet, an expert civil service, and a staggering catalogue of problems and ideas.

This is not, by any fair test, an unintellectual process. It involves a great deal more than physical strength, tactical skill, personal acquaintance and a telephone. It requires immense concentration on the facts of a great many issues at the same time, a quick knack of identifying and absorbing the essence of complicated and critical questions, and a limitless memory for those intimate personal and political facts that will move men to compromise.

There is much confusion on this point. Lyndon Johnson is not Dean Acheson, with a clear vision of the world and a carefully worked-out plan of the role America might play in the human story. But he clearly did not get where he is on a bag of tricks alone.

He does not concentrate on thinking programs through but on getting them through. He does not believe in "inevitable conflicts," or think in terms of tidy programs imposed or manipulated from the top. He is one of those old-fashioned, small "d" democrats who think that The People and their representatives, if presented with the facts, will find reasonable solutions. He sees politics as an exercise in adapting oneself to all sorts of people and situations, of discussing and bargaining with legitimate groups in search of a consensus.

His university really has been Capitol Hill, his classroom the committee hearings. He retains the memory of his experiences in Texas and in the Congress, but it would never occur to him to try to organize them into a system. Life to him is full of surprises, more so as the tempo of change increases, and he would no doubt support H. G. Wells's dictum that "to be honest, one must be inconsistent."

This, of course, only adds to the caricature of Johnson the manipulator. But there is another side to it. He is an incorrigible believer. He believes in everything that works. He shares all the popular ideals, assumptions and illusions of the nation. Kennedy was troubled by what he called the "myths" of the American past. Johnson loves them. Kennedy came to the White House wondering out loud whether a country governed such as ours could endure. Johnson could no more think or say that than he could denounce Lady Bird or the flag. He believes in the American system. He accepts it as he accepts the weather in his hill country of Texas: a little irritating and even cruel at times, but inevitable.

Similarly, he accepts the Congressional system the way it is—warts and all. Kennedy was in the Congress, Johnson is of it. He struggled to the top through the system and therefore thinks it's all right. He is not a critic of the elders of the Congress but their companion. He has lived with them for 30 years, spoken for them in their elections, stood up with them at their family weddings and christenings and funerals; drunk whiskey with them in Mr. Sam Rayburn's "board of education" hideaway in the House.

The pessimism and complexity of the modern world, accordingly, do not bother him. Unlike many of his intellectual critics, he is not paralyzed by excessive contemplation or doubt. He is all for the businessman making a pile, having made one himself. He believes in Horatio Alger's triumphant ragamuffin (who, after all, is Johnson). He believes in the hard doctrines of John Calvin and individual responsibility, and now that the planned deficit and the tax cut have increased prosperity, he even believes a little in John Maynard Keynes. He is fiercely patriotic. He genuinely believes that God looks out for Uncle Sam. He has no doubt that this nation was set apart to achieve good and noble purposes; that America is indeed the New Arcadia, or will be if he has his way.

This highly political, highly pragmatic and ceaselessly industrious approach, however, irritates a lot of people. Mr. Johnson is a hard, inconsiderate man, especially with his personal staff. He thinks of his staff as members of his family. At his ranch they eat all their meals with him, including his colored secretary. He showers them with presents, but he dominates their lives. He works night and day himself and he expects them to do the same. His personal considerations are not permitted to take precedence over the job; theirs are not expected to either.

It is interesting that the men of his own generation, who were his associates in the New Deal days, and whom he respects and consults on many of the most intimate questions of policy and personnel—Abe Fortas, Clark Clifford, James Rowe, and other friends such as former Secretary of the Treasury Robert Anderson and Donald Cook, the utilities expert in New York—have not joined his Administration. There are no doubt many reasons for this —maybe he wants it that way—but even some of these men prefer to work with him as outside advisers rather than under him as government servants.

This is not surprising. He is blunt and intolerant of mistakes, like his father whom he strongly resembles. Sometimes he is in a rush and will not take time to listen. Sometimes he will give hours to people who are embarrassed to use up so much of his time. On one occasion he may listen attentively and say very little. On another he may carry on a monologue which stuns rather than persuades the visitor.

This torrent of activity is deceptive. It gives the impression that he is impulsive, but nothing could be more misleading. All the talking, all the telephoning, all the expenditure of energy are generally part of an elaborate system of checking and double checking to be sure he knows all sides of the question before he moves. He has a catalogue of persons with whom he talks on each subject, some in and some out of government.

He knows these people extremely well and has them catalogued precisely in his mind. Each of them fits into a kind of Johnsonian political spectrum. "I know he regards me," explains one of his intimates, "as pessimistic and a little left of center and he judges what I say on this basis." If the answer given by the "pessimistic and left-of-center friend conforms to that pattern, the President will probably not spend much time talking to him. But if, for whatever reason, the answer comes back "optimistic" or a little conservative, the President will pay attention and start rechecking. He may go back over the list entirely to clarify this one point. But one way or another, he will pay attention to that surprising answer, like a scientist exploring some odd chemical reaction.

He has a horror of making mistakes. He is highly conscious even now of Franklin Roosevelt's Court-packing blunder after the election of 1936. President Kennedy's fiasco at the Bay of Pigs in Cuba is a nightmare to him. "Never move up your artillery," he says, "until you move up your ammunition." Like a majority leader who does not like to call up a bill until he is sure he has the votes, he does not easily make decisions as President without being reasonably sure of victory. This is why he has been so restrained in responding to the Communist pressures in Vietnam, and this, of course, is why he is under attack from those who think a President must sometimes move without being sure of victory and without being certain of popular acclaim.

Lyndon Johnson is not to be explained in the newspaper clippings of today but in the writings of the past. He came to the Presidency with more Government experience than any man in this century, but personally, he is a throw-back. He is a link between the Old Frontier of the days of William Jennings Bryan and the New Frontier days of John F. Kennedy.

When Frederick Jackson Turner came to the end of his long study of the influence of the American frontier on American character, he put himself to the task of defining the dominant human characteristics produced by frontier living, and in the process drew a word-portrait of Lyndon Johnson. He defined the frontier characteristics this way:

> That coarseness and strength combined with acuteness and inquisitiveness; that practical, inventive turn of mind, quick to find expedients; that masterful grasp of material things, lacking in the artistic but powerful to affect great ends; that restless, nervous energy; that dominant individualism, working for good or evil, and withal that buoyancy and exuberance which comes from freedom—these are the traits of the frontier or traits called out elsewhere because of the existence of the frontier.

In his attitudes toward his Government, likewise, Johnson retains a faith that was once more popular than it is today. The political critics of the present time wonder whether a man so preoccupied with political tactics can conceive of the programs essential to the well-being of a complicated modern society. They see the leader, or so it seems to me, in Churchillian or even in Gaullist terms as a man with a sharp vision of the world and his place in it, and with a precise plan for leading the nation toward his goals. This is not Johnson's way.

He retains the old faith that the *total society* will find the answers to its problems, not the President alone. "A President does not shape a new and personal vision of America," he said in his first State of the Union message after his election. "He collects it from the scattered hopes of the American past." Lord Bryce, in his monumental work, "The American Commonwealth," summed up this attitude 77 years ago.

> The American people, Bryce wrote, "have unbounded faith in what they call The People and in a democratic system of government . . . hence a further confidence that the people are sure to decide right in the long run. . . . If you ask an intelligent citizen why he so holds, he will answer that truth and justice are sure to make their way into the minds and consciences of the majority. This is deemed an axiom, and the more readily so deemed, because truth is identified with common sense, the quality which the average citizen is most confidently proud of possessing."

President Johnson believes in this today. He was brought up on it. He loves to tell of the days when his grandfather and uncle campaigned together in the same horse and buggy for a seat in the Texas State Legislature, one on the Populist ticket and the other on the Democratic ticket. His mother, who was a great influence on his life, gave him a scrapbook in 1954 four years before she died. On a scrap of lined paper inside, she wrote: "May he find in the lives that have gone into the making of his life fuller understanding of his traits of mind and heart, deep appreciation of his ancestry, and continuing stimulation and incentive to a rich and rewarding life."

From this background has come that deep sense of home and country, which Tocqueville noticed in so many Americans when he came to this country in the eighteen-thirties. "There is," he remarked, in "Democracy in America," "one sort of

patriotic attachment which principally arises from that instinctive, disinterested, and undefinable feeling which connects the affections of a man with his birthplace. This natural fondness is united with a taste for ancient customs and a reverence for traditions of the past; those who cherish it love their country as they love the mansion of their fathers."

President Johnson approached his first full term in much the same mood of nostalgia. The Presidency, he said, in his State of the Union Message, brings no gift of prophecy or foresight and the President's hardest task is not to do what's right but to know what's right.

"The answer was waiting for me in the land where I was born," he said. "It was once a barren land . . . but men came and worked and endured and built. . . . There was a dream . . . a dream of a continent to be conquered, a world to be won, a nation to be made. . . . Remembering this I knew the answer. . . ."

This connection between Johnson and the concepts of the frontier is startling, but is it relevant to the present time? The young intellectuals do not seem to think it is. The university and diplomatic worlds are dubious. Who, they ask, is to lead and articulate the new American Idea, so casually called the Great Society? Where will we get the synthesizing intelligence that will rally the Government and the nation and reduce diversity to identity? The President represents the popular characteristics of the ordinary people, but paradoxically, is not wildly popular, maybe because the people want to be represented by qualities better than their own.

This hurts Mr. Johnson but it does not change his mind, and it clearly cannot change his character. He thinks the concepts of the past are relevant to the present day. He believes we are still on the hard frontier of a wicked world, where men are bound to get hurt and sensitivities overrun. He does not feel that it can be won without faith, and the faith he sees and hopes to nourish is the faith of our fathers. He does not think it can be done without a vast collective effort and without unity. And this is not feeling and sentiment alone.

He believes in an apparent paradox—namely, that the very complexity, mobility and menace of the world today, which are causing so many problems, are also affecting all regions, and classes and nations, and therefore making it a little easier to bring about reconciliations between North and South, labor and management, rich and poor, the Congress and the White House, and even between the squabbling nations of the world. Accordingly, he feels that he is not trying to impose the past on the present, but merely trying to use the symbols of the past to create popular support for the essential innovations of the future.

Since his spectacular victory in November he has seemed more calm, as if he had tamed his inner demons at last. He is not a deeply religious man, and his attitude toward life was little changed by his heart attack in 1955, but it would be surprising if he were not now affected by the startling change in his fortunes.

At 45, he was convinced that he was as well prepared for the Presidency as any man in his party. At 52 he was denied the nomination because of what he regarded, with some bitterness, as prejudice against his Southern background. At 55 all was changed by the assassination of President Kennedy, precisely when Mr. Johnson had finally concluded he would never reach the White House.

This is the central paradox of his story. The things he planned and manipulated in pursuit of the Presidency failed, and the thing he did not plan—he took the Vice Presidency for the sake of the party and against the opposition of his wife—carried him in the end to the top.

He does not talk about the election now; he doesn't even analyze the results, as he analyzed the polls before the vote. He merely talks unity, and who is to say at this moment that he is wrong? "The art of free society," wrote Alfred North Whitehead, "consists first in the maintenance of the symbolic code, and secondly, in the fearlessness of revision. . . . Those societies which cannot combine reverence to their symbols with freedom of revision must ultimately decay."

This is Johnson's theme and method. He does not study these things; they are in his bones. Kennedy's purpose was to make men think; Johnson's is to make men act. Both were reformers but went about it in different ways. Kennedy demanded reforms by challenging the conformists; Johnson got Kennedy's reforms by seeming to be a conformist himself.

So let us pray. He may back into the future but he will do so consciously, for he believes there is a spirit and wisdom in America's past that will guide her wherever she goes.

12.   The Art of Politics

Rexford G. Tugwell

This very brief chapter from The Art of Politics *outlines some of the most important psychological and physical characteristics of the political man that Tugwell observed in Franklin D. Roosevelt, Luis Muñoz Marin, and Fiorello H. LaGuardia. The author is a professor at Southern Illinois University.*

* * *

I began by suggesting that the similarities among my three politicians were striking. I may even have given the impression that they might have been interchangeable. I could not support that contention if it was surface likenesses to which I referred; the three obviously led different lives in different places, they came from various social and economic environments, they had different educations and experiences, and they did not at all look alike. Yet let us see. Were even these surface characteristics as different as they at first seem?

Consider them physically. All were hearty, full-blooded types, vital, overflowing with energy, restless, driven by urges and ambitions long before these compulsions had any focus. They were destined to struggle and to rise, and there would be full and vital pleasure in all the incidents of their careers.

I venture to summarize their similarities:

They were unintellectual in the scientific sense.

They were strongly virile and attractive.

All were extroverts, enjoying sensual pleasures—eating, drinking, exercise, entertainment.

All were superb conversationalists; all knew the uses of parables.

All were insensitive to others' feelings except as concerned themselves, but their awareness of others' attitudes concerning themselves was phenomenal.

All seemed to have thick skins because they were abused, but this was only seeming: all were hurt and all were unforgiving; and all were anxious for approval.

All were ruthless in the sense of not reciprocating loyalty; they punished friends and rewarded enemies.

All had thick armor against probings. Not even those nearest to them knew their minds.

None held any traditions to be applicable to himself, though all were aware of them and made full use of their value to others.

They possessed talents for and used political techniques with faultless ease.

All were driven by an ambition to attain power in the political hierarchy, and all allowed it to dominate their lives.

This does not make them interchangeable. But it marks some of the characteristics of first-rank quality in the political field. And that is the point I wish to make.

13. The State Chairman

Joseph P. Lyford

Published as a case study for the Eagleton Institute of Politics, the excerpt printed here concerns the Chairman of the Democratic Party in Connecticut, John Bailey. Lyford, now with the Center for the Study of Democratic Institutions, ran as a candidate for Congress in 1952 and 1954 and has written about his effort to win the Congressman-at-large nomination in 1958 and the role played by John Bailey in the attempt. This selection covers Bailey's personality, his functions, motivations, responsibilities, and his powers in the state.

* * *

In a sense a map of Democratic politics in Connecticut is a map of John Moran Bailey. He has established a remarkable record of longevity in a job which in other states has a mortality rate similar to that of men who drive nitroglycerine trucks. Bailey has been chairman of the Democratic party since 1946. While he is a strict "organization man" today, the dim recesses of his own political history reveal that he was an insurgent and a local primary fighter in his time; as chairman of the Young Democrats he overthrew the Hartford regime of

From Joseph P. Lyford, *Candidate* (Eagleton Institute Case Study in Practical Politics, Case 9), pp. 4–6.

Tom Spellacy, Bailey's first political mentor. From then on it was inevitable that Bailey would take over leadership of the state organization. After becoming state chairman, Bailey strengthened his position by expert use of patronage and an unemotional, pragmatic approach to the problems of political organization peculiar to Connecticut.

Some of Bailey's motivations are obscure, but one of his main reasons for wanting to be state chairman is that he likes being an important politician. The financial benefits he derives from his position, which are considerable in terms of his own very successful law practice in Hartford, do not explain the seven-day weeks and thirteen-hour days he devotes to Democratic party affairs. A man of independent fortune, Bailey would be wealthy without politics; he would not be happy without politics. He enjoys politics the way he does golf, as an exhilarating game and as a competitive experience filled with a constant succession of improbable and unpredictable situations. He is a visible and active worrier. He often places his hand on his balding brow in desperation, but I suspect that he even enjoys this feeling—an enjoyment which perhaps rests upon the conviction that he will always end right side up. Bailey is a competitor; he likes to play against experts and preferably on new ground every time. The tougher the opposition and more excrutiating the difficulties the better.

He has been described as a "boss," the familiar term for the politician who stands at the top of a political organization. He does behave on the surface, frequently, like the stereotype of a "boss." His decisions can kill candidates or nominate them. Judges are appointed or disappointed as he sees fit. Dozens of varieties of patronage are dispensed only with his approval. But while Bailey may be a "boss," he is not an all-powerful dictator.

If Bailey has a motto, it might be a remark he once made to me: "You've gotta be where you've gotta be." Bailey, unlike a dictator, is under severe compulsions to act in certain ways, often against his own wishes. His function is to size up a given situation, figure out what the facts require him to do, and then do it—even if this requires the application of painful pressure on people who do not see things as he does. Bailey does not order politicians about capriciously; he tries to discover what course will lead most quickly to catastrophe and then avoid it by all means at hand. This approach enables him to defend his decisions with an air of helplessness which is most convincing. "What else can I do?" he asks, and there are few politicians who will not yield to the impulse to sympathize.

Bailey hates the sound of an angry politician, provided he is important, and will exert himself to keep such outcries to a minimum. His office is a truce tent, a forum, and a mediation chamber for the disgruntled. Any politician whose credentials have not expired can have his own interview with Bailey. The chairman spends part of his time listening, the other part talking—and even his talking is a pump-priming operation to get the other fellow to open up. He usually greets political visitors with "What do you hear about the situation?" This gambit makes the visitor feel he is important, or knows something Bailey does not, which is usually an illusion.

Bailey's function varies, depending on the party fortunes. When his party is out of office in the state, he is the final arbiter of party disputes. If, however, as is now the case, a Democrat sits in the governor's chair, the state chairman becomes his agent and adviser. In a sense this latter situation is more difficult for Bailey, because he may have to enforce decisions which are personally distasteful to him. But Bailey has never, so far as I can remember, abdicated his responsibilities as the governor's political executive officer. In 1949, when the then-Governor Chester Bowles decided to appoint William Benton to the United States Senate to fill the unexpired term of Raymond Baldwin, he passed over Bailey's own aspirations for the appointment. Informed of the decision by the governor, Bailey laid away his bitter disappointment and proceeded to convince recalcitrant Democratic politicians that Benton was the best possible man for the job. Bailey's relationship to Governor Ribicoff, a very different type of politician from Bowles, has been the same. If the Governor wants something, it is Bailey's job to see that it is done —whether or not he may have privately disagreed with the chief executive.

The myth that bosses are not only arrogant but efficient does not fit Bailey. Despite his shrewdness in escaping from individual crises, he is not an organizer. He can get things done, he can anticipate, but his techniques are often more improvised than calculated, and he is better at extricating himself from trouble than in keeping out of trouble. He plays by ear and, in Connecticut, it works beautifully. Bailey's ways are superbly suited to the peculiar character of Nutmeg Democrats. He herds the organization along with an imprecision and confusion which accords well with a party filled with cranky competing individuals, with personal ambitions which are consistent only in that they are always in conflict with each other. The Democratic party of Connecticut is certainly a functioning machine, but it is not well oiled. Under Bailey it creaks along, with many changes of course, accompanied by the loudest groans imaginable, many of them coming from Bailey himself. It is even inaccurate to say that the organization is "under" Bailey; often it is the other way around, with him down below somewhere looking at the wheels. But it is safe to make one generalization: he is always available, wherever he is, to receive suggestions as to how to keep the party headed toward November

victories and the promised land where there are enough political jobs for everybody.

If I were to attempt the impossible and click off Bailey's most striking personal characteristics, I would say that he is a journeyman psychologist, a poker player with a sense of humor, a listener, a collector, an executioner but not an executive, and a man with a natural preference for the top dog. He has no discernible prejudices—racial or religious—and he is dominated neither by considerations of personal friendship nor spite. Most important, he has been able, with very little effort, to avoid commitments to any philosophy of government whatsoever.

I know of nobody in Connecticut politics who would suggest that Bailey is in politics because of a burning desire to serve his fellow man or to promote a given set of government principles or ethics, and it would not be fair to suggest that he has ever attempted to cultivate such an impression. The business of a state chairman, as he sees it, is to remain state chairman. To remain state chairman means that under his direction the party must win elections and control as many jobs as it can. Judged in terms of these purposes, in recent years Bailey has been remarkably successful.

14. Two Negro Politicians: An Interpretation

James Q. Wilson

In this article James Q. Wilson, Professor of Government at Harvard University, describes two powerful political leaders— William Dawson and Adam Clayton Powell —whose constituencies are similar. The two Congressmen, however, function in very different ways. The author contends that

From the *Midwest Journal of Political Science*, vol. 4, no. 4 (November 1960), pp. 346–369, with footnotes deleted, by permission of Wayne State University Press.

these differences in political style are more closely related to the character of the party organizations involved, the incentives necessary to maintain these organizations, and the general political environment rather than to the different personalities of the two men.

* * *

This is an attempt to describe, and in part to account for, the differences between two powerful political leaders, whose constituencies are roughly similar. Although the two congressmen in question are well-known Negroes—Adam Clayton Powell, Jr. of New York and William L. Dawson of Chicago—the analysis of the character of their political life is not meant to explain their idiosyncratic features. It is hoped, rather, that these remarks will illuminate some of the central features of the role of any congressman. By choosing for study two men who, in many ways, are polar opposites but who at the same time share many of the same problems and resources, the contrasts between them can be made more vivid and the argument employed can be sketched in bold strokes.

Powell and Dawson are the most famous Negro Democratic congressmen. The former was first elected in 1944, the latter in 1942. Both represent districts that are almost entirely Negro in composition, and which have within them both appalling slums and expensive homes and apartments. Both are relatively senior members of the House of Representatives. Dawson is the chairman of the House Government Operations Committee; Powell is the second-ranking Democrat on the Education and Labor Committee and is a sub-committee chairman on the Interior Committee. Both have received national publicity, Powell more than Dawson, and both are well-known to their colleagues. Both tend to support the Democratic leadership of the House fairly consistently. On "party votes" (i.e., votes which pit a majority of

one party against a majority of the other party), neither Dawson nor Powell will as a rule vote against his party in more than two or three percent of the cases. Neither Dawson nor Powell has an especially good record of voting participation in House roll calls. Although Dawson is better than Powell in most sessions, both are well below the average for the House as a whole. Powell has on occasion been among the very lowest—sometimes *the* lowest—in voting participation, and rarely averages higher than 50 percent. Dawson has steadily increased his voting participation, rising from 38 percent in 1947–48 to 83 percent in 1958.

The similarities between the two men are, however, superficial. The differences are profound. Each has a unique political style which transcends issues, roll calls, or personal fortunes. The one is an orator, the other an organizer; one is flamboyant, the other is conservative; one is militant on the race question, the other is moderate. One seeks publicity and speaks almost always "on the record"; the other shuns publicity and speaks to interviewers only off the record. One is considered by most of his House colleagues to be demagogic and unreliable; the other has the confidence and respect of many influential congressmen. One raises the race issue on every occasion; the other goes out of his way to avoid discussing race or race questions. One is light-skinned, handsome, boyish, gregarious, fun-loving; the other is brown-skinned, aged, reserved, quiet. One spends his free time (of which he has a great deal) in world travel, entertaining, and night life; the other rarely travels, devotes himself completely to politics, and leads a home life carefully screened by privacy and silence. The two most prominent Negro politicians are radically dissimilar, avoid each other's company, speak disparagingly of one another, and elicit the most violent attitudes of love and hate from their many friends and enemies.

An explanation can be offered that will both account for many of these differences and suggest something of interest about the relationship of any political leader to his organization and his constituents. This explanation will endeavor to show that Powell and Dawson are not simply two interesting and perhaps unique men, but that they are also political leaders who have created and who seek to maintain two important kinds of political organizations. The creation and maintenance of these organizations places certain constraints on the actions of the leaders. The leaders' political styles reflect these constraints. It will be necessary, to make this argument plausible, to describe how these organizations were built, the nature of the political systems of which they are part, the maintenance needs these organizations have, and the implications these needs have for the political style of the leader.

We will argue, first, that the most important single factor in creating or modifying the political style of each leader is the character of the organization which supports the leader and the nature of the incentives which he must distribute to sustain it. Each political leader acts so as to maintain the strength of his organization. The strength of the organization is measured in terms of the number and size of the contributions to it, the extent to which a single undisputed leadership can control it, and the extent to which it can attain its collective goal (in this case, the retention of political office). To maintain the flow of contributions (the time, money, and energies of organization workers and the votes of the electorate), incentives must be distributed by the leader. In the case of Powell, these are largely intangible (non-material or "ideal") incentives; in the case of Dawson, these are largely tangible or material.

The second argument will be that the character of the organization which the leader must maintain is largely determined by the nature of the local political system. The aspects of that system most relevant here include the size and composition of the political districts and the relative strength and unity of the city-wide political organization. The maintenance of a Negro political organization is intimately bound up with the maintenance of the political system of the community as a whole.

POWELL

Adam Clayton Powell, Jr., was not, until the summer of 1959, a member of the regular party organization in New York City. When Powell sought to enter Congress in 1944, Tammany was a weakened machine. Eleven years of rule by LaGuardia, the adoption of a new city charter, and the extension of civil service had left the Tiger in a state of chronic malnutrition. The organization was shot through with factions and internecine warfare, both in Harlem and elsewhere. Rival leaders made competing alliances, broke them, and made new ones. The strength of the Manhattan organization declined, and other forces—such as the Bronx organization of Edward Flynn—rose to power. Few, inside or outside the organization, could depend on machine discipline or machine voting strength. Other bases of political power had to be found by those who sought a permanent and rising career in politics. Powell found his in the pulpit. He built his organization and his political following from outside the city machine. Although he received the endorsement of Tammany when he first ran for Congress in 1944, and subsequently until 1958, he felt he could not rely on either that endorsement or the efforts of the workers in the regular organization. The base of support for Powell was and is the Abyssinian Baptist Church, a church of perhaps 10,000 members that has existed since 1808. It was the church of his father, who retired in 1937. It is independent of any larger organization, and financially self-sustaining. In addition to the church, Powell was co-editor of a Harlem weekly, the *People's Voice*. In the stormy Harlem of the 1930's, Powell was a familiar and dramatic figure in and around the various Negro boycott movements, strikes, and protest demonstrations. He was opposed for the Democratic nomination for Congress in 1944 by the Negro who was then the most important Harlem district leader, but Tammany—either unsure of its ability to elect an alternative candidate, receptive to suggestions from other forces, or desirous of rebuking a rebellious district leader—chose to ignore the leader's protest and endorse Powell.

Powell created a personal organization. In part it was formed because Powell began his career from outside of the established organization, and in part it was necessary because even a position inside the Tammany machine was fraught with dangers and uncertainties. Whether outside or inside the organization, independent political strength was at least an advantage and probably a necessity. A church can be an ideal source of such strength. It directly recruits and organizes the masses, it can be financially independent, it has a variety of channels of communication throughout the community, and it has the luster of an indisputably good institution. In recent elections, Powell has been able to call upon as many as one thousand church workers for his campaigns, mostly volunteers. They are already organized through the elaborate committee structure and social service system of the church, and many of them hear Powell speak every Sunday. The church, in addition, has a paid bureaucracy of workers to provide the necessary staff. The appeals to these supporters are almost entirely intangible. The appeals are even larger than simply the exploitation of established race issues. They are centered around Powell as the personal embodiment, the projective personality, of the Negroes in his congregation. He is the vivid and colorful mani-

festation of their collective aspirations and expectations.

The use of intangible appeals in political organizations creates a set of constraints upon the user. When appeals are to principle, to lofty moral and racial goals, to the deepest wishes and fears of the listener, they enforce a logic upon the user which is compelling. Three important consequences of this kind of appeal can be mentioned.

First, these appeals tend to be "indivisible"; that is, they cannot easily be reduced to discrete units, given relative priorities, and dealt with apart from other aspects of the leader's career. Rather, they tend to function as a whole, a montage of interrelated ends and means, to which all phases of a leader's life must respond. Powell, for example, does not and probably could not divorce his career in Washington from his career in New York. His role as a congressman is inseparable from his role as a Harlem politician, Negro minister, and colorful personality. Politics for him is not a specific, but a general role, and the appeals upon which it is based are ramified and indivisible. Politics is "functionally diffuse." Powell's position as a congressman is an extension of his position as a Harlem leader. The two offices, in Washington and New York, are systematically related. Both receive a relatively large number of constituents. In Washington, four staff workers are in Powell's office; in New York, three. In Washington, Powell receives as many as five to eight hundred letters a week, perhaps 250 of which state personal problems or requests for information and services. In New York, his congressional office is almost indistinguishable from his church organization, both of which deal with a wide range of the needs and requests of his followers. The church has in its congregation an estimated ten percent of the registered voters in the Sixteenth Congressional District. Powell speaks to some four thousand people every Sunday, and upwards of one thousand persons come to the church or its community house every day of the week. There is little difference between voter and parishioner, between constituency and congregation.

The generality of Powell's political role is further suggested by the extent to which he intervenes in New York City political affairs in the same manner in which he intervenes in national affairs. Powell frequently makes public charges of race discrimination and injustice in Manhattan and he is not slow to attack the Mayor, the Police Commissioner, Carmine De Sapio, and other officials. Harlem is not simply a constituency which elects Powell to Congress; it is also a source of political issues. Powell's political style in part depends on the existence of an "enemy"—a source of alleged injustice against which Powell can direct his fire. Since his power has not been received from the political organization of the city, the organization is not immune from that fire.

On the other hand, Powell is usually not readily available in his district for receiving constituents. Although he maintains a congressional staff in Harlem which is closely linked with his church staff, he does not personally perform the services usual for a local political leader—hear complaints, requests, and demands from the voters who seek out their politicians directly. These services are provided by lieutenants.

The mingling of political, religious, and civic roles is seen in the organization of his headquarters. The secretary of the church's Board of Trustees acts as financial secretary of Powell's political club (the "Alfred Isaacs Democratic Club"). His congressional administrative assistant, charged with handling local political affairs, has an office adjacent to that of the church's full-time social worker, and the two share the task of dealing with voters-parishioners. The church, a $100,000-a-year enterprise, provided 600 to 1200 political volunteers at various stages of Powell's 1959 campaign for district leader and helped to raise the $30,000 necessary for the 1958 congressional campaign.

Second, intangible appeals tend to be endowed with a sacrosanct quality which renders them difficult to manipulate. This would be true whether the appeal is that of a charismatic leader with the "gift of grace" or of political principles which are invested with a sacred quality. There are undoubtedly elements of both charisma and ideology in Powell's appeal to his followers; how much of each would be difficult to assess. Although there would be important differences in detail, the general effect of either a charismatic or ideological appeal is that the leader becomes ill-suited for a bargaining role. As the manifestation of the private aspirations of individual Negroes, as the assertion of the great public ends of the race, or as the revelation of a prophetic, heroic, or exemplary personality, these appeals are endowed with a sacrosanct quality which makes both the leader and the ends he may represent superior to the leaders and goals of others. To compromise either the position of the leader or the essence of these goals would be to give way to morally inferior persons or demands; in short, it would be to corrupt them. To oppose Powell in an election is to take the side of evil, to be an "Uncle Tom," and to be a "field hand" on the "white man's plantation."

Paradoxically, this does not mean that Powell cannot escape his position on issues affecting the race which come before the local or national government. He can, and has, advanced and then dropped causes which involved race ends. Powell has frequently announced a dramatic move in local or national politics, but often little or nothing is in fact done. This was the case with his promised "boycott" of the 1952 presidential election and the independent political organization he promised in 1958.

Few followers seem disturbed by this. Powell's own explanation is that such moves, even if only threats, serve to keep Tammany and others "off balance."

It may even be that Powell could reverse himself on some important issue, relying on his personal standing with his followers to justify the move. Charisma would compensate for ideology where the latter had to be sacrificed. Such may have been the case, for example, when he joined with the other three Negro congressmen in voting against a Republican-sponsored civil rights amendment to the 1959 Housing Act on the grounds that it intended to defeat the bill by making it unacceptable to Southerners. Previously, he had sponsored and fought for a civil rights amendment to the federal education bill which, when adopted by the House, was followed by the defeat of the bill as a whole. But considered as a set of appeals, Powell's identification with race issues and aspirations leads to further and further commitments and reduces the opportunity for compromise or the deliberate choice of means. Means, in the words of another student of race and nationalism, always have an "end-component." Means cannot be selected simply on the basis of whether they are efficiently adapted to the attainment of given ends. Means are not valued merely on the basis of utility. Almost all means which might be used toward given ends have a value in and of themselves. Ends react on means, imbue them with value and render it difficult for a leader to be selective. The means Powell employs are precisely of this character. They involve defying the white man, asserting loudly the rights of Negroes, pressing for liberalizing legislation regardless of the costs to other values held by the society, and keeping the issues alive and hot.

Powell's political appeals lend themselves to campaigns based on the Negro ministry. The church is a vital part of Powell's base of support and, even though some ministers individually do not like Powell, most of them can be counted on to campaign in his behalf. It is principally through the mobilized resources of the Harlem ministry that Powell speaks to the people, addressing them from the pulpits of dozens of churches.

Third, Powell indulges his personal wants to an extraordinary extent. Powell stated in 1956 that his income was an estimated $115,000 a year—$40,000 a year earned by him as congressman and minister, and $75,000 earned by his wife (the noted jazz pianist, Hazel Scott). He owns fancy sports cars, several homes, and two boats. Since Powell does not hold his followers and workers by material benefits, they rarely feel cheated by his obvious material success. In part, the lack of resentment is probably due to the feelings of gratification less fortunate Negroes derive from the sight of Powell in expensive restaurants and night clubs. He is doing what many of them understandably would like to do. But in addition, his money and material benefits are not the basis of his political power. Since his organization is not built through the distribution of tangible rewards, Powell can possess an abnormally large share of such rewards without depriving his followers of what they feel ought to be theirs. They support him for other reasons and derive other rewards from his success.

DAWSON

Willam L. Dawson was at one time an expert and frequent user of many of the same kinds of appeals that now characterize Powell. As an insurgent Republican, seeking to force an entry into the regular organization in Chicago, Dawson was a well-known street-corner speaker with a magnetic personality. He built a personal following outside the machine, in part by holding out to them the hope of eventual material reward, and in part by arousing their interest in the race issues of the day and by appealing to their aspirations. After some success within the Republican Party (he served as an alderman from 1935 to 1939), Dawson joined the Democrats then under the leadership of Edward Kelly and Pat Nash. His entry into the party was the beginning of his first real career as a regular organization man, and it was the beginning of the end of his career as a purveyor of race rhetoric.

Kelly became mayor of Chicago at about the same time that LaGuardia became mayor of New York. The implications of this difference are far-reaching. LaGuardia took over a city administration under heavy attack from the reformers, and proceeded to hasten the rate of reform and further weaken the political machine that he had defeated. Kelly inherited a city administration and a political machine which were intact and in reasonably good health, and he proceeded to strengthen both. At the very time when Tammany was being starved, the Cook County Democracy was being feasted. In New York, the path to political power and success was becoming uncertain and strewn with traps; in Chicago, the same path was more clearly than ever becoming a private road belonging to the Democratic machine. Once inside such an organization, Dawson discovered that rhetorical or other intangible appeals were not only no longer useful, they could be a positive embarrassment. The stock of material incentives which the machine held —patronage and favors—was enormous and growing. Power came to him who could distribute them, and the right to distribute them was reserved to those in good standing with the organization. Remaining in such good standing means, among other things, not dividing or weakening the organization by raising issues which split the machine or which require it to act against its own best interests.

Dawson created an organization in his ward, and extended it to other Negro wards, which attracted and held its workers mostly through the opportunity for jobs. In turn, the organization began the slow and laborious task of altering the voting habits of a Negro population which had been firmly committed to the Republican party. In part the switch of allegiance was accomplished simply by exploiting the national trend among Negroes to the Democratic party, in part it was done by providing services and favors to voters, and in part it was done by bringing them into a complex and thorough set of organizations which clustered about the political machine —women's auxiliaries, youth groups, building and block organizations, and so on. By 1942 the organization was able to send Dawson to Congress by a slim majority (in fact, Dawson was unable to carry his own ward at the time), and then to control an aldermanic election by delivering a winning majority to an organization Democrat who was being challenged by a popular, non-organization Democrat. From that time on, the size of the organization's majorities grew steadily until they reached a stable level of about three-to-one, where they have remained ever since. In the process, Dawson acquired influence over four other Negro ward leaders.

Several consequences flow in part from the character of the organization of which Dawson is a leader and the nature of the rewards which must be distributed to sustain it.

First, tangible rewards tend to be divisible in a sense in which intangible ones are not. The distribution of material rewards can be kept separate from other aspects of the leader's position. His role as a local politician can become a fairly specific one, permitting him to play other roles without creating conflicts. There need be no inevitable connection between local political leadership in Chicago and congressional political activity in Washington, D.C. Few expectations about Dawson's performance and style as a congressman are created among his constituents or his workers. Indeed, Dawson has gone to considerable lengths to divorce his Chicago base of support from his Washington field of action. There is little contact between the Washington and the Chicago office. The staffs are separately recruited and separately organized. The flow of communications between the two centers is relatively small.

The ward headquarters in Chicago performs most in the services to constituents which are necessary; relatively few demands reach Washington. Dawson is to a greater extent than most other congressmen freed from constituency pressures, and he deliberately cultivates this situation. Dawson attends to his constituency assiduously, but in a manner entirely different from Powell. Dawson's Chicago headquarters are located in the very heart of the most depressed Negro area in a modest building. It is drab on the outside and plain on the inside, and deliberately so. It is accessible to the least advantaged constituent and nothing about the office is allowed to make the constituent feel he is out of his element or in unfamiliar surroundings. Dawson, when in Chicago (and he is there frequently), spends almost all his time in his ward office. No appointment is necessary to see him, and the visitor need not state his business to the receptionist. On the bench outside his office on a typical day might be found a police captain, a couple on relief, a young Negro lawyer, an unemployed man, a politician, and a university professor. When Dawson is not in the city, his place is taken by lieutenants who function in the same fashion. His Washington office and its work load are markedly smaller than Powell's, or indeed of other congressmen generally. Where Powell has four staff workers in his Washington office, Dawson has one; where Powell receives five to eight hundred letters a week, Dawson receives one hundred; where Powell replies to 250 "case letters" (requesting information or services) per

week, Dawson receives one-third as many. Where Powell mails out large numbers of *Record* reprints and other items, Dawson mails almost none.

Dawson cherishes his reputation as a congressman. He is the chairman of the House Government Operations Committee, one of the three or four largest and most powerful committees in the House. He is highly esteemed by almost all his colleagues, who go out of their way to compliment him and his committee. He enjoys the respect of many southerners as well as large numbers of liberal northern Democrats. He has built his committee since 1949 (when he became its chairman), and his success is measured by the most important yardstick used in government—the size of its budget. In the 81st Congress, it received $300,000; in the 85th, $1,175,000. Its staff is competent and largely free of purely patronage appointments; the proceedings of the committee reflect an attention to business and an aversion to simple publicity that is unusual.

Dawson conceives of his Chicago organization as a base of support which produces, without commitment to issues or similar appeals, automatic majorities for him and his slate. For his role as Chicago ward leader, Dawson has one set of attitudes and action. He is strong, sometimes ruthless; he brooks no rivals; he crushes opposition and the ambitions of men who would challenge him; and he insists on organizational loyalty. In Washington, he plays an entirely different role. There, he is a leader interested in good government and liberal measures. He presides over the committee with authority, but not harshly. He encourages junior colleagues to take on new responsibilities and rise in committee work. He does not feel that he has rivals or opponents, and is friendly with everyone. Although he has considerable power as a congressman, he rarely uses that power for political ends in Chicago. By and large, the political power he has assembled in

Washington is used for national goals, and only rarely for Chicago goals. Issues in Chicago affairs have arisen which were in some measure vulnerable to congressional intervention. He did not intervene.

One of the few themes common to both his local and national roles is the avoidance of race as a public issue. As in Chicago, so in Washington, Dawson rarely engages in a *public* discussion of race goals. He has not used his committee staff as a source of "race patronage." Only two of the fifty staff members are Negroes. It is explained that this reflects the shortage of qualified Negro personnel. The committee has wide jurisdiction, but rarely is its investigative power turned toward explicitly racial issues. Some members of the staff regret this. Many were unhappy about his opposition to the Powell Amendment in 1956. On that occasion he ignored the requests of the NAACP and the numerous representations made to him from people in his district and not only voted but spoke out against the civil rights amendment on the grounds that if it were adopted it would mean southern opposition would be aroused and there would be no federal education bill at all. Dawson, although on friendly terms with two of the three other Negro congressmen, does not confine his association to them. He seems to prefer his wide range of contacts with many congressmen, particularly the House leadership. Although he is not a militant advocate of race ends in Congress, since 1956 he has not voted against such matters on the floor. Dawson, personally, feels that his political power can best be used for the advancement of Negroes in ways other than pressing for legislative correction of racial abuses. He sees himself as promoting Negro interests by intervening on their behalf with the authorities, placing more Negroes in government, and demonstrating the achievements possible for a Negro leader.

The most important single source of controversy about Dawson is whether his political influence and position—which ad-

mittedly are rarely used publicly for race ends—are used in a private, unpublicized manner. Dawson and his supporters point to his intervention in many issues involving Negro rights. He has conferred with southern political leaders about Negro registration and segregation in party meetings and functions in the South. He intervened in the Emmet Till lynch case and moved to cut off the hostile, southern-led congressional investigation of school integration in Washington, D.C. All of these facts are difficult to document, given the secrecy which has surrounded them. The truth probably is that Dawson has had more effect than his critics allege and less than his most ardent supporters claim.

The other theme common to both Chicago and Washington is the extent to which Dawson shuns publicity. When Powell grants an interview, it is usually understood to be on the record; when Dawson does, it is almost always specified as off the record. Dawson's aversion to publicity is legendary, and goes far beyond that which is called for simply by prudence. He feels that he has been mistreated by an essentially hostile press, mostly in Chicago, that even friendly reporters are not allowed to print stories favorable to him, and that publicity invariably ends by embarrassing him or his political allies.

The *second* consequence of Dawson's position in an organization is the high degree of discretion he has on legislative matters. Dawson shuns race issues. His local organization meets weekly to hear Dawson and others speak; rarely is race a theme of their remarks. Dawson's attitude is that race progress must be made from within the party. If the organization can be persuaded to espouse race causes, well and good; if it cannot, then one must accept that fact as the inevitable cost of belonging. Dawson's view of appropriate race ends is largely confined to what has been termed elsewhere "welfare" ends—i.e., ends which are specific, direct, and tangible and which tend to improve the lot of the Negro without necessarily attaining some true measure of integration. Party, not racial unity is stressed.

Dawson has been challenged by individuals and voluntary associations such as the local NAACP for not taking more vigorous *public* stands on race issues such as lynching, the Democratic Party's platform on civil rights, and other matters. Dawson has been criticized in the Negro press. The important fact is that such challenges and criticisms account for little; his electoral strength is barely affected. Dawson, like Powell, is stronger than any single issue which might be used against him. He can survive almost any position he takes on any single issue. But unlike Powell, he need not devote himself to issues and aspirations. His freedom of choice in this matter is much wider. He can be far more deliberate in his choice of ends and means. He can devote himself almost entirely to the pursuit of other, non-racial goals without being penalized. His range of discretion regarding means to any important political ends is broad. This is true in part because he can afford the luxury of little or no publicity, and in part because he need not consider the extent to which the means he uses are endowed with value significance. Means, to Dawson, can be more completely instrumental than to Powell.

Nowhere is the contrast between the Dawson and Powell organizations more striking or important than in the differing roles of the Negro ministry. The ministry is politically significant only in those Negro communities where no independent base of political power exists—i.e., where there is no strong, patronage-oriented machine. Dawson has deliberately worked for twenty years to reduce or eliminate the role of the Negro minister as a political influence in Chicago, and he has in great part succeeded. A fundamental distinction between Negro political systems is whether they must work through existing mass organizations (churches and labor unions) or whether it is possible to organize the community *directly* for political ends. Dawson, to be sure, has ministerial allies, but he discourages the participation of ministers in politics for the most part. Nor is Powell "dependent" on the ministers. The relationship is symbiotic; each needs the other. The distinction is between one system in which the ends and basis of influence of the politician are relatively *independent* of other ends and bases of influence in the community (as in Chicago) and the alternative system in which political ends and influences are *implicated* in the community (as in New York).

Third, Dawson stands in an entirely different relationship to his followers and workers than does Powell. Because of the character of the incentives used by Dawson to hold their allegiance and maintain discipline, he is subject to a set of constraints from which Powell is largely exempt. The "status gap" between Powell and his supporters is manifestly greater than the disparity between Dawson and his followers. Powell, since he embodies the racial goals and private aspirations of many of his followers, can enrich his own position without weakening his stature—indeed, he may enhance it. Dawson leads a group of men who fundamentally, although not exclusively, are in politics for more tangible rewards. Dawson weakens his position by the extent to which he appears to gain at the expense of his followers. His supporters must be convinced that they can gain in proportion to the gains of Dawson. If Dawson gains disproportionately to his followers, he causes resentment, jealousy, and antagonisms.

This speaks to the question of the nature of Dawson's political skills. In part, of course, they are the skills of any leader of men—the ability to move other men to act in accordance with one's intentions. This requires arranging the situation so that the wants of individuals lead them to act toward the ends of the leader. A typical, but short-sighted, view as to the basis of a machine leader's power is that he "controls patronage." This is an insufficient and in part a misleading explanation. In reality, it says little more than that a man is powerful because he is powerful. The question remains, *why* has *he* been able to grasp and retain control of patronage for the purpose of sustaining his organization? If control of patronage were the only variable, then Negro politics in Chicago might be in a state of constant factional rivalry. The essential element in the use of tangible incentives to sustain political organizations is that the followers must never be allowed to feel that the gains of breaking with the leader outweigh the costs of such a break. The leader ought to create a pattern of expectations among his followers which he appears willing to satisfy even at his own expense.

This is made possible when the leader, such as Dawson, derives intangible rewards from a political system that produces tangible rewards for the followers. Dawson's gratifications are not in money and material perquisites, but in prestige, the sense of power, and the fun of the game. He lives austerely, drives second-hand cars, avoids ostentation, spends money freely on others, and generally minimizes the outward or material rewards of his position. He does not appear to be competing with his followers for the scarce material rewards of politics. Perhaps he could afford greater outward display than he does, but it seems clear that the lack of such display enhances his position.

CHICAGO AND NEW YORK

These differences between the two organizations can be accounted for largely by the differences in the political systems of which they are parts. In New York, the steady weakening of the Tammany organization which has gone on since 1933 has made it difficult for it to enforce its will on its members and impossible for it to turn back the challenge of a man like Powell. Further, Tammany attempted, during the LaGuardia-Fusion period, to govern Harlem from outside the district, through "absentee" leaders whose influence rested in part on keeping Negro political leadership divided and off balance. Tammany failed—in part through unwillingness and in part through lack of resources—to build a strong, centralized Negro leadership in Harlem. Powell now seeks to fill that void. After his election as a district leader (together with three other leaders allied with him) he sought to create a unified "Leadership Team" for Harlem. In January, 1960, Powell's group received control of the Tammany patronage in Harlem. Although he has now entered the regular organization, Powell's independent base of support and the paucity of the rewards Tammany can offer his followers means that Tammany needs Powell more than he needs it. All doubt on this manner was quickly dispelled when Powell made public attacks on New York political leaders for failing to give Negroes more representation in government, for denying Negroes patronage, for persecuting Borough President Hulan Jack (Powell's erstwhile political scapegoat), and for allowing police to drive out Negro numbers racketeers in favor of Italians.

Dawson's organization is a strong portion of a powerful city machine. The possibility of a Powell arising on Chicago's South Side is substantially reduced by this fact. In 1947–1955, an effort was made by a popular minister to become an independent political force in the community. He managed to serve two terms in the City Council as alderman of the Third Ward. But the Dawson organization defeated him in 1955 for several reasons—all of which are indicative of the differences in politics between Chicago and New York. The Dawson organization has available to it perhaps three times the amount of patronage available to comparable districts in Harlem. The independent had to fight, not a group of quarreling factions, but a single, organized opponent who was well-staffed with workers. The independent could gain relatively few civic allies; most were already committed to the strongest force in the community—the Dawson group. Although the independent was a minister, other ministers could not be mobilized as a solid group behind him. Finally, it was necessary in a city where the Democratic primary was invariably dominated by the regular organization for the independent to run as a Republican (where his sympathies happened to lie anyway) and this was a grave weakness in a community overwhelmingly Democratic. (Chicago's aldermanic elections are only nominally nonpartisan.) When the independent attempted to emulate Powell by moving from the city council to Congress, he had again to run as a Republican, and this was fatal.

Thus, the character of the political system into which Powell and Dawson moved in their formative years (the late 1930's and early 1940's) was of decisive importance in molding the kind of organization each created. Dawson found a strong, active apparatus in which he had to create a place for himself. Powell encountered a weak, divided organization which it was necessary neither to join nor to defeat.

SOME CONCLUSIONS

Two important congressmen with roughly comparable constituencies have been compared. Both men, it has been argued, act as if the maintenance of their organizations were their goal. Since the organizations and the incentives necessary to maintain them differ, the political styles of the two men differ.

One organization was created and is sustained by a system of ideal or non-material benefits. This has certain consequences. (1) The benefits are indivisible, and the role of the leader who dispenses them tends to become diffuse and general. All aspects of his career are treated as part of a whole, and all choices relate to a single set of values. (2) The benefits have a sacred component, and thus are difficult to compromise. Means used to attain them share in the moral or sacrosanct quality of the ends themselves; means can only with difficulty be regarded as purely instrumental. (3) The ideal benefits which followers share permit the leader to indulge himself in outward display without alienating them—indeed, he may enhance his position with them. The other organization was created and is sustained by a system of tangible rewards. Among the consequences of this are: (1) The rewards are divisible and may be isolated to the local organization. The role of the leader can be specific and compartmentalized. He may separate his base of support from his national field of action. (2) The absence of race or ideological appeals gives the leader a greater discretion as to the choice of ends to pursue. Means tend to be more thoroughly instrumental. Few of his actions are deliberately imbued with moral significance. (3) The power of the leader in part depends on his ability to satisfy his followers that they gain in proportion to him—that he does not gain at their expense. The "status-gap" between the leader and the led is relatively small.

Further, it has been argued that the character of the two organizations, and hence the nature of their maintenance needs, can be traced to the political systems of which they are parts. One political system (Chicago) has a single leadership which disposes of a large amount of patronage, is unified, and can control its own primaries with ease. The other (New York) has a leadership which constantly must meet challenges, has a short supply of patronage, and cannot invariably control its own primaries. In the latter Powell succeeded;

in the former, a Powell-like leader tried and failed.

This mode of analysis has an obvious shortcoming. A political style which may have been, at some early point, functional in terms of the needs of the situation, later tends to become temperamental. Political style tends to become the independent variable, *creating* in part the situation it had formerly served; that is, the image a leader creates of himself inevitably tends to react back on him and modify his behavior apart from what might be considered as the "objective" needs of the situation. Both Dawson and Powell undoubtedly carry many of their attributes to an unusual extreme, and settled habits have now replaced earlier experiments. But we need not linger too long on the problem of untangling the man from the situation, for however subtle a pattern of interaction exists between the two levels, the burdens of the analysis remains this: the political style of the two leaders is functional to the organization they must maintain and the position they hold within the larger political system of which they are part.

It is interesting to note the opinion of these men held by prominent Negroes in New York and Chicago. Publicly, both have been criticized and even attacked. The *Chicago Defender* was critical of Dawson in 1956; the New York *Amsterdam News* supported Powell's opponent in 1958. But public criticism is far rarer and much more gentle than the private criticism which can be found directed at both men. The followers are aligned in two intent and mutually exclusive camps. Neither man has anything like universal admiration from the Negro middle class or from Negro intellectuals. Both are criticized by many thoughtful Negroes: Dawson for doing nothing, Powell for being irresponsible. At the same time, both get grudging respect from most Negro civic leaders—Dawson because of his personal position, his stature, and his power; Powell because he is "not

afraid of the white man" and because he "stirs things up" and thus makes it easier for civic organizations to gain leverage against influential whites. The important aspect of the private praise and blame heaped on these men is that in the last analysis it is not concerned with ends or accomplishments. Neither leader has "accomplished" much in the way of legislation directed at race goals. Although Powell supporters criticize Dawson for "doing nothing," in fact, of course, Powell has no greater a list of accomplishments. And when pressed, many Negroes will concede this.

This means that most criticism of the two leaders centers on the nature of their political styles. In a situation in which *ends* are largely unattainable (at least by Negro action alone), *means* become all-important. On the basis of the means employed—the political style used—men make judgments as to the worth of the leader and his reputation. Means, in short, tend to become ends in themselves; what is important is not what you do, but how you do it. As pointed out earlier in another content, means acquire an "end-component" either because (a) ends are unattainable or (b) ends are morally endowed.

The relationship of leader to organization in these two cases raises interesting questions concerning the role of congressmen. It has often been assumed that one mark of the statesman is an interest in issues, rather than patronage, as the currency of politics. Schattschneider, for example, censures the "local bosses" because they are irresponsible and because they interfere in national politics to its detriment. The thrust of this paper is that, for a variety of reasons, a "boss" may deliberately separate his local and national roles. Further, he may use his local machine (a) to filter out constituency demands by satisfying them at the local level and (b) to sustain himself in office without extensive or irrevocable commitments on policy matters and without accepting the support of organized pressure groups. The very position of a person such as Dawson enables him, if he chooses, to disregard both the localistic demands of constituents and the demands of local or national pressure groups. The needs of the constituents can be met largely on an issue-free basis; the demands of the pressure groups can be ignored, as they can do little either to help or harm the leader. In theory, this leaves the congressman free to pursue the public interest, however he chooses to define it. Rather than constraining him and rendering him irresponsible, the existence of the local machine may liberate him and permit him to vote as his conscience dictates. Congressmen without such a powerful and non-ideological base of support may have much less discretion in such matters.

Aside from the theoretical advantages of such a position, there of course remains the empirical question whether a political leader who has risen through the ranks of a local machine would have any elevated view of the public interest. The way of life a machine creates for its members is such that it might render even its best leaders incapable of taking a broad and enlightened view of public affairs even though the organization enforces no constraints that would objectively prevent acting on the basis of such a view. In the psychological dimension of representation, there is a great variation in the roles played. Of all the Democrats in Congress supported by the Cook County organization, some take a narrow and routine view of their functions whereas others (such as Dawson) deliberately endeavor to act on the basis of an enlarged view of the functions of a congressman. No categorical judgments can be made on this point, but the interpretations presented in this study may suggest an approach to the re-examination of the impact of the constituency on the function of

representation and a re-evaluation of the role of the local machine in contemporary politics.

15. Characteristics of Party Leaders

Samuel C. Patterson

Professor Patterson of the State University of Iowa here analyzes the kinds of individuals who enter politics, who the activists are, how party organization affects the political process, and what impact parties and party leaders have on public policy. The article focuses on county party leaders in Oklahoma.

The author also explores the political background and experience of the leaders (more than half never served in political office), their degree of political aspiration (not exceptionally high), and their orientation (local). He finds that party leaders tend to be more organization-oriented where their party is dominant and more campaign-oriented where the other party is dominant.

* * *

Organized partisanship is one of the fundamental functional requisites for a democratic polity. The effective presentation of some kind of alternative to the electorate, even if it be only alternative personalities, requires organization. In the United States the organization of partisanship can be described loosely as a congeries of party activists and their followers at local, state, and national levels who are combined under the respective rubrics of the Republican and the Democratic parties. These combinations customarily compete

Reprinted from the *Western Political Quarterly,* vol. 16, no. 2 (June 1963), pp. 332–352, with footnote omissions, by permission of the University of Utah.

for political offices and their emoluments, nominating candidates and campaigning for their election. These are the commonplaces that depict the party battle in this country, and that lead to some of the central queries made about the political process: How are parties organized? What kind of individuals are recruited into politics? Who are the party activists? How does party organization affect the political process, and what impact do parties and party leaders have on public policy?

Some of these questions have been fathomed, and for them our body of knowledge is extensive. We know a great deal about the formal, and some about the informal organization of political parties. We have voluminous lore and data related to party operations in the processes of nominations, campaigns, and elections, and a considerable store of reliable knowledge on the nature and importance of party in the formulation of public policy.[1] What is more, in the last decade we have substantially improved our understanding of the kinds of individuals who get elected to public office, although our data are highly selective. Perhaps the most neglected area of research on political parties has been that of party leadership. V. O. Key, in his provocative account of state politics, has pointed out that "while a great deal of information has been assembled about the composition of the electoral followings of the parties, the character and structure of the leadership corps are matters about which reliable data are scant."

The data are scant, but not nonexistent. The vogue of the study of "machine" politics in cities in the 1930's produced analyses of precinct committeemen; Bone has suggested ways in which these data need to be updated in his study of Republican committeemen in Kings County, Washington. Sawyer has presented findings on the Michigan Democratic State Central Committee, and Frost has examined informal county party leadership in New Jersey. More studies of these kinds are badly needed, especially those that present or permit interparty, intraparty, and interstate comparisons.

Curiously, the level of party leadership that has been given least attention has been that of the county. We have in the standard treatments of political parties countless admonitions as to the significance of the county committee and its chairman. Yet we know very little about county party leaders. It is this deficit that the data presented in this paper seek to improve.

We know substantially more about sixty-odd million individuals who go to the polls to vote in presidential elections than we do about the three thousand county party chairmen in the several states who may occupy crucial positions in the party machinery. Thus our images of county party leaders are impressionistic and obscure. The county chairman may be pictured as the pliable hack of a state machine, the omnipotent dictator of a quaint and backward bailiwick, the bumbling conspirator

[1] The principal older studies of precinct committeemen are: Harold F. Gosnell, *Machine Politics: Chicago Model* (Chicago: University of Chicago Press, 1937); Sonya Forthal, *Cogwheels of Democracy: A Study of the Precinct Captain* (New York: William-Frederick Press, 1946); William E. Mosher, "Party and Government Control at the Grass Roots," *National Municipal Review,* 24 (January 1935), 15–18, 38; Leon Weaver, "Some Soundings in the Party System: Rural Precinct Committeemen," *American Political Science Review,* 34 (February 1940), 76–84. See also Wallace S. Sayre, "Personnel of Republican and Democratic Committees," *American Political Science Review,* 26 (April 1932), 360–62, and Austin Ranney and Willmore Kendall, *Democracy and the American Party System* (New York: Harcourt, Brace, 1956), pp. 239–41. Three recent studies have added significantly to our knowledge of the importance of local party leaders in elections. I refer to: Phillips Cutright and Peter H. Rossi, "Party Organization in Primary Elections," *American Journal of Sociology,* 64 (November 1958), 262–69; Phillips Cutright and Peter H. Rossi, "Grass Roots Politicians and the Vote," *American Sociological Review,* 23 (April 1958), 171–79; and Daniel Katz and Samuel J. Eldersveld, "The Impact of Local Party Activity upon the Electorate," *Public Opinion Quarterly,* 25 (Spring 1961), 1–24.

in the courthouse gang, or the ineffective and inactive politico whose only motivation for party leadership is personal or political self-enrichment through graft and patronage. Again, the county chairman may be pictured as a dedicated party activist, like Johnny Welsh,

> a wiry, well-preserved, gray-haired, sharp-tongued politician whose iron will and personal integrity had kept the local Democratic party functioning for more than a quarter of a century. When others of us were working abroad, he and his six sons were at home doing the dirty work of running a complex party organization. When the Democrats were in such low esteem locally that not even candidates could be found, Johnny Welsh ran for office. He made his living selling real estate, but his real occupation was politics, and he knew more about the workings of my county than any other man alive.[2]

None of these images is either completely true or false. Yet they do not help us very much in generalization about county party leaders.

The data to be presented here, while they do not shed light directly on the personalities of party leaders, contribute to our understanding of the characteristics of party leaders at the county level. Systematic empirical data were sought from county party leaders in one state to answer these questions: What kinds of party activists are recruited to the county party leadership role? How does the composition of this stratum of the party leadership corps compare with county leaders in other states? What kinds of previous political experience in terms of office-holding, characterize county party leaders? Is the county-leader position a linkage for its occupants to other political position, or not? Does the county leader conceive himself as playing an important part in the process of nominating candidates? How does the county leader conceptualize his job? The answers are much

[2] James A. Michener, *Report of the County Chairman* (New York: Random House, 1961), pp. 67–68.

more modest than the questions, and yet they are suggestive of the nature and functions of party leadership at the county level.

RESEARCH SITE AND PROCEDURE

The data for this analysis were gathered from Democratic and Republican county chairmen, Democratic co-chairmen, and Republican vice-chairmen in Oklahoma. In many ways Oklahoma is a valuable site for political research. The state was not extensively settled by whites until the territory was first opened in 1889. When the area was settled, migration into the territory came from two distinct parts of the country, and settlers brought with them different political traditions. The northwestern and north-central counties of Oklahoma were settled predominantly by people from the Midwest, while the southern and northeastern counties were settled mainly by Southerners. Those who moved across the border from Kansas brought with them their Republican political habits, while the Southerners brought to the southern part of the state (the southeastern counties are now identified as "Little Dixie") the Democratic political tradition. This intrastate sectional difference in the political tradition of Oklahoma voters still remains clearly identifiable in state politics. Republican political success, such as it is, is largely confined to the northern counties; and in the southern counties the Democratic party is dominant. These distinct political traditions are supported by cultural and economic differences between the two regions.

Oklahoma, in a real sense, spans the hazy line of demarcation between North and South. In gubernatorial and other state elections Oklahoma has been predominantly Democratic. Compared to other states it is proper to classify Oklahoma as a "one-party" Democratic state. On the other hand, Oklahoma is not properly written off as another one-party state like those of the

Old South. The Republican party has had electoral success in Oklahoma, however infrequently and tenuously. Once since Oklahoma entered the Union in 1907 the Republicans won a majority of the State House of Representatives, and nearly did so on another occasion. Three Republican United States Senators have been elected from Oklahoma, the last in 1942. Republican presidential electors have won in five presidential elections in the state. Eisenhower captured the Oklahoma electoral vote in both 1952 and 1956, and Nixon received a larger percentage of the two-party vote in Oklahoma than in any other state except Kansas and Nebraska. Even in gubernatorial and senatorial elections which have been won by Democrats, the Republican party in Oklahoma frequently has made a respectable showing. For instance, in two senatorial elections in the 1950's the Republican candidate polled nearly 45 percent of the vote, and in three pre-1962 contests for the governorship Republican candidates received more than 40 percent of the vote. In 1950 a Republican, Jo Ferguson, got nearly 49 percent of the vote, and in 1962 Republican Henry Bellmon won the governorship, becoming the state's first Republican chief executive. The principal explanation for the presidential success of the Republican party in Oklahoma and its difficulty in electing a governor may lie in the fact that gubernatorial elections are held in off-presidential years. Furthermore, the Republican party has a persistent base of strength in Tulsa and the remainder of the First Congressional District, where a Republican is regularly elected to the Congress.

The success of the Republican party in the three recent presidential elections, and the winning of the 1962 gubernatorial election, convinced many Oklahoma Republican leaders that a viable two-party system could be built in the state. The state Republican organization had been considerably revitalized and invigorated between 1959–62, most recently under the direction of state chairman (now governor) Henry Bellmon, a northern Oklahoma rancher. For the first time in Oklahoma history, the Republicans now had county party officers in nearly all of the state's seventy-seven counties, and efforts were devoted to precinct organizations in areas where no such activity had previously occurred. On the Democratic side, much the same process took place. Torpid, and under the direct control of the governor for many years, the Oklahoma Democratic party finally (though perhaps temporarily) became a political force independent of gubernatorial domination. This occurred, much to the consternation of some liberal Democrats, at the expense of reform Governor Howard Edmondson, and was widely interpreted as a victory for the Old Guard wing of the party. In fact, it went deeper than this; it reflected to a significant degree the efforts of organization Democrats (like state Chairman Gene McGill, also a rancher) to build a real party organization. Perhaps stimulated by the potential Republican challenge, the Democratic party showed more life in Oklahoma than it had for many years.

Thus our data stem from a state characterized by Democratic one-party control, but where there is a traditional basis of Republican strength. What is more, both party organizations were meaningful in the sense that the Democratic party was not languid and the Republican party was not defunct. While the Democrats could still count on winning most elections for state offices, their leaders now believed party organization was necessary to assure it. While the Republicans could not hope for sweeping electoral successes, the probabilities had markedly improved.

The instrument employed for the purpose of gathering data for this study was the mailed questionnaire. The two principal county party officers in every county where they existed were mailed a brief questionnaire in the summer, 1961, followed by a second mailing. About three-fourths (74.8 percent) of the questionnaires were returned. Democratic county leaders returned questionnaires in a somewhat higher proportion than Republican (Democrats, 76.9 percent; Republicans, 72.5 percent). A higher proportion of county chairmen returned questionnaires than did co- or vice-chairmen (Democratic chairmen, 77.6 percent; Republican chairmen, 78.9 percent; Democratic co-chairmen, 76.3 percent; Republican vice-chairmen, 65.2 percent). Obviously the small difference between parties in returning questionnaires stems mainly from the relatively lower proportion of returns among Republican vice-chairmen. There are no data available for all county party leaders on the basis of which to compare our large sample with the total population. A comparison of counties from whose county leaders questionnaires were returned with those whose leaders did not respond does not raise doubt about the validity of the sample. Based on the minimal comparisons which can be made, if there be any noticeable category of non-returners it is among party leaders in the most overwhelmingly Democratic counties where, presumably, the Democratic leadership is inactive and the Republican, wasting.

The questionnaire, of necessity a rather limited one, included questions relating to the respondents' social backgrounds, political experiences and aspirations, roles in state legislative nominations, perceived contacts with state legislators, and conceptions of their jobs as county party leaders. Clearly the mailed questionnaire device limits the scope and depth of data gathered. On the other hand, it has many advantages and the data gathered, if not definitive, are highly suggestive and of considerable value.

PROFILE

OF COUNTY PARTY LEADERS

Social background data for Oklahoma county party leaders are available for occupation, educational attainment, income and age. The first three of these variables are useful in the determination of the socioeconomic status of leaders, and are presented in Table I. The general proposition that is obvious from this table is that Oklahoma county party leaders tend to occupy high socioeconomic status. They tend to be employed in business or professional occupations, have high educational attainment, and command relatively high incomes. In marked contrast to the party committeemen in Chicago (in the 1930's), the Oklahoma county leader is a "man of parts" in his community. But the outstanding contrasts revealed by Table I are the differences between leaders of the two parties. Insofar as county leaders reflect the characteristics of the mass of party supporters, it certainly could not be maintained that the Republican party in Oklahoma is the party of business, managerial, and professional groups and the Democratic party the vehicle of the common man.

Our assumptions about the social background differences between party leaders in northern two-party states have been that (1) Republicans are employed in higher status occupations than Democrats; (2) Republicans have higher educational attainment than Democrats; (3) Republicans tend more than Democrats to be recruited from high-income categories; and (4) Republicans tend to be older than Democrats. Table I clearly indicates that for the first three of these hypotheses the reverse is true for Oklahoma county chairmen. In the case of age, the data are not presented because of a very high no response rate; but the fragmentary data bear out the same relationship with respect to age. In general, Oklahoma Democratic chairmen tend more than Republicans to come from high-status occupations, to have more education, to have higher incomes, and to be older.

This reversal of our usual expectations about interparty differences in the social background characteristics of party leaders is made more explicit in the interstate comparisons supplied in Tables II, III, and IV. Table II shows interparty breakdowns

TABLE I Occupational, Educational, and Income Characteristics
of Oklahoma County Party Leaders

	Democratic				Republican			
Characteristic	*Chairmen*		*Co-Chairmen*		*Chairmen*		*Vice-Chairmen*	
Occupation	*Number*	*Percent*	*Number*	*Percent*	*Number*	*Percent*	*Number*	*Percent*
Farmer–rancher	11	18.6	3	5.2	15	25.0	1	2.3
Businessman	13	22.0	9	15.5	12	20.0	4	9.3
Sales–clerical	6	10.2	4	6.9	8	13.3	4	9.3
Attorney	14	23.7	0		7	11.7	0	
Other professional	9	15.3	8	13.8	11	18.3	4	9.3
Public official	1	1.7	7	12.1	0		0	
Laborer	1	1.7	0		3	5.0	1	2.3
Housewife	1	1.7	26	44.8	0		29	67.4
Retired	2	3.4	1	1.7	2	3.3	0	
Other	1	1.7	0		1	1.7	0	
No response	0		0		1	1.7	0	
TOTAL	59	99.9	58	100.0	60	100.0	43	99.9
Educational Attainment								
Grade school	1	1.7	4	6.9	1	1.7	2	4.7
Some high school	4	6.8	6	10.3	6	10.0	4	9.3
High school diploma	6	10.2	11	19.0	15	25.0	10	23.3
Some college	17	28.8	21	36.2	12	20.0	20	46.5
College degree	9	15.3	14	24.1	14	23.3	4	9.3
Graduate degree	21	35.6	2	3.4	12	20.0	2	4.7
No response	1	1.7	0		0		1	2.3
TOTAL	59	100.1	58	99.9	60	100.0	43	100.1
Income								
Less than $4,000	1	1.7	15	25.9	8	13.3	8	18.6
$4,000 to $6,000	7	11.9	6	10.3	8	13.3	7	16.3
$6,000 to $8,000	5	8.5	10	17.3	10	16.7	4	9.3
$8,000 to $10,000	10	16.9	8	13.8	10	16.7	7	16.3
More than $10,000	34	57.6	15	25.9	23	38.3	14	32.6
No response	2	3.4	4	6.9	1	1.7	3	7.0
TOTAL	59	100.0	58	100.1	60	100.0	43	100.1

for county chairmen in Oklahoma, Kansas, and Wisconsin. Both Kansas and Wisconsin have been categorized as "one-party predominant" Republican states, although the classification for Wisconsin may be in need of revision. In any event, here are three states with different kinds of political structures: Oklahoma is one-party Democratic; Kansas, one-party Republican; and Wisconsin, in between—traditionally Republican, but moving in the two-party direction. The differences in the occupa-

tional characteristics of county chairmen in these three states are striking. Though not inscrutable, these data raise interesting questions about the impact of party dominance on the recruitment of party leaders. Oklahoma is deviant from Kansas and Wisconsin with respect to the occupational categories of farmer/rancher, businessman, sales/clerical, and attorney. In each case the occupational composition of the Oklahoma leadership corps is the reverse of those in the other two states. Kansas and

Oklahoma do not differ substantially in terms of professional occupations other than that of attorney. Similarly, in the manual-worker category Oklahoma and Kansas are parallel. Both differ markedly from Wisconsin in these categories in that a much higher proportion of Wisconsin Republican chairmen are in the "other professional" category than are Wisconsin Democratic chairmen. Also, while in Oklahoma and Kansas a higher percentage of Republican chairmen is in the laborer category than Democratic chairmen, in Wisconsin this condition is dramatically the reverse.

The explanation for some of these interstate differences is quite obvious. For instance, the more extensive industrial and manufacturing development of Wisconsin clearly explains the larger proportion of laborers and the smaller proportion of farmers among Wisconsin county chairmen in contrast to county leaders in Oklahoma and Kansas. That the interparty tendencies in Kansas and Wisconsin are largely similar, and generally dissimilar from Oklahoma, provides the interesting feature of Table II. Tables III and IV show education and income comparisons for both

parties' chairmen and co-chairmen in Oklahoma and Kansas. Here comparable data are not available for Wisconsin. However, they show that the generalizations which can be made for Oklahoma county leaders are the reverse of those which can be made for Kansas county leaders.

It seems likely that these interstate variations in the composition of Democratic and Republican county leadership are broadly related to the total political structures in the respective states, as well as to the differential compositions of the parties' supporters in these states. If we hypothesize that party leaders will tend to reflect in important ways the social characteristics of their supporters, then we can infer that interstate variations in party leadership reflect interstate differences in the electorates of the two parties. Unfortunately, we have no data describing the respective party supporters in these states. Whatever support we have for this hypothesis is based primarily on the national electorate and national political leaders, or on state legislators in predominantly urban two-party states. It seems doubtful that the Kansas and Oklahoma electorates as a whole differ very substantially, with the important ex-

TABLE II **Interstate Variations in the Occupational Backgrounds of County Party Chairmen**
(In Percentages)

Occupation	Oklahoma		Kansas		Wisconsin	
	Democratic	Republican	Democratic	Republican	Democratic	Republican
Farmer–rancher	18.6	25.0	28.8	14.5	15.6	3.1
Businessman	22.0	20.0	19.2	32.5	17.2	45.3
Sales–clerical	10.2	13.3	15.1	6.0	7.8	4.7
Attorney	23.7	11.7	13.7	27.7	18.8	29.7
Other professional	15.3	18.3	8.2	9.6	6.3	12.5
Laborer	1.7	5.0	1.4	3.6	23.4	0.0
Public official	1.7	0.0	1.4	1.2	1.6	0.0
Housewife	1.7	0.0	6.8	1.2	4.7	0.0
Retired	3.4	3.3	5.5	0.0	3.1	3.1
Other	1.7	1.7	0.0	0.0	0.0	0.0
No response	0.0	1.7	0.0	3.6	1.6	1.6
TOTAL	99.9	100.0	100.1	99.9	100.0	100.0
N's	59	60	73	83	64	64

TABLE III   Interstate Variations in the Educational Attainment
of County Party Leaders
(In Percentages)

| | OKLAHOMA | | | | KANSAS | | | |
| | Democratic | | Republican | | Democratic | | Republican | |
Education	Chairmen	Co-Chairmen	Chairmen	Vice-Chairmen	Chairmen	Vice-Chairmen	Chairmen	Vice-Chairmen
Grade school	1.7	6.9	1.7	4.7	12.3	3.7	7.2	8.1
Some high school	6.8	10.3	10.0	9.3	5.5	13.0	2.4	3.2
High school diploma	10.2	19.0	25.0	23.3	24.7	35.2	7.2	29.0
Some college	28.8	36.2	20.0	46.5	26.0	25.9	28.9	38.7
College degree	15.3	24.1	23.3	9.3	13.7	11.1	18.1	16.1
Graduate degree	35.6	3.4	20.0	4.7	13.7	11.1	32.5	3.2
No response	1.7	0.0	0.0	2.3	4.1	0.0	3.6	1.6
TOTAL	100.1	99.9	100.0	100.1	100.0	100.0	99.9	99.9
N's	59	58	60	43	73	54	83	62

TABLE IV   Interstate Variations in the Income
of County Party Leaders
(In Percentages)

| | OKLAHOMA | | | | | KANSAS | | | |
| | Democratic | | Republican | | | Democratic | | Republican | |
Income Range	Chairmen	Co-Chairmen	Chairmen	Vice-Chairmen	Income Range	Chairmen	Vice-Chairmen	Chairmen	Vice-Chairmen
Less than $4000	1.7	25.9	13.3	18.6	Less than $3000	19.2	27.8	6.0	24.2
$4000 to $6000	11.9	10.3	13.3	16.3	$3000 to $5000	17.8	29.6	9.6	19.4
$6000 to $8000	8.5	17.3	16.7	9.3	$5000 to $8000	20.5	11.1	19.3	9.7
$8000 to $10,000	16.9	13.8	16.7	16.3		17.8	7.4	13.3	4.8
More than $10,000	57.6	25.9	38.3	32.6		19.2	9.3	42.2	14.5
No response	3.4	6.9	1.7	7.0		5.5	14.8	9.6	27.4
TOTAL	100.0	100.1	100.0	100.1		100.0	100.0	100.0	100.0
N's	59	58	60	43		73	54	83	62

ception that Kansas voters tend to vote Republican and Oklahoma voters tend to vote Democratic. Thus it is pertinent to suggest the significance of party dominance in the recruitment of party leadership.

The channels of political success in Oklahoma have traditionally been through the machinery of the Democratic party; access to political power in Kansas has, except sporadically, been through identification with the Republican party. The active, ambitious, politically interested businessman, lawyer, or other professional man who is well educated and well paid could, in Oklahoma, best exploit his ambition or his talents in the Democratic party. In fact, his esteem in the community might have been seriously damaged if he became identified as a Republican. When political parties are long in power, and their support is widely diffused in the political system, the composition of their leadership corps is increasingly likely to reflect heavy infiltration of individuals in the higher socioeconomic categories. The "better people" in the community will tend to gravitate toward political power, whether the Republican or the Democratic party is dominant. And, added to these considerations, state Republican leaders have often had difficulty in finding a business or professional man in a given county who was available to serve as county chairman for the very simple reason that such a large proportion of them count themselves as Democrats.

POLITICAL EXPERIENCES OF COUNTY PARTY LEADERS

Factors other than the socioeconomic characteristics of party activists clearly affect the recruitment process for the selection of county leaders. The legitimacy of acquiring and holding a political position is affected by the degree to which indi-

viduals can claim to be of the community and by the incumbency of office. County party leaders tend to have been long-term residents of the counties in which they hold office, but also there tend to be important differences between the two parties' leadership corps insofar as length of residence and experience in office are concerned (see Table V). Democratic county party leadership in Oklahoma tends to be more "home grown" than Republican leadership. While a sizable proportion of Republican leaders, like most Democratic chairmen and co-chairmen, have lived in the counties twenty years or more, a number of the newly appointed Republican county leaders are newcomers, some of whom got their initiation into politics in other parts of the country. One finds in the ranks of Republican chairmen, for instance, a young geophysicist recently resident in the state whose previous political experience was as a precinct chairman in Whittier, California; a former attorney for the federal government who retired to his boyhood home and took up politics; a lawyer, an engineer, a sales manager, an office manager, and a

TABLE V   Length of Residence in County and Years in Office of Oklahoma County Party Leaders

	Democratic				Republican			
	Chairmen		Co-Chairmen		Chairmen		Vice-Chairmen	
Characteristic								
Years in County	Number	Percent	Number	Percent	Number	Percent	Number	Percent
Entire life	27	45.8	27	46.6	23	38.3	15	34.9
At least 20 years	23	38.9	21	36.2	14	23.3	14	32.6
At least 15 years	2	3.4	3	5.2	5	8.3	1	2.3
At least 10 years	4	6.8	6	10.3	8	13.3	5	11.6
At least 5 years	3	5.1	1	1.7	10	16.7	7	16.3
Less than 5 years	0		0		0		1	2.3
TOTAL	59	100.0	58	100.0	60	99.9	43	100.0
Years in Office								
Less than 1 year	6	10.2	1	1.7	29	48.3	20	46.5
1–2 years	22	37.3	26	44.8	20	33.3	10	23.3
3–5 years	13	22.0	20	34.5	4	6.7	9	20.9
6–10 years	13	20.0	10	17.3	6	10.0	3	7.0
More than 10 years	5	8.5	1	1.7	1	1.7	1	2.3
TOTAL	59	100.0	58	100.0	60	100.0	43	100.0

chemist new to the state and to politics. It is also manifest from Table V that more than a half of the Democratic county leaders have served in office three years or more, while more than half of the Republican leaders have served less than three years. The very large proportion of Republican leaders who have served less than a year results in part from the fact that the Republican party has only recently filled county leadership posts in many counties and reflects the organizational development of Oklahoma Republicanism.

An important feature of the political recruitment process is the operation of the principle of "availability." Leiserson points to the importance of this factor in observing how few elective politicians "come from a subordinate position in party organizations." Availability as a selective factor in the recruitment process operates in such a way, Leiserson suggests, as to limit the extent to which party leaders run for elective public office because "they recognize, and the leaders of constituency organizations know, that competent party work alone does not constitute a qualification for a place on a winning ticket."

Local party workers tend to restrict their sights to the city council or county board, or to other executive boards or offices which constitute an advancement in their local position, rather than to aspire to a role in state or national politics. Perhaps the highest level which the locally oriented party workers normally reach is the state legislature, where they can promote projects of concern to their districts and protect the interests of the local party and community.[3]

One approach to the examination of this hypothesis is by analysis of the party-organization experience of public officeholders. It may be equally useful to examine it from the point of view of the party leaders themselves. To what extent, for instance, have county party leaders held elective or appointive public office, or, incidentally, prior party office? And, to what extent do county leaders aspire to run for public office?

The Oklahoma data suggests, first of all, that previous position in party officialdom or the holding of public office may reduce the individual's availability for county party leadership. It is clear from Table VI that more than half of the county leaders in Oklahoma have never served in a previous political office, party or public. A higher proportion of Democratic chairmen has held public office for obvious reasons. Where county leaders have been elected to public office, or have served in other party offices, their experience has been predominantly at local levels. A tabulation of previous party and public offices held by county leaders, presented in Table VII, indicates that (1) those who have held party office tend to have held it at

[3] Avery Leiserson, *Parties and Politics: An Institutional and Behavioral Approach* (New York: Knopf, 1958), pp. 200–201.

TABLE VI   Political Experience of Oklahoma County Leaders

Type of Political Experience	Democratic				Republican			
	Chairmen		Co-Chairmen		Chairmen		Vice-Chairmen	
	Number	Percent	Number	Percent	Number	Percent	Number	Percent
Held other party office	8	13.6	18	31.0	13	21.7	15	34.9
Held public office	23	38.9	6	10.3	14	23.3	3	7.0
Held both other party office and public office	3	5.1	3	5.2	3	5.0	0	
Never held other party office or public office	25	42.4	31	53.4	30	50.0	25	58.1
TOTAL	59	100.0	58	99.9	60	100.0	43	100.0

TABLE VII Party and Public Offices Held
by Oklahoma County Party Leaders
(In Numbers)

Office	Democratic Leaders*	Republican Leaders*
Party office		
Precinct	24	16
County	3	9
District	5	5
State	1	9
YDems/YGOP/Women's clubs	7	6
TOTAL	40	45
Elective public office		
Municipal	16	10
County	15	6
State	3	1
National	0	0
TOTAL	34	17
Appointive public offices		
Municipal	2	0
County	11	3
State	7	0
National	2	1
TOTAL	20	4

* Each county leader was counted for each party or public office he held, which means, of course, that the total N's for this table are much higher than the total sample size. Though as Table VI indicates, few county leaders held both public and party office, a sizable number held more than one party office, or more than one public office.

the precinct level—successful precinct leaders are to some degree promoted up; (2) most county leaders who have held elective public office (and some hold such offices coterminous with party leadership) have done so at the municipal and county levels; and (3) those who have held appointive public office have done so at the county and state levels.

Of course, indications of offices held by county leaders, or evidence showing that a majority of party leaders had no previous office-holding experience, cannot themselves demonstrate that county leaders have not attempted to win office, or do not aspire to do so in the future. Losing an election is not as common for Democrats, and running for office is not as common for Republicans in Oklahoma as would be the case in

more competitive states. Oklahoma leaders were asked, "Have you ever been a losing candidate for elective public office?" Tabulation of positive responses shows the following percentages:

Democratic chairmen	16.9
Democratic co-chairmen	8.6
Republican chairmen	20.0
Republican vice-chairmen	9.3

Furthermore, nearly half of those who had been defeated for elective public office had also been elected, so a marked increase in candidacy is not indicated.

In addition, the degree of political aspiration among Oklahoma county leaders does not appear to be especially high. Here the data for Oklahoma county chairmen are illustrative, and the comparison with Epstein's Wisconsin data is particularly interesting. County leaders were asked about their political aspirations simply in terms of their intentions and their desires, and the percentage of positive responses is shown in Table VIII. In addition to the generally somewhat lower degree of political aspiration among Oklahoma county chairmen, the table further suggests the

TABLE VIII   Political Aspiration of County Chairmen
(In Percentages)

Political Aspiration	Oklahoma County Chairmen		Wisconsin County Chairmen	
	Democrats	Republicans	Democrats	Republicans
Intend to run for elective public office	13.6	20.0	34.4	15.6
Desire to run for elective public office	23.7	40.0	48.4	23.4
N's	59	60	64	64

function of party dominance for the political aspiration of party leaders. Minority party chairmen in both states register a higher degree of aspiration than majority chairmen. Candidacy should be a more important factor for minority party members; majority party activists aspiring to unseat party incumbents are not likely to be chosen, or to remain county chairmen.

More than 40 percent of the county chairmen in Oklahoma have not run for public office, do not intend to run, and do not desire to run; and in this Democratic and Republican chairmen do not differ significantly. Indeed, the county party leader seems "more likely to seek his fortune through his party connections, and to carve his niche in life in his local community," than to seek or aspire to candidacy for public office.

But the limited political aspirations and the local orientation of county party leaders ought not to obscure the important linkage the county leader provides between the local and the state and national party organizations. Epstein refers to the extent of county party leader participation in state and national party conventions as an elementary index of the degree to which county leaders play roles in state and national party organizations. This kind of activity among county chairmen in Oklahoma exists at a lower frequency than in Wisconsin, and to about the same extent as in Kansas. Although somewhat higher proportions of both Democratic and Republican chairmen have been delegates to a state convention in Oklahoma (Democratic chairmen, 89.8 percent; Republican chairmen, 86.7 percent), nearly the same proportions as in Kansas have been delegates or alternates to their party's national convention (Democratic chairmen, 23.7 percent; Republican chairmen, 8.3 percent). In Wisconsin substantially higher proportions of county chairmen have attended state conventions as delegates, and much higher proportions of Republican chairmen have been delegates to their national convention than in either Kansas or Oklahoma. In part the higher proportion of Democratic chairmen who have officially attended their national convention results from the larger membership of the Democratic convention. However, it does appear that, even so, grass-roots Democratic leaders tend to have a larger role in the deliberations of their national organization than Republicans.

THE ROLE OF THE
COUNTY PARTY LEADER

We have suggested up to this point that among county party leaders high-status occupations are most predominant, and that county leaders seem both to have had limited office-holding experience and only temperate aspiration for public office. We have inferred that the county leader, while to some extent supplying an important linkage between the local party organization and the state and national party machinery, tends to be tied primarily to his party's cause in his own locality. It is appropriate to ask what role the county leader plays in his locality. Some have examined the activities of party leaders in campaigns, and others have attempted to assess the role of party leaders in candidate selection. The latter course has been followed in this research.

County leaders were asked the question, "In your county, which of the following best describes what party leaders like yourself usually do with respect to the selection of party candidates for the Oklahoma state House of Representatives or state Senate?" The results are reported in Table IX. In general, county leaders seem to regard candidate selection activity as at least of some

importance in the performance of their role, although for about half of the Oklahoma county leaders such activity was confined to encouragement and persuasion. Republican leaders, especially county chairmen, were involved to a greater degree than Democratic leaders. Republicans in Oklahoma frequently find difficulty in convincing competent individuals to become their candidates, and much of their comment on questionnaires alluded to this difficulty. In one heavily Democratic county the Republican chairman said, "The Republican party has not had a candidate for the legislature for many years in [this] county . . . although individuals have been requested to run."

The county party leader's conception of his role in connection with candidate selection is clearly affected by the degree of political competitiveness in his county. The distribution arrayed in Table X needs to be interpreted in the light of the fact that all predominantly Republican coun-

TABLE IX Participation of Oklahoma County Party Leaders in Legislative Nominations

Nature of Participation	Democratic				Republican			
	Chairmen		Co-Chairmen		Chairmen		Vice-Chairmen	
	Number	Percent	Number	Percent	Number	Percent	Number	Percent
Actively seek well-qualified candidates	17	22.1	16	16.8	29	34.5	19	28.8
Persuade well-qualified individuals to run	11	14.3	16	16.8	12	14.3	9	13.6
Encourage well-qualified individuals to run	31	40.3	34	35.8	31	36.9	19	28.8
Try to persuade individuals not to enter the primary against a well-qualified candidate already in the race	7	9.0	15	15.8	5	6.0	4	6.1
No part at all; individual candidates just come forward on their own to run in the primary	10	13.0	13	13.7	3	3.6	11	16.7
No response	1	1.3	1	1.1	4	4.8	4	6.1
TOTAL RESPONSES*	77	100.0	95	100.0	84	100.1	66	100.1

* The total number of responses equals more than the sample size for each column because some individuals selected more than one type of participation, even though the questionnaire specified that the respondent select the *most important* type of participation.

**TABLE X   Participation in Candidate Selection
and Political Competitiveness of Counties
(In Percentages)**

	Democratic Leaders			Republican Leaders		
	Highly Competitive	*Semi- Competitive*	*One- Party*	*Highly Competitive*	*Semi- Competitive*	*One- Party*
Actively seek well-qualified candidates	23.5	18.9	16.3	30.6	37.2	22.2
Persuade well-qualified individuals to run	20.6	15.8	11.6	22.2	12.8	8.3
Encourage well-qualified individuals to run	35.3	35.8	44.2	36.1	30.8	36.1
Try to persuade individuals not to run	11.8	14.7	9.3	2.8	7.7	5.6
No part at all	5.9	14.7	16.3	5.6	6.4	19.4
No response	2.9	0.0	2.3	2.8	5.1	8.3
TOTAL	100.0	99.9	100.0	100.1	100.0	99.9
N's	34	95	43	36	78	36

ties are competitive, and all one-party counties are Democratic. The degree to which county leaders actively seek candidates for legislative elections clearly is reduced in one-party districts, where Democratic leaders may tend to remain neutral and Republican leaders may tend to feel helpless in the face of overwhelming odds. In fact, there is impressionistic evidence from the questionnaires of the boredom of some Democratic leaders and the feeling of futility on the part of some Republican leaders. Furthermore, there is a relation between county leaders who take no part at all in candidate selection and political competitiveness. In one-party districts considerable proportions of both Democratic and Republican leaders rely on encouragement of candidates to run.

Above and beyond the county leader's conception of his proper role in the process of candidate selection, and probably partly independent of it, is the party leader's conception of his basic function. The party leader in a democratic competitive system plays a very difficult role; and it may be more difficult when the process in which he is involved does not conform to his normative standards. Both parties' county

leaders, but especially the Republican's, frequently seem upset by the absence of two-party competitive standards. Many Republican leaders indicated that they went into politics in part to help build a two-party system in Oklahoma. But beyond this, conflicting demands on the party leader frequently lead him to orient his role in a particular direction. What are these conflicting demands? The political leader must constantly balance two very important demands on his ingenuity: he must maintain a viable political organization, and he must wage campaigns. Part of his function is introversive—he must create and maintain working party machinery; and part of his function is extraversive—he must successfully move the party machinery into operation in campaigns against the other party. These two role demands are sufficiently separate in theory as to make it reasonable to presume that some party leaders will be oriented primarily toward building their own party organizations, and that some will be oriented mainly in the direction of waging campaigns.

In an effort to examine the differential role orientations of Oklahoma county party leaders, we asked each one to explain the most important things a county leader should do in order to be most effective in his job. Accordingly, insofar as possible county leaders were classified as either *organization-oriented* or *campaign-oriented*. The organization-oriented county leader is one who sees his most important function as that of building and developing the party organization itself. He believes that he should maintain contact with and the loyalty of precinct chairmen, keep harmony in the county organization, coordinate with the district and state party leaders, encourage party members to be more active in party affairs, be fair and impartial with respect to primary candidates, and equitably and judiciously dispense the party patronage.

The campaign-oriented party leader is oriented principally in the direction of fighting the interparty battle. He thinks of his job primarily in terms of raising campaign funds, recruiting candidates to run in elections, preparing voter lists, urging citizens to register and vote, arranging party and public meetings for candidates and managing the party's campaign in his county.

That these broad role differentiations exist operationally is indicated by the data presented in Table XI. The considerable proportion of Republican chairmen who defined their role in other ways is a consequence in part of the large percentage of new Republican chairmen who could not succinctly define their job, or who did so in highly diffuse and universalistic terms. In

TABLE XI   Role Orientations of Oklahoma County Party Leaders

Role Orientation	Democratic				Republican			
	Chairmen		Co-Chairmen		Chairmen		Vice-Chairmen	
	Number	Percent	Number	Percent	Number	Percent	Number	Percent
Organization-oriented	21	35.6	25	43.1	23	38.3	11	25.6
Campaign-oriented	15	25.4	13	22.4	9	15.0	5	11.6
Both organization- and campaign-oriented	12	20.3	8	14.0	13	21.7	9	20.9
Other	2	3.4	6	10.3	13	21.7	6	13.9
No response	9	15.3	6	10.3	2	3.3	12	27.9
TOTAL	59	100.0	58	100.1	60	100.0	43	99.9

the case both of Republican and Democratic co- and vice-chairmen, many were not able to define their job at all, and some frankly admitted it on their questionnaires. Inadequate role definition on the part of county leaders in all probability reflects the generally low level of political competition, the incipiency of party organization in the state, and the incomplete performance on the part of state leaders in replacing incompetent leaders or in clearly defining their role for them. In general, Democratic leaders have a clearer conception of their role than Republican leaders. To some degree Democratic leaders are more campaign-oriented than Republicans.

The slightly greater organizational emphasis given by Republican leaders may be the result of temporary organizational demands in a party just beginning to build party machinery. In addition, it seems likely that the most effective county leader will be both organization- and campaign-oriented, that is, will effectively attempt to resolve his conflicting role demands; and if that be true the Republican leaders compare favorably with the Democratic leaders.

It was suggested earlier that these basic role conceptions may be partially independent of the activity of party leaders in candidate selection. When organization-oriented and campaign-oriented county leaders are compared on the basis of the nature of their participation in legislative nominations, the differences between them are not significant, although a somewhat higher proportion of campaign-oriented leaders *encourage* individuals to run, while a somewhat higher proportion of organization-oriented leaders plays no part at all in candidate selection.

It might be expected on a common-sense basis that party leaders in counties where their party is dominant should be more organization-oriented than in counties where the other party is dominant; that

party leaders in urban areas should be more campaign-oriented than in rural areas; and that party leaders should be more campaign oriented in competitive counties than in one-party counties. The Oklahoma data indicate that only the first of these propositions is wholly correct. A greater proportion of Democratic leaders in Democratic-dominant counties is organization-oriented than campaign-oriented, as is a greater proportion of Republican leaders in Republican-dominant counties (see Table XII). Party dominance is operationally defined as those counties in which the domi-

TABLE XII   Role Orientations of Oklahoma County Party Leaders and Party Dominance of Counties
(In Percentages)

Role Orientation	Democratic Leaders		Republican Leaders	
	Democratic-Dominant Counties	Republican-Dominant Counties	Democratic-Dominant Counties	Republican-Dominant Counties
Organization-oriented	65.1	50.0	68.4	75.0
Campaign-oriented	34.9	50.0	31.6	25.0
TOTAL	100.0	100.0	100.0	100.0
N's	63	10	38	8

nant party won at least 75 percent of the elections to the state House of Representatives between 1952 and 1958.

In the case of differences between urban and rural counties, urban party leaders appear on the whole to be somewhat more organization-oriented in Oklahoma. In the Republican case, however, the difference between urban and rural leaders is slight, while urban Democratic leaders tend to be substantially more organization-oriented than rural Democratic leaders. The urban-rural difference among Democratic leaders may not be too difficult to account for: in some rural areas in Oklahoma there has been, and still is, very little Democratic party organization at all, and in urban areas the patronage functions and the exploitation of party perquisites have sometimes

supplanted campaign activity on the part of party leaders.

Similarly, party leaders from counties characterized by differential political competitiveness do not differ in line with expectations. A very large proportion of Republican leaders in highly competitive counties (and this includes all the predominantly Republican counties) is organization-oriented. This may again be a ramification of the emphasis on party organization taking place in the Oklahoma Republican party. Again, more than half of the Republican leaders from Democratic one-party areas are campaign-oriented; and here it may be that Republican leaders have taken the campaigner role because of the impossibility of viable Republican organization, especially where campaigning alone seems to pay off in presidential elections. On the other hand, a higher proportion of Democratic leaders is campaign-oriented in highly competitive counties than in others.

CONCLUSION

Channels of access to political power are provided by party organizations. When the majority party is dominant in a political sub-system, high socioeconomic status elements of the population are likely to be inordinately represented among party leaders of the dominant party whether it be labeled Democratic or Republican. But county party leadership is not essentially a part of the recruitment pipeline for public office in the sense that few county leaders have held public office, and aspiration for elective public office is not particularly high among county leaders although minority party leaders have a higher aspiration for office. Finally, party leaders at the county level are differently oriented in their conceptions of their political leadership role, proportionately tending to be more organization-oriented where their party is dominant and more campaign oriented where the other party is dominant.

THE TOOLS OF POLITICS

16. Parties, Group Interests, and Campaign Finance: Michigan 1956

John P. White and John R. Owens

The Citizens' Research Foundation, for whom this study was written, is primarily concerned with the ways in which political parties are able to finance election campaigns. This particular publication concerns the 1956 election in Michigan, and the section reprinted here discusses the finance organizations of Michigan's political parties and their 1956 expenditures.

The money-raising method used by the Republicans, inspired by Arthur Summerfield, was a unified fund drive, with an independent administrative group doing the soliciting under the leadership of the Republican State Finance Committee. This method was eminently successful but created

a separate power structure in the party hierarchy.

The Democratic party also created a separate organization, but its state finance committee was firmly under the control of the party chairman. The Democrats raised money from large contributors and also ran a "Dollars for Democrats" drive. They benefited as well from labor sources. The report on financial expenditures in 1956 in Michigan alone shows that nearly three million dollars was expended, of which the Republicans raised three times as much as the Democrats.

* * *

In Michigan, as in other states, the formal party organization is prescribed by law in minute detail. Whatever may have been the motives of the framers of the relevant statutes, they did not include much consideration of the party organization as a fund-raising mechanism. In party finance (and in other areas of party activity) a net-

From "Parties, Group Interests, and Campaign Finance: Michigan 1956" (Princeton: Citizens' Research Foundation, 1960), pp. 11–20, with footnotes deleted, by permission of the Citizens' Research Foundation.

work of informal and extra-legal organizational activity has been grafted onto the skeleton of the legal party structure. A comparison of the party finance structure reveals that the contrasting electoral and financial power bases of the two parties have influenced the development of finance machinery.

Fund raising as a major organizational problem is a relatively recent phenomenon. Until the 1930's, the parties were largely financed by a combination of a few big party "angels," often office holders, and a broadly based patronage system, at least for the party in power at either national or state level. In both parties, candidates for top nominations were expected to provide most or all of the financial wherewithal to run their campaigns. But all this was changed drastically by a combination of depression, steeply rising income taxes, the increase in campaign costs, and since 1940, an iron-clad civil service system that virtually ended state patronage. Thus both parties had to force the pressing problem of finding new ways to raise money.

To the Republicans, the events of the thirties and early forties presented new opportunities as well as new problems. The emergence of a class-oriented politics during the New Deal period tended to solidify the support of business groups and individual businessmen behind the Republican party. The influence of liberal and radical elements in the Republican party, long a feature of Michigan's essentially one-party politics, was greatly reduced. Beginning in the 1930's, it made more sense to ask a businessman for a contribution to the Republican party. Previously his support would have gone to a faction or to individuals within the broad holding company that called itself the Republican party (or perhaps to the sometimes more conservative Democrats).

This potential reservoir of campaign contributors was outside the ranks of the party organization. By the same token, the leaders of the statutory party organization in the counties often had little or no rapport with the local business community. Michigan Republicans have attempted to solve this dilemma by setting up an extra-legal party organization that is designed primarily for the purpose of raising money from businessmen, and at the same time giving this financial constituency status and representation in the party organization.

The godfather of the new organization was Arthur Summerfield, who later became Postmaster General of the United States. Summerfield says the bitter reception accorded Wendell Willkie by the automobile workers of Flint in 1940 inspired him to enter Republican politics. Thereupon he considered ways and means of involving the business community of Michigan in the politics of the state, and the result of his labors was the well known "Summerfield plan" which has ever since been the basis of Republican finance organization in Michigan.

The Summerfield plan has two basic elements. One is the concept of the unified fund drive, borrowed from the experience of the community chest and similar groups. The idea is to centralize fund raising and to give assurance to the donor that he will not be solicited repeatedly by other units of the same or similar organizations. The second element involves the creation of an administrative hierarchy independent of the regular party organization, and with its own pattern of personal relationships, most of them involving businessmen raising money from other businessmen. Unification with the party organization is largely accomplished at the topmost level.

The capstone of the Republican finance organization is the Republican State Finance Committee, ostensibly an arm of the State Central Committee but in practice a coordinate body. The state finance director (currently Donald Ahrens, retired head of the Cadillac division of General Motors) is only nominally a subordinate of the chairman of the State Central Committee. Actually, he is in full charge of his aspect of the party's operations.

While the statutory party organization is built upon the county organizations of the eighty-three counties in the state, the finance organization operates through twenty regions, each headed by a regional director. There is also a director for each county within the region. In the more populous counties, the director is ordinarily not an official of the regular party organization, though in small rural counties one person may wear both party and finance committee hats. The budgetary process within the Republican party is a cooperative affair involving the political plans of the state chairman and the financial plans of the finance director. Regional and county quotas for fund drives are handed down through the channels of the finance organization.

The statewide domain of the Republican finance organization is, of course, slightly topheavy at the southeastern end of the state, where a single county finance organization, that of Wayne County, raises the bulk of all the money given to the Republican party. Politically, Wayne County is one of the most strongly Democratic areas in the United States, and even Dwight D. Eisenhower made no more than a rather feeble showing there. But it also houses such plush Republican suburbs as Grosse Pointe, and is the home county of many major contributors to the GOP. The Wayne County Republican Finance Committee is therefore the real foundation of the whole structure.

Under Michigan law, party organization in Wayne County is provided by six congressional district committees, having the same legal status as county committees in the outstate area. In the Wayne County finance organization, however, functional rather than geographical lines of organization are followed. During fund-raising campaigns, the small professional full-time staff and the executive committee of twenty

persons are augmented by a campaign committee of fifty members, including the members of the executive committee. This campaign committee is designed to represent the major groups from which financial support is to be expected. Solicitation of contributions is made through a divisional organization including such units as general manufacturing, automobile manufacturing, wholesalers and retailers, and similar occupational or business groupings.

This necessarily brief outline of the finance organization of the Republican party in Michigan should be sufficient to indicate some of the probable effects of the organization on the operation of the party itself. The system has some obvious advantages. It is, in more ways than one, businesslike. It goes after the money where the money is, using people who know how to get it. The centralized character of the system makes efficient budgetary techniques possible. It facilitates the redistribution of funds throughout the state in accordance with the needs of the party. It relieves the top party strategists from some of the most onerous and time consuming tasks, those associated with the problem of raising money.

For such advantages, a price must be paid. The erection of a virtually autonomous administrative hierarchy side by side with the regular party organization creates powerful potential competitors for influence over party policy. Both the regular party organization and the finance organization are structures of representation, but at a given time their respective constituencies may make conflicting demands on the party.

This was illustrated by the prolonged internal conflict which followed the rise to state power of the Eisenhower Republican faction, which gained control of the party organization following the 1952 elections. The more conservative Taft supporters, spearheaded by General Motors executives, reacted to this change in party leadership by going on a pocketbook strike which created severe financial problems for the party. The "modern" Republican state chairman, John Feikens, was *persona non grata* to General Motors, and would very likely have been displaced as state chairman in 1955 (after a crushing Republican defeat in the 1954 elections) had it not been that a very important part of the finance constituency, the Ford Motor Company, was in the Eisenhower camp. A temporary armistice was arranged in 1957, when Feikens' head was served up to his enemies, a General Motors executive (Donald Ahrens) was installed as head of the finance organization, but another "modern" Republican, Lawrence Lindemer, replaced Feikens as state chairman. In the 1956 campaign, General Motors executives were well represented in the ranks of major Republican contributors.

In the Democratic party, effective fundraising techniques are of even more recent vintage than those of the Republican party. The Democrats lost their last old time "angel" in 1932, when William A. Comstock announced to a shocked party that he had lost his fortune in the economic collapse, and could not again be counted on to finance his own gubernatorial candidacy, as he had in 1926, 1928, and 1930. Comstock was elected in 1932 anyway, but throughout the 1930's the Democrats operated on a financial shoestring. For a brief period they were able to capitalize on their newly acquired vote-getting power to finance party activity indirectly through a patronage machine under the leadership of Highway Commissioner and later Governor Murray Van Wagoner. The adoption of the civil service amendment to the Michigan Constitution system in 1940 put an end to that, and from 1942 to 1948 the party was in a state of extended financial collapse. In the ten years since the beginning of the G. Mennen Williams era, the financial situation of the Democratic party has improved greatly. It is unlikely that many other Dem-

ocratic state organizations are as relatively well financed as the Michigan Democratic party. But the Democrats, like the Republicans, have not escaped an organizational dualism that is a potential source of disharmony. However, the organizational management of interest group financial relationships has been quite different in the Democratic party.

We have observed that the Republicans institutionalized their financial relationships with the business community by setting up a separate administrative structure parallel to the regular party organization. A major reason for this course was obviously that the party itself had the task of integrating individual Republican contributors into the campaign organization. The Democrats, on the other hand, had an alliance with a very well organized group with strong traditions of independence and autonomy. Organized labor could and did form a close alliance with the Democrats, but there was never any question of organizational merger. Of course, the maintenance of separate formal organizations would not, in itself, disprove the "amalgamation" thesis. If the great bulk of labor's political money was turned over to the Democratic party, and if the party was substantially dependent for its campaign activity on that money, formal organizational separation would not be very meaningful.

As we shall demonstrate, available data indicate that the separation is far more than formal. In the first place, the Democratic party organization raises very substantial sums from non-labor sources. The state finance committee, which appears to be firmly controlled by the state chairman of the party organization, conducts a rather successful drive for large contributions. At the other end of the economic scale, the Democratic party organization, operating largely through the county committees, runs a vigorous "Dollars for Democrats" campaign which is parallel to, and perhaps to some extent competitive with labor's COPE dollar drives. As might be expected when a party holds all of the major state offices, the Democrats have made extensive use of *ad hoc* candidate and formally non-partisan committees (e.g., the "Re-Elect G. Mennen Williams Committee") to collect money from persons who wish, for one reason or another, to contribute to the campaign fund of a particular office holder. State Chairman Staebler suggests, however, that the Democrats are quite successful in preventing the "every man for himself" approach to fund raising and spending. Thus the state chairman is able to exercise a large measure of control over the funds spent by these nominally independent committees.

PARTY FINANCE IN 1956

Our analysis of campaign expenditure reports shows that a total of $2,885,517.69 was reported raised by both parties. This figure includes transfers of funds, and so does not involve double counting. It does not include the relatively small amounts raised by individual candidates for the state legislature or for county office. Of the grand total, Republicans raised almost exactly three times as much as Democrats: $2,166,-060.99 for the GOP and $719,456.70 by the Democrats.

Since slightly over three million persons voted in the 1956 election, this means that approximately one dollar was raised and spent for every ballot cast in the state. While this is a considerable sum, it does not appear high in relation to estimates of total national political spending in a presidential election year.

The ratio of Republican to Democratic expenditures conforms generally with the findings reported by Professor Heard. As his research indicates, in competitive two party states the Republican party tends to raise and spend more money than does the Democratic party. The three to one ratio of Republican to Democratic expendi-

tures in Michigan is higher than any comparison reported by Heard, but the explanation of this variation may be found in labor expenditures for Democratic candidates, which are made directly through union organization, and consequently never appear as entries in Democratic expenditure reports.

The impact of party and finance organization on fund raising and disbursal is indicated by our analysis of the sources and ultimate destination of funds. Sharply differing patterns emerge for each party. Tables 1 and 2 summarize the receipts of the two parties by organizational level. While the tabulation of receipts and disbursements in this fashion is useful, care must be exercised in its interpretation. Complete reliance on formal organizational level would make it appear that Democratic finance activities are highly centralized at the state level, while Republicans have a most decentralized operation. It is true that 71.5 per cent of the Democratic money was raised by the state central committee and other statewide committees, while only 13.3 per cent of the Republican money was collected by their Republican counterparts. However, closer analysis of the data demonstrates that the major difference between the parties is not in degree of centralization, but rather in degree of integration between the finance organization and the formal party organization. On the Democratic side, the major fund-raising organ was the state central committee, which collected 41.1 per cent of the total Democratic money. Another 30.4 per cent went to statewide candidates and to *ad hoc* committees at the state level. Interview data suggest that these latter fund-raising efforts were directed and controlled by the officers of the state central committee. Thus, the state leadership of the Democratic party organization clearly combined control of fund raising with other leadership tasks.

Republican fund raising was in reality no less centralized, but was not in the hands of

TABLE 1 Democratic Receipts and Expenditures, 1956

	Receipts				Expenditures					
	Receipts Reported	Transfers from Other Committees[a]	Adjusted Receipts	Pct.	Expenditures Reported	Transfers to Other Reporting State Committees	Transfers to Non-reporting State Committees	Transfers to National Committees	Adjusted Expenditures	Pct.
County committees	$144,406.82	$ 4,254.52	$140,152.30	19.5%	$121,054.62	$21,917.44		$ 150.25	$ 98,986.93	14.7%
Wayne county[b]	14,423.00	150.00	14,273.00	2.0	12,893.29				12,893.29	1.9
Outstate	129,983.82	4,104.52	125,879.30	17.5	108,161.33	21,917.44		150.25	86,093.64	12.8
State central committees	337,351.67	41,422.26	295,929.41	41.1	333,731.26	14,878.82	$1,489.00	52,665.35	264,748.09	39.3
Statewide candidates and committees	221,556.95	3,397.80	218,159.15	30.3	206,999.22	20,670.07	1,000.00	24,615.06	160,714.09	23.8
Congressional candidates and committees	74,207.59	8,991.75	65,215.84	9.1	71,044.83	600.00			70,404.83	10.4
Non-reporting committees[c]									79,869.66	11.8
TOTAL			$719,456.70	100.0%				$77,430.66	$674,723.60	100.0%

a Figures in this column deducted from Column 1 so as not to be counted twice.
b Outstate is defined as outside of Wayne County.
c Funds reported as transferred to national and state committees not reporting in Michigan.

TABLE 2 Republican Receipts and Expenditures, 1956[a]

	Receipts				Expenditures					
	Receipts Reported	Transfers from Other Committees	Adjusted Receipts	Pct.	Expenditures Reported	Transfers to Other Reporting State Committees	Transfers to Non-reporting State Committees	Transfers to National Committees	Adjusted Expenditures	Pct.
County committees	$1,829,418.24	$26,276.03	$1,803,142.21	83.3%	$1,807,585.26	$901,340.66	$58,000.00	$228,330.00	$619,914.60	29.4%
Wayne county[b]	1,130,144.98	3,219.90	1,126,925.08	52.0	1,177,253.03	634,263.00	58,000.00	183,380.00	301,610.03	14.3
Outstate[b]	699,273.26	23,056.13	676,217.13	31.3	630,332.23	267,077.66		44,950.00	318,304.57	15.1
State central committees	548,614.71 423,011.00[c] 971,625.71	832,605.66	139,020.05	6.4	553,700.52 386,330.00 940,080.52	49,728.32	19,050.00		871,252.20	41.4
Statewide candidates and committees	202,292.76	52,908.42	149,384.34	6.9	201,531.76	23,056.13		25,650.00	152,825.63	7.3
Congressional candidates and committees	186,849.39	62,335.00	74,514.39	3.4	129,831.99				129,821.99	6.2
Non-reporting committees									331,080.00	15.7
TOTAL			$2,166,060.99	100.0%				$253,980.00	$2,104,844.42	100.0%

a Reports of finance committees are consolidated with those of party committees in each category.

b Outstate is defined as outside of Wayne County.

c The Republican State Central Committee used an accounting device which eliminated from their gross receipts all funds ultimately used in the national campaign. Their report stated that the total of such funds was reported to the U.S. Senate Sub-Committee on Privileges and Elections. The figure given is that published by the Senate. See *Congressional Quarterly Almanac* (Washington: Congressional Quarterly News Features), XIII, 1957, p. 197.

the party's formal state leadership. The key unit in Republican fund raising was not the Republican State Central Committee, nor even the Republican State Finance Committee. It was rather the Wayne County Republican Finance Committee, which collected about half of all the Republican money. This ostensibly local committee, geographically and functionally separated from the formal state party leadership, and part of a separate finance hierarchy, is in reality the capstone of the Republican fund-raising structure.

If both parties are heavily dependent on a single unit of their organizational structure, the Republicans can, at the same time, lay claim to a relatively more important "grass roots" finance structure, in that their county committees (excluding Wayne County) produce a significantly greater share of total party revenue than the Democratic county committees. As Table 1 shows, all Democratic county committees raised only 19.5 per cent of Democratic funds, while the Republican county committees, even excluding Wayne County, raised almost a third of the much larger Republican total. The relative financial weakness of the county committees on the Democratic side may be viewed as a legacy of the one-party period in Michigan, in that much of the Democratic county organization is of recent vintage and is therefore lacking in fund-raising expertise.

There is a great disparity between the Democratic and Republican percentages of funds raised through candidate and other ad hoc committees. Almost a third of the Democratic money as compared with only 7 per cent for the Republicans was raised in this manner. Again, this may be related to the former minority status of the Democratic party. Historically, the Democratic party, as such, had little influence on public policy, and the occasional Democratic governor tended to assume an importance

greater than that of his party. Thus, individual candidates have always been more of a focal point of fund raising in the Democratic party than in the GOP. As we have suggested, this is merely a technique of fund raising, and does not appear to diminish the control of party finance by the state party leadership.

The expenditure of campaign funds displays patterns similar to those found in fund raising, except that the Republican state committees, unimportant as fund raisers, spend about the same proportion of party revenues as the Democratic State Central Committee. However, just as ad hoc committees at the state level are important Democratic fund raisers, they are also important spenders, with the result that 63.2 per cent of Democratic funds are spent at the state level, while only 48.7 per cent of Republican money is so expended. In keeping with their role in fund raising, the Republican county committees are much bigger spenders, both absolutely and relatively, than the Democratic county committees.

17.   Political Fund Raising and the Small Contributor: A Case Study

Richard F. Schier

This article is an analysis of the long-discussed proposal that political parties should be financed on a country-wide, voluntary basis. Professor Schier, of Franklin and Marshall College, outlines the results of such an attempt in Lancaster, Pennsylvania. Republicans outregister Democrats by over 50,000 persons in that area, and the problems of raising money for the Democratic

From the *Western Political Quarterly*, vol. 11, no. 1 (March 1958), pp. 104–112, with footnotes deleted, by permission of the University of Utah.

party in view of this situation are extremely difficult. The response to the Democratic drive was an average contribution of thirty-two cents per voter solicited.

Although the money amounts were not overwhelmingly large, the drive did serve to establish a list of known Democratic party contributors in a heavily Republican area. In addition, the soliciting of small sums helped to strengthen the image of the Democratic party as the party of the little man. It is also believed that such solicitation encourages increased voter participation at the polls. The fund raisers demonstrated in this case that from 10 to 15 percent of the money needed to finance a campaign can be raised by small contributions.

* * *

In recent years the increasing costs of American political campaigns consequent upon the growth of the mass media of communication have focused attention on the financial aspects of party activity. A University of North Carolina study estimated that the cost of nominating and electing all public officials in 1952 was approximately $140,000,000. It seems likely that the comparable figure for 1956 will approach $200,000,000. We now know with fair accuracy how this money is spent and we also know that much of it is raised in contributions of $100 or more. For instance, the same study estimated that in 1952 the Democrats raised 81 per cent of their funds in this way while such contributions accounted for 88 per cent of the Republican total. The phenomenon of sums of such magnitude being expended on so important a part of the political process is obviously deserving of the closest study. To date, however, students of government have almost completely ignored the 12 to 19 per cent of the parties' war chests which comes from small contributions.

Concern over the size of party treasuries together with perhaps excessive anxiety over the dangers inherent in very large contributions, has led to two recommendations for reform of this traditional reliance on large contributions. One proposal is substantially some kind of governmental subsidy to the parties. Other people have urged the parties to undertake a really serious effort to broaden the base of their financial support. It is, of course, possible to combine these two proposals through the medium of permitting tax deductions or credits for political contributions. It is ironic, however, that the suggestion that the parties appeal for smaller contributions from greater numbers of people is put forward before we have discovered whether significant numbers of them will in fact heed such appeals.

That political leaders have historically relied on large contributors for party funds is well known. What is not known, however, is whether this reliance is born of the knowledge that small contributions will not in general aggregate significant sums, or whether it is merely a product of an era in which expenses were not so large as to compel other sources to be explored. There is simply nothing in the literature of political science that gives any indication of the response to be expected from a really serious effort at mass financial solicitation by political parties. It seems generally admitted that Beardsley Ruml's widely advertised plan to finance the 1952 Democratic campaign with $5.00 contributions was a failure, but no precise figures on this attempt have ever been made public. It appears that the sum total of our knowledge on this matter is limited to an oft-quoted Gallup poll finding that most American families have never been asked for a political contribution, that in 1954 only one family out of eighteen made any political contribution at all, but that 31 per cent of them would give at least $5.00 if asked.

This paper is an effort to provide a moderately detailed case study of an attempt by a political party in one county to solicit its registered membership for political contributions. No pretense is made that the results of this effort are typical of what may be expected elsewhere, but since the precise method of solicitation was somewhat novel it would appear to be an experiment worthy of the attention of political scientists. This study, then, is presented in the hope that it will stimulate other and similar studies that will throw light on such questions as: Will registered party members give to their party? How much will they give? What proportion of a local party's expenses can be underwritten by small contributions? The answers to these questions have assumed increased importance since the announcement by the Democrats of their intention to institute a sustaining membership plan complete with party dues.

Lancaster County, Pennsylvania, the site of this study, is located in the southeastern corner of the state. It has a population of 234,717 according to the 1950 census and is 45.1 per cent urban. The county seat is the city of Lancaster with 63,774 residents, and there are four boroughs and three townships with populations greater than 5,000. The population is divided roughly in halves between those in agricultural and nonagricultural pursuits. Consistently Republican since its native son, James Buchanan, left the presidency, the 1956 party registration figures were: Republican, 80,882; Democratic, 29,657.

Early in 1956 a proposal was made to the Democratic party leaders for a selected solicitation of the party's membership for contributions for the 1956 campaign. After a period of discussion among the leadership it was decided to go ahead with the plan and appeal for funds to a select list of 3,000 party members. These 3,000 names represented party members who had, in connection with the 1955 local election, contributed $1.00 each in a fund-raising scheme in which their gift created the possibility

that fate might endow them with a new automobile. There was no way of knowing whether these names represented Democrats dedicated to the party's welfare or merely people who were prepared to regard a contribution of $1.00 as a hostage to the generosity of fortune. At worst, however, they were people who had demonstrated no hostility toward Democratic affluence and were, therefore, the best group available for the experiment.

A committee was accordingly established under the name of "Dues for Democracy" and the chairman of the Democratic County Committee assumed the chairmanship of the new committee. This decision was made deliberately, it being determined on the part of the proponents of the scheme that the whole effort should be toward *party* support and to emphasize that the Dues for Democracy Committee was a *party* committee. The title for the Committee, which served also as the title of the fund-raising plan, was chosen as being mellifluous and alliterative, as an accurate capsule description of the plan, and also, in reaction to the then-current Republican line, as an effort to capture for the Democratic party and the plan the adjectival connotation of "democratic."

The plan itself was outlined in a letter over the signature of the Committee chairman and mailed to each of the 3,000 voters on the list. Dated June 25, 1956, the letter opened with the heading "OIL AND POLITICS DON'T HAVE TO MIX. . . ." After reciting some of the costs of reaching the voter by mail, newspaper, and television the letter estimated the cost of "a frugal county campaign" at $30,000. The letter then described the problem posed by these figures in these words: "How does a political party bring its message to the electorate without mortgaging its integrity?" After urging that the voters must assume a responsibility for increasing campaign costs the plan itself was described: "Enclosed with this letter are five-postage-free envelopes. Please file these envelopes carefully in your desk, and at the first of each month beginning with July 1, 1956, enclose a single dollar bill in one of these envelopes and mail it out when you pay your other bills." The letter then pointed out that if these directions were followed a contribution of $5.00 could be made without hardship and concluded: "Democracy and political parties are inseparable. Is not the Democratic party worth 3¢ a day to you between July 1 and Election Day?"

The installment-plan character of the scheme was decided upon both because it was feared that a flat $5.00 contribution would be beyond the means of some party members and also because the enclosure of the five self-addressed, postage-free envelopes would constitute a kind of "gimmick" that would serve to attract attention and stimulate interest. The monthly-payment habit is by now deeply ingrained in our society and it was hoped that this might increase the number of participants by setting for them a kind of goal which could be reached by small and regular payments.

The letters were placed in the mail so as to be delivered in the last week of June. Simultaneously, an extensive program of publicity was outlined and news releases were prepared on the novel features of the drive. Since it was essential to maintain interest in the plan throughout the five months in which it was to be in operation, letters describing it were sent to Democrats prominent on both the state and national scene. Such personages as Governor Stevenson, Senator Kefauver, former President Truman, Mrs. Eleanor Roosevelt, National Chairman Butler, and many others were invited to comment on the "Dues for Democracy" idea in terms suitable for publication in a press release. The Committee filed these responses so as to permit releases at the beginning of each of the ensuing months.

At this point a development took place which transformed the whole experiment and greatly extended its scope. One of those who had been informed of the plan and asked to comment on it was Mr. Matthew McCloskey, a Philadelphian, and treasurer of the National Committee and chairman of the Finance Committee of the Pennsylvania Democratic party. Upon learning of the mechanics of the plan Mr. McCloskey telephoned the chairman of the Committee and urged that every registered Democrat in the county be solicited and, since the financial resources of the local party were hardly adequate for such a gamble with scarce funds, a sum of $1,500 was made available from the state party treasury by Mr. McCloskey to underwrite the experiment.

This decision to solicit on a county-wide basis was not made, therefore, until the very last days of June. It was essential, in view of the mechanics of the plan, to get the letter in the hands of the party's enrolled membership during the first week of July. Accordingly, it was decided that an additional 20,000 solicitation letters be printed, it being hoped that by skillful handling no more than one letter would be sent to each address and that in this way the entire registered membership of the party (29,657) could be reached with 20,000 letters. This hope proved to be illusory because sufficient care was not taken at the addressing stage to avoid such duplication and also because with many rural route addresses it was impossible to know whether they were the same residence. As a result the supply of envelopes and literature was exhausted before the voters' lists had been completely covered. In some voting districts no voters at all were circularized.

Moreover, the need for speed prevented processing the second mailing so as to eliminate those who had received the letter in the initial mailing. All that could be done was to append a postscript in the second printing of the letters urging the addressee to pass the letter on to a friend if he had already received such a letter. Because of this duplication and because of the duplication in addressing the second mailing, either unavoidably or through carelessness, not all Democratic registrants were reached. For the purpose of this study it will be assumed that 20,000 registered voters were solicited, but in many cases this involved both a husband and a wife. It was anticipated by the Committee that in most cases husband and wife would, if they contributed, accept only a single responsibility. This assumption proved to be mainly correct in the returns, but there were instances of both husband and wife making contributions. Some 9,000 of the registered Democrats were thus not reached directly, and it seems probable that in this way several thousand family units were omitted from the canvass.

A second decision was made at this time which was also prompted by the necessity for haste and which had a direct bearing on the profit shown by the contribution campaign. The volume of work involved in collating 20,000 letters with 100,000 contribution envelopes and stuffing, sealing and addressing the second mailing was deemed too great to be done in the time required by volunteer party help. This work was therefore contracted to the printing company and paid for by the Committee. This expense could normally be avoided by utilizing volunteer help, but time did not permit it in this instance. All of the second mailing was handled professionally and placed in the mail on July 7, 1956.

Response to the plan in the press was very favorable. One of the two large-circulation daily newspapers in the county printed an editorial praising the plan and also reprinted a commendatory editorial from the Philadelphia *Evening Bulletin*. Governor Leader of Pennsylvania praised the idea warmly and posed for a publicity picture with a member of the Committee accepting a dollar from him. Although interested almost exclusively in local pub-

licity for the plan, the Committee did secure outside recognition which it was able to convert into local news items. Drew Pearson mentioned the plan in his daily column. Congressman Eugene McCarthy of Minnesota also lauded the plan in an extension of remarks in the *Congressional Record*. For the most part, however, the Committee relied for periodical publicity on press releases based on the progress of the plan, the reaction of individual contributors, and endorsements of the plan communicated directly to the Committee.

Both in August and September follow-up postcards were addressed to delinquent contributors. These cards were sent only to those who had contributed to the drive but who had not made the contribution for that month. The cards expressed gratitude for the contribution received and reminded the contributor that another installment was now past due. During the first week of August the Committee also placed brief newspaper advertisements urging Democrats not to forget "Dues for Democracy." After the middle of September, however, no further reminders were addressed directly to contributors. By that time the political campaign was reaching its peak and it was felt that this activity would make the voters "politics conscious." Moreover, a great deal of publicity was being given to the financial plight of the Democrats on the national scene and the Committee hoped to profit locally from these appeals.

It is impossible to state whether the financial results achieved by the plan measured up to the expectations of local party leaders because they really did not know what to expect. The gross receipts of the scheme, received from 1,511 contributors, were $6,324 and these receipts were divided into the categories indicated in Table I. Assuming that 20,000 prospective contributors were reached, then a contribution of at least $1.00 was received from 7.6 per cent of those solicited. This percentage is lower than the Gallup poll result would lead us

TABLE I   Statement of Receipts by Contributors

Amount Contributed	Number of Contributors	Percentage of Contributors	Amount of Receipts	Percentage of Receipts
$1.00	253	16.7%	$ 253	4.0%
$2.00	174	11.5	$ 348	5.5
$3.00	154	10.2	$ 462	7.3
$4.00	164	10.9	$ 656	10.4
$5.00	625	41.4	$3,125	49.4
Over $5.00	141	9.3	$1,480	23.4

Total number of contributors 1,511   Total amount of receipts $6,324

to expect, but that poll was designed to measure family contributions; and since this mailing often reached more than one member of a family unit it is impossible to correct this figure for a valid comparison.

It can be seen from Table I that 23.4 per cent of the receipts of the plan came from persons whose total contribution was greater than $5.00. These contributions ranged from $6.00 to $50.00; their arithmetical average being $10.50 and the median contribution, $7.00. Many of the larger contributions, as the letters occasionally accompanying them indicated, were from people who had rarely if ever been asked for a political contribution, thoroughly approved of the plan, and sought to indicate their enthusiasm with a contribution larger than was requested.

It is also noteworthy that approximately 60 per cent of those contributing a total of $5.00 or more did so by means of a single contribution rather than using the installment method. This suggests that an appeal for a flat $5.00 contribution would not have been regarded by many contributors as excessive, but considerable revenue would have been lost, and perhaps more important, the number of voters participating in the plan would have been sharply reduced.

The expenses of administering the plan are indicated in Table II, below. It may be observed from this statement that the cost of duplicating the first mailing of 3,000 together with the cost of contracting the handling of the second mailing rather than doing this by volunteer party help reduced

TABLE II   Statement of Expenses

For original 3,000 mailing		
3,000 stamped envelopes (business size)	$109.62	
15,000 envelopes (return)	103.75	
3,000 letterheads	26.00	
Printing	18.00	
		$ 257.37
For second 20,000 mailing		
20,000 stamped envelopes (business size)	$730.80	
100,000 envelopes (return)	500.00	
20,000 letterheads	122.60	
Printing	58.15	
Addressing, collating, stuffing, etc.	936.98	
		$2,348.53
Newspaper advertising		$ 33.26
Postage (on returned envelopes)		111.84
Postcards (reminder notices)		32.00
TOTAL EXPENSES		$2,783.00

the net receipts of the drive by a substantial amount. The $257.37 spent on the original mailing plus the $936.98 spent for labor on the second mailing thus represents a sum of $1,194.35 which could be added to the net receipts of a future drive if adequate foresight were exercised.

Thus the plan produced a realized total of net receipts amounting to $3,541, this being the difference between gross receipts of $6,324 and total expenses of $2,783. When consideration is given to the nearly $1,200 spent through haste and duplication necessitated by inadequate planning it may be seen that the potential of such a program is considerable. It seems that of the voters reached in this particular drive the average contribution per voter solicited was approximately $0.32. The cost of contacting each voter may be estimated at approximately $0.08. When several thousands of registered party members are solicited the sum raised through this method can be of substantial help to a local party.

CONCLUSION

It should be remembered that the Lancaster "Dues for Democracy" plan was carried out in a presidential year. Thus the mass solicitation was conducted at a time when popular interest in politics is at its highest. Moreover, the Democratic National Committee was probably of assistance because of its nationwide appeals for small contributions. It is likely, however, that the national drive for funds by door-to-door solicitation carried out on "Dollars for Democrats" day, October 16, may have reduced the receipts of the local plan in that month. Registered Democrats who were participating in the local program and who were also solicited at their door may have omitted their mailed contribution that month. It is impossible to estimate the net effect of these two considerations so far as the receipts of the local plan were concerned.

More important, perhaps, than the sum realized for the 1956 campaign by the "Dues" plan is the acquisition of a mailing list of some 1,500 local party members who are proven contributors. It is the intention of the Committee to solicit only these known contributors for the local elections of 1957 and perhaps for one or two years thereafter. The receipts to be anticipated annually from solicitation of this list may prove to be of substantial assistance to the party because the large overhead associated with a mass mailing will be greatly reduced. Because of changes of address and population movement any mailing list can be used for only a few years. It seems probable that another mass mailing of all registered party members will again be necessary not later than 1960. For the local and state campaigns in the next three years reliance will be placed on the list of proven contributors.

There are advantages other than financial that accrue to a local party which employs such a mass solicitation. The letter requesting contributions can be a campaign document itself and a county-wide mailing to all registered party members thus serves a political purpose even for those voters who do not make a contribution. Moreover, all of the publicity associated with the "Dues for Democracy" plan redounded to the benefit of the party. One of the best electoral assets of the Democratic party is the widely held conviction that it is the party of the "little man." A campaign for small contributions helps to buttress this belief and thereby to strengthen the party's appeal.

Party leaders are also convinced that people who can be persuaded to contribute to the party can be relied upon to turn out and vote for the party on election day. This stems from the fact, amply attested to by the letters accompanying contributions, that such mass appeals help to create a sense of "belonging" among supporters who had not previously been asked for assistance in the party cause. Many voters seem to have been stimulated to a kind of proprietary interest in a party to which their affiliation had always been loose. Voting for the party on election day becomes for them an act in the nature of looking after their investment. It is impossible to measure the extent to which this feeling was aroused by the "Dues" campaign, but all members of the Committee agree that this is a feature of the plan which deserves emphasis. This result of mass solicitation was probably heightened by the installment character of this particular scheme which protracted the party member's obligation over a period of five months.

Even if the actual monetary return in this particular experiment was not as large as could be anticipated from the Gallup poll mentioned earlier, there can be no doubt that a very large proportion of the receipts represented money that the party would not otherwise have gotten. The majority of contributions came from contributors who were unknown to party leaders and regular financial supporters were urged not to use the "Dues" plan. It is the hope of the Committee that with repeated solicitations some of the contributors will become active party workers and future party leaders. This can be encouraged by using the contributor mailing list for notices and announcements of party activities such as rallies and dinners.

Sentiment among local party leaders is unanimous that this experiment in mass solicitation was an undoubted success. In an area where the Democratic party is seriously outnumbered and in a year when Mr. Eisenhower's presence on the ticket eroded the partisan zeal of many registered Democrats, the party nonetheless realized a substantial sum of money, enjoyed some highly favorable publicity, and also stimulated partisan enthusiasm in its followers. Receipts were certainly not sufficient to encourage the hope, without much further

citizen education, that such mass solicitation can substitute for the more traditional methods of party finance. Indeed, income from the "Dues" plan represented only about 10 per cent of the local party's budget for the year. Nonetheless this experiment took place at a time when the governorship of Pennsylvania was in Democratic hands and the party had access to funds much greater than it could hope for while in opposition. Such a mass solicitation program would have a truly significant importance in the lean years of being "out." Will Rogers once observed that politics "has got so expensive that it takes a lot of money even to get beat with." The Democratic party of Lancaster County, Pennsylvania, seems at least to have demonstrated that from 10 to 15 per cent of the money necessary "to get beat with" can be obtained in small contributions from a party's enrolled membership.

18. Polls and Politics in the United States

Louis Harris

Shortly before he left the field of private political polling, Louis Harris, who handled the Kennedy polling in 1960, described the role that has now been assumed by the private pollster in the planning of campaigns. The results and analyses of private polls are becoming more and more to be regarded as a source of counsel and intelligence for a political candidate. Harris does not believe, however, that private polling will ever take over in political planning, but suggests that professional politicians will continue to regard such advice in terms of professional consultation. Harris is con-

From the *Public Opinion Quarterly*, vol. 27, no. 1 (Spring 1963), pp. 3–8.

vinced that polling is most effective in terms of the use made of the results by the particular candidate, and he urges that results of polls be kept private when they have been privately conducted. Harris finds that the most important uses of polling for political purposes are in breaking down the political composition of a constituency, providing the public image held of a particular candidate, and thoroughly defining the issues.

* * *

Private polls have become an important part of the arsenal of weapons used in modern American political campaigns. Survey research is a powerful instrument of intelligence and counsel for the candidate running for office, whether for mayor, Congressman, U.S. Senator, Governor, or President. During the 1962 campaign it is likely that over two-thirds of the men running for the U.S. Senate had polls conducted for them, probably three-quarters of the candidates for Governor employed polling from a professional organization, and about one Congressional candidate in ten used survey research in his campaign for election. The reason for the disparity between Congressional and Senatorial use is primarily one of finances, rather than desire. Senatorial and gubernatorial campaigners can afford to pay for polls. Most Congressmen have such limited budgets that polling has been precluded up to now. This past year, however, the number of inquiries we received from Congressional candidates about polling for them exceeded the total number of polls we have conducted for Representatives over the years.

The role of the polls and the polltaker will vary, depending upon the professional employed and the candidate involved. A polltaker may go so far as to serve on the candidate's strategy committee as a professional advisor, privy to all the key decisions made, he may only be called in for special consulting from time to time, or he may simply provide some sort of written report of his survey, without any personal contact with the candidate or his campaign staff.

Three aspects of this new and important political instrument are worth closer inspection: first, how polls are put to use by candidates; second, where this development seems to be leading; and third, some of the sense and nonsense in current discussions about private political polling.

HOW POLLS ARE PUT TO USE BY CANDIDATES

Campaign entourages are noted for being either overoptimistic or overpessimistic: realistic appraisals of whether a candidate is ahead or behind are not often found. A poll will provide this realistic appraisal. Actually, however, this is one of the least useful functions of a poll, for unless a candidate knows what he can do about where he is, the information simply elates or deflates him. Nevertheless, no candidate will put out his good money for a survey without insisting on obtaining this information. Once he has it, he faces a quandary. If he is running ahead, he may feel pleased, but he is afraid to tell his staff for fear that his campaign workers will slacken their efforts. If he is running behind, he is somewhat discouraged, but he is likely to work all the harder; he still does not want to tell his workers in the vineyard for fear of discouraging them. If he is running nip and tuck, he is concerned, but again he is worried about shaking the confidence of his own workers.

During the 1960 campaign, Robert Kennedy discussed precisely this matter with us, reflecting the sentiments I have reported. As a consequence, our state-by-state reports went to only two men, the candidate himself and his brother, who was his campaign manager. Reports on the issues and key groups went to a larger number, including those handling speeches, scheduling, and campaign organization. In contrast, in the 1962 gubernatorial campaign in California, in which we were involved, our reports were always made verbally in the presence of a core staff group of six to ten people, including the candidate, whether the news was good or bad, and, I might add, the early news was not good for our client, although it got better as time went on.

Reporting the standings is simply a starting point, a superficial one at best. For, as V. O. Key has correctly observed, polls taken at a single point in time merely reflect the standings at that point in time. If the private poll is to be put to use effectively, then, perforce, the ultimate standings should be different. More than that, elections can shift in the course of a month, two weeks, one week, or even a few days. The 1958 standings in Ohio were changed completely in six weeks' time. The 1961 primary for Mayor of the City of New York was broken open in six weeks' time. The 1960 presidential primary in West Virginia was turned into a runaway in the last three days.

Ideally, the private polltaker should take his soundings on a continuing basis, beginning a good year before the election. However, this not only is expensive but is a difficult proposition to sell all but those candidates who are well informed about polls, their uses, and their limitations. On the other hand, one poll done in depth can often put a candidate on the victory track. In the 1958 Indiana Senatorial election, for example, neither the standings nor the issues varied by one percentage point in seven months' time, despite all the effort exerted by both candidates. Our three polls there were carbon copies of each other. But, obviously, we did not know this until the last of the three had been completed.

Candidates have told us that polls we have done for them are most valuable in three areas. The first fo these is the key group breakdowns that dissect the political anatomy of the constituency, indicating area differences, racial and religious patterns, nationality-group differences, occupational patterns (including unions and farm workers), differences by size of place, and how the vote in prior years is now dividing. Such a lay of the land is vital to a candidate, for it enables him to figure out just where he can put together his majority. It also tells him where he is failing to achieve a normal mark for a member of his political party. Polling, for example, confirmed the basic Kennedy strategy of 1960 of concentrating chiefly on the key industrial states rather than the argicultural and border states.

A second area of usefulness to a candidate is the indication the polls give of what an electorate thinks of him as a public figure —how many are familiar with his name, what they know of his record, what are the deficiencies of his performance. Such information, especially when it is negative, rarely reaches a candidate in the normal course of events. Voters tell polltakers things that not even the candidate's best friends would tell him. The polltaker, if he has courage and tact, is able to tell the candidate. In the course of our wanderings through the political hinterlands, we have had to tell candidates that they were considered spineless, arrogant, stuffed shirts, loudmouths, cold, poor speakers, or were just plain unknown. It can come as a shock to a U.S. Senator of six years' standing that a majority of his constituents are not sure who he is, or that he is thought to be the tool of labor unions or business interests.

A third area of useful information is the definition of issues. This is done in two principal ways: first, the voters are allowed to express in their own words the problems that they feel government should act upon; second, voters select from lists and reply to questions. We happen to believe that data from the mouths of voters are most valuable, for if people are allowed to express themselves in their own words then we have reason to believe that what they say has meaning in their own lives. It is reassuring when all the data point the same way, as often happens late in the campaigning, but when the types of data are in conflict, we will tend to trust the volunteered response more.

The issues thus defined are analyzed not only by key groups but, more importantly, by switchers—people who voted for one party in a previous election and now are switching to the other party in this election. This concept of switching is crucial, we believe. For when the electorate is analyzed by the hard-core vote for each candidate and the switchers for each candidate, then, indeed, we can see which issues are firming up the solid base of a candidate, which are bringing voters over to him, and which are losing him votes.

When armed with such fundamental information as issues of concern to switchers, a candidate may have a clearer perspective of the task facing him, but he still has to connect with the voters and make his own campaign. No poll I have ever been witness to has made the candidate a different man, has changed his position on an issue, has made him into what he is not. Especially with television, it is impossible to perform such transformations, even if it were proper. However, such polls can singularly alter the strategy of a candidate. They can tell him where to spend his time and money; which natural issues he has working for him, and which are boring the electorate to death; and how he can campaign most effectively. In all, we would estimate that polls cannot change an election more than 3 to 4 percentage points, but since most elections hover around the 50-50 mark, we would be less than frank not to admit that they can affect the outcome. More accurately stated, a candidate using polls effectively can alter the outcome.

WHERE THE GROWTH
OF PRIVATE POLLING WILL LEAD

Despite opposition to the use of private political polling, even within our own profession, its growth has continued unabated. And for good reason. Much as with market research before it, such polls pay off. They are helpful and by now have a proven track record—not that they are always right, and not that they cannot be misleading. They are subject to the same frailties as is any science-art, such as medicine, for example. We have on occasion been dead wrong in past elections and we will be dead wrong again. We have told some of our clients to pray when they hire us that this time we will not be wrong. But if a man stands a 50-50 chance of making the right decision by flipping a coin, and if he can be right 70 per cent of the time if he has some good native judgment going for him, then with polling instruments as now developed, polls should be right better than 90 per cent of the time. This is a better record than that of reporters, editors, political science professors, even sociologists, and perhaps soothsayers, without the use of survey research.

As we develop polltakers who better understand the mechanics, language, and Gestalt of politics, and as we develop candidates who are better informed about polls and social science research, inevitably the mating of the two professions will become more frequent and relations will become closer. The polltaker who is knowledgeable about politics will inevitably be invited to sit in on strategy meetings, mostly as a resource but also as a man of balanced judgment. The polltaker will more and more be in the position of recommending when and how many polls should be conducted for his client, rather than simply waiting for the political powers-that-be to call him and set the time schedule. This, too, is for the good, for if this tool is to be used to optimum advantage, the fullest and best thinking of the polltaker should be obtained.

SENSE AND NONSENSE ABOUT
PRIVATE POLLS AND POLITICS

First, let me state categorically that the day will not arrive when an army of polltakers will take over the political machinery of this country. Politicians with power have a singular way of not passing that power over to strangers, especially those who have been retained as professionals. Neither will the people allow this. What is more, politics is a full-time business for those in it, and, frankly, polltakers would starve if they tried to work at it full time.

It has been stated that a polltaker who sits in on strategy sessions will acquire a biased and warped point of view that will color his ultimate findings. But if there is any sense to the discipline of our method and our adherence to that discipline, then it is simply nonsense to believe that the social scientist who employs proper methodology will be swayed by emotion. What is more, the polltaker is hired specifically to be objective and to turn up the bad news wherever it is.

It has been stated that favorable polls are always leaked to give a candidate advantage in getting a bandwagon effect rolling or to line up a nomination. Long before polls were used, candidates tried to use whatever means they could to create such an effect. Yet leaks of polls are the exception rather than the rule. Of 514 political polls we have conducted since 1956, purported information from our polls has been published only 11 times. Wholly made up results about polls we never even conducted have found their way into the press 26 times that we know of. Should the polltaker take cognizance of every mention in the gossip columns and newspapers? I rather think not. It has been and is our policy, so stated in every report we deliver, that, if our clients leak any piece of information in the survey, we reserve the right to release the entire survey. That is why fewer than 1 per cent of our private poll results have ever become public. Some fellow-practitioners, it is true, have done polls paid for by partisan sources and put them out as impartial public polls; or have done private polls that have squirted out in partisan leaks; or, worse yet, have consented to the publication as campaign literature of parts

of polls that hide the essential weaknesses of the candidate and, to the contrary, make him out to be the strongest candidate. But I believe such charges have been grossly exaggerated and are the handiwork of those who believe the whole field should be indicted because of a few cases. To blow these cases out of proportion ill befits a discipline wedded to the proposition of cross-section sampling and balanced reporting.

Polls are having a profound effect on politics, and politics is having a profound effect on polls. But our free and democratic system will not be less free or less democratic as a result. At long last, the province of political research has come to include functional operations, and the worth of such polls is now appreciated most by the practitioners of politics. If the purpose of knowledge is to put it to use, then surely this is a desirable development. A book written in the 1930's entitled *Knowledge for What?* took a position since adopted by empiricists in every field of the social sciences. Now that political polling has found a functional home, I would strongly suggest that more energy be spent in trying to develop this infant art-science of ours in a positive direction than in deploring the development.

If, in some small way, such polling can reduce the number of irresponsibles who achieve high office, if it can make a candidate face the issues of concern to his electorate, if it can make the voice of the people a little clearer and more articulate, if it can make democracy function somewhat better in an hour when it is on trial, then, indeed, there will be a higher purpose in polling. But our first obligation is to report truth as we see it, to be professionals true to the discipline in our field, to develop the instruments of objectivity. We are not missionaries, but social scientists. We are not soothsayers, but reporters. We are also human beings, and we would hope that we apply our discipline with the sense of purpose and decency that has marked all great professions in the past.

19. The Public Relations Man in Party Politics

Stanley Kelley, Jr.

Professor Stanley Kelley, Jr., of the Department of Politics, Princeton University, considers the role of professional public relations in politics. This particular section from his book is concerned with the public relations man as he has emerged in party politics in this century. He characterizes the movement in party propaganda as one from press-agentry to public relations.

Kelley cites striking examples of the use of professional propagandists and summarizes the ways in which the activities of the public relations man impinges on the political process.

* * *

Something of the history of the public relations man in party politics has been separated out for independent treatment here. This is because of the subject's special pertinence to the purposes of this book, not because political party propaganda has been in fact isolated from developments in other areas. In a sense, early business public relations programs can be conceived as a borrowing of political tools by business from its partisan opponents. The further evolution of the programs then reacted back upon party politics, as industrial public relations and commercial advertising came to furnish standards by which to judge the efficiency of party propaganda efforts. Robert C. Brooks, writing in 1922, argued that:

> Considering the large sums constantly spent for political propaganda, it is rather remarkable that we have no better guides

in this field than certain traditional rules of thumb and the idiosyncrasies of the campaign manager in temporary command. By the employment of research methods similar to those applied in analyzing business concerns, efficiency experts should be able to throw light on the relative value of advertising, distributing documents, speakers' bureaus, and each of the other principal methods of campaigning.[1]

Pendleton Herring, in 1940, wrote that "In comparison with commercial advertising, political propaganda is still crude. The politician in this country has not taken advantage of . . . [the] . . . more subtle ways of manipulating public opinion." A prominent public relations counsel, finally, voices a similar sentiment: "Politicians in government still tend to think in terms of the printed word only and, as a result, depend upon newspapermen fresh out of the press . . . who know virtually nothing about all of the techniques of modern media mechanics or thought persuasion." But some politicians have taken note of such views, and the growing number of public relations men, specialized in politics and inspired by their commercial colleagues, is beginning to make such unfavorable comparisons no longer valid.

The political publicity man receives some, although quite sparse, mention in rather early works on American politics and political campaigning; and contemporary commentaries on political campaigns both before and after 1900 occasionally note the presence of newspapermen serving as press agents to candidates. As observed above, men who were important in the early stages of publicity developments in government and industry—men like Creel, Lee, and Parker—had also served politicians. A revealing letter written by California Senator Hiram Johnson in 1910 gave as

[1] Robert C. Brooks, *Political Parties and Electoral Problems* (New York: Harper, 1922), p. 327.

From Stanley Kelley, Jr., *Professional Public Relations and Political Power* (Baltimore: The Johns Hopkins Press, 1956), pp. 26–38, with footnote omissions, by permission of The Johns Hopkins Press.

"Three things . . . imperatively and immediately necessary with us" money, organization, and "a publicity bureau in charge of a skilled and competent newspaper man." Arthur C. Millspaugh, writing in 1917 of the party organizations in Michigan, observed that "Besides the executive committee . . . each party has usually had a speakers' bureau, a literary bureau, a treasurer, an assistant-secretary, sometimes a finance committee with its own chairman, and sometimes a publicity agent." By 1928, Frank Kent found the press agent to be a necessary, although obnoxious, element in the successful politician's entourage.

Perspective is gained if one compares the techniques of an early campaign with those of a modern one. Florence Weston has written a careful study of the presidential campaign of 1828, in which she gives considerable attention to the ways and means used to reach and convince the voter. At that time, political parties organized from the ward to the national level were only beginning to take form. Correspondence committees took charge of organizing public meetings, circularizing voters, and distributing pamphlets, handbills, cartoons, printed addresses, and party resolutions. "The use of mass meetings on a large scale," she observed, "was begun by the Jackson managers." Newspapers were used in a variety of ways: the parties maintained their own and founded new ones; they tried to increase the subscription lists of favorable "independent" papers and distributed copies of them free of charge; they made offers of presses to editors; distributed public printing in a way calculated to build friendships; and gave public jobs to men suggested by leading publishers. Well calculated though these tactics were, they are only slightly comparable to the maneuvers of the modern propagandist. In his book, *Publicity*, public relations man Herbert M. Baus lists over seventy-five *types* of modern publicity outlets, each requiring a special technique or techniques for effective use:

the campaign "blueprint," which the public relations man typically prepares, symbolizes the complexity of the factors with which he must deal. The Jackson managers needed no blueprint and the party newspaper editor was the period's nearest equivalent to the political public relations man.

It is probably accurate to characterize the movement in party propaganda, like that in business, as one from press agentry to public relations. A political press agent who has given a valuable account of his work is Frank Parker Stockbridge. Stockbridge was hired as Woodrow Wilson's pressman in 1911 and played a significant part in his pre-convention campaign for the presidency. This consisted of arranging Wilson's tour of the West, distributing information, speeches, and photographs to a large mailing list, getting out advance copy on Wilson's public addresses, and organizing press conferences for a candidate who was only reluctantly convinced of their value. Stockbridge, and apparently Wilson, came to see these tactics as a "repetition on a national scale" of Wilson's procedures in New Jersey where "he had gone over the heads of the politicians and appealed directly to the voters."

The first full-time, permanent publicity bureau of a political party seems to have been that organized by the Democrats after their defeat in the 1928 elections. The innovation had been recommended by Al Smith to ". . . develop the educational function of the minority party. . . ." John J. Raskob hired Charles Michelson to head the bureau, the appointment being officially announced on June 15, 1929. Raskob's ideas on the uses to which the bureau might be put may have been influenced by his experience as chairman of the finance committee of the General Motors Corporation, which by this time was already developing an extensive public relations program.

Both students of politics and practical politicians have expressed fears that the publicity resources available to government would lead to a permanent imbalance between the opposition party and the party in power. "The only way to meet the problem," Pendleton Herring has written, "is to grasp the weapons of the propagandist and to organize systematic counter-publicity." This is essentially what Michelson did, and in so doing, provided an example that has been followed and elaborated upon by minority Republicans in the period between 1932 and the election of Dwight D. Eisenhower.

Michelson came to political publicity via the newspaper world. He had had experience with two Hearst papers—the *San Francisco Examiner* and the *New York American.* "You may like or dislike William Randolph Hearst," he wrote, "but he was the nearest thing to a genius as an editor and publisher that I encountered. . . ." It is perhaps fair to say that Michelson's work with Hearst's papers where he developed an eye for the popular, the dramatic, and the circulation-building story, prepared him as the exponent of a kind of politics that had much in common with yellow journalism.

His initial efforts were not elaborate in conception. Essentially he considered his job one of making news that would hurt the Hoover Administration. He picked the tariff issue for treatment because "It was easy to get before the country a picture of slavish legislators closeted with the representatives of those industries whose owners had contributed most largely to the Hoover campaign fund and fixing the rates as they were told to do by Big Business." He fed statements to senators and congressmen whose names assured his material a place on the front page. He sent clipsheets of news items and editorial suggestions to newspapers. He circulated cartoons unfavorable to the Republicans with the permission of the newspapers which had originally published them. With the stock-market crash of 1929, his job became principally one of capitalizing on the social

unrest generated. He did it in terms of a rather primitive psychology which saw the beginnings of the Great Depression as the "Hoover panic" and the huddled tar-paper shacks of the unemployed as "Hoovervilles."

A short time after Michelson's publicity bureau began to function, the Republicans found it necessary to resort to a similar institution, which they put under the direction of another newspaperman, James L. West. At the bottom of the depression, Michelson was earning $25,000 yearly as the Democratic party's publicity man. In 1932, he became a part of the campaign's strategy board that included Roosevelt himself, and in this and the later campaigns of 1936 and 1940 the responsibility for much of the propaganda output of the party was centralized in his hands. Just as in an earlier period the career of Ivy Lee had dramatized the usefulness of the public relations counsel's talents to the captains of industry, so now did Charles Michelson's to the world of politics.

Developments in party propaganda since the organization of the Democratic publicity bureau in 1929 are almost as difficult to trace as those that preceded them. The subject is one that has not been adequately reported. The campaign of Alfred M. Landon, though poorly co-ordinated and in some respects ill conceived, set a new record for amounts of propaganda materials distributed. It was also highly influenced by the merchandising experience of business enterprise. The office of "Public Relations Director" was introduced for the first time into national party organization and Hill Blackett, a Chicago advertising man, was installed in it. Blackett drew upon his experience in commercial advertising in his use of radio, introduced a spot announcement campaign, put out campaign movies, sent out thousands of letters and post cards, and flooded the country with printed matter.

Because they called attention in a striking way to the presence of professional propagandists in politics, two other campaigns are worthy of notice. One of these was Upton Sinclair's race for the governorship of California in 1934. Socialist Sinclair surprised and frightened conservative politicians when he won a clear majority and the party's nomination in the Democratic gubernatorial primary. During both the primary and the general election campaigns his candidacy was forwarded not primarily by party groups but through the efforts of EPIC (End Poverty in California) clubs. The Republican organization, unaided, did not feel strong enough to meet the threat. The national advertising agency of Lord and Thomas, flanked by many other professional publicists, was put in general charge of anti-Sinclair propaganda. They were helped by the newspapers which were almost universally, and violently, opposed to the Democratic nominee. The movie industry threatened to leave the state in the event of his victory and put specially produced anti-Sinclair newsreels into all California theaters. When it was all over, Sinclair wrote bitterly that:

> When I first came to California, nineteen years ago, I met Harry Carr, of the Los Angeles "Times." Discussing journalism, he remarked to me: 'Sinclair, it has been so long since I have written anything I believed that I wouldn't know the feeling.' . . . There are hundreds of Harry Carrs in California journalism. There are thousands like him in another profession, that of advertising and publicity, where, of course, the concept of believing what one writes is unknown. It is interesting to note that when our big businessmen wanted to smash EPIC, the groups they relied upon were these two; also, of course, a few lawyers, who are hired to represent either side of any cause. It is notable that they used very few politicians. . . . When there is serious work to be done, and the plutocracy wants to be sure of getting its money's worth, they put their own people on the job.[2]

[2] Upton Sinclair, *Candidate for Governor and How I Got Licked* (New York: Rinehart, 1934), pp. 140–141.

Another impressive demonstration of the uses of publicity in politics was the pre-convention campaign of Wendell L. Willkie, in 1940. Willkie, so far as the general public was concerned, was an obscure figure a year before the convention. The real contestants for the Republican presidential nomination were thought to be Thomas E. Dewey, Robert A. Taft, and Arthur Vandenberg. While Willkie had few delegates pledged, he did have other advantages. He had the support of powerful businessmen like Thomas W. Lamont, of J. P. Morgan and Company, and Lewis Douglas, of the Mutual Life Insurance Company. He had the assistance of influential organs of the press: the Luce and Cowles publications, the *Saturday Evening Post,* and the *New York Herald Tribune.* Russell Davenport, managing editor of *Fortune,* left his post to work full time for Willkie and brought with him a whole group of enthusiastic professional public relations and advertising men—Steve Hannagan, Ned Stevenson, Fred Smith, Harry M. Shackleford, Chester La Roche, Ted Patrick, Thomas Ryan, and Stanley Resor. In mass circulation magazines, feature articles on Willkie began to appear as a part of a well timed publicity "build-up." Oren Root, Jr., figured prominently in organizing Willkie clubs and in circulating petitions booming the utility president's candidacy. As the convention date grew closer, newspapers were full of news on Willkie's under-dog campaign and the activities of his followers. As delegates assembled, businessmen among them got letters and telegrams by the dozens from big customers, and lawyers received them from clients.

The convention gave way and voted Willkie a sixth ballot nomination. John Chamberlain wrote, ". . . the Willkie strategy proved the Dewey-Taft-Joe Pew 'professionals' to be the real bunglers, the real amateurs." Wendell Willkie was, of course, no novice in matters of publicity. The utility interests, with which he was associated as president of Commonwealth and

Southern, had had a vast experience in the use of modern public relations techniques. Senator George Norris charged that it was this utility publicity machine that had "built" Wendell Willkie.

If, with presently available facts, it is not possible to judge with complete accuracy the full extent to which public relations men play a regular part in contemporary politics and political campaigns, it is clear that it is a widespread phenomenon. At the national level, both major parties have had publicity specialists since Michelson and West took up their respective duties. The present public relations departments of the Republican National Committee and the Republican Congressional Campaign Committee are, in effect, commercial public relations agencies performing political functions. While themselves offering propaganda services, they have encouraged each of their party's candidates to retain his own counsellor, and many of the administrative assistants of congressional office-holders are in reality public relations men. The Democratic National Committee likewise now advises Democratic candidates to retain professional advertising and publicity experts.

There can be little doubt, moreover, that parties and candidates have increasingly looked for the advice and help of the public relations specialist, if one accepts the testimony of party leaders and officials. Though a few of these forego any generalization (often because publicists have been attached to party organizations in their areas for a considerable period of time), more typical are comments like the following. From Washington: "You asked whether the use of public relations men in campaigns is increasing. In our part of the country it definitely is." From Minnesota: "I am sure that there is an upswing on the use of public relations men in political campaigns. This is becoming more evident in every campaign." From Michigan: "I would say that public relations men be-

came desirable adjuncts of political campaigns in Michigan from 1936 on. I pick that date only because I have in memory a man who handled a full campaign in that year and in the year succeeding I watched others operate in the same field. . . . In Michigan the use of public relations men in political campaigns is now fully accepted." From Ohio: "While I do not know if there is any great upsurge, the use of public relations counsel is becoming increasingly greater in political campaigns." From Kansas: "I wish to say that in my mind there is no question but what more advertising men and public relations men are being used in political campaigns." This judgment is affirmed by the further statements of party chairmen, secretaries, publicity directors, national committeemen, and public relations men in Arizona, Iowa, Massachusetts, Nevada, New Mexico, New Jersey, New York, California, Maryland, and Oregon.

It is also evident that public relations men are currently performing tasks for politicians at all levels of government. This is certainly true in New York. The same observations seem accurate of Washington, Oregon, Illinois, Michigan, Ohio, Pennsylvania, and Massachusetts. California is especially notable in this respect; an observer of politics there writes, "The real direction of a campaign is usually conducted by a paid expert or a public relations man." An advertising agency head in Iowa comments, "Not all aspirants to political positions as yet use the services of the professional publicizer but most successful ones do. . . ." The statement of a public relations man in the state of Washington deserves quotation at length, since the situation he describes is probably similar to that of many other places:

Most local elections, with the exception of the office of mayor in the larger cities, do not utilize the services of responsible and competent public relations and advertising people. The mayoralty campaigns usually do. The campaigns for most county officials, except in the very large counties, usually receive only second rate assistance. The same is true for all but the top state officers. Most congressional campaigns receive the service and advice of professional advertising and public relations people but very few of them receive top grade assistance. The campaigns for governor and U.S. senator almost invariably are assisted by qualified professional people. . . . Frankly, the kind of assistance given in most political campaigns, other than top level, are second rate practitioners picking up an odd dollar and usually contributing very little. . . . The two best campaigns in the State of Washington in the last election were the campaigns for senator, Henry Jackson, by the Wallace McKay agency and the campaign for Governor Langlie, handled by Frederick E. Baker and Associates.[3]

Beyond the extensive use of public relations counsels in Washington's political campaigns, the statement suggests that the skillful public relations man is most prominent as an actor in state-wide and national, rather than local, politics.

Summarizing the situation as it now seems to stand, we can make the following observations. At present, the activities of the public relations man impinge on the political process in a variety of ways. He helps clients adopt policies designed to earn public confidence and insure against governmental interference. He stages propaganda campaigns so that legislators will find it easier, or more difficult, to pass particular laws. He works to build men into public figures and to put them into the offices of government. He attempts to give political parties an advantageous publicity position. He manages campaigns for pressure groups desirous of putting initiative and referendum measures into the codes of public law. These kinds of participation by the public relations man in partisan politics are now frequent, and widespread geographically; they occur at all levels of government and are apparently

[3] From a letter to the writer.

increasing. As trends, they appear to be a part of a more general movement toward specialization in propaganda. The problem now becomes one of finding what it means for our system of government to have political discussion increasingly monopolized by members of a restricted skill group. . . .

20. Campaign Debates: Some Facts and Issues

Stanley Kelley, Jr.

Although President Johnson chose not to debate in the 1964 election, this article was written at the time that President Kennedy stated that he would be willing, even as an incumbent, to debate. The author, who is a Professor of Politics at Princeton University, devotes this article to three questions: (1) the kinds of political programs that would be preserved on television if debates were dropped, (2) how different program formats influence the way campaign issues are discussed, and (3) if debates are judged desirable, whether it would be best to suspend permanently Section 315 of the Federal Communications Act.

* * *

The Nixon-Kennedy joint television appearances aroused an extraordinary amount of interest among voters, they were widely believed to have had a crucial part in deciding the outcome of the 1960 election, and they were made possible by legislation only temporary in its effect. These facts virtually guaranteed that the role of such debates in 1964 would become a lively subject of speculation and controversy—and it has.

From the *Public Opinion Quarterly*, vol. 26, no. 3 (Fall 1962), pp. 351–366, with footnote omissions, by permission of the *Public Opinion Quarterly*.

The first steps toward determining that role have already been taken. President Kennedy has said unequivocally that he would be willing to debate his Republican opponent in 1964. The networks are eager to arrange a second series of joint appearances between major party candidates for President, if they can do so without incurring an obligation to give minor party candidates equal time. Two bills that would permanently suspend the application of section 315 of the Federal Communications Act to presidential and vice presidential campaigns (thus meeting the broadcasters' terms) have been introduced into the Congress. More recently the President, basing his proposal on a recommendation of his Commission on Campaign Costs, has asked the Congress for another temporary suspension of section 315 in 1964.

Those who decide whether there will be debates in 1964 may very well be deciding a great deal more: they may be deciding if debates are to become a permanent institution of presidential campaigns. If another round of debates attracts the kind of interest and attention that those of 1960 did, and if President Kennedy smashes the notion that an incumbent President is above debate, then it will be very difficult for any future presidential candidate to refuse to meet his opponent in face-to-face discussion, should his opponent challenge him to do so. And if debates become a regular feature of campaigns, they are likely also to become their dominant institution. A survey conducted by Elmo Roper for the Columbia Broadcasting System found that 44 per cent of the nation's voters believed that the Nixon-Kennedy debates had influenced their votes and about 5 per cent said they had made their final decision on the basis of the debates alone. No other campaign program or set of programs has ever elicited a comparable response.

The purpose of this article is to contribute to the already considerable discussion about the value of debates in campaigns by framing answers to three questions that have been given somewhat less attention than they deserve. First, if there are to be no television debates, what kinds of political programs will the medium be used for in the future? The merits or demerits of debates as a format for political discussion should be measured against those of probable alternative formats, not against the virtues of some ideal form of political discourse. Second, what kinds of differences in campaign discussion attend the use of different program formats? Third, assuming we want debates in presidential campaigns, is either the temporary or permanent suspension of section 315 necessarily the way we must go about getting them?

THE EMERGING CONVENTIONS OF CAMPAIGN TELEVISION

Network-controlled time. In 1960 the three television networks allocated a substantial amount of network-controlled time to reporting the presidential campaign and to appearances by the candidates. The campaign was given regular and extensive attention in newscasts, which often carried taped presentations of the candidates addressing rallies. The candidates and their wives were interviewed on "Person to Person," "Tonight," "Presidential Countdown," and "The Campaign and the Candidates." Kennedy, Henry Cabot Lodge, and Lyndon Johnson were all subjected to the rigors of "Meet the Press" and "Face the Nation," and Nixon, too, appeared on the former. "Eyewitness to History," "Election Countdown," and "The Campaign and the Candidates" featured reports on the progress of the campaign and speculation about the election's outcome. On two programs noncandidate representatives of the two campaign organizations gave their views on how things were going and on the virtues of their respective tickets. Exclusive of newscasts, the networks devoted some forty-one hours to campaign programs, more than half of them commercially sponsored.

This kind of programming of network-controlled time is probably a fair indication of things to come. If one disregards the debates, what the networks did in 1960 differs from what they had done in previous campaigns chiefly in that so many programs had appearances by the candidates as their main attraction. More than half did. The program formats used, however —the interview, the documentary, and the panel inquisition—were those long familiar in television public affairs programs. Because this was true, almost all the campaign telecasts of 1960 could have been offered even if section 315 had not been suspended: a 1959 amendment to 315 had already exempted from the application of the equal-time provision appearances by candidates on bona fide newscasts, bona fide news interviews, bona fide news documentaries, and on-the-spot coverage of bona fide news events. If section 315 is not suspended or revised by 1964, the long-standing aversion of broadcasters to equal-time claims by minor parties—at least valid ones—will further reinforce their already demonstrated preference for the tried and true formulas of public affairs broadcasting.

Paid time. By 1960 the use that politicians were making of paid time on television had begun to crystallize into relatively well-defined patterns. These can be expected to persist. This statement is not made on the basis of any simple faith that what has happened in the past is the best guide to what will happen in the future, but because the current use of television by campaigners reflects a developing consensus among them as to how the medium can best be made to serve their purposes.

In retrospect the approach that the rival campaign strategists took to television in the 1952 presidential race—the first in which television played a role of any significance—seems unimaginative, notwithstanding a statement at the time by the

Democrats that they planned to use it "in a more exciting, more dramatic way than any political party ever dreamed of. . . ." By far the greater number of programs sponsored by both parties were simply half-hour telecasts of speeches delivered at political rallies. Among the exceptions were the filmed documentaries that each side presented. In addition, Adlai Stevenson delivered a few fireside chats; Republican Governors appeared on an hour-long program; and the Republicans ended with a final night show that was a fast-paced, hour-long, three-network "report on the campaign" involving eighty-one switches from city to city and from live telecasting to film. In the campaign's closing days the Republicans saturated the air waves with spot announcements, reputedly spending somewhere between $800,000 and $1,500,000 in the effort. The Democrats roundly denounced this use of spots in 1952, but were in no position to do so in later years. The spot announcement has since won the secure respect of Democratic and Republican campaigners alike.

Some other trends in the use of television in United States presidential campaigns can be indicated quite briefly.

First, the parties have increasingly reserved their longer telecasts (those over five minutes in length) for appearances by their presidential and vice presidential candidates and by the incumbent President. In 1952 the candidates and the President were the principal speakers in 73 per cent of such telecasts. In 1956 and 1960 the comparable figures were 90 per cent and 88 per cent, respectively.

Second, the mean length of party telecasts has declined radically. In 1952 it was 29 minutes; in 1956, 13 minutes; and in 1960, 14 minutes. This decline was due mainly to the heavy use of the 5-minute "trailer" in the campaigns of 1956 and 1960: the modal length of party programs was 30 minutes in 1952; in 1956 and 1960, it was 5.

Third, the producers of party television programs have been engaged in an effort to make them visually interesting and to introduce audience participation, conflict, and other entertainment features into them. With a few notable exceptions most American politicians in television's early days used television as they had radio—they "gazed at their tables, script bound," as French politicians still did in 1958. By 1956 cue cards and the teleprompter had largely freed American politicians from scripts. They began to use visual aids and film clips. They tried panel discussions and interviews. They appeared with stars of the entertainment world: the most notable instance of this, perhaps, occurred during the 1956 campaign, when President Eisenhower was given a "surprise" party on his birthday, and entertainers rendered his favorite songs. They organized telethons: Vice President Nixon used this device on the last day of the 1960 campaign. They experimented with press conferences and programs modeled on press conferences: Nixon submitted to questioning from reporters in one show during the 1956 campaign; in another President Eisenhower held a "Citizens' Press Conference," where carefully selected citizens praised him and posed friendly questions.

What is to be made of this record? The most general explanation of the trends just outlined would seem to be this: They reflect the rational reaction of campaign strategists to what they have learned about the factors that affect the size and responses of audiences for political television. Most of their information about audience size and response has come to them from ratings, surveys, letters, and telephone calls. The inferences they have drawn from such data may not be entirely convincing to students of public opinion, but they have seemed sound enough to politicians to have influenced their behavior.

Audience survey data convinced politicians that voters are far more interested in hearing what candidates have to say for themselves than in hearing what other party leaders have to say for and about candidates—unless the "other party leader" is the President of the United States. In 1952 both the Republicans and the Democrats had numerous speakers who appeared on television on behalf of their respective party tickets: Robert A. Taft, Phillip Murray, Clare Boothe Luce, Walter Reuther, Herbert Hoover, and Wayne Morse, to name only a few of them. Now, the average audience for a Stevenson speech that year was approximately 3,620,000 television homes, and for an Eisenhower speech, over 4,120,000 television homes. Of speakers who were neither President nor candidates for the Presidency or Vice Presidency, only Senator Joseph R. McCarthy attracted an audience that equaled either of these averages. Most drew audiences that fell far below them. The Republicans took explicit notice of the lesson implicit in these facts. The later programming of both parties indicates that both had taken the lesson to heart.

Two additional conclusions that politicians have reached account for other features of television's use in recent campaigns, including the trend toward shorter programs and the innovations in program format. The first such conclusion is that undecided voters are the voters least likely to watch political television shows. This proposition, although it owes a good deal to intuition, squares with findings about the 1952 audiences reported by Janowitz and Marvick. It also conforms with more general findings about attention to campaign propaganda: Lazarsfeld and his associates reported in their Erie County study that "the people who already knew how they were going to vote read and listened to more campaign material than the people who still did not know how they would vote." R. S. Milne and H. C. Mackenzie made a similar observation in their study of voting in Bristol, England.

The other conclusion is that political television in its usual forms cannot effectively compete for audiences with commercial entertainment. Evidence to substantiate it accumulated rapidly. The 1952 conventions received considerably lower Nielsen ratings than the show, "I Love Lucy." In the 1952 campaign the two parties adopted different strategies in the purchase of television time, with a result that gave campaigners further food for thought. The Republicans, in an effort to minimize the competition of commercial entertainment, pre-empted the time periods of leading commercial programs. The Democrats hoped to build an audience for *political* television; they attempted to do so by presenting Adlai Stevenson in a series of programs regularly scheduled for 10:30 to 11:00 P.M. on Tuesdays and Thursdays. The Republicans were vindicated in the more pessimistic assumptions of their strategy when the rating services showed that both Stevenson and Eisenhower drew larger audiences when they appeared in pre-empted time periods.

They had not discovered any final solution to the politician's television problems, however, for party strategists soon learned that viewers were often highly annoyed when they turned to one of their favorite programs to find a political speech instead. Carroll Newton, the Republicans' chief time buyer, has reported, "I think the most phone calls we had during our campaign [the 1956 campaign] we got after displacing a very popular program and, while we were highly flattered at the number of calls, we found out that 98 per cent of them were disgruntled at us. . . ." He has reported also that half-hour political shows in 1956 drew audiences from 25 to 40 per cent smaller than those normal for the programs they replaced.

If one puts oneself in the campaigner's place, it is not difficult to see the significance of what has just been said. The campaigner wants to arouse the enthusiasm of his least enthusiastic partisans and to gain the support of the undecided voter. To do either of these things he must reach voters and he must please them. If it is true that voters, and undecided voters more than others, prefer entertainment to politics, two general strategies are open to him. The first is to attempt to locate and reach captive audiences. The second is to make politics entertaining.

Carroll Newton has forcefully advocated the first of these strategies and cogently stated its rationale and consequences:

> People are not as interested in politics and in candidates as they are in entertainment. Therefore, the audiences you enjoy will be largely determined by three factors: First, the size of the audience looking at the program immediately ahead of you; Second, the audience which normally every week tunes in for entertainment to the time period and the station you're buying for your political purpose; and Third, of course, the attraction value of the programs on other stations at the same time. . . . it is further significant that the ability of a political program to hold its audience varies in inverse proportion to its length. . . . I think you can conclude . . . that the people who are really interested will follow campaigns from every source there is. You don't have to worry about reaching them, but the people who aren't interested —you have got to slip up on them through the broadcasting media. You have to catch them when they are looking or listening to something else, if you want to reach them at all.[1]

Several prescriptions for action logically follow from these premises: (1) "Buy television at times when the largest number of people habitually use their receivers"; (2) "smaller units of time will reach more voters for your dollar," and, therefore, a large proportion of the television budget should be earmarked for spot announcements and 5-minute trailers, which are effective because voters "have to listen before they can get up and switch them off"; and

[1] In an address to Republican state chairmen, June 1958.

(3) "Devote all the time you buy to issues of real significance [as determined by surveys] and present your point of view so simply that even the viewers who don't give a damn will understand what you're talking about."

Newton's views are peculiar neither to himself nor to Republicans. The Democrats have been making essentially the same recommendations to their candidates as those just quoted. They, too, have noted that the candidate's principal competition on television is the entertainment program. They have advised against half-hour shows. They value the spot announcement that presents a simple and memorable slogan. They have advised against giving advance notice of trailers on the grounds that such notice is more likely to repel than to attract voters.

The attempt to attract audiences by making politics entertaining has been pursued with considerably less determination than has been brought to the search for captive audiences. This is undoubtedly true in part because many politicians have been unable to see clearly how they might exploit the entertainment values inherent in political discourse. Many have been aware that a speech growing out of a dramatic situation—Nixon's 1952 speech defending his use of a specially subscribed fund is the best and almost the only example—could compete effectively for audiences with commercial shows. It is not apparent, however, how such situations might be contrived as a part of a conscious strategy.

But there is another reason for the politician's hesitation to adopt this strategy. Conflict is the most obvious entertainment appeal of political campaigns. The panel discussions, the interviews, and the "press conferences" have been very tentative and very timid steps toward tapping this appeal. Genuine conflict cannot be injected into political programs, however, without incurring one very heavy cost—that of exposing one's audience to an opposing point of view, forcefully presented. When this is not done but only simulated, the program is very likely to elicit a feeling similar to that expressed about a show in which Conservative Ministers were questioned by British editors—"it resembled a board meeting with the directors being questioned by a group of keen but generally sympathetic shareholders."

SOME CONSEQUENCES OF PROGRAM FORMAT

The import of all this for campaign television in a future that does not include debates can be summarized as follows: both the networks and campaigners will devote the lion's share of the time they control to presenting the candidates, and for basically the same reasons. The candidates are the headliners of the electoral drama. The networks will devote another large block of time to shows that explore the question, "Who is winning?" Television news departments have discovered, as newspapers did before them, that a sizable section of the mass media audience is interested in the game aspects of elections. The networks will rely primarily on the newscast, the interview, the documentary, and the panel program as formats within which to present campaign discussion. Paid political programs, on the average, will be much shorter than those presented in network-controlled time. They will use a variety of formats, but the spot announcement, the trailer, the short speech, and the friendly interview are almost certain to be among those used most heavily.

What would debates add? An answer to this question can be suggested by comparing discussion as it occurred in the Nixon-Kennedy joint appearances with the discussion made available to viewing audiences via televised speeches, interviews, and panel programs in 1960.

In the four joint appearances the candidates explicitly acknowledged agreement on a number of points. This was in contrast to their behavior on other campaign programs. The candidate-debaters quickly established that their differences were about means and not ends, about the kinds of programs needed to reach goals, not about the goals themselves. Nixon stated, in addition, that he had no quarrel with Kennedy's views on several substantive issues of importance: internal security, the need to extend economic assistance to underdeveloped countries, the defense of Berlin, and the significance that voters should attach to the religious affiliation of the candidates. Kennedy said that he could find no fault with Nixon's stand on summit meetings.

In his nondebate appearances on television Kennedy acknowledged agreement with Nixon only once: in the course of an interview with Chet Huntley and David Brinkley, he refused to criticize Nixon's intervention in, or handling of, the steel strike. Nixon in his speeches emphasized—as he did in the debates—his agreement with Kennedy that neither candidate's religious affiliation should play any part in voters' decisions. He noted also that "my opponent, of course, has programs in these same fields . . . ," thus implicitly admitting that he differed with him principally on the way to meet problems, not on what problems needed to be met. The other instances in which Nixon declared himself to be of one mind with his opponent, however, were really backhanded attacks. Toward the end of the campaign, for instance, he stated repeatedly that Kennedy had finally come to agree with his (Nixon's) stand on Quemoy and Matsu, on Cuba, and on what the proper course of action should have been in the U-2 affair. Then he would go on to say, by way of comment on his opponent's alleged change of heart. "When you're a candidate you can say something, make a mistake, and correct it the next day and nobody is the worse for it. But when you're President of the United States, when you speak or act as President, it's for keeps. . . . I believe . . . my opponent would have

risked war or surrender for the United States in those particular areas."

Of course, it is not unusual for presidential candidates to be in agreement on a considerable number of issues and certainly not unusual for them to be in agreement on the basic goals of public policy. What is rare is for them to admit that they agree. How can one account for the seeming tendency of the debates to evoke such admissions? The most plausible explanation would seem to be this: with the candidates' views exposed, side by side as it were, the fact of their agreement on many issues was obvious. Both found it more difficult, therefore, to maintain the kind of pretense that many candidates seem to think useful and frequently adopt in solo appearances—the pretense that the candidate who is speaking is the only one who really cares about the problems of the aged, the unemployed, school-age children, or farmers; who is interested in containing communism or winning the approval of neutral nations; or who is concerned about economic growth. Thus debates may help to identify for the voter those issues on which rival candidates do not disagree, making it easier for him to center his attention on those issues on which they do.

Once two men, each asking to be preferred to the other for the office of President, admit that they do not differ on the goals of public policy, they place themselves under some compulsion to say by what means they propose to reach those goals. In the debates Nixon and Kennedy did put themselves in this position. And they made relatively explicit statements about what ought to be done about problems of labor-management relations, education, medical care to the aged, civil rights, agriculture, depletion allowances, nuclear testing, fiscal affairs, and some aspects of foreign relations.

The specificity with which Kennedy described what he would do about various problems in the debates contrasted sharply with his discussions of programs in his speeches. In the latter he typically dwelt on the blunders of the past, the problems of the present, and his hopes for the future. He made it abundantly clear that he wanted to get the country moving again, but he was exceedingly vague about how he proposed to do so. A speech of September 20 gives an indication of the kind of program suggestions that Kennedy advanced in most of his speeches. The next President, he said, should be

> prepared in the first three months of his office to send to the Congress messages that will deal with wiping out poverty here in the United States, which will deal with the problems of full employment, of a higher minimum wage, of better social security for our older citizens, more slum clearance, and aid to depressed areas, more help for the marginal farmer and the sharecropper, a concentrated drive on illiteracy, improved distribution of surplus foods because over 4 million Americans wait every month for those surplus food packages, and a better economic break for all Americans regardless of where they live and regardless of their economic status.[2]

Nixon's speeches spelled out his programs in somewhat more precise terms than did his rival's, but it is fair to say that both candidates specified their program intentions in the debates on a greater number of issues than they did in their televised speeches, and usually to a greater extent on any given issue.

Thus the debates seem to have had some tendency to overcome the inclination—often remarked—of campaigners to say little about method and much about goals. If debates work this way, the fact has some interesting implications for any future debates between an incumbent President and his challenger. An incumbent is necessarily identified with a record, and a record necessarily involves having made decisions on concrete and controversial issues. A challenger, pointing to past errors and

promising to do better, can hope to exploit dissatisfaction with the record in groups of quite diverse interests, provided he does not go into too much detail about changes he would make. An incumbent who used the debate situation to challenge the challenger, forcing him to get down to specifics, could greatly lessen the efficacy of this strategy.

Students of campaigning have frequently noted the tendency of candidates to raise points against the opposition while ignoring points raised against them, to attack more than they defend, to join issues—not with each other—but with opponents of their own creation. This tendency was probably less pronounced in the 1960 campaign than it has been in some previous ones. Kennedy, in his speeches, rarely contrasted any point of view he espoused with one taken by Nixon, and still more rarely did he attempt to answer any of Nixon's charges. Nixon, however, quite frequently and quite explicitly attempted to counter a number of the principal Kennedy themes. He would declare, "they say that . . . America has been standing still for the last 7½ years" and then go on to give evidence that "Anyone who says America has been standing still hasn't been traveling around America." He contrasted his and Kennedy's views on the possibility of a recession, the proper approach to take to the farm problem, aid to depressed areas, medical care for the aged, and many other questions.

Nixon's tendency to cast many of his speeches in a "Now, they say" and "Now, I say" form may simply have reflected his peculiar approach to campaign speaking, but this is not the only explanation that can be plausibly offered for it. The candidates in 1960, unlike those in earlier campaigns, could be sure that a very large proportion of their audiences had been exposed to the principal arguments of the other side. They had been exposed to them in the debates. Nixon's 1960 style may simply have reflected his recognition of

[2] *Freedom of Communications*, Report of a Subcommittee of the Senate Committee on Interstate and Foreign Commerce 87th Cong., 1st sess., I, 297.

this fact. On several occasions, when he was drawing a distinction between his position and that of Kennedy, he told his audience that the American people had had the opportunity in the debates to see how Kennedy would have made decisions and that they should test him by the record he had made there.

Even for Nixon and certainly for Kennedy, however, attack and defense were more nearly balanced in the debates than they were in the speeches. The format of the debates—question, answer, comment on answer—made this almost inevitable. Thus the debates brought out the other side of a number of issues that remained one-sided in the speeches. Two examples may suffice to illustrate this point.

Nixon, in his speeches, made much of the fact that Kennedy (just after the U-2 incident and the collapse of the Paris summit conference in May of 1960) had suggested that President Eisenhower could have apologized for the U-2 flights. In his speeches, Kennedy ignored this attack. He could hardly do so, however, when debate panelist Edward P. Morgan asked, "Senator, last May in Oregon you discussed the possibilities of sending apologies or regrets to Khrushchev over the U-2 incident. Do you think now that that would have done any good? Did you think so then?" In response, Kennedy said that he did think an expression of regrets would have been in order and that the U-2 flights—though proper as a security measure—were not in accordance with international law. An expression of regrets, he argued, would have been in accordance with international custom and should have been offered if the Administration felt the summit conference could have been saved. He went on:

the point that is always left out is the fact that we expressed regrets to Castro this winter, that we expressed regrets—the Eisenhower administration expressed regrets—for a flight over Southern Russia in 1958. We expressed regrets for a flight over Eastern Germany under this administra-tion. The Soviet Union in 1955 expressed regrets to us over the Bering Sea incident. The Chinese Communists expressed regrets to us over a plane incident in 1956.[3]

Discussion of medical care for the aged in the debates also led to an elaboration of both sides of this issue and a clarification of it. Kennedy advocated a medical care program for the aged "tied to social security." Nixon, too, had a medical care program had been offered as an amend-tioned by Kennedy)—one not financed by a social security tax and one that would have offered all persons over sixty-five a choice among a government-sponsored insurance plan, a private plan, or no plan at all. Nixon charged in his speeches, and Kennedy ignored the charge, that the Kennedy program was inadequate because it would do nothing for 3 million people not covered by social security. When Nixon made the same charge in the course of the first debate, however, Kennedy called attention to the fact that his medical care program had been offered as an amendment to the Kerr bill, which provided assistance for persons not eligible for social security benefits.

It will have been noticed that so far we have compared discussion in the debates chiefly with that in speeches by the candidates. We have done so because this comparison yields clearer contrasts, on the whole, than a comparison of discussion in the debates with that in the interviews and panel programs presented on network-controlled time. Yet even here there were some differences worthy of note.

In the interviews there was a difference in the kinds of issues discussed. Debate panelists canvassed much the same range of topics that the candidates covered in their speeches. Interviewers did not. They were prone to ask personal questions—how the candidate had become interested in politics, what satisfactions he found in political life, how the lives of his wife and

---

[3] *Freedom of Communications*, III, 148.

children were affected by his career, how he felt the campaign was progressing. Interviewers' questions were personal in another sense also—they tried to get the candidates to talk about other leaders in their respective parties. Nixon was questioned about his relationship with Governor Nelson Rockefeller, Kennedy about his with Adlai Stevenson and Dean Acheson. Unlike that of the debates, the atmosphere of the interviews was relaxed, although interviewers generally served up one or two tough questions to their guests. Walter Cronkite, for instance, after allowing Kennedy to discourse on how he felt about mudslinging, asked the future President, "Does the thing that used to come up occasionally about softness toward McCarthyism, does that bother you at all—personally?" On "The Campaign and the Candidates," where David Brinkley and Chet Huntley were the interviewers, Nixon was made to wriggle perceptibly in responding to: "I would gather, then, that we might expect, if you are elected, 4 more years of the kind of leadership we have had in the last 8, roughly the same, in terms of vigor, aggressiveness, tone, and character of the Presidency."

The two panel shows, "Meet the Press" and "Face the Nation," had formats very like that employed for the joint appearances. Their panelists explored much the same kinds of issues that were raised in the debates, although, with less time, they explored fewer. And they played a somewhat different role in discussion than the debate panelists did. They cross-questioned candidates, frequently in an effort to deflate issues.

For example, Lawrence Spivak asked Nixon—who had voted against a Democratic bill that would have given aid to the states to pay the salaries of public school teachers—if he favored Federal aid to education. Nixon said he did, if such aid were for financing school construction. He then went on to say, "The moment you in effect have the Federal Government paying our teachers in whole or in part, in our public schools, you inevitably give to the Federal Government power to set standards for teachers and to control what is taught. . . ." Then:

MR. SPIVAK: Why should we get Federal controls if we give aid for teachers' salaries and not get it if we give aid for buildings? I mean, haven't we got the imagination to set up a system where we give the money to the localities and allow them to dispense it as they need it?

VICE PRESIDENT NIXON: It is an altogether different thing. When we give money for buildings, even here we say we are not going to have standards. But let's say we did have standards; the classrooms have to be a certain size. That is one thing. When you set standards for teaching, what they teach, what subjects can be taught, what they have to meet, this is an altogether different thing. We are talking in the one instance about control of the mind. We are talking in the other instances of control over matter, and there is a very great difference. One means control of the whole system itself.

MR. SPIVAK: Yes, but Mr. Vice President, why do we have to set standards? Why can't we give them aid just as we give it to them for buildings, and let them set their own standards?

VICE PRESIDENT NIXON: This would be an ideal, provided you could reach it. But the history of aid of any type, where aid is given in fields of this sort, has inevitably been that once you aid the next step is control, and I feel that the risk is so great that a position must be taken against it.[4]

Debate panelists, unable to cross-question and switching from subject to subject as their individual interests dictated, played a less useful role in discussion than did their counterparts on "Meet the Press" and "Face the Nation." Often their presence seemed to be frustrating a desire on the part of the candidates to put issues into sharper focus. In the third and fourth debates, in fact, Nixon and Kennedy began to talk past the panelists, each giving only perfunctory answers to some questions in order to use his

[4] *Freedom of Communications*, III, 17.

allocated time to respond to some argument the other had made.

In one respect the debates differed from all other campaign programs, even the panel programs. They showed a far greater capacity to attract audiences and to hold the attention of audiences. Why this should have been the case can only be a matter of speculation, but several factors were probably important: (1) the entertainment value of the debates was greater than that of other campaign programs, (2) they got a great deal of advance publicity, (3) they were an economical way for any citizen who felt that he had a civic duty to hear both sides before voting to discharge that duty, (4) they monopolized the airwaves during the times they were shown. But whatever the causes for the enormous audiences that the debates drew, the consequence of their having drawn them was that the two major party candidates were able to put reasonable adequate statements of their respective cases before an audience that included virtually the entire electorate. The well-known tendency of voters to expose themselves selectively to partisan propaganda was effectively countered.

REGARDING THE MEANS

As has already been noted, proponents of future debates are recommending the suspension of section 315. The only difference of opinion among most of them seems to be about whether suspension should be permanent or temporary.

This state of affairs calls for a brief comment. First of all, whatever else it would do, suspension of section 315 would make it possible for broadcasters to indulge partisan biases in allocating time among candidates. Advocates of permanent suspension are apparently convinced that the performance of the broadcasting industry

in 1960 is an adequate answer to this objection. Those who favor temporary suspension want further evidence. Yet what broadcasters do under a temporary suspension can never really be a reliable indication of the way they would conduct themselves under a permanent suspension. The broadcasting industry wants to be free of section 315: temporary suspension—with an implied promise of permanent suspension—puts them on good behavior. Moreover, if those who will evaluate the fairness of broadcasting practices have standards that enable them to make such an evaluation, why do they not write those standards into the law?

Second, suspension of section 315 is certainly not the only way to make campaign debates possible. Simply exempting appearances of candidates in debates from the provisions of section 315, as their appearances on newscasts and news interview programs are now exempted, would serve that purpose equally well. So would revising section 315 to make its equal time provisions applicable only to major party candidates in general elections and to leading candidates in nomination contests, as Thomson has suggested. So would a measure that distinguished between leading and minor candidates for nominations and between major and minor party candidates in elections, drawn to require substantially equal treatment for candidates falling into any one of these categories, while establishing some permissible degree of inequality as between candidates falling into different categories.

To debate or not to debate, to suspend or not to suspend, are separable issues. That campaign debates may be a valuable addition to the repertory of campaign techniques is a spurious justification for the methods now being considered to encourage them.

III. PARTY ORGANIZATION
Donald G. Herzberg

The two-party system is rooted in the election of the President, Vice President, and the members of Congress by the people. The execution of national and state elections has required the growth of a number of customs, usages, and laws that informally constitute the party system.

The founders of the Constitution had apparently hoped to avoid the hazards of a party system, but in this respect, as in some others, their hopes have been frustrated. The American party system is an integral, vital part of our Constitution.

Within this country there are vast differences in patterns of party organizations. The safest generalization would be that there are practically as many patterns of party organization as there are organizations. Within the framework of law and custom, the way in which political organizations behave depends upon a number of factors and the interplay of these factors, a characteristic similar, in many respects, to the observation of molecular activity under a high-powered microscope.

First, political behavior relates to the period of time in the electoral life cycle of a particular organization. The most important task facing any political organization is the winning of elections. Everything else an organization does is secondary. Its whole pace and style is geared to that special occasion known as election day—be it a primary or a general election. This essential fact of political life causes a natural electoral life cycle, and there are great differences within a political organization, depending upon where it is in relation to the cycle. The Middlesex County, New Jersey, Democratic organization is a vastly different operation the October preceding a presidential election from what it is the January following the election. It is also different the weeks preceding a primary from what it is the weeks before a general election. It is essential to the understanding of the political process to take into account this life cycle.

A second factor that determines the political behavior of a particular organization is the relative success or nonsuccess of the organization in the essential task of winning elections. A party organization that consistently supports the party's candidates successfully at the polls is a very different kind of organization from one that is rarely successful or from one that wins and loses about an equal number of elections. Obviously, the success of any political organization at any level is directly related to the impact of the competing party organization and the opportunities for potential political control of the area. Thus the organizational state of the Republican party in Chicago is directly affected by the successful party machinery controlled by Democratic Mayor Daley. The relationship between competing party organizations in a highly competitive district will be different from that found in a one-party district.

The relationship of a party organization to other political organizations within the same party is a third factor. A local party organization that consistently wins, that supports the county and state party organizations in primaries, and that performs other party duties with loyalty is clearly in a better position to work out its financial needs and patronage choices than an organization that fails to do these things. A successful organization is also likely to have more to say about the choice of candidates. In New York State, for example, the internal relations of various organizations in the Democratic party were exposed to public view when John English, backed by the power of his fast-growing Nassau County organization, supported Robert Kennedy's bid for the Senate nomination. The newer Democratic power groups in the state, aligned with several other power blocs, were able to determine the selection of Kennedy over what are believed to be the protests of Mayor Wagner, who had thus far dominated the party.

A fourth factor in the pattern of party organization is the relationship of the organization to the formal government, all levels of government. For example, the Cook County, Illinois, Democratic party has a relationship with the national government when there is a Democratic President—perhaps a President indebted, in part, to that organization for his nomination or his election or both. Clearly there is a relationship between the Cook County organization and the Illinois statehouse.

A fifth factor affecting the behavior of party organizations concerns how the organizations are influenced by nonpolitical organizations—ethnic, religious, economic, and other groups. The lore of the "balanced" ticket in American politics is ample evidence of the power of some of these groups. In New York City mayoral appointments, consideration is given the special-groups factor, and the same is true for the selection of candidates for city office by both parties. Recently when state Senator Constance Motley was endorsed for the Manhattan borough presidency by Mayor Wagner, newspaper editorials commented that this post was now regarded as a "Negro office" in order to give recognition to the political power of that group in the city. A party organization that fails to respond to such pressures will be in a different power position from one that does respond.

On occasion a political organization that has responded in the past to these group pressures and has held the dominant political power can be defeated at the polls if the other political party puts forth candidates that respond to other equally strong pressure-group appeals. A case in point is the candidacy of Jacob Javits in New York on the Republican ticket, which won away many normally Democratic Jewish voters. This naturally changed the power position of the Democratic party in the state.

The influence of individual personalities on political organizations is a sixth factor to be considered. A strong personality in command of the party machinery may not only deeply affect his own organization but his influence may extend to other parts of the political system in his state and elsewhere. John Bailey, for example, the dominant figure of Connecticut Democratic politics for a number of years, has had tremendous influence on the nature of Democratic party organization at the local level. Bailey developed strong city organizations, ran registration drives in Hartford and New Haven, and developed strong and loyal local political leadership across the state. Simultaneously, the Republican state and local organizations, in attempting to do him battle, reflected his organizational influence and talents (13). A Ray Bliss in Ohio, putting his particular stamp on the Ohio Republican organization, built the kind of reputation there that led Republicans to ask him to attempt to bring back the national party from the depths of the 1964 defeat. The kinds of organizational change that the Republican National Committee is presently undergoing are a reflection of Bliss' personal methods and organizational needs.

The seventh and final factor, and in a sense the one from which all other factors stem, is the nature of the rules of the game in American politics. Because these rules are largely informal and unwritten, party organizations are often not as they appear. Party officials who legally hold power are often no more than stand-ins for others who actually hold the power. The men who wield the real power do not usually appear in the organization chart. The formal and legal decision-making process may be no more than a process for confirming decisions that have already been reached informally.

All of the foregoing factors and their interplay in any given locale determine the nature of the party organization. They account for the fact that the party organization differs from the more traditional, neatly ordered pyramid organization. The arrangement of political party units on a federal, state, and local level —the simple order is national committee, state committee, county committee, municipal committees, and the local precinct organization—is, in fact, not a reality. In practice, the power more often flows up from the locality than down from the national level. Rarely does authority and power descend the line of command from level to level, and often the determining voice in a community is a combination of one or more levels—the precinct, the city, the county, or even the state. In New Jersey in 1965, a special selection committee was chosen to screen potential Republican gubernatorial nominees in order that the defeat-torn party might present a united front—and one candidate—in the primary, the very primary in which the Republican voters are supposed to choose their nominee. The fluidity of power, the shifting base of decision making, and the imprecise chain of command are characteristics of party organizations all over the country, because the organizations are no more than a reflection of varying patterns of power. It is these factors that have produced the essence of American politics: a two-party system in which the competition is almost never equal. It is on this political fact, on these patterns of inequally competing election districts, that attention should be turned in order to understand the nature of our varied party organizations.

When the basic units of party politics, the almost 176,000 precincts throughout the United States, are examined individually, it is discovered that, in the great majority of them, one of the two parties is so dominant that it consistently receives over 55 percent of the vote for all or almost all of the offices contested. Only in occasional elections do the parties at the precinct level compete on anything like equal terms. When neither party dominates by more than 55 percent of the vote, these precincts are likely to be in a temporary state of flux. Eventually they will settle down, with one of the two parties assuming dominance.

These units of one-party power are clusters of political organization. Further proof of the clustering of party power is found in the growing number of congressional districts that both parties concede to be "safe districts," districts in which the incumbent holds his seat by more than 55 percent of the vote. Thus it is seen that two-party competition in the United States is essentially comprised of clusters of one-party areas in competition with other clusters of one-party areas. In some states, this competition between dominant one-party clusters may produce a genuine, competitive two-party system at the state level.

Large urban areas provide another example of the clustering of precincts. Most big cities are Democratic. An examination of Philadelphia, for example, shows that most of the precincts are heavily Democratic. (In addition, the few precincts in which the Republicans dominate are Republican by greater than 55 percent of the vote.) These big-city organizations, like Philadelphia or Chicago or Jersey City, have tended to dominate and to have great influence on the Democratic parties at the state level. On the other hand, Republican city organizations, overwhelmed as they normally are, have had little influence on Republican state parties. Instead, Republican state organizations have tended in the past to be influenced by rural, small-town, and suburban organizations, the very areas that have had little influence in Democratic party organization at the state level.

Today, however, it appears that the clusters of one-party areas may be shifting, and these shifts have grave implications for the future of party politics in the United States. The changes in cluster patterns are being accelerated by the rapid growth of the suburbs, as well as by the Supreme Court decisions on reapportionment of state legislatures. Over the nation as a whole, new voting patterns of urban and suburban precincts may foretell vast changes in the nature of the two-party system.

New York state presents an interesting example of this change. Traditionally, the competition between the two parties in the state was Democratic New York City against the upstate Republican areas, a classification that is somewhat oversimplified because of enclaves of Democratic strength in Albany, Buffalo, and, occasionally, in other upstate cities. The state Democratic party, however, was dominated in its leadership and policies by New York City. In the election of 1964, however, many traditional Republican areas shifted, giving a great victory to the Democrats, including control of the New York legislature for the first time since the midthirties. In the struggle to elect the leaders of the legislature, it became evident that there were new areas of Democratic power that were unwilling to continue in the old pattern of New York-centered leadership. A bitter power struggle developed, which was resolved only temporarily by the intervention of the Republican minority who voted with the New York City Democrats in choosing Democratic leaders. This struggle left the state party in shambles. The situation was further complicated in March 1965 when the apportionment plan passed in late December by the previously Republican controlled legislature was ruled unconstitutional, thus giving the Democratic majority the additional headache of reapportionment. Under a temporary plan, in 1965 the Democrats lost control of the State Senate while retaining control of the State Assembly.

So far suburban areas have not been completely mastered by either political party. Neither the technique of the big-city machine nor that of the rural political organization has proved effective in suburban America.

It is also clear that suburban areas all over the country will emerge in the next decade as the most important political battlegrounds. It is here that the political process can be revitalized. From the demands of the suburban voter a new kind of party system could evolve. Many of these voters are of the generation that grew up accustomed to the Roosevelt programs of social security and other welfare provisions, and they have tended to retain this Democratic allegiance. The Kennedy assassination placed a somewhat different emphasis on the 1964 election, but it was clearly demonstrated that the Goldwater program was overwhelmingly rejected by the majority of Americans. The kind of rebuilding done by the Republican party over the next few years—in view of the portents of the electoral coalition that won Johnson his landslide victory—will largely determine the future political complexion of the suburbs and other areas that have recently been in a state of flux. Not since the Civil War has there been such an opportunity for political parties to reform themselves to be responsive to the needs of the people. The job presented to the Democrats in 1966 as the majority party differs from that confronting the Republicans in 1966 as the minority party. The Republican National Committee is formally in new hands, but leadership of the party is decentralized. Individual candidacies in 1965— the gubernatorial election in New Jersey, the mayoralty election in New York, and the special legislative elections—presented an opportunity for the Republicans to adapt their organization, their candidates, and their image to the changing political scene. The flexible nature of party organization permits such adaptation, nationally, at the state level, and locally. The Democrats, on the other hand, control the major machinery of government, and their task is to maintain and extend that control. Political party organizations are adaptable to these problems.

21. The Democratic National Committee in the Campaign of 1960

Daniel M. Ogden, Jr.

This very brief essay on the Democratic National Committee, written by a former member of the faculty at Washington State University, illustrates the varied approaches and the changing nature of the national committee and the national chairman in the preconvention, campaign, and transition phases of a presidential election year. The article outlines the shifting power base as political power changes hands, and the author demonstrates that the committee method is geared to the particular electoral status of "in" or "out" party—performing differently for an incumbent than for an aspirant President.

* * *

To the Democratic National Committee, the campaign of 1960 brought both victory and basic organizational changes. In the year from February 1960 to February 1961 three successive national chairmen provided three very different concepts of administrative leadership and of the proper role of the chairman. During the same period, the basic theory guiding committee activity was changed from the "party responsibility" concept of American parties to the "arena of compromise" theory. In adjusting to the campaign and readjusting to electoral vic-

From the *Western Political Quarterly*, vol. 14, supplement (September 1961), pp. 27–28, by permission of the University of Utah.

tory, the committee staff was twice reorganized and nearly completely replaced. Many of the early programs were abandoned or substantially altered.

THE PRE-CONVENTION COMMITTEE

The pre-convention National Committee was led by Paul M. Butler, a determined advocate of the "party responsibility" theory who believed that the national chairman should be his party's spokesman when it is out of executive office. But Butler also attempted to exercise personal, minute direction over every phase of National Committee activity. The staff accordingly was organized primarily to move the party toward "responsibility."

The designation of Henry M. Jackson as chairman at the close of the Democratic National Convention of 1960 meant the victory of Butler's opponents within the party. After he left office July 16, 1960, Mr. Butler was not consulted about the affairs of the National Committee. After the election, his works were swiftly undone.

THE COMMITTEE DURING THE CAMPAIGN

The Democratic presidential campaign of 1960 was an integrated organizational enterprise. But the agreement to use the National Committee as the integrative unit created a basic organizational problem. The well-established Kennedy family campaign organization had long before designated Robert Kennedy as campaign manager. It had no place for a national chairman who also exercised effective internal management controls. The upshot was that Robert Kennedy ran the national committee while Chairman Jackson went on tour to campaign for the ticket; the party theory issue was submerged in the task of winning the election; and the committee was reorganized to fit the campaign needs.

Campaign coordinators from the Kennedy pre-convention staff were appointed to oversee the key units of the Committee and to maintain informal personal liaison with each other as the need arose. Otherwise, formal organizational arrangements were kept at a minimum to avoid red tape and to encourage quick action.

The National Committee had not possessed the divisional units essential for a presidential campaign. Its Department of Organization was geared to training, not campaign management. It had no scheduling office, and no speech-writing department. Its research division was not equipped to do deep research for a presidential candidate. Consequently, the Kennedy staff itself took over the essential campaign functions and the pre-convention committee staff was merged with it where useful. New teams provided organizational leadership, scheduling, advertising materials, and contacts with organized special interests.

THE POST-ELECTION COMMITTEE

Between election day and the inauguration of President Kennedy, the National Committee faced four principal tasks: First, it had to screen prospective appointees for federal office. Second, it had to begin the task of paying off the $3,820,000 deficit. An inaugural-eve spectacular entertainment program, organized by Frank Sinatra, was the first principal effort. Third, it had to reduce its staff and readjust its services to support a president in office. Fourth, it had to assist the official Inaugural Committee in the organization, publicity, and staging of the ceremony and its accompanying events.

The Kennedy team turned its major attention to the first task, although the publicity division worked with the Inaugural Committee. Treasurer McCloskey turned the attention of his Finance Department to the second. The third goal was accomplished by releasing all the temporary personnel and firing most of the permanent staff of the National Committee. Only the pre-convention Kennedy team, which was scheduled to go into the Administration, and the Finance Department remained intact. Many of the discharged people were promptly employed by the Inaugural Committee and thereby furnished the needed coordination and liaison.

The staff changes did reduce payroll, eliminate the most controversial works of Paul Butler, and make clear the rejection of reforms derived from the "party responsibility" theory. But the changes appear to have been taken without an eye to the services the National Committee must render to state and local committees between elections and during a period in which the incumbent National Chairman had announced that he would resign at the next Committee meeting.

The National Committee meeting of January 21, therefore, appears not only to have selected James Bailey of Connecticut as the new national chairman, but also to have confirmed the repudiation of the "party responsibility" theory and of the works of Paul Butler. It further made clear that henceforth the President, not the national chairman, will be the party's spokesman. Upon the new chairman it also placed the responsibility of repaying the huge campaign deficit and the unfinished task of building sound party organization from the precinct level up. To this latter end, Mr. Bailey surely will find that he and other party leaders must re-think the decision to close the Department of Political Organization. The Department's carefully developed precinct workers' training programs, county leadership workshops, and regional leadership conferences offer a major opportunity for constructive service in the improvement of the Democratic party.

22.   Strategists for 1962 and 1964

David S. Broder

David Broder, a veteran Washington Star *correspondent, examines the power positions of the respective national committees and the effect of their electoral status upon their policies, personnel, and operations. Using the 1961 chairmen as examples, John Bailey of the Democratic National Committee and William E. Miller of the Republican National Committee, Broder describes the changes that occurred within both committees when the White House went to the Democrats in 1960 and the Republicans became a minority party in both the legislative and executive branches. This article demonstrates the flexibility of national party power and mode of operation.*

*   *   *

In this autumn of apprehension, one of the more curious and yet comforting sights in Washington is that of the chairmen of the Democratic and Republican national committees going about their customary business of plotting each other's ruin.

Others may fret away their time worrying about this week's challenge in the United Nations or next month's showdown in Berlin, but John M. Bailey, the Democratic chairman, and Representative William E. Miller, the Republican, daily affirm their faith in the future by devising stratagems for a national election that is still more than a year away.

To some, their activities may seem as irrelevant and irritating as the cries of a persistent peanut vendor during the ninth inning of the seventh game of the world series. A great many Americans are suspi-

From The New York *Times* Magazine (October 15, 1961), p. 26+. © 1961 by The New York Times Company. Reprinted by permission.

cious of full-time, year-round politicians, anyway, and when a genuine crisis threatens, they readily endorse suggestions that "politics" be suspended. Even those citizens wise enough to understand that you can hardly dispense with "politics" without surrendering democracy might have difficulty explaining what it is that keeps Chairmen Bailey and Miller hopping these days.

The jobs they hold are among the least understood in American politics—and for a very good reason. There simply is no handbook of the powers and duties of a national party chairman. At various times in recent years, the party chairmanship has been an empty title, or the focus of great intra-party power struggles, or the seat of unrivaled power and influence. The chairmanship is what each chairman is able to make it, as Bailey and Miller, both novices this year, are rapidly learning.

About the only thing any two party chairmen have in common is their responsibility to win the next election. Probably the best way to explain what is involved in that assignment is to spin a little myth:

Suppose you dream for a moment that you are asked one day to lead a band in a national music competition scheduled for next fall. You will have about 500 men playing for you in various places around the country and each of these principal performers will have supporting players under his own direction. You'll find out later who the performers are. You can tell them what music you would like to hear, but they will have the final say on what they play. There will be no rehearsals, but for about six weeks before the competition, they will all be playing full blast and you will do what you can to get them in tune. Then, on the appointed day, anyone who has heard them—and even those who haven't—can vote to decide which is the best band.

How does it strike you? Not exactly your cup of tea? Well, if you substitute Con-

gressional and gubernatorial candidates for the musicians in this script, and make Bailey and Miller the conductors of the rival bands, you have a fair notion of what their job entails. The way in which they are proceeding tells a lot not just about the talents of the two chairmen but about two opposing conceptions of what it takes to be a successful political manager these days.

John M. Bailey is the perfect embodiment of the "old-fashioned" or "backroom" approach to political management. He is a "boss"—but, unlike most past "bosses" of his party, he is in politics not for the money but for the fun. A Harvard graduate and an independently wealthy Hartford lawyer, Bailey, now 56, has made politics his seven-day-a-week hobby for the past thirty years. Unlike such other wealthy Connecticut Democrats as Chester Bowles and William Benton, Bailey's interest has always been in political machinations rather than the policy side of government.

Defeated in his only try for public office more than twenty years ago, he has since devoted himself to mastering the techniques of political management, an area in which he has become so proficient that Connecticut Democrats have acquiesced for fourteen years in his being the nominator of candidates, the distributor of patronage, the enforcer of discipline and the Democratic Governor's chief lobbyist.

The most powerful state chairman in his party and the senior in experience, Bailey is also one of the most popular professionals in the business. For all his mastery of the arts of political skulduggery, he has retained the amateur's wide-eyed enthusiasm for politics as a game. In his uninhibited private conversations, he dwells not on his past triumphs, which have been many, but on the delightful oddities of human behavior that have turned up in the stress of a long series of campaigns.

Bailey and his Connecticut sidekick, Abraham A. Ribicoff, were early and important Kennedy backers, and when the

President named Bailey as national chairman last January, there were many who expected him to play a role on the national scene comparable to that which he has played—and still plays—as Connecticut's party chairman. In fact, though the national title is bigger, his power in Washington is considerably less sweeping than it is in Hartford and falls substantially short of what such former national chairmen as Jim Farley and Paul Butler exercised.

This reflects no lack of capacity on Bailey's part, but rather a deliberate decision by Mr. Kennedy to limit his party chairman's role. The President definitely did not want anyone at Democratic headquarters making policy pronouncements, as Butler tried to do during the years his party was out of the White House.

Mr. Kennedy knew it would never occur to Bailey to state a viewpoint contrary to that of the White House, but just to make it absolutely plain that the party, as such, would have no further voice in policy-making, the Butler-created Democratic Advisory Council was abolished and the public affairs and research sections of the national committee, which had flourished under his chairmanship, were pared to the bone.

Similarly, the President felt no desire or obligation to give Bailey as free a rein in running party affairs as Farley had enjoyed under Roosevelt. Unlike Farley, who could fairly claim chief credit for F. D. R.'s nomination, Bailey was a subordinate to Robert Kennedy throughout the 1960 campaign. Even today, when a showdown comes on staffing the national committee, it is the Attorney General who has the final word.

Also unlike Farley, Bailey has been given neither a Cabinet post nor the final control of patronage. Following the custom of former President Eisenhower—a custom which many Republicans blame for the weakening of the G. O. P. during his incumbency— President Kennedy has kept his party chairman outside his official family.

Control of Federal patronage has been lodged not in the national committee but in the White House, where it has been used more often to grease the ways for the Kennedy legislative program than to reward, inspire or strengthen the Democratic party in the fifty states.

Some Democrats find in this pattern of events evidence for their belief that the Kennedys, from the very beginning, have been interested in the Democratic party only as a vehicle for their own ambitions. However, the official explanation, in which Bailey joins, is that the strategy for winning the 1962 and 1964 elections is simply to make the Kennedy Administration look as good as possible.

If the President is a success, if he keeps the peace and if he persuades Congress to redeem his campaign pledges, then the belief is that every Democratic candidate everywhere can ride to victory on his coattails.

In this scheme of things, the job of the national chairman and his staff is to keep the party organizations in the states happy and to service their needs. So far as Bailey is concerned, keeping them happy means spending hours each week listening to their patronage complaints and doing what he can at the White House to satisfy them.

The service function includes providing speakers for their fund-raising dinners, helping out on local campaigns when requested (as he and his aides are doing now in the New Jersey gubernatorial race) and keeping the precinct workers informed, through the weekly party newspaper and other publicity, of the achievements of the Kennedy Administration.

It is a job that Bailey appears to find congenial, even though it scarcely taxes his skills to the limit. When the President met his national chairman at a party recently, he asked him, "John, what have you been doing with yourself?"

"I've been keeping out of trouble," Bailey replied. "You haven't had to repudiate a thing I've said."

Keeping out of trouble is definitely not one of Republican Chairman William E. Miller's assignments. His chief task, an inescapable one for the leader of the "outs," is to make the opposition arguments heard against what has been called "the giant loudspeaker" of the Presidency.

To win an audience for his party's viewpoint, the opposition chairman first must attract attention to himself, and there is no surer way of doing this than to make himself a controversial figure. Miller was chosen by the Republicans last June precisely because of his talent for controversy.

In picking him, the members of the Republican National Committee and the party's most powerful leaders—Eisenhower, Nixon, Rockefeller and Goldwater—made a deliberate choice of an exponent of the "modern" or "public relations" approach to political management over a "traditional" or "back-room" operator.

The man they turned down for Miller was Ohio state chairman Ray C. Bliss, who has often and accurately been called the John Bailey of the Republican party. Like Bailey, Bliss is a shrewd and successful manipulator who is as ill at ease on the public platform as he is at home in a closed-door caucus.

Miller, by contrast, has limited experience in running a headquarters but abundant ability to hold his own in any public forum. A crack debater at Notre Dame, he has been in sequence, a prosecutor at the Nuremberg trials, a district attorney in his native Niagara County, N.Y., and a successful six-time candidate for the House. (His district was carried handily by Mr. Kennedy last November.)

A conservative in domestic affairs and an internationalist, Miller was part of the group of young Republicans who overthrew Joe Martin in 1959 and made Charles Halleck the Republican leader of the House. Halleck, in turn, made the tough, intense, 47-year-old New Yorker chairman of the Republican Congressional Campaign Committee in 1960 and backed him strongly for the party chairmanship this year.

In the relatively few months he has been in office, three things have become plain about Miller's effort to sell Republicanism to the country.

First, he conceives of the "sales campaign" in much broader terms than have most previous practitioners of political public relations. It will include plenty of direct political propaganda—a field in which the G. O. P. already outproduces the Democrats—and plenty of public speaking by the chairman. But it will also embrace intensive efforts to recruit brighter and more articulate candidates (five teams of Republican Congressmen are roaming the country this fall, looking for likely prospects), the hiring of special operatives to promote Republican programs among Negroes, union men, farmers, nationality groups and other "special constituencies," and field work to build organization strength in problem areas like the big cities.

Second, the Miller-directed sales program will be much more frankly partisan than anything the Republicans have seen in recent years. The three national chairmen who served Mr. Eisenhower played down party loyalty and appealed to "discerning Democrats" to put aside their normal allegiance and vote for the General. By contrast, Miller is, as Bailey described him in a recent speech, "a bare-knuckle, slam-bang partisan."

It was Miller, a Catholic himself, who accused the Kennedy forces of using "bigotry in reverse" to win Catholic votes in the last campaign and it was Miller who suggested last June that Mr. Kennedy might be meeting Khrushchev in Vienna "to negotiate some under-the-table deal in order to increase his prestige." Despite the President's current high standing in the polls, the Republican chairman is convinced that the G. O. P. can cut the New Frontier down to size if only it attacks frequently and vigorously enough.

He is also convinced—and this is the third salient characteristic of his sales program—that Republicans must emphasize their diversity and breadth of appeal, rather than strive for doctrinal purity. This is the key to Miller's whole approach to the 1962 campaign and it is this element in his thinking that his critics have found most difficult to grasp.

While others may see an irreconcilable conflict in the diverse views of Nixon, Goldwater and Rockefeller, Miller delights in the fact that he can use all three of them in the fight to regain control of the House next year. Some have called him "another Paul Butler," but in fact he believes that "no national chairman can claim a mandate to determine the position of his party on any issue" and he has rejected all proposals to create a Republican equivalent of Butler's Democratic Advisory Council.

What Miller is anxious to do is "use the agency of the national committee to broaden the base of party leadership and keep it from being a closed shop." He has pressured insistently but so far unsuccessfully for inclusion of other Congressmen on "Ev and Charlie's" weekly televised press conference not because he has any dissatisfaction with the leadership abilities of Dirksen and Halleck but because he wants the country reminded there are other Republicans around, as well.

He hopes soon to set up a meeting of Republican governors under his aegis, not because he is anxious to promote another round in the traditional battle between the state houses and the Congress for control of party affairs but because he regards the governors as unexploited Republican resources.

Miller's advice to the state and local organizations for the 1962 campaign is to "nominate the best man for your district,

the one whose ideas have the most appeal for your voters." When he is criticized for inconsistency in campaigning for an ultra-conservative, state-rights Republican in the South and a liberal, internationally minded Republican in the North, his reply is characteristically blunt:

> As long as the Democrats control Congress by electing a Jim Eastland in Mississippi and an Adam Powell in New York and win a national election with a ticket like Kennedy and Johnson, I'm damned if I see why I should apologize for the differences within the Republican party.

So far this year, Miller and the Republicans appear to have had the better of the political infighting. Miller's quick steps to overhaul the national committee staff and his strong partisan rhetoric have visibly stiffened the backbones of the Republican regulars. His insistence that Republican candidates should speak in the ideological accents of their states and districts, rather than echoing some prescribed party philosophy, strikes most observers as a sensible strategy for a Congressional election, even though some of them are skeptical of the value of his across-the-board condemnation of the Kennedy Administration.

Bailey, on the other hand, has had some difficulty regearing his headquarters for the task the President assigned him. He has been frustrated by local feuds and local bosses in seeking some of his objectives and has been only partially successful in keeping patronage fights from dissipating the organization strength he himself helped develop in 1960. He has not yet established firm liaison with the issue-oriented and volunteer-manned parties of the Midwest and West, whose style of politics is alien to him. There are many who doubt that Mr. Kennedy's personal popularity will be as big a force in 1962's state and Congressional races as Bailey thinks, though it is obviously a Democratic asset.

In their only head-to-head battle, on a national television show, Miller routed Bailey, but this was a battlefield that was bound to show off Miller's strength as a stand-up debater and conceal Bailey's essential skill as a political operator. Republicans were elated at the result and Bailey was disgusted.

"Those guys," he said, referring to the television interviewers, "asked me about Cuba. What the hell do I know about Cuba? As far as I'm concerned, their asking me about Cuba is about as sensible as their getting Dean Rusk up there and asking him about Congressman Breeding's chances of beating the Republican gerrymander in Kansas. I'll go on their shows if they want to talk about politics, but I'm no damned foreign-policy expert."

Bailey figures, and many observers agree, that the Democrats will begin to score more heavily as next year's election approaches. Miller and other Republicans from General Eisenhower on down are already engaged in an all-out assault on the Democratic position, while Bailey has most of his strength in reserve.

Still untapped are the President's personal campaigning ability, the power of Congress and the Executive branch to deliver politically vital programs and projects to specific states and districts and the precinct strength that accrues to the Democrats from their alliance with labor and their control of two-thirds of the units of state and local government.

The real tests for both chairmen lie ahead. Next fall, the rival bands will sound off, and on election day, either Bailey or Miller will be hailed as the Toscanini of his trade, while the other side goes out to look for a new conductor.

23. The Republican Party in Illinois

Clayton D. Ford

Clayton Ford, Director of the School of Government at Principia College, has written about the organization of the Republican party in a state that has both strong rural and urban influences. The informal structure and leadership is also taken into consideration.

* * *

Political parties in Illinois are minutely regulated by the state statutes. The structure of the parties is set forth in detail, and their test of membership, methods of nominating and electing candidates to public office, and convention machinery are specified in the laws. This statutory prescription provides the framework in which the formal and informal aspects of party action take place.

Membership in the Illinois Republican party is loosely defined, individually declared by requesting a Republican primary ballot. No test of party membership other than this is required. Membership can be ascertained only if one has access to the permanent registration forms deposited in the office of the county clerk or election board. Although the statute prohibits a person from changing his party affiliation for a 23-month period, he might never again support the party after a primary declaration.

HOW PARTY OFFICERS ARE CHOSEN

The "grass roots" officer of the party is the precinct committeeman in all parts of the state except Cook County. There the

From Lois M. Pelekoudas, ed., *Illinois Political Parties* (final papers of the Assembly on Illinois Political Parties, 1960), pp. 65–70, with footnotes deleted, by permission of the author and the Institute of Government and Public Affairs of the University of Illinois.

ward committeeman in the City of Chicago and the township committeeman in the remainder of the county serve as the party base. Committeemen are elected at the primary election, those from the downstate precincts for a two-year term, and those from Cook County for a four-year term. Thus, at the party primary the Republican voter elects the party worker.

These committeemen form the hard core of party organization, for it is upon them that the success or failure of the party's effort depends. Mitigating against the urgency of strong party allegiance or discipline is the choosing of committeemen by election. Anyone presenting a petition signed by ten Republican voters in his precinct may have his name placed upon the ballot. If he is elected, he may or may not serve the party well. There is no way to remove him until the next primary. Republican committeemen are not under pressure to produce results to the same degree as are those of the Democratic party, and have in numerous instances been less vigorous or less bound to party discipline.

A somewhat different situation prevails in Cook County, for in Chicago precinct captains and workers in each ward are appointed by the ward committeeman, and precinct captains in the township organizations in the rest of the county are appointed by the township committeemen. The appointed workers have a greater stake in the party organization and tend to work harder than those elected in the downstate areas. The organization in Cook County and Chicago tends toward more cohesiveness in the prosaic duties of precinct work than is evident downstate.

The statutes further provide for the election of other party officials, all of whom are less important, in the estimation of the author, than are the precinct, ward, or township committeemen.

Representative district committeemen are elected for a two-year term from all the representative districts except those in Cook County. Where the district is composed of three or more counties or parts of counties, a committeeman is elected from each county or part of a county; if the district is made up of two counties or parts of counties, three are elected for the district, two from the county or part of a county polling the largest number of votes in the primary. The former is illustrated by the 52nd district, which is composed of five counties, Jersey, Macoupin, Montgomery, Christian, and Shelby; the latter by the 39th district, Rock Island and Mercer counties. If the district comprises only one county, like the 36th district, Du Page County, three members elected from the district form the representative district committee. In Cook County, again the exception, township and ward committeemen in each representative district function as district committeemen. State central committeemen are elected for a four-year term at the primary, one from each congressional district, or 25 in all.

Although a representative committeeman or a state central committeeman is elected from a relatively large electoral area, his importance as a party worker is limited. Most are unknown to the rank and file of the party, and they perform their functions unheralded. Here again it may be emphasized that the precinct, ward, or township committeeman mans the most active party groups.

ORGANIZATION AND FUNCTIONS OF PARTY COMMITTEES

The party officials elected in the primary are formed into a series of committees. The township committee, which consists of all the precinct committeemen in the township, functions only to determine the time and place for holding the biennial caucus for the nomination of candidates for office in those townships that do not use petitions or primaries for nominations. Many townships include only a single precinct, in which case the committeeman alone performs this function.

The municipal committee, composed of the precinct committeemen in downstate municipalities or the ward or township committeemen in Chicago and Cook County, performs a vital job for the party if the municipal elections are partisan. The municipal committee may become an important factor in the party's activity in the state, and may even challenge the position of a county committee.

This latter group, the county central committee, is generally the most active functioning organization of the party, exercising vigorous control over party activities in the county. The success of Republican fortunes in a county may be determined by the effectiveness of the work of the committeemen and the leadership of the county chairman, who is the strongest individual in the party system. In fact, a county chairman who has the support of his committee, especially in a populous county, can determine the fortunes of nominees, local and state. The bailiwick of the county chairman is limited by the county boundaries, but in a populous county his control goes beyond the county, and in many instances his influence extends further than that of the chairman of the state central committee.

The number of functions performed by the county chairman adds to his political status. In a congressional district comprising more than one county, the county chairmen and the state central committeeman, who serves as chairman, make up the congressional committee. The importance this committee may have was shown in the election of 1958, when the Republican candidate for Congress in the 20th district died ten days before the election. The county chairmen met and put forth another candidate. In addition, county chairmen serve on the state senatorial district committees, which have the power to nominate a candidate in case of a vacancy. The powers accruing to the county chairman from his posi-

tion on these committees, plus the fact that the Republican state central committee and its chairman have little effect in the counties, congressional districts, or senatorial districts, give him added influence. The existence and influence of the Republican County Chairmen's Association, a group not authorized by statute, also attests to the importance of these officials. Where county chairmen in small counties cooperate, they present a very strong force in party affairs, and in some instances may counter the influence of county chairmen for more populous counties, particularly since the chairmen of large, urbanized counties, such as Cook, St. Clair, Madison, and Peoria, are not noted for cooperation. It is a generally accepted idea that the Republican county chairman is a more powerful and important cog in the party machinery than is his Democratic counterpart.

The other local party organization is composed of all representative committeemen in each district. The representative committee decides 70 days prior to the April primary the number of candidates that the Republicans will nominate in the district for the state House of Representatives. Each party may nominate three under the cumulative voting procedures, but few districts do. The usual number is two, and sometimes only one is nominated.

In light of the actual influence of the county chairmen, as noted above, the comment that the state central committee "has precedence over all other committees" is somewhat misleading. This committee, made up of the 25 state central committeemen, has formal supervision over affairs relating to statewide nominations and elections of party candidates. This function is, of course, highly significant, but often the county chairmen, especially when they cooperate, assume more authority over state elections than do the state central committee and its chairman. Evidence of the weakness of the state central committee is a bill

(S.B. 887), apparently stemming from the Republican County Chairmen's Association, proposed in the 1957 General Assembly to abolish the office of state central committeeman, and provide instead a committee formed of county chairmen and, for Cook County, ward and township committeemen. The bill was not passed, but did get through a second reading in the Senate before it was stricken.

In short, the Republican state central committee, because of its formal power, has the potential for control over the party in Illinois, yet it has not used it. Its Democratic counterpart serves its party much more effectively in producing a cohesive, smoothly running machine.

PARTY CONVENTIONS:
LOCAL, STATE, AND NATIONAL

Since the primary is the major device for selecting nominees for public office in Illinois, the county and state conventions are unimportant and ineffective. However, they are still used. In the county conventions, each precinct committeeman possesses one vote for each Republican ballot cast in his precinct at the preceding primary, which he, in turn, casts for the officers of the county central committee and for delegates to the state convention. In many of the smaller county committees, the process of electing delegates to the state convention resolves itself into finding those that want to go, and it is usually fairly difficult to find enough to fill the allotment of one delegate per 500 votes or fraction thereof cast for the Republican party at the primary. In Chicago and Cook County the convention to elect delegates is a ward or township one.

The state convention has few functions to perform: making a state platform, which very few of the party workers ever see; nominating candidates for electors in the presidential and vice-presidential electoral college elections; nominating candidates for trustees of the University of Illinois; and selecting delegates-at-large and alternates for the national convention. Usually, these functions are perfunctory, and the leadership of the Governor, if he is a Republican, is in evidence.

Candidates for the Supreme Court districts and the judicial circuits are nominated in conventions, and here the basic operations toward the selection of candidates are sparked by the county chairmen. Their position is paramount and their influence vital. Qualifications of candidates mean little, but the posturing of the chairmen means a lot.

The state Republican party is a part of the national party, and chooses one woman and one man to be elected to the Republican national committee at each national convention. When Illinois has elected a Republican Governor or when its last electoral vote was Republican, the chairman of the state central committee also becomes a member of the national committee. The selection of the national committeeman and woman is left to the state's delegation to the national convention. Very often the delegation is controlled by the Governor, and therefore the members selected for the national committee represent his influence. Or, if one of Illinois' United States Senators is a Republican, he may be an influence. Often the national committeeman and woman are not outstanding leaders in the party, but instead represent blocs within the party then in control. Where a powerful national committeeman is found, his influence more often than not is exerted in the background. To a large degree the importance of any state's representation on the national committee is in proportion to its electoral vote. Since Illinois possesses one of the larger electoral votes, it has influence, provided it has leadership to equal it.

For the 1956 Republican national convention, two delegates and two alternates were elected from each congressional district in Illinois. Candidates for delegate may support a known presidential candidate, or keep very quiet about their preferences. Individuals running for delegate may or may not be well known. Unless alerted by the county chairman, many precinct committeemen know little about the candidates for delegate. In some cases, even the county chairmen do not know them. The delegates-at-large and their alternates are most carefully selected in convention, and the cohesiveness of the whole delegation stems from the leadership of the Governor or Senator.

ACTUAL LEADERSHIP
IN THE REPUBLICAN PARTY

During the past few years the leadership exerted by the state central committee has been rather weak. The committee is often unknown to the precinct committeemen, and does not inspire the party organization with leadership that would produce vital action or develop strong party harmony.

The resulting diffusion of authority has forced leadership of the party into the hands of strong state candidates or officials. The Governor, a Republican, exercises stronger leadership than any party official. Although his leadership is sometimes challenged, in general it may be assumed that a candidate for state office, as well as candidates for Congress and for the United States Senate, is only infrequently nominated without either his nod or his tacit approval. When the Republicans are not in power, the candidate for the gubernatorial nomination may have enough personal appeal to dictate certain approval of other nominees.

To get authority over the party, the office-holder uses many devices to build prestige, such as putting county chairmen on the state payroll for giving key workers prestige jobs in repayment for work done. It has been reported that over half of the Republican county chairmen have state jobs. This condition is not found to the same extent in the Democratic party, where the leadership of the state central committee chairman is more effective. Strong leadership among Democratic legislators is also effective. Leadership from these two sources supplements and sometimes replaces the leadership of a Democratic Governor.

The Republican party in Illinois is not a strong, solid organization. Rather than having a well-developed party with responsibility located in a strong hierarchy, the Republicans have carved out enclaves of independent power that in many instances show internal conflict instead of cooperation. Within a county, strife for party control often takes precedence over the general party good. Where no single party leader is strong enough to crack down on dissident groups, chaos is common, even though it means the election of Democratic officials. No strong state leader has emerged to provide inspiring leadership. The Governor approximates it, but the structural weaknesses of the party prevent him from exercising strong leadership. In spite of this, the Republicans have been able to control vital state offices.

24.   The Democratic Party
in Illinois

Thomas W. Tearney

This article, in conjunction with the foregoing selection by Clayton Ford, emphasizes the difficulties confronting the two major party organizations in a state in which rural and urban influences are strong. Neither party has perfected an organization capable of mastering both aspects of American political life.

From Lois M. Pelekoudas, ed., *Illinois Political Parties* (final papers of the Assembly on Illinois Political Parties, 1960), pp. 71–73, with footnotes deleted, by permission of the Institute of Government and Public Affairs of the University of Illinois.

The formal structure of the Democratic party in the State of Illinois is an intricate network of committees, conventions, and officers, for the most part defined by statute. Party organization is closely tied to certain levels of election organization. The various committees, conventions, and officers do not, in theory, law, or fact, form a neat, pyramidal, hierarchical pattern, with lines of responsibility and authority clearly established. The most concrete example of this is that the members of the state central committee are elected directly by the primary voters in congressional districts, but each congressional district has its own so-called congressional committee, made up of all the chairmen of all the county central committees within its boundaries. Each county central committee, in turn, consists of all the ward, township, and precinct committeemen in the county, and elects its own chairman.

In other words, the pattern appears fairly neat and hierarchical up to the top of the pyramid—the state central committee. This committee in no sense emerges from the committees further down, and, indeed, it results from an entirely different process of selection. None of the committees has any legal power, control, or influence over any of the other entities, except in the sense that what one committee may decide influences the actions of another committee.

INFORMAL STRUCTURE AND LEADERSHIP

These brief comments only highlight that structure of the Democratic party wherein the leaders of the party must function. However, any discussion of the structure would not be complete without a few explanatory inquiries which convert this legal, impersonal structure into a living political party.

Democratic voting strength in Illinois is concentrated mainly in a few urban centers, and, although the party is definitely competitive on a statewide basis, only infrequently has a Democratic state administration actually been elected. Consequently, there is not now, and usually has not been, an elected state official who can exert leadership over the state Democratic party like the present Republican Governor does over his party. Statewide leadership thus falls to the appropriate party officials—i.e., the state central committee—much more than it does in the Republican party.

However, real leadership in the party tends to gravitate toward the leaders of the strong Democratic urban organizations, particularly to the leader of the Chicago organization. Thus, at the present time, the mayor of Chicago is generally recognized as the *de facto* leader of the Illinois Democratic party, with his leadership resting quite frankly on the number of votes the Chicago organization can amass in the general election and, especially, in the primary. It is even doubtful whether a Democratic Governor could seriously challenge the leader of the Chicago organization for leadership of the party, since in any primary contest—and nominations for all key offices are decided in the primary—the person who controls most of the votes will have the most to say about candidates. In fact, there has been a tendency to have very little competition in the Democratic primary; slate-making of nominees is done by the party leadership before the primary, and most potential candidates seem to feel that unless they get the nod from the organization, it is useless to run in the primary.

The leadership of the Chicago mayor is occasionally challenged by downstate leaders and even by dissatisfied Cook County Democrats. Two recent developments among Illinois Democrats—the formation of the Democratic Federation of Illinois and the establishment of a Democratic County Chairmen's Association— might be interpreted as, in the first case, a protest against "machine domination" of the party, and in the second, a move to strengthen and coordinate downstate county chairmen to balance the power of the Chicago organization. There is no evidence, however, that the Democratic County Chairmen's Association is, or will soon become, nearly as important as its Republican counterpart.

Most of the problems within the Illinois Democratic party arise from its bifurcation. Although some of the county Democratic organizations operate in highly competitive districts, the usual pattern has been for the Chicago and East St. Louis organizations to be almost always successful, and for most of the downstate organizations to be almost always unsuccessful. The weaker downstate organizations can get no patronage unless a Democratic Governor is elected, and in many cases their only function, besides the sending of a representative to the Illinois General Assembly, is to cut down the opposition majority so that state Democratic candidates will have a better chance. On the other hand, the strong urban organizations operate with a great deal of patronage at their disposal, and can maintain their strength without having a Democratic administration in Springfield. On a statewide basis, it is the piling up of large majorities by these strong organizations that permits state candidates to be elected.

This extreme difference in situation and consequently in function causes misunderstandings between leaders from the majority and minority areas, and has brought about an informal understanding, usually adhered to, that nominees for state offices will be split evenly between Chicago and downstate. This kind of situation, of course, also exists within the Republican party, which is strong in less populated counties but weak in major urban areas.

The major problem, then, is: how can leadership be satisfactorily provided in the Democratic party on a statewide basis? Whether any state leadership can be pro-vided, of course, depends largely upon the attitude of the strong urban organizations toward the rest of the state, and up to now no concentrated attempts to build up weak organizations and broaden the base, area-wise, of Democratic leadership has become evident.

25.   Patronage in New York State 1955–1959

Daniel P. Moynihan and James Q. Wilson

The following selection studies the deliberate use of patronage by former Governor Averell Harriman of New York in order to obtain and maintain control of the Democratic party. Daniel Moynihan is a former Assistant Secretary of Labor, and James Wilson is Professor of Government, Harvard University.

* * *

When Averell Harriman became Governor of New York on January 1, 1955, the Democrats assumed power in Albany for the first time in twelve years. With Harriman came his newly appointed Secretary of State, Carmine G. De Sapio, leader of Tammany Hall, Democratic National Committeeman, and widely described as the architect of the Democratic resurgence. Harriman, however, had only barely won the election, and such unity as the party had achieved during the campaign was evanescent at best. The Democratic Party was very much alive, but its energies were woefully centripetal. The cleavages ranged from the most primitive thrusts of tribal warfare between Italians and Irish to the

From the *American Political Science Review*, vol. 58, no. 2 (June 1964), pp. 286–301, with foot-notes deleted.

most elegant ideological concerns of middle- and upper-class liberal Protestants and Jews. The election had deepened some conflicts, raised others, and settled none. The ancient Irish hegemony was giving way before pressure from Italians within the regular party organization and reform liberals as yet outside it. The very ticket on which Harriman ran was symptomatic of the times—for the first time in decades it had no Irish Catholic running for a major executive office and, at the same time, a magic name in New York politics—Roosevelt—had been relegated to a subordinate place on the list after a bitter, clamorous effort by young liberals (who later were to be the backbone of a major reform assault on Tammany) to win the gubernatorial nomination for the son of the former President.

Under any circumstances, the allocation of jobs by a new state administration is a matter of keen interest to party members; under these circumstances, however, patronage was of crucial importance. Not, of course, because Democratic voters or rank-and-file party workers were standing hungrily in line. In New York, as elsewhere, low-paying state jobs were no longer attractive to most voters or to many party workers; in any case, not very many such jobs were available at the state level. Rather, patronage was important because those selected for the top offices would set the tone for the entire administration and thus significantly affect its chances for success in both its legislative program and its bid for re-election, and because the awarding of jobs could possibly alter the distribution of power within the party, rewarding some party leaders favored by the administration and penalizing others.

From the outset, then, at least two goals were to be served by the allocation of jobs —staffing the government with competent and attractive administrators, and acquiring and consolidating power over the party apparatus. These goals were obviously not always compatible, particularly when there

was a chronic shortage of men whose qualifications would make their appointment contribute to the attainment of the first of these ends.

In a sense, the first goal could be looked upon as voter-serving and the second as party-serving. In those bygone days in which the mass of voters, at least in the big cities, had a personalistic and localistic view of politics, there may have been little conflict between these two goals. If the immigrant voter judged the party as a whole largely in terms of a local party leader who offered him friendship, service and favors in exchange for his vote, then more patronage for the party leader meant more opportunities for "buying" (with either tangible or intangible gratifications) the loyalty of the voter. Assuming that the local leader was rational and that he was usually threatened by intra-party competition, the greater his success in extracting influence and patronage from the party, the greater the largesse he could and would distribute to his constituents. As voters abandoned the immigrant political ethic, they began to judge the party in terms of issues, community-wide or state-wide programs, and the quality, (honesty, efficiency, "glamour" and impartiality) of its elective officials. The allocation of jobs that was voter-serving (*e.g.*, appointing "blue-ribbon" officials and "expert" administrators) was often an allocation which was no longer party-serving as well. A job given to a blue-ribbon bureaucrat would often (though not always) be a job taken away from a county or district leader.

This study is an analysis of the efforts of one administration to discover and apply guidelines for patronage decisions which would optimize the attainment of two potentially conflicting goals. It can be argued that stating the problem in this way exaggerates the element of rationality in the process. In part this is deliberate: for purposes of analysis, we postulate two goals and seek to discover to what extent action was "rationally" directed at their attainment. If we can account for all the acts of the patronage-dispensers on the (perhaps false) assumption that they acted "as if" they intended to maximize certain goals, then no other "explanation" of their behavior is (we argue) necessary. But in part there are good grounds for asserting that to some extent a quest for rationality was *in fact* a motive for much that was done. From the personal involvement of one of the authors in the patronage process, we are left with little doubt that the principal participants deliberately sought to use patronage both to staff the government competently and to acquire and maintain control over the state party. Their efforts in this direction were perhaps even more deliberate than one might ordinarily expect because at least one key participant had a quasi-intellectual approach to the problem: by habit and style, he sought to systematize the process and to make it bureaucratically rational (*i.e.*, to settle specific cases by reference to general rules). This, of course, makes the New York case somewhat atypical. Furthermore, maintenance of the party organization in the face of competing claims for very scarce resources led the job dispensers to formulate general rules and to keep detailed records in order to defend their actions. Rationality (or what could plausibly be described as such) was not only intrinsically important (the dispensers wanted to maximize certain goals), it came to be extrinsically important as well (the dispensers wanted to be able to settle arguments and justify their discretionary acts by "objective," superficially non-arbitrary decision rules).

This study does not deal with all forms of patronage. Judicial patronage—particularly the selection of judges—was of great interest to the party; however, it was not handled by Governor Harriman's patronage aide, but by his Counsel. The patronage of the Attorney-General's office was no doubt substantial, but we have no direct

knowledge of it. Finally, the awarding of contracts—particularly highway contracts —was potentially of enormous importance, but however political considerations may have influenced it, no records were kept.

I. THE ORGANIZATION OF PATRONAGE

The allocation of patronage was a joint effort of public and party officials, among whom the governor was preeminent. He almost always had the formal authority to appoint (or, where legislative confirmation was required, to nominate) and thus his agreement was essential. Governor Harriman did not, at least in the area of job patronage, abdicate his authority and thus he was something more than a "titular" head (although something less than an undisputed head) of the state Democratic party.

As liaison with the party organization, the governor assigned a lawyer, Milton D. Stewart, who was on the payroll of the office of the Governor's Counsel. He was a clearance point for administration officials dealing with the party and party leaders dealing with the administration. Although he had other duties as well, allocating patronage became his chief responsibility. As he told an interviewer,

> it is hard to believe how much *time* goes to patronage—more time on that than on any other single thing. And that was about as true for the governor as it was for me. It is simply nondelegable—for constitutional, legal, or political reasons.

The process of awarding a job began either with a candidate or a vacancy. It did not begin *de novo,* however, but rather on the basis of some hastily learned behavior. To a great extent the uncertainty which afflicts a new administration in handling patronage (or any other important matter) is reduced by trying to learn how the previous administration did it—in this case, the Republican administration of Governor Thomas E. Dewey. Harriman's staff thus inherited, willy-nilly, many of the procedures for handling patronage left to them by the Republicans. By and large, they found these procedures reasonable.

If the process began with a vacancy, the commissioner (*i.e.*, the cabinet-level department head) would first discuss the matter with Stewart. If the commissioner had some one in mind for the vacancy, if he were strong-willed and persuasive, and if he had a plausible candidate, he would often get his way, even against party pressures. Stewart was the "litmus paper": if the commissioner's arguments could stand up against Stewart's pressure on behalf of party regularity and the party nominee, the commissioner would usually prevail.

If the commissioner had no candidate, or had a poor one, or if the party was advancing a candidate for whom a place had to be found, Stewart would consult the party leaders. Each of New York's sixty-two counties had a county Democratic leader; to deal with all of them individually would have been difficult. More importantly, it would have been destructive of certain principles of hierarchy deeply cherished by party officials. Two key party leaders were selected for the handling of all patronage matters. For the five counties comprising New York City, Carmine De Sapio was the channel; for most of the fifty-seven counties outside New York City, State Chairman Michael Prendergast was the channel. This arrangement was modified by the right of each county leader to appeal a patronage decision directly to the governor and by the fact that the most powerful upstate leaders bypassed Prendergast and went to the Governor's office directly. Another modification was even more important: Prendergast was selected for the post of State Chairman by Harriman. He had little authority beyond what the other would grant him and thus was the junior partner within the party leadership. Stewart, on behalf of the governor, negotiated appointments

with De Sapio and Prendergast who in turn negotiated with the county leaders—and often with many other sources of nominees.

De Sapio's special role in the process was only partly due to the fact that he was Democratic National Committeeman (after all, the governor—with some effort—could probably have replaced him in that job if he had wanted to); more important, it was the result of the fact that Harriman owed him his nomination, respected his judgment, and acknowledged the fact that among New York City Democratic leaders he was *primus inter pares*.

To get a job in the Harriman administration a man or woman had first of all to be capable of performing it. In the higher posts the standards of performance attained were considerable, an achievement made possible in part by the supply of political executives who had served in Washington under Presidents Roosevelt and Truman. A sustained effort was made, however, to extend these standards throughout the government. Thus letters regularly went out to Democratic county chairmen stating, *e.g.*, that such and such a member of the Board of Visitors of a local state hospital had been recorded absent in a number of recent meetings of the Board, and that this was not the understanding on which the appointment, albeit honorary and unpaid, had been made. Similarly it was made explicit with many who might think otherwise that a full forty-hour week was expected of all appointees. Unless he were a lawyer, the appointee had to give up outside jobs and—in cases of doubtful merit —he had to submit in advance a signed but undated letter of resignation.

There was no strong tradition of corruption in New York State government, but it did exist. In general, the Harriman administration knew enough about the political process to know where the greatest dangers of corruption were to be encountered and what could best be done to prevent it. As an example, the State Liquor Authority was given particular attention. It had been corrupt under the preceding Republican administration and became corrupt again under the succeeding Republican administration. With great care Harriman chose as Chairman of the Authority, not a "good government" type, but a Tammany judge who combined the highest ethical standards with a native understanding of the occasions of sin. Whatever the reason (and good luck was surely an important factor) the administration survived four years without scandal in the upper reaches of the S.L.A. —or elsewhere.

II. PATRONAGE AND SPONSORSHIP

Every patronage appointee has a "sponsor" who makes or approves the applicant's claim on the job and to whose account the job is "charged." Generally speaking, the Harriman administration made a determined effort to make the Democratic party the chief sponsor for patronage. There was little "anti-patronage" feeling evident among his aides; even among the young liberals, a strong sense of loyalty to the party prevailed.

By and large, the Democrats fared well. Table I shows the distribution of jobs by primary sponsor. In some cases an applicant had more than one chief sponsor (for

TABLE I Patronage Appointments in New York State, 1955–1959, by Sponsor

Sponsor	Appointment	
	Number	Percent
Democratic Party		
nominated	1,190	61.8
cleared	214	12.1
TOTAL PARTY	1,304	73.9
Personal, nonparty	281	15.9
Republican Party	81	4.6
Labor unions	55	3.1
Liberal Party	28	1.6
Other, miscellaneous	16	0.9
TOTAL	1,765	100.0

example, both the Democratic State Committee and the A.F. of L.) but in general the records of Harriman's patronage office list only one primary sponsor for each job dispensed. The table shows, not surprisingly, that the Democratic Party received the bulk of the jobs—nearly three-fourths of the total of 1,765. Personal, non-party appointments were the second largest group, amounting to nearly one-sixth of the total. All other sources accounted for scarcely more than one-tenth of all jobs. Among these other sources, however, there were some interesting relationships. Republicans accounted for more jobs than either organized labor or the Liberal Party, despite the fact that the latter two groups were, in general, strong supporters of Democratic party nominees (Governor Harriman polled 264,093 votes on the Liberal line). Liberal party jobholders were outnumbered by Republicans by almost three-to-one and by labor union jobholders by almost two-to-one.

The dominance of the Democratic party in the patronage process is exaggerated by these figures, however. In many cases, party clearance by the local county leader was purely *pro forma*. Many appointees—often ex-federal administrators available as a result of the Eisenhower victory of 1952— were asked to obtain the approval of their Democratic county leader even though they had never before met him, had not lived in their home county for several years, and had done little or nothing for the party in their county. This *"post facto* clearance" was usually granted—if for no other reason than that the local leader had nobody else to recommend for the job who would meet the qualifications laid down by the administration in Albany—because he liked the idea of being "consulted" about seemingly important matters, and because he feared appearing powerless if the job went anyway to the man he refused to clear. The prospective appointee would, in the typical case, have to be an outspoken critic of the local leader in order to fail of clearance except in those cases where the leader had his own favorite whose candidacy he was actively pressing.

About one-sixth of all Democratic party jobs (214 out of the 1,304) were of this character. As Table I indicates, "party cleared" (as opposed to "party nominated") candidates accounted for about one-eighth (12.1 per cent) of all state jobs under Harriman. This means that appointees who were actually the *nominees* of Democratic party leaders were about three-fifths (61.8 per cent) of the total. The rather empty formality which often characterized "party clearances" was not without its consequences, however. Not only did it make it easier for Harriman's patronage office to "recognize" many county leaders who otherwise would have felt left out of the new administration, but it frequently placed young jobholders in contact with their local party leaders for the first time. A certain premium often attached to an appointee's ability to speak with an air of political sophistication of "my leader"; many young

and able workers were first recruited into the party organization by this otherwise token clearance.

A further qualification is introduced into this picture of Democratic party strength when the dollar value of the jobs distributed among the various primary sponsors is indicated (see Table II). Although the Democratic party nominated or cleared between half and three-fourths of the appointees in each job category, the 1,304 jobs it was given were concentrated in the lower-paying and minor honorific categories. Nearly half of all party jobs either paid less than $5,000 each per year or were lesser honorary appointments which paid nothing. By contrast, Liberal party jobs were concentrated in the higher pay brackets. Nearly one-third of its total paid more than $12,000 a year and two-fifths paid over $9,000 a year; none of its jobs were in the lowest pay category and, of its honorific appointments, over twice as many were major as were minor. The distribution of jobs given to organized labor was similar to that of the Democratic party, the heaviest

TABLE II   Patronage Appointments in New York State, 1955–1959, by Sponsors and Job Value

Sponsor	Salaried Posts				Honorific Posts		
	Agency Head, Department Head, Board Member (over $12,000)	$9,000 to $12,000 per Year	$5,000 to $9,000 per Year	Under $5,000 per Year	Major	Minor	Total
	%	%	%	%	%	%	
Democratic Party (nominated and cleared)	12.1	5.9	19.6	12.7	14.1	35.5	100.0
Personal and nonparty	15.1	4.6	14.9	2.5	30.6	32.4	100.0
Republican Party	9.9	0	1.2	2.5	44.4	42.0	100.0
Labor unions	7.4	1.9	44.4	3.7	33.3	9.3	100.0
Liberal Party	31.0	10.3	13.8	0	31.0	13.8	100.0
Other, miscellaneous	6.3	6.3	0	75.0	0	12.5	100.0
All sponsors	12.6	5.3	18.5	10.7	18.9	34.0	100.0

Total number of appointments = 1765.

concentration being in the $5,000-to-$9,000-a-year category. It had the smallest percentage of jobs in the highest pay bracket (7.4 per cent as compared to 12.1 per cent for the Democrats and 31.0 per cent for the Liberals) but, unlike the party, had its honorific appointments concentrated in the more prestigious posts.

This Table also indicates the reason for the surprisingly large number of Republicans in the Harriman administration. Of their 81 jobs, only eleven paid any salary. The vast majority—over 86 per cent—of all Republican jobs were honorific. These honorific posts were typically on various boards and commissions where, by law or custom, Republican representation was required or where the governor felt a Republican appointment would enhance his "voter-serving"—even nonpartisan—image. Thus, although the Liberal Party was outnumbered by both the Republicans and the unions in the ranks of the Harriman administration, its jobs were—in pay terms at least—the most desirable.

The personal, non-party appointments of the Governor were, generally speaking, either high-paying staff, cabinet, and sub-cabinet posts (15 per cent) or honorific posts (63 per cent). He made fewer low-paying appointments than any group except the Liberal Party.

Despite all these qualifications, however, the position of the Democratic party in the patronage process was still very strong. Although the distribution of Democratic jobs, to a greater extent than the jobs of other sponsoring organizations, was skewed in the direction of lower-paying and lesser honorific posts, the Party still nominated or cleared from 70 to almost 88 per cent of the appointees in every category except one (major honorific). From one point of view, this distribution was probably quite rational. Party patronage was greatest in the least visible jobs; among the more visible cabinet and major honorific posts, the party "gave away" a considerable number (nearly one-third of the cabinet posts and nearly one-half of the major honorific appointments) to the personal appointees of Governor Harriman and to the Liberal and Republican parties. If we assume that personal and non-Democratic party appointments could as a group be more easily justified (regardless of the merits of individual appointees) as appointments based on "merit" and "nonpartisan qualifications," then such appointments could be looked upon as a measure of the extent to which the Democratic party was willing to meet "voter-serving" expectations at the price of "party-serving" expectations. Whether such sacrifices were subjectively experienced as "rational" by party leaders is, of course another matter. In all likelihood, all but the highest leaders most closely identified with the Harriman administration resented every job that went to a non-Democrat.

III. PATRONAGE, PARTY AND REGION

The question of organizational sponsorship was only one of the problems for the patronage dispensers. Another of comparable importance involved geographic distribution. Particularly within the Democratic party, but to some extent within other sponsoring organizations as well, the jobs had to be distributed around the state so as to satisfy all major regions. In its simplest form, the choice was between New York City and "upstate"—the latter referring broadly to any of the fifty-seven counties outside the five which comprise New York City. Upstate, of course, is far from being a homogeneous area. It includes several subregions: the four suburban counties near New York City, the upstate Democratic strongholds (such as Albany, Erie, and Monroe counties, which contain important industrial cities), and the heavily Republican rural and small-town counties which make up the largest part of the total.

Upstate versus downstate. Table III shows the percentage of each sponsoring organization's jobs which were given to

TABLE III   Percentage of Patronage Appointments from New York City, by Sponsor and Job Value*

Sponsor	Salaried Posts				Honorific Posts		Total
	Agency Head, Dept. Head, Board Member (over $12,000 per Year)	$9,000 to $12,000 per Year	$5,000 to $9,000 per Year	Under $5,000 per Year	Major	Minor	
	%	%	%	%	%	%	%
Democratic Party (nominated and sponsored)	58.2	40.3	35.9	9.6	32.1	13.6	27.1
Personal and nonparty	64.3	77.0	59.5	71.5	52.3	41.8	53.5
Republican Party	37.5	0	0	0	25.0	17.2	21.0
Labor unions	60.0	100.0	16.7	100.0	50.0	40.0	93.1
Liberal Party	100.0	50.0	100.0	93.0	100.0	100.0	38.2
Other, miscellaneous	0	100.0	0	9.1	0	100.0	60.0
All							32.5

* In each cell, the number represents the percentage of all jobs in that category which were given to New York City residents. The percentages thus do not add to 100, either across or down.

people from New York City, arranged by job category. In total the City is greatly under-represented. Although it produced 54.8 per cent of the Democratic vote in 1954, the City received only 32.5 per cent of the 1,765 jobs dispensed by the Harriman administration. The under-representation was even worse for appointees sponsored by the Democratic party. Even though the party structure in New York City dominates the statewide party (New York City Democrats control both the Democratic state convention and the Democratic delegation to the state legislature), it received only 27.1 per cent of the Party's jobs; nearly three-fourths of the Party's jobs went to Democrats living elsewhere in the state.

An examination of this regional distribution by job value indicates where the City's losses occurred. Table III shows for the Democratic party a consistently positive correlation between the value of the job and the probability that it would be awarded to a New York City resident: the

higher the salary of the job (or the higher the prestige of the honorific appointment), the greater the percentage of those jobs which went to City Democrats. Candidates sponsored by one of the five county organizations in New York City got 58.2 per cent of all cabinet and subcabinet posts paying over $12,000 a year; similarly, they got 23.1 per cent of all major honorific appointments but only 13.6 per cent of the minor honorific posts. Yet though City Democrats lost out primarily in the competition for lesser jobs, even among the best paying posts they barely won a share comparable to their share of the Harriman vote. On the other hand, over half of Harriman's personal and nonparty appointments went to New York City; in the two highest-paid categories, the City got between two-thirds and three-fourths.

Almost all the Liberal party appointees were from the City, and with good reason: the party scarcely exists outside the metropolitan area. Republicans, by contrast, were almost entirely from upstate even though the City produced 30 per cent of the statewide Republican vote. To the extent that this distribution of Republican jobs was the result of calculation by the Harriman administration, it probably made good sense. Giving most of the Republican jobs to upstate counties where, in most cases, the Republican party was firmly entrenched anyway probably did less damage to the Democratic party organization (and more importantly, to Democratic party morale) than would have been done if the Republicans were appointed from New York City where they would have been both more visible to most Democratic workers and more likely to help strengthen a weak but potentially dangerous Republican organization.

One reason why New York City Democrats failed to obtain a proportional share of the lowest-paying jobs was that such jobs were, on the whole, less attractive to party workers in the City than to workers elsewhere. The lowest-paid jobs are often not located in or near New York City, but in the state capital (Albany) or in scattered locations through the state (on highway and other construction projects, for example). Few New Yorkers are likely to move to another part of the state to accept a patronage job worth less than $5,000 a year. In addition, better jobs are likely to be available from local patronage (jobs in the Democratic city administration or in the Democratic-controlled local judiciary).

Elsewhere in the state, however, the demand for such jobs was significant. The last old-fashioned political machine of any consequence in New York State was the O'Connel organization in Albany. In 1960 Albany had the highest ratio of municipal employees to inhabitants (16.3 per thousand population) and the lowest average monthly pay ($203 per city employee) of any city in the state. Enough people lived off non-merit municipal employment in Albany to support a flourishing and powerful politi-

cal machine. To the members of such a machine, a job paying less than $5,000 a year was often quite attractive: furthermore, since they lived in the state capital, many of the jobs were within easy reach. As a result of these considerations, Albany county (which includes the city) received a disproportionately large share of all jobs, but particularly of low-paying ones.

There were other reasons for upstate dominance, particularly among low-paying jobs. Although the five New York City Democratic leaders—so long as they are united—can afford to ignore upstate Democratic leaders, they can never be certain they will be united. Indeed, Democratic leaders in the City fight among themselves almost as often as they fight the Republicans. Thus, each county leader from the City has an interest in developing and maintaining upstate allies. Furthermore, there are many areas in upstate New York where the Democrats have been out of power since the Civil War (they are still paying the price of the Copperhead opposition). In addition, they had been starved by twelve years of Republican domination in Albany. Harriman and De Sapio wanted to build up party strength in those areas (both had statewide and national ambitions which led them to act differently from county leaders); to this end, patronage was deliberately awarded upstate in order to recruit attractive candidates for local office, strengthen party organization, and undercut party leaders whose compromises with Republican power were deemed excessive.

Allocation among counties. To the Harriman administration, the problem of finding a way to distribute Democratic party jobs among the sixty-two county leaders was of great importance. How these jobs were distributed was crucially relevant to the distribution of power within the party, the prospects for party unity, the allegiance of party leaders (and their legislative representatives) to the Governor and his program, and the extent to which Carmine

De Sapio would be able to maintain his position as *de facto* party leader.

Depending on the goal sought, several decision rules were possible. If the Harriman administration had wanted, for example, to reward the party faithful and punish the heretics, it could have decided to give jobs to those party leaders most important in winning the nomination for Harriman or (what was often the same thing) those likely to be most influential in insuring his renomination. If the administration sought to use patronage to maximize its vote, it might have given the most and the best jobs to county leaders whose organizations were most likely to be stimulated by patronage and whose Democratic voters were most likely to respond at the polls to the local activities of an energetic organization. Or, to take a third possibility, if the administration wanted to improve the prospects of its legislation, it might have given its jobs to county leaders whose assemblymen and state senators were most influential in the legislature—including, if need be, to Republicans.

Perhaps because it wanted to do all these things (and more) at once and thus could do none entirely, or perhaps because it did not know exactly which of these ends it most wanted to attain, the administration attempted to balance the many and conflicting claims of county leaders for a share of the patronage. As in many such cases, it is more important that the principle be plausible than that it be reasonable. Since both population and Democratic voting strength were very unequally dispersed throughout the state, jobs would be "fairly" distributed if they were allocated in accordance with each county's contribution to the statewide Democratic vote for governor in 1954. Stated another way, the chief concern of the patronage dispensers was not in "economizing" but in "equity." That is, they were less preoccupied with discovering the proper allocation of resources to maximize the attainment of some goal than with adjusting competing claims "fairly." In the

words of one aide to the governor, the chief task in patronage allocation was to "equalize dissatisfaction" and "minimize the number of complaints." The elaborate statistical records (described below) were kept to prove to county leaders that the administration was being "fair" and (what was more important) to enable the county leaders to "prove" to their followers that they were getting all the jobs to which they were entitled. No county leader wishes to appear weak and ineffectual to his organization; the patronage records were useful "cover" to forestall challenges to his authority within the county. Whatever was wrong with the allocation rule developed, it served the needs of organizational maintenance because it appeared to be nonarbitrary and susceptible to statistical precision.

Not all jobs could be handled in this way, in part because (as previously noted) not all counties had any use for the lowest paying jobs. Thus, the distributional rule was applied, for the most part, only to jobs paying $6,000 or more a year. Finally, and most importantly, *all* jobs—whether party jobs or not—were made subject to this geographic rule, in part because it often enabled the administration to make a virtue out of a necessity (if a job had to go a certain county anyway—perhaps to meet the residence requirement of a particular board or commission—then it was advantageous to "charge" that job to the local leader's quota).

Table IV is based on the allocation of *all* jobs, party and nonparty, paying over $6,000 a year, among the state's counties. Of the sixty-two counties (fifty-three upstate, five in New York City and four which were New York City suburbs), only ten received no jobs at all, and these were among the very lowest in Democratic votes. The rank-order coefficient of correlation (Kendall's *tau,* corrected for ties) between votes and jobs for all counties is +.818.

In general, as already noted, New York City was underrepresented; the suburban and upstate counties were overrepresented.

TABLE IV **Counties of New York State, Showing Percentage of 1954 Democratic Vote for Governor and Percentage of All Patronage Jobs Paying over $6,000 per Year**

County and Region	Percentage of Democratic Vote	Percentage of Jobs over $6,000 (N = 556)	County and Region	Percentage of Democratic Vote	Percentage of Jobs over $6,000 (N = 556)
New York City:	*54.84*	*47.53*	Hamilton	0.02	0.00
Kings (Brooklyn)	18.79	12.83	Herkimer	0.38	0.38
New York (Manhattan)	12.70	18.30	Jefferson	0.37	0.00
Bronx	11.57	6.41	Lewis	0.10	0.00
Queens	10.65	9.05	Livington	0.22	0.18
Richmond (Staten Island)	1.13	0.94	Madison	0.19	0.38
			Monroe	3.87	3.39
Suburbs of New York City:	*11.24*	*13.01*	Montgomery	0.47	0.38
Nassau	5.28	5.28	Niagara	1.07	0.75
Rockland	0.55	1.32	Oneida	1.62	1.88
Suffolk	1.66	1.13	Onondaga	2.14	1.83
Westchester	3.75	5.28	Ontario	0.28	0.00
			Orange	0.78	0.94
			Orleans	0.13	0.00
Upstate:	*33.63*	*39.27*	Oswego	0.39	0.56
Albany	3.32	6.60	Otsego	0.26	0.18
Allegany	0.14	0.00	Putnam	0.18	0.38
Broome	0.79	1.13	Rensselear	1.10	2.64
Cattaraugus	0.38	0.38	St. Lawrence	0.44	0.38
Cayuga	0.44	0.18	Saratoga	0.46	0.75
Chanango	0.13	0.38	Schenectady	0.97	1.13
Chatauqua	0.71	0.00	Schoharie	0.15	0.18
Chemung	0.49	0.38	Schuyler	0.06	0.18
Clinton	0.31	0.56	Seneca	0.15	0.00
Columbia	0.26	0.56	Steuben	0.38	0.18
Cortland	0.13	0.75	Sullivan	0.34	0.18
Delaware	0.18	0.18	Tioga	0.11	0.38
Dutchess	0.69	0.94	Tompkins	0.19	0.56
Erie	6.40	5.09	Ulster	0.57	0.56
Essex	0.15	0.00	Warren	0.18	0.18
Franklin	0.20	0.56	Washington	0.22	0.75
Fulton	0.28	0.18	Wayne	0.22	0.00
Greene	0.20	0.18	Wyoming	0.14	0.18
Genesee	0.23	0.38	Yates	0.05	0.38
			TOTAL	99.71	99.81

This table does not correspond precisely to Tables I, II, III. The Harriman records were kept in such a way that, for calculating mode of sponsorship, ethnicity, religion, and other factors, the dividing line between low-paying and better-paying jobs was at $5000. In this table, the dividing line was $6000. No significant error is introduced by this discrepancy. For example, New York City had 44 per cent of all jobs over $5000, but 47.5 per cent of all jobs over $6000: *the lower the cutting point, the greater the difference between jobs and votes.* In this table, the higher cutting point has been used. (Totals do not add to 100.0 because of rounding.)

Overall, this under-representation was not great and could perhaps be explained by random factors. Within New York City, however, the disparity was much greater. Manhattan (*i.e.,* New York County) had far more than its share of jobs; Brooklyn and the Bronx had far less. These relationships can be conveniently expressed by dividing each county's percentage of all jobs by its percentage of Democratic votes in 1954. The resulting ratios, if less than 1.0, indicate the extent to which the county was underrepresented; if greater than 1.0, the extent to which it was overrepresented:

Manhattan	1.44
Staten Island	0.92
Queens	0.85
Brooklyn	0.68
Bronx	0.55

The two New York City counties which were (and are) the most heavily Democratic and which had the strongest Democratic party organizations—Brooklyn and the Bronx—received the least return in terms of patronage jobs. One reason for this may be that Carmine De Sapio, the *de facto* party leader in the state under Governor Harriman, was also, of course, the leader of the Manhattan Democratic party organization (*i.e.*, Tammany Hall); he might be expected to favor appointees from his own county. Of equal or greater importance, however, was that Manhattan undoubtedly harbors a disproportionate share of the wealth, talent and prestige in New York City. One would expect Manhattan to be heavily overrepresented among personal, nonparty appointments where talent or prestige is the chief consideration (although we have no direct evidence, this seems to be the case); what is interesting is the extent to which, even among *party* appointments, the need to meet voter-serving expectations resulted in costs being imposed on certain strong party organizations.

One cannot, of course, assume that Manhattanites were any more likely to be "qualified" in any technical sense than, say Brooklynites. Indeed, if by "qualified" one means prior knowledge of and experience in state administration, practically no appointee was "qualified" (only *one* cabinet member, the Commissioner of Correction, had had any previous experience in state government). "Qualified" in fact meant something broader and vaguer than experience—it meant professional stature, a reputation for probity, success in business or other levels of government, a "clean" record, and the like. People with these attributes are, it is reasonable to believe, somewhat more concentrated in Manhattan than Brooklyn.

We have no detailed information on how jobs were allocated *within* the various counties except that the Democratic party county leaders did not hesitate to take care of themselves. By the end of the Harriman administration, one-third of all county leaders were on the state payroll in one form or another.

Almost all the 1,304 party-sponsored appointments we have discussed so far were "exempt" jobs, free of civil-service restrictions and therefore legally available to the party, or "non-competitive" jobs for which examinations are not feasible. Exempt jobs, mostly to be found at the policy-making level, were only a tiny fraction—about 1 percent—of all state jobs. Two other classes of jobs were more numerous but, in many ways, less valuable; laborers and the regular competitive civil service.

Most of the laborer jobs were in the Department of Public Works (DPW) which had (in June, 1958) 3,083 fulltime laborers. As much as possible, these were given to Democrats through regular party channels. This was a limited possibility, however, for the jobs simply were not in great demand —they were not sinecures, the pay was low, and they were often inconveniently located. As a result, Republicans were not laid off wholesale. For example, in 1956, two years after the Harriman election, fifty-six laborers were employed in the Binghamton area by the DPW, of whom fewer than half (twenty-three) were Democrats; of the remainder, eleven were avowed Republicans and twenty-two were not enrolled in any party.

In the competitive civil service were found the great majority of state jobs. Here administration policy was complicated. In general, the rule was to favor Democrats in every way possible in those departments in which favoritism had "traditionally" been shown by the party in power and where it could be done without violating any explicit regulations or impairing the competence of the service. Many familiar techniques were employed to this end: Democrats were favored with "temporary" appointments (where no examinations are required), with provisional appointments (where no eligible list exists and examination is eventually required), and with the discretion permitted to the "rule of three." This last rule permits supervisors to select from the top three eligible applicants on the civil service list; where possible, an effort was made to select Democrats.

In all this, the Civil Service Commission and its staff were willing participants, so long as no great violence was done to the general principle of "fitness." Nine departments were subject to this kind of political interference, the most important of which were Public Works, Taxation and Finance, Correction, and Conservation. The others were Agriculture and Markets, Labor, State, the Division of Veterans' Affairs, and the Rent Control Commission. Other departments were emphatically not subjected to such intervention, including Education, Health, Social Welfare, Mental Hygiene, and the State Police, even though the administration was often under considerable pressure from party leaders to relax these restrictions.

The reason for sacrificing party interests in some departments and not in others was complex. Generally speaking, party intrusion into a department is most likely to cause an adverse popular reaction when the department is the province of a well organized profession which is able and willing to resist intrusion publicly on the ground that it violates "professional standards." Educators, doctors, psychiatrists, social workers, and public health officers effec-tively control their departments and these departments, in turn, are perceived by voters as being agencies in which "neutral competence" and "expertise" ought to prevail. The Harriman administration could (and did) justify to party leaders its decision to respect these expectations on the grounds that "this is what the Republicans did." In one sense the struggle between the professions and the party for control over (or influence in) certain departments was resolved by the administration in favor of the professions and justified to the party on grounds of party competition—to intrude where the Republicans had not intruded would create an "issue."

IV. PATRONAGE AND "RECOGNITION"

"Recognizing" certain groups in the community by appointing some of their members to office has long been thought to be a principal function of patronage. Such recognition supposedly binds members of various racial, religious and nationality groups more closely to the party, or wins them away from a rival party by conferring on them the symbolic and vicarious satisfaction of seeing "one of their own" given prestige, power, and income. It is at the very least debatable how relevant today such "recognition" is to the groups of voters who are supposed to be benefitted. It seems to us quite likely that the principle of racial and religious balance was more important to the Harriman administration than it was to the electorate; some few votes may be changed, or some loyalties reinforced, by "recognition," but—in the absence of any evidence one way or the other —we assert they are few indeed.

This raises the question of why the Harriman administration acted as if such recognition was important. That it did so act is beyond question—great efforts were extended to "recognize" certain groups and careful records were kept of the racial and religious identity of the appointees. To a great extent, of course, claims for nationality recognition advanced by party leaders are simply cover for their own claims. When an Italian county leader, for example, complains that a recent appointment should have gone to an Italian, what he often means is that it should have gone to him or his organization. Some nationality groups demand jobs directly (the Poles were a conspicuous example during the Harriman administration); more typically, such claims are made on behalf of nationality groups by politicians who may or may not have any real commitments to the principle of ethnic recognition.

Despite their use as "cover," ethnic claims were often taken seriously by the patronage dispensers for several reasons. First, county and assembly district leaders were themselves faced with struggles for power which in turn were motivated by (or masked as) claims for ethnic recognition. Italian or Negro insurgents challenging an Irish district leader created a problem which the Irish leader would often attempt to deal with by asking for a job for the Italian or Negro insurgent (or one of his backers) to "keep them happy."

Second, certain groups least assimilated politically (notably the Negroes and the Poles) made organized demands on politicians for symbolic recognition. When a Negro or Pole was appointed, there was no doubt in anyone's mind that it was *because* he was a Negro or Pole (albeit hopefully an able one) that he got the job. By contrast, Jews are least likely to claim jobs for persons *qua* Jews; indeed, Jewish liberals in the Democratic party often are at pains to make clear their belief in the impropriety or even immorality of ethnic recognition as a basis for personnel decisions. Between these two extremes, claims for jobs for Irish and Italian candidates were most likely to come from politicians, not from ethnic organizations, and to be "cover" for their own interests.

Third, ethnic claims are a kind of political shorthand used to convey a sense of general political identity even when ethnicity is not the most important component of that identity. When a post in the field of mental health is to be filled by a brilliant, politically liberal, Vienna-trained psychoanalyst from Manhattan, it is inconceivable that the candidate would turn out to be anything but a Jew. Thus, when professional politicians—for whose vocabularies ethnic labels are extremely important—say that the job must go "to the Jews," they often mean not to a Jew *qua* Jew but to a person with "Jewish" professional, intellectual, residential and ideological attributes. Similarly, filling a prison warden's job with an experienced man means, almost invariably, filling it with an Irish Catholic conservative because men experienced in law enforcement and prison work are largely of that sort; as a result, politicians tend to regard such posts as "belonging" to the Irish.

Finally, ethnic and religious recognition was of great importance, not so much because of the maintenance needs of the party or of ethnic pressure groups, but because of the maintenance needs of agencies of the state government. Each of the various departments, boards, and commissions which are responsible for substantive policy areas is obliged to appear legitimate in the eyes of the special constituency which it serves. To forestall organized opposition, to anticipate possible vetoes, and to win consent for its policies, almost every agency organizes itself in such a way as to co-opt at least one representative of every significant group likely to be affected by its policies. A kind of syndicalism comes to envelop virtually all these agencies, and once established, it becomes sanctified by tradition. In this "agency syndicalism" three categories of interest are typically represented: regional, occupational, and ethnic.

Ethnicity and occupation became critically important considerations to Harriman's patronage dispensers, in our view, as much because of agency syndicalism as because of party pressure. Several examples could be offered. For instance, the Department of Social Welfare sent a letter to the patronage office two weeks after Harriman took office in which it described in the frankest terms the "qualifications" (*i.e.*, the occupational and ethnic identities) which should govern any appointments to the fifteen-member State Board of Social Welfare:

> There are longstanding traditions as to the composition of the membership of the Board. For instance, the members are divided religiously as follows: 7 Protestants, 5 Catholics, 3 Jews. There is always one Negro member of the Board. It is customary to have 10 men and five women on the Board. There has been a longstanding custom of having two doctors on the Board; presently one of these is a psychoanalyst. . . . It has been the custom for Governors to reappoint members to enable them to serve the full extent of their 10-year legal period.

Accordingly, Harriman decided to retain as chairman of the Welfare Board a Buffalo Protestant Republican whom Governor Dewey had appointed a few weeks earlier. With regard to the three vacancies on the Board (one of which had been filled with a recess appointment by Dewey), Harriman deferred to the organization constituencies of the Board. Two vacancies "belonged" to Catholics. Almost immediately after the inauguration, the Roman Catholic Bishop of Albany, in his capacity as Chairman of the New York State Catholic Welfare Committee, recommended to Harriman that the two Catholic vacancies be filled with a Catholic woman from Albany and a Catholic grain merchant from Buffalo. (The latter had the additional, perhaps not coincidental, attraction of being the son-in-law of a former Democratic county chairman of Erie County.) The proposals of the Bishop and his Committee were quickly accepted.

The third vacancy caused considerable difficulty and was not filled for a year. One woman from upstate was proposed by the Democratic State Committee and endorsed by the Business and Professional Women's Clubs of New York. The Commissioner (the professional director) of the Department of Social Welfare objected on the ground that the vacancy should go to a male Protestant; the candidate was a female Catholic. Further inquiry showed that, although indisputably female, the candidate was not quite a Catholic: she was married to an Italian Catholic, but was herself a Protestant. She was shunted aside (the following year she was made a member of the Mental Hygiene Council) in favor of an upstate male Protestant lawyer who was nominated by his Democratic county chairman.

Competing ethnic claims, like others, had to be balanced. These claims were seen primarily in terms of five categories, which, in rough order of preference, were Irish, Protestant, Jews, Italians, and Negroes. Table V shows the number and percentage of all jobs awarded to each of the five groups. It should be noted that the largest single group consists of people who either were not identified by ethnicity or were members of very small groups—*e.g.*, Puerto Ricans, Hungarians, Greeks, etc.

This Table is obviously based on a combination of racial, nationality, and religious

TABLE V   Patronage Appointments in New York State, 1955–1959, by Ethnicity and Religion of Recipient

Ethnicity or Religion	Appointments	
	Number	*Percent*
Irish	415	23.5
Protestants	313	17.7
Jews	284	16.1
Italians	107	6.1
Negroes	41	2.3
Miscellaneous and unclassified	605	34.3
TOTAL	1,765	100.0

identifications; in this it reflects the perceptions of the politicians themselves. Each category might be thought of as consisting of a dominant and a recessive trait—although everyone had both a nationality (or racial) and a religious identity, one or the other was perceived as the dominant one. Thus, Irish always meant Catholic as well, the Protestants from Ireland having for the most part ceased to think of themselves as Irish in view of the, to them, more fundamental distinction of religion. Protestant usually meant English or Scottish, although Scandinavians and Protestant Irish might also be given this label. For Jews, the distinction is religious and cultural; nationality differences tended to be overlooked by the party leaders (although perhaps of great importance to the Jews themselves). German Jews and East European Jews are generally treated as one category for patronage purposes. Italians are identified by nationality, not by religion; as a result, many prominent Italian politicians (such as Judge Ferdinand Pecora, whom De Sapio backed for Mayor in 1949, and Charles Poletti, who was once Lieutenant Governor and briefly Governor) are in fact Protestants. Negroes of course are identified by race, although in New York City at that time a certain preference could be discerned for Negro Catholics (*e.g.*, Hulan Jack, formerly Borough President of Manhattan).

As one would expect, the largest single ethnic group in patronage offices was the Irish; as one might not expect, however, their dominance was far less than is often supposed. They held less than a quarter of all jobs, and nearly four-fifths (78.2 per cent) of those went to upstate Irish. The New York City Irish were outnumbered two-to-one by the Jews and pressed hard by the Italians, despite the fact that during most of this time four of the five Democratic county leaders from New York City and the Democratic minority leaders in both houses of the state legislature were

Irish. None of the really important political figures in the administration was Irish (none, certainly, who had the influence of Paul Appleby, the Director of the Budget); a few able commissioners were Irish, but these tended to be men like Edward T. Dickinson, who was a Yale man and part Italian anyway. As one chief Harriman aide, himself an Irishman, phrased it, "the Irish appointees tended to be nice fellows, but neither hungry nor energetic, living rather too much on a reputation other men had won for their breed." The ablest Irish had gone on to other things.

The Italian applicants were not lacking in energy but they were often deficient in experience. Italians were above all cohesive, often without regard to party lines, and they had in Carmine De Sapio a kinsman whose rise in the party had been in great part due to his support among Italian district leaders. But not only did their lack of experience in government reduce their numbers in the administration, they were also probably hindered by their own leader. De Sapio was assured of Italian support anyway; he had to use his scarce resources to buy support elsewhere (chiefly, it appears, among the Jews), and in any case, he had no wish to encourage competitors for dominance in the Italian community.

Table VI summarizes the ethnic composition of the patronage appointments by kind of job and job value. It suggests the standing of the various groups in the party (and perhaps in society). The Italians and Negroes were much more heavily concentrated in the lower-paying jobs (under $9,000 per year)—nearly half the jobs for these two groups were in that category. By contrast, only about a fourth of the Jewish and Protestant jobs were in that bracket. The Protestants particularly were concentrated in the honorific jobs (60 per cent of their appointments paid prestige but no money); only 22.4 per cent of the Italian and 34.1 per cent of the Negro jobs were of this kind. In part the Protestant (and by

TABLE VI Patronage Appointments in New York State, 1955–1959, by Ethnicity and Job Value (Miscellaneous and Unclassified Omitted)

Ethnicity	Salaried Posts				Honorific Posts		Total
	Agency Head, Dept. Head, Board Member (over $12,000 per Year)	*$9,000 to $12,000 per Year*	*$5,000 to $9,000 per Year*	*Under $5,000 per Year*	*Major*	*Minor*	
	%	%	%	%	%	%	%
Irish	14.5	5.8	21.9	16.4	13.0	28.4	100.0
Protestants	12.9	4.3	12.9	9.8	18.8	41.2	100.0
Jews	18.3	9.9	22.9	6.7	20.1	22.2	100.0
Italians	21.5	8.4	34.6	13.1	6.5	15.9	100.0
Negroes	12.2	4.9	41.5	7.3	19.5	14.6	100.0

that we mean, of course, white Anglo-Saxon Protestant) concentration in honorific jobs reflects the fact that such people are more likely to be Republicans; and Republicans, for reasons already mentioned, were given a disproportionate share of these posts. We suggest that it is also due to the fact that Protestants are perceived as more likely than Italians or Negroes to confer legitimacy, in the eyes of the community, on the board or commission.

One interesting case is that of the Germans, who in these tables are classified under "miscellaneous," not because their numbers were small (there were 94 "German" appointments, more than twice the number of Negroes) but because they were not perceived by the politicians as a relevant category. There were no "German" politicians in evidence during the Harriman administration and no "German" demands were made either from within the party or by outside groups. An indication of this lack of political identity is the fact that the official patronage records listed only sixteen Germans when in fact our independent count shows ninety-four of probable German extraction. Much has been written about how ethnic groups *acquire* a sense of political identity; little, if anything, has been said about why a group, such as the German-Americans, either fails to acquire such an identity or, if it is ac-

quired, then loses it. Undoubtedly, the explanation would involve a consideration of the relatively early period of German migration to this country, their very rapid socio-economic progress, their religious heterogeneity, and the enormous and divisive impact of two world wars.

V. PATRONAGE AND POWER

Patronage has many functions—indeed, it was precisely the great number of such functions that led the Harriman administration, inevitably, to attempt to serve many and often conflicting goals in the allocation of jobs. One function—that of using patronage to win votes from voters—which might be appropriate to a big-city political machine was obviously irrelevant here. There were simply too few jobs and too many voters, most of whom were not interested in working on, say, a state highway project. Another function—that of supporting rank-and-file party workers—was relevant, but not directly to the Harriman administration. Supporting workers who would ring doorbells was a job for county and district leaders; to Harriman's staff, the problem was not to "spend" patronage in a way that would maximize the vote such paid workers would produce, but to spend it in a way that would (in part) satisfy party leaders, most of whom had no organization and no workers to speak of. One important function remains: that of assembling power, within the government and within the party.

Whatever else he may have wanted, Governor Harriman surely desired to have enough power over the state government to have a reasonable chance of putting into effect the policies he favored and of making certain that the routine business of government was carried on with reasonable efficiency and honesty. Patronage was one means of attaining these objectives, but a limited means. Many important programs were in the hands of boards and commissions and, although Harriman might have been able to wield considerable influence over many of them if he had been willing to accept the costs, the costs were high. Most boards had well organized constituencies and clientele groups which saw the boards as in fact if not in law agencies independent of the governor. The professional staffs of these boards usually concurred in this view. *De facto* independence was protected by informal but rigid representational formulas—"agency syndicalism"—which could only be violated at great risk of organized opposition to the administration from prestigious groups who would have a convenient anathema, "political meddling," to pronounce on Harriman's efforts. Patronage under such circumstances had only a very limited utility as a means of assembling power.

Despite these limitations, Harriman and the party leaders intended to use patronage (as well as other means) to assert control over the statewide party and to a certain degree they succeeded. By the judicious clearing of appointments through one leader rather than his rival, the men in Albany were able to influence the choice of local candidates for elective office. In several upstate cities, men now prominent in state politics were given important nominations because the Harriman administration used its patronage power to eliminate or mollify local leadership objections to these nominations. In a curious way, these patronage appointments were important as much for their symbolic as for their practical value: a by-passed leader not only loses control over the income of a particular person, he also (and perhaps more importantly) loses legitimacy in the eyes of his followers.

Harriman used patronage in this way because he wanted attractive, vigorous candidates on the ticket with him when he ran for reelection; De Sapio supported him because he wanted to consolidate his influence with county and district leaders. Two things prevented these two men from retaining control of the party: certain claimants for a share in the party's leadership could not be dealt with by patronage, and at a crucial moment the two leaders could not agree between themselves.

Harriman's election in 1954, like Mayor Robert Wagner's in 1953, was the product of a complicated alliance among the Democratic county leaders of New York City (of whom De Sapio was only one), the Liberal party, certain trade unions, and a wide variety of liberals and "reformers," most of whom were only beginning to organize. Once in office, the regular Democratic party organization was unrepresentative of this electoral coalition. The county leaders throughout the state were still for the most part the heirs of Al Smith; there was little in common between these men and the other, newer elements in the alliance. Although Harriman and De Sapio worked together, they represented these contrasting elements (however little either may have wished it!). This latent tension was revealed by the composition of the administration. The personal staff and chief aides of the governor were, to a considerable extent, young men who were Harriman's personal, nonparty appointees—party cleared rather than party nominated. Ethnically, they were Protestant and Jewish; ideologically, they were of the liberal left. The cabinet, by contrast, consisted largely of men who were party nominated, who were Catholic or Jewish, and who were ideologically either neutral or conservative. The cleavage in both political style and political goals was considerable (*e.g.,* the insistence of the Insurance Commissioner—a cabinet level party nominee—that insurance license applicants have a security clearance was utterly incomprehensible to the liberals on the Governor's staff). Many of the heads of line departments and bureaus, as a result, did not always attach overriding importance to the necessity of working with the Governor—much less with his staff. Given both their background and their sponsorship, such men found themselves more comfortable working with the legislature and were easily distracted by matters of importance to the locality from which they came. The governor's staff, in turn, often failed to appreciate the importance of such matters.

This dichotomy persisted and grew more serious as the activity of the newer, nontraditional elements within the alliance increased. These newer elements—particularly New York City liberals who were beginning to organize reform clubs in the Manhattan assembly districts—could not be dealt with effectively by patronage even if the party leaders had been so inclined. (Certain reform leaders might have welcomed the jobs and assumed the constraints that accompanied them, but in most cases their followers in the reform clubs would have regarded such behavior as an intolerable "sellout.")

The crisis in the Democratic party might have been postponed (in the long run, it could not have been avoided) had Harriman and De Sapio acted in concert. But at the disastrous 1958 state convention in Buffalo, the alliance collapsed. After Mayor Wagner refused to run, the regular leaders favored as the Democratic nominee for

United States Senator the esteemed District Attorney of New York County (Manhattan), in part to get an Irish Catholic back on the statewide ticket (there had been none in 1954) and in part to repudiate what they regarded as the presumptuous claims of the Jewish and Protestant reform groups in New York City. Harriman, seeking to have on the ticket with him a candidate of national stature, and recognizing the pivotal power of the new groups, backed Thomas Finletter, a Protestant reform leader.

In the convention balloting that followed, the regular party leaders—the beneficiaries of Harriman administration patronage—easily overwhelmed the governor in the convention voting. Whereupon the Democratic ticket was just as easily overwhelmed at the polls. Patronage has increased the cohesion of the regular party, but that party did not yet contain all the elements of the electoral alliance on which it depended for victory.

26.   Patronage and Party

Frank J. Sorauf

This article is the result of much research and thought concerning the uses of patronage. The author raises some questions about the usefulness of patronage to the party, particularly in view of new knowledge about the political process. He examines the main assumptions that underlie the rationalization that patronage is a political bastion: (1) the ability of parties to administer patronage; (2) the necessity of patronage for effective parties; (3) the vitality of patronage as a reward or incentive; (4) the single use or purpose of patronage; and (5)

From the *Midwest Journal of Political Science*, vol. 3, no. 2 (May 1959), pp. 115–126, with footnote omissions, by permission of Wayne State University Press.

the nature of the party using the patronage. Sorauf's conclusion is that the acceptance of conventional assumptions about patronage may reflect a type of intellectual lag between present realities and earlier urban circumstances under which patronage flourished. Patronage survives as a political tool, Sorauf concludes, and as a means of protest by local centers of political power.

The author is Professor of Political Science at the University of Minnesota.

* * *

It was not long ago that political scientists reacted instinctively against political patronage much as they reacted against slavery, aggressive war, and divine right monarchy. Reminders of that older, more moral day linger even today—in, for instance, the activities of civic and better-government organizations, and in the Library of Congress's subject classification of "spoils system" under "corruption (in politics)." But I suspect that the issue of patronage, even among those scholars not yet willing to endorse or condone it, is no longer the highly-charged moral issue it once was.

Undoubtedly the rise in prestige and status that political parties have enjoyed has done a great deal to elevate the institution of patronage to semi-respectability, at least among academics. In this era of strong, positive government, scholars have seized upon the party as an instrument through which discipline and responsibility may be achieved within the Leviathan. Party joins with government to generate the political power for achieving broad social ends. The stock of patronage rises concurrently with party's prestige on the general assumption that patronage is essential to a strong and vital party organization. In brief, we have succumbed to the lean but forceful logic of George Washington Plunkitt:

First, this great and glorious country was built up by the political parties; second, parties can't hold together if their workers don't get the offices when they win; third, if the parties go to pieces, the government they built up must go to pieces, too; fourth, then there'll be h——l to pay.[1]

There doubtless remain other reasons for the decline in the crusading enthusiasm against patronage. The whole thrust of the political science of this generation has been toward a realistic acceptance of the political facts of life, a willingness to study and participate in grass-roots politics. The interest of political scientists in programs such as that of the Citizenship Clearing House is indicative. Furthermore, patronage no longer dominates public personnel policy as once it did, and consequently it does not present a problem of the magnitude it did.

Where patronage remains today, two chief justifications or rationales generally support it. In the first place, its friends argue that patronage remains an essential aid to party responsibility and control of public policy. Republicans after 1952 bemoaned their inability to appoint a full "Republican team" to top administrative posts in Washington; the removal of some 130,000 jobs from Civil Service protection was said to be a move to restore unity to policymaking at the national level. Secondly, it is widely held that patronage contributes to, and may even be vital to, an energetic party system by providing a system of rewards and incentives for party service. It is this second justification that furnishes the focus of this paper.

The brief observations that follow grow out of research and thought about the uses of patronage and are concerned mainly with at least raising some questions about the assumed values and utilities of patronage to the party. Patronage has for long remained a tail tied to the kite of party; once its importance to party was conceded, its fortunes rose with those of party. To attack patronage was to challenge party

[1] William Riordon, *Plunkitt of Tammany Hall* (New York: Knopf, 1948), p. 18.

and to appear to be burning the barn to kill the mice. It seems to me likely, however, that the basic political usefulness of patronage as either reward or incentive may be overestimated or misunderstood. At any rate the traditional justification of the benefits of patronage to party demands a re-evaluation in the light of new knowledge about the political process and recent developments in parties and politics in America. The main body of this paper contains brief examinations of the more important assumptions underlying (and, in fact, creating) the more explicit rationalization of patronage as a bastion of party. They are set down in the conviction that it ill behooves political science to accept any untested assumptions, much less public policy based on them.

THE ASSUMPTIONS

(1) The ability of parties to administer patronage

In the first place, one may seriously question the implicit assumption that the parties are able to use the patronage at their disposal. "The fiction prevails," writes V. O. Key, "that while party leaders may not always manage the public service well they are wizards in the conduct of party business." Too often we fail to realize that the effective administration of a patronage system demands administrative skills that very few county chairmen or precinct leaders can command. The unyielding application of political criteria, the systematic extraction of partisan service, and the ruthless firing that follows election victories require a high degree of administrative will and finesse. Especially in the small, closely-knit rural and small-town areas across the country the use of patronage becomes even more difficult and unlikely. Ties of friendship, blood, and community militate against the political discipline essential to the administration of patronage. The resulting

lax and ineffective use of political jobs, the failure to appoint jobholders and supervise their activities with only the welfare of the party in mind, points to the possibility that one may very well need more of the arts of public administration to run a patronage than a civil service system.

Furthermore, patronage systems offer just one more example of an old social fact—just as it takes money to make money, it takes political power to achieve greater power. The party long out of office and desperately in need of new reservoirs of strength is precisely the party that, should it suddenly find itself in office, would be least able to use patronage for rebuilding. Weak parties lack the discipline, the trained leadership, and the surplus of potential jobholders to use the system to their maximum advantage. It is, in other words, the dominant party that can muster the discipline and strength necessary to administer the apparatus of patronage. So capably do the strong build on strength that one is tempted to say that patronage does not build parties quite so much as parties build patronage systems.

(2) The necessity of patronage for effective parties

Students of politics and parties have too often accepted without empirical evidence the assumption that a certain amount of patronage is vital to the parties as a motivator of political activity. But the fact remains that in states such as Wisconsin political parties have survived and achieved a certain measure of strength and discipline without the inducement of political appointments. Patronage is not, in brief, a universal concomitant of the political process; it is rooted deeply in a particular set of social conditions and traditions.

The implication that party loyalties and activity rest on so slender a reed as the promise of political spoils is at least open to question. Recent studies have indicated that ties to the major parties rest heavily on the conserving force of tradition and on the present appeal of candidates and issues. At least some of this traditional and programmatic loyalty has been converted into work for the party. A generation or two ago patronage flourished among the uprooted, illiterate, and unassimilated groups in the urban centers of America. Without political tradition and involvement in the issues of the day, and constantly beset by economic insecurity, they could be wooed and their political allegiance shaped by offers of political reward. Patronage was under these circumstances a valuable aid in the pragmatic majority-building of American politics.

Rather than universalize the importance of patronage to party, however, one might suggest that its role is declining and that it survives in many places as a mere shadow of its former self. The politics of Messrs. Plunkitt and Dooley have been curtailed by the political education and assimilation of migrant and foreign-born populations. Furthermore, with the help of the mass communications media the parties have created loyalties to candidates by retailing their personalities to all corners of the political cosmos. And by centralizing political issues and appeals, the parties have diminished the importance of the local political activity that patronage once bought. Since the 1930's American parties have also become involved in social and economic politics to an extent quite new in our politics and have attracted new attention to the relevance of policy alternatives. Finally, one should mention that well-organized interest groups, such as labor unions, have begun to provide the parties with an alternate source of political workers. The result has been an inevitable decline in the necessity of patronage to the political party.

At the same time that party dependence on patronage has, as I have indicated above, declined steadily, the incidence of patronage has itself declined. Government, for instance, has stolen much of patronage's social and charitable function with its social welfare programs. Steadier economic prosperity, and the expansion of educational opportunities, have reduced the importance of patronage as job security. The need for greater specialization and skills within the public service has in its way contributed to the waning of patronage. But whatever the reason, the most casual glance will indicate the recession of patronage in our time, and that decline in itself—accompanied by no perceptible weakening of the parties—may be taken as evidence that the classic rationale for patronage no longer has the same validity it might once have had.

(3) The vitality of patronage as reward or incentive

Implicit in the whole argument on behalf of the patronage system is the assumption, related to the previous one, that the political job offers inducement enough to spur men to give money or service to the party. Unless the job carries high value and desirability as a reward, it can hardly serve as either "payment for past work or incentive for new labors." Many more empirical studies must be made to determine the value of patronage as a political reward. Is it the main or only motive behind political activity? Does the patronage holder perform political service for the party? Does he even vote the party ticket, and does he lead his family, friends, and neighbors to the polls as well? Is patronage, in other words, a really effective means for securing organization and campaign activity for the party? The answer is at least uncertain.

In the first place, the poor pay and generally dismal future prospects that attend most patronage jobs discourage many potential jobholders. Especially in a period of full employment, qualified men and women can find more attractive career possibilities than those which patronage systems offer. More especially, the upper social, economic, and educational levels on which the parties increasingly rely for leadership will find little to tempt them in patronage as it exists in most states today. As a result most patronage jobs fall to the lower skill groups who also lack the political skills the parties need. Political jobs in many areas, because of low pay and the considerable insecurity involved, have been consequently debased as a political currency. They simply cannot attract first-rate political leadership nor extract party service from what jobholders they attract. Where pay is low, the worker may well feel that he "owes" nothing for his salary other than a good day's work. Very possibly, too, he may not be fully aware of the rationale and obligations of the system. As unlikely as it might seem to the sophisticated, he may recognize the party as the appointing agency without understanding his informal debt to it in return for the job.

Undesirable as these jobs may be in times of full employment, they might conceivably become attractive in a period of recession or in a pocket of high unemployment. But, paradoxically, in those very areas of economic hardship where the political job achieves its greatest desirability, the job insecurity also works to the party's disadvantage. A man removed from his position for partisan reasons may find it difficult or impossible to obtain re-employment, particularly if he is beyond his 40's, and he may turn against party and patronage in a rage of disenchantment that more than destroys any gratitude he may have had for the initial appointment. Employment and economic security no longer are accepted as the subjects of political charity that patronage would have them, and dismissal for political reasons strikes the average employee today as unfair, if not immoral. Thus, the very conditions that give a political job its greatest value on appointment

probably create the greatest hostility at dismissal, a hostility directed not only at the "other party," but at politics and patronage in general as well.

(4) The single use or purpose of patronage

We tend to assume (and, indeed, this paper has thus far assumed) that patronage serves only the function of reward for the recipient's past or future service to the party. Even at that, parties often must choose between patronage as either reward or as incentive. Were the Republicans after 1952, for instance, to reward the defecting Democrats for Eisenhower in the South or were they to use available patronage to build a Republican party in the South? But the greatest dilemmas facing a party in the administration of a patronage system may arise from the presence of nonpolitical uses or purposes of patronage.

For instance, patronage may become an inverted reward system, rewarding the rewarder rather than the recipient. The mere opportunity to dispense patronage favors may soothe and flatter the ego of the party official to an extent great enough to reward him for his work on behalf of the party. But when the disposal of political jobs becomes the private suzerainty of the local politico, and when he gives the jobs to friends, relatives, and neighbors rather than to the politically worthy, he destroys the value of patronage as a device for enlisting party workers. In this respect I recall often being told by party officers that they cared not who really made the patronage appointments so long as the appearances of their dispensation were maintained, and so long as they could carry the word to the lucky recipient and claim his gratitude.

The patronage system may also, surprisingly, serve a combination recruitment and "civil service" function. While at heart patronage and merit may be incompatible personnel selection systems, political parties may have to make their peace with efficiency and capability in administration. The party whose appointees, for instance, maintain a rural road network has a genuine political interest in maintaining public approval of the road system. It may have to compromise the use of patronage as reward by appointing and retaining skilled employees, regardless of their political qualifications, for the road crews. Even where this sort of *ad hoc* merit system does not flourish, the party at least functions as a decentralized, local recruitment and job placement agency.

Under usual conditions, therefore, patronage fills many roles. Within any system some balance and compromise among conflicting goals and claims must be struck. What emerges within any patronage system is in reality many systems: some of the more attractive positions may actually serve as rewards, or possibly for policy coordination; some of the most specialized may be subsumed into a quasi-merit system; and some of local concern may be set aside for the self-satisfaction of the local party hierarchy.

(5) The nature of the party using patronage

No scholar of any perception would indulge himself in the illusion that American political parties are great unified, monolithic structures. Yet, we assume all too often that "the party" benefits from the use of patronage, that "the party" curries favor with its appointments. What we overlook is that only one organ of the party is apt to gain from any one specific political appointment. And it is a matter of vital concern in understanding the effects of patronage to know just which party organ or leader, on what level of the party structure, reaps the reward. Patronage, therefore, by bolstering local centers of power and entrenching the political lords in their local fiefs, by preventing unity on candidates and policy, may be used as a weapon in intra-party

squabbles just as easily as it may be used to create intra-party cohesion or vitality.

To state the assumption another way, we assume, contrary to the preponderance of evidence, that political patries have just one internal interest. They indeed have many interests, and patronage may serve one to the detriment of others. The very existence of the institution of "senatorial courtesy" illustrates the way between national party and state party over the use of federal patronage. And just five years ago Leonard Hall was chosen national chairman of the Republican party only after he had assured the national committee of the party a greater voice in the distribution of the GOP patronage. In any event, patronage, like any other form of partisan power, may be used in destructive, internal wars as well as in the great interparty battles.

IN CONCLUSION

These remarks on the assumptions undergirding a patronage system indicate how we build a somewhat unreal image of patronage. The result is a view of patronage that dwells on its political uses, while ignoring its inadequacies and disadvantages. It has been largely on the basis of this simplifield and overly charitable appraisal of the political values of patronage that the system has been weighed against merit systems. One could even suggest that in addition to overestimating the political constructiveness of patronage, we underestimate its power to destroy both itself and partisan strength.

The self-destructive tendencies of patronage are most virulent when patronage is laxly administered. Where only some workers are replaced following a change of parties, the group replaced will in most instances be the group that has been politically the most active. In other words, the workers who have been least identified with the appointing party become most acceptable to a new administration; accordingly, the apolitical and the "bi-political" survive. Such lessons are not lost on workers who realize they can cheaply purchase job security with political inactivity. A denaturing of patronage results.

Similarly, the retention of workers for personal reasons or for reasons of skill and experience works the same havoc on the patronage system. When personal rather than party considerations dictate political job-giving, as they so often do in closely-knit communities, the political nature of the job is obscured, as is the political obligation and discipline that it demands. Eventually, the very political essence of the positions becomes unclear and impotent. Community expectations about patronage are reshaped and altered, and woe then to him who tries to reestablish a tight political rein over the patronage positions. In fact, anything less than the greatest virtuosity in the management of spoils will invite these self-destructive tendencies. That fact represents the truth in the oft-quoted plaint of the party functionary that with each political appointment he makes nine enemies and one ingrate.

This willingness to accept the conventional assumptions about patronage may reflect some sort of "intellectual lag." The assumptions were no doubt truer 20 or 30 years ago and in the heyday of spoils than they are today. Much of the writing on patronage stems from that period and reflects not only the times but the particular urban conditions under which patronage flourished most vigorously. Political scientists and students of public administration have failed in this respect to heed the advice of the historian to reformulate their generalizations for their own generation. Their failure to do so may be due in part to the decline of patronage and to the triumph of merit civil service systems. But it may also be the result of the delicacy and touchiness of the subject; they may fear to tread where ordinarily voluble politicians become silent and evasive. So, the land in which "fat cats" eat "pie" and in which public servants are "maced" remains largely *terra incognita* for academic political science.

One final problem remains. If the rewards of patronage are so meager and the problems so great, why do parties fight to maintain the patronage system? Political leaders deprecate the value of patronage both publicly and privately, yet do little to divest themselves of it. Their reasons are no doubt complex, and one can only tentatively suggest a few. The parties need the strength of patronage, however minor and irregular it might be, and they realize, as does any great nation, that in matters of empire one does not willingly surrender even the most barren desert. Above all, patronage has generally been the political way of life and the political ally of the local centers of political power in their losing battle for political superiority in America. It survives to a great extent in their protest against the growth of national politics and centralized parties in the United States.

27. The Direct Primary and Party Structure: A Study of State Legislative Nominations

V. O. Key, Jr.

Primaries, instituted as part of the progressive reform movement, were regarded as a means of widening the scope of the democratic process. In their effects, however, they have weakened democracy by limiting a competitive party system. V. O. Key, Jr.,

From *The American Political Science Review,* vol. 48, no. 1 (March 1954), pp. 1–26, with footnotes deleted.

late Professor of Government at Harvard University, here shows how party organizations have been rendered less powerful and how party competition has been restricted.

* * *

Some analysts blame the direct primary for the supposedly parlous state of the American party system; others assert that nominating procedures do not affect parties at all. The literature abounds with more or less judicious, and conflicting, estimates of the consequences of the primary mode of nomination. In fact, our present knowledge provides little basis for confident appraisal of the effects of the direct primary. This article reports an attack on a small part of the problem, viz., state legislative nominations in two-party states, by explicit methods of analysis, whose use may both make possible a minor substantive contribution as well as demonstrate the appalling amount of work necessary for a provisional solution of even the smallest aspect of the broad problem.

To cope with questions about the consequences of particular institutional arrangements requires both a working theory and a means of observation to determine whether it fits the facts. For lack of a better concept, the problem of the effects of the primary method of nomination may be regarded as a special case of the broader question of the nature of the interaction between formal and informal organization. An old and basic proposition of political science warns that formal institutional arrangements may cloak radically different informal patterns of behavior. Thus, the actual position of the British monarch diverges from the nominal.

Recognition of the divergence between actual and formally prescribed patterns of practice opened lines of observation that have yielded indispensable insights. The fruitfulness of inquiries based on the assumption of disparities between nominal and actual, however, has also led to an exaggeration of the insignificance of formal arrangements. In some circles the view prevails that informal organization governs all and that formal organization deserves no attention. The familiar debate over this matter deserves only an irreverent disregard because it usually concerns the wrong question. Common knowledge testifies to the fact that political practices do not invariably follow formal prescriptions. On the other hand, the contention that formal arrangements are without effect on behavior patterns is like arguing that the rule book has no bearing on the way the ball game is played. The real problem is not one of either-or; it is one of identifying differentiations among types of situations in which varying sorts of interactions occur between formal arrangements and informal organization.

The direct primary nomination procedure may be regarded, at least in the type of situation with which we are concerned, as a formal procedure superimposed over a pre-existing informal organization. In its bearing on the informal organization of parties and of power-seeking activity, direct primary legislation is largely permissive rather than prescriptive. It permits pre-existing cliques and hierarchies to utilize a new procedure; it also opens the door to activity by new groups, new aspirants to power. It changes the rules of the game and creates within the field of political action opportunities for types of political behavior different from those prevailing before its adoption. The extent to which those opportunities are utilized—and thus modify or displace pre-existing behavior patterns—represents the extent of the consequences of the "formal procedure" in altering "informal behavior."

In this pattern of interaction between formal and informal both sides of the equation are variables. The formal procedure of nomination itself may be by convention or primary, with gradations in between.

The informal political organization itself may possess a wide variety of characteristics. Obviously the extent of the effects of formal procedure will depend not only on its own character but also in part on the nature of the informal structure of power and patterns of action into which it is installed. For that reason a primary procedure may have radically different consequences, within similar time periods, in relation to a tightly knit party hierarchy than in relation to an amorphous politics with a sketchy power structure.

While hypotheses about the effects of the use of the direct primary nomination procedure may be formulated readily enough, their systematic testing against experiences raises difficult problems of observation and analysis. So many variables are involved in even the simplest political process that their disentanglement to create a basis for reflection on the significance of particular factors in the whole complex often taxes both energy and ingenuity. Although voting returns report only limited observations of the electoral process, they are readily available for many jurisdictions over a long period of time. Nominations of state legislators, since there are many of them, provide data in sufficient quantity to permit the differentiation of nominations under many types of circumstances and the identification of variables associated with particular types of behavior.

I

A first step toward an attack on the question of the relation between formal procedure and informal organization consists of an analysis of the utilization of the direct primary in state legislative nominations. That analysis will identify features of party behavior that exist under the primary system and raise the question whether they can be attributed to that system itself. In this description of the primary system its workings may be checked against a model that probably corresponds roughly to the broad expectations of early advocates of the primary. According to this model more or less spontaneous candidacies in the primaries would permit "the people," or more particularly the mass of the party, to choose between candidates. Thus, competition within each party would precede competition between candidates of opposing parties at the general election. In a perfectly balanced competitive situation each legislative district of a state would be characterized not only by competition at the general election but also by rivalry in each of the party primaries.

A basic departure from the crude model consists in the variation among legislative districts in the degree to which they approach an even competition between parties. Although the form of the distribution varies from state to state and from time to time, districts range from those whose electorate is overwhelmingly committed to one party, through those that are closely divided, to those that are in high degree attached to the other party. Moreover, at individual elections the movement of districts from party to party tends to be largely in one direction. If the general shift of sentiment is to the Republicans, they capture districts that were Democratic by a narrow margin at the preceding election, but they lose few if any districts they already held. Or a similar selective movement occurs in the other direction. Table I, which relates the 1946 election of the Missouri House of Representatives to that of 1948, illustrates this observation. In 1948 the Democrats lost no district they had carried in 1946; they gained mainly seats that Republicans had won by a relatively narrow margin in 1946.

This variation in the competitiveness of legislative districts, which is partially shown in Table I, turns out to be most useful in analysis of the workings of the primary. Instead of there being a couple of Republicans who vie for their party's nomination and a pair of Democrats who contend for

TABLE I   Party Fortunes in Legislative Races in Relation to Vote at Preceding Election: Republican and Democratic Victories in 1948 Missouri House Elections Related to Distribution of Legislative Districts According to Democratic Percentage of 1946 Popular Vote

Percent Democratic, 1946	Number of seats 1946 (1)	Democratic, 1948		Republican, 1948	
		Number (2)	Percent (2) of (1)	Number (3)	Percent (3) of (1)
0	14	2	14.3	12	85.7
10–29.9	13	0	0.0	13	100.0
30–34.9	8	1	12.5	7	87.5
35–39.9	21	7	33.3	14	66.7
40–44.9	20	11	55.0	9	45.0
45–49.9	23	19	82.6	4	17.4
50–99.9	39	39	100.0	0	0.0
100	16	16	100.0	0	0.0

the right to oppose the Republican nominee, it turns out that a great many nominations go by default. The extent to which a party's nominations are contested in the primary by two or more aspirants apparently depends in large measure on the prospects for victory for the nominee in the general election. Uncontested nominations for legislative posts are almost the rule in those districts in which a party's cause seems hopeless, while a large proportion of nominations will be contested in relatively sure districts. A type situation is described by the graphs in Figure 1 which relate the proportions of nominations contested by two or more candidates in primaries for the Missouri House of Representatives to the division of the vote in the subsequent general election. The division of the district vote at the general election itself may be regarded, post facto, as a rough measure of expectations about the outcome of elections.

Although the increase in the incidence of primary competition as the prospects for party victory improve, demonstrated by Figure 1, probably recurs from state to state, the proportion of all nominations contested varies from state to state with a variety of factors. Table II, with its data on Indiana's 1948 primary, indicates that in

Indiana, as in Missouri, the greatest propensity to compete for a party's nominations occurs in those districts in which the nominees have the greatest assurance of victory in the general election. The table also reveals a considerably higher incidence of competition—with general election strength held constant—in Indiana than in Missouri. That difference doubtless points to basic differences in the political

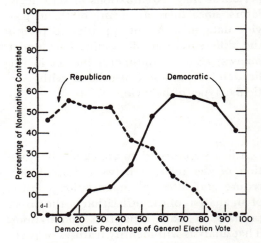

Fig. 1 Primary competition and the prospects for general election victory: relation between proportion of nominations contested and percentage of general election vote polled by Republican and Democratic nominees for Missouri House of Representatives, 1942–1950.

TABLE II   Primary Contests in Relation to General Election Vote:
Proportions of Democratic and Republican Legislative Nominations
Contested, Indiana, 1948 in Relation to 1948 General Election Vote
in Legislative Districts

Nominees' General Election Percentage	Democratic		Republican	
	Number of Nominations[a]	Percent Contested	Number of Nominations	Percent Contested
Under 40	3	0.0	9	44.4
40–44.9	14	7.1	21	61.9
45–49.9	18	33.3	30	76.7
50–54.9	30	76.7	18	66.7
55–59.9	20	85.0	13	84.6
60 and over	11	81.8	8	87.5

[a] Included are those nominations made by party committee rather than by primary. Such nominations are in effect classified in the percentage computations as uncontested.

structures of the two states, one of which is that a larger proportion of the Indiana districts is closely contested. Table II incidentally suggests some of the limits of the actual vote as a measure of the expectation of victory; note that the Republicans competed for nominations to a large proportion of those seats which they lost by a small margin, perhaps in part a reflection of the rosiness of Republican expectations before the 1948 upset.

The high degree of association between primary competition and the prospect for general election victory points to another deviation from our crude model. Instead of lively competition in all primaries of both parties, the prediction now would be that simultaneous contests for both nominations would occur chiefly in those districts regarded as more or less evenly balanced between the two parties at the general election. In districts thought to be relatively safe for either party, competition for nominations would tend to be restricted to the primary of the dominant party. These expectations are on the whole fulfilled by the data of Table III relating to the Indiana primaries of 1948 and 1950. While the

TABLE III   Primary Contests, According to Party Primary in Which
They Occurred: Contests for Nominations for Indiana House
of Representatives, Single-Member Districts, 1948–1950,
According to General Election Vote for Nominees

Democratic Percentage General Election	Districts	Percent of Nominations Contested in			
		Both Primaries	Neither Primary	Democratic Only	Republican Only
0	5	0.0	0.0	0.0	100.0
30–34.9	5	0.0	0.0	0.0	100.0
35–39.9	11	9.1	36.4	0.0	54.5
40–44.0	29	24.1	31.0	3.4	41.4
45–49.9	33	15.1	33.3	6.1	45.4
50–54.9	30	36.6	23.3	26.7	13.3
55–59.9	13	15.4	23.1	53.8	7.7
60–64	4	75.0	0.0	0.0	25.0
100	2	0.0	0.0	100.0	0.0

distribution in the table indicates that factors other than the estimate of the chances for victory may induce competition, save for an erratic exception consisting of a cell of small numbers simultaneous competition in both primaries tended to be most common in relatively close districts. The data of Table III clearly point to the tendency for primary competition in safe districts to be limited to the primaries of the dominant party.

While the preceding analyses account for a considerable part of the variation among districts in competition for party nomination, they also leave some of the variation unexplained. Factors other than prospects for victory also induce or discourage competition in primaries. The supposition that "one good term deserves another" suggests a test of whether primaries in which incumbents seek renomination are less likely to be contested than are those in which no incumbent is in the race, with prospects for party victory held constant. A test of the hypothesis appears in Figure 2 which records an analysis of the primaries of both parties in Missouri for the years 1946, 1948, and 1950. A less extensive collection of Ohio data is analyzed in Table IV. The data of Figure 2 and Table IV indicate that, at least in the safe districts as we have defined them, primaries in which incum-

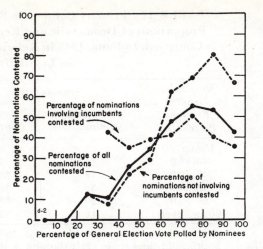

Fig. 2 Incumbents and primary competition: competition in primaries involving incumbents and in primaries involving no incumbents with comparable prospects of general election victory, Missouri House of Representatives, 1946–1950.

bents seek renomination are less likely to involve competition than are those in which no incumbent is running. The Missouri data, however, reveal a higher rate of competition for incumbents in the lower ranges of party strength than in primaries involving no incumbents in districts similar in party strength at the general election. Districts in which the incumbents' party polled but 30 to 40 percent of the general election vote obviously underwent a wide swing in popular vote from the preceding

TABLE IV Incumbency and Competition for Legislative Nominations: Proportion of Ohio House Republican Primaries in Single-Member Districts Contested in 1948, When Incumbents Involved and Not Involved

| Republican Percentage General Election, 1948 | PRIMARY INVOLVING | | | |
| | Incumbents | | No Incumbents | |
	Nominations	Percent Contested	Nominations	Percent Contested
30–39	2	100.0	3	0.0
40–49	10	20.0	5	80.0
50–59	19	47.4	6	83.3
60–69	6	50.0	0	0.0
70–79	2	0.0	0	0.0
100	20	40.0	3	66.6
TOTAL	59	40.7	17	64.7

election and probably differed in some important respects from those in which the party had no incumbent but polled the same small vote at the general election. A better measure of expectation of party victory in the two types of districts would probably remove the discrepancy from the data in these lower ranges.

While a larger sample would probably reveal more regular relations than those in Table IV, examination of the data for other states suggests caution in the ascription of uniform significance to incumbency in relation to primary competition. The extent to which incumbents seek renomination and the customary public attitudes about the candidacies of incumbents no doubt differ from state to state and even from locality to locality. In any case in the

data presented "incumbency" probably masks a more inclusive type of relation between the aspirant for nomination and his constituency and perhaps between him and other potential candidates. There may be a common denominator or denominators between uncontested incumbents and uncontested non-incumbents.

While several factors associated with primary competition have been identified other variables doubtless exist. Demographic characteristics of districts may be more or less conducive to primary competition, and, indeed, to political competition generally. Rural districts may, for example, be less given to political commotion than highly urbanized ones. A test of this supposition appears in Table V. That table compares rates of competition in urban and

TABLE V   Urbanism and Contests in Primaries Involving No Incumbents: Democratic Primaries to Nominate for Missouri House of Representatives, 1948

Democratic Percentage in General Election	NOMINATIONS IN DISTRICTS					
	Under 50% Urban		Over 50% Urban		Total	
	Number	*Percent Contested*	*Number*	*Percent Contested*	*Number*	*Percent Contested*
Under 50	33	3.0	7	28.5	40	7.5
Over 50	28	17.8	25	56.0	53	35.8
TOTAL	61	9.8	32	50.0	93	22.6

rural districts in Missouri primaries involving no incumbents, and thereby excludes from the comparison differences associated with incumbency. A sharp difference may be seen to exist in the proportions of such primaries contested in districts under 50 percent urban and in those over 50 percent urban, with the more placid politics in the rural districts.

A telescoped table such as Table V, with its broad categories, is rightly suspect. A further test of the ruralism-urbanism relation is provided by the more detailed breakdown for the Ohio Republican and Democratic primaries of 1948 which appears in Table VI. That table exhibits some irregu-

larities which would probably disappear by the analysis of a larger number of cases, but generally, within similar ranges of party strength, a higher incidence of primary competition occurs in the more urbanized districts. A lingering doubt remains about the nature of the association between urbanism and competition. It seems clear that the relation between urban population percentage and propensity to compete is not linear. Moreover, metropolitan political systems in which no competition occurs in primaries are common enough. The multiplicity of centers of power and of aspiration in highly urbanized areas may, however, require the application of greater effort,

TABLE VI   Urbanism and Contests in Primaries: Contests
in Ohio Republican and Democratic Primaries to Nominate
for State House of Representatives, 1948, in Relation to Nominees' Strength
in General Election and to Urbanism of District*

Nominees' General Election Percentage of District Vote	NOMINATIONS IN DISTRICTS					
	Under 50% Urban		Over 50% Urban		Total	
	Number	*Percent Contested*	*Number*	*Percent Contested*	*Number*	*Percent Contested*
25–29	2	0.0	0		2	0.0
30–39	8	25.0	8	50.0	16	37.5
40–49	26	15.4	66	66.7	92	52.2
50–59	26	40.6	67	73.1	93	68.8
60–69	8	50.0	7	42.9	15	46.7
70–74	2	0.0	0		2	0.0
100	21	33.3	4	75.0	25	40.0

* In counties electing two or more members at large, nominations were regarded as uncontested
to the extent that the number of aspirants for nominations was less than twice the number
of nominations to be made. In the computation of the percentage of the two-party general
election vote for candidates in such counties a base was obtained by addition of the vote of a
winning candidate to the vote of the highest losing candidate of the opposite party.

ingenuity, and resources to monopolize
party position than in otherwise comparable but predominantly rural areas.

A final question about the incidence of
competition for nomination needs to be
raised. The preceding analyses have compared different districts at one primary.
The fact that electoral decision is actually
pushed back in many instances to the uncontested majority primary may lead to the
conclusion that many such districts rarely
have genuine political competition, whereas in an earlier day in every district candidates of the parties regularly did battle
in the general election. Perhaps what occurs
is that with the decay of party institutions
whose reason for being is to do battle every
two years, competition tends to occur less
frequently than the two-year election interval. When an incumbent retires, when an
issue happens to divide the community, or
when the body politic undergoes disturbance for one reason or another, a contest
will develop in the primary. Such events do
not occur with the regularity of elections.
To test these notions the history of indi-

vidual districts must be traced through several primaries. Figure 3 records an analysis
of individual Missouri districts through the

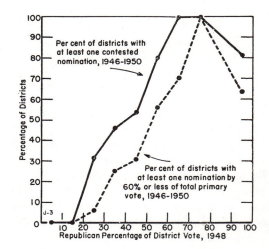

Fig. 3 Incidence of competition in three successive primaries: proportion of districts with
Republican nominations for Missouri House of
Representatives contested at least once in primaries of 1946, 1948, and 1950, and proportions
contested closely at least once, related to Republican percentage of district general election
vote, 1948.

three Republican primaries of 1946, 1948, and 1950. Those districts were identified in which at least one contest occurred in the three primaries as well as those in which at least one "close" contest took place. On the assumption that the incidence of these conditions would vary with party strength, the districts were grouped according to their Republican percentage in the legislative race in the general election of 1948.

When the districts are followed through these three primaries, as may be seen from Figure 3, a much higher proportion of the districts have primary contests in at least one of the primaries than in a single year. Yet the relation between party strength and the incidence of primary competition emerges even more sharply than in the earlier analyses. All this suggests that such factors as urbanism and incumbency may affect the frequency of primary competition but that in the long run the incidence of primary competition is a function chiefly of the prospects for victory in the general election.

If Figure 3 is viewed from a different angle, it throws light on another question. From Figure 1 and other similar analyses based on individual primaries the conclusion might follow that among the sure districts for each party there were many in which the "organization" was so strong that no aspirant dared challenge its man in the primary while in many others the "organization" was so weak that a primary fight occurred. An analysis of several primaries in sequence, as that of Figure 3, indicates that in most of the safe districts the "organization" either is not strong enough to prevent occasional serious challenge or makes use of the primary to settle its internal disputes. Attention to the time aspect of the matter, at least in this instance, modifies the inference of "organization" invincibility that might be drawn from the absence of contest in a considerable number of districts at a single primary.

II

The salient fact that emerges from all this is that competition for popular primary endorsement is concentrated in the districts relatively sure for one party. This association between primary competition and expectation of party victory appears to outweigh other factors that bear on the incidence of competition in the nominating process. The primary procedure, to a varying extent, transfers popular decision from the general election to the primary of the party that has the advantage in voting strength in the district.

These findings return us to the broad problem stated at the outset, viz., whether the primary, by changing the rules of the game, has had consequences for the informal organization of party and of power-seeking activity generally. Does the channeling of actual decision into the primary of the stronger party, by its impact election after election over a considerable period, alter the role and structure of the inner party cliques within the legislative districts; attract voter interest to the primary of the party with the advantage in the general election; tend to bring to the ranks of the stronger party the politically ambitious; and perhaps lead to the atrophy of the informal district leadership once vested with the function of putting forward minority candidates?

While the location of the variations in incidence of primary competition provides material for discussion of such questions, their systematic testing encounters most difficult problems of analysis, quite apart from the problem of obtaining relevant data. If consequences for informal practices flow from the primary, the chances are that they accumulate so gradually that they would be beyond capture by field observation unless it were prolonged for a generation. Yet some inferences may be drawn from the elections data.

The "machine" is said to control nominations as always save that it acts through the primary rather than the convention. Even the data presented to this point compel modification of that view at least with respect to the types of nomination under examination. Consider in particular Figure 3, especially as it describes the incidence and nature of primary competition in districts where the expectation of general election victory for the party is high. If in most such districts a close primary contest occurs at frequent intervals, the position and role of the "machine" or inner party clique in the district must have been radically altered by the forces loosed and the opportunities created by the primary procedure. Such an interpretation rests on assumptions about the power of the inner clique in settling nominations in pre-primary days. Even, however, if it should be supposed that the "machine" wins every close primary contest, the fact remains that it is frequently seriously challenged. If appropriate pre-primary information could be had, the chances are that it would point to a trend toward a weakening of political leadership within the stronger party in the districts, and to at least a net decline in cohesion of the inner core of the stronger party, with, of course, local exceptions.

If the attention of voters and the efforts of aspirants to leadership roles tend to be attracted to the primary of the majority party in legislative districts, the forecast would be that over time a larger proportion of districts would become "sure" districts. In a state in which districts were more or less normally distributed (i.e., a frequency distribution of districts according to party division of the general election popular vote assumed roughly the form of the normal curve of error), relatively more districts would become sure for both Democrats and Republicans. In a state with a skewed distribution of legislative districts, the proportion of sure districts would increase for whichever party had the advantage in safe districts at the outset. In either case the proportion of districts genuinely competitive between the parties would decline. The effects of these tendencies would be perceptible, of course, only in the absence of countervailing forces.

A test of these propositions appears in Figure 4, which compares the distribution

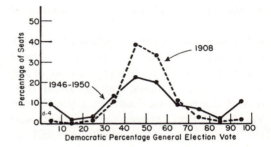

Fig. 4 Pre-primary and post-primary contrasts: distribution of Missouri House districts, 1908 and 1946–48–50 combined, according to percentage division of district general election vote on representatives.

of Missouri House districts according to the percentage division of the two-party vote in 1908, the first year of operation under the direct primary law, and in 1946, 1948, and 1950 combined. Observe that the distribution of districts became more widely dispersed between 1908 and 1950. At one end of the scale Republicans came to win, usually without contest, a block of seats; at the other end of the scale, the number of seats that went to the Democrats by default increased. The proportion of districts clustered about the 50-50 point declined. Whether or not the direct primary was the cause of it all, a point to be weighed shortly, a sharp change occurred in the district distribution in the period 1908–1950.

A word needs to be said about the rationale for the comparison of two distributions so far separated in time. The assumption is that informal habits of political action—the activity of organizational cliques, the loyalty of electors to party symbols, and so forth—are altered only gradually, if at all, by such matters as primary procedures. Patterns of political action have a very considerable durability. If this is true, the effects of the direct primary procedure on political practice become visible only after a political generation or so, not after an election or two. It is, of course, perilous to assume that the two distributions at 1908 and 1946–50 represent observations of two points in a long-term, straight-line trend. Such examination as was made of the intervening period suggests that the change represented by Figure 4 is secular.

The broadened dispersion of Missouri districts between 1908 and 1948 shown in Figure 4 flows principally from the failure of parties to put forward candidates in some districts. Nevertheless, a check ought to be made to determine whether a tendency exists for voters to desert their party on local candidates in order, as the saying goes, "to have a voice in local affairs." Some voters thus might register in the dominant local party, participate in its primaries, vote for the local candidate in the general election, yet remain loyal to the state and national ticket of the opposite party. If

such a tendency prevails, in weak Democratic districts the Democratic legislative candidate would run behind the presidential or gubernatorial candidate; in strong Democratic districts the Democratic legislative candidate would run ahead of the presidential or gubernatorial candidate. These disparities would presumably be most marked in states using the office-bloc ballot.

To test these questions the analysis of the 1948 Massachusetts primary in Table VII was made. No uniform tendency appears for the voters to behave according to the hypotheses stated. The Massachusetts data, however, may not adequately test the question, for the relations in the table undoubtedly are influenced by factors other than the two variables whose relationship is in question and the cases are few. A similar analysis of the 1948 Missouri election, in which the party-column ballot was used, revealed a closer matching of party division of the vote for governor and for legislator in those districts in which both parties had legislative nominees. The upshot seems to be that when there is a legislative candidate on the ballot, he is likely,

TABLE VII Relationship between Democratic Presidential Vote and Vote for Democratic Legislative Candidates in Massachusetts Single-Member Districts, 1948

District's Democratic Presidential Percentage 1948	Number of Districts	Mean Democratic Percentage, Districts with Legislative Contests		Districts with None	
		Presidential Vote	Legislative Vote	Democratic Legislative Candidate	Republican Legislative Candidate
10–19	1			1	0
20–29	4			4	0
30–39	15	36.5	39.6	7	0
40–49	27	44.8	41.4	13	1
50–59	15	54.8	59.2	0	1
60–69	12	64.4	64.9	0	1
70–79	15	76.6	67.3	0	6
80–89	7	84.0	73.3[a]	0	6

[a] Only one district is included in this cell.

on the average, to run about as strongly as the head of the ticket in the types of situations examined.

The inference follows, from the discussion of Table VII, that the type of broadening dispersion of legislative districts recorded in Figure 4 does not flow primarily from a movement of voters from party to party but more from the atrophy of party leadership in the districts. That atrophy manifests itself in many districts in a failure to put forward candidates. This state of affairs exists not only in districts overwhelmingly attached to one party or another but also in districts in which minority legislative candidates would poll quite respectable votes and even on some occasions have a chance to win. The chances are also that the districts that show up in this analysis—those without enough of a party apparatus to turn up a candidate—differ only in degree of party decay from other districts in which the party has a self-appointed candidate. If so, our indicators detect only a part of the disintegration of party that has occurred.

Another check on the question of whether voter desertion or organizational atrophy underlies the widening dispersion of legislative districts may be made by considering the data recorded in Figure 5 concerning the single-member districts of Ohio and Indiana for 1908 and 1948. The distributions for these states are of considerable interest because they suggest an entirely unexpected clue to the nature of the relation between primary and party organization. The contrast between the 1908 and 1948 Ohio distributions resembles that previously shown to exist between similarly separated Missouri distributions. The Ohio distribution, however, curled up only at the Republican end of the spectrum which reflects in part a difference between the party systems of Ohio and Missouri. On the other hand, the Indiana distribution changed comparatively little between 1908 and 1948. It flattened out somewhat but in 1948 a large proportion of the districts remained in the 60–40 range in general election vote (83.1 percent against 93.2 percent in 1908), i.e., they were carried by a ratio of 3 to 2 or less. Figure 5 also provides a minimum measure of the effect of party "organization" in maintaining the 1948 Indiana distribution close to that of 1908. Shown there is the form the 1948 Indiana distribution would have taken if

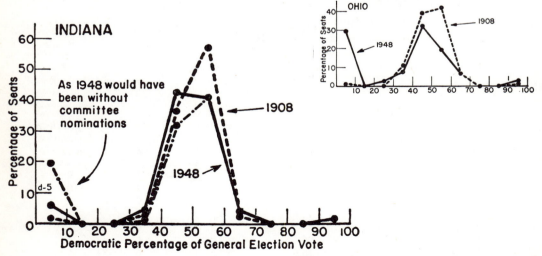

Fig. 5 Pre-primary and post-primary contrasts: distribution of single-member house districts, 1908 and 1948, Ohio and Indiana, according to party division of district general election vote for representative.

one regarded as uncontested those districts in which the nominee was named by party committee rather than by primary.

The contrasts between the Indiana and Ohio patterns suggest a reformulation of our notions about the bearing of primary procedures on the vitality of informal party groups and cliques. Indiana nominates its state legislative candidates by direct primary; its candidates for governor, United States senatorships, and other state-wide offices, by state convention. Ohio, on the contrary, nominates for state as well as for local offices by direct primary, although it uses conventions to draft platforms. The necessities of state nominating convention operation may stimulate the maintenance in all localities of party leadership cliques with at least the capacity to round up delegates to the state convention. A delegate from a county 20 percent Democratic weighs as heavily as one from a county 80 percent Democratic. Thus stimulated, the activity of party cliques may carry over into the recruitment of legislative candidates. On the other hand, similar external forces may not sustain the same degree of inner-core activity in all districts when a state nominates for state office by direct primary. The hypothesis, thus, might become that the atrophy of local or district party cliques derives not solely from local factors but more significantly from the erosion of the organizational superstructure that once linked local minorities to central points of power within the state. Or, conversely, that local minority cliques once gained vitality from their linkage with state leadership and from the functions they performed vis-à-vis that leadership.

If the primaries so far dissected are representative, minority party cliques in sure legislative districts have tended to decay since the introduction of the direct primary. The vexing problem is how to establish whether the primary had anything to do with that development. From the beginnings of agitation about the primary, 1900–

1910, to the present a variety of factors have been operative, all of which might be supposed to have had some effect on the system of informal groupings which make up a "party."

If party atrophy in legislative constituencies is associated with statewide and local nomination by primary, the same sort of local decay of leadership cliques would not occur in states which retain the convention system for both state and local nominations. Since the use of the primary is so widespread, comparative experience from convention states is scarce. Connecticut, however, remains a more or less simon-pure convention state and its record may be laid alongside the data thus far presented. Figure 6 shows the distribution of Connecticut

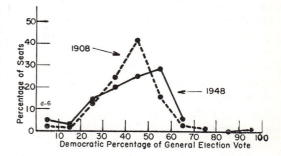

Fig. 6 Sustained party competition for legislative seats: distribution of Connecticut House seats according to party division of district general election vote for representative, 1908 and 1948.

legislative seats according to the party division of the general election vote in 1908 and 1948. While the 1948 distribution, in comparison with 1908, flattens out a bit, it does so only in parallel with the shift in general party complexion of the districts as measured by their presidential vote. Moreover, the proportion of seats in the 40–60 range in 1948 differs very little from that of 1908. If attention is centered on the districts carried by one or the other party by default, striking differences appear between Connecticut and Indiana and the other states on which data have been presented. The proportions of seats uncontested at the general election were as follows:

	1908	1948
Connecticut, all seats	2.4%	4.8%
Indiana, all seats	1.0	5.0
Indiana, single-member districts	1.4	7.6
Ohio, all seats	1.8	18.5
Ohio, single-member districts	2.6	32.1
Missouri, all seats	1.4	21.4

In these contrasts, the Connecticut distributions reflect the least movement of districts into the uncontested category. In Indiana, which retains the state nominating convention but uses the primary for local nominations, the rise in the proportion of uncontested seats has been comparatively small. On the other hand, in those states in which both state and local candidates are nominated by primary, sharp rises have occurred in the proportions of seats won without general election contest.

In the absence of contrary explanations for these different tendencies, they could be attributed to the effects of the direct primary and, perhaps more particularly, to the state-wide primary with its reduction of the necessity for the maintenance of going local party cliques in all counties for the operation of the state nominating convention. The problem then becomes one of whether an explanation other than the institutional one can be found for the differences in behavior of Connecticut and the full-fledged primary states. A genuinely rigorous demonstration of the association between primary procedures and organizational decay requires the exclusion of all other explanations of the differing behavior of the two types of states.

An alternative explanation of the broadening dispersion of legislative districts could rest on the theory that party competition has roots deep in the social structure of the state. The specific hypothesis might be that in our primary states the move-

ments of population, from country to city, from city to suburb, and so forth, had nicely sorted out Democrats and Republicans among districts to make the cause of one or the other party hopeless in many districts with a consequent disappearance of minority candidates. Meanwhile, in the convention states the demographic trends might not have been such as to destroy the bases for party competition in many districts by this sort of polarization.

If this hypothesis were correct, it would be expected that the distribution of districts according to their presidential vote would have undergone a transformation similar to that of the distribution according to the division of legislative vote. The proportions of districts overwhelmingly Democratic or Republican in presidential voting would have increased sharply. Checks on the states analyzed indicate that the spreading of the legislative distribution 1908–1948 is not simply a reflection of alteration in the presidential distribution. Illustrative is Figure 7 which shows the distributions of Ohio single-member districts according to the Democratic percentage of the presidential vote in 1908 and 1948. Compare this with the legislative distributions for the same districts in Figure 5. The Missouri data are similar. The conclusion seems clear that if in such states there were

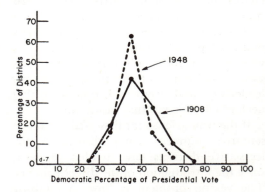

Fig. 7 Sustained party competition in presidential politics: distribution of Ohio single-member districts according to division of their presidential vote, 1908 and 1948.

enough of a party organization in each district to bestir itself to put up a candidate and to campaign a bit, the current legislative distributions would more nearly resemble the presidential.

Another type of check on the general point is provided by Figure 8 which shows

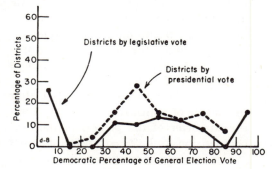

Fig. 8 Contrasts in presidential and legislative competition: distribution of Massachusetts single-member House districts according to division of district presidential and legislative vote, 1948.

the distribution of Massachusetts single-member legislative districts according to the division of their legislative and presidential vote at a single election, that of 1948. At both ends of the distribution the minority party does not put up either enough candidates or enough of a fight to realize its potential in the legislative voting. While a realignment of voters may in some instances produce an alteration of the distribution of legislative seats quite independently of the primary, it seems apparent that that factor does not account entirely for the changes examined here although it may well have been of some effect.

Several other explanations, in addition to nominating practices, could be offered for the differences between 1908 and 1948 legislative distributions. Thus, the introduction of the popular election of senators may have eliminated centers of state leadership that took steps to assure that a legislative candidate ran in almost every district. While this constitutional change probably

was of significance for the organization of state politics, had it been controlling the Connecticut party organization would have atrophied in a manner similar to the state organizations in states using the direct primary. Another explanation, and one more difficult to cope with, is the theory that the informal structures of the Connecticut party system have always had a strength exceeding that of the other states with which it has been compared. Otherwise the Connecticut organization would not have been capable of preventing the imposition of a mandatory direct primary system while other state organizations succumbed to the demand for reform. Unless the retention of the convention system alone be regarded as proof, the supposition would be extremely difficult to test. Another possibility is that over the past forty years those groups disposed to seek office and those groups able to support office-seekers have gravitated toward the Republican party. Nobody is left, so the argument goes, to run for office in many districts under the Democratic banner even though there may be a good many Democratic voters left. If this were the explanation of the tendency in the primary states, the same sort of trend would also probably exist and be felt in Connecticut. It is also possible that such a movement of leadership strata, if it has occurred, may have been, especially among office seekers, at least in part a consequence of the primary system itself.

III

The data make it difficult to reject the hypothesis that the creation by direct primary legislation of new channels to power, more readily accessible and less readily monopolized than antecedent procedures, operates over the long run to modify the nature of the informal structure of party leadership in bi-party systems. The inferences about the effects of informal party structure have, to be sure, been based largely on the indirect evidence of the presence, absence, or performance of candidates. That evidence deserves weight on the principle that where there are no bear tracks there are no bear. Yet the conclusions should be limited to the time and to the type of situation under examination and perhaps even to the specific cases studied. In particular, the observations should not be projected to primary nominations in large jurisdictions. Moreover, the examination of local nominations points to statewide party procedure and organization as a significant determinant of the character of political competition within the districts. Inquiry in that direction would complement and perhaps modify the conclusions. Furthermore, on many questions the data dealt with here can yield no information. The findings boil down about to the following:

1. The transfer, to a considerable extent, of the actual popular choice to the majority party primary probably has brought a basic change in the role and structure of the inner party leadership within the majority party in such legislative districts. Such a conclusion must rest on the assumption that in pre-primary days inner party cliques had a relatively free hand in nominations. That state of affairs must be contrasted with the genuine competition for popular favor that appears at majority party primaries, although the level and regularity with which it is sustained differ from district to district with factors such as closeness of the general election vote. The data tell little about the workings of party cliques within majority districts, other than that if or when they exist they do not ordinarily operate without at least occasional serious challenge.

2. The direct primary leaves a clearer trail in its effects on the minority party. Over the long run there seems to be associated with the primary a tendency for the district party cliques and leadership in the minority party to atrophy. The comparative analysis suggests that a critical factor underlying this drying up of local leadership is not the local primary alone but the combination of the local primary with the alterations in the structure and place of state leadership involved in the abandonment of the state nominating convention. This special case of organizational atrophy may be subsumed under the more general proposition that institutional decay follows deprivation of function.

3. These two broad effects combined alter the nature of political competitors, if not the character of the process of political competition itself. The transfer of actual choice to majority primaries, to the extent that it occurs, affects the monopoly of opposition enjoyed by the minority party, which, Schattschneider asserts, "is the most important asset of the second party." The function of opposition comes to be carried out in considerable measure by candidates within the majority party primary. If carried to its extreme, this process would destroy the minority. More commonly the atrophy of leadership of the second party may leave it less well equipped to perform the function of governance at critical moments when it is willy-nilly swept into office. All this rests on the assumption that the preservation of the monopoly of opposition and the exercise of the rights and duties of that monopoly build and prepare leadership for responsibility.

4. Prudence dictates some hedge about the method of analysis and the interpretations that flow from it. Given the complexity of the sort of political phenomena with which we are concerned, it would be a wise conjecture that the institutional variable is only one of a bundle of factors or causes explicative of the contrasts that appear in different states and in the same state at different

times. Variations in the proportions of these unidentified variables might even on occasion produce results that diverge from those in the states examined here and thereby lead to the identification of factors significant but not perceived in the situations examined here. An increase, for example, in the effort devoted to the development and maintenance of a state-wide integrated party system might offset institutional depressants of party life that operate when such effort remains more or less constant.

5. A word of caution for party reformers is in order. If the assumption is correct that changes in informal patterns of action occur only gradually, repeal of the mandatory primary laws would by no means restore tomorrow the party structure existent before their adoption. So firmly established are the forms and practices of direct primaries that probably in many constituencies even in the absence of statutory mandate they would be continued. Only over a longer term could significant alterations in informal party structure be expected to follow a change in nominating procedures.

28. The Changing Pattern of Urban Party Politics

Fred I. Greenstein

The following selection explores the nature of the old-style party organization—the disciplined and largely autonomous local political parties that sprang up in the urban areas in the nineteenth century. The circumstances under which these organizations disappeared and the effect of the New Deal in reducing the necessity for party-oriented welfare programs and services are also considered. The author has taught at Yale University and is presently with the Department of Government at Wesleyan University.

* * *

ABSTRACT: Disciplined urban party organizations, capable of controlling politics and government in their communities, have been one of our more interesting indigenous political growths. This political form probably could not have arisen in the United States had it not been for certain broad cultural patterns, such as the absence of strong traditional authorities. These cultural patterns were necessary but not sufficient for the growth of party machines. The immediate determinants were the organizational requirements of urban growth, the inability of existing city governments to meet these requirements, the presence of a market—among both businessmen and voters—for the services of the old-style politician, and the existence of free suffrage. Old-style urban parties have declined only partly as a consequence of direct attacks upon them. A variety of social and political changes have sapped the resources of old-style parties and, in many communities, have reduced voter interest in those resources still available to the parties. Further insight into the functions of old-style parties may be had by looking at certain of their present-day alternatives—the politics of nonpartisanship and new-style reform politics within the Democratic party.

Highly organized urban political parties are generally conceded to be one of America's distinctive contributions to mankind's repertory of political forms. Just as the two major national parties in the United States are almost universally described in terms of their *disorganization*—their lack of an

From *The Annals of the American Academy of Political and Social Science,* vol. 353 (May 1964), pp. 1–13, with footnote omissions.

authoritative command structure—the municipal parties have, until recently, been characterized by most observers in terms of their hierarchical strength. E. E. Schattschneider once summarized this state of affairs in the memorable image of a truncated pyramid: a party system which is weak and ghostlike at the top and solid at the bottom.

This essay deals with the disciplined, largely autonomous local political parties which sprang up in many American cities in the nineteenth century. Much of the literature on these political configurations is heavily pejorative, concerned more with excoriation than explanation. Even the basic nomenclature, "boss" and "machine," is laden with negative connotations, although recently there has been a turn toward nostalgic romanticization of the "vanishing breed" of city bosses.[1]

Here, for reasons which I shall indicate, the attempt shall be to delineate rather than to pass moral judgment: What was the nature of old-style urban party organization? Why did this political pattern develop and how did it operate? What contributed to its short-run persistence in the face of reform campaigns? Under what circumstances have such organizations disappeared and under what circumstances have they continued into the present day—or even undergone renaissances? What are the present-day descendents of old-style urban party organizations?

Analytic delineation invariably involves oversimplification. This is doubly necessary in the present case, because our knowledge of the distribution of types of local party organization is scant. We have no census of local political parties, either for today or for the putative heyday of bosses and machines. And there is reason to believe that observers have exaggerated the ubiquity of tightly organized urban political parties in past generations, as well as underestimated somewhat their contemporary prevalence.

OLD-STYLE PARTY ORGANIZATION: DEFINITIONAL CHARACTERISTICS

Ranney and Kendall have persuasively argued that the imprecision and negative connotations of terms like "boss" destroy their usefulness. What, beyond semantic confusion, they ask, can come from classifying politicians into "bosses" versus "leaders"? Such a distinction leads to fruitless preoccupation with the purity of politicians' motives rather than the actuality of their behavior; it overestimates the degree to which figures of the past such as Richard Croker, William Tweed, and Frank Hague were free of public constraints; and it obscures the fact that *all* effective political leaders, whether or not they are popularly labeled as bosses, use quite similar techniques and resources.

Granting these points, it still seems that a recognizable and noteworthy historical phenomenon is hinted at by the venerable terms "boss" and "machine." If the overtones of these terms make us reluctant to use them, we might simply speak of an "old style" of party organization with the following characteristics:

1. There is a disciplined party hierarchy led by a single executive or a unified board of directors.
2. The party exercises effective control over nomination to public office, and, through this, it controls the public officials of the municipality.
3. The party leadership—which quite often is of lower-class social origins—usually does not hold public office and sometimes does not even hold formal party office. At any rate official position is not the primary source of the leadership's strength.

[1] Among the better-known accounts are Frank R. Kent, *The Great Game of Politics* (Garden City, N.Y., 1923, rev. ed., 1930); Sonya Forthall, *Cogwheels of Democracy* (New York, 1946); Harold F. Gosnell, *Machine Politics* (Chicago, 1937); and the many case studies of individual bosses. For a recent romanticization, see Edwin O'Connor's novel, *The Last Hurrah* (Boston, 1956).

4. Rather, a cadre of loyal party officials and workers, as well as a core of voters, is maintained by a mixture of material rewards and *nonideological* psychic rewards—such as personal and ethnic recognition, camaraderie, and the like.

THE RISE OF OLD-STYLE PARTY ORGANIZATION

This pattern of politics, Schattschneider comments, "is as American as the jazz band . . . China, Mexico, South America, and southern Italy at various times have produced figures who played roles remotely like that of the American boss, but England, France, Germany, and the lesser democracies of Europe have exhibited no tendency to develop this form of political organization in modern times."[2] What then accounted for the development of old-style party organization in the United States?

The Crokers, Tweeds, and Hagues and their organizations probably could not have arisen if certain broad preconditions had not existed in American society and culture. These include the tradition of free-wheeling individualism and pragmatic opportunism, which developed in a prosperous, sprawling new society unrestrained by feudalism, aristocracy, monarchy, an established church, and other traditional authorities. This is the state of affairs which has been commented on by countless observers, even before de Tocqueville, and which has been used to explain such disparate phenomena as the failure of socialism to take hold in the United States, the recurrence of popularly based assaults on civil liberties, and even the peculiarly corrosive form which was taken by American slavery.[3]

It also is possible to identify five more direct determinants of the form that urban party organization took in the nineteenth

century, three of them consequences of the Industrial Revolution and two of them results of political institutions and traditions which preceded industrialization.

Massive urban expansion

Over a relatively brief span of years, beginning in the mid-nineteenth century, industrial and commercial growth led to a spectacular rise in the number and proportion of Americans concentrated in cities. A thumbnail sketch of urban expansion may be had by simply noting the population of urban and rural areas for each of the twenty-year periods from 1840 to 1920:

	Urban Population	Rural Population
	(in Millions)	
1840	1.8	15.2
1860	6.2	25.2
1880	14.1	36.0
1900	30.1	45.8
1920	54.2	51.6

These statistics follow the old Census Bureau classification of areas exceeding 2,500 in population as urban. Growth of larger metropolitan units was even more striking. In 1840 slightly over 300,000 Americans lived in cities—or, rather, a single city, New York—with more than a quarter of a million residents; by 1920 there were twenty-four cities of this size, containing approximately 21 million Americans.

The sheer mechanics of supporting urban populations of this magnitude are, of course, radically different from the requirements of rural life. There must be extensive transportation arrangements; urban dwellers are as dependent upon a constant inflow of food and other commodities as an infant is on the ministrations of adults. A host of new administrative functions must be performed as the population becomes urbanized: street construction and maintenance, bridges, lighting, interurban transportation, sanitary arrangements, firefighting, police protection, and so forth.

[2] E. E. Schattschneider, *Party Government* (New York: Holt, Rinehart and Winston, 1942), p. 106.

[3] See, for example, Edward A. Shils, *The Torment of Secrecy* (Glencoe, Ill., 1956) and Stanley M. Elkins, *Slavery* (Chicago, 1959). Reprinted with an Introduction by Nathan Glazer (New York, 1963).

Overwhelming demands suddenly are placed on governments which, hitherto, were able to operate with a minimum of effort and activity.

Disorganized forms of urban government

The forms of government which had evolved in nineteenth-century America were scarcely suitable for meeting the demands of mushrooming cities. Governmental structures reflected a mixture of Jacksonian direct democracy and Madisonian checks and balances. Cities had a multitude of elected officials (sometimes they were elected annually), weak executives, large and unwieldly councils and boards. The formal organization of the cities placed officials in a position permitting and, in fact, encouraging them to checkmate each other's efforts to make and execute policies. Since each official was elected by appealing to his own peculiar constituency and had little incentive to co-operate with his associates, the difficulties caused by the formal limitations of government were exacerbated. In a period when the requirements for governmental action were increasing geometrically, this was a prescription for chaos.

Needs of businessmen

A third aspect of mid-nineteenth-century American society which contributed to the formation of old-style party organizations was the needs of businessmen. There was an increasing number of merchants, industrialists, and other businessmen, licit and illicit, who needed—and were willing to pay for—the appropriate responses from city governments. Some businessmen wanted to operate unrestrained by municipal authority. Others desired street-railway franchises, paving contracts, construction work, and other transactions connected with the very growth of the cities themselves.

Needs of dependent populations

The needs of the bulk of the nineteenth-century urban population were not for profits but for the simple wherewithal to survive and maintain a modicum of dignity. It is difficult in the relatively affluent society of our day to appreciate the vicissitudes of urban life several generations ago: the low wages, long hours, tedious and hazardous working conditions, and lack of security which were the lot of most citizens. Even for native-born Americans, life often was nasty and brutish. But many urbanites were first- and second-generation immigrants who, in addition to their other difficulties, had to face an alien culture and language. Between the Civil War and the First World War, the United States managed somehow to absorb 25 million foreigners.

Unrestricted suffrage

Urban dwellers were not totally without resources for their own advancement. The American tradition of unrestricted male franchise was, in the long run, to work to their advantage. Although it doubtless is true that few city dwellers of the day were aware of the importance of their right to vote, politicians *were* aware of this. Because even the lowliest of citizens was, or could become, a voter, a class of politicians developed building upon the four conditions referred to above: the requirements of organizing urban life, the inability of existing governments to meet these requirements, and the presence of businessmen willing to pay for governmental services and of dependent voting populations in need of security from the uncertainties of their existence.

The old-style urban party leader was as much a product of his time and social setting as was the rising capitalist of the Gilded Age. Building on the conditions and needs of the day, the politician had mainly to supply his own ingenuity and co-ordinating ability in order to tie together the machinery of urban government. If a cohesive party organization could control nominations and elect its own agents to office, the formal fragmentation of government no longer would stand in the way of municipal activity. The votes of large blocs of dependent citizens were sufficient to control nominations and win elections. And the financial support of those who sought to transact business with the city, as well as the revenues and resources of the city government, made it possible to win votes. The enterprising politician who could succeed in governing a city on this basis was a broker *par excellence;* generous brokers' commissions were the rule of the day.

The importance of out-and-out vote-buying on election day as a source of voter support can easily be overestimated. Party organizations curried the favor of voters on a year-long basis. In a day when "better" citizens espoused philosophical variants of Social Darwinism, urban politicians thought in terms of an old-fashioned conception of the welfare state. In the familiar words of Tammany sachem George Washington Plunkitt:

> What holds your grip on your district is to go right down among the poor families and help them in the different ways they need help. I've got a regular system for this. If there's a fire in Ninth, Tenth or Eleventh Avenue, for example, any hour of the day or night, I'm usually there with some of my election district captains as soon as the fire engines. If a family is burned out I don't ask whether they are Republicans or Democrats, and I don't refer them to the Charity Organization Society, which would investigate their case in a month or two and decide they were worthy of help about the time they are dead from starvation. I just get quarters for them, buy clothes for them if their clothes were burned up, and fix them up til they get things runnin' again. It's philanthropy, but it's politics, too—mighty good politics. Who can tell how many votes one of these fires bring me? The poor are the most grateful people in the world, and, let me tell you, they have more friends in their neighborhoods than the rich have in theirs.[4]

[4] William L. Riordon, *Plunkitt of Tammany Hall* (originally published in 1905; republished New York, 1948 and New York, 1963; quotations are from the 1963 edition), pp. 27–28.

With numerous patronage appointees (holders not only of city jobs but also of jobs with concerns doing business with the city), party organizations could readily administer this sort of an informal relief program. And, unlike many latter-day charitable and governmental relief programs, the party's activities did not stop with the provision of mere physical assistance.

> I know every man, woman and child in the Fifteenth District, except them that's been born this summer—and I know some of them, too. I know what they like and what they don't like, what they are strong at and what they are weak in, and I reach them by approachin' at the right side.
>
> For instance, here's how I gather in the young men. I hear of a young feller that's proud of his voice, thinks that he can sing fine. I ask him to come around to Washington Hall and join our Glee Club. He comes and sings, and he's a follower of Plunkitt for life. Another young feller gains a reputation as a baseball player in a vacant lot. I bring him into our baseball club. That fixes him. You'll find him workin' for my ticket at the polls next election day. Then there's the feller that likes rowin' on the river, the young feller that makes a name as a waltzer on his block, the young feller that's handy with his dukes—I rope them all in by givin' them opportunities to show themselves off. I don't trouble them with political arguments. I just study human nature and act accordin'.[5]

This passage reflects some of the ways in which party activities might be geared to the *individual* interests of voters. *Group* interests were at least as important. As each new nationality arrived in the city, politicians rather rapidly accommodated to it and brought it into the mainstream of political participation. Parties were concerned with the votes of immigrants virtually from the time of their arrival. Dockside naturalization and voter enrollment was not unknown.

But if the purpose of the politicians was to use the immigrants, it soon became clear that the tables could be turned. In Provi-

[5] *Ibid.,* pp. 25–26.

dence, Rhode Island, for example, a careful study of the assimilation of immigrant groups into local politics shows that, within thirty years after the arrival of the first representative of a group in the city, it began to be represented in the councils of one or both parties. Eventually, both of the local parties came to be dominated by representatives of the newer stocks. Thus, in 1864 no Irish names appear on the lists of Democratic committeemen in Providence; by 1876 about a third of the names were Irish; by the turn of the century, three-quarters were Irish. In time, the Republican party became the domain of politicians of Italian ancestry. Perhaps the most dramatic example to date of urban party politics as an avenue of upward social mobility was in the antecedents of President Kennedy, whose great-grandfather was an impoverished refugee of the Irish potato famine, his grandfather a saloon keeper and a classical old-time urban political leader, his father a multimillionnaire businessman, presidential advisor, and ambassador to the Court of St. James.

When the range of consequences of old-time party organizations is seen, it becomes apparent why moral judgments of "the boss and the machine" are likely to be inadequate. These organizations often were responsible for incredible corruption, but they also—sometimes through the very same activities—helped incorporate new groups into American society and aided them up the social ladder. The parties frequently mismanaged urban growth on a grand scale, but they *did* manage urban growth at a time when other instrumentalities for governing the cities were inadequate. They plied voters, who might otherwise have organized more aggressively to advance their interests, with Thanksgiving Day turkeys and buckets of coal. But, by siphoning off discontent and softening the law, they probably contributed to the generally pacific tenor of American politics. It seems fruitless to attempt to capture this

complexity in a single moral judgment. One can scarcely weigh the incorporation of immigrant groups against the proliferation of corruption and strike an over-all balance.

WHY REFORMERS WERE "MORNIN' GLORIES"

Stimulated by high taxes and reports of corruption and mismanagement on a grand scale, antiboss reform movements led by the more prosperous elements of the cities, became increasingly common late in the nineteenth century. Compared with the regular party politicians of their day, reformers were mere fly-by-night dilettantes —"mornin' glories." They lacked the discipline and the staying power to mount a year-long program of activities. Perhaps more important, the values of the reformers were remote from—in fact, inconsistent with—the values of the citizens whose support would be needed to keep reform administrations in office. Reformers ordinarily saw low taxes and business-like management of the cities as the exclusive aim of government. To the sweatshop worker, grinding out a marginal existence, these aims were at best meaningless, at worst direct attacks on the one agency of society which seemed to have his interests at heart.

THE DECLINE OF OLD-STYLE PARTY ORGANIZATION

Although in the short run old-style party organizations were marvelously immune to the attacks of reformers, in recent decades the demise of this political form has been widely acclaimed. Because of the absence of reliable trend data, we cannot document "the decline of the machine" with precision. The decline does seem to have taken place, although only partly as a direct consequence of attempts to reform urban politics. Events have conspired to sap the traditional resources used to build voter support and to make voters less interested in these resources which the parties still command.

Decline in the resources of old-style urban politicians

Most obviously, job patronage is no longer available in as great a quantity as it once was. At the federal level and in a good many of the states (as well as numerous cities), the bulk of jobs are filled by civil service procedures. Under these circumstances, the most a party politician may be able to do is seek some minor form of preferment for an otherwise qualified job applicant. Furthermore, the technical requirements of many appointive positions are sufficiently complex to make it inexpedient to fill them with unqualified personnel. And private concerns doing business with the cities are not as likely to be sources of patronage in a day when the franchises have been given out and the concessions granted.

Beyond this, many modern governmental techniques—accounting and auditing requirements, procedures for letting bids, purchasing procedures, even the existence of a federal income tax—restrict the opportunities for dishonest and "honest" graft. Some of these procedures were not instituted with the explicit purpose of hampering the parties. Legislation designed deliberately to weaken parties *has,* however, been enacted—for example, nomination by direct primary and non-partisan local elections, in which party labels are not indicated on the ballot. Where other conditions are consistent with tight party organization, techniques of this sort seem not to have been especially effective; old-style parties are perfectly capable of controlling nominations in primaries, or of persisting in formally nonpartisan jurisdictions. But, together with the other party weakening factors, explicit anti-party legislation seems to have taken its toll.

DECLINE OF VOTER INTEREST IN REWARDS AVAILABLE TO THE PARTIES

Even today it is estimated that the mayor of Chicago has at his disposal 6,000 to 10,000 city patronage jobs. And there are many ways of circumventing good government, antiparty legislation. An additional element in the decline of old-style organization is the increasing disinterest of many citizens in the rewards at the disposal of party politicians. Once upon a time, for example, the decennial federal census was a boon to those local politicians whose party happened to be in control of the White House at census time. The temporary job of door-to-door federal census enumerator was quite a satisfactory reward for the party faithful. In 1960 in many localities, party politicians found census patronage more bother than boon; the wages for this task compared poorly with private wages, and few voters were willing to put in the time and leg work. Other traditional patronage jobs—custodial work in city buildings, employment with departments of sanitation, street repair jobs—were becoming equally undesirable, due to rising levels of income, education, and job security.

An important watershed seems to have been the New Deal, which provided the impetus, at state and local levels as well as the federal level, for increased governmental preoccupation with citizen welfare. The welfare programs of party organizations were undercut by direct and indirect effects of social security, minimum wage legislation, relief programs, and collective bargaining. And, as often has been noted, the parties themselves, by contributing to the social rise of underprivileged groups, helped to develop the values and aspirations which were to make these citizens skeptical of the more blatant manifestations of machine politics.

VARIETIES OF CONTEMPORARY
URBAN POLITICS

Nationally in 1956, the Survey Research Center found that only 10 per cent of a cross section of citizens reported being contacted personally by political party workers during that year's presidential campaign. Even if we consider only nonsouthern cities of over 100,000 population, the percentage is still a good bit less than 20. This is a far cry from the situation which would obtain if party organizations were well developed and assiduous. But national statistics conceal a good bit of local variation. A survey of Detroit voters found that only 6 per cent of the public remembered having been approached by political party workers; in fact, less than a fifth of those interviewed even knew that there *were* party precinct officials in their district. Reports from a number of other cities—for example, Seattle and Minneapolis—show a similar vacuum in party activity.

In New Haven, Connecticut, in contrast, 60 per cent of the voters interviewed in a 1959 survey reported having been contacted by party workers. The continuing importance of parties in the politics of this municipality has been documented at length by Robert A. Dahl and his associates. New Haven's Mayor Richard C. Lee was able to obtain support for a massive urban redevelopment program, in spite of the many obstacles in the way of favorable action on such programs elsewhere, in large part because of the capacity of an old-style party organization to weld together the government of a city with an extremely "weak" formal charter. Lee commanded a substantial majority on the board of aldermen and, during the crucial period for ratification of the program, was as confident of the votes of Democratic aldermen as a British Prime Minister is of his parliamentary majority. Lee was far from being a mere creative creature of the party organization which was so helpful to him, but he also was effectively vetoed by the party when he attempted to bring about governmental reforms which would have made the mayor less dependent upon the organization to obtain positive action.

Further evidence of the persistence of old-style party activities came from a number of other studies conducted in the late 1950's. For example, in 1957 party leaders from eight New Jersey counties reported performing a wide range of traditional party services, in response to an ingeniously worded questionnaire administered by Professor Richard T. Frost.

Services Performed
by New Jersey Politicians

The Service	Percentage Performing It "Often"
Helping deserving people get public jobs	72
Showing people how to get their social security benefits, welfare, unemployment compensation, etc.	54
Helping citizens who are in difficulty with the law. Do you help get them straightened out?	62

There was even some evidence in the 1950's of a rebirth of old-style urban party activities—for example, in the once Republican-dominated city of Philadelphia, where an effective Democratic old-style organization was put together. Often old-style organizations seem to exist in portions of contemporary cities, especially the low-income tions. These, like the reform groups to be described below, serve as factions in citywide politics.

Why old-style politics persists in some settings but not others is not fully clear. An impressionistic survey of the scattered evidence suggests, as might be expected, that the older pattern continues in those localities which most resemble the situations which originally spawned strong local parties in the nineteenth century. Eastern industrial cities, such as New Haven, Philadelphia, and many of the New Jersey cities, have sizable low-income groups in need of traditional party services. In many of these areas, the legal impediments to party activity also are minimal: Connecticut, for example, was the last state in the union to adopt direct primary legislation, and nonpartisan local election systems are, in general, less common in industrial cities than in cities without much manufacturing activity. Cities in which weak, disorganized parties are reported—like Seattle, Minneapolis and even Detroit (which, of course, *is* a manufacturing center of some importance)—are quite often cities in which nonpartisan institutions have been adopted.

SOME NEW-STYLE URBAN POLITICAL PATTERNS

In conclusion, we may note two of the styles of politics which have been reported in contemporary localities where old-style organizations have become weak or nonexistent: the politics of nonpartisanship and the new "reform" factions within some urban Democratic parties. Both patterns are of considerable intrinsic interest to students of local government. And, as contrasting political forms, they provide us with further perspective on the strengths and weaknesses of old-style urban politics.

The politics of nonpartisanship

The nonpartisan ballot now is in force in 66 per cent of American cities over 25,000 in population. Numerous styles of politics seem to take place beneath the facade of nonpartisanship. In some communities, when party labels are eliminated from the ballot, the old parties continue to operate much as they have in the past; in other communities, new local parties spring up to contest the nonpartisan elections. Finally, nonpartisanship often takes the form intended by its founders: no organized groups contest elections; voters choose from a more or less self-selected array of candidates.

In the last of these cases, although nonpartisanship has its intended effect, it also seems to have had—a recent body of literature suggests—a number of unintended side effects. One of these is voter confusion. Without the familiar device of party labels to aid in selecting candidates, voters may find it difficult to select from among the sometimes substantial list of names on the ballot. Under these circumstances, a bonus in votes often goes to candidates with a familiar sounding name—incumbents are likely to be re-elected, for example—or even candidates with a favorable position on the ballot. In addition, campaigning and other personal contacts with voters become less common, because candidates no longer have the financial resources and personnel of a party organization at their disposal and therefore are dependent upon personal financing or backing from interest groups in the community.

Nonpartisan electoral practices, where effective, also seem to increase the influence of the mass media on voters; in the absence of campaigning, party canvassing, and party labels, voters become highly dependent for information as well as advice on the press, radio, and television. Normally, mass communications have rather limited effects on people's behavior compared with face-to-face communication such as canvassing by party workers. Under nonpartisan circumstances, however, he who controls the press is likely to have much more direct and substantial effect on the public.

Ironically, the "theory" of nonpartisanship argues that by eliminating parties a barrier between citizens and their officials will be removed. In fact, nonpartisanship often attentuates the citizen's connections with the political system.

The reform Democrats

The doctrine of nonpartisanship is mostly a product of the Progressive era. While nonpartisan local political systems continue to be adopted and, in fact, have become more common in recent decades, most of the impetus for this development results from the desire of communities to adopt city-manager systems. Nonpartisanship simply is part of the package which normally goes along with the popular city-manager system.

A newer phenomenon on the urban political scene is the development, especially since the 1952 presidential campaign, of ideologically motivated grass-roots party organizations within the Democratic party. The ideology in question is liberalism: most of the reform organizations are led and staffed by college-educated intellectuals, many of whom were activated politically by the candidacy of Adlai Stevenson. In a few localities, there also have been grass-roots Republican organizations motivated by ideological considerations: in the Republican case, Goldwater conservatism.

New-style reformers differ in two major ways from old-style reformers: their ideological concerns extend beyond a preoccupation with governmental efficiency alone (they favor racial integration and improved housing and sometimes devote much of their energy to advocating "liberal" causes at the national level); secondly their strategy is to work within and take control of the parties, rather than to reject the legitimacy of parties. They do resemble old-style reformers in their preoccupation with the evils of "bossism" and machine politics.

There also is an important resemblance between the new reform politician and the old-style organization man the reformer seeks to replace. In both cases, very much unlike the situation which seems to be stimulated by nonpartisanship, the politician emphasizes extensive face-to-face contact with voters. Where reformers have been successful, it often has been by beating the boss at his own game of canvassing the election district, registering and keeping track of voters, and getting them to the polls.

But much of the day-to-day style of the traditional urban politician is clearly distasteful to the new reformers: they have generally eschewed the use of patronage and, with the exceptions of campaigns for housing code enforcement, they have avoided the extensive service operations to voters and interest groups which were central to old-style party organizations. For example, when election district captains and other officials of the Greenwich Village Independent Democrats, the reform group which deposed New York Democrat County Leader Carmine De Sapio in his own election district, were asked the same set of questions about their activities used in the New Jersey study, strikingly different responses were made.

Services Performed by New York Reform Democrats[a]

The Service	Percentage Performing It "Often"
Helping deserving people get public jobs	0
Showing people how to get their social security benefits, welfare, unemployment compensation, etc.	5
Helping citizens who are in difficulty with the law. Do you help get them straightened out?	6

a Vernon M. Goetcheus, *The Village Independent Democrats: A Study in the Politics of the New Reformers* (unpublished senior distinction thesis, Honors College, Wesleyan University, 1963), pp. 65–66.

The successes of this class of newstyle urban party politician have vindicated a portion of the classical strategy of urban party politics, the extensive reliance upon canvassing and other personal relations, and also have shown that under some circumstances it is possible to organize such activities with virtually no reliance on patronage and other material rewards. The reformers have tapped a pool of political activists used by parties elsewhere in the world—for example, in Great Britain—but not a normal part of the American scene.

One might say that the reformers have "discovered" the British Labor constituency parties.

It is where material resources available to the parties are limited, for example, California, and where voter interest in these resources is low, that the new reformers are successful. In practice, however, the latter condition has confined the effectiveness of the reform Democrats largely to the more prosperous sections of cities; neither their style nor their programs seem to be successful in lower-class districts. The areas of reform Democratic strength are generally *not* the areas which contribute greatly to Democratic pluralities in the cities. And, in many cities, the reformers' clientele is progressively diminishing as higher-income citizens move outward to the suburbs. Therefore, though fascinating and illuminating, the new reform movement must at least for the moment be considered as little more than a single manifestation in a panorama of urban political practices.

CONCLUSION

The degree to which *old-style* urban party organizations will continue to be a part of this panorama is uncertain. Changes in the social composition of the cities promise to be a major factor in the future of urban politics. If, as seems possible, many cities become lower-class, nonwhite enclaves, we can be confident that there will be a continuing market for the services of the service-oriented old-style politician. Whether or not this is the case, many lessons can be culled from the history of party politics during the years of growth of the American cities—lessons which are relevant, for example, to studying the politics of urbanization elsewhere in the world. In the nineteenth century, after all, the United States was an "emerging," "modernizing" nation, facing the problems of stability and democracy which are now being faced by countless newer nations.

29. Reform and Organization Politics in Philadelphia

James Reichley

This extract is from a book on Philadelphia politics—reform and organization—by James Reichley, who is presently serving on the staff of Governor William Scranton of Pennsylvania. This section deals with the nature and characteristics of the men involved in the reform movement of the Democratic party in Philadelphia. The author examines in detail two leaders, Richardson Dilworth and Joseph Clark, and discusses the difficulties of building a permanent organization on the "good-government" ideal. He concludes that the inability of the reform organization, generally, to succeed itself is due to the short-term nature of its goals and reforms and the failure of the movement to adapt itself to a broader, long-range social image.

* * *

How do the committeemen in these divisions control their voters? Interviews with a number of them indicate that they do so by acting as "go-betweens" for their constituents with the police and other agencies of government, and also by such acts of good-fellowship as doling out numerous small loans to the needy—practically everybody—in their divisions. "I hardly ever give a man more than a quarter or 50 cents at a single time," says one committeeman, "but I've got some fellows in my division

From James Reichley, *The Art of Government: Reform and Organization Politics in Philadelphia* (New York: Fund for the Republic, 1959), pp. 100–116, with footnotes deleted.

who hit me for as much as 25 dollars that way in the course of a year."

The collaboration between the effective committeeman and the magistrate in his district, who has first jurisdiction over the petty crimes for which residents of the "Tenderloin" seem to have a great weakness, is likely to be very close. The minority-party magistrates (one-third of the total) are particularly vulnerable to the committeeman's pressure because they must be in the upper half of their slate to be elected; a few aggrieved committeemen whose constituents have received ungenerous treatment in the magistrate's court may easily consign him to oblivion on election day. The police force today is not the committeeman's goon squad that it was in the days when the police were appointed primarily as enforcers of the will of the majority party, but it is still widely believed, particularly among Negroes, that committeemen "can keep you on the right side of the police."

The days of the turkey on the doorstep from the committeeman at Christmas time and the ton of coal in the cellar for new arrivals in the division are pretty definitely gone forever—there is not the return in politics any more to pay for such largesse —but the committeeman is still usually willing to carry a man for a while who is down on his luck. Some committeemen continue to hold court in their homes or offices at regular times when their constituents may call with problems, personal as well as political; but, again, the days seem gone when a great many committeemen were a combination of legal guide, warlord, and father confessor to the inhabitants of their divisions. The weakening of the committeeman system was caused, in part, by the arrival on the scene of majorities of second- and third-generation Americans who had less need of extra-legal assistance in dealing with government than did their immigrant forebears; in part by steps toward the rationalization of local government that have

made many of the committeeman's services obsolete; and in part by the growth of the federal government, which is largely out of the committeeman's reach, as an agency for welfare and relief. In part, too—so the old committeemen say—by the gradual passing away of the heroic breed of committeemen itself.

Nevertheless, as we have seen, there still remain divisions in the city where a committeeman is able to control absolutely from one to two hundred voters. In these divisions, one is told, the loyal voters say that they belong "to the party of Joe Burke" (or whatever their committeeman's name may be) and change their label from Republican to Democrat whenever Burke decides to change his. There appear to be about 200 such white divisions in the city and 300 more such Negro divisions, with the difference that many of the Negro committeemen (or the white committeemen who still often man largely colored divisions) could probably not persuade the majority of their constituents, under present conditions, to move from the Democratic to the Republican party. The other thousand-odd divisions are either independent or those in which there are "bad" committeemen—those who do not work at their jobs of taking care of their constituents and therefore have no control over the vote.

If each of the controlled divisions is allowed 100 voters firmly loyal to their committeeman, these divisions together can turn in a core of 50,000 votes for the organization. Since even a "bad" committeeman or one who is located in an independent division is expected to control at least ten votes among his family and friends, the remaining precincts should add a minimum of 20,000 votes to the organization's beginning total. This means that the organization has a rock-bottom vote of 70,000 on the voting machines before the election gets under way. Extra jobholders and committeemen like those in the 13th ward, 5th precinct, who can account for 200 or more votes, easily boost the organization's starting advantage to 100,000. In a primary election, which rarely attracts more than 200,000 voters in either party even when there is an important fight, such an early lead would obviously be decisive. In a general election it need not necessarily be so, particularly if the opposition party can account for some controlled divisions of its own (as the Democrats could in the late Forties) and has committeemen working actively in all or nearly all of the city's precincts. But, even then, when the sure vote is added to the theoretically independent but actually unshakably habitual voters whom each party can count upon, the resulting margin is very difficult to overcome.

The loyalty of the committeemen to the organization is best assured, as we have seen, by the organization's ability to bestow desirable government jobs and to distribute funds to its workers on election day. Other than that, what manner of men are these who make politics their life's work? In the first place the majority of them don't; the "bad" committeemen and most of those in the independent wards generally have some other means of gaining a livelihood and play at politics for the extra dollars, prestige, and fellowship that it may bring to them. The professionals, the "boys," are a breed apart from these, as they are a breed apart from most of the human race. Keeping hours that often resemble a doctor's schedule, managing negotiations with the government that would make even a lawyer shudder, listening to gales of shapeless oratory that might try the wits of a clergyman, they are men with a vocation as certain as any on this earth.

To begin with, they are men not especially fond of hard labor as a rule; they have, that is, a hankering for a soft life in the sense of not keeping regular hours, not doing much actual work, remaining more or less permanently in the pleasant morasses

of conversation. Their claim that they give more time and at least nervous energy to their jobs than most men do is nevertheless valid: Their task of bridging the gulf between the individual and his government, or at least of seeming to do so, forces on them endless small duties which take them to all corners of the city at all hours of the day and night. They are usually gregarious, vocal, good-natured, as one would expect, although every now and then one runs across a committeeman, often effective in his own division, who is close-mouthed or possesses a sour disposition. Many of them are suspicious of strangers (perhaps in memory of some comrade who opened his mouth or his books too freely to treacherous journalists, reformers, or congressional investigators) and as testy as a gang of feudal knights about the deference and perquisites to which their positions entitle them (reflecting the rigid hierarchy in which they exist). Often they have inherited their trade from fathers, uncles, and grandfathers who were magistrates, congressmen, city commissioners.

They are one and all men who, as one of the most able of them told me after searching his mind for the reason why he had chosen his profession, "love politics." What does it mean to "love politics"? It might mean just to love people or it might mean to love the special skills that are involved in successful government; in some cases it does mean one or both of these things, but in most cases it means something more.

The "boys," when one thinks of them, are strikingly different in their origins—Irish, Jewish, Italian, Negro—but yet they are strangely homogeneous as a group. There may be more significance to the predominant absence of white Protestants from their number than the Protestant concentration on the rewards of private enterprise would indicate. It may be that Northern European Protestants by and large lack or else have suppressed the motivation that causes men to "love politics." What could this motivation be? Money? In part, certainly. The "boys" as a rule, if they manage to stay on the winning side, make money out of politics—out of petty graft, out of pay-offs from the racketeers, out of their insurance or contracting or legal businesses that benefit from their knowledge of how the government is spending its money and their ability to manipulate the direction of its expenditures, out of the salaries which for some public offices are by no means meagre ($12,000 nowadays to a councilman in Philadelphia). But one has heard them complain often enough and with apparent sincerity that if only they would devote the time to selling insurance or practicing law that they give to politics they would be far wealthier and see more of their wives and families besides, and one cannot believe that money alone keeps them in public life. Why, then, don't they get out? "Because," they say, "I love politics." What can it mean? The game, the maneuvering, the excitement? Partly. But there is more to it than that.

One explanation of their motivation would locate the "boys'" essential urge in the factor known as "prestige." The truth is, many intellectuals and many members of the upper class who have come in contact with politicians argue that, for the Irish, Jewish, Italian bright boys who pursue it, politics is a "status-conferring" occupation. The Bill Greens and the Victor Blancs and the Aus Meehans, they point out, could no doubt have earned wealth and even the respect of their fellow-men by selling insurance, practicing law, and the like. But the one thing that they could not earn in these ways is "place" in the community. Politics gives them that. As successful politicians, they can demand deference from the greatest capitalists, the toughest union leaders, the oldest of the old families. The Protestants, on the other hand, the argument continues, have "place" conferred upon them as their natural birthrights, and many may rise in

society through the practice of the more normal professions; it is for this reason that so few Protestants are to be found in the dirty trade of politics.

There is much truth, I believe, to this theory: It explains the remarkable similarity between the Irish, Jewish, and Italian faces gathered around the tables in the Bellevue at lunch time; it explains the difference of these men from the folks who remain back in the neighborhoods from which they have come and also from their ethnic brothers who have risen in the world through business or the professions; it explains the financial sacrifices that many of them actually make to remain in public life. They constitute a separate class—very nearly a governing class—in most of our large cities. They form a circle of consciously powerful men, united in their determination to hold control over the community and in their conviction that loyalty to the organization is the way in which this control is most readily achieved.

It is this class, incidentally, that men like Dilworth and Joe Clark seem mainly to hate. Accusations that Dilworth is "anti-Italian" or "anti-Semitic" are obviously absurd. He has displayed clear sympathy for the minority groups as such, and he has many friends among lawyers and intellectuals from these groups who have risen along the path of Ivy League education. But he is, as is Clark (who is more careful about displaying his hostilities), anti-something: he is anti-"boys." He *says* that he is against them because they give the city bad government, but one suspects a rancor that lies deeper than that. A large part of what he dislikes, one feels, is their pushy manner, their arrogance, the way in which they hang together, their very existence as a class which without any particular qualifications or background has in some sense dared to challenge his own.

We may, then, accept the "prestige" explanation for participation in politics as being largely correct. It goes far to tell us why men devote their lives to the service of an organization that can be demanding as any church. And yet . . . and yet . . . does it really tell us what men mean when they say that they "love politics"? Do they really mean only that they love prestige and status? I suggest that it is at this point that the prestige theory fails. It explains the initiating energy but not the emotional satisfaction that politics seems to bring to its practitioners. I propose to defer exploration of this ultimate motivation for political activity to the final section of this study.

In the meantime, however, we must answer John Bucci's claim that the organization brings "the services of government to the largest possible number of people." The answer is both yes and no, or rather the answer depends on the situation of the city of which one is speaking. It is perfectly true that in Philadelphia before 1951 the committeemen were the effective means of communication between City Hall and the great majority of the city's residents. It is also true that the committeemen brought a certain democracy into the distribution of the city's services which the presumably more cold-minded civil servants who have been taking over their role since 1951 do not provide. Decisions at the present time tend to be made more on the basis of what the people "need" than of what they want or think they want, and this tendency carried to extremes can certainly be coercive to the will of the citizen.

But it is also true that this system of communication and this political democracy, so far as it went, were purchased at a very high price. The organization run by the "boys" is likely to be resistant to technical improvement in the means of government which reduces the number of patronage jobs; the opposite side of its democracy is its availability to anti-social forces which can buy its favors; concern for

its powers leads it to discourage popular interest in government and to cloak public affairs in a blanket of secrecy; its tendency to maintain itself by favors rather than by performance in the public good produces in the long run the sort of chaos that engulfed the Republicans in the late Forties. There is no reason to believe that the price to be paid for rule by the present Democratic organization would be any less than that which was exacted during the reign of the old GOP machine. It is the tragedy of the Bill Greens, the Emmanuel Weinbergs, the Sammy Roses, the Louis Amarandos, as of the Aus Meehans and the Bill Meades, that, though they are men who genuinely "love politics," they tend always to corrupt and destroy the very art of government to which they have devoted their careers. A few of them become thieves; many of them become loafers; almost all of them end by being "enemies of the people" whom I believe they have truly sought to serve.

Democracy is a difficult form of government, and I do not know that we have really learned how to make it work most effectively for the public good. The "organization" can no doubt be eliminated as a political institution if it is deprived of patronage and the ability to perform favors (as was once done in California), but the result is the loss of the only true means that we have yet developed to communicate to the seats of the mighty in government the sentiments of the great mass of citizens as individuals (not as anonymous respondents to public-opinion polls or as members of herd-like pressure groups) and to give these sentiments a genuine role in the formulation of public policy. The price of maintaining the organization based on patronage and favors, on the other hand, seems to be waste, inequity, inefficiency, corruption, and the sort of slimy transactions that have over the years given such a bad name to politics in the United States.

REFORM

Reform, it has been said, is what we have in America in place of ideology. Political participation by those not professionally involved in politics is built around periodic attacks on the alleged corruption in government. Unfortunately, these attacks in most areas turn out to be few and far between, and the reform doctrine does not supply the kind of motivation that would keep the greater part of the population politically activated during the long dry spells between uprisings. What is the reason for this failure of "reform" to produce permanent interest in politics, and is there any possibility that it will in the future perform a function of social integration as well as eliminate the abuses at which it is primarily aimed? To answer these questions it will first be necessary to examine the nature of the reform idea.

Let us begin by turning back to the years immediately following the end of the Second World War when reform politics in Philadelphia was chiefly an exciting brew being passed from lip to lip among a little band of idealists in the city's gentleman's clubs and intellectual associations. A part of the nature of this mixture we have already suggested: Dislocated aristocrats were turning to politics as a means of winning back their own from the managerial class that was displacing them in practical life.

How was this strictly upper-class motivation, and the genuine social idealism that undoubtedly accompanied it, translated into a battle-cry that activated citizens of Philadelphia by the thousands to enlist in the army of reform? In the first place, of course, the reform spirit received its mass base by allying itself with the downtrodden city Democratic organization which had been waiting through almost half of the twentieth century for the logic of urban politics finally to sweep the local offices into the grasp of the party of the working

man. But what was the aspect of the reform spirit that the Democratic politicians at last accepted, and how was it that this aspect was for a time not only acceptable but actually popular with the henchmen of the minority party organization? A clue to the answer to this question may be found in the story of the actual binding of the Democratic and reform causes.

Early in 1947, Michael Bradley, the then chairman of the Democratic city committee and a leading proponent of alliance between his party and the reformers, gave consideration to four possible reform candidates for mayor: Walter Phillips, a leisured member of the upper class who had led the city planning crusade; Joseph S. Clark, a dabbler in Democratic politics over the years and anxious to be "rung in on things" since his return from the wars; Richardson Dilworth, a flamboyant war hero hovering on the outskirts of the city's old society; and Lewis Stevens, a starchy Philadelphia lawyer and leading lay figure in the Presbyterian Church of Pennsylvania. Phillips had gained attention through his association with city planning, Clark through advocacy of civil-service reform, Stevens through his religious activities, and Dilworth through his publicly expressed intention to "throw the crooks out of City Hall." With little hesitation, the Democratic city chairman chose Dilworth. Emotional moralizing over the alleged corruption of the opposition, it seems clear, was the element of the reform program that most appealed to the organization Democrats. Had they not for years been threatening to "throw the rascals out"?

Dilworth's campaign in 1947 and virtually every campaign he has waged since that time have been built around the image of himself as prosecutor of the "crooks" whom he has sought to represent as the leaders of the GOP. (A young lawyer, a typical "clean-cut" Republican member of the legal fraternity with no trace of underworld connections, tells of having asked

Dilworth in the early Fifties a rather difficult but fair question at one of his street-corner rallies, to which the reformer replied in rasping tones, "Young man, may I ask what numbers bank you represent?") This strategy paid off at the polls, not so much in 1947 as Michael Bradley had hoped it might, but particularly in 1949 and 1951 after the newspapers had exposed the fact that there was indeed a good deal of corruption in the Republican administration of City Hall.

More recently, such an approach has been somewhat undermined by the fact that it has become Dilworth's own Democratic party that controls the city administration, but the reform leader, seeking to maintain his stance as champion of the only aspect of the reform movement that has seemed much to interest him, has pretty broadly suggested, particularly during the Blanc campaign, that even under Democratic rule City Hall still has its share of crooks and that these would be likely to run riot were it not for the vigilant efforts of Richardson Dilworth. "I seem," he says, "to see the same faces in the corridors here that I saw eight years ago."

Unfortunately, the image of crook-catcher has been a little dimmed by the circumstances that Dilworth has in point of fact caught rather few crooks (the numbers racket, for instance, his special target, seems to thrive as much as ever throughout the city), and that his sometimes very courageous stands against the Democratic organization have usually been followed by back-sliding attempts to get back into the good graces of its leaders. The present mayor, it would seem, has been demoralizingly trapped between a desire to avoid Clark's outright defiance of the organization and a wish to be at the same time regarded in the public mind as the organization's reforming nemesis.

The spirit of Clark and of Walter Phillips, which dominated the first reform administration elected in 1951, may be said, in the long run, to have channeled the reform impulse in Philadelphia more successfully than Dilworth's moral preachments against the rascals in City Hall. This spirit, expressing the typical American mid-twentieth century philosophy of "good government," is less moral than institutional and economic. When Clark moved into the mayor's office in 1951, he directed, with the assistance of Phillips and the three governmental technicians who composed his cabinet, a thorough overhaul of the city's financial structure, its system of record, the operation of almost all its departments, and the entire decision-making process within the municipal hierarchy. At the same time, the new administration devoted serious attention to long-range problems like urban renewal and traffic control which had been almost completely neglected by its hand-to-mouth predecessors. Electronic machines appeared in City Hall to perform efficiently the tasks of recording that generations of ward-heelers had carried out with doubtful competence; trained economists brought fiscal sophistication to a budget that previously had been planned on the level of inky-ledgered arithmetic; employees hired under civil service replaced a large number of the party workers who formerly had given irregular service at their nominal jobs; great housing and commercial developments began to spring up in all parts of the city.

So complete were the changes made at this time that it is most unlikely that the return of any conceivable Democratic or Republican machine administration could alter many of the most important of them. It is probably true, as Lennox Moak, who served as first director of finance under Clark and now is director of the Pennsylvania Economy League in Philadelphia, says: "The reforms that will stick are the reforms that we made in the city's institutions. I cannot believe that any organization would willfully put bad policies in place of good policies in areas where its patronage and so forth are not affected. The normal organization, once it gets into power, does things 'as they have always been done.' They will most probably in nine cases out of ten follow the precedents that we laid down for them." The city of Philadelphia will never return to the condition in which Joe Clark found it. With the single vital exception of civil service (ironically, Clark's special concern) the reforms that he and his collaborators made can almost certainly not be undone. And yet, in at least one respect, the Clark-Phillips school of institutional reform has been even less successful than the "throw-the-rascals-out" approach practiced by Richardson Dilworth.

"The problem that we have never solved is the problem of continuity," admitted Joe Clark in the summer of 1958. It is perfectly true that neither he nor Dilworth has constructed the kind of city-wide organization that could give any sort of permanence to the spirit as distinguished from the institutions of reform in city politics. Beyond a handful of activists in City Hall and the ADA, the reform movement appears to have lost all cohesiveness in the city; the Democratic organization, almost universally regarded as a "bunch of political bums," is universally rolling into power. This is due partly to certain biases within the spirit of reform. Before turning to these, however, it will be well to attempt to determine how much of the failure is due to the personalities of the two reform leaders themselves.

Despite their shared upper-class background and their common interest in reform, Richardson Dilworth and Joseph S. Clark are about as unlike as two men in public life can be. Dilworth is the warm, all-too-human, relatively simple extrovert in politics; Clark, in contrast, is reserved, reflective, some say cunning, complex, the thinker as politician. Dilworth seems to require heavy doses of admiration if not adulation from his sizable entourage; Clark, a loner by temperament, is sometimes ac-cused of being difficult to work with. The current mayor, despite his retinue of supporters, runs what is in the last analysis a one-man show; all persons who deal with the city government are used to receiving phone calls from him in which pending problems are often settled in a few minutes of personal negotiation. The former mayor was a man of the staff who operated through his subordinates whenever he could; many of the people who now are consulted by Dilworth several times a month never had a personal conversation with Clark during his four years in office.

Dilworth rather resembles one of those heroes of F. Scott Fitzgerald, who came out of the Middle-Western gentry to be educated and make a name in the patrician East. Like them, he is charming, generous, unstable, not remarkably scrupulous, brave, ambitious, fond of high living, eager to make a splash, and fundamentally innocent. Dilworth, one feels, is forever playing out a role that he has only half understood, concentrating on the show while frequently growing bored with the substance. Like them, too, he seems to be motivated by an odd and not entirely ignoble idealism— the restless yearning to realize "the Platonic ideal of himself." It is harder to find a literary parallel for Clark. He is more tough-minded than the heroes of John Marquand whose background he shares, and he is more ambitious than the philosophic upstate squires created by James Cozzens (the Arthur Winner of Philadelphia is, in some ways, Walter Phillips). The truth is that he is the product of an upper class more deeply rooted in time than those which American novelists have usually got around to describing. To find his model one must probably turn to such European writers as Conrad, Stendhal, or Tolstoy; perhaps, even, it is in that crafty creator of a commonwealth, Shakespeare's King Henry IV, that one discerns his features most clearly.

In attitudes toward government Dilworth seems at first the more conservative, but on further thought one realizes that he is merely the more conventional (T.R. riding forth for another loud and fairly ineffectual crack at the forces of political unrighteousness). Senator Clark, who is frequently accused of being a radical, may on the other hand be "the most conservative leader in American public life today," as a friend of his calls him, but, if so, it is the calculated conservatism of Disraeli rather than the visceral conservatism of Burke. The Senator has given ample evidence for his attachment to such nonradical concepts as class, authority, and tradition, but he appears to believe that these concepts can be preserved in the modern world only with the assent of the mass of ordinary human beings. He has thus become the aristocratic leader of the commons against the "oligarchs" who seek to diminish the formal government so that their wills may be informally absolute in their private baronies.

Were (or are) either or both of these two most fascinating individuals capable of building an organization that might carry on the good-government ideal after they themselves have passed out of public life or at least out of intimate connection with city politics? Certainly they would have had great difficulties—Dilworth perhaps because he is too much the prima donna anxious to win quick victories and big headlines rather than to attempt any fundamental restoration of civic life, Clark perhaps because the very ruthlessness and cold intelligence that have made him personally strong tend to alienate him from the camaraderie and fellow-feeling that form the indispensable mortar to any enduring political organization. All the same, both possess great natural talents—an unfeigned fondness for humanity in the case of Dilworth, a lucid understanding of human nature in the case of Clark—which might well have suited them for the gigantic task of creating a permanent reform

movement in the city. That both have so signally failed to do so (and with them the somewhat more earnest reformers like Phillips, not to mention the Republican public-relations reformers like Longstreth and Pomeroy) is, I think, partly due to the good-government philosophy itself which all have in one way or another represented.

This philosophy, in both its moral and its economic forms, seems to be oriented toward particular projects rather than toward any broad social image. It promises to perform certain worthwhile tasks of government, whether throwing the crooks out of City Hall or providing a more efficient means of circulating downtown traffic, instead of seeking to understand and to satisfy the fundamental needs of human beings. It takes the needs of human beings as given, and sets out to eliminate obstacles to the relief of these needs which it detects in the framework of society (like crooks) or which have been created by society's own rapid expansion (like street congestion). These objectives, even the moral ones, seem finally to be reducible to an economic view of the nature of man: Crooks are bad because they steal the taxpayers' money; traffic congestion is bad because it is strangling the economic life of the city; city planning is good because it provides an orderly means for the development of metropolitan commerce (though with city planning of the Bacon-Phillips kind, it must be admitted, a humanistic note is often struck).

The social implications and shortcomings of such a view will be discussed later. Here it may be pointed out that the economic view, coupled with a prevailing individualism which insists that government must limit itself to removing the obstacles to fulfillment of the economic needs of the population rather than undertake to fulfill them itself, makes difficult if not impossible any sustained, large-scale political effort dedicated to the objective of "reform." The declared purpose of reform is the solution of this or that economic problem; when the problem is solved or when it has turned into a bore, the whole reason for the effort has collapsed. The possibility of "continuity" in the reform movement therefore becomes slim, and before very long it is "the same faces" of the organization politicians or ones very much like them that again begin to appear in the halls of government.

A little more than seventy years ago two young Philadelphia gentlemen, Mr. E. P. Allinson and Mr. B. Penrose, wrote a little book called *City Government in Philadelphia* in which, discussing the ultimate failure of a recent reform campaign in their city, they observed:

> In its nature, however, the remedy was esoteric and revolutionary, and therefore necessarily ephemeral. It would not retain the spoils system and therefore attract the workers. Its candidates, when elected, often betrayed it and went over to the regulars, who, they foresaw, had more staying qualities. Its members became tired of the thankless task of spending time and money in what must be a continuous, unending battle. The people became restive, and refused their support to what jarred on their conservative ideas, and what they were pleased to call the dictation of an autocratic, self-constituted body. The cry was raised, "Who made thee a ruler and judge over us?"

Mr. B. Penrose, having learned his lesson, went on to become U.S. Senator Boies Penrose, the mighty and unidealistic boss of the Pennsylvania Republican machine.

On a fall afternoon in 1947, twenty-five years after Penrose had died, Richardson Dilworth, then campaigning for the first time for mayor of Philadelphia, told a rally of students on the campus of the University of Pennsylvania: "If I am elected, I will control the Democratic city organization because it will be completely dependent on me. The Democratic organization will

be my organization, the organization of reform." The modern politician has stuck by the cause of reform with greater tenacity and firmer dedication than did the old Republican boss; all the same, he has not succeeded in turning his party into "the organization of reform." In the end, almost certainly, it will be the "regulars" who will have "more staying qualities," and the government of Philadelphia, institutionally improved and technologically modernized though it may be, will again slip away from the citizens who are its proper custodians and into the grip of a political machine strikingly similar to that from which Dilworth and his collaborators rescued it in 1951.

30.   The Suburban Boss

Robert C. Wood

This selection from Robert C. Wood, Under Secretary of Housing and Urban Development, contrasts the suburban and the urban political situation and places particular emphasis on the power position of the suburban boss.

In most nonpartisan communities, the conditions that encourage nonpartisanship also tend to restrain local political leadership. The services performed by the urban boss are not necessarily the same as those of his counterpart in suburban areas, where the residents, in contrast to those in cities, are psychologically, economically, and institutionally oriented toward independence. The suburban party leader assumes importance in that he serves as a link with the county and state political organizations, works at recruiting candidates, and often is involved in political maneuvers of a far more lively and sophisticated nature than those confronting the urban boss.

From Robert C. Wood, *Suburbia, Its People and Politics* (Boston: Houghton Mifflin Company, 1959), pp. 167–175.

THE SUBURBAN BOSS

The conclusion that few citizens are capable of living up to their own ideology is not startling. The same sort of gap between the aspirations and practice of democracy exists almost everywhere in the United States. Yet the ineffectuality of citizen direction and control in many suburbs indicates a quite different pattern of decision-making and manipulation from that existing in other localities. In cities and rural areas the vacuum between constituency and government is usually filled by avowed political leaders; in suburbia, this alternative is typically not available. In a nonpartisan community the professional politician very seldom appears, and when he does, he operates under special circumstances.

It is true that some suburbs feature highly partisan and professionally organized elections; the Jersey City of the late Mayor Hague was, technically speaking, a suburb. Party competition can be strenuous in those outlying municipalities undergoing rapid changes in the character of their populations, as is the case in several suburbs around New York. Some suburbs attract the politically ambitious or idealistic, who chafe under the restraints of the city organization and hope for more successful or rewarding political careers outside the city limits. Occasionally, as Charles Adrian has made clear in his study of a Detroit suburb, a single political figure appears to dominate a municipality, especially when the suburb is industrial in character. Nonpartisanship is only a major and not a universal feature of suburban politics, and even its doctrines can be turned against themselves to produce a strong man.

Nonetheless, in most suburban municipalities, and especially in residential ones, the same conditions of suburban life that encourage nonpartisanship restrain the exercise of local political leadership as it is commonly understood. By his very migration, the suburbanite proclaims the fact that he does not need the help of the politician in managing his personal affairs. He is, as Louis Harris points out, no longer looking for handouts, jobs, or entry into the kingdom of American citizenship. He does not even require the intercession of a higher authority between the landlord and himself: his residential finance problems are with the institutionalized forces of the bank, the Federal Housing Authority, and the Veterans' Administration. Undoubtedly, personal adjustments and favoritism take place in the process of financing a new suburban home, but this complicated pattern of corruption involves collusion between sectors of private business and federal agencies more frequently than between local officials. A bank lawyer or vice-president, a federal employee, as Congressional investigations testify, are often more strategically located than a suburban political leader. Studying the results of his fifty-seven county investigations, Janosik concluded, "Traditional and flagrant types of political favoritism, such as interceding with law enforcement officers or conferring unofficial health and welfare benefits have never played an important role in suburban politics and do not today."

With the traditional function of the party leader as a dispenser of favors absent from the suburban environment, other community characteristics make the development of effective party control more difficult. In the residential suburbs it is harder to put together an effective ward organization, both because of the spatial dispersion of the community and the unpopularity of party associations as such. As far as votes are concerned, patronage no longer has substantial appeal, access to the welfare rolls is not a major aim of the middle class residents, and fewer suburbanites are likely to be engaged in illicit enterprises that require the connivance of the local police for their existence.

It is also more difficult, by reason of the

limited size and scope of suburban government, to generate the pressures and inducements to finance a healthy machine. In the city, an alert boss can subject small or large business to pressures via the assessment, licensing, and regulatory routes; in the suburb, business is likely to reverse the process, for the wealth and income it offers to the community is likely to result in public concessions in the form of zoning, inspection and service adjustments rather than the payment of private tribute. Even in large industrial suburbs, the psychological influence of nonpartisanship, the generally higher income status of the population, and above all, the yearning for respectability, make the rule of the boss more difficult. The nonpartisan basis of local elections requires that the activities of a would-be boss be especially subtle, and the standard techniques for appealing to groups and classes and for manipulating voting procedures are not countenanced.

The same forces of respectability, prosperity, and the limited potential for outright corruption work against the appearance of the rural machine. The strength of the courthouse gang depends essentially on amateur administration and relative community poverty. As municipal professionalization increases, opportunity for juggling tax assessments, making special contractual arrangements, farming out legal business, and manipulating property records decreases. The fees which the clerk or sheriff once found a comfortable increment to his other occupations are abolished; once these officials are put on a regular salary, the temptation to contrive phony events to bring additional fees diminishes.

The necessity for "getting the county's business" also declines: the lawyer no longer finds that service to the local government is a major part of his income and competition for official favors diminishes. Both the rise of the professional administrator and the decline of the community as a place of business remove the local government from a favored position as the dispenser of munificence. Undoubtedly, special favors in real estate and legal businesses continue, and special exceptions in the use of the police power are made. But these gifts can rarely be translated into votes. The suburban man remains psychologically, economically, and institutionally oriented toward independence.

The suburban "boss," when he appears, then, bears little resemblance to the traditional American image. This is not surprising, of course, for the political machine as typically understood has lost ground throughout the nation. Generally, however, the place of the boss has been taken by the party leader, a term denoting a man more interested in the fortunes of the organization than in personal prerogatives and power. It is in this respect that suburban politics begin to diverge from those of other localities.

A suburban party leader is needed in the general party framework. Someone is required to maintain contact with the state organization, to recruit candidates for the state legislature and for Congress, and to claim for his suburb the proper share of favors and appointments. Since the suburban government has extensive dealings with the state, in education, welfare, and most especially, highways, a man who knows his way around the capital is useful. Since both parties face today a growing problem of maintaining a semblance of grassroots organization, they have an interest in promoting devoted party work at the suburban level. In this sense, quite frequently a local party leader appears, usually at the county level, where the ties to the state government are most direct, and sometimes he receives, deservedly or not, the appellation of boss.

The circumstances surrounding suburban party leadership, however, place the leader in a position that is both more comfortable and more restrained than his urban or rural counterpart. His job is made easy in the sense that the vote that he is expected to deliver generally delivers itself. Situated as he is in a community preponderantly of one party whose members are indoctrinated with the responsibility of good citizenship, he faces neither the possibility of sporadic minority uprising nor the obstacles that physical distance and personal apathy impose on the rural organization. He can generally count on a good turnout at the polls without much effort on his part; he does not need to stimulate interest by dispensing money or liquor, rounding up jobs in the county highway department, or providing transportation to the voting booth. Impersonal means of communication—flyers, mimeographed letters, and posters—suffice to inform his party members of the dangers that await them if the opposition triumphs in Washington or at the state and county levels.

To a considerable degree, then, the leader can talk issues rather than provide personal favors, however much he may distort and exaggerate their substance. Alternatively, he can devote himself to protecting the residents of his jurisdiction from invasion by what appears to be an undesirable wave of immigrants from the city or surrounding municipality. In either case, however, he is more likely to reflect adroitly his constituency's sentiments than to shape them. Demands for vigorous and disciplined action on the leader's part correspondingly diminish, for in a very real sense he has the best of two worlds: the small town homogeneity that creates a party consensus quite naturally, coupled with the sense of civic obligation which brings voters to the polls largely on their own initiative.

At the same time the suburban party leader is likely to work under restrictions which his urban and rural colleagues do not share. They live in an environment in which traditionally local offices are used as

stepping stones for more responsible party posts. Party leaders are expected to indicate their preferences for local offices and an association between active party work and local office-holding is viewed as natural. In the New York political world of Carmine De Sapio, the Chicago of Mayor Daley or Senator Byrd's Virginia, municipal, county and state offices are tied together by the operation of the party, and politics at these levels blend. In this environment, the limitations of urban political activity are most usually determined by the growing professionalism of the city's bureaucracy.

In the suburbs, however, the party leader intervenes extensively in local nonpartisan affairs below the county level, somewhat at his peril. While a few are influential in local affairs in the same ways as their urban and rural counterparts, more typically the ethos of nonpartisanship makes their involvement more dangerous. The local candidate is considered suspect if he is too obviously an outpost of the party organization for state and county activities. It is frequently best for a local official to belong to the right party but not to be prominent in it. So Janosik reports that, particularly in the newer and less densely settled suburbs, "the independence of the voter is so fierce that the extent of political activity on election day is the distribution of small sample ballots at the polls and occasionally bringing an elderly lady to the polls . . . Political workers of both parties in these sections assert that the electorate resents the slightest attempt to encourage a citizen to avail himself of the right to vote, much less induce him to support a particular party. The voters' adherence to political independence compels party activity of an oblique nature, quite different from that associated with party organization."

Under these circumstances, a party leader is usually well advised to remain aloof from municipal, town, or village elections and to allow opposing candidates to fight it out for themselves, as long as they both come from the ranks of his own party. He comes to expect and even to encourage local government uninfluenced by partisan considerations. At the minimum, he undertakes to strike a pose of neutrality and to insist that nonpartisan efficiency is his ultimate local goal.

Although his philosophy of conscious self-restraint relieves the party leader of considerable headaches, it may occasionally pose some problems. Apart from the obvious fact that he is not in control over all aspects of political activity in the way other party leaders may be, the restrictions make it more difficult to grant rewards for party fidelity and to recruit new blood. The leader still has the obligation of caring for the struggling young lawyer who in ten years may make a good Congressman, and he still needs money for campaign coffers, especially when his suburb does not encompass the entire electoral district in question.

Generally, the leader finds the solution to the first difficulty in the appointive and usually uncontested offices which special districts provide. No one really cares who mounts the guard over Fire District 37 or who belongs to the commission that runs the garbage district. Only lawyers are aware of the counsel jobs authorized for the multitude of special jurisdictions and only lawyers are qualified to fill them. The very number of local units in the suburbs, abetted by the conviction that the public need not be concerned with technical services, gives the leader a certain leeway in patronage of a high type, which does not arouse nonpartisan indignation. Quite frequently this patronage is all he needs in the environment of middle class respectability.

So far as money is concerned, the state today operates the major highway programs and the award of really important construction contracts is often apart from local control. As long as the leader makes sure that his suburb is adequately provided for in state allocations and that local contractors receive their just due, he is likely to find campaign funds available. So long as he exercises the deciding vote in judicial appointments, he is satisfying the major aspirations of the suburban legal talent he needs in order to make his limited party organization work. All these matters are not the direct concern of local government, and his power here does not bring forth charges that grassroots democracy is being prostituted. To be sure, there are advantages if the local officials heed party requests, and certainly partisan considerations are at times bootlegged into local administration and policy, but the suburban "boss" does not absolutely require them to fulfill party obligations.

By and large, then, the party leader represents an additional dimension to suburban politics, standing beside but to quite a degree apart from local government. The two worlds are defined by the boundary line of nonpartisanship, and to the degree that the local government is not party-oriented, the partisan leader may actually be strengthened. The contrast with the old boss whose image lingers on in many voters' minds, is a point in his favor, and in the sphere where party activity is acceptable, the leader may find voluntary converts simply because he steers clear of local activities. Operating primarily within the party framework, supplying occasional assistance in local affairs but more generally oriented to the state level, he is able to receive credit both for the good government he does not control and for the big majorities he does not produce. In his own world of inter-governmental relations and a few ambitious personalities, an intimate knowledge of law and administrative procedure in state departments and an accurate feeling for the temper of his suburb are better sources of strength than popular and flamboyant action in behalf of the discontented.

In the final analysis, the specter of a dominant political personality is not a particularly realistic one in suburbia. Outlooks, institutions, and election habits work against this sort of development, with the party leader tolerated only within his own backyard, or if accepted, severely restrained in the demands he can impose upon the locality. But the absence of a single personality does not mean the absence of politics by personality. On the contrary, since the environment discourages formally organized political activity, politics by personality is about the only kind that exists.

In place of the outright politician, the professional who works full time at his job, residents look to "wheels" to spark civic affairs—men and women who engage in politics as their avocation, and occasionally as their recreation. Sometimes regarded as conscientious citizens, sometimes as simply incurable extroverts finding release for their energies, the amateur dabblers in public affairs shape local party policy. The pattern of politics which emerges from their efforts often provokes intricate maneuverings among competing groups, lively conflict and sharp disagreements; and it is volatile and complex. But it is rarely partisan in the accepted sense of the word—and it is seldom managed by the professional politician which the city breeds.

IV. THE ELECTORAL PROCESS

Gerald M. Pomper

The American electoral process is an exercise in the building of party and public coalitions. Existing in a pluralist environment, the parties are not monoliths but coalitions of diverse groups. Moreover, they are not permanent coalitions but alliances which must be constantly re-created and rebuilt. Nominating candidates and campaigning for their election comprise the processes by which a party builds its coalition, within which it hopes to include a majority of the citizenry.

There is a logic to the electoral process. The logic may not meet standards of philosophic rationality, but it does provide an explanation for many of the vagaries in American electoral politics. The key axiom in this system of political logic is that coalitions are built by bargaining. Bargaining is necessary because no group, no party, no set of leaders possesses sufficient force to compel majority support. To be sure, force is not completely unknown in American politics. When employed, it is usually in order to exclude participants from the system altogether, as Negroes are still prevented from voting in some Southern counties. Among those who have gained entrance to the system, however, direct force is rarely applied.

Those who aspire to power must gain consent. The methods they use will certainly vary, but, whatever the methods, they are employed in an environment of relative freedom, in which support must be won rather than compelled. Individuals may be persuaded, cajoled, browbeaten, bribed, seduced, or convinced—but they retain the option to spurn these attentions. Bargaining is the essential process of the system; authoritarian command is largely absent.

The necessity for bargaining is evident throughout electoral politics and explains some of the characteristics of politics that appear peculiar in isolation. One such characteristic is the "balanced ticket," with candidates deliberately selected to include representatives of various religious and ethnic groups. This principle ought not to be condemned as a denial of "100 percent Americanism." Instead, it should be understood as a means of uniting disparate groups in a common cause. To take another case, the policy pledges made in party platforms or campaign speeches need not be viewed as meaningless utterances doomed to oblivion. Rather, they may be analyzed as one of the inducements parties offer to those whose support they seek.

The process of coalition building is uninterrupted. It takes place within the party organization as well as in the party's attempt to win public support, after as well as before elections, in minority as well as in majority parties. We have already discussed the varied coalitions that exist within the party organizations.

278

In its public aspect, the process of building coalitions is most evident in the processes of nominating, campaigning, and electing candidates for President. The nomination of a presidential candidate requires the building of a majority coalition within a discordant and decentralized party. The campaign and the election of the chosen candidate requires a far larger alliance. In this case a majority must be constructed from an electorate heterogeneous in composition, generally unconcerned with political questions, and resistant to party arguments and blandishments.

THE NOMINATING COALITION

A nominating coalition is not simply constituted by a majority of the delegates to the national convention. A candidate must also seek support among the various groups that comprise that house of many mansions, the American party. One important group is the national party leadership, such as the incumbent President or past Presidents, congressional leaders, or members of the national committee. No individual within this group is in a position to dictate a choice of candidate (other than a President seeking his own renomination), nor is the group as a whole likely to have undisputed control of the party. However, some degree of support from this group is essential.

A party coalition extends beyond professional politicians. It also includes interest groups that are crucial to the success of the party. While each of the two major parties is an amalgam of the significant interests in the nation, the relative importance of a particular group varies from one to the other. The Republicans, for example, include farm, labor and minority interests, but industrial and financial groups are particularly powerful. It was presumably these interests that were included within the "Eastern establishment," a group supposedly defeated by the Goldwater faction in 1964. In fact, however, these interests were divided or apathetic toward the Arizona Senator. No candidate would be likely to win against their united opposition.

Within the Democratic party a wide variety of groups maintain an uneasy but apparently durable coexistence, and a presidential candidate must seek their support as well. He must consult the leaders of organized labor, particularly the national AFL-CIO and the larger industrial unions. Other vital interests include liberal ideologists as well as liberal contributors of campaign funds, civil rights organizations, and traditionally Democratic businessmen in such industries as tobacco, oil, and entertainment. Of course, only a rare candidate will gain support from all of these interests.

Increasingly, a candidate in either party needs backing from voters outside of the organized party or interest groups. With the development of the mass media, especially television, it is possible to reach the voters directly. Public opinion polls and presidential primaries provide indexes of the electoral magnetism of the candidates. These developments have transformed the nominating campaign. It is now conducted beyond the quiet and comparative privacy of the smoke-filled room, through the network news interview, the street-corner handshaking tour, and the speech-writing session. A major result has been frequent success for the visible, popular, and extroverted candidate and the decline of the dark horse and compromise choice.

From the first days until the final decision, the candidate must seek the support of the state parties—of their leaders and their delegations to the national convention. In the more restrictive politics of the nineteenth century, the state parties monopolized presidential nominating decisions. Although these groups still cast the official votes at the national convention, their decisions are now influenced by the expressed opinions of other groups within the party. A candidate favored only by state parties would be unlikely to win nomination. On the other hand, as shown by the Goldwater victory, support within the states is the essential foundation of a majority coalition.

To gain the support of these various groups, a candidate must bargain. A wide variety of possible lures is available. He may appeal solely to the personal interests of delegates, offering them such rewards as personal recognition, money, or public office. Perhaps more frequent is an appeal to the individual political interests of party personnel. Policy and ideology are important to convention delegates, as McClosky, Hoffman, and O'Hara have shown above (4). A candidate can therefore gain support by taking positions with which a delegate is in sympathy. Similarly, for unselfish reasons, the delegate may be convinced by a particular candidate that he would be best fitted to occupy the presidency.

Such individual appeals undoubtedly affect nominating decisions. In most years, however, we would expect individual bargains and preferences favoring one candidate to be balanced by those favoring another. Of more general significance are political goals held by larger groups. Each of these groups has particular interests it wishes to promote. An interest group would like a candidate who espouses its particular doctrines. A state party anxiously seeks a nominee popular in its own area who can thereby contribute to the success of the local ticket. Competing factions would like to be assured of due recognition and of a reasonable share of whatever spoils are available for distribution.

Over and above their particular interests, all groups share certain common goals. In the bargaining, the single greatest appeal a candidate can have is the likelihood that he will win the Presidency. Control of the executive branch of government is an inviting prospect to the parties. Policy direction and office, personal, material, and emotional satisfactions as well as local "coat-tail" victories, are all likely to follow. Only a thoroughly alienated faction will resist this lure. If national success is doubtful or unlikely, all factions will seek to win the favor of the candidate who finally wins the nomination and thereby share in the control of the party. All share an interest in preserving the identity and unity of the national party itself.

The dynamics of the nominating convention, as analyzed by Nelson Polsby (32), stem from the conflicts between these groups and their goals. There rarely is conflict over the renomination of an incumbent President because this action is consonant with the personal, particular, and general interests of the party. In other cases, it is unlikely that any one candidate can satisfy all of these demands. Obviously, offices promised to one group cannot honestly be pledged to a second. A position on a policy question that brings support from one interest often creates opposition from another.

The goals themselves may be in conflict. Common goals, such as party unity, may be subordinated to particular ones, such as factional victory, and individual preferences may be considered more important than political success. Thus, in 1964, the Republicans chose a candidate who met their ideological desires. He was also a candidate, however, who was doomed to disappoint their presumed goals of party unity and victory in state and national contests.

BUILDING THE NOMINATING COALITION

Bargaining is a two-way process, involving an exchange of resources and the mutual satisfaction of goals. On one side of the relationship are the party groups. Their principal resource is the support they can provide to capture the nomination. They will trade this resource in exchange for the satisfaction of their stated and various goals. On the other side is the candidate and his faction. His goal is obvious—the nomination. His resources include the political rewards at his disposal, his ideology, and his influence with other politicians. As a candidate acquires support, this becomes a resource in itself. Nothing succeeds like success, and a candidate who appears to be a likely winner will attract additional support from those who want to be in the winning camp.

Perhaps the most crucial resource for a candidate is popularity. If the candidate is popular, then the party has a chance of winning the election and thereby reaping the other goals it seeks. Much of the nominating process is an attempt to prove popularity and to make bargains on the basis of this asset. The party groups, for their part, seek evidence of popularity and will be heavily influenced in their eventual choice by their opinions on the candidates' public standing.

All resources must be acquired, developed, and proved. This process encompasses a series of periods. The preconvention period is increasingly critical. Even before a formal declaration of candidacy, the groundwork for success must be laid. The initial coalition is recruited at this time among national and state party leaders, interest groups, financial sponsors, and organizational cadres. A strategy is developed, indicating the possible sources of support and the means of gaining victory.[1]

The nominating campaign becomes more open, extensive, and intensive with an official announcement of candidacy and entrance into presidential primary elections. Participation in these contests has become almost obligatory for any serious candidate. The importance of the primaries does not derive fundamentally from the delegate votes that can be collected. Although any support is desirable, the maximum number of votes at stake amount to fewer than a quarter of the total at the convention. Victory in a primary, however, can be used to gain other resources and bargaining advantages. A candidate will receive increased attention from the mass media and from the electorate. Politicians in other states will take him more seriously and may be converted to his cause.

Primaries demonstrate more than the popularity of the candidate. They also are a test of his skill, courage, and judgment. The diversity of the legal regulations governing primaries demands a series of decisions from the candidate as to whether and where to enter them. The tensions of the campaign reveal his qualifications under fire. The extended trial period provides an opportunity for

[1] See Theodore H. White, *The Making of the President 1960* (New York: Atheneum, 1961), chaps. 2 and 3, for a description of this preliminary period in 1960.

voters to reevaluate their preferences, for candidates to modify their strategies, and for the party thoroughly to consider its selection.[2]

More generally, the preconvention period provides a large and continuing stream of information. Primary defeats will eliminate some candidates, simplifying the choice. The popularity and other resources available to the aspirants will become clearer, and the bargaining options available to the party groups will also be more clearly defined. A series of primary victories and personal successes, such as those of John Kennedy in 1960, can effectively foreclose the party's choice. A mixed record, such as that of Barry Goldwater, results in a de-emphasis of the resource of popularity. As alternatives are clarified, as resources are developed, as bargains are made, the composition of the nominating coalition becomes increasingly precise.

The final construction of the coalition takes place at the nominating convention. In recent years, the discretion of the delegates has been sharply limited. More than one ballot has not been required to name a presidential candidate of either party since 1952. Where doubt remains, convention processes are available to provide greater information to party groups and to clarify their resources and goals. Concluding bargains then follow.

The state delegations are likely to be the crucial party group at the convention. They will still be seeking to satisfy their various goals. Some information relevant to the satisfaction of these goals will have been supplied during the preconvention period. Delegates should know the popularity of the candidates, for example, both nationally and in their states. Where information is lacking, it will probably concern the identity of the winner and the rewards a state delegation may expect for supporting him.

Most delegations would like to be included in the winning coalition. Bandwagons for an individual candidate are an indication of the winner and may stimulate additional support as party groups try to avoid being left behind in the rush. Most bandwagons, however, are artificially stimulated by the candidate involved. Delegates seek more definite indications of the drift of sentiment than an emotional floor demonstration or a barrage of inspired news stories.

Tests of strength are a more reliable index of convention politics. The vote on credentials, convention officers, or the platform can indicate the degree and sources of strength of different factions. A similar effect can follow from a nominating ballot in a deadlocked convention. With this additional information, bargaining can proceed.

"Deals" are a direct means of creating a majority coalition. Through factional agreements, the goals of different party groups can be satisfied. A candidate may make concessions on policy, or the distribution of patronage may be clarified, and the unity of the party cemented. The platform may be amended to mollify one state, for example, or the vice-presidential nominee may be selected from a defeated faction. "Deals" are not always explicit; only rarely are they venal in character. Most commonly, a group is assured that its interests will be protected and its requests considered.

As the nominating convention completes its work, the first part of the coalition-building process has been completed. From a large variety of national and state

[2] Paul T. David, Ralph M. Goldman, and Richard C. Bain, *The Politics of National Party Conventions,* rev. ed. (New York: Random House, Vintage, 1964), pp. 22–23.

party leaders, interests, and voting groups, a majority has been built within the party. The candidate then attempts to build the larger majority from an electorate of 110 million voters.

THE ELECTORAL COALITION

The electoral coalition is sharply different from the nominating coalition, although one follows from the other. Previously, the general electorate was important chiefly as a resource in the bargaining process. Now the voters become the chief object of attention. The numbers involved are strikingly different as well. Building the nominating coalition, even though an involved process, still concerns only a small fraction of the voting public. The campaign, however, is designed to win the support of tens of millions. There must be more of everything: money, time, staff, speeches, travel. This quantitative difference also creates qualitative differences.[3] A distinct technology is necessary. Indirect communication is substituted for individual contact. The logic of intraparty bargaining is replaced by the uncertainties of dealing with a varied electorate.

The resources of the voters in this period are obvious enough—their votes. To be sure, there are other resources a candidate would like to win, such as financial contributions, personal endorsements, and campaigning zeal. These are sought from the relatively small proportion of the public that has the requisite interest, affluence, time, and energy. To capture them, the candidate will establish a "citizens'" campaign group which parallels or even displaces the formal party organization. He will devote a proportion of his time to private cocktail parties for those sufficiently vain or altruistic to pay $1000 for membership in a "President's Club." Interest groups will be consulted and assured of the candidate's sympathy for their aims. Barnstorming tours are likely, not especially to reach a few thousand voters but to raise the morale of the local campaign organizations. A "summit" conference of factional leaders may be necessary to consolidate party unity.

The chief resource, however, remains the votes of the public. In exchange for its votes, the public has a number of goals it seeks to satisfy, but these are not necessarily mutually compatible, unchanging or unchangeable, or easily discernible to the candidate. Much of the campaign, in fact, is an attempt to discover, influence, and satisfy these goals in exchange for the endorsement of the voters.

An individual voter may have entirely selfish goals—a patronage position, a bribe, a government pension. Candidates can achieve only limited support in this way. There cannot conceivably be sufficient resources available to them, or to the government they hope to lead, to win a majority in this way. Moreover, the opposing candidate could match most offers of this sort if he were so inclined.

Instead of inefficiently seeking individual votes in this manner, a candidate can appeal to large groups of voters by means of policy initiatives. Proposals may be made to extend social security, maintain a military installation important to the local economy, or protect the oil-depletion allowance. Many people will endorse a policy and its sponsor even if its benefits to them are uncertain, indirect,

[3] See E. E. Schattschneider, *The Semi-Sovereign People* (New York: Holt, Rinehart and Winston, 1960), *passim*.

or intangible. Welfare expenditures may be supported by persons of wealth. International affairs usually do not affect the voters personally, but they may still cast ballots on the basis of American foreign policies.

It is possible for both candidates to offer similar policy incentives to the voters and to try to match one another in the bargaining for votes. A complete duplication is unlikely, however. Since some policies are inherently mutually exclusive, the candidates must choose between alternatives. Neither can they be certain which policies are likely to win the greatest support. The candidates must calculate and guess, and the probability is low that they will both determine that the same set of policies is to their advantage. Moreover, they are not free agents. In their public lives, and in building their coalitions, they have made certain policy commitments. The party they lead has an historical identity and a position on vital issues that cannot be easily reversed. Rather than duplicate one another, the parties will stress their own presumed strengths.

Policies represent hard choices for the candidates because they alienate as well as attract support. Additionally, the voters are not commonly very concerned about issue positions. The candidates, therefore, will attempt to satisfy other goals. Some votes can be gained by a vague, rather than specific, position on issues. Ideology or party loyalty can be employed for this purpose, as the candidate proclaims his devotion to "conservatism" or "Democratic party principles," without specifying their content. This method can be an efficient use of his resources because he risks less loss of support by keeping his appeals vague. Ambiguous slogans can also attract voters without restricting the candidate. Few voters would oppose "the full dinner pail" or "the great society."[4]

Psychological appeals may also be employed. Most voters have a loyalty to one or the other party and usually gain emotional satisfaction from "their" party's victory. A candidate will use party loyalty when it is to his advantage. Since the majority of the voters identify with the Democrats, a candidate of that party will stress party loyalty. A Republican, on the other hand, must attempt to weaken these attachments, by emphasizing nonpartisan goals or by claiming that his opponent is not a "true" Democrat.

Personality has become increasingly important among campaign assets. Public relations experts and "image makers" have become essential members of the candidate's staff. Personality appeals have the advantage of being unrelated, essentially, to public policy questions. They do not obligate the candidate greatly and so cost him little. Presenting an attractive personality, moreover, is relatively simple in an era of indirect communication and psychological research. It became evident that personality can be an effective means of winning the electorate as early as William Harrison's "log cabin and hard cider" campaign of 1840.

BUILDING THE ELECTORAL COALITION

It is clearly impossible for a candidate to satisfy all the goals of all the voters. To win even a majority involves efforts that are hazardous, necessarily hesitant, and often futile. Pervading all party efforts is uncertainty. Doubts are persistent as to how to conclude the electoral bargain. The candidate cannot fully know

---

[4] For a thorough analysis of such party appeals, see Anthony Downs, *An Economic Theory of Democracy* (New York: Harper & Row, 1957), especially chaps. 4, 7, and 8.

which incentives will be most appealing and which goals the voters will be most eager to satisfy. The possible influences on the voters are apparent, but the particular influences vary from one election to the next, thereby providing both the problem and the opportunity for the parties.

The best methods of reaching the voters are also uncertain. Is the low unit cost and broad reach of television, for example, more important than the personal intimacy and interaction achieved through barnstorming? A particular policy stand may gain some votes, but it is possible that it will lose still more. While all politicians will agree that half the effort of any campaign is wasted, they remain in doubt as to which half is expendable.

In most campaigns, in fact, all efforts are wasted, in the sense that the formal campaign period has not changed the result from what could have been predicted at the outset. Yet, sometimes votes and results are changed and campaigning may matter, as in the narrow Kennedy victory in 1960. The candidate can never know in advance whether he is doomed to defeat or certain of victory. He does not know how to avoid the one or insure the other. If his efforts seem inefficient, irrational, or futile, this is not unusual in human affairs.

One course open to the candidates is to influence the turnout of voters. The candidate seeks those appeals more likely to bring his supporters to the polls, without arousing the opposition equally. Appeals can be made as well to previous nonvoters. Without a past record of political activity, this group may be more susceptible to campaign influence. A potential vote of some forty million is available, far more than the relatively few independent or faithless voters who change parties from one election to the next.

In recent years, great stress has been laid on registration campaigns and proselytizing among nonvoters. The unsuccessful Goldwater effort in 1964 was directed toward an assumed "silent conservative vote." By contrast, part of the success of the Johnson campaign was due to a large increase in voting among Negroes. Historically, changes in the composition of the electorate may have been more significant for party success than direct appeals to previous voters. The coalition that elected Andrew Jackson was created through the establishment of white, male suffrage. Similarly, the period of Democratic ascendancy after 1928 was founded on the large increase in voting among assimilating immigrant groups.

The influence of the campaign among other potential voters is limited. In any particular election year, the bulk of the electorate has already determined its position on issues, its party loyalties, and its evaluations of individual personalities. The most common effect of campaigns is simply reinforcement of the existing preferences. In such cases, as shown by Berelson, Lazarsfeld, and McPhee (38), the campaign is basically a conservative force that strengthens established coalitions, rather than creating new ones. In fewer instances, the campaign activates latent preferences for a party and candidate or, in the smallest group, converts voters from one side to the other.

The course for the candidate is to reinforce and activate those preferences that favor him and to convert (or ignore) the other voters. To do this, he must discover and emphasize the goals held by the electorate that favor his candidacy. The choice of appeals is influenced by basic political conditions. A Democratic candidate is more likely to emphasize party loyalty. He will also tend to stress liberal social welfare policies. Surveys and past elections have shown that the voters approve such policies and that they are more trustful of the Democrats on these matters. A Republican will tend to de-emphasize party loyalty and tangible goals. Instead, intangibles, ideology, and personality are likely to be put forward. The formula for GOP success is a well-liked candidate—such as Dwight Eisenhower—invoking such general themes as "Korea, corruption, and communism."

A candidate does not have unlimited discretion in his choice of appeals. If some issue concerns the voters he must deal with it as best he can. John Kennedy would probably have preferred to avoid discussing his religion publicly, but the concern over his Catholic faith forced him to confront a group of Protestant ministers in 1960. Unexpected events or opposition charges will occur during the campaign and call for a reaction. Nor can a candidate use all appeals equally well. Some men are relatively lacking in personality, others find certain proposals objectionable, and all are restrained by their own and their party's previous commitments. No Democrat would propose extended restrictions on labor unions, nor would a Republican advocate repeal of the Taft-Hartley Act.

The goals to which candidates appeal are also closely related to the methods they employ. Campaigning conducted largely through precinct canvassing will place greater emphasis on the appeals of personal friendship, direct material gain, and party loyalties. Indirect campaigning through the mass media requires a shift in emphasis. More weight will be placed on policy positions and the personality or "image" of the candidate, as shown by the television debates of 1960 (20).

Within these limits, a candidate may choose his appeals. Polls, visceral impressions, and even computers are consulted in an effort to discover the concerns of the electorate. The arts of persuasion and propaganda are employed to convince the voters that the nominee can satisfy their goals. An attempt may be made to educate or convert the voters, and to change their goals, as in Adlai Stevenson's attempt to "talk sense to the American people," in 1952. A candidate may even deliberately court defeat by holding to a personal but unpopular ideology, as did Goldwater in 1964.

The candidate ultimately must decide which appeals he will employ. As he makes his choices, he is also defining the nature of the coalition he seeks. A policy position on behalf of civil rights restricts the number and influence of segregationists in his camp, and an emphasis on party loyalty reduces his appeal to members of the opposition. As he makes his choices, he is also providing information to the voters about his personal qualities. Prominent among the voters' goals is the desire for competence in the Presidency. The pressures of the campaign provide a vital insight into the abilities of the candidates. Even more than in the nominating period, they must prove their mettle under fire.

When all of the bargains have been concluded by the candidate and all of the decisions made by the voters, one party emerges with a majority coalition. The coalition is quickened to life by one man's ambition; it grows by consultation and contract; and it ends with one man, again, in the seat of national power. To gain this power, however, others must be satisfied, and the goals of many interests and individuals must be accomplished. With undisciplined parties and a heterogeneous population, such bargaining is indispensable if American society is to conduct its affairs in freedom. The coalition-building process is the ultimate safeguard of popular control and democratic government.

PRESIDENTIAL NOMINATIONS

31. The Nomination Game

Republican National Committee

This light piece describes the strategies and tactics employed in winning a presidential nomination, with emphasis on the viewpoint of the candidates themselves. It realistically summarizes the practical politics of the national convention system. It may be, however, that many of these accepted rules of the game are in the process of considerable change, as nominations come to be more subject to new pressures.

* * *

This is a game played every four years by two groups of Americans, the Ins and the Outs. It involves more than a thousand pieces. The object of the game is to obtain a majority of the pieces at the stage of the game known as balloting. When that occurs, the game is over and the player possessing all these pieces is designated as the Nominee. In general the game should be played so that at each stage one increases the number of pieces in his possession. Otherwise, observers of the game conclude that the player is never likely to win. He is then in danger of losing his pieces to another player.

THE PLAYERS

Incumbent President. This is the most important player among the Ins. Because of the skill which he has exhibited in previous games, he occupies a privileged position. If he has played the Game once before, he is permitted to compete in the Game again. When he does so he begins at the finish line and is declared to be once more the Nominee. This discourages other players. If he has played the Game on two previous occasions, he may not compete again himself but may be of considerable assistance to another player. If he picks another player as his favorite, he can often transfer control of enough pieces to this other player to enable him to get the nomination. This also discourages other players, but is not as certain to prevent them from playing as when the Incumbent President is in the running himself.

Crown prince. This is the player picked by an incumbent President to receive the nomination. He usually is someone very closely associated with the Incumbent President, a person the Incumbent President regards as capable of carrying on his policies. A Crown Prince should show that he is a dynamic individual who has ideas of his own even though he is completely devoted to the programs of the Incumbent President. This balancing act requires considerable skill, and is not really necessary if the Incumbent President has sufficient control over the Delegate pieces to transfer them to the Crown Prince.

Senator. Things are much livelier when the Outs play the Nomination Game. With neither an Incumbent President nor a Crown Prince around, more players are apt to enter. Some of these are known as Senators. A Senator plays the Nomination Game by taking stands on important issues and attacking the President for failing to develop satisfactory policies. Although a Senator spends some time in Washington so as to appear on television programs originating in the Capital, he spends more time on airplanes going to one place or another to make speeches. This increases a Senator's

From the *Republican Report,* vol. 3, no. 2 (February 1964), pp. 2–4, by permission of the Republican National Committee.

chances of obtaining new Delegate pieces. A Senator cannot win the Nomination Game by doing committee work or other important things in the Senate, but if he works very hard at his job and is highly regarded by his colleagues, he sometimes wins the Consolation Prize.

Governor. A Governor of a large important state plays the Nomination game by doing a good job in Stateville. This enables him to make speeches pointing to the effective program which has been carried out in Stateville, contrasting this with the ill advised policies of the President. He mentions this whenever he makes speeches around the country. Sometimes a Governor stays in Stateville and issues periodic statements that he is not going to play the Nomination Game. Then his friends have to make the speeches contrasting the good job being done in Stateville with the ineffective program of the President.

Titular leader. A Titular Leader is a person who has successfully played the Nomination Game four years before but who happens to live at the wrong address. (Any address other than 1600 Pennsylvania Avenue is considered to be the wrong address.) His past success permits him to be introduced as the Titular Leader of his party whenever he makes speeches. This is very useful, and has enabled two recent contestants to win the Nomination Game a second time. It is, however, considered safer to live at the correct address. Then you are introduced as the President of the United States, and are able to play the Nomination Game with the Ins instead of the Outs.

General. A General makes quite different moves from the players discussed thus far. He begins at an early age by attending West Point and emerging as a Second Lieutenant. Many years then pass while he becomes a Lieutenant Colonel. If it happens that the nation gets involved in a war, and he is promoted to the command of a victorious army, he is likely to become openly involved in the Nomination Game. Otherwise he remains a Lieutenant Colonel whose name is misspelled by newspapers.

Popular figure. A player may enter the game if he has done very well in some non-political occupation, if he is, for example, a distinguished lawyer, corporation executive, ambassador, or college president. If he wishes to play the Nomination Game, his picture should appear on the covers of as many national magazines as possible together with stories to the effect that the wisdom he has shown in his chosen profession implies an ability to lead the country. Hence it is essential that such a player obtain the services of a good press agent who can build him up to the status of a Popular Figure.

Dark horse. A Dark Horse also plays the Nomination Game in a very special way. He becomes an active player in the Game only when it becomes apparent that none of the favorites are going to win. Until that time it is necessary that he avoid making anyone angry, anyone, that is, in his own party. This causes Dark Horses to be very quiet while the Nomination Game is being played. Most are so unobtrusive that they are completely forgotten. In fact, it has been forty years since a Dark Horse won the Nomination Game.

PARTY LEADERS

The contestants play the Nomination Game with the assistance of party leaders. The party leaders who are involved in the Nomination Game are those who control some of the Delegate pieces. Some states have a single party leader who controls all of his state's Delegate pieces. Occasionally states have been known to have as many as fifty party leaders, each of whom has control over a single Delegate piece. This causes a certain amount of confusion, but it is very interesting to observers because of the intricate strategy it requires.

Party leaders often do not care who wins the Nomination Game. If they are playing with the Ins, they have been told who is going to win the Game. If they are playing with the Outs, they want to arrange things so they can play as Ins next time. But beyond this, they are principally concerned with the problems confronting them in their own states. They want a candidate who will support policies which are popular in their state. They make their views clear to the players. The players in turn bargain for their support by trying to show that their ideas will be popular in the party leader's state. This is referred to in the Nomination Game as making a commitment. The party leaders become attached to the fortunes of some particular player, and the player makes certain commitments to the party leaders. The party leaders try to guess who the winner is going to be, and then bargain with him for their Delegate pieces at a time when the player will be willing to make many promises for control of the Delegate pieces. (It does no good for a party leader to reach an agreement with a losing player as he cannot carry out his promises.) The players try to convince the party leaders that they are going to win the Nomination Game, for which reason it would be wise for the party leaders to transfer control of their Delegate pieces without requesting any commitments from them. Players dream of winning the Game without making a single commitment. This is the same as receiving a kick off in your end zone and running it back to the opponent's end zone without a tackler touching you. It requires speed and good foot work.

THE DELEGATE PIECES

Part of the fascination of the Nomination Game is that the pieces with which the Game is going to be played are themselves selected in the early stages of the game. Each state is allotted a certain number of at-large pieces and a certain number of district pieces. All states are given a minimum number of pieces so their party leaders

can take part in the game, and the states whose party leaders have been successful are given a number of bonus pieces so they can have more bargaining power.

Each state decides for itself how it is going to select its pieces. In a few states, this job is entrusted to the party leaders themselves. Other states select their pieces in a state convention, and still others hold primary elections for this purpose. Some of the primary states turn over control of the pieces to one of the players; others select their pieces by vote, but permit the party leaders to award control of the pieces to whatever player they see fit. This is a very complicated process. Sometimes a player thinks he is very popular in a particular state, but discovers that another player has control of that state's pieces. Players should keep a sharp eye on the rule book during this stage of the game.

THE GAMBITS

Entry. A player is permitted to enter the Nomination Game after he has logged the required number of hours flying around the country, and after a number of party leaders encourage him to play the Game.

Foreign travel. At a very early stage, the player should make one or more trips abroad. He should visit areas affected by foreign policy crises, and then issue a statement to the effect that the United States and the Free World face a critical situation there. (The player could make the same statement in Stateville, but he would not get nearly as much press coverage.) It is important for the player to have pictures taken when he is talking with foreign dignitaries. These can be used later in the Nomination Game as evidence that he understands world problems.

Pollsmanship. The best move for a player is to have polls published showing that he is the most popular person in his own party, and that he is more popular than the most popular player in the other party. This is difficult to arrange for more than one person, so the other players must react differently to the polls. Everyone but the front-runner should point out that the front-runner "peaked too early" and that his strength will not last. Another move is to produce polls which show that your own standing is constantly increasing. This is easiest to do if one begins with a very low standing in the polls. (This low position, however, should not be maintained for too long a time.) If all else fails, the polls can be denounced as "mere popularity contests."

Announcement. At some stage each player is expected to make a public declaration that he is playing the Game. This is preceded by a number of statements urging the individual to become a candidate. These come from party leaders who are supporting this particular player. The player responds for some time by saying that he is not a candidate. (Such a Non-Announcement is more advantageous than an Announcement since it can be repeated a number of times.) The Announcement, however, cannot be indefinitely delayed because other players will use a too-often-repeated Non-Announcement as a tactic to gain Delegate Pieces themselves. Therefore the player eventually holds a press conference at which time he states that he is giving in to the many demands which have been coming from all parts of the nation, and that he is, in fact, playing the Game.

Primaries. Each player must decide whether he wants to try to acquire pieces in primary elections. If he wins the primary elections, this increases his bargaining power with other party leaders. But if he loses any primary elections, other players at once say that he is not going to win the Game and start competing for the pieces he already has. The player therefore selects primaries where he thinks he may make a good showing, and stays out of the others. If he estimates his chances as less than even, he usually does not campaign but arranges for Delegates to be run "without his con-

sent." If he believes his chances are even or better than even, he does everything he can to build up support in the state and shakes hands with every voter he can find. Meanwhile he says that he is "facing an uphill battle" in the state, and is always "pleasantly surprised" if he wins.

Conventions. District and state conventions attract less attention in the press, and are sometimes forgotten by observers of the Nomination Game. They are, however, quite important. A player can acquire more pieces at conventions than he can in primaries. Whereas primaries require campaigns to obtain as many votes as possible, conventions call for the intensive cultivation of the delegates. Occasionally a player will make trips to the state to speak at the conventions. If he does not, he should see to it that party leaders who are supporting him attend the convention with a view to convincing the delegates that the states' pieces should be given to him.

Arrival at the convention city. There was a time when the players did not go to the Convention City at all. Now many players go to the city where the final rounds of the Game are to be played. Their arrival is announced well in advance. The player should be met at the airport, driven to his hotel, and welcomed at the hotel by cheering crowds. Although normal curiosity will often produce a good sized crowd, this should not be relied upon. Workers supporting the player should crowd around the entrance to his hotel carrying large signs. This is important for television coverage.

Platform. The platform is a document which gives the reasons why an In or Out should be elected. In general, the In's platform points to all of the wonderful things the President has accomplished, while the Out's deplores the fact that the In's haven't been able to do anything. The details of this platform may be embarrassing to a player if it says that his party stands for policies which are unacceptable to him. If the player has friends on the platform committee, he ought to let them know that he is unhappy about the platform they are writing. If the player does not have friends on the platform committee, he should skip this move and go directly to credentials.

Credentials. This move determines which pieces are going to be counted in the balloting. It sometimes happens that states have chosen more than one set of Delegate pieces. The rules prohibit this, and the credentials committee must decide which set is going to be used. If two or three players have almost the same number of pieces, this can be vital to the chances of the players. If a player has a number of friends on the credentials committee, he should praise the impartiality and fairness of this committee. If he lacks friends on the committee, he often demands that the determination be made on the floor of the convention.

Test vote. This is a preliminary count of the number of pieces which each player has. It may come about in a variety of ways. It may involve the platform, or concern a decision about credentials, or appeal a ruling of the chair. The important thing is that it should be on an issue which will maximize the number of pieces in the player's possession. If a player is successful in making this move, it is much easier for him to acquire further pieces prior to the balloting.

Balloting. This is the final counting of the pieces in the possession of each player, the pay-off of the entire Nomination Game. The counting will continue until one of the players has a majority of the votes. If a player is thought to have almost a majority of the votes, he should try to exhibit such a majority on a very early ballot. Otherwise party leaders who had made commitments to him on the assumption that he was going to win the Game are likely to start switching their pieces to some other player. If one does not have enough pieces to win on an

early ballot, he should try to hold his pieces until it is evident that the players with more pieces are not going to win. At this stage he can begin to bargain with other players for control of their pieces. This continues until it is evident that none of the players who had a substantial number of pieces before the balloting began will be able to get a majority. This is called a deadlock, and at this point the more important party leaders get together and decide which one of the Dark Horses will be the Nominee. Regardless of the stage of the balloting at which he was selected, the Nominee then goes directly to Election Game.

32. Decision Making at the National Conventions

Nelson W. Polsby

Although national conventions may appear to be carnivals or bedlams, there is an underlying logic to their procedures and decisions. In the following article, Nelson Polsby, Professor of Government, Wesleyan University, adduces a series of propositions about the behavior of the delegates, leaders, and candidates. Convention participants operate under the basic principle that victory is the goal of a political party. Their behavior in particular instances follows from this primary axiom.

* * *

Our national conventions are famous for puzzling casual observers, both foreign and domestic. It therefore seems especially worthwhile to show that a great many convention practices and events can be related to basic rules and circumstances of American politics.

From the *Western Political Quarterly*, vol. 13, no. 3 (September 1960), pp. 609–617, with footnotes deleted, by permission of the University of Utah.

THE CONVENTION
AS A SOCIAL SYSTEM

1. *Delegates to national conventions are expected to behave in a way that will maximize their political power; that is, they are politicians.*

The rational dice player will place his bets in accordance with his chances of winning under the rules of the game he is playing. Similarly, the "rational" delegate will be expected to be reasonably well informed about how his behavior affects his chances of achieving his goals, and will behave in accordance with his information, his position in the game, and the goals he is intent upon achieving.

The goal "political power" can for our purposes be specified as the ability to make decisions, or to influence the making of decisions of government. Instrumental to this is the achievement of access to those offices and officials empowered to make governmental decisions, and instrumental to access, in turn, is the ability to staff the government, either by selecting officials to fill appointive offices (patronage) or by significantly influencing the nomination and election of elected officials. Since the latter are usually empowered to make appointments, access to this class of officials is often instrumental to the dispensation of patronage. "Access" we may define as the opportunity to press claims upon decision-makers. This does not imply that those who have more access are more successful in pressing their claims, but it is generally supposed that claims have a better chance of realization when they are presented repeatedly and auspiciously to decision-makers.

It may be well to emphasize that the term "politician" refers to but one of many roles that individuals play, and it is only insofar as these individuals are delegates to national conventions that they need be considered politicians here. If delegates are politicians in other contexts—members of Congress, for example—this fact may be expected to have impact on their behavior in the convention situation, and may predict channels of communication in the convention. This proposition, however, merely defines the frame of values within which delegates will be expected to calculate their gains and costs.

2. *At each level of government, party organization is controlled by the elected chief executive.*

Parties are organizations devoted to maximizing political power. At each level of government, the elected chief executive (mayor, governor, President) generally has the most political power, and as a result the party organizations depend more upon access to chief executives than on any other source for their political power. In addition, parties are accountable for the activities of chief executives elected with their endorsement. Accountability means that when the party endorses a man, it designates him as its agent before the electorate. The fortunes of the party depend on the success of party candidates. Candidates come and go, but parties and electorates remain, and it is assumed that the actions of a party's men in office will in the long run determine the extent and location of the party's appeal within the electorate, and its record of success at the polls.

Just as the party is greatly dependent, at any moment, upon its incumbent officeholders for its political power, these officeholders in turn often have great discretion in the distribution of indulgences to the party, and it is expected that they will seek to strengthen themselves within the party organization by the judicious dispensation of favors and patronage. This suggests that the elected chief executive comes closer than any other individual to possessing unilateral controls over the party organization, and that these unilateral controls may be used by the chief executive to impose his own preferences on the party organization.

We may consider it axiomatic that the presidency possesses more political power than any other national office, and that the governorship possesses more political power than any other state office. If we also take account of the fact that the national government as compared with state and local governments dominates American political life in the scope, comprehensiveness, and immediacy of its powers, we may deduce the following additional propositions: (1) the Presidency possesses more political power than any other office; (2) access to the Presidency is the most efficient means for politicians to realize their goals; and (3) the choice of a presidential candidate is the single decision dominating the national convention. If the powers of the President vis à vis the national party organization are all that previous propositions assert, they should be reflected in his control of a national convention.

3. *An incumbent President runs national conventions of his party hierarchically, if he chooses to do so.*

The presidential power over national conventions has historically extended to (1) the right to renomination, or to designate the party nominee, effectively exercised in seventeen of the nineteen conventions since the Civil War in which the President interested himself in the outcome; (2) the power to dictate the party platform; (3) the power to designate the officers of the convention; (4) the power to select many delegates—especially potent in the case of Republican delegations from the one-party Democratic South, where Republican Presidents, until the passage of the Hatch Act, drew upon a corporal's guard of federal patronage appointees to man this sizable convention bloc.

National conventions which are run hierarchically seem to be subject to the same costs of calculation and control as are most other hierarchies. Just as hierarchical price-fixing will tend to misrepresent real costs, this type of decision-making in conventions has historically miscalculated the bounds of the framework of consent within which the political party must function. Party accountability and federal patronage are powerful incentives to co-operation with the President, but this power is not unlimited. This was demonstrated when, in 1912 and 1948, several delegations walked out of national conventions and set up splinter parties to protest hierarchical decisions which threatened to inflict severe deprivations on factional and sectional politicians who acquiesced to them. This suggests that party splinters are much more likely to occur when a party is in power than when a party is out of power, as a possible consequence of hierarchical decision-making.

4. *A relatively few party leaders control the decisions of a large proportion of the delegates to conventions.*

Delegates to national conventions are chosen, after all, as representatives of the several state party organizations, apportioned according to a formula laid down by action of previous national conventions. While it is true that official decisions are made by majority vote of delegates, American party organizations are centralized at state and local levels. This means that such hierarchical controls as actually exist on the state and local levels will assert themselves in the national convention. Since the probabilities are fairly good that both major parties at any given time will have succeeded in electing a substantial number of governors and mayors of important cities, the chances are likewise fairly good that a substantial number of delegates will be controlled hierarchically. The tendency toward centralization is formally aided by the so-called unit rule, providing that a majority vote of a state delegation shall determine the way in which the vote of the entire delegation shall be cast.

The decision to adopt the unit rule is a difficult one for state political leaders faced with an intense, dissident minority within their delegations. While adoption of unit voting assures them of a solid bloc of votes with which they can bargain, hard feelings may linger on within the state. When a minority element within a state is strong enough to gain representation on a convention delegation, muzzling it by imposition of the unit rule is seldom wise. The unit rule is used to best advantage by those delegations whose members generally feel more strongly about preserving the bargaining advantages of a bloc vote than they do about any particular candidate. In a delegation firmly committed to a particular aspirant, the unit rule is superfluous. It is sometimes avoided by a leader who wants to reward delegates who stick together on the delegation's first choice. He releases them to vote as they individually please on their second choice, if the first choice is removed from contention. Hence state delegations governed by the unit rule are most often likely to be relatively uncommitted in their presidential preferences, and comparatively homogeneous in their political outlooks and allegiances. The following conclusions may therefore be drawn: (1) state delegations tend to be hierarchically controlled by state political leaders; (2) the chief political leader of state delegations will be the governor, or his agent; (3) if a state delegation puts forward a favorite son candidate, there is a higher probability that he will be the governor of the state than any other person; and (4) presidential nominees are more likely to be governors than any other persons.

These propositions all rest upon assumptions about who is likely to control access to political power. There may be significant deviations from these propositions in real life, however. For example, there are a few instances in recent years where party leaders controlled a majority of a state's delegation in opposition to the governor of the same party. Usually, the governor, if he is not a state's favorite son, is still the leader of the delegation and is likely to be allied with the favorite son as well. An example of this would be Governor Orville Freeman, who has long been a close ally of Minnesota's favorite son, Senator Humphrey. No doubt some of these coalitions between the leaders of a state are shotgun marriages, as may have been the case among Tennessee's Democrats in 1956, but for the purposes of the convention, these alliances seem to hold together despite centrifugal impulses.

5. *Politicians will have different preferences among those presidential aspirants having a chance of winning election.*

This proposition follows from the fact that politicians desire to maximize access to governmental decision-makers. But the probability is very high that they will differ in their relations with the various aspirants to the Presidency. A politician will naturally favor a presidential hopeful from his own state, or an aspirant with whom he has been on close personal or professional terms. Each presidential aspirant begins the convention with a cluster of connections of this sort with delegates and delegation leaders. The predispositions of delegates toward candidates are shaped by their expectations of access to them, which may depend upon historical accidents, ideological affinities, and/or explicit "deals."

6. *In the absence of hierarchical control by an incumbent President, decision-making at conventions is co-ordinated by a process of bargaining among party leaders.*

We may think of bargaining as a method by which activities are co-ordinated in situations where controls between individuals are bilateral or multilateral and approach equality. Bargainers may differ as to their goals. They are presumed to harbor the expectation that participating in the bargaining process (1) will aid them in achieving their goals and (2) will inform them of the goals and tactics of others, which in turn may help them in attaining their goals. Prerequisites to bargaining may be summarized as (1) non-hierarchical controls;

(2) interdependence of bargainers; (3) disagreement among bargainers; and (4) expectation of gain.

When the President is of the opposite party, or chooses not to control the convention hierarchically, the convention becomes a bargaining system because no other political leader is in a position to control the national convention unilaterally. The interdependence of party leaders may be established by reference to the rule of American politics which provides that the voters may replace the elected officials of one party with those of another at general elections. In order to mobilize enough nationwide support to elect a President, party leaders from a large number of constituencies must be satisfied with the nominee. Without agreement on a nominee, none is likely to enjoy access to the eventual President; hence party leaders are interdependent and expect to gain from the outcome of the bargain. Because of the different access to different aspirants which delegates carry with them into the convention the preferences of delegates are likely initially to disagree.

Politicians seek to maximize their own political power, but in order to do so, must maximize the potential vote for candidates whom they sponsor. The more leaders who agree on a candidate, the more interest groups and state party organizations there are working for the election of the candidate; consequently, the greater are the chances that the candidate will win election and provide those politicians who supported him with access to political power. Therefore, we may postulate the following: (1) Party unity is perceived by politicians as prerequisite to the achievement of their goals. (2) Unless party leaders achieve a consensus among themselves, the chances are diminished that they will be able to elect a President. (3) Parties tend to nominate candidates who are (a) at the least, not obnoxious to, (b) at the most, attractive to, as many interest groups as possible. (4)

Party platforms tend to be broad and vague. (5) Sanctions open to a dissident party faction revolve around its ability to destroy party unity.

7. *The parties are in direct competition for many of the same votes.*

Voters and interest groups are distributed between and outside the two parties, and parties must of necessity build a nationwide coalition of votes to win the Presidency. Politicians are uncertain as to the exact distribution of presidential preferences among groups in the population, however, and must make nominations and write platforms with the broadest possible constituency in mind. The two parties thus compete for many of the same politically neutral, apathetic, ambivalent and/or uncommitted interest groups and voters. Therefore, (1) party platforms tend to be similar, though not identical, and (2) presidential candidates are likely to come from states having a large electoral vote and which are politically competitive. This last proposition follows partly from what has been said above, with the addition of the electoral college rules which distribute presidential votes by states roughly according to population and give the whole electoral vote of a state to any candidate winning a majority within the state.

8. *Vice presidential nominees are calculated to help the party achieve the Presidency.*

Party nominees for President and Vice-President always appear on the ballot together and are elected together. A vote for one is always a vote for the other. Yet the Vice President occupies a post in the legislative branch of the government which is formally honorific, and his powers and activities in the executive branch are determined by the President. The electoral interdependence of the two offices gives politicians an opportunity to gather votes for the Presidency, and from this we can deduce the criteria for the selection of the Vice President. A vice-presidential nominee must have the same qualities as a presidential nominee, with two additions: (a) he must possess those desirable qualities the presidential nominee lacks, and (b) he must be acceptable to the presidential nominee.

As we have seen, the selection of a presidential nominee is the business which dominates the convention. From this follow: (1) The importance of decisions preceding the presidential nomination in the convention is entirely dependent upon the implications of the outcomes for the presidential nomination. (2) Decisions not taken unanimously which precede the presidential nomination in the convention are tests of strength between party factions divided as to the presidential nomination.

THE STRATEGIES
OF PARTICIPANTS

The one route to political power open to all delegates in the convention is to contribute to the majority essential for the nomination of the man they believe will be the winner. This explains the so-called "band wagon" behavior, which can be seen in operation at many conventions.

1. *When delegates believe that one presidential aspirant is certain of nomination, they will attempt to record themselves as voting for that aspirant as quickly as possible. Delegates committed to a favorite son candidate will trade their votes for access to the candidate they think most likely to win nomination.*

Note the differences in the two statements above. In the first, delegates know which candidate will win, and hope to earn his gratitude by voting for him. In the corollary, delegates are less certain of the outcome, hence their commitment to an aspirant is more costly for the aspirant, who often makes explicit promises of access to delegates in return for their support.

2. *The most important consideration for a politician in choosing a presidential nominee is the expectation that he will win election.*

Clearly, if a candidate is given no chance of winning election, access to him is not instrumental to politicians' goals. Presidential aspirants claim victory and stimulate manifestations of public enthusiasm and support for themselves as a means of convincing delegates that they will win nomination and election. This follows from delegate behavior in the decision-making process outlined above. If delegates, because of their uncertainty about what other delegates will do, often are driven to band wagon behavior, the rational presidential aspirant will try to capitalize on this fact. The votes of a majority of delegates are indispensable to nomination, and, as we have seen, a prerequisite to getting these votes is the ability to stimulate the expectation of victory, that is, to generate a band wagon.

3. *Unexpected losses in primary elections usually doom an aspirant's chance of nomination, so the rational aspirant enters only those primaries he thinks he can win.*

Primary elections function largely as a means by which politicians inform themselves about the relative popularity of presidential aspirants. The expectations of delegates are of critical importance in determining the nominee, as the propositions above show, and the strategies of aspirants respond to these conditions. Some aspirants play a somewhat different game from the maximizing behavior postulated in the above proposition. An aspirant from a state with relatively few electoral votes and who has only a few votes from outside his state initially pledged to him may find it necessary to enter primaries where his chances are questionable, in order to come into the convention with enough first ballot votes pledged to him so that he is considered seriously for the nomination. Without this minimum number of votes, the aspirant from the small state stands little chance of consideration. He takes a chance on primaries not to maintain a preconvention record of success (since this is of little utility to him), but because he has nothing to lose.

4. *An aspirant who leads in votes for the nomination must actually win nomination by a certain point in time, after which his chances of eventually winning decline precipitously, even though he remains in the lead for the time being.*

This follows from the fact that much delegate support is given candidates because of the expectation of victory. When this victory falls short of quick materialization, delegates may question their initial judgment. Thus, the longer a candidate remains in the lead without starting a band wagon, the greater the chance that his supporters will reassess his chances of victory, and vote for someone else. In order to achieve access, delegates must support the eventual winner before he achieves a majority, as a general rule. They are therefore guided by what they expect other delegates to do, and are constantly on the alert to change their expectations to conform to the latest information. This information may be nothing more substantial than a rumor, which quickly takes on the status of a self-fulfilling prophecy, as delegates stampede in response to expectations—quickly realized—about how other delegates will respond. I have previously pointed out the costs of hierarchy in convention decision-making. In the fragmented situation there are also costs, since there is no guarantee that nominations made in this situation will reflect the best judgment of delegates or leaders, or even their second-best judgment as to the most acceptable party nominee. This is the case because delegates may stampede on reliable or unreliable information, with effects that may be highly prejudicial to the party's chances to elect a President.

Aspirants sometimes combine their voting strength in the convention in order to prevent a front-running candidate from gaining a majority. They will then negotiate the nomination among themselves. If the front-runner's victory promises other aspirants insufficient access, they may defeat him by preventing a band wagon in his favor. The rational aspirant who leads but lacks a majority will promise access to leaders representing the requisite number of votes. This is the rational response to the expectation that no band wagon will appear, unstimulated. The front-runner may reasonably expect to win without cost (i.e., without making such promises) unless leaders of opposing factions reach agreement on a ticket, and appear likely to combine against him. Early front-runners often win nominations, precisely because they face a divided opposition.

5. *There are conditions under which a rational delegate will vote for a candidate other than the probable winner, according to his calculations.*

If a politician is without hope of obtaining access to a particular candidate, for any of a variety of reasons, then there is no reason for voting for him, even if the politician calculates that the candidate is the probable winner. A second condition under which this obtains has already been mentioned. By withholding his vote temporarily from the probable winner, the delegate may obtain firm promises of access. A third condition may be classed as an irrationality, namely the force of primary law in some states which commits delegates to a candidate regardless of the promises of access other candidates make to the delegation. Since delegates may be released by the candidate they are bound by law to support, this transfers to the candidate significant bargaining power which may provide him with the access to more probable winners usually accorded to politicians within state delegations. Politicians bound by primary law are thus often severely handicapped in the bargaining process.

33. Rationality and Decision Making: The Illinois Democratic Delegation of 1960

James A. Robinson

The basic units of decision making at national conventions are the state delegations. James Robinson, Professor of Political Science, Ohio State University, observed the Illinois Democratic delegation in 1960. His article describes the relations between leaders and followers in a hierarchical organization and the overwhelming importance of electoral victory as a goal for both groups. He concludes by defending the rationality of the convention process.

* * *

This paper is not a comprehensive critique of the convention but instead reports data on one delegation relevant to one criterion likely to be on any list of standards for evaluating the convention system. This criterion is rationality. Rationality is a word with many usages, but in spite of its ambiguity, most people will surely say that the process for making a decision or nominating a president ought to be rational. For our purposes, we may define a rational nominating procedure as one which selects candidates with qualifications similar to those required by the office. Nothing about the presidency requires that the chief executive have a full head of hair, so we could say that any nominating process which discriminated against baldness per se would be non-rational. . . .

WHO WERE THE DELEGATES?

The delegation was chosen by a combination of two methods. Each of the 25 congressional districts elected two delegates and two alternates in the April primary. Each of these delegates had one vote. The remaining votes were allotted to 38 delegates-at-large chosen at the party state convention in late May. At the same time, 18 alternates-at-large were selected by the convention.

In the primaries, a few delegates ran committed to particular candidates. One who did was Paul Powell, Speaker of the Illinois House of Representatives, who committed himself to Senator Stuart Symington. In the 13th district, which embraces part of Cook County and runs along the lake shore to the Wisconsin border, a candidate pledged to Chester Bowles ran a poor third. In most parts of the state, however, delegates ran uncommitted to any particular candidate, and many of these apparently ran with the blessing of the state or local party organization leadership.

Half of the elected delegates were chosen in contested primaries with low rates of voter turnout, and many held party positions, public office, or were candidates for office at the time of their selection as delegates. Of the 12 contested districts, only two fell within Cook County where party organization is observably more disciplined than the rest of the state. But even in the contested districts, voting was lighter for delegates than for other offices. Data are available for nine of these and the difference between total vote for delegate and the total vote for all offices ranged from 16 percent to 33 percent.

Virtually all of the delegates had a record of prior activity in local, state, or national politics. Several well-known people were chosen by the state convention as delegates-at-large without any request on their part or without any advance notice by the party leaders. These were at-large delegates, each of whom had one-half vote and included such figures as former Governor Adlai E. Stevenson and Senator Paul H. Douglas.

From Paul Tillett, ed., *Inside Politics: The National Conventions, 1960* (New Brunswick: Rutgers —The State University, 1962), pp. 240–251, with footnotes deleted, by permission of Rutgers— The State University.

More than half of the delegates held party or government positions. Data are not available on the occupations of all delegates, but 51 of the 88 occupied or aspired to positions over which party leaders possessed discretion or nomination or appointment. In these circumstances, it is not surprising that the leadership exerted a high degree of control. The only possibility of a split lay in the cleavage between the leaders in Cook County and those downstate, including Paul Powell, John Stelle, former governor, and Scott Lucas, former United States Senator.

DELEGATE PARTICIPATION

Several indicators reveal the low degree of individual delegate participation in Illinois. The first sign was the response among delegates to the nationwide CBS telecast prior to the convention on what the convention floor and the proceedings on the floor would be like. The network in Chicago invited all Illinois delegates and alternates to a special showing. Thirty-two responded that they planned to attend; only seven did. A second indicator is the number of absentees among the delegation during sessions of the convention. Although no exact count could be made, the many vacant seats during the proceedings of the convention made the delegation conspicuous. A third indicator of a low level of involvement among individual delegates is the observed reactions to such convention activities as demonstrations following the nomination of candidates. When Senator Kennedy was nominated, Mayor Daley marched through the convention hall carrying the Illinois standard and wearing a Kennedy hat, and there was considerable cheering among people sitting in the Illinois delegation. With this exception, and one other, Illinois delegates neither participated in nor reacted visibly to the demonstrations.

The further exception took place during the demonstration for Adlai Stevenson.

About half of the Illinois delegates were on their feet during the prolonged demonstration for their governor, but they were not standing or cheering for Stevenson. In fact, those who participated waved Kennedy signs and many cheered "we want Kennedy" rather than "we want Stevenson." . . .

THE PRESIDENTIAL DECISION

Many have remarked that Senator Kennedy's campaign for the presidency began the afternoon during the 1956 convention when he narrowly lost the vice presidential nomination. If this be so, it is relevant to recall that Illinois gave an overwhelming majority of its 64 votes that day to Senator Kennedy. Inasmuch as 40 of the 69 votes in the 1960 convention had been members of the 1956 delegation, a substantial portion of the Illinois delegates had previously voted for Kennedy.

During the first half of 1960, the newspaper speculation was that Mayor Daley again hoped to be for Senator Kennedy, but the Mayor did not commit himself publicly prior to the convention. Throughout the spring, speculation also held that regardless of the Mayor's preference, there would be considerable downstate support for Senator Symington. In February, even before the delegation was chosen, political reporters thought they could find 20 votes for the Missouri neighbor.

During the spring and early summer, party leaders had various opportunities to hear something of individual delegates' preferences. These opportunities included the state convention at Springfield, visits around the state during the primary campaign, and other political conversations. Delegation leaders say that they did not ask delegates their preferences or put pressure on them for a particular candidate, but that as they talked with them, they learned of the growing favor for Senator Kennedy. Kennedy visited the state more often than any other candidate and drew exceptionally large crowds downstate even in bad winter weather. Symington and Hubert Humphrey made occasional stops in the state, but Lyndon Johnson came only once and then for a non-political speech. Kennedy's crowds indicated to delegates and local precinct committeemen that he might run well in their areas. This, added to Symington's failure to make noticeable gains in other states, helped Kennedy at Symington's expense.

On June 16, the Kennedy staff issued a state-by-state survey of their strength and claimed 57 votes in Illinois. The same week former Governor Stelle was said to be discouraged about Symington's prospects. Outwardly, Speaker Powell remained confident, nevertheless, and said he expected 18 to 20 votes for Symington.

In the Stevenson camp, it was believed that Kennedy would receive a minimum of 49 votes. Symington would have 13, Stevenson 4, and they believed 3 were still undecided the day before the caucus.

Meanwhile, Chicago papers predicted 50 to 56½ would go to Kennedy. This was on the strength of what Mayor Daley was expected to do, because many delegates declined to answer reporters' polls, stating that they would follow the Mayor's judgment. Just before the caucus the delegation leaders themselves expected about 55 votes for Kennedy, 6 or 7 for Symington, 2 for Stevenson, and perhaps 2 for Johnson. This, then was the situation when the Illinois delegation caucused.

CAUCUS

The Sunday afternoon caucus was closed to the press and to representatives of candidates. Mayor Daley spoke for about fifteen minutes reviewing Senator Kennedy's qualifications for the nomination with overriding emphasis on the Senator's vote getting prowess, his excellent organization, and his capacity to help Democratic candidates up and down the ticket.

The Mayor noted that some delegates had been elected pledged to other candidates and their promises should be respected by all. However, he hoped that every delegate who honestly could, would support Kennedy, and that the Senator would obtain the overwhelming endorsement from Illinois.

Following the Mayor's speech, 21 delegates and alternates arose to speak in behalf of candidates. Former Senator Lucas, who had been Majority Leader of the Senate, pointed out that he should probably be for Senator Johnson, who had succeeded him as Majority Leader. He knew the great burdens of that office; he knew the responsibilities it required; and he had great admiration for the man who now held it. But he did not believe that Johnson could be elected. He thought the perfect candidate was Senator Symington who, he emphasized, had "no political scars." Another speech for Senator Symington was made by Speaker Powell who explained that he had promised President Truman that he would support Senator Symington. He did not intend to go back on his promise as long as Symington was a candidate. . . .

The theme recurring most often was Kennedy's strength as a candidate and the help he would bring to the state and local tickets. References to his youth were almost all defensive and apologetic. The apology, however, was sometimes turned to an advantage, as in the case of a prominent elder party official who said that the older generation had not done very well with the world and that perhaps it was time to turn to the younger generation.

With the exception of the two references to the labor issue, there were few reasons which related directly to issues or to the responsibilities of the presidency. That is not to say that sometime during the speeches references were not made to other issues, the most frequent ones being to civil rights and to the great needs of the country and the current international situation; but these were never the major themes of individual speeches. What concerned delegates the most was who would win in November, and more particularly, who would most help the state and county tickets in Illinois. On this question Senator Kennedy clearly had the advantage. As the Mayor emphasized, the Senator had won seven primaries, and this figure was repeated by other speakers.

When the roll was called, 59½ votes were given to Kennedy, 6½ for Symington, 2 for Stevenson, and one delegate passed. All those who voted for Symington were from downstate, but not all downstate delegates supported Symington. Governor Stelle split from Speaker Powell and Senator Lucas, and voted for Kennedy, an action which the *Chicago Tribune* interpreted as an assist to Mr. Arvey's desire to be re-elected national committeeman. Others from downstate joined Kennedy because as George Saal, the sheriff of Tazewell County, told a reporter: "Shucks, I want to be with a winner." . . .

EXTERNAL INFLUENCES

After the caucus, the Kennedy floor managers had checked daily to see that there would be no depreciation in their ranks. When the delegation met on the floor, one could see members of the Kennedy family and the Kennedy campaign organization very much in evidence around the Illinois delegation, many brought there because one of the six Kennedy telephones on the convention floor was installed at a corner of the delegation. Also visiting the delegation from time to time was R. Sargent Shriver, Jr., a brother-in-law of Senator Kennedy, and President of the Chicago Board of Education. Mr. Shriver's wife, Eunice, a sister of Senator Kennedy and other sisters also appeared, presumably, as a Kennedy campaign worker said, to distract them. Representative Charles Brown, Symington's campaign manager, came to

talk to Speaker Powell, Colonel Arvey, and other delegates.

Stevenson forces made the most evident attempt to influence the delegation. In Los Angeles the delegation had received thousands of telegrams from Stevenson supporters in and out of Illinois. The state chairman received a telephone call at 11 p.m. on the Saturday night before the convention from an individual in Long Island, New York, who had once resided in Illinois. It was two o'clock in the morning when the call was placed from New York, and the message was that it would be morally wrong for the Illinois delegation to support, and the convention to nominate, any candidate other than Stevenson. Throughout the week, the secretary of the Party received telegrams, opened them and passed them to their addressees. All bore essentially the same message—vote for Stevenson. One alternate, on receiving such a telegram, crumpled it in disgust and threw it to the floor. Not long before the balloting took place on Wednesday night, Stevenson supporters rushed on the floor with a copy of a United Press International dispatch quoting a statement by a Western Union official that the company had received more than 25,000 telegrams endorsing candidates since the first floor demonstration for Stevenson. UPI said the deluge of telegrams was so heavy that it had impeded the outgoing press traffic which was then more than a million words a day. Although the Western Union spokesman declined to divulge the count for each candidate, it revealed that the telegrams were running heavily in favor of Stevenson.

These telegrams did little to influence the attitudes or the behavior of the Illinois delegation in Stevenson's favor. The delegation was not only firmly for Kennedy but was firmly opposed to Stevenson and seemed to become confirmed in this stance as the telegrams flowed in. Many were not amused, but annoyed, and some remarked on the naivete of anyone who believed that he could influence the decision of the delegation by something as anonymous and indirect as a telegram.

A second effort by the Stevenson campaign organization to influence the decision of the delegation in particular and the convention in general was the visit by Stevenson to the convention floor on Tuesday night. Stevenson called the state chairman of the Illinois party at noon and advised him that he would be coming that evening. The party chairman, Mr. Ronan, and Stevenson's alternate, Mr. O'Keefe, met him off the floor and escorted him through the press and admirers to the delegation. This was interpreted within and among the members of the Illinois delegation as a withdrawal from candidacy for the presidency. They noted that it was customary for candidates to remain off the floor and away from the proceedings. This, of course, was not at all the intent of Stevenson or his campaign managers. He was urged to make such a visit for the purpose of giving renewed impetus to his campaign and encourage his sometimes disappointed supporters. . . .

All external efforts to influence the Illinois delegation had no discernible effect. The decision reached Sunday remained firm, except for the slight increase in Kennedy support which Mayor Daley's efforts had secured.

The Illinois leader also attempted to assist Kennedy in other ways. He tried, for example, to induce Stevenson to second Kennedy's nomination, arguing that because Kennedy had nominated Stevenson in 1956, it would be appropriate for Stevenson to second the Senator's nomination in 1960. This effort, however, came to naught.

Few other states were as solid for Kennedy as was Illinois, and it was doubtless appropriate that Mayor Daley should be among those called to the rostrum to be on the reception committee when Kennedy came out to deliver a short speech following his nomination. But before the presidential choice was final, the Mayor was already at work with leaders of other delegations to try to get a favorable candidate for the vice presidency.

ILLINOIS PARTICIPATION IN THE VICE PRESIDENTIAL DECISION

The leadership of the delegation favored Senator Symington for vice president, and as early as Tuesday Mayor Daley was involved in conferences concerning the second place on the ticket. Newspaper reports linked him with Carmine DeSapio of New York, Governor David Lawrence of Pennsylvania, and Governor Michael V. DiSalle of Ohio, in urging the nomination of Senator Symington.

Daley and other Illinois leaders backed Symington for the same reason they supported Kennedy: they believed that he would help the party's state and local candidates. In a television interview after the nomination of Senator Johnson, Senator Lucas reaffirmed his support for Symington, again noting that of all the candidates he had "no political scars." Powell, who had indicated that he thought Mayor Daley had done all he could to get the nomination for Symington, thought that Johnson would cost the ticket as many as 75,000 or 100,000 votes in Illinois.

But the nomination of Johnson was certainly acceptable to the delegation, who reasoned that while he might not run strongly in the northern parts of the state, he would surely be an asset to the party in the more conservative and rural downstate Illinois. Congressman William Dawson, one of the leaders in Negro politics in the state, vice president of the Democratic National Committee, and long an influential member of the House, was asked by Mayor Daley to second Johnson's nomination. On Friday, after Johnson's nomination on Thursday night, Representative Dawson gathered together a number of Negro leaders at the Biltmore Hotel to hear Johnson speak on civil rights. There is no question, then, that Lyndon Johnson was an acceptable vice presidential candidate to the Illinois leadership.

The leadership reached the vice presidential decision without a caucus. When the time for balloting arrived on Thursday night, fewer Illinois delegates were on the floor than at any previous time in the convention. Friends and guests of the delegates who previously had been in the galleries took the places on the floor. To a man they rose to applaud Dawson as he went to the rostrum to second the nomination of Johnson.

CONCLUSION

It would be easy to interpret the lack of participation, listlessness, and sheep-like behavior of the Illinois delegates as a failure of representative democracy. That sort of criticism should not be drawn from this description. The unity of the Illinois delegation was, of course, a function of the strength and capacity of its professional party organization. The success of a president in carrying out his and the party's program depends upon his capacity to marshal the kind of political support which Kennedy was able to obtain from Daley and the Illinois delegation.

A second characteristic of this delegation is similar to one which could be observed in other delegations. This is that the major reason which brought Illinois to Senator Kennedy's side was that Kennedy was expected to deliver the largest number of votes in November. This was not the only or the sufficient condition for winning Daley and his colleagues to Kennedy's candidacy. There were other reasons that they were disposed to support Kennedy, but it seems clear that what made it possible for Illinois to support Kennedy in such strength was that he more than any other

candidate had proved his electoral magnetism.

It is easy to regard the behavior of the Illinois delegation as an example of non-rational decision-making. The model, which many of our textbooks and commentators still retain, holds that the individual voter and the individual delegate evaluate (or should) presidential nominees in terms of their positions on the issues and their administrative qualifications. To be sure, other delegations, notably Michigan and the District of Columbia, gave great weight to candidates' stands on issues. Illinois was not uninterested in these questions, too, as witness the leadership's tentative search for a vice presidential nominee who would appeal to a wide variety of interests in the state, interests, reflected in political issues. Yet among the Illinois delegates and their leadership, concern for the administrative capacities and the stands on issues of the candidates seemed clearly secondary to their belief that Kennedy promised to be a winning candidate in Illinois.

Surely, however, the ability to win and to help local candidates are related to the requirements of the presidency. If the president must call upon the state party leaders for support in adopting his programs, he may surely be expected to help the local party organizations.

Moreover, to the political professionals, the machine which Kennedy organized was a remarkable demonstration of leadership. While one might prefer that more weight be given to factors other than the capacity to win in November, one could hardly deny that this factor is directly related to the needs of the office. Indeed, it is one sign of skill as a leader. If a rational nominating process is defined as one which focuses on factors related to the qualifications for the office, this delegation acted rationally when it gave great weight to the electoral strength of the candidates for president and vice president.

34. Caucuses of 1860

Murat Halstead

Convention tactics, "deals" and hilarity, are neither novel nor noxious. It was through such activities that Abraham Lincoln was first nominated by the Republicans in 1860, as reported at the time by Cincinnati Enquirer *reporter Murat Halstead. This selection recounts how Lincoln's friends defeated the front-runner of the convention, William Seward of New York, while outflanking other candidates such as Simon Cameron of Pennsylvania and Salmon Chase and Benjamin Wade of Ohio.*

* * *

The New Yorkers here are of a class unknown to Western Republican politicians. They can drink as much whiskey, swear as loud and long, sing as bad songs, and "get up and howl" as ferociously as any crowd of Democrats you ever heard, or heard of. They are opposed, as they say, "to being too d——d virtuous." They hoot at the idea that Seward could not sweep all the Northern States, and swear that he would have a party in every slave State, in less than a year, that would clean out the disunionists, from shore to shore. They slap each other on the back with the emphasis of delight when they meet, and rip out "How *are* you?" with a "How are you hoss?" style, that would do honor to Old Kaintuck on a bust. At night those of them who are not engaged at caucusing, are doing that which ill-tutored youths call "raising h——l generally."

Wherever you find them, the New York politicians, of whatever party, are a peculiar people.

The Seward men have been in high feather. They entertain no particle of doubt of his nomination in the morning. They have a champagne supper in their rooms at the Richmond House to-night, and have bands of music serenading the various delegations at their quarters. Three hundred bottles of champagne are said to have been cracked at the Richmond. This may be an exaggeration, but I am not inclined to think the quantity overstated, for it flowed freely as water.

The delegation here is a queer compound. There is a party of tolerably rough fellows, of whom Tom Hyer is leader, and there is Thurlow Weed (called Lord Thurlow by his friends), Moses H. Grinnell, James Watson Webb, Gov. Morgan, Gen. Nye, George W. Curtis, and others of the strong men of the State, in commerce, political jobbing, and in literature—first class men in their respective positions, and each with his work to do according to his ability. In the face of such "irrepressibles," the conservative expediency men—Greeley, the Blairs, the Republican candidates for Governor in Pennsylvania, Indiana, and Illinois —are hard pressed, sorely perplexed, and despondent. . . .

Every one of the forty thousand men in attendance upon the Chicago Convention will testify that at midnight of Thursday-Friday night, the universal impression was that Seward's success was certain.

The New Yorkers were exultant. Their bands were playing, and the champagne flowing at their head-quarters as after a victory.

But there was much done after midnight and before the Convention assembled on Friday morning. There were hundreds of Pennsylvanians, Indianians and Illinoisans, who never closed their eyes that night. I saw Henry S. Lane at one o'clock, pale and haggard, with cane under his arm, walking as if for a wager, from one caucus-room to another, at the Tremont House. He had been toiling with desperation to bring the

From Murat Halstead, *Caucuses of 1860* (Columbus: Follett, Foster & Co., 1860).

Indiana delegation to go as a unit for Lincoln. And then in connection with others, he had been operating to bring the Vermonters and Virginians to the point of deserting Seward. Vermont would certainly cast her electoral vote for any candidate who could be nominated, and Virginia as certainly against any candidate. The object was to bring the delegates of those States to consider success rather than Seward, and join with the battle-ground States—as Pennsylvania, New Jersey, Indiana, and Illinois insisted upon calling themselves. This was finally done, the fatal break in Seward's strength having been made in Vermont and Virginia, destroying at once, when it appeared, his power in the New England and the slave State delegations. But the work was not yet done. The Pennsylvanians had been fed upon meat, such that they presented themselves at Chicago with the presumption that they had only to say what they wished, and receive the indorsement of the Convention. And they were for Cameron. He was the only man, they a thousand times said, who would certainly carry Pennsylvania. They were astonished, alarmed, and maddened to find public opinion settling down upon Seward and Lincoln, and that one or the other must be nominated. They saw that Lincoln was understood to be the only man to defeat Seward, and thinking themselves capable of holding that balance of power, so much depended upon, and so deceptive on those occasions, stood out against the Lincoln combination. Upon some of the delegation, Seward operations had been performed with perceptible effect. The Seward men had stated that the talk of not carrying Pennsylvania was all nonsense. Seward had a good Tariff record, and his friends would spend money enough in the State to carry it against any Democratic candidate who was a possibility. The flood of Seward money promised for Pennsylvania was not without efficacy. The phrase used was, that Seward's friends "would *spend oceans of money.*"

The Wade movement died before this time. It had a brilliant and formidable appearance for a while; but the fact that it originated at Washington was against it, and the bitterness of those delegates from Ohio, who would not in any event go for any man from that State other than Chase, and who declared war to the knife against Wade, and as a second choice were for Lincoln or Seward, stifled the Wade project.

It does not appear by the record that "old Ben. Wade" ever stood a chance for the place now occupied by "old Abe Lincoln." If his friends in Ohio could have brought the friends of Mr. Chase to agree, that the delegation should vote as a unit every time as the majority should direct, Wade might have been the nominee, and instead of hearing so much of some of the exploits of Mr. Lincoln in rail-splitting, when a farmer's boy, we should have information concerning the labors of Ben. Wade on the Erie Canal, where he handled a spade. While touching the Wade movement as developed in the delegation from Ohio, it is proper to give as an explanatory note the fact, that at least six gentlemen from Ohio, who were engaged in it, were understood to have aspirations for the Senate, and to be regarding Mr. Wade's chair in the Senate-chamber with covetous glances. These gentlemen were D. K. Carter, Joshua R. Giddings, C. P. Wolcott, William Dennison, Jr., Tom Corwin, and Columbus Delano.

The cry of a want of availability which was from the start raised against Seward, now took a more definite form than heretofore. It was reported, and with a well-understood purpose, that the Republican candidates for Governor in Indiana, Illinois and Pennsylvania would resign, if Seward were nominated. Whether they really meant it or not, the rumor was well circulated, and the effect produced was as if they had been earnest. Henry S. Lane, candidate in Indiana, did say something of the kind. He asserted hundreds of times that the nomination of Seward would be death to him, and that he might in that case just as well give up the canvass. He did not feel like expending his time and money in carrying on a hopeless campaign, and would be disposed to abandon the contest.

The Chicago Press and Tribune of Friday morning contained a last appeal to the Convention not to nominate Seward. It was evidently written in a despairing state of mind, and it simply begged that Seward should not be nominated. The Cameron men, discovering there was absolutely no hope for their man, but that either Seward or Lincoln would be nominated, and that speedily, and being a calculating company, were persuaded to throw their strength for Lincoln at such a time as to have credit of his nomination if it were made. There was much difficulty, however, in arriving at this conclusion, and the wheels of the machine did not at any time in Pennsylvania run smooth. On nearly every ballot, Pennsylvania was not in readiness when her name was called, and her retirements for consultation became a joke.

The Seward men generally abounded in confidence Friday morning. The air was full of rumors of the caucusing the night before, but the opposition of the doubtful States to Seward was an old story; and after the distress of Pennsylvania, Indiana & Co., on the subject of Seward's availability, had been so freely and ineffectually expressed from the start, it was not imagined their protests would suddenly become effective. The Sewardites marched as usual from their head-quarters at the Richmond House after their magnificent band, which was brilliantly uniformed—epaulets shining on their shoulders, and white and scarlet feathers waving from their caps—marched under the orders of recognized leaders, in a style that would have done credit to many volunteer military companies. They were about a thousand strong, and protracting their march a little too far, were not all able to get into the wigwam. This was

their first misfortune. They were not where they could scream with the best effect in responding to the mention of the name of William H. Seward. . . .

The applause, when Mr. Evarts named Seward, was enthusiastic. When Mr. Judd named Lincoln, the response was prodigious, rising and raging far beyond the Seward shriek. Presently, upon Caleb B. Smith seconding the nomination of Lincoln, the response was absolutely terrific. It now became the Seward men to make another effort, and when Blair of Michigan seconded his nomination,

> At once there rose so wild a yell,
> Within that dark and narrow dell;
> As all the fiends from heaven that fell
> Had pealed the banner cry of hell.

The effect was startling. Hundreds of persons stopped their ears in pain. The shouting was absolutely frantic, shrill and wild. No Camanches, no panthers ever struck a higher note, or gave screams with more infernal intensity. Looking from the stage over the vast amphitheatre, nothing was to be seen below but thousands of hats —a black, mighty swarm of hats—flying with the velocity of hornets over a mass of human heads, most of the mouths of which were open. Above, all around the galleries, hats and handkerchiefs were flying in the tempest together. The wonder of the thing was, that the Seward outside pressure should, so far from New York, be so powerful.

Now the Lincoln men had to try it again, and as Mr. Delano of Ohio, on behalf "of a portion of the delegation of that State," seconded the nomination of Lincoln, the uproar was beyond description. Imagine all the hogs ever slaughtered in Cincinnati giving their death squeals together, a score of big steam whistles going (steam at 160 lbs. per inch), and you conceive something of the same nature. I thought the Seward yell could not be surpassed; but the Lincoln boys were clearly ahead, and feeling their victory, as there was a lull in the storm, took deep breaths all round, and gave a concentrated shriek that was positively awful, and accompanied it with stamping that made every plank and pillar in the building quiver.

Henry S. Lane of Indiana leaped upon a table, and swinging hat and cane, performed like an acrobat. The presumption is, he shrieked with the rest, as his mouth was desperately wide open; but no one will ever be able to testify that he has positive knowledge of the fact that he made a particle of noise. His individual voice was lost in the aggregate hurricane.

The New York, Michigan and Wisconsin delegations sat together, and were in this tempest very quiet. Many of their faces whitened as the Lincoln *yawp* swelled into a wild hosanna of victory.

The Convention now proceeded to business. The New England States were called first, and it was manifest that Seward had not the strength that had been claimed for him there. Maine gave nearly half her vote for Lincoln. New Hampshire gave seven out of her ten votes for Lincoln. Vermont gave her vote to her Senator Collamer, which was understood to be merely complimentary. It appeared, however, that her delegation was hostile or indifferent to Seward, otherwise there would have been no complimentary vote to another. Massachusetts was divided. Rhode Island and Connecticut did not give Seward a vote. So much for the caucusing the night before. Mr. Evarts of New York rose and gave the vote of that State, calmly, but with a swelling tone of pride in his voice—"The State of *New York* casts her *seventy votes* for *William H. Seward!*" The seventy votes was a plumper, and there was slight applause, and that rustle and vibration in the audience indicating a sensation. The most significant vote was that of Virginia, which had been expected solid for Seward, and which now gave him but eight and gave Lincoln fourteen. The New Yorkers looked significantly at each other as this was an-

nounced. Then Indiana gave her twenty-six votes for Lincoln. This solid vote was a startler, and the keen little eyes of Henry S. Lane glittered as it was given. He was responsible for it. It was his opinion that the man of all the land to carry the State of Indiana, was Judge John McLean. He also thought Bates had eminent qualifications. But when he found that the contest was between Seward and Lincoln, he worked for the latter as if life itself depended upon success. The division of the first vote caused a fall in Seward stock. It was seen that Lincoln, Cameron and Bates had the strength to defeat Seward, and it was known that the greater part of the Chase vote would go for Lincoln. . . .

The Secretary announced the vote:

William H. Seward, of New York	173½
Abraham Lincoln, of Illinois	102
Edward Bates, of Missouri	48
Simon Cameron, of Pennsylvania	50½
John McLean, of Ohio	12
Salmon P. Chase, of Ohio	49
Benjamin F. Wade, of Ohio	3
William L. Dayton, of New Jersey	14
John M. Reed, of Pennsylvania	1
Jacob Collamer, of Vermont	10
Charles Sumner, of Massachusetts	1
John C. Fremont, of California	1

Whole number of votes cast, 465; necessary to a choice, 233.

The Convention proceeded to a second ballot. Every man was fiercely enlisted in the struggle. The partisans of the various candidates were strung up to such a pitch of excitement as to render them incapable of patience, and the cries of "Call the roll" were fairly hissed through their teeth. The first gain for Lincoln was in New Hampshire. The Chase and the Fremont vote from that State were given him. His next gain was the whole vote of Vermont. This was a blighting blow upon the Seward interest. The New Yorkers started as if an Orsini bomb had exploded. And presently the Cameron vote of Pennsylvania was thrown for Lincoln, increasing his strength forty-four votes. The fate of the day was now determined. New York saw "checkmate" next move, and sullenly proceeded with the game, assuming unconsciousness of her inevitable doom. On this ballot Lincoln gained seventy-nine votes! Seward had 184½ votes; Lincoln 181. . . .

It now dawned upon the multitude, that the presumption entertained the night before, that the Seward men would have every thing their own way, was a mistake. Even persons unused to making the calculations and considering the combinations attendant upon such scenes, could not fail to observe that while the strength of Seward and Lincoln was almost even at the moment, the reserved votes, by which the contest must be decided, were inclined to the latter. There, for instance, was the Bates vote, thirty-five; the McLean vote, eight; the Dayton vote, ten—all impending for Lincoln—and forty-two Chase votes, the greater part going the same way. . . .

While the third ballot was taken amid excitement that tested the nerves, the fatal defection from Seward in New England still further appeared—four votes going over from Seward to Lincoln in Massachusetts. The latter received four additional votes from Pennsylvania and fifteen additional votes from Ohio. It was whispered about—"Lincoln's the coming man—will be nominated this ballot." When the roll of States and Territories had been called, I had ceased to give attention to any votes but those for Lincoln, and had his vote added up as it was given. The number of votes necessary to a choice were two hundred and thirty-three, and I saw under my pencil as the Lincoln column was completed, the figures 231½—one vote and a half to give him the nomination. In a moment the fact was whispered about. A hundred pencils had told the same story. The news went over the house wonderfully, and there was a pause. There are always men anxious to distinguish themselves on such occasions. There is nothing that politicians like better than a crisis. I looked up to see who would be the man to give the decisive vote. The man for the crisis in the Cincinnati Convention—all will remember —was Col. Preston of Kentucky. He broke the Douglas line and precipitated the nomination of Buchanan, and was rewarded with a foreign mission. In about ten ticks of a watch, Cartter of Ohio was up. I had imagined Ohio would be slippery enough for the crisis. And sure enough! Every eye was on Cartter, and every body who understood the matter at all, knew what he was about to do. He is a large man with rather striking features, a shock of bristling black hair, large and shining eyes, and is terribly marked with the small-pox. He has also an impediment in his speech, which amounts to a stutter; and his selection as chairman of the Ohio delegation was, considering its condition, altogether appropriate. He had been quite noisy during the sessions of the Convention, but had never commanded, when mounting his chair, such attention as now. He said, "I rise (eh), Mr. Chairman (eh), to announce the change of four votes of Ohio from Mr. Chase to Mr. Lincoln." The deed was done. There was a moment's silence. The nerves of the thousands, which through the hours of suspense had been subjected to terrible tension, relaxed, and as deep breaths of relief were taken, there was a noise in the wigwam like the rush of a great wind, in the van of a storm—and in another breath, the storm was there. There were thousands cheering with the energy of insanity.

A man who had been on the roof, and was engaged in communicating the results of the ballotings to the mighty mass of outsiders, now demanded by gestures at the sky-light over the stage, to know what had happened. One of the Secretaries, with a tally sheet in his hands, shouted—"Fire the Salute! Abe Lincoln is nominated!"

35. On the Superiority of National Conventions

Aaron B. Wildavsky

National conventions are not held in very high esteem by most Americans, and a majority, according to public opinion polls, would favor their replacement by a national primary. Aaron Wildavsky, Professor of Political Science at the University of California, Berkeley, here argues against any substitution. Measuring the convention system by six common criteria, he finds it superior to any alternative and a contribution to the maintenance of a moderate and democratic two-party system.

* * *

No one will deny that presidential nominating conventions are peculiar.[1] After all, they perform a peculiar function. The task of the convention is to unite a party which is not inherently united, behind a popular candidate who is unpopular with many delegates, in order to speak for all the people after battling half of them in an election. It would be surprising if a political institution which must accomplish these goals did not reflect some of the contradictions it is designed to embody.

The critics of national conventions[2] find them gay when they should be solemn, vulgar when they should be genteel. In a word, they find the conventions somehow too American. The reforms proposed by these critics suggest that grave decisions should be made at a solemn convention or that the convention system should be abolished entirely. Yet we shall see that every major change suggested has the unfortunate result of leading to consequences much worse than the evils they are supposed to remedy.

In order to evaluate national conventions, and the alternatives to them, we need a set of goals which most Americans would accept as desirable and important. The following six standards appear to meet this test: any method for nominating presidents should: 1. aid in preserving the two-party system; 2. help secure vigorous competition between the parties; 3. maintain some degree of cohesion and agreement within the parties; 4. produce candidates who have some likelihood of winning voter support; 5. lead to the choice of good men; 6. result in the acceptance of candidates as legitimate.

Let us first evaluate the alternatives to national conventions to see if they are superior to the existing system.

A national primary has often been suggested. This, however, would have serious disadvantages. It is quite probable that as many as ten candidates might obtain enough signatures on nominating petitions to get on the ballot. Nor would it be surprising if they divided the vote equally.

[1] One of the earliest and still one of the best discussions of conventions is found in M. Ostrogorski, *Democracy and the Organization of Political Parties* (New York, 1911). For a comprehensive survey of a single convention see Paul David, Malcolm Moos, and Ralph Goldman, *Presidential Nominating Politics in 1952*, Vols. I through V. A vast amount of data about conventions is presented in Paul David, Ralph Goldman, Richard Bain, *The Politics of National Party Conventions* (Washington, D.C., 1959).

[2] Conventions have been subject to criticism for many years and in many places. A brief introduc-

tion to this literature might include James (Lord) Bryce, *The American Commonwealth* (New York, 1891); M. Ostrogorski, *op. cit.;* Louise Overacker, *The Presidential Primary* (New York, 1926); E. E. Schattschneider, *Party Government* (New York, 1942); American Political Science Association, Committee on Political Parties, *Toward a More Responsible Two-Party System* (1950); Estes Kefauver, "Indictment of the Political Convention," *New York Times Magazine,* March 16, 1954; Stephen K. Bailey, *The Condition of Our National Parties* (New York, 1959).

From the *Review of Politics*, vol. 24, no. 3 (July 1962), pp. 307–319, with footnote omissions, by permission of the *Review of Politics*.

The victor would then have to be chosen in a special run-off primary. By following this procedure, the United States might have to restrict its presidential candidates to wealthy athletes: no poor man could ever raise the millions required for the nominating petition, the first primary, the run-off primary, and the national election; and no one who was not superbly conditioned could survive the pace of all these campaigns.

National primaries might also lead to the collapse of the party system as we know it. It is not unusual for a party to remain in office for a long period of time. If state experience with primaries is any guide, this would result in a movement of interested voters into the primary of the winning party where their votes would count more. As voters deserted the losing party, it would be largely the die-hards who were left. They would nominate candidates who pleased them but who could not win the election because they were unrepresentative of a majority of the nation. Eventually, the losing party would atrophy, thus seriously weakening the two-party system and the prospects of competition among the parties. The winning party would soon show signs of internal weakness as a consequence of the lack of opposition necessary to keep it unified.

A national primary is also likely to lead to the appearance of extremist candidates and demagogues who, unrestrained by allegiance to any permanent party organization, have little to lose by stirring up mass hatreds or making absurd promises. A Huey Long or a Joe McCarthy would have found a fertile field in a national primary, an opportunity sufficient to raise the temperature of American politics to explosive levels even if he did not win. The convention system rules out these extremists by placing responsibility in the hands of party leaders who have a permanent stake in maintaining the good name and integrity of their organization. Some insight into this prob-

lem may be had by looking at the situation in several southern states where most voters have moved to the democratic primary and where victory in that primary is tantamount to election. The result is a chaotic factional politics in which there are few or no permanent party leaders, the distinction between the "ins" and "outs" becomes blurred, it is difficult to hold anyone responsible, and demagogues arise who make use of this situation by strident appeals, usually of a racist variety. This functional theory of demagoguery (in which extreme personality takes the place of party in giving even a minimal structure to state politics) should give pause to the advocates of a national primary. . . .

Perhaps, it may be argued, what is required is not some radically new method of nominating candidates, but reform of some of the more obnoxious practices of the present system. High on the list of objectionable practices would be the secret gathering of party leaders in the smoke-filled room. Some liken this to a political opium den where a few irresponsible men, hidden from public view, stealthily determine the destiny of the nation. Yet it is difficult to see who, other than the party's influential leaders, should be entrusted with the delicate task of finding a candidate to meet the majority preference. Since the head-on clash of strength on the convention floor has not resolved the question, the only alternatives would be continued deadlock, anarchy among scores of leaderless delegates, splitting the party into rival factions, or some process of accommodation.

Let us suppose that the smoke-filled room were abolished and with it all behind-the-scenes negotiations. All parleys would then be held in public, before the delegates and millions of television viewers. As a result, the participants would spend their time scoring points against each other in order to impress the folks back home. The claim that bargaining was going on would be a sham, since the participants would not really be communicating with each other. No compromises would be possible, lest the leaders be accused by their followers of selling out to the other side. Once a stalemate existed, it would be practically impossible to break and the party would probably disintegrate into warring factions.

An extensive system of state primaries in which delegates were legally compelled to vote for the victorious candidate would lead to the disappearance of the smoke-filled room without any formal action. As the delegates could not change their positions, there would be little point in bringing their leaders together for private consultations. Sharply increasing the number of pledged delegates would introduce such rigidity into the convention that it would perpetually be faced with stalemates which could not be overcome because no one would be in a position to switch his support. . . .

Some critics object to the convention's stress on picking a winner rather than "the best man" regardless of his popularity. Now this is a rather strange doctrine in a democracy where it is presumed that it is the people who should decide who is best for them and communicate this decision in an election. Only in dictatorial countries do a set of leaders arrogate unto themselves the right to determine who is best, independently of the popular preference. An unpopular man can hardly win a free election. An unpopular President can hardly secure the support he needs to accomplish his goals. We deceive ourselves when we treat popularity as an evil condition instead of a necessary element for obtaining consent in democratic politics.

Although popularity is obviously a necessary condition for nomination, it should not be the only condition. The guideline for purposes of nomination should be to nominate the best of the popular candidates. But "best" is a slippery word. A great deal of what we mean by best in politics is "best for us" or "best represents our policy

preferences." And this can hardly be held up as an objective criterion. What is meant by "best" in this context are certain personal qualities such as experience, intelligence, and decisiveness. Nevertheless, it is doubtful whether an extreme conservative would prefer a highly intelligent radical to a moderately intelligent candidate who shared the conservative's policy preferences. Personal qualities are clearly subject to discount based on the compatibility of interests between the voter and the candidate.

Insofar as the "best man" criterion has a residue of meaning, I believe that it has been followed in recent times. Looking at the candidates of both parties since 1940—Roosevelt, Truman, Stevenson, Kennedy for the Democrats, and Willkie, Dewey, Eisenhower, Nixon for the Republicans—there is not one man among them who could not be said to have had some outstanding qualities or experience for the White House. Without bothering to make a formal declaration of the fact, American political leaders and their followers have apparently agreed to alter the requirements of availability. They have restricted their choice to those popular candidates who give promise of measuring up to the formidable task of the President as preserver of the nation and maintainer of prosperity. The nominee whose sole virtue is his innocuousness or pleasant smile seems to have disappeared.

It has been alleged, however, that this criterion has been violated because nominations have come to be determined by popularity, that is, by expressions of mass preferences as reported in polls and state primaries.[3] Merely defining the candidate who won the nomination as most popular is not sufficient to prove the thesis; it must be shown that the voters agreed who was the most popular candidate, that this was communicated to the delegates, and that

[3] William Carleton, "The Revolution in the Presidential Nominating Convention," *Political Science Quarterly*, Vol. LXXII (June, 1957), 224–240.

they nominated him. It would be hard to say that William Howard Taft, Warren Harding, Alfred Landon, Wendell Willkie and Thomas Dewey, to name a few, were indisputably the most popular Republican candidates. Dwight Eisenhower might fit in this category (though he had to fight for the nomination) but he represents just one case and is counterbalanced by Theodore Roosevelt's failure to obtain the nomination in 1912. There is no evidence to suggest that, among Democratic candidates, Woodrow Wilson was more popular than Champ Clark in 1912, that James M. Cox and John Davis fit the most popular category, or that Franklin Roosevelt could have been placed there with certainty before his first nomination. If anyone was most popular in 1952 it was Estes Kefauver and not Adlai Stevenson.

A surface view of the situation in 1960 might suggest that John F. Kennedy's nomination was due to an irresistible current of public opinion. Obviously, Kennedy's excellent organization and the difficulty of refusing the nomination to a Catholic who had won important primaries must be taken into account. Furthermore, the Republican experience suggests another important factor. We never discovered whether or not Nelson Rockefeller was more popular with the voting public than Richard Nixon because the latter had such strong support among party professionals that the former decided it was not worth running. A crucial difference between the two conventions was that there was no Democrat to oppose Kennedy who could claim a widespread preference among party leaders as was the case with Nixon in the Republican Party.

To be sure, popularity as evidenced through victory in primaries is important. But the unpledged delegates, comprising some two-thirds of the total, may use their judgment to disregard this factor as they did in nominating Willkie and Stevenson who entered no primaries. The significance of primaries derives not nearly so much from the delegates they bring to an aspirant's side as from the indication they give that he is likely to win the election. The candidate who feels that he already has considerable delegate strength would be foolish to enter a primary unless he was quite certain he could win. All he can gain is a few additional votes but he can lose his existing support by a bad showing that would be interpreted to mean he could not win the election. Naturally, primaries are the vehicles of candidates who must make positive demonstrations of support in order to be considered and are hardly worse off by losing than if they had not entered at all. Candidates who are strong at the outset can pick and choose the one or two primaries they wish to enter and can use the most favorable circumstances to defeat their opponents. It does not seem too great an emphasis on popularity to ask that an aspirant be able to win at least one or two primaries. Alternately, it does not seem too shocking that the candidate who wins all the contested primaries, as Kennedy did, should be given prime consideration.

No doubt the primaries, though held in different sections of the country and in different kinds of states (Wisconsin, California, West Virginia) are by no means a perfect representation of the electorate. Yet this is a rather peculiar argument coming from those who wish to downgrade the importance of primaries; for if primaries were truly representative of the nation their importance would be enormously enhanced. How could the nomination be denied to a candidate who had apparently proved that he had the support of a majority of a very large and accurate sample of the voting population?

The conclusion I would draw is that the primaries, together with other methods of delegate selection which gives predominance to party activists, provide a desirable balance between popularity and other considerations which party leaders deem important. Without denying an element of popular participation, the decision is ultimately thrown into the hands of the men who ought to make it if we want a strong party system—the party leaders. . . .

Although I hope to have avoided the error of assuming that whatever is is right, the superiority of national conventions to the available alternatives is clearly demonstrable. Only the convention permits us to realize in large measure all the six goals— the two-party system, party competition, some degree of internal cohesion, candidates attractive to voters, good men, and acceptance of nominees as legitimate— which we postulated earlier would commonly be accepted as desirable. We get good candidates but not extremists who would threaten our liberties or convert our parties into exclusive clubs for party ideologists. Leaders are motivated to choose popular candidates who will help maintain vigorous competition between the parties but who are unlikely to split them into warring factions. The element of popular participation is strong enough to impress itself upon party leaders but not sufficiently powerful to take the choice out of their hands. The convention is sufficiently open to excite great national interest but it is not led into perpetual stalemate by pseudo-bargaining in public. Voters have a choice between conservative and liberal tendencies —a choice which is not absolute because a two-party system can be maintained only if both parties moderate their views in order to appeal to the large population groups in the country. In all these ways, national conventions make an essential contribution to the maintenance of the peculiarly American political system, a contribution which could not be made by any competitive mechanism now on the horizon. It would be interesting to speculate on the reasons why a political institution,

which no one consciously set out to create in its present form, should have evolved in such a way that the delicate balance between its parts serves us so well.

36. Patterns in the Nominating Process

Paul T. David, Ralph M. Goldman, and Richard C. Bain

While each national convention has its unique elements, there are patterns and trends that become apparent with the passage of time. In the following study, the authors find five types of nominations. A distinct trend away from bargaining among small groups of party leaders is evident. Contemporary nominations tend to be won by unchallenged national leaders or by candidates of distinctive intraparty factions. The results of the 1964 conventions provide further evidence of these directions. The senior author, Paul T. David, is Professor of Political Science at the University of Virginia.

* * *

The act of nominating a presidential candidate is primarily a choice of group leadership—the age-old problem of apostolic succession that has had to be solved in one way or another by every human organization that has managed to replace its first leader. The patterns of choice employed by a given organization tend to recur, since their number is obviously limited first of all by the purpose and conditions of the choice, and second by the group

From Paul T. David, Ralph M. Goldman, and Richard C. Bain, *The Politics of National Party Conventions,* a condensation originally published by The Brookings Institution (Copyright 1960, 1964 by the Brookings Institution. First Vintage Edition, March 1964).

characteristics of the choosers. Obviously, too, purpose and characteristics may change if the organization is long-surviving.

In the nominating process, there are two main conditions of choice—the first when an existing party leadership is simply confirmed or rejected, the second when the previous leadership is not available or has been rejected—within each of which various patterns may operate. . . . Here it is proposed to classify all of the nominations since 1832 in accordance with the type of power center that in each case seemed to be most effective. The comparisons that can then be made between the patterns common since 1896 and those of the earlier period have importance as guide lines to possible future developments in the nominating process.

PATTERNS IN CONFIRMATION OF LEADERSHIP

In three situations the presidential nomination simply confirms (or rejects) an existing party leadership: the renomination of a President who was elected directly to the office; the nomination for a full term of a President who, originally elected as a Vice President, succeeded to the Presidency through death of the incumbent; the renomination of a titular leader.

Presidents who had been elected directly to the office have generally been far more successful in obtaining renomination than either of the other two classes of party leader, as Tables 1 and 2 indicate. At the beginning of the convention system,

TABLE 1   Success and Failure in Achieving Renomination

Retired Voluntarily at End of One Term[a]	Sought Renomination Unsuccessfully	Renominated Once or More
Presidents Elected Directly to the Office		
Democratic Party		
Polk, 1848	Pierce, 1856	Jackson, 1832
Buchanan, 1860		Van Buren, 1840
		Cleveland, 1888
		Wilson, 1916
		F. D. Roosevelt, 1936,
		1940, 1944
National Republican, Whig, and Republican Parties		
Hayes, 1880	None	Lincoln, 1864
		Grant, 1872
		B. Harrison, 1892
		McKinley, 1900
		Taft, 1912
		Hoover, 1932
		Eisenhower, 1956
Presidents Elected Initially as Vice Presidents		
Democratic Party		
None	None	Truman, 1948
National Republican, Whig, and Republican Parties		
None	Tyler, 1844	T. Roosevelt, 1904
	Fillmore, 1852	Coolidge, 1924
	Johnson, 1868	
	Arthur, 1884	

[a] The year given in this column is that in which the President would have been required to seek renomination had he not decided to retire.

**TABLE 2   Success and Failure in Achieving Renomination—
Titular Leaders Who Had Suffered Electoral Defeat**

Did Not Seek Renomination in Party Convention Next Following Defeat[a]	Sought Renomination Unsuccessfully	Renominated Once or More
Democratic Party		
McClellan, 1868	Van Buren, 1844[b]	Cleveland, 1892[b]
Seymour, 1872	Cass, 1852	Bryan, 1900, 1908
Tilden, 1880	Smith, 1932	Stevenson, 1956
Hancock, 1884		
Bryan, 1904,[c] 1912		
Cox, 1924		
Davis, 1928		
Stevenson, 1960[c]		
National Republican, Whig, and Republican Parties		
Clay, 1836[d]	Clay, 1848	Dewey, 1948
Scott, 1856[e]	Willkie, 1944	
Frémont, 1860		
Blaine, 1888		
Harrison, B. 1896[b]		
Taft, 1916[b]		
Hughes, 1920		
Hoover, 1936[b]		
Landon, 1940		
Dewey, 1952[c]		

[a] In this column the year given is the one in which the titular leader would have been required to seek renomination had he not decided to retire.
[b] Had served one term as President and had failed of re-election for a second term.
[c] Had previously been nominated and defeated twice when declining to stand for a third consecutive nomination.
[d] The National Republican party disintegrated after holding one convention and made no further nomination.
[e] The Whig party disintegrated after losing with Scott and held no national convention in 1856.

Andrew Jackson (1832) and Martin Van Buren (1840) were renominated to succeed themselves; after that no further instance occurred until 1864. This was an era of one-term Presidencies and of frequent rejection of the President as party leader. With Abraham Lincoln and Ulysses S. Grant, the two-term tradition was restored. By 1892, even as weak a President as Benjamin Harrison was able to secure renomination in the face of factional opposition—although perhaps in part because the supporters of William McKinley expected a party defeat and wished to save their man for 1896.

Since then it has been assumed that a regularly elected President is entitled to his party's nomination for a second term. Contesting candidacies have rarely been even discussed, unless the President's own availability was for some reason in doubt. The conflict over the renomination of President William Howard Taft in 1912 is the only outstanding exception.

The seven Vice Presidents up to 1960 who became President through death of the previous incumbents sought nominations for the next full term as President. That President Lyndon B. Johnson will also do so is a reasonable assumption. Of the four nineteenth-century cases shown in Table 1, not one was able to secure the nomination. . . .

The change in practice was striking when it came, and the growing power of the Presidency was probably mainly responsible. Each of the three Vice Presidents succeeding to the Presidency from 1896 to 1960 won nomination for the next full presidential term, and won the election as well. The strength of Theodore Roosevelt as a popular leader was doubtless a factor in the timing of the change, but by 1924 even a Calvin Coolidge could be nominated for the full term without much opposition. In the Democratic party, where the problem had arisen only once, the claim to the nomination was successfully maintained by President Harry S Truman in 1948. There now seems to be general agreement among political leaders, political writers, and the public that a Vice President succeeding to the Presidency automatically becomes the leader of his party and will be a strong candidate for the next nomination.

Titular leaders have also gained strength in recent decades, as Table 2 shows, and this also is probably related to the new power status of the Presidency, which confers importance on any candidate for the office. For a long period the possibility of renomination was remote for almost all defeated major-party candidates; in the present century the trend has been the other way. . . .

William Jennings Bryan was the first to achieve renomination in either party without benefit of a previous term in the White House. In the Republican party, no defeated presidential candidate tried—at least openly—for a second nomination until the 1940's. Wendell Wilkie's attempt came to grief in the primaries of 1944; Dewey's try in 1948 succeeded. Adlai Stevenson won renomination in the Democratic party in 1956 after a period in which no one since Bryan had done so. In both parties the basis has been laid for the claim that a defeated candidate is entitled to another try if he has made a good race.

PATTERNS
IN LEADERSHIP SUCCESSION

When a previous party leader is unavailable, or has been rejected, any one of four major patterns of succession may operate, with variations in each. The instances are brought together in Table 3.

Inheritance

Inheritance by an understudy or by an outstanding member of the previous leadership group is a common form of succession in most organizations, but it has not happened often in presidential nominations under the convention system. The in-party cases of Martin Van Buren in 1836, William Howard Taft in 1908, Herbert Hoover in 1928, and Richard Nixon in 1960 are the clearest examples of the type. Henry Clay's second nomination in 1844, although classified here as an in-party case, was not greatly different from his first nomination in 1832, in view of the circumstances prevailing during the Tyler administration. Al Smith's nomination in 1928 was similarly the result of high availability in an out-party situation where no other powerful figure was willing to contest the nomination.

Inner group selection

Processes of inner group selection can be said to occur at times in American national parties, but only if the term "inner group" is given a rather special meaning. As noted earlier, the American parties do not ordinarily have any single or genuinely cohesive inner group that is dominant for all party affairs, except in the party in power when leadership has become firmly centered in

**TABLE 3   Patterns of Leadership Succession through Nominations
in National Party Conventions[a]**

Inheritance	Inner Group Selection	Compromise in Stalemate	Factional Victory
Party in Power			
Van Buren (D), 1836	Cass (D), 1848	Hayes (R), 1876	Scott (W), 1852
Clay (W), 1844	Grant (R), 1868	Garfield (R), 1880	Buchanan (D), 1856
Taft (R), 1908			Douglas (D), 1860
Hoover (R), 1928			Blaine (R), 1884
Nixon (R), 1960			Bryan (D), 1896
			Cox (D), 1920
			Stevenson (D), 1952
Party Out of Power			
Clay (NR), 1832	Frémont (R), 1856	Polk (D), 1844	W. H. Harrison (W), 1840
Smith (D), 1928	McClellan (D), 1864	Pierce (D), 1852	Taylor (W), 1848
	Greeley (D), 1872	Seymour (D), 1868	Lincoln (R), 1860
	Hancock (D), 1880	Harding (R), 1920	Tilden (D), 1876
	Cleveland (D), 1884	Davis (D), 1924	B. Harrison (R), 1888
	Parker (D), 1904		McKinley (R), 1896
	Hughes (R), 1916		Wilson (D), 1912
	Landon (R), 1936		F. D. Roosevelt (D), 1932
			Willkie (R), 1940
			Dewey (R), 1944
			Eisenhower (R), 1952
			Kennedy (D), 1960

[a] The symbols after each name indicate the party making the nomination: Democratic (D), Republican (R), National Republican (NR), Whig (W).

the President. But there have been occasions when the dominant leaders of the various party factions have seemed disposed to work together informally on a sort of federated basis in reaching agreement on the next nomination—with the "federation" not usually lasting long when the convention is over, and especially if the candidate loses. . . .

Most of the cases identified as inner group selection occurred in a party out of power, and most of these out-party cases took place under conditions of some party weakness. . . .

Despite the relative success of Grant and Cleveland in winning elections, and the eminence and near-win of Justice Hughes, it appears evident that the pattern of inner group selection, as employed by the American parties, has been remarkably unsuccessful in recruiting candidates who could

win elections or provide party leadership. This may be, however, mainly a sign of the conditions under which this pattern of nominations has occurred.

Compromise in stalemate

Seven compromise candidates have been chosen in stalemated conventions, four Democrats and three Republicans. Two of the seven—Rutherford B. Hayes (1876) and James A. Garfield (1880)—were the nominees of a party in power; both won. In each case, the incumbent President refrained from making any noteworthy effort to influence the succession and the convention was badly split, with the strongest faction supporting a front-runner who fell short of a majority.

In each of the other five cases, all in a party out of power, the eventual compromise candidate was acceptable to all of the major factions represented in the convention. The nomination was thus a major act of interfactional conciliation. James K. Polk (1844) and Franklin Pierce (1852) were each nominated after attempts to renominate the previous titular leader had reached a stalemate; both won election. The other three nominations all occurred in factional situations where the previous titular leader had lost all standing or had specifically taken himself out of the running. Only Warren G. Harding won election.

Most of the seven have been considered "dark horse" nominees, that peculiar appellation of American politics. There is no generally agreed definition of what constitutes a "dark horse," but on its face, the term seems to imply an unanticipated or minor candidate whose victory was a surprise. Sidney Hyman, writing in the *New York Times* in 1955, held that in the oral tradition of American politics the authentic dark horses were but five: Polk, Pierce, Hayes, Garfield, and Davis, to whom he would add Harding and Wendell Willkie. But since Willkie had been campaigning vigorously for several months before the convention and was the avowed candidate of an important aggregation of party supporters, he would seem the most highly illuminated dark horse in history. In any event, he was not a compromise candidate in a situation of convention deadlock, as were Harding and Horatio Seymour, both of whom have often been regarded as dark horse candidates.

Factional victory

Factional victory can occur in a party in power when there is a successful attempt to deny renomination to an incumbent President, or when a retiring President is defeated in an attempt to control the succession, declines an active role, or finds no satisfactory candidate to back, thus leaving the way open for what is called an "open" convention.

Among the cases classified here as reflecting factional victory in in-party situations,

those of Winfield Scott, James Buchanan, and James G. Blaine represented defeat for an incumbent President who was seeking renomination. Stephen A. Douglas was nominated despite the opposition of the incumbent President, Buchanan, who was not himself running for renomination; William Jennings Bryan was the nominee of the forces most opposed to the Cleveland administration. James M. Cox was nominated in a situation in which the administration had deliberately adopted a hands-off policy, Adlai E. Stevenson in one where the administration had been unable to find an adequate candidate before the convention, with Stevenson originally refusing to serve as an understudy to President Truman. Among the seven in-party cases, Buchanan was the only election winner.

Factional warfare is especially common in out-party situations, where it has led to compromise after stalemate in about one third of the cases. Where the struggle has led to factional victory, it has sometimes involved a form of insurgency in which renomination was denied a titular leader. More often, the victory has simply been the outcome of a contest among coordinate factions, no one of which was clearly in control of the party leadership. . . .

A recognized factional leader generally takes an active part in the strategy. He must fight openly against the field, and is usually limited to first-choice votes, for he will usually have at least one unbending opponent. An outsider is a passenger on a band wagon operated by the faction. He has a better chance to pick up second-choice votes at the convention, and to court the independent voters in the election campaign.

CONTINUITY AND CHANGE IN THE PATTERNS OF NOMINATION

If the sixty-five nominations are recapitulated as for the periods 1832–1892 and 1896–1960, first by major party, then by in-power and out-power status, as in Tables 4 and 5 the patterns that emerge have special interest in connection with the study of long-term changes in the nominating process and the party system. The periods divide the total experience under the convention system of nominations into two nearly equal portions, the breaking point coinciding with the critical election year of 1896.

TABLE 4 Patterns in Major-Party Presidential Nominations Since 1832; by Major Parties[a]

Type of Nomination	Democratic		Republican[b]		Major-Party Total	
	1832–1892	1896–1960	1832–1892	1896–1960	1832–1892	1896–1960
A. Confirmation	4	8	3	7	7	15
B. Inheritance	1	1	2	3	3	4
C. Inner group selection	5	1	2	2	7	3
D. Compromise in stalemate	3	1	2	1	5	3
E. Factional victory	3	6	6	4	9	10
TOTAL	16	17	15	17	31	34

a Data from the previous tables.
b Includes National Republican and Whig.

TABLE 5 Patterns in Major-Party Presidential Nominations Since 1832; by In-Power and Out-of-Power Status of the Parties[a]

Type of Nomination	Party in Power		Party Out of Power	
	1832–1892	1896–1960	1832–1892	1896–1960
A. Confirmation	6	11	1	4
B. Inheritance	2	3	1	1
C. Inner group selection	2	0	5	3
D. Compromise in stalemate	2	0	3	2
E. Factional victory	4	3	5	7
TOTAL	16	17	15	17

a "In-power" and "out-power" status was determined in accordance with whether the currently incumbent President had been elected on the party ticket. The result is anomalous to the extent that it classifies the Whig party as holding power during John Tyler's administration, and the Republican party during Andrew Johnson's; but the result would be even more anomalous if the Democratic party were regarded as holding power in those instances.

The patterns of the future

In all analytical work based upon small numbers of cases it is necessary to guard against inferences that may have no basis other than purely random variations in the numbers. There is also danger in projecting into the future the observed trends of the past, however well ascertained. A projection of trends on the basis of the figures of Tables 4 and 5 alone would be hazardous indeed, but, in the total historical context, the figures mainly have the effect of clarifying and solidifying what would otherwise be much more vague.

Probably the simplest prediction that can be made is that first-term Presidents who have been elected directly to the office will, when willing and available, continue to secure party renominations with a high degree of unanimity, as they have since 1864, and will continue to be extremely strong election contenders. . . .

Vice Presidents who succeed to the Presidency through death of the incumbent will probably continue to secure nomination for a second term with little difficulty, as they have since 1904. Succession by the death of the President will cause less disruption of party and governmental affairs in the future, to the extent that increasing attention is given to factional and personal compatibility between the presidential and vice-presidential candidates of each party. However, the new doctrine on the selection of Vice Presidents has not yet been fully accepted.

The future of the titular leaders as candidates for the Presidency is full of uncertainties and imponderables. It seems likely that the position of the titular leadership will continue to be strengthened, and this may be favorable to continued success in the pursuit of the party nominations. But these tendencies could be delayed or even reversed unless some titular leader eventually wins election as well as renomination.

In making predictions about the choice of new leadership the situation of the in-party must be distinguished from that of the out-party and a divided vote, has become much less common in the party in power than in the party out of power. But conflict over the succession will probably continue to occur from time to time even in the party in power, as long as the Democratic and Republican parties are no more internally cohesive than they are at present.

Factional candidates in a party out of power will probably continue to achieve nominations with considerable frequency, unless the titular leadership is greatly strengthened, and perhaps even if it is. The successful candidates who drive through to out-party factional nominations within ten years or less after they first become prominent have a type of glamour that can be extremely useful. If the factional infighting does not become too severe, the contest may serve to demonstrate party vitality and to publicize the eventual candidate. Such candidates should continue to have good chances for electoral victory.

Inner group nominations will probably be much less heard of in the future, unless there is a return to a party imbalance so extreme that the out-party becomes a minority in which the recruitment of suitable candidates is difficult.

The compromise or dark horse nominees have been reserved for final treatment because they are, as a group, perhaps the most interesting, and also the most crucial when the nominating process is being appraised. It is the group that is most generally cited when the convention system is under attack. The fact that even one Harding could be nominated under the convention system is to many critics a sufficient argument for substituting a national primary as the nominating instrument.

But all the other compromise candidates except John W. Davis, who was defeated, are figures of ancient party history. It is easy to argue that they were the only possible solution—the price of union—at a time when politics was fiercely sectional and factional passions ran high. Yet the parties may thereby have missed performing an essential function—that of giving the voters alternatives through which national issues could have been solved. Be that as it may, dark horse candidates seem to be a vanishing type, just as most of the conditions conducive to their candidacies have disappeared.

The nominating habits of the major parties have developed over the years under the impact of changes in the structure of government, and in the kind of political issues at stake—and sometimes under the impact of personalities and personal decisions. The main purpose of the convention system from the first has been to select candidates in such a way as to unite the party for the election.

The nominating patterns identified in this chapter represent the tactics variously chosen by political leaders who sought both to press for the results they desired and to avoid breaking up the party. Usually a consensus has been achieved. Those who were disappointed were not so bitter as to walk out; the party held together; and the chance of victory in the election was not thrown away. On other occasions the con-sensus failed and the party was split—whereupon the voters took a hand in the election and taught the warring political leaders the value of compromise, unity, and the integrity of the two-party system.

THE CAMPAIGN

37. The Organization and Functions of Campaigns

Alexander Heard

The nature of campaigning has changed historically. In our first elections, direct appeals to the voters were considered improper, while modern campaigns require immense amounts of personal stamina, money, time, and professional skills. Alexander Heard, chancellor of Vanderbilt University and a leading student of political finance, here traces the evolution of campaigns. He then assesses their cost and value in a democracy.

* * *

Although entirely unlike in external appearance, election campaigns may serve identical political functions. In their consequences, the torchlit, whooped-up speakings of 1860 may not differ from the klieglit, souped-up broadcasts of 1960. Boisterous campaigning at a crossroads tavern in one century may be equivalent to a televised carnival in another. The requirements for an effective television personality have been lampooned; but it has not been shown that these, while different, are more deleterious to political debate than the bull-horn voice and chautauqua talents that prospered in another era. One gathers that Mr. Lincoln's anecdotes, not all of which presumably were original with him, illuminated some issues and obscured some. Mr. Eisenhower's capsule simplifications of public problems, not all of which presumably were original with others, achieved the same ends.

If political campaigns are functional, their functions may well be accomplished by different means under different conditions. Processes of communications and organization may change without altering significantly the functions themselves. To see the meaning of trends in campaign expenditures is harder than to detect the trends.

CAMPAIGN TRENDS

A change in American campaign habits always arouses foreboding. In the election of 1836 William Henry Harrison made the first public appeal by a presidential candidate that resembled a modern campaign speech. During the next four years the novel practice grew, and Representative John Quincy Adams, himself once a president, recorded his exasperation in his *Memoirs*:

> Here is a revolution in the habits and manners of the people. Where will it end? . . .
>
> Electioneering for the Presidency has spread its contagion to the President himself, to his now only competitor, to his immediate predecessor. . . .

From · Alexander Heard, *The Costs of Democracy: Financing American Political Campaigns* (Chapel Hill: University of North Carolina Press, 1960), pp. 400–403, 405–411, 426–428, by permission of the University of North Carolina Press.

One of the most remarkable peculiarities of the present time is that the principal leaders of the political parties are travelling about the country from State to State, and holding forth, like Methodist preachers, hour after hour, to assembled multitudes, under the broad canopy of heaven.

Nearly a century later, speaking through the president of the Southern Publishers Association, newspapers protested the growing use of radio broadcasting by the major parties. The arrival of television and the campaign airplane stimulated a fresh splash of commentary, some of it hopeful, but most of it apprehensive. Ability to gauge the consequences of changed campaign practices is severely limited. It is difficult enough to discern the effects on voters of particular campaign appeals. It is even more difficult to understand the import for the political system of altered ways of making the appeals.

The evolution of campaigns

American national campaigning has evolved through five broad periods, as measured by the things for which money has been spent.

Limited public campaigning characterized the Republic's first third century. Before the time of Jackson and Harrison, the presidential contest was a relatively staid procedure in both tempo and scope. The visible exertions of the candidates were slight, although organizational work was often of prime importance. Most of the canvassing, as it was called, took the form of preachments by supporters from stump and pulpit, of debate in the highly partisan press, of private correspondence, and of persuasive activities on election day. There was no lack of raucous contention for lesser offices, with due attention to the frailties of voters, but the suffrage was limited and the focus of presidential politics was as often on legislatures as on the people.

The torchlight era commenced with Jackson's election, symbolic of a shift in political power from the leadership of the eastern patriciate. The controversies surrounding Old Hickory deepened political competition. The United States Bank spent heavily in the campaign of 1832, but Jackson appealed directly to the masses against the "Money Monster." They understood and showed it in torchlight processions and hickory-pole raisings. The hard-cider campaign of 1840 demonstrated in full swing a new style of canvassing that would last until the end of the century.

The presidential stump speech grew in importance. After its first use by Harrison, other candidates occasionally took to the hustings, notably Douglas, Bell, and Breckenridge in 1860—but not Lincoln. Garfield spoke 70 times during the 1880 campaign, the most active stumper since Harrison and the only one aside from Tippecanoe to get elected. Not until 1928 did speeches by candidates on tour become a fixture of presidential campaigning.

Campaigning has always been concerned with two basic processes: communications and organization. Public attitudes are sensed and asserted in various ways, but chiefly through these processes are efforts made to mobilize popular support. In the flamboyant campaigning of the torchlight period, the emphasis lay on organization. Financial demands mounted and both parties began to draw on wealthy backers for funds. The municipal machine became the hallmark of American politics. These organizations sold their influence, and individuals sold their votes, on a massive scale. Appeals to the electorate were made through newspapers, broadsides, processions, public speaking, but field activities consumed the giant share of national and state campaign budgets, and election-day expenses consumed the largest share of local budgets. Travelling organizers arranged the support of local leaders, plotted ways to corral votes, negotiated the tactics of personalities and issues. It was said that in 1896 the Republican national committee hired 1,400 organizers and sent them wherever they were most needed.

The era of campaign literature began in 1880. Handbills and other printed materials had been campaign fixtures for decades, but a mounting number of printing presses and a fall in the price of paper produced an unprecedented torrent of printed words. In 1896, the Republican national committee alone was said to have distributed from its headquarters 300,000,-000 pieces, weighing, somebody calculated, 2,000 tons. The torches literally went out that year, marking a transition to modern political-campaigning methods. Printed words came to supplement fiery oratory. The new century brought sharply mounting expenditures for communications, i.e., campaign publicity. Pollack reported in 1926 that the combined costs of advertising candidates, and printing and distributing their speeches and other tracts, constituted the most important item of campaign expense at national, state, and local levels. During the years 1912–24, something like 40 percent of total expenditures went for newspaper and periodical advertising, news bureau services, outdoor billboards, lithographs, and the printing and sending of campaign literature. The profession of advertising grew, along with mass mailings and other techniques facilitating access to large publics. Politics followed business in making use of them.

Radio campaigning produced a sudden decline in 1928 of expenditures for newspaper advertising by the two national committees. Radio had been used but slightly in 1924, and at small cost to the parties. Four years later it emerged as a major campaign innovation, to remain until 1952 the distinctive medium of communications characterizing those years.

Television campaigning, after a limited initiation in 1948, began its dominance of campaign communications in 1952.

The displacement principle

Throughout the history of campaigning, a process of displacement has gone on. As new forms of campaigning develop, they displace older ones. It has already been suggested that the cost of national-level campaigning did not increase between the 1920's and 1950's, if allowances are made for changes in the price level and in the size of the electorate. Moreover, at the end of that period, publicity as a whole consumed no larger share of national campaign-committee expenditures, about one-half, than it had at the beginning. Yet in 1952, two-thirds of communications costs were attributable to radio and television, whereas in 1920 there had been no significant charges for these items. Expenditures were made for other kinds of communications. Even in 1928, in fact, radio accounted for only 18 and 10 percent, respectively, of the expenses of the Democratic and Republican national committees. In other words, by 1952 broadcasting had significantly *displaced* other publicity devices in the campaign budgets of the national campaign organizations.

Between 1952 and 1956, however, the story was different. Radio and television broadcasting by *national-level* campaign groups not only further displaced other media of publicity but had the additional effect of increasing total costs. The percentages of total direct expenditures and the dollar amounts are shown on page 324. For both parties, the percentage and the dollars spent for broadcasting went up, and the percentage and the dollars spent for other types of publicity went down. The percentage also went down in both cases for the remaining campaign costs, although only in the case of the Democrats did the dollar outlays decline. The fall in these

		1952		
	Rep.	*Dem.*	*Other*	*Total*
Radio and TV:	31%	34%	16%	30%
(in millions)	$2.0	$1.5	$0.2	$3.7
Other publicity:	16%	18%	33%	19%
(in millions)	$1.1	$0.8	$0.5	$2.4
Other expenditures:	53%	48%	51%	51%
(in millions)	$3.5	$2.2	$0.7	$6.4
TOTAL:	100%	100%	100%	100%
(in millions)	$6.6	$4.5	$1.4	$12.5

		1956		
	Rep.	*Dem.*	*Other*	*Total*
Radio and TV:	37%	41%	11%	36%
(in millions)	$2.8	$1.7	$0.1	$4.6
Other publicity:	12%	17%	37%	16%
(in millions)	$1.0	$0.7	$0.4	$2.1
Other expenditures:	51%	42%	52%	48%
(in millions)	$3.8	$1.7	$0.6	$6.1
TOTAL:	100%	100%	100%	100%
(in millions)	$7.6	$4.1	$1.1	$12.8

categories was nevertheless not sufficient to offset the broadcasting increases. . . .

Politicians campaign at all governmental levels and for many offices. The changes that take place in campaign practices, however, do not occur equally in all kinds of elections. Many local candidates have been left relatively untouched by the shift from printed publicity to radio and television. For them, personal canvassing continues the chief requisite for success.

Campaigns are more likely to be altered by new media of communications in large constituencies. In large constituencies, also, changes in population and in social patterns are more likely to require new modes of campaign organization. Presidential campaigns seem to register most readily the innovations that periodically occur. The significance of such changes is more difficult to discern than the changes themselves, but what is true of presidential politics will often be true to varying extents of lesser offices.

Television: new medium, old process?

In 1960, the United States found itself deep in an era of mass communications

campaigning. The era had commenced at the end of the previous century, and its most notable current manifestation was television. What the coming of television means to American politics and American society has been the subject of much foreboding and much optimism. The impact on the structure of American values and on the ability of the United States to understand its problems and meet them with consensus might well prove profound. Yet its impact on voting behavior was uncertain, and some of its other presumed consequences might be more apparent than real. Innovations in campaign practice have always prompted grave predictions by those accustomed to the old ways.

A large proportion of the people of the United States unquestionably follow politics over television; when questioned in polls, a large share of them assign it as the most important source of their campaign information. Not all the consequences claimed for its use might be as portentous, however, as seemed to some at first. It was pointed out, for example, that television enabled candidates to become quickly "known" throughout large constituencies.

Adlai Stevenson was declared by many to have benefited accordingly in 1952. Nonetheless, the United States across its history has chosen many successful presidents who were not personally exhibited to a large share of the voters. Moreover, 56 years before, and sans microphones, William Jennings Bryan at the age of 36 had converted himself into a national figure in an equally short period of time.

It has been observed, too, that the speed and coverage of television also served Richard Nixon well in 1952. The vice presidential candidate was able to answer the Nixon Fund charges promptly, personally, and before a large audience. That the medium would reduce the incidence of campaign slander—the meaning some of Mr. Nixon's supporters saw in the episode —was, however, by no means assured. Critics held that the very tactics employed by Mr. Nixon then and on other occasions corrupted political debate. But the one-way feature of mass communications has always tempted ardent campaigners down lines less permissible in face-to-face colloquies. At the turn of the century, quantities of defamatory falsehoods, called "roorbacks," were printed and distributed in ways designed to influence the ignorant and thwart an adequate rejoinder. Some individuals clearly prospered before the television cameras. That Stevenson and Nixon and others possessed a set of personal skills denied other men less suited to the contemporary medium did not, however, seem significant. The same was true in other days, in the days of Franklin Roosevelt's radio voice, of Theodore Roosevelt's boisterous phrase-making, of Thomas Jefferson's agile pen. The types of persons equipped for successful political careers alter with the changing requirements of campaigning. It is difficult to see why at any given moment the random distribution of political talents would favor one politically significant group over another. It is difficult to conclude that the poor have

fewer spokesmen or the rich are ridden over because the personal qualities that elected the father will hardly help the son.

The subtle and the lasting effects of television campaigning might in the end prove numerous and profound. As many feared, ability to project personality might, through television campaigning, acquire a primacy hitherto unknown. In the meantime, certain characteristics of the mass communications campaigning that had commenced half a century earlier were visibly accentuated by the use of the new medium. At one time, a candidate's organization consisted principally of a small group of personal aides and a set of treaties with other political leaders. As the importance of publicity mounted, the character of the campaign skills required and the ways they were assembled changed. Organization continued crucial as a campaign function, but the decline of old-style political machines and the growth of direct communications between candidates and voters evidenced the ascending significance of communications, especially its financial significance. The changes were, basically, technological in origin. Inventions in transportation and communications affected campaigning directly and underlay most of the profound alterations that occurred in social organization, in the character of the electorate, and in the nature of political issues. These forces combined to revolutionize the machinery of campaigning and its cost and to touch deeply other aspects of party procedure. Certain of these were especially noteworthy.

More than a Pheidippides needed

Pheidippides fell dead as he reached the outskirts of Athens. Modern mass communications have converted many presidential campaigns into marathon races, imposing an astonishing personal burden upon presidential candidates. Hard work is no novelty for American politicians, but candidates for high office have important responsibilities to meet, including the maintenance of good health, if they are to serve well the offices to which they are chosen. It was anomalous that as the ease of communicating to the electorate improved, the labor devoted to doing so increased. In the first year of full radio campaigning, 1928, stump speaking by the candidates became a *standard* feature of presidential campaigns. Curiously enough, television further increased the pressure on candidates to travel, and with the airplane, the time saved in the air multiplied the demands upon the candidates instead of reducing them. Not even his immense popularity and severe illnesses excused President Eisenhower from the stump in 1956, but rather they seemed to make his personal appearances necessary. In 1896, William Jennings Bryan, in an unprecedented orgy of oratory, travelled more than 18,000 miles to deliver some 600 speeches to 5,000,000 people in person. In 1956, Adlai Stevenson, who could be seen and heard by many times his number by going before a television camera—and on numerous occasions was—felt compelled to travel twice the distance by plane, train, and car.

The pressures on presidential candidates to hit the hustings stem from several sources. The spread of competition among the states increases the interest local and national leaders feel in their personal appearances. The visits made by Eisenhower and Stevenson to the South in 1952 and 1956 reflected a trend in evidence elsewhere. Candidates running simultaneously for other positions often want the leaders of the party ticket to visit their states—pleas likely to be treated with respect when the candiates might later assist in presidential relations with Congress. The airplane has limited the ability of the presidential aspirant and his managers to say no. They can no longer plead lack of time. Moreover, to be broadcast, a speech must be made. A hall of howling partisans adds

punch. So candidates accept some of the sounding boards offered to them, and to avoid favoritism they race off to others. The mobility resulting from technological developments leads political interests of all types to press claims for the personal attention of candidates. The growth of organized interest groups has both reflected and created increased demands on government. The plight of the presidential candidate is not solely a product of planes and mikes but of a more complex structure of political interests as well.

The result of it all is a cruel, grueling personal experience that exhausts the candidate. The pace of his day and the multiplicity of his decisions exceed the capacities of the best. (They led one candidate to call his party's nominee for Congress by the name of an opponent, and another after a speech in Bethlehem to thank the good people of Allentown.) Decisions taken and commitments made in the heat of a campaign are always difficult enough. In a day when domestic politics and foreign policy are seldom separate, the campaign no longer constitutes a backyard play that can be forgotten as soon as it is over. Like a president, a presidential candidate needs to be informed, to be alert, to make decisions under such conditions that he may reasonably be held responsible for them. The organizational and staffing needs of the White House finally received attention; the corresponding needs of presidential candidates require attention too.

An era of specialists

Detailed study of the purposes for which modern campaign funds are used reveals a high degree of specialization in campaign operations. Campaign organizations are neither large nor complex by the standards of contemporary administrative structures in government and business, but the thousands of pages of itemized campaign payments reported for each election emphasize the multiplicity of goods and services called into use. The proliferation of skills employed in the political process extends beyond campaign organizations to all reaches of party candidate activities.

As a result of this division of labor, a politician becomes a difficult person to define—which reveals, incidentally, that the door to political activity is open to a wide variety of persons. The concept of the politician as a mediator among conflicting interests embraces the broad functions of parties and factions. But not all individuals significantly active in parties and campaigns are engaged directly in mediating roles, nor are they all clothed with the ultimate attributes of political leadership, power, representativeness, accountability. In common parlance, all candidates, their managers, and party officers are accepted as politicians, although job descriptions of what even they actually do in different settings would expose many variations. In addition, necessary cogs in the wheels of modern politics include diverse types such as jingle writers, stage directors, public opinion pollsters, advance men, statistical researchers, precinct bosses, interest-group leaders, public relations advisers, contributors, solicitors, finance chairmen, career accountants, field representatives, confidential alter egos, advisers on an infinite number of special policy areas, the head of a women's division, and the head of a Negro division. These just begin the list that makes the campaign organization of the mid-twentieth century a wholly different phenomenon from that which sought Mr. Buchanan's election in 1856 or Judge Parker's in 1904.

Campaign effectiveness and party bureaucracy

Waste of money has been acute in political campaigns as far back as the record runs. It is not simply that money may stick to the fingers through which it passes (or rather, through which it does not pass). Men of experience have at one time or an-

other estimated that a fourth, a half, even a larger proportion of campaign expenditures went down a useless drain. Administrative inefficiencies have been gross (symbolized at the end of the last century by the million copies of a document directed to organized labor in New York that were printed without a union label, only to be junked and printed again). Political inefficiencies, more important to the effectiveness of the election process, have taken the form of poor judgments, piqued feelings, unneeded commitments, wretched failures to capitalize on opportunities to build public support. Most campaign headquarters are welters of confusion, a state of affairs inherent in modern conditions of campaigning.

The probabilities and penalties of campaign inefficiency have reached new peaks with the arrival of television. There is a new premium on campaign planning and efficient management. The large costs of network television, to be met in advance, alone require a new kind of timing in the planning and launching of campaigns. Failure to anticipate television needs apparently cost Republicans $300,000 to $400,000 in 1952. Pre-emption and other charges could have been avoided by advance arrangements, although it might be argued that the money was well spent if it permitted the Republicans to capture a significant part of the audience of the choice commercial shows whose time was pre-empted. The preparation required by modern campaigns often must commence before candidates are chosen, a condition, it may be well to remember, that makes difficult the shortening of campaigns.

Few if any party organizations possess the staff necessary to supply the technical and professional skills called for in modern campaigns. To fill this void, and in some localities to help fill larger voids created by generally weak party organizations, public relations people and others from outside the party structure have often stepped in.

They claim to offer a steady set of diverse and expert skills that cannot be developed and sustained by party organizations. The parties are not, however, entirely devoid of stable administrative staffs. . . .

WHAT SHOULD CAMPAIGNS COST?

In the present state of the craft, there is no conclusive answer. Despite vigorous criticism of the volume of campaign expenditures, no one has designed a model campaign that fixes optimum levels of expenditure under specified conditions. As a matter of fact, not much is said explicitly about what an election campaign ought to accomplish. Campaign theory goes little beyond the general notion that a well-informed electorate will behave more wisely than an ill-informed one.

Two-bits per vote

The difficulties of defining and determining total expenditures in particular campaigns have already been emphasized. In most localities, nevertheless, there is a limited sector of total costs that candidates or their backers must "see" a reasonable chance of meeting before a campaign can be undertaken. This is the money that must be assembled for use through one or more central headquarters. In many states, local campaign organizations are expected to raise and spend their own funds. In others, especially in primary campaigns, a state headquarters may help finance local campaign operations. The headquarters money must be raised by the candidate or his group of immediate supporters. In most campaigns, once they are underway, modest funds flow automatically to all significant candidates. But to launch a campaign and to keep its central organs functioning require a basic amount of money, and this is the money that must be seen at the outset.

Types of expenditures and levels of costs vary with the office sought, the locale, the candidate, the character of the competition, local financing habits, and other factors alluded to earlier. Yet *headquarters'* expenditures for statewide races in most of the country in the mid-1950's ran between 10 and 25 cents for every vote cast. Using information gathered informally by interview as well as from official reports, this range seemed to obtain in such states as Connecticut, New York, Virginia, Illinois, Montana, Oregon, and California. (In several southern primaries, where heavy subventions were made to local campaign organizations from headquarters funds, the cost might run three or four times as high.) Candidates in all states may spend both more and less than the sums mentioned, but these sums are representative under typical conditions.

As long as present conditions obtain, sums on this order must be taken into account in legislative proposals for subsidizing or limiting state campaign costs. Except for those cases where large-scale local-level financing is required through state headquarters, 25 cents per vote cast is a reasonable working maximum of the money needed—or at least spent. For all national-level campaign committees combined in a presidential contest, the corresponding expenditures per party came to about one-half that amount in 1952 and 1956.

Is it worth it?

During the discussion of campaign costs that followed the 1956 elections, Louis Graves, a veteran southern newspaper editor, declared that most campaign money is wasted: "Ninety-five per cent . . . would be a low estimate of the waste. The voters could get all the information about issues that would do them any good, all that they could possibly understand, if the two parties would just agree, or be compelled by law, to limit their appeals for votes to a few amply circulated newspaper statements and a few radio and television broadcasts in the five or six weeks before the election." Thus is raised a central query. How useful, how functional, is the money that is spent?

The efforts made by public relations firms to rationalize political campaigning are normally guided by one criterion: the efficient influencing of voters. The energies they and others direct toward influencing voters, however, accomplish other purposes as well. There are latent as well as manifest functions in the use of campaign money. Campaigning is inescapable in a system of popular elections, so that candidates and parties may display themselves, their records, and their views to the scrutiny of the electorate. But the process achieves more than the election of some candidates and the defeat of others.

The socially useful functions of political parties are numerous, and election campaigning contributes substantially to many of them. They are part of what the nation buys with its election money and should be remembered in assessing the social utility of campaign expenditures.

The public and private discussion generated by election campaigns serves to organize agreement and disagreement on public matters. The campaign is a necessary part of the process by which parties and groups reach agreements within themselves and focus the disagreements that separate them. This process in turn is integral to the long-run processes through which public matters are aired, information about them is distributed, and conflicts about them are reconciled or put on the shelf. The political campaign is one of the chief means by which parties achieve the functions claimed for them in American society. An American election campaign is more than a contest between candidates. It is a forum for the representation of interests in which a significant share of the citizenry feels involved. It is one way the country goes about making up its mind about its common concerns. The sums required to facilitate this discussion and to encourage the myriad of narrower debates that proceed within it exceed

those sufficient for candidates and parties to present their programs and personalities.

Large numbers of people relate themselves to their government through the activities of campaigns. They need not ring door bells nor make speeches to become importantly involved in the processes of self-government. The campaign and its surrounding events are, in fact, the one occasion that presses citizens to address themselves to the totality of their government. At other times they are concerned with the property-tax rate, a regulatory commission, a minimum-wage statute, the exercise of public domain, the decision of a revenue officer, the fate of a son overseas. These and other *particular* concerns thrust the citizen at random points into contact with the governments under which he lives. The political campaign asks him to think in larger categories of public concern; it asks him to decide what candidates—usually, which one of two candidates—will, on balance, serve his total interests best. To do this launches a harmonizing, reconciling process within individuals by which consciously or subconsciously they themselves decide what things are most important to them. Faced by the alternative candidates and parties they may perceive the depth or the absence of the choices before them. The processes that go on within individuals are stimulated by the variety and volume of communications that reach them. Some are touched by one medium, others by many; the bombardment of repetitive political messages of a campaign may stimulate *internal* self-governing processes of individuals that otherwise would lie dormant.

The vexed vent their wrongs, can have their say, or hear another say it for them. Their competitive and combative energies find outlet, vicariously and actively, in the conduct and excesses of campaigning. A campaign is sublimated violence and is part of the election process that achieves peaceful transition of authority. As such, those who enter the lists, and some of those whose support they seek and represent, exert or spend themselves to the maximum for victory. The psychological adjustments achieved by campaigns may require greater expenditures than needed for an informed and rational voting decision.

A unity of community, moreover, is bred by common campaign experiences. The bonds woven in politics run to allies. But the bonds even cross battle lines to link opponents with a sense of mutual fate. Old political enemies, like old prizefighters, often stand arm in arm, linked by a private bond more personal than they share with their own lieutenants. Thomas Jefferson and John Adams were even closer after their years of rivalry than before. Despite the raucous charges and frequent bitterness, the typical, eventual result of American elections is a greater sense of unity. Seldom does dispute cut deep enough to vitiate a sense of common process and confidence in it.

It seems likely, too, that the volume and character of communications stimulated by political campaigns contribute to a general sense of community. Sense of community must be fortified periodically if the common tasks of a community are to be met effectively. The mass media lace all hamlets, all cities, all sections of all states together in a common net of information, emotion, dispute. Many feel they are on their way to hell in a hack, but at least for the larger problems everybody is in the same hack. No pretense is offered that electioneering is an unblemished, golden vessel; on the contrary, the confusion of election processes may well contribute to the condition described by Joseph A. Schumpeter as the "reduced sense of responsibility and the absence of effective volition" characterizing many American citizens. The point is that political cam-

paigns serve functions not apparent to the unaided eye and whose value cannot be measured solely in dollars and cents.

38.   Political Effects of the Campaign

Bernard R. Berelson, Paul F. Lazarsfeld, and William N. McPhee

Voting research indicates that the principal results of campaigns are reinforcement and activation of previous party commitments, rather than the conversion of the voters. The following study of the 1948 campaign in Elmira, New York, shows how President Truman achieved his upset victory by the revival of the Democratic party majority forged in the New Deal. The authors have conducted their research through the Columbia University Bureau of Applied Social Research.

* * *

TREND AND PATTERN OF PARTY PREFERENCE

The stability of votes

The Republicans made substantial gains in Elmira from 1944 to June, 1948, lost ground during the campaign, and ended up on election day just where they were in 1944 (Chart I). The timing of such gains and losses is crucial. An election is partly a race against time as well as against the opposition. What matters is who is ahead on election day. If Elmira is representative,

PERCENTAGE REPUBLICAN OF TWO-PARTY VOTE (OR INTENTION)

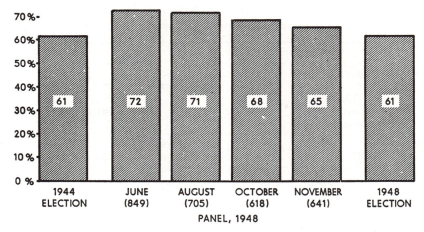

Chart I The Republicans gained between campaigns, lost during the campaign, and ended up even.*

* These figures include all cases at the specified interview. The distribution of votes does not change more than 2 percentage points if the cases are restricted only to those respondents interviewed in all four waves, thus eliminating the possible effect of mortality. A total of 181 of an additional 238 cases, designated by the sampling plan but not interviewed in June or thereafter in the panel, were found in a November follow-up to be disproportionately Democratic. Had they been included, the "unofficial" figures above would be about 2 points less Republican (and thus nearer the official returns), but presumably the trend would have been similar.

Dewey's lead seemed sufficient to have won as late as two weeks before election day. And, assuming that the Republicans were sensing the Truman trend and would have taken strong steps against it, Dewey may have won a few weeks after election day.[1]

In contrast to some European practices, American political campaigns are arbitrarily designated "slices" of time out of a historical process, and election day is the terminal point for the wavering of voters. History can hang not only on a candidate's timing, as in the unusual 1948 case, but also on the timing of issues and events during the period. For example, the tensions attending the Berlin blockade raised fears of war, and rising prices increased sentiment for price control (Table 1). Less

[1] Elmira being a Republican city, Dewey's support in that city was greater than his support in the nation—*Editor's note.*

than one-third of the respondents shifted from one side to the other, but they shifted overwhelmingly in the direction "imposed" by the course of events. The timing of these "natural" events seemed to contribute to Dewey's high point in June and to Truman's rally in November—beyond the generating effect of party propaganda itself (though, of course, the propaganda exploited the events).

Yet, unstable political year as it was compared to such election years as 1924 or 1944, the trends that make all the difference historically are relatively small statistically. Votes are much more stable, as expressions of preference, than opinions on issues. The gross and the net changes in vote, from interview to interview, are much less than the corresponding shift on the issues (Table 2). Whereas the turnover in Table 1 is 32 percent and 28 percent, in Table 2 it is

TABLE 1 Turnover in Opinion during the Campaign
Reveals the Effect of External Events
(Only Respondents with Opinions Both Times)

June	October (Percent)			June	August (Percent)		
	Expect War within Ten Years	Do Not	Total		For Price Control	Against Price Control	Total
Expect war in ten years	32	8	40	For price control	38	4	42
Do not	24	36	60	Against price control	24	34	58
TOTAL	56	44	100 (604)	TOTAL	62	38	100 (782)

TABLE 2 Turnover in Vote during the Campaign
Is Not Particularly High
(Only Respondents with Positions Both Times)

June	August (Percent)			August	October (Percent)			October	November (Percent)		
	Rep.	Dem.	Total		Rep.	Dem.	Total		Rep.	Dem.	Total
Rep.	67	6	73	Rep.	68	3	71	Rep.	66	4	70
Dem.	5	22	27	Dem.	1	28	29	Dem.	1	29	30
TOTAL	72	28	100 (641)	TOTAL	69	31	100 (543)	TOTAL	67	33	100 (552)

11 percent, 4 percent, and 5 percent. In all repetitive measures of political (or, for that matter, other) preferences, people shift back and forth to a greater or lesser extent. By measures of either gross turnover or net trend, vote intentions were more stable than subsidiary opinions in 1948 Elmira. They were less subject to manipulation by the circumstances of the moment and presumably more deeply rooted in the voters' personal predispositions and social surroundings.

In some senses, votes and opinions on issues are not comparable at all in stability. For example, if votes are considered as "average" or summary expressions of a multitude of smaller judgments moving in different directions, then obviously the average is more stable than the parts. Moreover, votes undoubtedly move on larger time scales than current-issue opinions. For many people, votes are not perceived as decisions to be made in each specific election. For them, voting traditions are not changed much more often than careers are chosen, religions drifted into or away from, or tastes revised.

Something like a long-term "standing decision," in V. O. Key's term, seemed to be the case, especially among the Republican voters of Republican Elmira in Republican upstate New York. Most of those who eventually voted Republican had been that way all along without any change during the campaign. Even half of the unstable Democratic minority in the town had been constant during the 1948 campaign (Chart II). (Yet voters who were in both camps during the campaign were more likely to vote Democratic on election day—or, rather, eventual Democrats were more likely to have been in the other party at some point.)

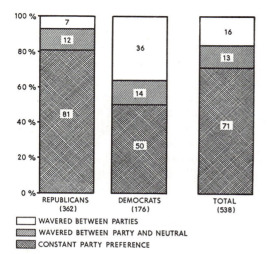

In making later decisions, the Democrats of Elmira showed greater signs of instability, the reasons for which we shall examine in some detail later. For the moment, however, the differences between the two parties (in what was an unstable year for the Democrats) should not obscure the fact that about two-thirds of those who voted in November had *not* shifted position at all—had not so much as wavered to a neutral viewpoint from June (*before* the conventions) to November. Votes do not change easily, at least during a campaign.

Constants and changers

What kinds of votes do change? The people who change most *during* a campaign are the people who changed most *between* campaigns. Among 1948 voters those who intended in June to vote as they had in 1944 were remarkably stable; fully 96 percent of them (both parties) carried through in November as intended in June. Moreover, of those who were undecided in June, three-fourths returned to their former party. But those supporting a different party in June, 1948, from that supported in the 1944 election were the least stable of all: almost 40 per cent of them returned to their former position. Political preferences are highly self-maintaining; when they start to change, the influences making them what they were reassert themselves and press for a "return to normalcy."

More generally, changers of vote are characterized not only by inconsistencies in the past but by inconsistencies in their present position on subsidiary political matters. It is the people with "cross-pressured" opinions on the issues or candidates or parties—that is, opinions or views simultaneously supporting different sides—who are more likely to be unstable in their voting position during the campaign. Accepting one stand by a given party but not another, or identifying with a given party but rejecting its stand on a given issue— such "contradictions" weaken the voter's

Chart II Most voters remained constant throughout the campaign; those shifting between parties ended up Democratic.

It follows that the time of final decisions, that point after which the voter does not change his intention, occurred *prior* to the campaign for most voters—and thus no "real decision" was made *in* the campaign in the sense of waiting to consider alternatives. Again, this was especially the pattern among the socially supported, traditional Republican majority in Elmira (Chart III).

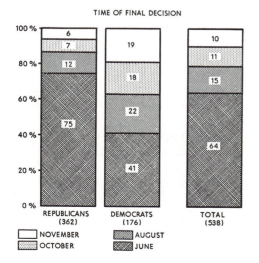

Chart III The time of final decision was much earlier for Republican voters than for Democrats.

stability. Quite reasonably, if he has a foot in each camp, he is more likely to move between them—or to the midway position of indecision.

How do people get into inconsistent and unstable positions? In part they do so because of conflicting currents in the particular historical situation and the almost inherent contradictions of any two-party system in a complex, pluralistic society. But for many voters such inconsistency of opinion, and the resultant fringe of instability surrounding the solid core of more stable American votes, arises simply from not caring much one way or the other about the election. Stability in vote is characteristic of those interested in politics and instability of those not particularly interested. Since the bulk of each party's votes move only sluggishly if at all, the short-term change that "decides" close elections is disproportionately located among those closer to the border line of disinterest.

To summarize some properties of voting changes: first, they are often reversals of earlier attempts to change; second, they are associated with analogous inconsistencies in supporting attitudes at the given time; and, third, they are more likely to occur among those who do not really care about the election. . . .

COMPONENTS
OF THE DEMOCRATIC TREND

The trend to Truman was by no means made up of a random sample of Elmirans. It consisted mainly of two types of voters— one defined by political characteristics and the other by socioeconomic ones.

On the political side the trend was composed primarily of former Democratic voters (and secondarily of former neutrals or new voters). Just two-thirds of those who changed to Truman during the campaign and voted for him on election day were Roosevelt supporters in 1944, and nearly all the rest supported neither side in 1944.

Only 5 percent of the changers to Truman came from 1944 Republicans. In short, there was a rally into the Truman Fair Deal camp of former supporters of the Roosevelt New Deal, plus neutrals and new voters who had hesitated. Those who had voted against Roosevelt in 1944 did not respond to Truman in 1948. His support came from voters with a Democratic voting history, or at least a non-Republican history. The campaign trends, then, were less of a conversion than a rally.

On the socioeconomic side the Truman rally was composed of voters with working-class or ambivalent—but not business-class—sympathies.

Indexes of Elmira data can be formed to represent a variety of concepts that occur in theories about socioeconomic "classes" (e.g., objective socioeconomic position, subjective class identification, class-related ideology of a general sort, and specific reactions to current political symbols in this sphere). No matter which index is used, party preference varies with socioeconomic dispositions. More than that, when these interrelated class indexes are combined, campaign trends are seen as a function not only of their joint effect but also of *inconsistency* or *ambivalence* among them. About two-thirds of the changers to Truman were either working class or ambivalent in their sympathies. The latter were especially likely to shift to the Democratic side—more even than people with firmer attachments to the class position associated with the Democratic vote.

Now the rallying of earlier political loyalties and of class sentiments were not independent of each other. Each was, in fact, a condition for the operation of the other. Only those former Democrats with tendencies toward the working-class position in socioeconomic affairs responded to Truman's appeal during the campaign proper. And the response to his socioeconomic arguments occurred only among those who had supported or at least had not voted against the Roosevelt New Deal (Chart IV). Once the candidates were nominated and the campaign proper was on, the trend to the Democrats was composed of voters without Republican voting histories and without clear business-class sentiments. Almost all the Democratic increase came from the other groups, those with some already-existing affinity for the New Deal party and the socioeconomic interests it represented. Where there were business-class sympathies or previous Republican voting histories, the response was effectively blocked.

In short, the mere location of 1948 trends suggests (1) the rallying of previously demoralized *party* loyalties through (2) reactivation of *socioeconomic* interests and sympathies. In the remainder of this analysis of the shift to Truman, we shall deal *only with respondents who could be expected to respond to such a rally* (boxed cells, Chart IV). They were "potential Democrats," and our concern is with what happened to them rather than with the quite different situation of the 1944 Republican and/or business classes.

DEMORALIZATION
OF THE NEW DEAL MAJORITY

If 1948 was a rally of voters who "should" have been Democratic all along, why had they *left* the party? The potential for change is always present in a two-party democratic system. It is there simply because new events bring new problems and

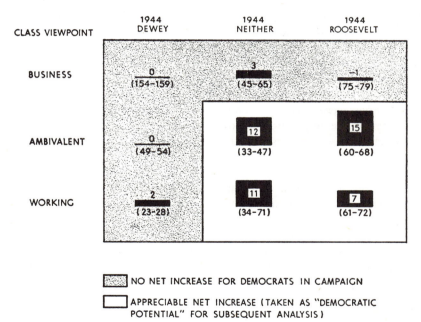

PERCENTAGE POINTS GAIN IN DEMOCRATIC VOTE (TWO-PARTY)
FROM AUGUST TO ELECTION*

CLASS VIEWPOINT	1944 DEWEY	1944 NEITHER	1944 ROOSEVELT
BUSINESS	0 (154-159)	3 (45-65)	-1 (75-79)
AMBIVALENT	0 (49-54)	12 (33-47)	15 (60-68)
WORKING	2 (23-28)	11 (34-71)	7 (61-72)

▨ NO NET INCREASE FOR DEMOCRATS IN CAMPAIGN

☐ APPRECIABLE NET INCREASE (TAKEN AS "DEMOCRATIC POTENTIAL" FOR SUBSEQUENT ANALYSIS)

Chart IV The shift to Truman was related to class dispositions and political loyalties.*

* Boxed cells, locating the significant Democratic gains in the campaign, define the universe of *"potential Democrats"* or *"Democratic potential"* discussed in the text. The cell entry is, again, the difference in percentage points between the proportion for Truman at the beginning and at the end of his campaign. For reasons that will become clear in the text, the June–August trends at the time of Truman's nomination were confused, and we use August–November data here.

new leaders to deal with them. And these were the central conditions explaining the "defection" to the Republicans of potential Democrats at the beginning of the 1948 campaign. First, the Democratic leader was in disfavor (even within his own party) and, second, new issues attracted (the Democrats would say "distracted") the voters. We take up the former problem first.

The problem of succession

President Truman's difficulties symbolize the historically significant problem of political succession: how does a political party replace a strong leader? In this instance, after a brief honeymoon period, the replacement of a magnetic leader (President Roosevelt) by the almost necessarily less impressive man who is next in line stimulated party demoralization. This was clearly one of the chief elements in the Democratic situation of 1948. In Elmira the image of Truman was not particularly encouraging; Democrats were much more favorably inclined to Dewey than Republicans to Truman. In fact, twice as many favorable terms as unfavorable ones were used by Democrats to characterize the opposition candidate after his nomination in August. On the national scene Truman's popularity had fallen regularly for nearly two years following his inauguration, and after a short rise it had gone down again by the summer of 1948.

Among all Elmira voters, and in particular among the potential Democrats (as defined above), there was a marked correlation between the image of Truman and vote. Those with a favorable image of Truman were strong for him; those with an unfavorable image were strong against him. And this relationship carried over to *change* in vote. Many potential Democrats were less than happy about Truman's nomination. While most of the defectors had already left the party by June, the very fact of Truman's nomination seemed to repel

still more of them between June and August—those who had hoped for other nominations or who had not previously thought much about who would be nominated.

Yet, while Truman may have had special troubles of his own, his difficulties were probably typical of political successors who attempt to hold together an already disintegrating majority coalition after the passing of the original leader. Whatever the case, however, part of the Republican strength at the start of the 1948 campaign was attributable to the dissatisfaction of potential Democrats with Truman the candidate.

The problem of distraction

The second major element in the demoralization of the Democratic potential is also an integral part of the rise and fall of political majorities. As the years go by and a political movement like the New Deal matures, new problems (e.g., war and its aftermath) accumulate beyond the set of problems (e.g., socioeconomic reform) that originally characterized the movement. They bring to the fore a new set of issues that often crosscut the original set and hence complicate and disturb the political majority, which in a two-party system is necessarily an alliance of divergent elements.

In Elmira in June, 1948, few voters were concerned with the labor-consumer ("class") issues that had been at the heart of Democratic victories since 1932. When asked about the disagreements between the two parties, the Democratic potential was either apathetic or concerned with other issues, mainly those dealing with international affairs. As a Democrat might put it, the Democratic potential was "confused" or "led astray" by the day's topical problems.

And such dispersion of attention onto different issues had its effect upon vote intentions. When voters are not attentive to a given set of issues, they tend to overlook their related values and interests. For example, there was a marked difference in Democratic vote between those to whom labor-consumer or "class" issues were salient in June and those to whom they were not (and this result holds with 1944 vote and class position controlled). Thus "distraction" from socioeconomic issues was associated in June, 1948, with defections from the Democratic party among those normally its supporters. With the socioeconomic interests underlying the New Deal majorities in abeyance, at least for the time being, different problems brought different criteria and inclinations into operation on the vote decision. And again the effect of this "distraction" upon vote carried over from June to August: those to whom class

issues were not salient became *less* Democratic by August than those of the same June intention who were conscious of class issues (Chart V).

In summary, the Democratic potential was (1) vulnerable after the loss of its long-time leader and (2) subject to distraction of attention away from traditional rallying issues and interests of the party. The first difficulty centered around President Truman himself or, more generally, around the problem of effecting a smooth political succession. The second difficulty centered around the loss of socioeconomic class issues or, more generally, around the problem of maintaining the core of a political program or ideology against the pressure of new events. These are interrelated matters, and

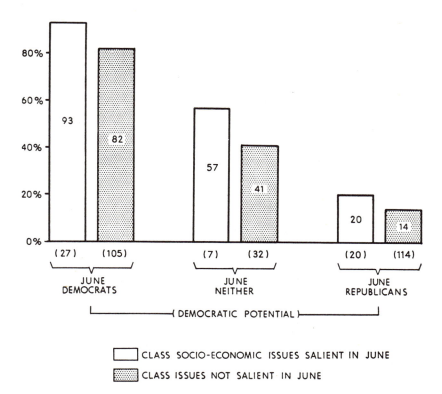

PERCENTAGE DEMOCRATIC OF TWO-PARTY INTENTIONS IN AUGUST

Chart V Change in vote from June to August reflected "distraction" from class issues.

the Democratic demoralization of mid-summer in 1948 can be summed up in the statement that both the old political loyalties and the socioeconomic interests on which the New Deal had flourished had, under changing conditions, lost their original strength.

But that demoralization did not continue in force throughout the campaign. The Democrats regained enough of their former support to make the difference between defeat and victory. And that brings us to our third and, of course, most important question.

THE FAIR DEAL RALLY

Why did a sizable portion of the Democratic potential return to the fold? In terms of our previous analysis there are two possibilities. First, it may have been that people came to like President Truman better, thus allowing old Democratic political loyalties to come back into force. He may, so to speak, have "sold himself" as Roosevelt's successor. Or, second, the focus of attention may have changed away from Truman and the distracting issues and back to the socioeconomic class issues of the times, thus enabling the interests, values, and "prejudices" associated with these issues to reassert their force.

To state the alternative hypotheses more generally, voters may have kept the *same standards* of judgment, that is, considering which person they wanted, but adopted a *different evaluation* within such standards (e.g., they may have come to like Truman better). Or they may have kept the *same evaluation* of the candidates but shifted to *different standards* (e.g., from judging "the man" to judging "the issues"). Was it a change in evaluation or a change in standards?

Image and saliency

To evaluate the two hypotheses, let us start with the voters' image of Truman.

Among Democratic-inclined voters, was there a major change in evaluation of Truman? Actually, from August to October there was almost no change at all in what potential Democrats thought of him as a candidate. The voters' image of the President had been built up over a period of years, including three years as chief executive, and it was not subject to much manipulation during the few months of the campaign. Truman's campaign made no net change in what people thought of him as a candidate. The trend toward Truman in vote intention was greater than the trend toward acceptance of Truman personally. People came to vote for Truman faster than they came to like him.

Now, to consider the alternative, there *was* a sharp shift in the saliency of "class" issues for the voters. The campaign was characterized by a resurgence of attention to socioeconomic matters, at the expense of international affairs. The image of Truman did not change, but the image of what was important in the campaign—and perhaps even the image of what Truman stood for—*did* change to a dominance of socioeconomic issues. . . .

The trend in vote further clarifies the matter. The voters within the Democratic potential who did *not* have a favorable image of Truman in *either* August or October nevertheless increased in intention to vote for him. The trend to Truman was concentrated among those who had *not* previously liked him, nor did they like him even when they changed to his side. (While the trend is sharp among those whose image improved, they are few in number.) Improved opinions of Truman were not the dominant feature of the rally; they were less changed than simply overridden. Vote trends were *negatively* related to images of what was being voted for!

However, saliency of "class" issues had a *positive* relation to the trend. The increase in Democratic support from June to October came largely in relation to the saliency, and to an *increase* in the saliency, of economic labor-consumer "class" issues (Chart VI). The net trends prior to October were concentrated among the people for whom class issues were or became salient in this period. The voting trends were negligible among the cases who had not focused on them by October. We have here, then, a relationship consisting of *simultaneous* trends in the focus of attention and in the voting rally of potential Democrats.

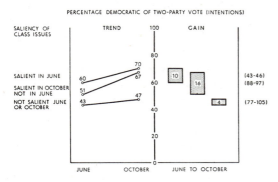

PERCENTAGE DEMOCRATIC OF TWO-PARTY VOTE (INTENTIONS)

Chart VI   The sharpest increase in Democratic vote intentions came from those to whom class issues were salient.*

* Here the largest number of changers to Truman came from those who increased saliency, as sample sizes indicate.

Now if such simultaneity of change is the case, then those who had *already* made socioeconomic issues their focus of attention at the peak of the campaign would not change their votes further in the final weeks. Instead, the additional net recruitment of Democratic strength might be expected to come from among those who had not previously "got the point" of the Democratic campaign, that is, who had not previously seen these socioeconomic issues as the main point of the argument. Such indeed may have been the case; at least it was the previously "dormant" cases who moved *after* October. The intensifying campaign of the last two weeks presumably brought home to them what was already clear to others.

Reasons for change

Now these trends summarize many small shifts of a compensating nature. But taken in the aggregate, like time-series data, they indicate a *timing* of the Democratic rally corresponding to the timing of attention to these class issues, perhaps even to the delayed Democratic voting reaction of those who did not recognize such issues to the very end. Thus, one might infer from these data alone than an important role was played by these issues in the Democratic rally, just as their *absence* had evidently played a role in the earlier demoralization of the Democratic party.

Fortunately, we have additional evidence of the role of the issues in the direct reports of the people who changed votes. All those who made some kind of a voting change (either from nonvoting to a party or from one party to the opposition) were especially questioned as to "why" they had done so. A classification of the political content of the reasons given for these changes, made independent of and prior to this analysis, clearly shows the same result: a marked shift in the basis of decision from the matter of personality to that of class issues. In their own reasons for change to Truman the respondents reveal a marked shift in the standard by which they were judging the campaign.

The comments of the changers give the flavor of the arguments effective at the close of the campaign:

> I was waiting for Dewey to give an opinion on the Taft-Hartley Law. I work in a plant, and I am against it. When I heard him in that speech in Pittsburgh, he said that the Taft-Hartley Law was good for both labor and management, but it might have to have some changes. He didn't enumerate those changes, so I went to the other side, because I was dead set against the law . . . and I know Truman will fight against it. [A fifty-year-old tool-and-die maker, Republican in August.]

> Truman is the only man for labor. We have had better Presidents than Truman,

but he is the best man running now because he is for labor. [A sixty-five-year-old machinist, changing to Truman.]

[I'll vote for Truman] because the Democrats have always been better for the working people. [A secretary, changing to Truman.]

A modern presidential campaign is won or lost on the basis of a multitude of appeals, and a variety of "explanations" can thus be abstracted out of the total phenomenon. But in our data it seems clear that an impending defeat for the Democratic party was staved off by a refocusing of attention on the socioeconomic concerns which had originally played such a large role in building that party's majority in the 1930's. While an improving appreciation of Truman was partly involved in the process, we are led on several grounds to discount this idea as the primary notion explaining the 1948 campaign trends. We are led, rather, to conclude that such a trend was subsidiary to the shift in attention and in standards of judgment, *away* from Truman's personal difficulties and other problems that had inhibited the Democratic vote prior to the campaign and *toward* another focus of attention more favorable to the Democrats, namely, a focus on class issues. The rally was due more to a change in standard than to a change in evaluation.

39. To Be a Politician

Stimson Bullitt

The demands on candidates in a campaign are increasingly severe. Beset by uncertainty, hopeful of victory but sensing defeat, the candidate attempts to find some comfort in electioneering itself. The flavor and problems of campaigning are described here by *Stimson Bullitt, a Seattle lawyer and former Democratic candidate for Congress. He also raises some questions concerning the educational value of campaigns.*

* * *

Forgetting that they themselves compose the jury, people sometimes regard their favorite candidate as their champion engaged in a trial by combat to vindicate their principles and interests. To describe a campaign as a "race" or "fight" is inaccurate because the efforts of a competitor seldom are decisive. A politician, unlike a general or an athlete, never can be invincible, except within a constituency which constitutes a sinecure. Furthermore, a candidate cannot even be sure that his campaigning will change the election result, while a lawyer in a lawsuit knows at least that a diligent pursuit of proven methods of preparation and trial will raise the odds of success, even if the outcome hinges on the image of some half-forgotten experience in the mind of a judge.

Scientists refuse to accept an hypothesis until they have verified it by exhaustive examination of all available evidence which may prove or disprove it, and they continue to discard each successive hypothesis as it fails to meet their tests. By contrast, a politician must act on his hypotheses, which are tested only by looking backward on his acts. A candidate cannot even experiment. Because no one knows what works in a campaign, money is spent beyond the point of diminishing returns. To meet similar efforts of the opposition all advertising and propaganda devices are used—billboards, radio, TV, sound trucks, newspaper ads, letter writing or telephone committee programs, handbills, bus cards. No one dares to omit any approach. Every cartridge must be fired because among the multitude of blanks one may be a bullet.

Some urge an attitude of Olympian reserve, a few sonorous pronouncements of fundamental principle. Some claim a catalogue of documented facts is just the thing to woo the inscrutable voter. Others insist the only way is to put a hammer lock on the opponent and roll around in the sawdust. Many think a speech ought to be what Napoleon said a constitution should be, short and obscure. A member of the State Senate for many years, who has never lost an election, told me how he campaigns in his district door to door: "You tell your host or hostess who you are and declare in forthright tones, 'I'm here to talk with you about our State government; you may not agree with me but at least you will know where I stand.' Then you sit down in the living room, listen to him or her and agree!" When a fellow named Gillespie Craighead ran for Congress in Seattle he asserted he was the only man in the race who could prove he was sane; then he would display his certificate of discharge from a mental hospital. He received several thousand votes, but a former U.S. Senator beat him.

A common mistake of post-mortems is to assert that a certain event or a stand or mannerism of a candidate caused him to win or lose. Often no one knows whether its effect was plus, minus, or zero, whether the election result was because of this factor or despite it. Spectacular events, whether a dramatic proposal, an attack, or something in the news outside the campaign, are like a revolving door. They win some voters and lose others. A disclosure that a candidate's brother committed suicide in a mental hospital will cause some voters to doubt the candidate's own mental strength and health, while others will be drawn to him by sympathy and repelled by his opponent's cruelty. Another example is the matter of Grover Cleveland's bastard in the 1884 campaign. The net balance in these cases remains unknown in both direction and amount, and even if correctly estimated, such a factor still could not be called the

sole cause of the result. It was merely one of many causes of which the election is the algebraic sum. Where the margin was close, this factor could be called the cause only to the extent that the result would not have happened but for it, like the horseshoe nail that caused the kingdom's loss.

Each voter makes up his mind by the delicate resolution of several factors, some unconscious and all variable. No test has been devised for campaign methods or strategy, and little can be done to determine the effects of other factors. To know the effect of each thing he is doing and saying is a candidate's dearest wish. If he knew where pay dirt was he could concentrate there instead of digging all over the countryside. But he proceeds in ignorance. Not even his friends can be relied on to tell him all they know, which is less than is revealed by the scientific opinion polls, themselves inadequate as political weather vanes. A man will freely tell which fender styling he prefers. Often enough to be statistically useful, he will say for whom he plans to vote, and then keep his word. But he will not or cannot tell why. In testing the effects of campaign methods there are too many deviating, indeterminable factors. The interviewed voter may not have been affected by any speech or slogan, yet may feel that unless he says he was, he will be thought an ignoramus. He may have been affected by a certain campaign act but when asked about it he may forget either the act or the effect or both. He may or may not still be affected by it in his decision on election day, and he may not vote. The effect of what one side does may be canceled out in his final decision by what the other side does later. He may not be able to sift the campaign acts which repel him or attract him. Seldom when a man speaks to a stranger about some deep and subtle thought within him is he articulate enough to say what he means or candid enough to mean what he says. He may try to tell the interrogator what he thinks the other would like to hear, or he may refuse to talk at all. A candidate does not know whether he is throwing balls or strikes.

By their impact just before an election, poll figures tend to bring to pass their own predictions. When the polls become more accurate about opinion, as distinguished from voting intention, where the margin of error is already small, not only will they directly affect the results, they also will alter campaign methods. Candidates will watch the reports and try to reflect them exactly. If response to the public wishes expressed in the reports was the only action taken, candidates would be left even with each other. So candidates will try to think up an appealing novelty, guess the errors in the polls, or guess how opinion will change between the sampling and the election, and will try to be the first in harmony with it. This will be like playing the stock market in trying to anticipate the trend or to out-guess the experts, although the game is even more elusive because it is based alto-gether on slippery elements of opinion, while in the market the starting point, at least, rests on solid measurement of eco-nomic fact. A market speculator first will guess the future effects of economic forces, then what other speculators think about these forces, then what may be the expec-tations of other speculators about each other. Keynes wrote that some imaginative minds carry this process to the fifth or sixth degree. By contrast, a candidate's duopoly relationship with his opponent seems to call for simpler calculations, especially since he can predict the other's actions more ac-curately than he can the thoughts of an un-known voter. Before long the polls and other studies may be able to tell him cur-rent attitudes above or below the surface of many voters' minds. But they may avail him little because voters are becoming more like speculators in basing their opinions on the attitudes of others, who do the same. In-stead of splashing around in this quick-

silver he may resort to asserting his own ideas again. . . .

The time when a politician should be most responsive is during a campaign and the period of warming up to it. Unpopular stands are better made long before, and soon after, a campaign. A short period lim-its the chances for circumstances to prove the soundness of an unpopular action, and a candidate's courage will receive little ac-claim unless and until his decision has be-come popular because generally regarded as having been right. If you are going to op-pose the wishes of the people whom you represent you had better not go before them for endorsement until either they have had a chance to forget the apparent injury or circumstances have been allowed to show that you never injured them at all.

The tumult and passion of adversary pro-ceedings make a campaign an unsatisfac-tory occasion to win acceptance of a new idea, although it will do to introduce one. It is hard to get original proposals accepted any time. And in campaigns the natural re-sistance to a new idea, rational disagree-ment based on its defects and opposition hostility and ridicule unrelated to its worth, combine to place a burden of proof too heavy for an advocate to overcome. Ideal-ists or those who favor affirmative thought are often disappointed with candidates who do not go beyond a few of the genuine is-sues of the day except to engage in personal criticism or argue issues which would be dead if only both sides would drop them. In fact, a candidate who proposes some-thing new is often irresponsible or vision-ary. If he proposes an original creative plan, no matter how sound, he is likely a dreamer to think he will get anywhere with it in the campaign. If he makes out that he has in-vented some inexpensive marvel which will bring joy to all, he is either a fool or a fake.

Because a campaign makes impossible a dip beneath the surface, not only the advance of a new idea but teaching of any kind is more effective between campaigns. To paraphrase Mark Antony when he knocked on Cleopatra's door, a candidate says, "I didn't come to teach." In a campaign, people are not interested in theory. The lessons are more often moral than intellectual. People want to know *what* a candidate proposes to do about pending specific problems. In quiet times, one can descend to fundamentals and tell *why*. People then will listen longer to a reasoned explanation and apply a smaller discount to the speaker's words as colored in a way to serve himself. But despite the fact that the teaching process is less efficient during a campaign than at other times, the value of education and the large size of the audience justify making education the main function of a campaign, provided this emphasis will not result in losing the election, that is, provided one is either way behind or way ahead.

A common cause of such a noncompetitive situation, which would justify the use of a campaign for educational purposes, is a legislature's boundary revision, creating a series of Alabamas and Vermonts, thus giving contentment to incumbents by relieving them of job insecurity and to the party organizations by assuring each of winning some prizes every time; but such an arrangement stagnates politics by suppressing competition and it curtails the citizens' choice.

On occasions when there is no real contest except in measure of disagreement, if a candidate is an odds-on choice to win, he can transmit his ideas effectively. Little opposition interrupts him; he receives the respectful attention of those who know he is going to be an officeholder and thus important, and of those who admire winners; the greatest advantage is that he can obtain sufficient contributions to satisfy quite avaricious dreams. If he is thought to be a sure loser he can reach the voters only with his own time and money, for he will receive little help from his party and nothing from private groups or persons. Even if he is thought to be both noble and eloquent, those of the idealists who have money to give prefer to help a candidate of equal merit who has a chance to win. Lovers of lost causes will not help him because they are content already to see him headed for defeat.

Among those who run for office, it is widely thought that little good can be done one's fellow men unless one wins. What General MacArthur said, "There is no substitute for victory," is only half true. Some candidates aim at both halves. So far as he is heard, seen, and understood, a candidate is a moral and intellectual teacher for better or worse. Like most means, a campaign is also in itself an end. It gives a chance to demonstrate virtue, to declare, defend, and illuminate the truth, and to do the statesman's duty to guide, to elevate and to instruct. . . .

Except in one-party states, general elections for important offices tend to be statistically close. The majority often does not exceed the scientific opinion polls' margin of error, so that there is yet no certain way to foretell the result. Until the moment of truth, a candidate does not know whether he is the bullfighter or the bull.

The uncertainty of politics dismays a person used to systematic plans. The loss of spontaneity through thinking of the next thing is a defect of modern life. Everyone has to consider the morrow. No one can do as the lilies of the field. Foresight is compulsory because one falls by the wayside if he fails to use it as everyone else does. Yet in a campaign it is difficult to plan one's steps. One is denied both the carefree joy of spontaneity and the security and certainty of foresight. Politics is an art and it is played by ear, though politicians often wish that they could use with profit more scientific method in the conduct of their work.

As generals are said to prepare for the last war, so election campaigns are planned with excessive attention to undigested lessons of history. The thinking of a candidate's advisers resembles that of scholastic philosophers, long on speculation and short on verified facts. The members of a strategy committee tend to be boosters rather than detached critics, a command group instead of a staff. Sometimes a candidate feels like a steer being groomed for a 4-H Club contest. His council is more likely to give him encouragement than guidance. For example, once in the Bronx Coliseum a powerful Negro from Brooklyn was hitting me hard; I clutched him and looked over his shoulder at a spectator who pounded on the ring apron as he shouted, "Pretend he's a Harvard man!"

For candidates, campaigns are like a war. There are comradeship, sacrifice, warmth of loyalty given and received, and moments of glory, fulfillment, and fear. Absence from home strains domestic ties, and clan ties are strained by taking sides. It is dirty and expensive. When it is over, this alien experience drops quickly out of mind, despite the remaining scars and debt. The heat of battle intensifies a candidate's combative spirit. Exhaustion weakens his power to decide. The necessity to act in haste under conflicting pressures and on confusing information makes his decisions less the result of reflection or belief than of character, habit, and chance. Unless his friends restrain him he may throw away both his purse and his good name. His friends' advice colors his acts more than when he is not on such a headlong chase. The counselors of even the most bullheaded candidate do much to set a campaign's tone. The choice of levelheaded, honorable advisers improves his chances to finish the race without regret or shame.

The hardest campaign is the first. After that the path is familiar, and there is the momentum of supporters, friends, and a well-known name. Among candidates before a campaign starts there is an eager, apprehensive wait; hurry and busy strategic moves off stage. As in the early rounds in a poker hand, the response and strength of possible opponents and the presence of support are tested by experimental bluffs. Next to the wait from the closing of the polls until the returns begin, the highest suspense in a campaign is when a candidate declares himself. He climbs to the battlements and blows his trumpet, then peers out to see how many men at arms come running to rally round his flag.

He has to be alert to tricks which can be important even though in form they resemble a practical joke. When Ed Munro, a high-principled politician, ran for county office in a northwest state, an Indian who had the same surname filed against him in the primary. This tactic would split his vote enough to give the nomination to his other chief opponent (who presumably had induced this filing). Before the names had been put on the voting machines, the second Munro withdrew when told that such a deception was a felony, and therefore if he stayed in the race he would be the only candidate guaranteed to spend some time in the county courthouse. Ed's friends had found this man after a desperate hunt. He was hard to find because he had been sleeping in a tree.

At the start a candidate's efforts are concentrated within his party. As the scale and formality of the campaign increase, the target shifts to the general public. On these early occasions, before his audience is critical and large, a candidate's material is tested. There is a chance to sharpen gags, expand lines, and cut what falls dead. It is like opening in New Haven before New York.

At repeated party meetings, the candidate grinds out his stock recital to a crowd of the faithful who know him well. Most of them could prompt him if he faltered. Attendance gains him little except to invigorate their working spirit and to avoid provoking their hostility by the appearance of a snub. Senator Henry Jackson has adopted the sensible practice of saying good-by to his friends at the beginning of a campaign, after he has told them that he loves them but that he will be busy for a while in their common cause. Some candidates take the easy but ineffectual course of campaigning mainly within party groups. Like the salesmen who go to the golf course to cultivate their friends instead of making calls on strangers, these candidates either fool themselves or yield to the temptation to stay where the going is smooth.

Local public meetings held to enable the community to hear the candidates often waste the time of both audience and speaker. Each candidate is stalled for part of an evening waiting his turn to speak to a few people. He faces an audience numbed by the beating of incessant waves of oratory. A succession of brief individual interviews is more effective in enabling citizens to know something of his opinions and catch the flavor of his personality. Despite the wasted time, public meetings are justified in the case of candidates for some of the smaller offices because these meetings furnish almost the only means for voters to observe these candidates.

On cold nights a man of lukewarm faith was wont to point to a framed prayer on the wall and say, "Lord, them's my sentiments," as he jumped under the covers. By this means a candidate can declare his platform when allowed only a few minutes to speak. He states his accord with what another politician stands for. He names the man whose platform is more like his own than that of any other person among those whose platforms the audience already knows. An even more common practice is for the candidate to try to identify himself with a victorious figure who sometimes blesses his party mates who are reaching for his coattails from lower on the ladder.

An important factor is personal contact, which inspires those who meet a candidate to recommend him to others. To use this multiplier principle, the rings spreading from where a stone fell in a pool, timing is of the essence. Contacts made in the days just before election have slight worth because time does not permit the multiplier to operate, and without the multiplier's effect the number of persons a candidate can meet even in a whole campaign is too small to matter in a large constituency. Early in a campaign, except for an incumbent who is news in himself, public interest has not developed enough intensity to make the multiplier go. The candidate is less a subject of interest and may be less well known. People have less desire to talk to others about having met him. In most cases, therefore, shaking hands with a multitude is most effective during the month before the week before election day.

A wide personal acquaintanceship acquired before the campaign is a help. "My sister-in-law is a friend of Wheelhorse, the fellow who's running for the legislature. She knew him even before he went into politics" —magic words.

Probably the most effective campaign acts are those performed between campaigns. The volleys and thunders of a campaign raise a voter's resistance and obscure his sight. A Chief Justice of the Alabama Supreme Court kept on his office wall pictures of George Washington and John Marshall and an autographed photograph and letter from Jim Farley, congratulating him on his election. It was the only congratulation he had received after the general election, an uneventful day in those parts, as all the handshakes and other letters had come when he was nominated.

The functions of some offices fail to inspire ardor, either sacrificial or pugnacious. One who runs for governor or mayor often is surrounded by those whose assistance is given on condition of an implied reward.

But a candidate for Congress has so little patronage in prospect that few self-seekers repel him by their presence or embarrass him by their aid. Many persons uninterested in favors from him warm and uplift him by faithful work on his behalf.

In campaigns people work as volunteers to obtain several satisfactions. Some are a step toward fulfillment of a wish expressed through a conviction; that is, an attempt to assert or defend a principle or advance or protect an interest. Other satisfactions are directly emotional. There is the common experience in an adventure and membership in a common effort. There is the purgative from close observance of dramatic conflict, operating on people who themselves are peaceable.

A further motive applies to young people. They do simple work such as handing out folders but they get to hang around the headquarters and consort with the candidate and some of his lieutenants. Their own views on policy may be heard and sometimes even listened to. They learn plans before their execution and feel themselves participants in matters more important than would be allowed them in the ordinary course of life. They are more flattered than older people to be allowed to fraternize with these men and women. They finish armed with anecdotes to entertain their peers.

A campaign is a revolving circus which bewilders actors and spectators alike. Blocks of votes are cast against (or for) a candidate for contradictory reasons, sometimes both wrong. Candidates who succeed in their effort to please everyone may get some votes because they are thought to be for the common man and others for being against him. The same things may be thought of their more clumsy opponents with the opposite results. In one campaign I was attacked as both a Bourbon and a Red. As a member of the commission which had drafted the proposed County Charter which was to be on the ballot, I supported its adoption in unison with the solid, "good government" elements of the business community. I was called a reactionary, both for the stand itself and by reason of the syllogism, common in campaigns, that since things equal to the same thing are equal to each other, persons who take the same side must be alike. In a conversation overheard on the bus a man told another he was going to vote against the Charter because Bullitt helped write it, "so probably it's a left-wing document."

The ferocity and violence of a rough campaign generate passionate animosity in a candidate's heart and inspire deep gratitude to those who bear arms in his cause. The rationality of a campaign tends to vary inversely with its length. Candidates and parties may have much in common, but it is on the basis of the differences that the voters make their choice. The sides start close together. They are driven to magnify existing differences and to invent new ones. As they draw farther apart verbally they provoke each other to greater excess. The separation grows by geometric progression until each side approaches nonsense land.

In contrast to an average citizen, a candidate is too busy with detail to be aware of an election's historic import. He is too elated by enthusiastic treatment or too concerned with what to say to a hostile or indifferent audience to think of community or national destiny. In a speech he may say "the world (nation, state) is watching what we do here," without realizing that this may be the truth.

A candidate may see that he is going to lose if he does not delude himself and the margin is wide enough to be discerned. His helpers can drop out and cut their losses, but, like a player far behind near the end of a game, he is obliged by an unwritten rule of sport to keep giving the old college try.

He must go out to meet people, yet reserve enough time to rest, relax, and think, so that he can give a fresh and lively performance before the mass media. Stevenson's fall campaign in 1956 suffered from the preceding grind of state primaries and soliciting delegates.

Like a prisoner, the candidate marks off the calendar squares until the day when he is to be executed or paroled. On election day he feels like the man who had to open one of two blank doors. Behind one is a maiden, behind the other a tiger. To the candidate's friends, however, the contrast in alternatives may not be sharp. Often they are uncertain what fate to wish for him, whether to win, or to be spared the pains and, to them, degradation of public life. Thinking of him as though his body were to be tested for service by the Army or as though his mind were to be examined at a sanity hearing in court, the friends are in doubt whether to support his hopes, his vows, his rights, or his welfare.

A politician is almost by definition a man who enjoys people. But near the close of a campaign he has been surfeited by them. He resents his enemies. He is exasperated by his friends' proprietary demands, irritated by the importunities of his acquaintances, and weary of his own persistent approaches to strangers. He has had enough of the human race. He does not become a misanthrope but longs to be a forest fire lookout. He would rather be rude than President. But after the election his enjoyment of people soon revives when he is rested and free from the compulsion to persuade, impress, or please. Although spent, some defeated candidates soon begin to think like a baseball fan—"Wait till next year."

For certain happy warriors, many of them celebrated, campaigns are not nights in a cement mixer but trips to the country. Like Antaeus when he touched the earth, these buoyant spirits, by contact with their fellow men, are strengthened and refreshed. On election eve they turn in with dark-encircled sparkling eyes.

* * *

40. The Goldwater Campaign of 1964

The New York Times

The campaign of 1964 was the most unusual in recent history. It evidenced an uncharacteristic intensity, emotionalism, and ideological emphasis. The three articles that follow, by New York Times correspondents, portray the quality of that campaign and some of the factors that contributed to the overwhelming Democratic victory. In a more general sense, they also indicate the uncertainty, cross-pressures, strategies, and sheer luck that characterize all American political campaigns.

* * *

The Goldwater Whistle-Stop Tour

Russell Baker

ABOARD GOLDWATER CAMPAIGN TRAIN, Oct. 3—Senator Barry Goldwater's train tour of the Middle West this week has dramatized the peculiar political paradox of the electronic-nuclear age.

The closer the politicians get to the people, the harder it is to tell what's going on. The problem was illustrated the other day in Frankfort, Ind., a town of 15,000 persons that seemed to have turned out half its population to hear the Republican nominee for President.

Selections from The New York *Times* (October 11, 1964); *Times Talk*, vol. 17, no. 8 (October 1964), pp. 4–5; The New York *Times* (November 11, 1964). © 1964 by The New York Times Company. Reprinted by permission.

As the Senator ran through a half-dozen of his stock campaign themes, the big crowd responded with the kind of cheers that warm a politician's heart. What the Senator did not know, however, was that most of the cheering thousands could not have heard a word he said.

The public address system on the rear platform of his private car was too weak to project his voice more than 30 yards beyond the platform. And so, whatever else the bulk of the crowd may have been cheering, it could not possibly have been the message the Senator had brought to Frankfort. It was a small mystery, but it typified the larger quandary a Presidential candidate faces in the age of coast-to-coast television, scientific polling and mass-mind manipulation: Shall a candidate tie his fate to the electronic tube, the cosmetician, the opinion sample and the computer, or shall we rely on the old flesh-and-blood contacts?

All the evidence of the last week suggests that the intimate whistle-stop campaign, which worked for Harry S. Truman in 1948, may be better for the candidate's morale than for anything else.

All polls tell Mr. Goldwater that he is in deep difficulty, but all through Ohio, Indiana and Illinois his trainside crowds have been big. Not enormous and not tumultuous, to be sure, but large enough and sympathetic enough to cheer a candidate with the suspicion that the polls might just possibly be wrong.

But do the crowds mean anything in terms of voting patterns? It is a mystery. Large proportions of them have consisted of schoolchildren let out of classes to get an object lesson in civics. Were they screaming their family devotion to conservatism or merely shouting their joy at escaping the schoolhouse? It is a mystery.

QUESTION OF HECKLING

And what about the adults? Does their turnout reflect a grass-roots uprising against foreign aid and medical care or merely the strength of Republican machinery in traditional Republican territory? It is a mystery.

And what of the unusually heavy heckling given Senator Goldwater through Ohio? Some of the anti-Goldwater signs that faced him from the crowds were more violent than anything a Presidential candidate has had to face in the last generation.

"Help Goldwater Stamp Out Peace," seemed a popular favorite. In Springfield there was "Goldwater Is Like Polluted Water—Stinks." And in Athens: "Closed Heart, Closed Mind, Barry Is No Friend of Mine."

In Indiana there was a woman heaving apples at the train. "That's what you'll be selling if he's elected," she cried. And as the train ran through rural Ohio, children stood in the fields giving it the thumbs-down gesture.

THE MYSTERY THICKENS

How seriously is the heckling to be taken? Does it reflect a popular revolt against the party in a Republican stronghold, or is it merely the work of a well-organized Democratic campaign to demoralize the Senator? It is a mystery.

The trouble with train campaigning is that everything quickly becomes a mystery. The local politicians climb aboard at each stop and tell you what they want to believe, but they inevitably end up talking about the polls, which tell them something else.

There is no time to talk to people in the crowds and, in an age when everybody pins his faith on the scientifically structured opinion sample rather than the random voter, there seems little point in canvassing the audience.

Is the audience swayed by the Senator's message? It is a mystery. "Did you like his speech?" a woman in Crown Point, Ind., was asked the other night.

"It was wonderful," she said.

"What did you like about it?"

The woman looked puzzled, turned to her companion, shrugged, then smiled and said, "Everything."

Would she have been just as thrilled if he had confined himself to reciting the alphabet? Very possibly.

HAS A RELAXING WEEK

The Senator himself is said to have enjoyed the week and to have found it relaxing. The flesh-and-blood contact seemed to give him a lift, and his rear-platform speeches frequently seemed so relaxed that the audience, which had come to hear him raise the hair on the back of its neck, stood along the tracks looking anesthetized.

His rhetoric runs to powerful statement, and in the newspapers he seems fierce as he accuses the President of arm-twisting, blackmailing, lying and "softness on Communism"—four charges he repeated consistently all week.

His delivery, however, is so gentlemanly, so matter-of-fact, that he rarely stirs the powerful juices of crowd passion or evokes the animal roar that tells the politician he has hit the jugular. And when he introduces Mrs. Goldwater—"a grandmother I've been married to for 30 years"—the tableau of gentle domesticity gives the tiger image its coup de grâce.

Through most of the week, the Senator has struggled to destroy the charge that he is too impulsive and too war-minded to be trusted with control of the country's nuclear arsenal.

Would the entire week's work be better done with a single nationwide television appearance? The question really comes down to whether the whistle-stop campaign puts the modern candidate too close to the people for his own good. It is a mystery.

"On Nov. 3 you're going to get your country back," the Senator has been telling crowd after crowd, and the crowds invariably roar.

But the unanswerable question right now is whether the roar comes from just another crowd or from a scientifically structured opinion sample.

Insulted on the railroad, away from the latest polls, it's hard even to make a guess.

The Barry—Mohr Profile

Charles Mohr

When I reported for work at The New York Times last Jan. 2, I was given a tour of the third floor by that reporter's reporter, Abe Rosenthal. I was also given what diplomats call a tour of the horizon. Abe's orientation course was designed to make me familiar with The Times and fit to serve it away from home base. According to the regimen outlined I would work on the city staff for a while. I would spend some time in the culture, sports and business departments. I would sit a week on each of the three major desks and perhaps in the bullpen. I would do some night rewrite. It occurred to me that when all this was finished I would know more about The Times than Abe himself knew. That was Monday. On Friday, a smiling Abe made the long walk to my rear row desk to let me know that I was being loaned to Harrison Salisbury to cover Sen. Barry M. Goldwater—"for a while."

Ten months and 100 hotel laundry bills later, I am still covering Barry Goldwater. Except for an eight-week period in the spring, I have covered almost nothing else.

One measure of the length of my assignment is that the able, expert men in the 43rd Street recording room no longer laugh when I begin to dictate a story. My slug ("Barry—Mohr") used to strike them as a very funny pun. All they ever say now is "hang up when you're finished."

To answer a key question quickly, it has been a thoroughly enjoyable assignment. I felt from the start that Goldwater was not just a politician, but a political phenomenon. The whole premise of his campaign is unique, and I doubt his like will be seen again for many decades. The other day on a campaign train Teddy White remarked, "You realize, of course, that we will be dining out on this campaign for years." The store of American political anecdote has been greatly enriched by Goldwater, and I was lucky to be on hand for the whole show, not just part of it.

There have been annoyances, of course. One of the most maddening is the habit of some people of identifying me with the candidate. I have had to listen to many outraged rebuttals of Goldwater statements before I was able to shout, "Wait a minute, I'm not responsible for Goldwater." Some other persons seem to regard me as omniscient when they ask me to explain why Goldwater does what he does. I can not supply answers for unfathomable questions.

Goldwater is pleasant company—when he is in the mood. One of the most pleasant days I can recall came last February in Arizona. The press veterans, of which I am one, ate lunch at Goldwater's house. We then piled into two light airplanes and flew to Nogales—on the Sonora border—because Barry wanted to take us to a Mexican restaurant called "La Cavernax" on the Mexican side. Many marguerita cocktails were consumed. A Mariachi band was hired to serenade us. The talk was good as it can be when a man is thoroughly happy in his environment, which Barry Goldwater was. We bought tequilla at bargain rates.

And late that night we flew back to Phoenix. An N.B.C. soundman had recorded the Mariachi music and when we landed he put the tape recorder down under one wing and we all listened nostalgically to the high, wavering trumpet and the guitars. The tequilla bottle began to pass in a circle and Peggy Goldwater took her pulls along with the rest of us. "Play it again," Barry would say. When his wife began to tug at his arm he refused to leave. He didn't want to end that chilly desert night, and neither did we.

But he can be careless of other people's feelings at times and he is a thoroughly independent man. When he feels like acting withdrawn or brusque, he does exactly that. The early intimacy has ended as the campaign approaches its climax. There are too many strangers in the press corps now, and Goldwater cannot be comfortable with strangers.

One thing that may not be well understood is that, for the most part, Goldwater's campaign staff has also been excellent company. They are not right wing ogres. And they show more intellectual tolerance than any men in politics I have ever met. They can be joked with and joked about without losing their tempers. The stories and "Q" heads which you are certain will annoy them usually draw spontaneous praise as showing "insight." I do not know why they behave this way and I am not certain it will survive a possible debacle on Nov. 3, but it is true now.

However, Goldwater's speechwriter, Karl Hess, is not one of my fans. He was the unnamed source of an erroneous "periscope" item in Newsweek which reported that Goldwater believed that of all the press only David Halberstam and Carl Greenburg of The Los Angeles Times had been "fair."

My fellow reporters thought this was funny. Halberstam thought it was funny. So did I. All I could say to David was that at least Madame Nhu liked me better than she did him.

I have been fortunate in that I do not receive much of the violent hate mail which many Goldwater supporters love to send to newspapers. I am moving around so much it may not catch up with me. However, one man (or woman?) on Long Island has been sending me postcards regularly ever since January. I have never answered any of them because I have never been able to make out *one* word of the script. The writer's emotions will remain forever a mystery to me, unless he (or she) buys a typewriter.

Journalistically, the assignment has been a somewhat unusual one. Most politicians repeat themselves shamelessly—and, while they talk a lot, they don't say much.

Goldwater, as everyone knows, says the damndest things and he says them every day. When people say to me, "You must get tired of hearing the same speech over and over," I either gape or laugh. There are very few Goldwater speeches that don't surprise me. This means you never have to scratch for a lead. But it also means that you are hard put to find space for color or for the instant political analysis which a campaign story usually needs.

But since Goldwater is the most "ideological" Presidential candidate in memory, I am convinced that the question of what he says has been and remains the heart of this election contest. I have stuck pretty doggedly to "said today" leads because I felt I had to.

But when the color comes, it comes in a cascade. To me the high point of the whole campaign remains the frosty night in New Hampshire when we were informed that Goldwater would participate in a torchlight parade.

And here he came, sitting with an embarrassed and foolish grin in a pony cart pulled by a grotesquely small horse. Ahead of him was a high school drum and bugle corps dressed in Indian feather bonnets, playing "Blue Moon." And ahead of them was a pudgy high school girl, with blue and frozen knees, carrying, of all things, a United Nations flag.

I also remember the night in Glendora, Cal., when a wild-eyed Goldwater fan rushed up to one of the Senator's aides and gasped out: "You've got to warn the Senator, right away. There are men out there taking down every word he says."

One of the things about Goldwater is that everything he says does not get into The New York Times. There is just not space enough for it, and my notebooks are full of truly remarkable statements that would have been the lead with an ordinary candidate, but that ended on the cutting room floor.

One night in Reno, Nev., Goldwater was asked if he had made a certain statement on nuclear weapons. He was angry and he said, "I would never say that, even in my most lucid moments."

We all get tired. The physical abuse of this campaign has been notable because it has been so prolonged. An 11-pound Olivetti seems to weigh 90 pounds these days. But I'm not complaining. I wouldn't have missed it for anything. I wouldn't ask to be relieved—not even in my most lucid moments.

The 1964 Campaign

Senator Barry Goldwater lost the 1964 election in the vain hope that a huge conservative vote awaited his call.

Even during the campaign, Senator Goldwater appeared to many observers to be throwing away his chances of winning.

He did it, in the main, by permitting and even aiding in his own isolation from the Republican party. It was a minority party when the campaign started, and its deliberate fragmentation, which President Johnson skillfully abetted, ended all hope of any majority-producing coalition.

Despite the fact that it was never widely believed that Senator Goldwater had a real chance to win, he dominated the American political scene all year.

He dominated for two primary reasons. He presented to ordinary voters in both parties, in a form sometimes direct, sometimes obscure, disturbing questions about matters directly affecting them. He also offered the voters a choice, a choice of making a major political shift to the right.

SAW THREAT TO BENEFITS

To many, he seemed to threaten personal benefits like Social Security. To others, he seemed to suggest nuclear war as a conceivable line of policy. To still others, he conveyed the idea that he would slow, or at least not push, the Negro drive for civil rights.

Tennesseans were told he favored selling the Tennessee Valley Authority; old people were convinced he would leave their care to their children. Something about the Senator's supporters, notably the John Birch Society, created a distinct unease in the minds of minority groups and civil libertarians.

Because he raised these questions in voters' minds, Mr. Goldwater raised an even more sweeping question in the minds of Republican leaders, professionals, financiers and philosophers.

To them, he seemed to present the painful prospect of a major ideological shift to the right, a fundamental break with the domestic political course of the last 30 years, a return to the policy of nationalistic isolation from the world.

Barry Goldwater began his Presidential campaign Jan. 3 with the belief that there was a strong conservative tide running—a growing number of voters who challenged, as he did, the "mainstream" and who wanted "a choice, not an echo."

THE HERO OF THE RIGHT

In his 12 years in the Senate, he became the Republican party's most popular speaker and, with his mild manner, good looks, charm and stands against liberal causes, the unquestioned hero of the right.

Mr. Goldwater was convinced that he could count on at least about 45 percent of the vote and make a respectable showing for his cause, but even he was not sure

he could capture the Republican party from what he once called the "mysterious clique in the East."

It turned out that he was wrong on both counts. Moderate Republican leadership had atrophied and his nomination was simple, even in the face of the numerous mistakes he made and the frequent setbacks he suffered. But his type of conservatism did not seem to attract the conservatism of New England Yankees, the small towns of the Middle West or the city suburbs.

His formal announcement was followed by three political debacles. First, he suggested that Social Security be made voluntary. Then he said he would consider threatening to sever diplomatic relations with the Soviet Union to force sweeping concessions in Eastern Europe. And, in his first major speech, he suggested that the poor were to blame for their own poverty.

HOPED FOR A CHANGE

Men like Senator Norris Cotton, of New Hampshire, who had staked their prestige on supporting Mr. Goldwater, were appalled. But they thought that he would modify his style and message.

In this they were mistaken. Although he made many contradictory and complex changes in the wording of his "policies," he never really changed the aggressively conservative tone of his campaign.

In the New Hampshire primary, Mr. Goldwater used almost no written speeches, held frequent news conferences and everywhere solicited questions from his audiences. He talked more and said much more that was controversial than do most Presidential candidates. His advisers later called it a case of "overexposure."

The damage from Mr. Goldwater's New Hampshire defeat proved not much of a setback to his campaign for the nomination. But it had an enormous effect in creating fears about and hostility to him and in giving him a reputation of a "trigger-happy hip-shooter" and a man indifferent to welfare problems.

Mr. Goldwater's managers were not really relying on the primaries. They were good organizers and administrators. They had a plan, and they had an experienced hand in F. Clifton White of New York to carry it out.

Mr. White's concept was sound. Goldwater campaign officials sought to influence every state convention that would select delegates to the national convention. Attention also was given to Congressional district caucuses and even to precinct meetings.

In essence, the plan was not simply to woo political leaders but also to install ideologically dedicated Goldwater supporters in key positions.

Much groundwork had been laid by a "Draft Goldwater" committee in 1963 in gaining control of Republican organizations. The "new" Republicans of the South were natural allies and had already won their delegate fights. In retrospect, the nomination was never in doubt.

Mr. Goldwater needed California to clinch his delegate majority. He needed it, too, to show that he could win popular support in a major state.

The Senator left it to his well-organized precinct organizations to save the primary. This they did, giving him a majority of slightly more than 51 percent.

The effect on the party's professional politicians was stunning. They had not prepared themselves to fight Mr. Goldwater because they thought he would somehow "beat himself." Now they had to decide what to do.

SCRANTON MOVE FAILS

Almost farcial events followed. In the face of vacillation by former President Dwight D. Eisenhower and indecision by Governors William W. Scranton of Pennsylvania and George Romney of Michigan, the Republican Governors, few of whom backed the Senator, took only timid steps. Mr. Goldwater almost contemptuously refused even to discuss party policy with them at the Governors Conference.

On June 12, Mr. Scranton announced his candidacy with a slashing attack on Mr. Goldwater that exceeded anything the Democrats have since said.

But it was far too late, and the nomination of Senator Goldwater at San Francisco was an anticlimax.

In his hour of triumph, however, Mr. Goldwater—again challenging American political tradition—offered no quarter to his opponents. His acceptance speech was a hard-line conservative appeal containing the famous phrase that extremism in the defense of liberty was no vice.

From the moment he spoke in the Cow Palace, evoking the frenzied cheers of the conservatives and the worst fears of the moderates, his chance of unifying his party and shaping it in the conservative mold was gone.

FINDS NEED FOR UNITY

Nevertheless, it became clear to the Senator that he needed a united national party.

To Hershey, Pa., on Aug. 12, Mr. Goldwater summoned the established leaders of the party—the great majority of whom were his political enemies—and made, at last, a conciliatory speech.

When he formally opened his campaign Sept. 3, he continued the "Spirit of Hershey," promising that he would "go slowly" in cutting the Government down to size and that the Government's social and economic commitments would be honored.

But within a few days the Senator was campaigning in an even more conservative manner than he had in New Hampshire.

Thus, no lasting effort was made to unify the party.

The Democrats hastened to exploit the developing split.

President Johnson himself was the master strategist of the Democratic campaign. He called the shots, whether it was directing the writing of a major speech or a snap decision on the speaker's platform to tear the speech up. Much as he criticized his opposition for impulsiveness, the President demonstrated time and again in his campaigning that he operated from instinct.

The President's great talent, his confidants believe, is using his judgment and restraint to bring divergent groups together.

In shaping his campaign strategy, he wanted victory by a huge margin, an overwhelming mandate. In private conversations, the President expressed a deep-seated fear, not of Senator Goldwater himself, but of the men in the Senator's camp.

TWO BASIC QUESTIONS

Mr. Johnson believed that the American people possessed a strong sense of their times and the choices confronting them, and that they would respond to a candidate who gave reasoned answers to the questions uppermost in their minds. These questions, he felt, could be reduced to:

Peace or war.

Future well-being.

In shaping his campaign strategy, the President found in Senator Goldwater an antagonist who made his problem easy.

Mr. Goldwater made it clear that his campaign would be based on dissent. Mr. Johnson, from the moment he succeeded to the Presidency, had called for national unity.

INVITATION TO REPUBLICANS

Mr. Goldwater could be counted on for hard negative criticism of the Administration. Mr. Johnson espoused positivism,

holding out a vision of prosperous progress at home and peace abroad.

Mr. Goldwater could be counted upon to mount a personal campaign. Mr. Johnson had commanded Congress "to always debate principles, never debate personalities."

Mr. Goldwater took an uncompromising stance that made it difficult to unify his party. Mr. Johnson invited Republicans to join with the Democrats.

Mr. Goldwater indicated his aloofness from the voter, disdaining mingling with the crowds. "Meeting the people" became the most distinctive characteristic of the President's campaign.

In short, the Goldwater campaign appeared to the Johnson strategists to be vulnerable in almost every sector.

In the President's camp, there was one major blunder ascribed to the Republican strategists. That was their calculation that the President would lose his self-control under extreme pressure. Intimates knew that the greater the pressure, the more restrained the President became, and the more his self-assurance grew.

President Johnson concentrated most on a talk that would widen and perpetuate the split between Senator Goldwater and the Republican moderates. His splitting technique was based on repeated taps on a wedge rather than massive strokes.

WEDGE TAPPED SUBTLY

In the beginning, the entry of the wedge was so subtle as to be scarcely recognizable.

"I have come here today," he said in Detroit on Labor Day, "to pledge that, if all Americans will stand united, we will keep moving. This country is not going to turn its back on the future. This country is not going to turn from unity to hostility, from understanding to hate."

Everywhere, the President sounded his unity theme, wooed Republican votes with high praises for bipartisanship and pictured his opponent as an outcast in his own political community.

But it was not until the cleavage between the Senator and his party was plain that Mr. Johnson slapped him with direct insult, and then only rarely. In mid-October at Reno, Nev., he said:

"One candidate is roaming around the country saying what a terrible thing the Government is. Somebody better tell him that most Americans are not ready to trade the American Eagle in for a plucked bantam rooster."

For the most part, however, the anti-Goldwater campaign was based on tactics of ridicule for his policies without humiliation to his person. When the Senator accused the President of being "soft on communism," Mr. Johnson gave the softest possible answer and said he thought even Senator Goldwater would back away from such a line after thinking it over.

Mr. Johnson, meanwhile hewed close to his basic strategy, reciting the record of his Administration, the nation's prosperity, his "responsibility" in the face of crisis, and most of all, the quest for peace and coexistence. And he "visited with the people."

His dead-run campaigning to the finish line was as hard and determined as any in history. He ran as though it were a close race.

Oct. 14 was the low point of the Johnson campaign. Early that evening, the White House announced that a Presidential aide, Walter W. Jenkins, was in a hospital with nervous exhaustion. Then the account of his morals arrests came out. Later that night, in New York, Mr. Jenkins's resignation was announced.

JOHNSON OFF HIS STRIDE

All that day, in New Jersey and in Pennsylvania, the President was off his stride. He gave the crowds what amounted to a brush-off. The gloom in his camp was ascribed to fatigue from the rigors of his Western trip earlier in the week.

The next day he went back at it in upstate New York, but an incredible stroke of luck played into his hands. The Jenkins case was crowded out of the headlines by the ouster of Nikita S. Khrushchev as Soviet Premier and the test explosion of an atomic device in Communist China.

On Oct. 18, the President took to nationwide television, and while he gave his countrymen reassurance against a crisis, he also precipitated an argument by the Goldwater people over equal television time that further diverted public attention from the Jenkins case.

Mr. Johnson got the breaks, but he also showed how to capitalize on them. For a week thereafter, the President slacked off his campaign activities and gave the nation an image of a President hard at work in his office. Only once from Oct. 16 to Oct. 24 did he hit the campaign trail, and then swiftly into Ohio, Illinois and Missouri, returning immediately to Washington.

The low point of the campaign was safely passed. From there on, the movement was upward.

V. *VOTING AND ELECTIONS*

Gerald M. Pomper

Voting and elections are the crucial elements of democratic government. Popular elections do not guarantee popular control, it is true, as demonstrated by modern totalitarianism. Still, there is no other reliable foundation for such control. Despite their importance, however, the nature and function of popular elections are unclear.

Analysis of the voting process has been dominated by classic democratic theory. Three principal postulates of democratic theory, as developed over the centuries, are relevant here. First, voting is conceived to be an individual act. The citizen votes on the basis of personal judgments, in relative isolation from social influences. Second, votes are decided on the basis of issues and the public good. The citizen supports those candidates and policies that he believes will advance the total interests of society and not necessarily his own particular interests.

> Each man . . . wills the general good in his own interest, as strongly as any one else. What the people is asked is not exactly whether it approves or rejects [a] proposal, but whether it is in conformity with the general will, which is their will. Each man, in giving his vote, states his opinion on that point; and the general will is found by counting votes.[1]

The third principle is a logical extension of the others. If voting is an individual matter and decided on the basis of issues, a majority vote indicates support for particular policies. Once voters have expressed their opinion on public issues, the officials of government are under a "mandate" to implement the chosen policies. Elections are thus seen as a means of determining the actions of government.

Considerable evidence is now available that the character of voting is different from what it was assumed to be in the traditional debate over democracy. Contrary to the first postulate of classic theory, individuals do not decide their votes in isolation. Rather, voting is a social act. The voter is dependent upon others for his information, for much of his perceptions of candidates and issues, and indeed for his basic party loyalty in most cases. He will be influenced by his group memberships, such as his class, religion, and ethnic affiliation. If voters were acting as isolated individuals, we would expect no more than chance differences in the partisan loyalties of different groups. There would be approximately equal percentages of Democrats, for example, among manual and white-collar workers, Catholics and Protestants, urbanites and suburbanites, Negroes and Caucasians, grade-school graduates and college alumni, those descended from

---

[1] Jean Jacques Rousseau, *The Social Contract and the Discourses* (New York: Dutton, Everyman, 1950), pp. 103, 106.

southern and eastern European emigrants and those with progenitors from northern and western Europe. In fact, significant differences exist. In each of the stated pairs of groups, there are substantially more Democrats in the first group than in the second.

It is also evident that voting is not decided on the basis of issues alone, nor are voters greatly concerned with discerning the "general will." No more than 15 percent of the electorate can be considered to be "ideological," casting its vote on the basis of an overarching approach to public questions. Most electoral decisions are made on narrower grounds. Where questions of public policy are involved at all, the voter is most likely to be influenced by a particular issue that affects him, or the groups with which he identifies, rather than more general interests.[2]

In many cases, moreover, issues are totally irrelevant to the vote. Individuals are not greatly interested in, or knowledgeable about, government. Their perception of issues is clouded and their concern is limited. Given the complexity of government, and the many immediate demands on the limited time and abilities of individuals, these results are hardly surprising.

A pointed illustration of the lack of public interest in issues is provided by the proposed "Bricker amendment" to the Constitution. A subject of intense controversy in the 1950s, the amendment would have sharply restricted the President's treaty-making powers. Despite the controversy and a dramatic Senate debate, 84 percent of the voters never formed an opinion on the subject.[3] Even the small minority who had an opinion would have been unlikely to vote on the basis of this single issue.

We must also doubt traditional assumptions about the function of elections. With voters unaware or uninterested in election issues, a meaningful "mandate" is unlikely. Typically, parties do not offer pledges sufficiently distinct and specific to establish such a relationship. Even if, for example, the voters had been concerned about the Bricker amendment, they would have found it difficult to express their concern through a partisan choice. In most instances, a party will include voters who favor both sides of a specific controversy, as well as a probable majority who are not concerned with the issue at all. If only a minority supports a particular policy, there is no effective "mandate."[4]

Traditional assumptions about the character of voting in a democracy have not been demonstrated in practice. Popular elections have also failed to confirm the fears of the opponents of democracy. From the time of Plato, antidemocratic theorists have predicted doom in a society permitting universal suffrage. The selfish rule of the mob would foster unstable government, it was argued. Public officials would be subject to the close control of transient popular majorities. Government policies would change with each new fancy of the voters. As the heritage of the past was disregarded, chaos would be substituted for order. "Democracies have ever been spectacles of turbulence and contention," wrote Madison, "and have in general been as short in their lives as they have been violent in their deaths."[5]

[2] Angus Campbell, *et al., The American Voter* (New York: Wiley, 1960), chaps. 8–10.

[3] V. O. Key, Jr., *Public Opinion and American Democracy* (New York: Knopf, 1961), pp. 82–84.

[4] See Leon D. Epstein, "Electoral Decision and Policy Mandate: An Empirical Example," *Public Opinion Quarterly,* vol. 28 (Winter 1964), pp. 564–572.

[5] James Madison, *The Federalist,* no. 10 (New York: Random House, Modern Library, 1941), p. 58.

Modern antidemocrats have taken further comfort from the evidence of voting studies. They have used these studies to argue that "the mass" is incapable of self-government and that power should be monopolized or manipulated by "the elite." This is the common premise of groups such as the "hidden persuaders" of the public relations industry, the Communist advocates of "people's democracy," and the submissive authoritarians of the John Birch Society.

The available evidence does require us to abandon the traditional theory of voting and elections. It does not, however, require us to accept the arguments of the antidemocrats. Voting has not led to instability, demagoguery, and doom. Indeed, modern democracies have proved to be more stable than competitive political systems. Voting studies also do not require us to accept the elitist conceptions of the modern antidemocrats. These findings prove neither the incapacity of the general electorate nor the superiority of the would-be elite.

What is needed is a more informed explanation of voting, not the abandonment of the principle of universal suffrage. We must recast our empirical theory to take account of the established evidence. If our expectations become more realistic, they will be more likely to be fulfilled. Ultimately, however, a preference for democracy must be based on moral choices independent of and more basic than any empirical investigations.

THE CHARACTER OF THE VOTE

Stability is the dominant characteristic of democratic voting. This is contrary to the expectations of both democratic and antidemocratic theorists. The former expected the voter to examine his position individually and rationally at each election, changing his vote as the times demanded. In fact, the voter is more likely to persist in past habits. Antidemocrats expected universal suffrage to promote instability, as policy reflected the ephemeral moods of the electorate. In fact, the stability of the individual vote is paralleled by the stability of the total political system based on voting. A fraction of the electorate may be agitated by a particular grievance or favor some radical policy, but most voters will be unaffected. The great size and bulk of the electorate tends to absorb, moderate, and insulate the total polity from social upheavals.

Voting is stable in character and stabilizing in its effects. This statement is manifested in many specific instances. As one example, we can examine some differences between voters and nonvoters. Those who vote more frequently also tend to become attached to a particular party, and the more often a person votes the more he is likely to become a committed Democrat or Republican. Change in the political system, then, is not likely to come from those who are habitual voters.

Those who ordinarily do not vote are more flexible. If they can be aroused to participate in a particular election, they can affect great changes. In an extreme case, such as in pre-Nazi Germany, these individuals may even constitute a threat to the democratic system. Hitler gained a disproportionate amount of his support from those previously apathetic toward politics. Those already accustomed to voting were "immunized," so to speak, against radicalism.[6] Less

---

[6] See Seymour M. Lipset, *Political Man* (New York: Doubleday, 1960), pp. 216–219, and William N. McPhee and William A. Glaser, *Public Opinion and Congressional Elections* (New York: Free Press of Glencoe, 1962), chap. 6.

violent changes may also be accomplished by appeals to nonvoters. The Eisenhower success of 1952 and the Johnson victory of 1964 are illustrative. Both gained great support from previously apathetic citizens.

Stability is also evident in the partisan choice of voters. Persistent party loyalty is clearly evident in American elections. At least three-fourths of the voters identify with one of the two major parties. Considering the high status accorded to independence in American political norms, this is an impressively high figure. Even among the remaining group, most individuals do, in fact, lean toward one party or the other. Those free of any attachment to a major party constitute less than a tenth of the electorate, and these individuals tend to be the least interested, the least informed, and the least likely to vote.

Michigan University voting studies (41) indicate the depth of these loyalties. Voters retain their party loyalties over long periods of time. In the postwar period, despite major social changes and the alternation of power between the parties, the Democrats have retained a lead of more than 3–2 over the Republicans in party identification. Voters have been persistent in their voting habits as well, with a large majority always or almost always voting for the party of their constant choice.

Party loyalties also persist between generations. Most voters gain their partisan views as children within the intimate family, in much the same way as they learn manners and grow up in a particular religion. As early as the fourth grade most children identify with a party.[7] During their lifetimes, some will change their loyalties, but close to 80 percent will continue in the party of their parents. Over the course of many decades, this loyalty will continue from one generation to the next. The persistence of partisan choice can be illustrated as well by electoral maps, which show the distribution of the vote in regions, states, and counties. Thus the process of political transmission has resulted in long-term Democratic party support in the South and Republican strength in the Great Plains.

Attachment to party exists independently of other factors. Loyalty to the Democratic party, for example, is not the same as being a manual worker or a Catholic. There are many persons who share these social characteristics who are Republicans, as well as many Democrats who are businessmen or Protestants. Similarly, policy preferences do not clearly differentiate the voters. Opinions on public policies divide voters within as well as between the parties. To be sure, there are relations between party loyalties and these other factors. Catholics and manual workers do tend to be Democrats, as do those favoring more liberal social welfare policies. The relation, however, is not one of direct cause and effect.

Loyalty to party, then, is widespread, persistent, and autonomous. For the individual voter, his fealty provides a stable reference point amidst the confusing stimuli of the political world. It relieves him of the impossible task of assimilating all the information required for a fully rational choice. With a pre-existing commitment, the voter does not approach each election with an open mind or an empty head. His perception of the candidates and issues will be conditioned by this loyalty. Some distortion of the real world will ensue, possibly resulting in a less-informed decision. Any such distortion and consequent ills, however, are

[7] Fred I. Greenstein, "The Benevolent Leader: Children's Images of Political Authority," *American Political Science Review*, vol. 54 (December 1960), pp. 934–943.

balanced by the saving of the voter's time, effort, and anxiety in arriving at a decision.

In the total political system, party loyalty promotes stability. Voters are not likely suddenly and drastically to change these preferences. New or radical movements will be obstructed by lack of interest and slowed by inertia. The established parties are reasonably assured of survival and of a large proportion of the vote. With this stake in the existing system, they are unlikely to favor drastic change.

Any particular election takes place within a context of overall stability in party identifications.

> Every American election summons the individual voter to weigh the past against the future. . . . Each of the great tribal communities of American life is split between Republicans and Democrats in different proportions; but these different proportions are among the most enduring realities in our political system.[8]

In his decision, the voter begins, in V. O. Key's words, with a "standing decision" to support his party. This decision is not irrevocable, and voters do change their party loyalties, both on a long-term and short-run basis. A long-term change affects not only a particular vote but the basic party identification itself. Such reversals result from many causes. Each generation is inevitably unique in the problems it faces and the policies it favors. In a mobile society like the United States, moreover, children often differ significantly from their parents in their social characteristics. They are likely to have a different degree of education, to hold different jobs, and to live in different regions. Certainly events differ from one generation to the next, changing the environment in which party loyalties are maintained or revised.

The voter is also subject to short-term influences. Without changing his basic party identification, he may still abandon his party in a particular election. The "standing decision" may be reversed by the particular events, issues, personalities, and appeals of a campaign. Thus, in the 1950s, most Americans continued to regard themselves as Democrats, and few crossed over the party line permanently. Nevertheless, millions of self-styled Democrats voted for the Republicans on the basis of the specific political factors of the time—the personal appeal of Eisenhower, an unfavorable reaction to the Korean War, and the Truman Administration, and approval of "peace and prosperity" in 1956. When these temporary factors were no longer present, the voters returned to their established party loyalties, electing John Kennedy and Lyndon Johnson.

The stability of the vote results from more than individual preferences. It is also founded on the loyalties and influences of the groups to which the individual voter belongs. The family is the most important unit, of course, but here we refer to broader categories such as social classes, religious denominations, and ethnic communities, as well as to formal organizations such as unions, churches, and fraternal societies. Groups serve as additional reference points for the individual voter. They provide information and standards by which he may judge candidates and issues. The effects of membership are most apparent among individuals closely identified with a group. A useful example is the influence of religion in the 1960 election. In that year, Democrats were most likely to vote

---

[8] Theodore H. White, *The Making of the President 1960* (New York: Atheneum, 1961), pp. 211–212.

against the Catholic candidate of their party if they were closely identified with Protestantism (as measured by church attendance). To put it another way, Protestant Democrats who were most loyal to their church were also least loyal to their party in 1960. On the other hand, even among regular Protestant church-goers, a majority of Democrats still voted for Kennedy. Party loyalty remained more basic than religious affiliation.[9]

As in the case of individuals, groups tend to demonstrate an inherited party loyalty. They therefore act as a stabilizing influence, transmitting values from old members to new ones and from one generation to the next. The individual's attachment to his social groups reinforces established party loyalties and deters change. The origin of party loyalties, however, is rarely a simple causal relationship. Philosophical or ideological values may provide a partial explanation in some cases. The preference of Protestants for the Republican party, for example, may be related to the emphasis of their church on individual salvation, a position akin to Republican distrust of social planning.

This kind of a relationship is, at best, tenuous and indirect. Loyalties to American parties have probably been created or changed in more mundane ways. We would suggest three kinds of origins. Policy is one basis. Groups have supported those parties that, in turn, have supported their aims or granted them political recognition. Another source is the conflict between groups, as antagonistic elements adhere to opposing parties. A third cause of group loyalty is reaction to major social events or catastrophes. However formed, attachments are transmitted within families and groups even after the specific causes are irrelevant or forgotten.

Negro voters illustrate all of these influences. Negroes were solidly Republican after the Civil War, as a result of Emancipation and Reconstruction. This party preference was reinforced by group conflicts, particularly in the native Southern states of most Negroes. In that region, the Democrats constituted the party of white supremacy, leaving the Negro no alternative to the GOP. These feelings were reversed, however, by the Depression and the New Deal. The economic catastrophe was particularly severe on Negroes, and the New Deal particularly beneficial, because of the position of this group at the bottom of the economic ladder. Increasingly after the Depression, Negroes became loyal Democrats. This loyalty reached its acme in 1964, when some 96 percent of nonwhites voted for Johnson. In this election, group conflict had come to reinforce the Democratic party preference. The Republicans nominated a candidate opposed to civil rights legislation and supported by segregationists. The Negro vote had come full cycle.

As the history of Negro voting illustrates, group loyalties are not fixed. Over time, rapid or evolutionary change is likely. Similarly, a group will vary in its voting from one campaign to the next. Particular elections will tend to stress particular group loyalties and to relegate others to a lesser position. The candidacy of a Catholic in 1960 made religious affiliations more relevant to the vote. In 1964, as the contest centered on economic and racial issues, social class and ethnic affiliation became more important. Sociological characteristics do not determine the vote, either in all elections or in any particular contest. Voting remains a political decision.

[9] See Philip E. Converse *et al.,* "Stability and Change in 1960: A Reinstating Election," *American Political Science Review,* vol. 55 (June 1961), pp. 269–280.

THE SIGNIFICANCE OF ELECTIONS

Individual and group voting evidences considerable stability. If we now turn to the general effects of elections, we again find considerable continuity. This is particularly evident if we disregard the transient aspects of elections, victory and defeat for particular individuals, and instead concentrate on the balance of parties resulting from voting.

Typically, in any historical period, one of the two major parties is predominant in the political system and can expect to win most presidential elections. Within an historical era, party loyalties remain stable. This does not mean that the dominant party is certain of victory, but that it can be expected to win any given election in the absence of unusual circumstances, such as a very popular candidate receiving the nomination of the minority party or a split in the ranks of the majority. Elections in this period have been characterized by Michigan University researchers (48) as "maintaining" or "deviating," depending on whether the election is won or lost by the established majority party.

American political history can be seen as a series of such periods, or cycles, each approximately thirty years or a generation in duration. The dates of the cycles are not always precisely obvious, and there is certainly no political or mathematical determinism that necessitates a new cycle every thirty years. With these reservations in mind, we may analytically group American elections into five such periods. The names of the President elected at the beginning of each period and the approximate dates are (1) Jefferson, 1800–1824; (2) Jackson, 1828–1860; (3) Lincoln, 1864–1892; (4) McKinley, 1896–1928; (5) Franklin Roosevelt, 1932–1960(?).

There are certain similarities among these cycles. Within each, the minority party was able to win no more than two Presidential elections. Each ended with a confused election, characterized by the growth of third parties, the election of a President with a minority of the popular vote, or uncertainty in voter loyalties.

Elections at the beginning of a cycle also evidence similarities. There is a rapid growth in turnout and in the vote of the nascent majority party. A change in the character of the vote can be seen, as demonstrated by the support for the parties from different geographical areas and social groups. In such an election, there is not a universal trend in the direction of one party, but some elements of the population will tend toward one and others will tend in the opposite direction. The final result will be a decisive victory for one party.

A new cycle is initiated by the coming of a new generation of voters. After some thirty years, the electorate is transformed as children replace their parents in the voting booth. Responding to new issues and new group memberships, they may evidence a changed party loyalty. This replacement of one generation by another is a continuous process, to be sure, and political loyalties are constantly in flux, indirectly affected by each birth and death, each location of an industrial plant or suburban subdivision. Partisanship may change slowly, as voting groups engage in a process of "secular realignment." The party balance may also be rapidly transformed. In a "critical election" (49), the result is a lasting realignment of voter loyalties. With this change, a new equilibrium is established between the parties and a new cycle begins. In some cases, a new cycle involves a change in the identity of the majority party, as in Democratic ascension in the New Deal period. In other cases, the same party remains dominant, but with an altered basis of support, as in the case of the Republican party after the election of 1896.

In analyzing the present party balance, we lack the advantages of historical hindsight. It is obvious that the Democratic party is now dominant, but it is not clear exactly when it became the majority. Although the first party victory did not come until 1932, the signs of realignment were clearly evident in 1928. In that year, turnout increased by 25 percent, and the Democratic vote nearly doubled. Much new support was gained, particularly in the Northeastern cities, while Southern support was lost. Roosevelt brought victory to the party in 1932, but little realignment was evident in that year. If we must choose an election that marks the triumph of the Democrats, 1936 may well be the best choice.

It is not clear whether the Democratic majority created by Roosevelt persists or if the party's present position is the result of recent realignment. By 1960, signs of change in the electorate were evident. However, most voting seemed to be an affirmation of old loyalties, and there clearly was not the decisive victory one would expect in a critical election. The election of 1964 may be a clearer case. As we would expect, the outcome was decisive, bringing the Democrats into overwhelming control nationally and in most states. Some signs of a realigning election were lacking in 1964, however. Voting turnout barely increased. Almost all sections and population groups tended toward increased support of the Democrats compared to 1960. Substantial change was obvious only among Negroes and white Southerners, who markedly increased their vote for the Democrats and Republicans respectively. We shall probably have to await the presidential results in 1968 and 1972 before reaching firm conclusions.[10]

The partisan results of elections are further evidence of stability. In most elections, the balance of parties is retained. Eventually, however, the old partisan balance becomes outdated, based on issues and group alignments that are no longer viable. In a particular election, a new choice is presented, as the parties change their appeal, candidates, or composition. Most voters still retain their party loyalties despite the changed conditions. However, responding to the new choice, a crucial marginal group changes its party loyalties. The system becomes stabilized again as a new equilibrium is established, more representative of the electorate and more relevant to its concerns.

In selecting a party, voters also choose policies, but this is not a direct selection of specific programs. Only on rare occasions, as in 1964, do the parties present sharply different programs. Even on such occasions, we cannot be confident which of the many issues involved in partisan debate was most important to the voters, or, indeed, if issues were of importance at all. Nevertheless, voting does exert a substantial influence on public policy.

One basic effect of voting is to limit the proposals and actions of government. Certain policies will not be followed because of the check of popular elections. The conduct of American public officials and the issues raised by parties and candidates are thereby restricted within a narrow range. Radical and extremist proposals are excluded from consideration. No American government,

[10] One interesting thesis concerning realignment in 1964 is David Danzig, "Conservatism after Goldwater," *Commentary*, vol. 39 (March 1965), pp. 31–37.

for example, would confiscate the savings of its citizens or export food while its own people were in want—but these policies have been followed by Communist governments free from direct electoral influence.[11] American parties may disagree on the desirability of federal aid to education, but there is no disagreement on the more important issue of the desirability of a tax-supported public school system.

Elections serve to channel political discussion and public policy. The process is unlike that postulated by the theory of mandates. The voter does not initiate policies. His actions are of a negative character, disapproving and electorally punishing those who depart abruptly or considerably from established practice. The total effect of voting is seen as stabilizing, resulting in the continuity of government programs.

Voters further control policies by the judgments they make in elections on the conduct and policies of officials. This judgment is usually made retrospectively, rather than prospectively. The electorate does not choose the policies it wishes in advance. Rather, it indicates its areas of concern, expresses its satisfaction and dissatisfaction with the men and methods of the past, and then endows a group with the power to deal with the problems. In the next election, it judges the results achieved by this group.

The first two elections of Franklin Roosevelt are illustrative. In 1932, in the midst of the Depression, the voters repudiated the Republican Administration of Herbert Hoover. There was no evident meaning to this electoral verdict in terms of specific governmental programs. The Democratic platform was contradictory, pledging both broad welfare measures to deal with unemployment and a 25 percent reduction in federal expenditures. Few voters had read the platform, however. Their vote for F. D. R. was an expression of need rather than the endorsement of any detailed way of handling that need. In the following election, in 1936, the voters did have specific measures to judge. The New Deal had been created and had brought significant changes in American life. By the overwhelming endorsement of Roosevelt in that election and the concomitant realignment of party loyalties the voters retrospectively approved these changes. Given this endorsement, both parties accepted the changes made by the New Deal and they became permanent American institutions.

Many elections, possibly most, are not even as clear as the generalized verdicts of 1932 and 1936. "The vocabulary of the voice of the people consists mainly of the words 'yes' and 'no'; and at times one cannot be certain which word is being uttered."[12] The effect is to leave public officials with a considerable degree of discretion in the selection of policies, in contrast to the theory of electoral mandates. Officials must not overstep the boundaries of accepted policies, and they must try to promote satisfaction among the voters, striving for such general goals as "peace and prosperity." The choice of means to accomplish these goals, however, is left to the officials. The final outcome is a stable balance. Government is kept responsible, but is free from constant popular intervention.[13]

[11] Nelson W. Polsby and Aaron B. Wildavsky, *Presidential Elections* (New York: Scribner's, 1964), p. 199.

[12] V. O. Key, Jr., *Politics, Parties and Pressure Groups*, 5th ed. (New York: Crowell, 1964), p. 544.

[13] For further analysis, see Talcott Parsons, " 'Voting' and the Equilibrium of the American Political System," in Eugene Burdick and Arthur J. Brodbeck, *American Voting Behavior* (New York: Free Press of Glencoe, 1959), pp. 80–120.

Voting results both in the choice of leaders and in the indirect and general choice of policy. These two results are related. The voters choose not only specific individuals but they also select a coalition—created through the nominating and campaigning processes. The composition, goals, and appeals of this coalition will determine the specific content of policy. The voters confer legitimacy on this coalition, giving it the right to govern by means of its endorsement in a popular election. They reserve to themselves the power to review periodically the accomplishments of this coalition, to enter or leave it, to continue it in office, or to displace it with a different coalition.

Stability is characteristic of the entire electoral system. The individual voter is stable in his party and group loyalties. The party balance is stable over long periods of time. Public policy is stabilized by the limits placed on governing coalitions. Officials do not change their programs with every passing popular fancy, but do so when discontent becomes widespread. Voting and elections do not follow the traditional model. Over time, however, the voters do control their government and its policies. Democracy is not simple, direct, or automatic—but it does exist in an environment of competitive political parties.

THE VOTING DECISION

41. The Impact and Development of Party Identification

Angus Campbell, Philip E. Converse, Warren E. Miller, and Donald E. Stokes

Since 1948, the University of Michigan's Survey Research Center has conducted interviews with a nation-wide, representative sample of the electorate. These surveys have become a prime source of knowledge of electoral behavior. The following selection, by members of the Center, emphasizes the effect of party identification, which has been found to be the single most important influence on the vote. Developed early in life, party loyalty is likely to persist in the face of all but the most dramatic social events. In a specific election, however, because of short-term influences, a voter may desert his party.

* * *

A general observation about the political behavior of Americans is that their partisan preferences show great stability between elections. Key speaks of the "standing decision" to support one party or the other, and this same phenomenon soon catches the eye of any student of electoral behavior. Its mark is readily seen in aggregate election statistics. For virtually any collection of states, counties, wards, precincts, or other political units one may care to examine, the correlation of the party division of the vote in successive elections is likely to be high. Often a change of candidates and a broad alteration in the nature of the issues disturb very little the relative partisanship of a set of electoral units, which suggests that great numbers of voters have party attachments that persist through time.

The fact that attachments of this sort are widely held is confirmed by survey data on individual people. In a survey interview most of our citizens freely classify themselves as Republicans or Democrats and indicate that these loyalties have persisted

From Angus Campbell, Philip E. Converse, Warren E. Miller, and Donald E. Stokes, *The American Voter*, abr. ed. (New York: John Wiley and Sons, 1964), pp. 67–72, 80–83, 86–93.

through a number of elections. Few factors are of greater importance for our national elections than the lasting attachment of tens of millions of Americans to one of the parties. These loyalties establish a basic division of electoral strength within which the competition of particular campaigns takes place. And they are an important factor in assuring the stability of the party system itself.

THE CONCEPT
AND MEASUREMENT
OF PARTY IDENTIFICATION

Only in the exceptional case does the sense of individual attachment to party reflect a formal membership or an active connection with a party apparatus. Nor does it simply denote a voting record, although the influence of party allegiance on electoral behavior is strong. Generally this tie is a psychological identification, which can persist without legal recognition or evidence of formal membership and even without a consistent record of party support. Most Americans have this sense of attachment with one party or the other. And for the individual who does, the strength and direction of party identification are facts of central importance in accounting for attitude and behavior.

The importance of stable partisan loyalties has been universally recognized in electoral studies, but the manner in which they should be defined and measured has been a subject of some disagreement. In keeping with the conception of party identification as a psychological tie, these orientations have been measured in our research by asking individuals to describe their own partisan loyalties. Some studies, however, have chosen to measure stable partisan orientations in terms of an individual's past voting record or in terms of his attitude on a set of partisan issues. We have not measured party attachments in terms of the vote or the evaluation of partisan

issues precisely because we are interested in exploring the *influence* of party identification on voting behavior and its immediate determinants. When an independent measure of party identification is used, it is clear that even strong party adherents at times may think and act in contradiction to their party allegiance. We could never establish the conditions under which this will occur if lasting partisan orientations were measured in terms of the behavior they are thought to affect.

Our measurement of party identification rests fundamentally on self-classification. Since 1952 we have asked repeated cross sections of the national population a sequence of questions inviting the individual to state the direction and strength of his partisan orientation.[1] The dimension presupposed by these questions appears to have psychological reality for virtually the entire electorate. The partisan self-image of all but the few individuals who disclaim any involvement in politics permits us to place each person in these samples on a continuum of partisanship extending from strongly Republican to strongly Democratic. The sequence of questions we have asked also allows us to distinguish the Independents who lean toward one of the parties from those who think of themselves as having no partisan coloration whatever.

The measure these methods yield has served our analysis of party identification in a versatile fashion. To assess both the direction and intensity of partisan attachments it can be used to array our samples

[1] The initial question was this: "Generally speaking, do you think of yourself as a Republican, a Democrat, an Independent, or what?" Those who classified themselves as Republicans or Democrats were also asked, "Would you call yourself a strong (Republican, Democrat) or not very strong (Republican, Democrat)?" Those who classified themselves as Independents were asked this additional question: "Do you think of yourself as closer to the Republican or Democratic Party?" The concept itself was first discussed in George Belknap and Angus Campbell, "Political Party Identification and Attitudes toward Foreign Policy," *Public Opinion Quarterly*, XV (Winter 1952), 601–623.

across the seven categories shown in Table 1, which gives the distribution of party identification in the electorate during the years from 1952 to 1958.

In using these techniques of measurement we do not suppose that every person who describes himself as an Independent is indicating simply his lack of positive attrac-

TABLE 1   The Distribution of Party Identification

	Oct. 1952	Sept. 1953	Oct. 1954	Apr. 1956	Oct. 1956	Nov. 1957	Oct. 1958
Strong Republicans	13%	15%	13%	14%	15%	10%	13%
Weak Republicans	14	15	14	18	14	16	16
Independent Republicans	7	6	6	6	8	6	4
Independents	5	4	7	3	9	8	8
Independent Democrats	10	8	9	6	7	7	7
Weak Democrats	25	23	25	24	23	26	24
Strong Democrats	22	22	22	19	21	21	23
Apolitical, don't know	4	7	4	10	3	6	5
TOTAL	100%	100%	100%	100%	100%	100%	100%
Number of cases	1614	1023	1139	1731	1772	1488	1269

tion to one of the parties. Some of these people undoubtedly are actually repelled by the parties or by partisanship itself and value their position as Independents. Certainly independence of party is an ideal of some currency in our society, and it seems likely that a portion of those who call themselves Independents are not merely reporting the absence of identification with one of the major parties.

Sometimes it is said that a good number of those who call themselves Independents have simply adopted a label that conceals a genuine psychological commitment to one party or the other. Accordingly, it is argued that a person's voting record gives a more accurate statement of his party attachment than does his own self-description. Our samples doubtless include some of these undercover partisans, and we have incorporated in our measure of party identification a means of distinguishing Independents who say they lean toward one of the parties from Independents who say they do not. We do not think that the problem of measurement presented by the concealed partisan is large. Rather it seems to us much less troublesome than the problems that

follow if psychological ties to party are measured in terms of the vote.

This question can be illuminated a good deal by an examination of the consistency of party voting among those of different degrees of party identification, as is done in Table 2. The proportion of persons consistently supporting one party varies by more than sixty percentage points between strong party identifiers and complete Independents. For the problem of the undercover partisan, the troublesome figure in Table 2 is the 16 per cent of full Independents who have voted for the candidates of one party only.[2] The importance of this figure diminishes when we remember that some of these persons have voted in very few presidential elections and could have supported one party consistently because of the way their votes fell, free of the influence of a genuine party tie.

[2] In this discussion we assume that the concealed partisan is less likely to distort his voting record than his description of his party attachment; that is, we assume that what the undercover partisan values is chiefly the designation "Independent." To the extent this is untrue the analysis of voting consistency by strength of party identification fails to enhance our understanding.

A simple test of this hypothesis is made in Table 3 by separating persons who have come of voting age relatively recently from those who have been of voting age for a greater number of elections. Plainly, the length of time a person had had to develop a variable voting record influences the likelihood that he will report that he has voted for the candidates of more than one party, whatever the strength of his party identification. But among complete Independents the proportion of people thirty-five years old or older who could reasonably be called concealed party identifiers is now reduced to 11 percent. A detailed inspection of these cases shows that a number of these individuals have voted in relatively few elections and have had little opportunity to

TABLE 2 Relation of Strength of Party Identification to Partisan Regularity in Voting for President, 1956[a]

	Strong Party Identifiers	Weak Party Identifiers	Independents Leaning to Party	Independents
Voted always or mostly for same party	82%	60%	36%	16%
Voted for different parties	18	40	64	84
TOTAL	100%	100%	100%	100%
Number of cases	546	527	189	115

[a] The question used to establish party consistency of voting was this: "Have you always voted for the same party or have you voted for different parties for President?"

TABLE 3 Relation of Strength of Party Identification to Partisan Regularity in Voting for President, by Age Groups, 1956

Age	Strong Party Identifiers	Weak Party Identifiers	Independents Leaning to Party	Independents
21 to 34				
Voted always or mostly for same party	91%	78%	60%	33%
Voted for different parties	9	22	40	67
TOTAL	100%	100%	100%	100%
Number of cases	104	120	53	21
35 and above				
Voted always or mostly for same party	80%	55%	26%	11%
Voted for different parties	20	45	74	89
TOTAL	100%	100%	100%	100%
Number of cases	440	405	136	93

form an inconsistent voting record. When the frequency of voting turnout is considered, the proportion of extreme Independents who have voted only for the candidates of one party is not greater than we would expect it to be by chance alone.

The measurement of party identification in the period of our research shows how different a picture of partisan allegiance voting behavior and self-description can give. Despite the substantial Republican majorities in the elections of 1952 and 1956, the percentages of Table 1 make clear that the Democratic Party enjoyed a three-to-two advantage in the division of party identification within the electorate in these same years.[3] Moreover, Table 1 documents the stability of this division of party loyalty in a period whose electoral history might suggest widespread change. Except for the shifting size of the group of respondents refusing to be assigned any position on the party scale, there is not a single variation between successive distributions of party identification that could not be laid to sampling error.

The great stability of partisan loyalties is supported, too, by what we can learn from recall data about the personal history of party identification. We have asked successive samples of the electorate a series of questions permitting us to reconstruct whether an individual who accepts a party designation has experienced a prior change in his party identification. The responses give impressive evidence of the constancy of party allegiance.

The fact that nearly everyone in our samples could be placed on a unitary dimension of party identification and that the idea of prior movements on this dimension was immediately understood are themselves important findings about the nature of party support within the electorate. In view

of the loose, federated structure of American parties it was not obvious in advance that people could respond to party in these undifferentiated terms. Apparently the positive and negative feelings that millions of individuals have toward the parties are the result of orientations of a diffuse and generalized character that have a common psychological meaning even though there may be a good deal of variation in the way party is perceived. . . .

PARTY IDENTIFICATION AND ELECTORAL CHOICE

The role of general partisan orientations in molding attitudes toward the elements of politics is thus very clear. As a consequence of this role, party identification has a profound impact on behavior. A sense of its impact may be gained if we . . . express the probability that a given individual would vote in a given partisan direction. From the strength and direction of attitudes toward the various elements of politics we could order the individuals in our samples according to the probability of their voting Republican. That is, we could form an array extending from those most likely to vote Democratic to those most likely to vote Republican. Let us now make explicit the impact party identification has on behavior through its influence on attitude, by showing a separate array for each of five groups defined by our party identification scale. For each of the distributions shown in Fig. 1, the horizontal dimension is the probability an individual will vote Republican; to the left this probability is low (that is, the likelihood the individual will vote Democratic is high), and to the right the probability that the individual will vote Republican is high. The effect of party is seen at once in the changing location of the distributions along this probability dimension as we consider successively Strong Democrats, Weak Democrats, Independents, Weak Republicans, and Strong

---

[3] Because Republican identifiers voted with somewhat greater frequency than Democratic identifiers in these years, the Democratic edge in party allegiance was slightly less among voters.

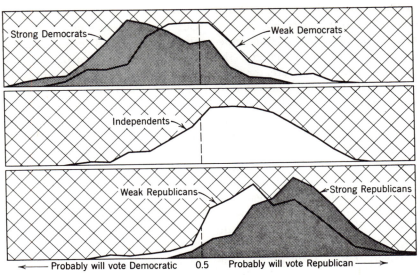

Probability of voting Republican calculated
from evaluations of elements of National Politics

Fig. 1 Probable direction of vote by party identification groups, 1956.

Republicans. The moving positions of these arrays show clearly the impact of party identification on the forces governing behavior.

The properties of Fig. 1 serve also to demonstrate once again that party allegiance is not the sole determinant of the attitudes supporting behavior. In the election of 1956 all five of these arrays were "biased" in the Republican direction in the sense that many more strong or weak Democrats than strong or weak Republicans are seen to be probable voters for the opposite party and fewer Independents are probable democratic voters than are probable Republican voters. Evidently in this election powerful antecedent factors other than party allegiance influenced in a direction favorable to the Republican Party the psychological forces acting on behavior.

The distributions of Fig. 1 foreshadow the division of the presidential vote within the several party identification groups in the election of 1956. In view of the dependence of voting choice on the psychological forces we have treated, these probability arrays lead us to expect extreme differences in the division of the vote across the party groups. They lead us to expect, too, that the Republican Party had an advantage in this election in securing the votes of Independents and of persons identifying with the opposite party. Both these expectations are confirmed by Table 4.

Differences in the motivational forces acting on voters of contrasting party loyalties lead us to expect wide differences between party groups in the division of the presidential vote. Yet the variability of the vote shown in Table 4 is so extreme that it naturally raises the question whether party identification does not have a residual effect on behavior apart from its impact through the attitudes it influences so profoundly. That this residual effect is small is indicated by the fact that adding party identification to the set of attitude variables from which we have predicted behavior brings only a slight improvement in explanation of either the sense of statistical estimation or that of

TABLE 4   Relation of Party Identification to Presidential Vote

	Strong Demo- crats	Weak Demo- crats	Inde- pendents	Weak Repub- licans	Strong Repub- licans
1952					
Republican	16%	38%	67%	94%	99%
Democratic	84	62	33	6	1
	100%	100%	100%	100%	100%
Number of cases	262	274	269	171	199
1956					
Republican	15%	37%	73%	93%	99%
Democratic	85	63	27	7	1
	100%	100%	100%	100%	100%
Number of cases	286	270	305	194	211

the discrimination of actual Republican voters from actual Democratic voters.[4] The improvement that *is* found we attribute primarily to the role of party identification in motivating directly the behavior of persons who are without a well-developed image of the things to which their vote re-

[4] Incorporating party identification in the statistical model used for prediction in Chapter 3 increases the multiple correlation with voting choice from 0.72 to 0.74 in the election of 1952 and from 0.71 to 0.73 in the election of 1956. In each year the addition of this factor raises less than 2 per cent the number of persons who could be correctly classified as Republican or Democratic voters.

lates. For them, the connection of party identification and behavior may not be mediated by attitudes toward the political objects this behavior concerns. As a result, knowing their stable partisan loyalties improves our ability to predict behavior more than it does for individuals who have formed stronger evaluations of the things toward which the vote is directed.

The nature of this difference—and of our conception of the place of party identification in the forces leading to the vote—can be made clearer if we examine, in Table 5, the behavior of individuals whose attitudes

TABLE 5   Relation of Degree of Attitude Development to Direction in which Conflict of Party Identification and Partisan Evaluations Is Resolved in Voting[a]

	Those Who Have Formed Evaluations		Those Who Have Formed No Eval- uations at All
	That Are Well- Developed	That Are Poorly Developed	
Vote agrees with party identification	20%	47%	75%
Vote fails to agree with party identification	80	53	25
TOTAL	100%	100%	100%
Number of cases	143	164	36

[a] Figures in this table are based on a combination of data from the 1952 and 1956 election samples.

toward the current elements of politics contradict their sense of party identification. Among those who have a strong evaluative image of the elements of presidential politics, behavior coincides with these evaluations in 80 per cent of the cases. The fact that party allegiance prevails in only one-fifth of these cases is the more remarkable if we keep in mind the very strong relationship of party identification to the vote across the electorate as a whole. Among those who have a less clear evaluative image of the objects of politics, behavior coincides with party identification in a much greater proportion of cases. For these people the relation of party allegiance to behavior does seem to be mediated less by evaluations of political objects, although a good half of even these persons act in accord with the evaluations they have formed, rather than in accord with their party loyalties. Table 5 also describes the behavior of the very small group of individuals in our samples who identify with one of the parties yet who appear on our standard measures to have no perceptions of current political objects whatever. This is the group for which we would expect the causal sequence connecting party allegiance, attitudes toward the elements of politics, and the voting act to be most severely truncated. With evaluations of political objects playing no apparent intervening role between partisan allegiance and behavior, 75 per cent of these people simply vote their party loyalties at the polls. . . .

ORIGINS OF PARTY IDENTIFICATION

When we examine the evidence on the manner in which party attachment develops and changes during the lifetime of the individual citizen, we find a picture characterized more by stability than by change— not by rigid, immutable fixation on one party rather than the other, but by a persistent adherence and a resistance to contrary influence.

Early politicization

At the time we meet the respondents of our surveys they have reached the minimum voting age, and most of them are considerably beyond it. The only information we can obtain about their political experience in their pre-adult years depends on their recall. Hyman's review of the literature on "political socialization" brings together the available data to extend our understanding of this important stage of political growth.[5] It is apparent from his presentation that an orientation toward political affairs typically begins before the individual attains voting age and that this orientation strongly reflects his immediate social milieu, in particular his family.

Our own data are entirely consistent with this conclusion. The high degree of correspondence between the partisan preference of our respondents with that which they report for their parents may be taken as a rough measure of the extent to which partisanship is passed from one generation to the next.[6] This correspondence is somewhat higher among those people who report one or both of their parents as having been "actively concerned" with politics than among those whose parents were not politically active. If we make the reasonable assumption that in the "active" homes the political views of the parents were more frequently and intensely cognized by the children than in the inactive homes, we should of course expect to find these views more faithfully reproduced in these children when they reach adult years. In contrast, we find that persons from inactive homes, especially those with no clear political orientation, tend strongly toward nonpartisan positions themselves. For a large

[5] Herbert Hyman, *Political Socialization* (New York: Free Press of Glencoe, 1959).

[6] There are obvious weaknesses in this measure. Some of our respondents had undoubtedly carried an "inherited" party identification into early adulthood but had changed by the time we interviewed them.

proportion of the electorate the orientation toward politics expressed in our measure of party identification has its origins in the early family years. We are not able to trace the history of these families to find an explanation of why the homes of some people were politically oriented and others were not. Such homes appear to exist in all social strata, less frequently in some than in others, of course.

The persistence of partisanship

The extent to which pre-adult experience shapes the individual's political future may be judged from the constancy with which most people hold to the partisan orientation they have at the time they enter the electorate. When we ask people to recall their first presidential vote, for example, we discover that of those who can remember their first vote for President two thirds still identify with the same party they first voted for. A majority (56 per cent) of these presidential voters have never crossed party lines; they have always supported their party's candidate.

A direct assessment of the stability with which the average citizen holds to his political orientation may be obtained from his report on whether he has ever identified himself differently than he does at present. The picture is generally one of firm but not immovable attachment. The greatest mobility (32%) is found among those people whose party attachment is weakest; the strongly identified are least likely to have changed sides (only 7% of strong Democrats, and 15% of strong Republicans).

It is apparent from these various pieces of evidence that identification with political parties, once established, is an attachment which is not easily changed. Some members of the electorate do not form strong party attachments, however, and they make up a sufficiently large proportion of the population to permit the short-term influence of political forces associated with issues and candidates to play a significant role in de-

termining the outcome of specific elections. Even strong identifiers are not impervious to such influences, and, as we shall see, occasional cataclysmic national events have had the power to produce substantial realignment in long-standing divisions of political sentiment.

FLUCTUATIONS IN PARTY IDENTIFICATION

Changes in public attitudes may be classified according to the type of stimulus that produces them. We may speak of *personal forces*, which move individuals selectively without reference to the larger social categories to which they belong, or of *social forces*, which move large sections of the population more or less simultaneously. Personal forces produce changes that vary in an uncorrelated way from individual to individual and do not have a significant impact on the prevailing pattern of attitudes, even though the total proportion of people shifting their position may be sizable. Social forces influence large numbers of people in similar ways and may produce substantial realignments of the total distribution of attitudes.[7]

Changes produced by personal forces

A variety of circumstances in the life of the ordinary citizen have political significance for him as a person without having any accompanying implications for broader groups. When we examine the reports of those of our respondents who shifted parties for reasons that appear to be entirely individual, we find that their change in partisanship tended to be associated with a change in their social milieu. A marriage, a new job, or a change in neighborhood may

[7] This formulation closely resembles a model for the explanation of attitude changes developed by George Katona. See his "Attitude Change: Instability of Response and Acquisition of Experience" ("*Psychological Monographs*," Vol. 72, No. 10; Washington, D.C.: American Psychological Association, Inc., 1958).

place a person under strong social pressure to conform to political values different from his own. Close personal relationships are usually associated with common political identifications in American society, and discrepancies tend to create strain, especially if the conflicting political views are strongly held.

Of the 20 per cent of our respondents who say they have changed party affiliation during their lifetime only about one in six explains this change as a result of personal influence. Considering the high degree of mobility in American society, one might have anticipated that changes of this kind would be more numerous. The movements of large numbers of people from the farm to the city, from the city to the suburbs, from region to region, and from one employment situation to another undoubtedly result in profound differences in their manner of living. But none of these movements necessarily implies a change in one's immediate surroundings. As we know, there are large representations of both parties at virtually all social and occupational levels and it would not be surprising for a person of either political persuasion to find himself among copartisans in almost any new situation into which he moved. We would, in fact, expect him to seek out such associates. Only in certain special groups, such as labor union members in mass industry in Northern metropolitan centers or high income business owners and executives, do we find such strong consensus of political belief that a dissenter might find himself in a lonely position.

Changes produced by social forces

Although the changes resulting from purely personal circumstances may be expected to occur about as often in one partisan direction as the other, changes brought about by experiences shared in common are likely to be cumulative. If these experiences are sufficiently intense and suf-ficiently widespread, their political consequences may be profound.

Social forces create cumulative changes, but these changes need not disturb the prevailing balance of party strength. If the stimulus to which the public is subjected strikes different segments of the electorate in ways that have contrasting political implications, the resulting shifts in partisanship may change the makeup of each party's support without altering the relative proportions supporting each party. The impact of social forces may also have quite a different character, producing systematic movements from one party to the other that are not offset by movements in the opposite direction. There are two general types of public experience that appear to have this quality: those experiences associated with great national crises and, less obviously, those associated with progress through the life cycle. There have been two occasions when national crises have shaken prevailing political loyalties so violently that they reversed the balance of party strength throughout the country.

The political upheaval associated with the Civil War imposed a regional dimension on the partisan attachments of the American electorate. The violent reaction in the East and Midwest to the passage of the Kansas-Nebraska Act in 1854 led to the creation of the Republican Party, committed to resisting the extension of the "great moral, social, and political evil" of slavery. The Free Soil movement, taken up as a major principle by the Republican Party, and the Homestead Act of 1862 created a resource of rural Republican strength throughout the Northern and Western areas. Within a short period the political contours of the nation had been drastically reshaped. The South, which in prewar years had divided its votes in proportions similar to those of the North, became the Solid South. Northern communities that had been Democratic turned Republican and remained so for decades. The distribution of partisan attachments in the nation today, a century after the Civil War, follows the same regional lines laid down at that time.

The second national crisis that reshaped the political profile of the nation took place during the lifetime of most of our respondents, and we can see directly the impact of that event in their lives. The economic collapse that befell the nation during the administration of Herbert Hoover swept out of office a party that had dominated national politics since the election of William McKinley in 1896. The scope of the reversal of the party fortunes that followed 1932 is amply documented by the election statistics. In the early years of the New Deal there was a swing to the Democratic ticket, which was felt in varying degrees throughout the country. The tide then receded, and those areas that had been centers of Republican strength returned to Republican majorities. But the Republican Party did not regain the national majority that it had obviously had prior to 1932. When we ask from what levels of society the Democratic Party drew this new strength,

we find from our survey data and from the aggregative election figures that the impact of the events of that period appears to have been felt most strongly by the youth, the economically underprivileged, and the minority groups.

Youth. Our inquiries into the political histories of our respondents lead us to believe that a larger component of the Democratic gain came from young voters entering the electorate and older people who had previously failed to vote than from Republicans who defected from their party.

A demonstration of the impact of the depression on the people reaching voting age at that time is given in Fig. 2. We have here arrayed our respondents by age group according to the party identification they reported at the time of our interview with them. Those members of the present electorate who came of age during the 1920's have a lower proportion of Democratic identifiers than do any of the groups that entered the electorate in later years. The sharp increase in Democratic identification among those who reached their majority at the end of this decade or during the early 1930's does not represent the total shift toward

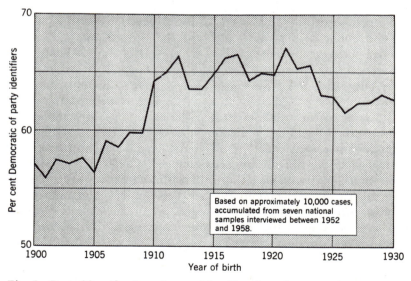

Based on approximately 10,000 cases, accumulated from seven national samples interviewed between 1952 and 1958.

Fig. 2   Party identification of party identifiers born between 1900 and 1930.

the Democratic Party at that time, but it does show the proportion of that shift that has persisted over the intervening years to the present time.

Economic groups. The appeal of the New Deal was unquestionably strongly economic in character; it had, after all, been brought into being in the midst of the greatest economic catastrophe in American history. Mr. Roosevelt spoke about the "forgotten man" and sponsored a program of social legislation that his critics regarded as outright socialism. It is difficult to estimate how much influence all this had on the economic composition of the followings of the two parties, but it can be said with assurance that the economic and class distinctions between the two parties increased during this period. Such associations as had existed prior to the Depression between the less favored sections of the electorate and the Democratic Party were undoubtedly greatly enhanced.

On the basis of extensive analysis of the election returns from 1932 and 1936 Key offers these "educated guesses." "The policies of the New Deal brought in 1936 substantial new support from their beneficiaries. Metropolitan, industrial workers turned in heavy Democratic majorities. The unemployed, and those who feared they might become unemployed, voted Democratic in higher degree. Organized labor moved more solidly into the Democratic ranks."[8]

Our surveys do not go backward in time sufficiently for us to follow the political changes at the various economic levels during the Depression period, but the impact of the Depression is unmistakable in the images of the parties that we find in the public mind long after that tragic decade had passed. The association of the Republican Party with economic depression was one of the strongest features of the picture the public held of that party at the time of our 1952 study. Through their twenty years out of office the Republican Party could not erase the memory that lingered in many minds of the hardships of the Depression nor rid itself of the onus of responsibility for them.

Minority groups. The impact of the Depression and the New Deal was not exclusively economic. The philosophy of the Roosevelt Administration contained a strong element of social equalitarianism, which gave it a special appeal to religious and racial minorities who had reason to feel themselves discriminated against. Catholics have had a long history of association with the Democratic Party. During the Eisenhower elections there were substantial defections among Catholics to the Republican nominee, but even at that time Catholics were more likely (5–2) to consider themselves Democrats than Republicans.

The Jewish minority comprises one of the most Democratic groups to be found in the electorate; Democratic Jews outnumber Republican Jews in the order of 4–1. During the 1920's the vote in heavily Jewish districts of the Eastern metropolises ran as high as 80 per cent Republican.[9] Although vote is not the same as party identification, it can scarcely be doubted that the orientation of this group toward the two parties was substantially altered during the 1930's. We may surmise that the rise of the Nazi dictatorship in Germany and the opposition of the Roosevelt Administration to it must have played an important role in this change. Whatever the cause, the shift of Jewish allegiancies to the Democratic Party was one of the most impressive of the several group movements in political preference during the Roosevelt period.

[8] V. O. Key, *Politics, Parties, and Pressure Groups* (4th ed., Thomas Y. Crowell Company, New York, 1958), p. 578.

[9] Lawrence H. Fuchs, *The Political Behavior of American Jews* (New York: Free Press of Glencoe, 1956), p. 56. See also Oscar Handlin, *The Uprooted* (Boston: Little Brown, 1951), p. 216.

Prior to the 1930's, so far as we can tell from election statistics, the prevailing political preference among Negroes was Republican. This was a consequence, of course, of the Civil War and the attachment of Negroes to the party of Lincoln. During the 1930's politics took on a different significance to the Negro tenth of the electorate. It is impossible to know whether the shift of Negro allegiances to the Democratic standard from the traditions inherited from earlier generations occurred as the reactions of individual Negroes to the personalities and events of the times or as a mass movement resulting largely from the mobilization of Negro sentiment by an articulate leadership. No doubt both of these circumstances were present. In any case, the conversion of Negroes to the Democratic Party was very substantial. During the Eisenhower period Democratically identified Negroes outnumbered Republican Negroes by a margin of 3–1. . . .

Intensity of identification. We find a steady increase in strong party attachments as we move through successive age levels, demonstrating the presence of age-related influences that are obviously not random. Young people, just entering the electorate, are more likely than any of the older age groups to call themselves Independents. This proportion drops among people in their late twenties and thirties and is accompanied by a proportionate increase in the number of strong identifiers. The older half of the electorate are clearly more likely to show a strong party attachment, with the most extreme position of all held by those people over 65 years old, a group that now constitutes approximately one twelfth of our adult population; 50 per cent of this age group are strong party identifiers, compared with 24 per cent of those 21 to 24 years of age. . . .

42. The Role of Social Class in American Voting Behavior

Robert R. Alford

While many Americans believe theirs is a "classless society," voting research has shown moderate, but distinct, differences in the party preferences of blue-collar and white-collar workers. Robert Alford, Professor of Sociology at the University of Wisconsin, finds that these differences continue to be as evident today as in the past and that they exist independently of religious or regional factors.

* * *

Social class and political behavior are probably not as closely associated in the United States as in some other Anglo-American countries. The parties in the United States are not explicitly linked to class-organizations and do not appeal for support on the basis of class. Nevertheless, the parties are seen by the electorate as linked to specific class-interests, and undoubtedly many people vote in accordance with an image of the parties as representing their economic interests. A number of characteristics of American society and its political system undoubtedly reduce the relation of class and vote. The enormous size of the country, its division into fifty states with real degrees of sovereignty, tremendous ethnic and religious diversity, combined with the decentralized party structure, all reduce the salience of *national* class-divisions as the main basis for party cleavages. That national class-divisions still exist, and divide the parties even as distinctly as they do, is a measure of the degree of economic and political integration the nation has achieved.

From the *Western Political Quarterly*, vol. 26, no. 1 (March 1963), pp. 180–194, with footnote omissions, by permission of the University of Utah.

The diversity of support for the political parties has been shown by a series of studies of voting. The initial study, setting a pattern for subsequent studies both in the United States and Great Britain, was *The People's Choice,* a survey of voting in Sandusky, Ohio, in the 1940 presidential election. Since this was a study of only one northern city and its environs, the regional economic and political diversity of the United States presumably did not affect voting behavior. Still, not only social class differences, but religious and rural-urban differences, were found crucially to affect the political loyalties of voters. Being in a low-income group, a Catholic, or an urban resident, all predisposed a voter toward the Democrats; being in a high-income group, a Protestant, or a rural resident predisposed a voter toward the Republicans. The consequences of "contradictory" social characteristics presumably pushing people in opposite political directions—the now classic notion of "cross-pressures"—were the main focus of this study. The point here is that a relatively high proportion of persons in Sandusky was under cross-pressures, indicating that the diversity of sources of political loyalties is great in the United States.[1]

The main problem of this article will be neither to explain the existence of such class-bases of support as exist for the national political parties in the United States nor to show the diversity of support besides that based upon class; but rather to examine, by means of survey data, whether the relation of social class to voting has declined since the 1930's, and in which religious or regional groups.

Despite the diversity of support for the parties, American political parties are both perceived as supported by, and actually are supported by, persons at different occupational, educational, and income levels, although there is a sizable minority that votes for the "other" party. The voting studies have also made this point clearly, and there is no need to go into details. The authors of a study of the 1954 Congressional election summarized their results as follows:

> Our data make it evident that a number of the major population categories have a persistent inclination toward one or the other of the two parties. The major theme of this group orientation in voting is social class. The prestige groups—educational, economic—are the most dependable sources of Republican support, while the laborers, Negroes, unemployed, and other low-income and low-education groups are the strongest sources of the Democratic vote.[2]

And the parties can be distinguished as representing Left and Right positions. According to Max Beloff:

> If we take the simple view that there is, other things being equal, likely to be one party of the rich and one party of the poor, the Republicans fill the bill for the former, and outside the South, the Democrats fill it for the latter. The former accept roughly the justice of the present distribution of worldly goods between classes and regions; the latter by and large welcome government intervention to alter it.[3]

The phrases "by and large" and "other things being equal" hide a multitude of

---

[1] Other such voting studies are: B. Berelson, P. Lazarsfeld, and W. McPhee, *Voting* (Chicago: University of Chicago Press, 1954), and a series of studies done by the Survey Research Center at the University of Michigan, beginning with the presidential election of 1948. These are reported in A. Campbell, G. Gurin, and W. E. Miller, *The Voter Decides* (Evanston: Row, Peterson, 1954); Angus Campbell and Homer C. Cooper, *Group Differences in Attitudes and Votes* (Ann Arbor: Survey Research Center, University of Michigan, 1956), and A. Campbell, P. E. Converse, W. E. Miller, and D. E. Stokes, *The American Voter* (New York: Wiley, 1960). For a summary of the findings of many voting studies, see S. M. Lipset, *Political Man* (New York: Doubleday, 1960), Chaps, 7, 8, and 9.

[2] Campbell and Cooper, *op. cit.,* p. 35.

[3] Max Beloff, *The American Federal Government* (New York: Oxford University Press, 1959), pp. 157–58.

contradictions in the policies and voting patterns of Democratic and Republican legislators, but if that statement is accepted as substantially correct (and no effort to verify it will be made here), then the class-bases of the major American parties are understandable. Another compilation of poll data from seven national polls conducted from 1944 to 1952 found that two-and-a-half times as many business and professional people thought the Republicans best serve their interests as thought the Democrats do, and that seven times as many unskilled workers and four times as many skilled workers thought the Democrats best serve their interests as thought the Republicans do. Whether or not the parties actually serve their interests better is, of course, not proved by these images of the parties, but this evidence at least shows that American voting behavior is roughly in line with voters' conceptions of their own interests.

But, has the association of class and vote declined since the 1930's? It is by now a commonplace notion that the salience of class for voting was less in the prosperous 1950's than it was in the depressed 1930's. The political scientist V. O. Key, Jr., for example, has asserted that

> . . . perhaps in the election of 1936 the party division most nearly coincided with differences of income and occupation. That coincidence declined, as class-relevant questions faded from the forefront, and in 1952 and 1956 Republicans won substantial support in the lower-income groups.[4]

A recent study actually found a decline of class-voting in the period 1948 to 1956, which seemingly documents the decreasing importance of social class for voting behavior. The authors of *The American Voter* computed an index of "status-polarization" which showed that the correlation between the occupational status of respondents and their partisan vote in three separate na-

tional surveys in 1948, 1952 and 1956 dropped from 0.44 to 0.26 to 0.12. According to the authors:

> The most striking feature of the polarization trend in the recent past has been the steady and rapid depolarization between 1948 and 1956. This decline occurred in a postwar period when the nation was enjoying a striking ascent to prosperity and a consequent release from the pressing economic concerns that had characterized the Depression.[5]

The way that this decline of "status-polarization" is explained is also relevant here, because the authors infer that changes have taken place since the 1930's, although they have no specific evidence on such changes. A substitute for this is evidence on the status-polarization (or class-voting, the term which I shall henceforth use, to avoid confusion) among different age-groups. In their 1948 and 1952 surveys, a marked "depression-effect" was found. Persons in their twenties and thirties during the depression of the 1930's (presumably those most affected by it) exhibited the highest level of class-voting. In 1956, this was not evident, and the authors conclude that this illustrates the "fading effects of the Depression."

It may be noted here that this finding of highest class-voting among the Depression generation does not contradict the usual inference that persons in such a generation should be more similar in their political attitudes and behavior than persons not sharing this common experience. Another study of American voting behavior, specifically focused upon the problem of generational differences, found that the Depression generation (taking those who were born in the period 1913–22 as the Depression gen-

---

[4] V. O. Key, Jr., *Politics, Parties and Pressure Groups* (4th ed.; New York: Crowell, 1958), p. 274.

[5] Campbell, *et al., The American Voter*, p. 347. The method of computing the index of status polarization is identical to that used for the index of class-voting to be described later. I use the different terms because of a different theoretical concern, with long-term rather than short-term fluctuations of the effect of various social factors upon voting.

eration) was likely to be more Democratic, regardless of sex, occupation, income, or other social differences. In spite of the Michigan finding that manual and nonmanual strata in the Depression generation are farther apart in their voting patterns than any other age group, political consensus is still present. Both strata were affected similarly by major political currents. These two findings indicate the relative independence of the absolute level of vote for a party from the degree of political divergence of classes.

But the Michigan results may not reflect actual voting patterns in the 1930's. Remember that their results are for persons interviewed in the 1940's and 1950's, divided by age. Whether age-differences at one point in time truly reflect past behavior and the differential impact of a historical crisis upon persons at different ages when the crisis occurs is an inference which may or may not be justified. Data to be presented may clarify the real patterns of class-voting and change in those patterns since the 1930's.

The decline of class-voting between 1948 and 1956 is thus linked by the authors of *The American Voter* to "increasing prosperity and fading memories of the Great Depression of the 1930's." These two factors should imply a continuing decrease of class-voting since the 1930's. But, the authors must account for another empirical finding of their own, that class-voting was lower in 1944 than in 1948, after which it dropped almost linearly. They suggest that variations in the importance of domestic economic versus foreign-policy issues account for this change. When economic issues are important, class-voting tends to rise; when noneconomic issues such as foreign policy are important, class-voting tends to drop. " . . . war is a basic public concern that may eclipse those problems of domestic economics leading to cleavage among status interest groups."[6] The authors thus infer what the patterns of class-voting *might* have

been during the 1930's. Presumably class-voting should have been high in the elections of 1932 and 1936, when class issues were dominant. With World War II, "national" issues superseded class ones, and class-voting should have been lower in 1940 and 1944. As they put it, "polarization tendencies carrying over from the Great Depression may have been dampened as a result of the national crisis posed by the Second World War, rebounding upward after that conflict was concluded." Domestic economic issues again became important, resulting in the rise of class-voting in 1948. After this peak, "the renewal of the threat of global war and the outbreak of hostilities in Korea may have acted, in concert with increasing prosperity, to depress the level of status polarization [class-voting] once again."[7]

The inferences thus made are logical ones from the data available to the authors of that study, and are relevant to one of the main problems of concern here: whether class-voting has declined since the 1930's. This particular problem is not of major concern to these authors, since they are focusing upon "short-term" fluctuations. These inferences as to declining class-voting certainly imply that a long-term decline of the importance of social class in the support of the American parties has taken place. But has it?

TRENDS IN CLASS-VOTING IN THE UNITED STATES SINCE THE 1930's

Although fluctuations in the level of class-voting have occurred in the period 1936 to 1960, there is some evidence that no consistent decline of class-voting has occurred. Before the evidence for this conclusion is presented, a brief amplification of the assumptions upon which the manipulation of the data is based is in order.

In estimating the importance of the class bases of politics, shifts to the Right or to

---

[6] Campbell, *et al., The American Voter*, p. 361.   [7] *Ibid.*

the Left should be minimized, because they blur the differences between social strata. In such political systems as the Anglo-American two-party ones, not just the United States, political shifts usually occur in the same *direction* in all politically relevant social groups, although not always to the same degree. Such a shift to the Right as the Eisenhower victories in 1952 and 1956 could conceivably be regarded as a decline in the importance of social class as a determinant of political behavior. It is probably true that a large vote for Eisenhower among workers meant that class-identifications were less important in those elections than in 1948, for example. But, my contention is that only if the *gap* between manual and nonmanual support of a party has lessened, can one speak meaningfully of a decline of class-voting. The data presented in *The American Voter* show without question that not only did all social groups vote more Republican in 1952 and 1956 than they did in 1948, but that underneath this shift to the Right, social classes moved closer together *in addition*. But, was this part of a long-term decline of the importance of the class-bases of politics? Or was this only a fluctuation within the "normal range" of change of the

class-bases of American politics, given the social and political structure of American society?

The data to be presented are derived from varied sources—University of Michigan Survey Research Center surveys for the years 1948 and 1952 and Gallup and Roper surveys for the other years. Results from a total of fifteen surveys were tabulated from the IBM cards, and are shown in Figure 1. It must be emphasized that there is no intention here of implying that the data gathered by the Gallup and Roper polling organizations (especially from surveys prior to 1948) are as reliable as those gathered by the Survey Research Center. The latter uses probability samples whereas Gallup and Roper use quota samples, for which a sampling error cannot be computed, and into which the biases of interviewers enter to a far larger degree. Nevertheless, no other data are available for national samples prior to 1948, and the problems of sampling error, particularly the underrepresentation of workers in the early years of polling, are compensated for somewhat by the initial control for class.

Figure 1 shows the level of Democratic voting among manual and nonmanual occupational strata from 1936 to 1960. The

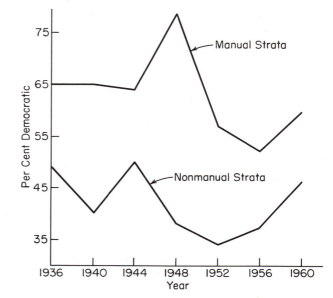

Fig. 1 Class voting in the United States, 1936–1960.

gap or "distance" between the two lines may be considered to be an index of the level of class-voting in the American political system, and will be so termed henceforth (class-voting in 1948 was thus +41 percentage points, in a Michigan survey). Considerable shifting in the Democratic vote is evident, although class-voting was not sharply different in the 1950's from its level in the 1930's. About two-thirds of the manual workers voted Democratic in the three elections between 1936 and 1944; their Democratic vote rose sharply in 1948, dropped just as sharply in 1952 and 1956, then rose back to about 60 per cent in 1960. Among the middle class, the Democratic vote stayed between 40 and 50 per cent between 1936 and 1944, dropped below 40 in the following three elections, and rose again to 46 per cent in 1960. The only election in which both strata moved in sharply opposite directions was 1948, which might be termed a "non-consensual election." If that election had been chosen as the beginning of a time series, the end of class-voting might have been predicted, but

data for the longer period indicate that 1948 was exceptional. The "range" of class-voting has been in this period between 15 and 25 percentage points, except for the 1948 election.

No pattern of consistent decline of class-voting is thus evident, and its level only reached that of Britain and Australia in the 1948 election. Nor has the level dropped to the average Canadian level in any election. It may be concluded from the evidence presented in Figure 1 that there has been no substantial shift in the class bases of American politics since the 1930's, despite the prosperity since World War II, and despite the shifts to the Right in the Eisenhower era.

These data also permit some evaluation of the thesis of the authors of *The American Voter* concerning the causes of short-term fluctuations of class-voting. Class-voting was not high in 1936; quite the contrary. Two separate national Gallup samples in 1936 show that class-voting was as low in that year as in any subsequent one. Table I shows that this low level was due

TABLE I   Rank Order of United States Regions in the Level of Class-Voting, 1944–1960*

Region	Frequency of Rank							Rank Index Score
	1	2	3	4	5	6	7	
West Central	5	1	1					10
Mountain	1	3	1	1			1	14
New England	1	1	3		1†		1†	24
East Central	1†	1†	1	1	2	1		26
Pacific		1	4	2				28
Middle Atlantic					2	5		40
South		1†			1	2	3	40

* An index of class-voting was computed for each survey by subtracting the proportion of persons in nonmanual occupations preferring the Democratic party from the proportion of persons in manual occupations preferring the same party. See R. Alford, "A Suggested Index of the Relation of Voting to Social Class," *Public Opinion Quarterly*, 26 (1962), 417–25, for discussion of the range of variation of the index in two-party systems, and problems of applicability and computation. The rank index score was computed by multiplying the number of the rank by the number of times a given region appeared in that rank. Ties were counted twice, then the next rank was skipped. Regions correspond to the census classification of states.
† These cases indicate the deviations found in 1960 surveys from the usual pattern. There were two surveys for each of the years 1956 and 1960.

to a high Democratic vote among persons in nonmanual occupations. All social strata felt the "need for a change" and voted Democratic accordingly. Social classes were not polarized further by the class issues of the 1930's, but pulled over to the party that promised change.

Why the "depression-generation" in the later surveys conducted by the Michigan Survey Research Center exhibited more class-voting is an interesting question, but one which cannot be explored here. Possibly during such a period of crisis a consensus emerged on the proper political path. But, after the crisis was over, the *memory* of the crisis assumed a different meaning for different social strata. For workers, the memory may have reinforced their Democratic allegiances. For the middle class, it may have reinforced their Republican attachments, since the actual legislation carried out in the crisis period furthered the centralization of government which they oppose when accepting Republican ideology.

Thus, the inference in *The American Voter* that class-voting is likely to be higher in elections in which domestic economic issues are salient is weakened by some data from 1936. Its inference is also weakened by the rise of class-voting in 1940, an election in which presumably the issues of foreign policy were dominant, rather than class ones. The drop in 1944 is also not consistent, since by that time the issues of national interest were abating, and domestic conflicts were again assuming importance. But the point is not to debate the salience of different issues in different elections. A reliable conclusion demands much more subtle evidence than is available here. The main point is that there is no evidence that class-voting is declining.

Before we can accept the conclusion that class-voting has not declined, it is important to consider where it may have declined, or where it may have actually increased. Trends in various regions of the United

States, as well as among various religious groups, may offer a clue as to the future role of social class in American politics. It is not at all clear, for example, that class-voting will remain as low as it is. The disappearance of the loyalties of middle-class Southerners to the Democratic party, when and if it occurs, may mean a rise of class-voting, and therefore a realignment of the social bases of the parties more along class lines. And the possible dwindling of special religious and ethnic loyalties to the parties may have similar consequences. Clinton Rossiter has suggested that in the future

the influence of class on political behavior and allegiance may become even more visible than it is today, especially as the influences of ethnology and religion fade ever so slowly but steadily from view. . . . We are still a long way from the class struggle in American politics, but that does not mean that class consciousness is a negligible factor. To the contrary, it must inevitably become a more important factor as Americans become ever more alert to the rewards and symbols of status.[8]

The specific questions which can be answered from the survey data include the following: Has class-voting declined or increased in any United States region, and does this change seem to be related to any pervasive social changes taking place, such as urbanization or industrialization? We might expect that if any trend toward the political reintegration of the South is evident, class-voting might have increased in that region since the early 1940's. On the other hand, in the most urbanized and older regions, such as New England, we might see a decline of class-voting, and these two trends might cancel each other out, to produce the over-all lack of change. Or, we might find that class-voting is higher in the urban South than in the rest of that area, and infer that this is a sign of impending change of the social bases of Southern

[8] Clinton Rossiter, *Parties and Politics in America* (Ithaca: Cornell University Press, 1960), p. 166.

politics, and an omen of a future national realignment more along class lines.

Similarly, trends in the class-voting patterns of Protestants and Catholics may foreshadow the future. It is possible that class-voting has dropped among Protestants but increased among Catholics, to cancel each other out, as far as an over-all index is concerned. The diversity of politics in the United States implies that a single measure of the importance of a single factor for voting behavior is almost meaningless, unless the relationship is examined in various other subgroups of the population.

REGIONALISM AND CLASS-VOTING

The sectional character of American politics is a commonplace, and does not need documentation here. Not only the South, but many states have had a traditional alignment with one of the major parties. This has meant that each of the parties has long cherished a sectional stronghold, within which the other party had little chance of winning legislative representation.

> In 1904 less than one-seventh of the population of the U.S. lived in states in which the parties contested the election on relatively equal terms, while in 1920 only about 12 million out of 105 million Americans lived in states in which they had a choice between the two major parties both of which had some chance of winning.[9]

And, as V. O. Key puts it:

> Sectionalism . . . contributes to the multi-class composition of each of the major parties, a characteristic bewildering to those who regard only a class politics as "natural." A politics that arrays the people of one section against those of another pulls into one party men of all social strata. A common interest bound the southern banker, merchant, cotton farmer

and wage earner together against the northern combination of finance, manufacturing and segments of industrial labor.[10]

One major question which can be answered by survey data is whether class-voting is actually substantially lower in areas such as the South. The second major question of concern here is, of course, whether class-voting has declined in any major region, or whether it has increased, particularly in the South. Since the South is the chief example of political regionalism, and since its domination of the Congress has important political consequences for the nation, its special voting patterns will be of primary interest in my discussion of regionalism.

Southern politics is a one-party politics, dominated by extremely conservative elements, which distort the national party pattern by introducing a Right bias within the Democratic party, the major Left party of the nation. The dominance of Southerners on key committees determining which legislature shall come before the whole House of Representatives, a dominance due to their long seniority and lack of opposition, is some measure of the dominant role of the South in the American political system. It is therefore of both practical and theoretical importance if the regional loyalties of Southerners are being replaced by political cleavages similar to those in other regions.

In these selected surveys (selected only in the sense that the regional data were available), the over-all level of class-voting varied between +14 and +22 percentage points, while the highest level achieved in any region was +35 (in the Mountain states in 1952) and the lowest was −1 (New England in 1960 in one survey). Unfortunately, sampling error is so great for particular regional figures that trends within regions cannot be regarded as reliable, and the few

9 E. E. Schattschneider, "United States: The Functional Approach to Party Government," in Sigmund Neumann (ed.), *Modern Political Parties* (Chicago: University of Chicago Press, 1955), pp. 203–204.

10 Key, *op. cit.*, p. 267.

generalizations to be offered must be regarded as speculative. An attempt to discern some regular difference among regions in the average level of class-voting is presented in Table I.

Table I lists the number of times each region was found in the certain rank when the level of class-voting was computed for each region. It is noteworthy that most of the sharpest deviations were found in 1960 surveys, particularly in regions where a pro-Catholic or anti-Catholic effect might have been expected: New England and the South.

The political diversity of the United States is shown by the high degree of variation in class-voting over time within and between the major regions of the country. (The data showing changes over time will not be presented in detail.) The Eisenhower and Kennedy elections did not mark a dwindling of this difference, but an intensification of it. If the single survey available for 1948 is representative of the electoral shifts in that year, the major regions, save for the "Mountain" area, drew closer together in that year—a "class election—than in any other between 1944 and 1956. No apparent dwindling of the political diversity of America's regions appears in the original data, and no apparent trend toward the reintegration of the South.

Since the focus of this article is not upon explaining variations in regional political patterns, no detailed exploration of the regularities shown in Table I can be undertaken. It seems probable, however, that this is no accident, and that certain historical and structural features of these regions could be found that would account for these differences. The consistently low level of class-voting in the South is no surprise, and easily explained. But why does the West North Central region exhibit almost the highest consistent pattern of class-voting? These are the Midwest agrarian states, largely Republican (Minnesota, Iowa, Mis-

souri, North and South Dakota, Nebraska, and Kansas). Clearly this is not a "regionalism" like that of the South, because both strata are not pulled over to a single party. On the contrary, the Democratic vote of manual workers is usually above the average, that of nonmanuals usually below. For some of these states, the high level of class-voting may reflect the historical patterns of agrarian revolts, expressed through the NonPartisan League in North Dakota, and the Socialist traditions of Minnesota. (It must be noted that these data do not include farmers, but only persons in manual and nonmanual occupations.)

The vacillations of the Mountain region (the strip along the Rocky Mountains from Montana to New Mexico) are not so easily laid to a particular historical tradition, and may merely reflect the small number of cases (the fewest in any region), or the heterogeneity of the region. Part of this vacillation may be due to its frontier character. Further research might be able to pin down some of the reasons for this and other regional regularities of political behavior.

Although no evidence has been found from national surveys that the South, at least, is becoming more like other regions in level of class-voting—and therefore is losing its special regional allegiance to the Democratic party—other kinds of evidence indicate that such a change may be imminent. The Republican vote has steadily climbed in the South, and may be derived from middle-class more than from working-class persons.

Also, to some extent Southern political distinctiveness may be due to its character as a "backward" area, and not to true differences in the allegiances of similar kinds of voters. Some evidence to this effect is that urban Republicanism in the South has become quite similar to urban Republicanism elsewhere.[11] The higher Democratic

[11] See Donald S. Strong, *Urban Republicanism in the South* (University of Alabama, Bureau of Pub-

percentages may increasingly come from rural Democratic loyalties (which are Republican elsewhere), and which will be as hard to change as any rural traditionalisms.

The authors of *The American Voter* note that "generally speaking, status polarization is lower in the South than in other regions of the nation," but their data show that "between 1952 and 1956 . . . when levels of [status-polarization] were declining elsewhere, there was an actual increase of polarization in the South, from a coefficient not much above zero to a point of clear significance in 1956." In a footnote they suggest that "this trend may reflect growing industrialization and urbanization in the South, processes that are likely in the long run to blur traditional differences in political behavior generally." This suggestion reflects a hypothesis which this writer shares: class-voting should increase if and when the influence of traditional regional, ethnic, and religious loyalties to party dwindles.

---

lic Administration, 1960), for an ecological study of several Southern cities. The author concluded that "prosperous southerners are now showing the same political preferences as their economic counterparts outside the South. Here one may see the abandonment of ancient loyalties forged a century ago and their replacement by voting based on calculations of class advantage" (p. 57).

Also, "status voting was more prevalent among *weak* party identifiers than among strong in the South in 1952," with a smaller but consistent such relationship in 1956. This might indicate that persons who are breaking away from their Democratic identifications are predominantly middle class, and are the voters who both are least strongly identified with the Democrats and are those whose shift to the Republicans accounts for the increasing class-voting (or status-polarization) in the South in 1952 and 1956 shown by *The American Voter* data.

RELIGION AND CLASS VOTING

The continuing diversity of American politics is shown not only by regional but also by religious differences in class-voting. As before, the question is: has class-voting dropped among either Protestants or Catholics, and what possible significance do shifts in class-voting among either religious grouping have for a future trend?

Evidence from six surveys in five different presidential elections indicates that class-voting may be declining slightly among Protestants, but that nonclass factors affect the voting behavior of Catholics so much that no clear trend exists. Figure 2 shows

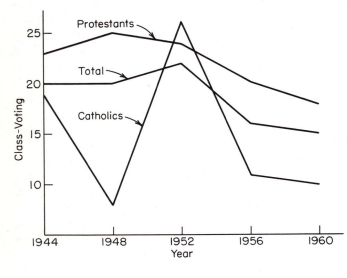

Fig. 2 Class voting among Protestants and Catholics, United States, 1944–1960.

the vacillations of class-voting among Catholics and an apparent slight decline among Protestants. (See Table I for the method of computing the index of class-voting.)

No *sharp* decline is found among Protestants, and the margin for error is such that we must conclude that for Protestants as well as for the total electorate in the United States, there is no evidence of any change in class-voting. As a matter of fact, the Protestant level is more consistent than the Catholic, and implies that much of the vacillation of class-voting, possibly even in earlier years, is due to a higher level of political shifting among Catholics than among Protestants.

Protestants have exhibited a higher level of class-voting than Catholics in each election except in 1952. The general pattern is consistent with the presumed ethnic and minority sentiments among Catholics which override class sentiments as a basis for political loyalties. If only the 1944, 1948 and 1952 data were available, it would appear that Protestants and Catholics were becoming just alike in their levels of class-voting, since a pattern of convergence is evident which culminated in actual higher class-voting among Catholics than among Protestants in 1952. This change was due to a rise among the former, not a drop among the latter. More specifically, it was due to a pull of the Catholic middle class over to the Republican nominee.

The 1952 election was the only one in which the religious deviation of both manual and nonmanual Catholics was about equal. In all of the other surveys, Catholic nonmanuals were much farther from Protestant nonmanuals than Catholic manuals were from Protestant manuals. Catholicism seems in the United States to have more political consequences for persons in nonmanual occupations than for manual workers. Just because nonmanual occupations are less identified as a particular social class (nonmanual occupations are less homogeneous than working-class

occupations), nonclass loyalties and identifications of various kinds affect the political behavior of persons in nonmanual occupations more easily. But, in 1952, this possible process affecting religious voting failed to operate. Nonmanual persons in different religions were, in this period only, more alike than manual persons in different religions. In 1956 and 1960, they returned to the usual pattern. This 1952 deviation may have been due to the "strong foreign policy appeal to the ethnic groups, especially the Catholics and Germans." These data indicate that such an appeal, if it were the cause of this Republican shift among the middle-class Catholics, did not affect Catholic workers, tied to the Democrats by both class and religious loyalties, and therefore class-voting among Catholics increased to a point above that of the Protestants for the only time in a fourteen-year period.

Whether class is defined objectively or subjectively, class-voting was higher in 1952 among Catholics than among Protestants, as Table II shows. Although the Democratic vote within similar strata, defined *both* by subjective and objective class, was higher for Catholics than for Protestants (except among nonmanual middle-class identifiers, among whom the Democratic vote was uniformly low), both objective and subjective class made more difference for the politics of the Catholics than of the Protestants. Holding occupation constant, the association of subjective class identification with voting was higher among Catholics than among Protestants. Holding subjective class identification constant, the association of occupation and voting was higher among Catholics than among Protestants. This is additional evidence that the lack of difference between Catholics and Protestants in 1952 was not spurious, and that politics of persons in different religions were more alike in that year than in others before or since.

In 1960, class-voting among Catholics did not change appreciably from its 1956 level,

TABLE II Per cent Voting Democratic among Protestants and Catholics, within Manual and Nonmanual Occupations Identifying Themselves as Working Class or Middle Class, United States, 1952*

(per cent)

| Occupation | Subjective Class Identification | | | Subjective |
	Total	Working	Middle	Class voting
	Protestants			
Manual	52 (422)	54 (334)	39 (88)	+15
Nonmanual	29 (330)	45 (126)	23 (185)	+22
Objective Class-voting	+23	+9	+16	
TOTAL		52 (440)	25 (273)	+27
	Catholics			
Manual	65 (184)	68 (144)	47 (34)	+21
Nonmanual	38 (98)	52 (46)	22 (50)	+30
Objective Class-voting	+27	+16	+25	
TOTAL		64 (190)	32 (84)	+32

* Michigan 1952 Survey, reported in *The Voter Decides, op. cit.* These tabulations do not appear in the book. The totals do not add up because persons declaring that there were no classes in the United States are not included. Further analysis of the same survey which considers the effect of class-identification upon political behavior appears in H. Eulau, *Class and Party in the Eisenhower Years* (New York: The Free Press of Glencoe, 1962). Eulau uses a different index of class, so that his results are not comparable.

but the association of religion and voting went up sharply, undoubtedly because of the candidacy of a Catholic for President. Even manual Protestants did not give the Democratic candidate a majority. Whether the victory of a Catholic candidate will finally end Catholic minority-consciousness is an open question. Peter H. Odegard suggests that "minority" consciousness may be the chief cause of the Catholic deviation.

As consciousness of "minority" status declines for any religious group, one may assume that other factors than religion will play a larger and larger role in determining voting behavior. That is to say, as intensity of religious identity or distinction declines, economic and social status may be expected to increase in importance in explaining voting behavior. As this occurs among American Catholics and Jews, their party preferences will be less and less influenced by religion and more and more by other factors. They should then become

distinguishable from the preferences of others of the same or similar economic and social status, regardless of religious affiliation.[12]

Although certainly this argument is a plausible one, and should hold for the regional as well as the religious deviations from class-voting in the United States, no evidence of a consistent increase of class-voting or a decline of the religious deviation is as yet manifest. It might be noted that only among nonmanual persons identifying themselves as middle class did the religious difference in voting behavior disappear, as is indicated by Table II. Not only objectively higher status, but a subjective sense of being part of the "great middle class" is required to rid Catholics

[12] Peter H. Odegard, "Catholicism and Elections in the United States," in P. H. Odegard (ed.), *Religion and Politics* (Published for the Eagleton Institute of Politics at Rutgers, the State University, by Oceana Publications, 1960), pp. 120–121.

of their sense of minority-consciousness, and, as a consequence, their disproportionately Democratic loyalties.

Obviously much more could be said about variations in class-voting among different groups in the American electorate, but the concern of this article has been to see whether any consistent pattern of decline or increase of class-voting was evident in general, and within various regions and within the two major religious divisions, Protestant and Catholic.

CONCLUSIONS

No evidence of either a decline of class-voting, or any substantial change in the pattern of class-voting among major United States regions or religious groups has been found. The diversity of American politics, remarked on by most political observers, remains as great as ever. Some signs of regional economic and political integration have been cited, which may mean the pulling of the South into line with other parts of the country, but the outcome is not yet visible in any increase of class-voting in that region. The 1960 election marked the greatest difference since 1944 of Protestant and Catholic voting behavior, even when similar occupational groups were compared, and therefore there is no sign yet of any decline of this source of nonclass voting.

But, despite this continuing diversity, the opposite side of the coin should also be stressed. Data from a number of surveys from 1936 to 1960 have shown no unmistakable decline of class-voting in the United States, despite the move to the Right in the Eisenhower period. As S. M. Lipset has said, "such factors as occupational status, income and the class character of the district in which people live probably distinguish the support of the two major parties more clearly now than at any other period in American history since the Civil War."

Therefore, and the data already presented reinforce this conclusion, there has not yet been a "secular realignment" of the class bases of the political parties in the United States, in V. O. Key's phrase.

Another incidental conclusion of this attempt to investigate changes of patterns of voting over time is that surveys over as wide a time-span as possible must be taken into account when attempting to assess not only political change, but also the particular behavior of a social group. The exceptional behavior of middle-class Catholics in 1952 is a case in point. If the only evidence for their political behavior were taken from that election, many false generalizations concerning the decline of religious deviations could be erected. Especially when the political realignment of entire social groups (rather than the voting shifts of individuals) is the research focus, as many surveys as possible over a broad range of time are necessary.

The lack of any consistent decline of class-voting does not necessarily mean that class loyalties and consciousness have remained strong. Workers might continue to vote Democratic and businessmen Republican, but the sense of identification of this behavior with class-interests might be becoming obscure and weak. Such a change could occur within both parties and social classes: the parties themselves could be moving ever closer together in their platforms and appeals, and/or occupational groups could be moving closer together in their values, styles of life, and political perspectives. An important line of research is implied by these possible changes: what changes of political values and attitudes can take place *without* any substantial shift in the actual political alignment of a social group? The data on class-voting give no direct clue to these changes, but they give pause to the easy conclusion that the Eisenhower swing and postwar prosperity of the United States greatly modified the class differential in voting behavior.

43.   How Big Is the Bloc Vote?

Seymour Martin Lipset

Religious and ethnic group loyalties are another vital influence on voting. On the basis of history, interests, and philosophical values, these groups tend to identify with one of the two major parties. Seymour Lipset, Professor of Sociology, the University of California, Berkeley, traces the development of the attachment of "minorities" and speculates on the possible consequences of the increasing support of the Democratic party evident among all of these groups in recent elections. The actual division of "the bloc vote" in 1964 is detailed by Louis Harris (46).

* * *

To speak and write of bloc voting on a religious, racial or ethnic basis has been deprecated alike by politicians and by the leaders of the groups involved. But why, in this day and age, some people object to the idea that bloc voting exists while others, recognizing that there are such blocs, consider their behavior undemocratic or un-American, is difficult to understand.

Although bloc voting may seem to violate the democratic *mythos* about rational man, most politicians have always known what all great observers of American life, from Tocqueville, Bryce and Ostrogorski to Brogan, have noted—that Americans differ in their voting behavior not only according to whether they are poorer or richer, rural or urban, Northerners or Southerners but also because they are of different religious, racial and ethnic backgrounds.

What is meant by the term "bloc"? Basically, a bloc is a group of people who have a "consciousness of kind," who react to others having the same identifying characteristics with the feeling, "He is one of mine." This does not mean that a bloc is monolithic, that group members vote only for others in their group What it does imply, however, is that membership in a bloc, particularly of a religious or ethnic character, is a major influence on political behavior.

Thus we have the deep study of bloc trends this year. Public opinion polls suggest that over 90 percent of Jews and Negroes will support President Johnson. It also appears from such surveys that about three-quarters of the Catholic vote will go to the national Democratic ticket, despite the nomination of a Catholic as the Republican Vice-Presidential candidate.

Why should Catholics be much more likely to vote for Johnson and Humphrey than for Goldwater and Miller? The answer lies not only in the candidates themselves, but also in the long-term association between Catholics and Democrats.

From Jefferson's day to Lyndon Johnson's, the principal vehicle for Catholic expression and recognition in politics has been the Democratic party. In 1960, at the end of the Eisenhower era but before the Kennedy nomination, over 80 percent of the Catholic members of Congress were Democrats. One-quarter of all Democrats in Congress were Catholics, as contrasted with but 7 percent among Republicans. If we compare, as political scientist Peter Odegard did, appointments to the Federal judiciary under Republican Presidents Harding, Coolidge and Hoover with those made by Democrats Roosevelt and Truman, we find that one of every four judges appointed by the Democrats was a Catholic, as contrasted with but one of every 25 designated by the Republicans.

Clearly, the Democratic party has played a considerable role in helping to raise the status of the Irish and other Catholic groups. From the early 19th century onward, most immigrant Catholic ethnic groups found the local Democratic parties to be of considerable assistance in obtaining jobs and power. The Federalists, Whigs and Republicans were the parties of the social, economic and religious Establishment, composed largely of persons of Anglo-Saxon background. With rare exceptions, these parties showed little interest or ability in helping the lowly immigrants who settled in the cities. And as these parties of the privileged saw the immigrants providing massive infusions of new Democratic votes, they often openly campaigned for restrictions on the political rights of the foreign-born, thus welding them and their offspring even closer to the Democrats.

The predominant identification of Catholics with one party in the 19th century did not matter too much, since they were not that large a segment of the electorate. Today, however, Catholics constitute over one-quarter of the eligible voters, and their continuing commitment to the Democratic party makes the job of electing a Republican extremely difficult.

But Catholic attachment to the Democratic party, long after the end of massive immigration and the decline of Catholic slum ghettos, cannot be explained by historic loyalties alone. Continuity would seem, in part, to be related to the congruence between the positions fostered by the Democratic party in recent decades and certain values endemic in Catholic teachings.

As early as 1917, Catholic bishops in the United States called for a more heavily graduated income tax, social security, unemployment insurance and minimum-wage legislation. Whether such pronouncements affect the laity is difficult to demonstrate, but voting studies have shown that Catholics are not only more Democratic, they are also much more likely to favor trade unions and welfare measures than are socially and economically comparable Protestants. Even Republican Catholics have been found to be, on the average, more favorable to welfare-state or New Deal measures than their Protestant co-partisans.

Jews constitute but 3 to 4 percent of the eligible electorate, but since they are concentrated in a few large states, such as New York, Illinois, Pennsylvania and California, they are in a position to influence considerably the politics of key states with many electoral votes. And their strong liberal propensities give to the Democrats a sizable number of needed middle-class votes and financial contributions.

Much has been written seeking to account for the reformist propensities of Jews, even among many of the well-to-do. To a considerable extent this behavior would seem to reflect the fact that Jews, even when wealthy, have suffered social discrimination at the hands of non-Jewish privileged classes. Although anti-Semitic attitudes and behavior are now at a low ebb, one finds that many of the élite city clubs, as well as many suburban country clubs, do not admit Jews to membership. These clubs tend to be overwhelmingly Republican in their membership. Such discrimination places even wealthy Jews among the out-groups, and helps them to continue to identify with others who are low in the stratification system.

There is also the fact that Jewish values, as developed under the pressure of living as a persecuted minority for two millenia, have emphasized the responsibility of the privileged to help others. The pattern of philanthropic giving, which shows much higher contributions by Jews to both Jewish and non-Jewish causes than is usually found among non-Jews in the same economic bracket, reflects the great strength of community responsibility felt by Jews. And such values seem also to stimulate support for the party which favors the welfare state, which presses for community help to the underprivileged.

To these general factors must be added the specific conditions in 1964 that have made the Jews more predisposed to vote Democratic than ever before: the civil-rights issue and the visible presence of extreme rightists in the Goldwater movement.

For most Jews, the civil-rights cause is as much theirs as it is the Negroes'. He who hates the Negro, the Catholic or the foreign-born is probably also anti-Semitic. The Nazi experience is obviously still the most crucial historical event in the minds of Jews; extreme rightists, whether anti-Semitic or not, are seen as threats to the democratic process and consequently a danger to Jews. Hence the phenomenon in this election year that seemingly most Jewish conservatives and Republicans will vote for Johnson and Humphrey.

Negroes, who make up about 11 percent of the population, represent somewhat less than that percentage of the electorate. Their overwhelming backing for the Democratic ticket in 1964 is clearly linked to party differences on the civil-rights issue, with most Negro Republican leaders the country over supporting Johnson and Humphrey because of Senator Goldwater's attitude on the Civil Rights Bill and the conscious effort to recruit segregationist support in the South.

Although in the recent decades we have become accustomed to counting Negroes as a bulwark of the Democratic party, this voting pattern is relatively new. From the Civil War to 1932, studies of the vote of Negro residential districts show that they voted Republican for the most part. The G.O.P. was the party of Lincoln, the party that freed the slaves, and insofar as racial issues entered into elections before the New Deal, the party that supported the Negro's cause.

The shift from the Republican to the Democratic camp occurred largely between 1932 and 1936. Federally financed relief and public-works programs established during the first Roosevelt Administration gave money and employment to a large section of the Northern Negro population, and gave such help in nondiscriminatory fashion. Labor unions, closely identified with the Democrats, organized large numbers of Negro workers for the first time in history in the late thirties. And gradually the Democratic party took over the role of advocate of the Negro's social and economic rights.

What about the voting patterns of the white Protestant majority—now a declining majority in relation to the total electorate? Clearly, if they had ever voted as a predominant bloc, the party they backed would have had a permanent majority. But various factors have divided the Protestants. In addition to class and ethnic cleavages, the most visible factor, of course, has been sectional; the South, until recently, was one of the most Protestant and Democratic parts of the country.

Class and sectional factors apart, white Anglo-Saxon Protestants—the so-called WASPs—would seem to have been developing tendencies toward bloclike links to the Republicans. Various historians have documented trends in this direction in the 19th century, when the WASPs were still a majority nationally.

Thus, a study of British immigration after the Civil War shows that many British immigrants joined the Republican party because cities were often controlled by an Irish-Catholic-dominated Democratic party, and Democratic officeholders were wont to give strong support to the cause of Irish independence. More recently, students of urban New England politics, communities in which those of old-stock Anglo-Saxon Protestant background find themselves in a small minority, suggest that they have been behaving much like a self-conscious minority ethnic group, usually backing Republicans but showing a disposition, like other deeply self-conscious minorities, to break away and support Democratic candidates from their own ethnic group.

Many observers have called attention to the processes through which Protestantism, particularly in its ascetic forms, has contributed to individualism, self-reliance, feelings of personal responsibility for success and failure, and interpretation of social evils in terms of individual moral failings. Catholicism, on the other hand, has tended to stress community responsibility and does not stress as much the responsibility of the individual for the moral consequences of action.

A survey of the values of Protestants and Catholics by a sociologist, Gerhard Lenski, reports that when comparing members of these two broad religious communities, holding class background and length of family immigrant history constant, Protestants are more likely to have positive feelings toward hard work, to be less active in trade unions, to expect to agree with businessmen rather than with unions on various issues, and to be critical of installment buying. Data from Gallup surveys indicate that as recently as 1959, one-third of all Protestants as compared with 9 percent of Catholics favored a national law prohibiting the sale of liquor.

These varying attitudes of Catholics and Protestants, especially Protestants adhering to the historic sectarian groups, may incline the Protestants to oppose the welfare state and the Democrats, much as Catholic and Jewish values may press *their* adherents to accept liberal political principles.

Foreign policy issues, particularly those revolving around entry into the two World Wars and relations with the Soviet Union, have had visible effects on the voting patterns of different ethnic groups. Harding's great victory in 1920 was in large part a result of his picking up support from normally Democratic ethnic groups who had opposed entry into World War I or resented the treatment of their ancestral mother country in the Versailles Treaty. Similarly, in the late 1930's and the 1940's, national groups were pressed in different political directions by their attitudes toward Germany, Italy, and the Soviet Union.

Past elections show how parties may pick up needed support from groups normally predisposed against them by fostering policies or nominating candidates who appeal to the values or interests of the given group. In New York, for example, Governor Dewey, running for re-election, was able to carry Harlem by a small majority after signing the first state fair-employment law enacted in the country. But though New York Negroes rewarded Dewey in the state election, they voted overwhelmingly against him for President in 1948.

Senator Jacob Javits of New York, a liberal Republican with a very favorable record on civil rights and welfare issues, has been able to make strong inroads into Jewish and Negro Democratic strongholds whenever he has run for election. His strength cannot be credited primarily to the fact that he himself is Jewish. Other Jews running as Republicans against non-Jewish Democrats have frequently been defeated by large majorities in Jewish districts. A major example of this occurred in the New York City mayoralty election in 1945, when Jonah Goldstein, running as a Republican, was trounced in Jewish and Catholic areas alike by William O'Dwyer.

Today, all signs point to a large segment of New York Jews, perhaps a good majority, voting for Senator Keating against Robert Kennedy. Interviews with Jewish and other liberally disposed voters indicate that they are moved by Senator Keating's seeming liberalism in his pre- and post-convention opposition to the candidacy of Senator Goldwater. Voting blocs can be split when a party normally opposed by the bloc moves in the direction of the values of the bloc; they are no more immutable than patterns of class voting.

Whether or not one deplores bloc voting, the fact remains that it will continue to affect American politics. No party can afford to ignore such groups; yet the Goldwater Republicans would seem to be doing so.

Negroes, Catholics and Jews constitute about 40 percent of the American population today. Collectively, they will probably give Lyndon Johnson a larger majority than any other candidate has ever achieved among them. At the moment it would appear that of this 40 percent, over three-quarters—constituting more than 30 percent of the entire electorate—will back Johnson and Humphrey. Less than one-quarter of these three blocs, or less than 10 percent of the total voting population, favor Goldwater and Miller.

If this estimate is correct, then the Democrats need but one out of every three Protestant voters to have 50 percent of the voters. Any votes above that figure will add to their majority. In fact, all available evidence suggests that the Democratic Presidential ticket may secure *a majority of white Protestant votes,* coming disproportionately from trade-unionists, intellectuals, government employes and white-collar workers in large industry, in that order.

There is strong evidence from opinion surveys, both academic and non-academic alike, that the Democrats were gradually gaining in Protestant backing long before the Goldwater nomination. At the same time, they have not been losing their religious, ethnic and racial bloc support. The welfare program of the Democrats has an appeal to many Protestants, particularly workers and farmers. And the growth of education and general cosmopolitanism has greatly increased the number of white Prot-

estants who join the minorities in seeing the Negro's claim for equality as a moral one which must be acknowledged by government action.

The growing weakness of the Republicans among Protestants was concealed in 1960 by the considerable antipathy which many of them had to backing a Catholic president. The real meaning of the 1960 vote may be seen by comparing the votes of religious groups in the Congressional elections of 1958 and the Presidential contest of 1960.

In the former year, without Kennedy on the ticket or in the White House, Democratic Congressional candidates outside the South took over 70 percent of the Catholic vote, as much or more among Jews and Negroes, and apparently slightly less than half of the white Protestant electorate. Two years later, with a Catholic heading up the ticket, over 80 percent of the Catholics voted Democratic, but only about one-third of the Protestants. Seemingly, approximately one out of seven Protestants who favored Democrats in the 1958 Congressional elections voted against Kennedy in 1960. But in 1964, as I have already suggested, Lyndon Johnson should equal or surpass Kennedy's vote among the Catholic-Jewish-Negro segment of the population while also gaining a majority among white Protestants.

All this suggests, of course, the same result as the evidence adduced so far by pollsters and political analysts about 1964 suggests—an overwhelming majority for Johnson and Humphrey. If the analysis is correct, it also points up the long-term problem faced by the Republican party if it is not to go the way of the Federalists and the Whigs: Either it must modify its program and image so as to appeal to groups which now decisively reject it, or else it must reconcile itself to a permanent minority status.

44. Registration in Forrest County, Mississippi

U.S. Civil Rights Commission

Negro voting has become a subject of major legal and political interest in the nation, as evidenced by the voting rights law of 1965. Discriminatory literacy tests have restricted voting by Negroes in the past and have stimulated national action to correct this unfair treatment. The following selection is a strictly factual presentation by the U.S. Civil Rights Commission of registration practices in one of the "hard-core" areas of the South.

* * *

The following is the data with respect to the accepted white applicants. The answers to the questions are in the applicants own words, including errors, if any.

The application of Henry Lambert, white, dated June 2, 1962, was accepted by the registrar despite the utter nonsense which he wrote in question 19 as his interpretation for section 118 of the Mississippi Constitution.

Lambert copied section 118 as follows:

"The governor shall receive for his service such compensation as may be fixed by law, which shall neither be increased or diminished during his term of office."

His interpretation was:

"The people shall provide the necessery funds and money to help the governor to promoting and carried the laws, of, Mississippi.

"And it is the Dutis of a citezen of Mississippi to financl and help for poyer for the right Govermnient.

"The State of Mississippi shall maked cermcery The Salary for Govemor of the state the laws shall be the sane as long of his terms be. for a foursece terms."

The application of Ericcelle Pearce, white, dated May 28, 1962, was accepted by the registrar. The registrar told her where to sign her application form. Many Negroes were rejected for failing to sign the form. The registrar also told her to add the phrase "to uphold the law" in her answer to question 20 which requires a statement of the duties and obligations of citizenship.

The following is the data with respect to the rejected Negro applicants. Question 19 is the answer the Negro has given to the constitutional section he was asked to interpret. Question 20 is the answer to the question asking that the duties and obligations of citizenship be stated.

The answers to the questions are in the applicants' own words, including errors, if any.

The application form of David P. Roberson dated April 18, 1962, was rejected. In the oath part of the application form he omitted his election district and he failed to sign the form. (On a subsequent form David P. Roberson was rejected for failing to put his specific street address in answer to question 9. The registrar did not seek out the April 18 form which contains this information as he did in Lewis' case with respect to his residence.) Roberson, a Negro high-school teacher, completed his master's degree work in 1962–63 on a National Science Foundation Scholarship at Cornell University.

He was required to interpret the following section of the Mississippi Constitution:

"Sec. 100. No obligation or liability of any person, association, or corporation held or owned by this State, or levee board, or any county, city, or town therefore, shall ever be remitted, released, or postponed, or in any way diminished by the legislature,

From the *Congressional Record,* Daily ed., 88th Congress, 2d Session (April 1, 1964), vol. 110, pp. 6528–6530.

nor shall such liability or obligation be extinguished except by payment thereof into the proper treasury; nor shall such liability or obligation be exchanged or transferred except upon payment of its face value; but this shall not be construed to prevent the legislature from providing by general law for the compromise of doubtful claims."

Roberson, answer to question 19, section 100: "This section of the constitution states that the legislature do not have the power to take from any citizen, nor organization their obligation or liabilities by an act that would (seem) to please some organization or individual but if it be the case that such liabilities or obligation are situation where a compromise is in order the legislature can then act.

"It further states that just payment is the only way in which those obligations can be meet unless a compromise of its values is considered.

"The above section had reference to obligation or liability to the state, levee board, county, city town, etc."

Answer to question 20: "The duties and obligations of citizenship under a constitutional form of government are many. Some are (1) To obey the laws set forth (2) participate in activities that will serve to make the community a better place to live in such as (a) attending church regularly (b) working with boy-scotting units (c) aiding these who cannot help themselves (d) encouraging obedience of the law (f) voting. These are not all but the duties are endless."

The application form of Wayne Sutton dated April 23, 1962, was rejected. He failed to properly put his election district in the oath part and failed to sign his name on the form.

Mr. Sutton is a Negro elementary schoolteacher in Hattiesburg.

He was required to interpret section 124 of the Mississippi Constitution:

"SEC. 124. In all criminal and penal cases, excepting those of treason and impeachment, the Governor shall have power to grant reprieves and pardons, to remit fines, and in cases of forfeiture, to stay the collection until the end of the next session of the legislature, and by and with the consent of the senate to remit forfeitures. In cases of treason he shall have power to grant reprieves, and by and with consent of the senate, but may respite the sentence until the end of the next session of the legislature; but no pardon shall be granted before conviction; and in cases of felony, after conviction no pardon shall be granted until the applicant therefor shall have published for thirty days, in some newspaper in the county where the crime was committed, and in case there be no newspaper published in said county, then in an adjoining county, his petition for pardon, setting forth therein the reasons why such pardon should be granted."

Wayne Sutton, answer to question 19: "Section 124 of the Mississippi Constitution states that in all criminal and penal cases the Governor will have the power to grant reprieves and pardon and to remit fines. In the case, of forfeitures, to hold the collection until the end of the end of the next session of the legislature, and with the consent of the senate to remit forfeitures. In the cases of treason he shall have the power to grant reprieves and by and with the consent of the senate, but may delay the sentence until the end of the next session of the legislature. No pardon will be granted before conviction. In the cases of felony, after conviction no pardon will be given until the applicant will (have) published for 30 days in the county newspaper where the crime was committed. And if there is no newspaper, it shall be published in an adjoining county. His partition or pardon giving the reason why the pardon shall be granted."

Answer to question 20: "A citizen shall uphold the laws of his county, city, State and Nation. A citizen shall take an active part in civic and community affairs."

The application of Robert Lynwood Lewis dated April 18, 1962, was rejected. In question 8 Lewis stated that he had resided in Mississippi for 6 years. The registrar sought out a prior rejected application dated September 29, 1961, in which Lewis' answer to this question was 28 years. Lewis also did not sign the application form at the bottom. The registrar did not ask Lewis about this inconsistency, and the residence requirement in Mississippi is only 2 years. Lewis is a Negro high schoolteacher; he has a graduate degree.

He was also required to interpret the following section of the Mississippi Constitution:

"SEC. 160. And in addition to the jurisdiction heretofore exercised by the chancery court in suits to try title and to cancel deed and other clouds upon title to real estate, it shall have jurisdiction in such cases to decree possession, and to displace possession; to decree rents and compensation for improvements and taxes; and in all cases where said court heretofore exercised jurisdiction, auxiliary to courts of common law, it may exercise such jurisdiction to grant the relief sought, although the legal remedy may not have been exhausted or the legal title established by a suit at law."

Lewis, March 1960, answer to question 19: "My interpretation—from a layman's point-of-view: The section states that the chancery court doesn't only jurisdiction to try titles and cancel deed and other matters relating to titles of real estate, but it also have power to decree possession and to displace possession, to decree rent and compensation for improvements and taxes. It may also grant relief to auxially courts when sought even of the legal remedy have not been exhausted or the legal title established the law suit."

Answer to question 20: "I think that under constitutional government a citizens obligation is to uphold the local, state, and federal government—to support it in any way possible."

The application form of Wayne Kelly Pittman dated April 25, 1962, was rejected with the notation that he had been convicted in 1934. He is a minister and completed 1 year of college.

Reverend Pittman had previously obtained a restoration of his civil rights by a special act of the Mississippi Legislature and he so advised the registrar and showed him the certified copy of the bill signed by the governor restoring his civil rights which explicitly included the right of suffrage. The registrar required him to complete an application form prior to registering.

He received section 17 to interpret.

"SEC. 17. Private property shall not be taken or damaged for public use, except on due compensation being first made to the owner or owners thereof, in a manner to be prescribed by law; and whenever an attempt is made to take private property for a use alleged to be public, the question whether the contemplated use be public shall be a judicial question, and, as such, determined without regard to legislative assertion that the use is public."

Wayne Pittman, answer to question 19: "The owner or owners of private property shall be paid for their property as provided by law, whenever such property has been taken for public use.

"The courts will determine whether the question is, or is not, justifiable, or not, and that the existing legislative laws and assertions have any bearing upon (local) (sized) private property when same shall be (sout) for public use. The court or courts must decide whether or not the public usage of the private property shall be for the best interest of the community and general welfare of all concerned."

Answer to question 20: "A citizen should take end active part in all welfares of the Government qualify and vote in all elections. Uphold and obey the laws of the local, state, and federal government."

The application form of James Avon Cohen dated April 24, 1962, was rejected.

He failed to complete the general oath and failed to sign the form.

Mr. Cohen is a pharmacist in a Negro drugstore in Hattiesburg, Miss.; he has a bachelor's degree in pharmacy.

He was required to interpret section 89 of the Mississippi Constitution:

"SEC. 89. There shall be appointed in each house of the legislature a standing committee on local and private legislation; the house committee to consist of seven representatives, and the senate committee of five senators. No local or private bill shall be passed by either house until it shall have been referred to said committee thereof, and shall have been reported back with a recommendation in writing that it do pass, stating affirmatively the reasons therefor, and why the end to be accomplished should not be reached by a general law, or by a proceeding in court; or if the recommendation of the committee be that the bill do not pass, then it shall not pass the house to which it is so reported unless it be voted for by a majority of all members elected thereto. If a bill is passed in conformity to the requirements hereof, other than such as are prohibited in the next section, the courts shall not, because of its local, special, or private nature, refuse to enforce it."

James Avon Cohen, answer to question 19: "My interpretation of this the 89 section of the Miss. Constitution is that in each house of legislature a standing committee shall be appointed on both local and private legislation. The house committee will consist of 7 representatives and the senate committee of 5 senators. No local or private bill shall be passed by either house until it has been referred to by the committee thereof and reported back with a recommendation in writing the result of the action on said bill.

"If a bill is passed to the stated require-ment hereof the courts shall not refuse to enforce it regardless if it is of local, special, or private nature."

Answer to question 20: "I believe that a citizen under a this form of government should be loyal to the duties and obligations of that government. He must realize that he or she is a part of that government, and the whole is not whole than its parts."

The application form of Leonard P. Ponder dated April 24, 1962, was rejected. He failed to put his specific address in question 9 and did not sign the final line of the application form.

Mr. Ponder is a Negro minister who has completed 2 years of college. He was required to interpret section 17 of the Mississippi constitution:

"Sec. 17. Private property shall not be taken or damaged for public use, except on due compensation being first made to the owner or owners thereof, in a manner to be prescribed by law; and whenever an attempt is made to take private property for a use alleged to be public, the question whether the contemplated use be public shall be a judicial question, and, as such, determined without regard to legislative assertion that the use is public."

Answer to question 19: "The property owned by any person or persons shall not be taken or damaged for public use without the owner or owners be paid or satisfaction be made in accordance with the law and when an attempt is made to take private property to be used for public it shall be determined by law without regard to assertion that the use is public."

Answer to question 20: "One of the duties and obligations of citizenship is to support the sanitation and health of the community where you live. To pay all due taxes and to abide by and uphold the law of the state."

45. Political Theory and the Voting Studies

Eugene Burdick

*Empirical voting research has severely un-
dermined much of traditional democratic
theory. The uninterested and generally
uninformed party loyalist described in
these studies is sharply different from the
rational, concerned citizen postulated in
the past. Commenting on three voting
studies, Eugene Burdick, late professor of
Political Science at the University of California, Berkeley, described the resulting
problems of political theory. He then advanced some tentative means of reconciling
facts and values. The apathy and limited
knowledge found by the voting studies, he
suggested, may actually promote a stable
democracy.*

* * *

THE "CITIZEN" OF DEMOCRATIC THEORY AND THE "VOTER"

Rationality

Central to almost every democratic
theory has been the idea of the essential
rationality of the citizen. Locke conceived
this rationality to be so durable that in his
famous "state of nature," autonomous
rational men were reasonably happy. Indeed each, being possessed of rationality,
was able to exercise a form of "executive
power" and the over-all effect was one of
harmony—blemished only by occasional
miscalculations. Locke further conceived
that man lost none of his rationality when
the civil society was formed. He wrote that

men entered civil society "only with an
intention in every one the better to preserve himself, his liberty and property for
no rational creature can be supposed to
change his condition with an intention to
be worse."

Very little in classical democratic theory
refuted Locke. Rousseau, despite the recent uncertainty about his work, was
firmly in the tradition which viewed political man as rational. If the eighteenth century was optimistic in this regard the
nineteenth was even more so. The Utili-
tarians saw man not only as rational, but
they thought that his moral life could be
made scientific and orderly. For Bentham
the state was nothing more than a means
by which the pains and pleasures of each
perceiving and rational individual could
be remorselessly added and subtracted
and the "felicific calculus" of the entire
society computed. Adam Smith might
sound an eccentric warning about the non-
rationality of humans, but as late as 1890
Sidgwick had to "demonstrate" that "unreasonable action" was possible. The American tradition was essentially the same.
Although a number of the Founding Fathers had reservations, both public and
private, about the limits of reason, the
necessity to argue a theory of rights also
drove them to embrace, at least, a modified
theory of rational political man. When
Paine remarked immodestly that he was
"unconnected with any party, and under
no sort of Influence, public or private, but
the influence of reason and principle," he
expressed a dominant mood.

The "voter" who emerges from the studies discussed in this book has little of the
rationality of the "citizen" of democratic
theory. Even when rationality is given a
minimum definition the American voter
does not meet the test. If rationality is
defined merely as the possession of the

information necessary to make a decision, ratiocination on that information, and the *self-conscious* evolution of a decision, the voter is, by and large, not rational. In Elmira over a third of the respondents knew correctly only one stand taken by Dewey and Truman on issues of the utmost gravity. In the Michigan study only a third of the respondents were "greatly interested in the election" and only a fifth thought it made a "good deal" of difference who won. There is also ample evidence that the perception of the political world was highly selective and often inaccurate, e.g., the respondent "saw" what he wanted to see, even if this defied common sense and the stated position of a candidate.

This is not to argue that the voter is irrational. It will be indicated below that his interest in politics is so slight that his behavior in this field is no true test of his rationality. But he most surely acts unrationally in his political choices; the voter of the Elmira and Michigan studies quite obviously is incapable of the kind of rationality which Locke expected of him, to say nothing of his ability to make the kind of intricate "felicific calculus" which Bentham required of his citizen.

Political nature of man

The citizen of classical democratic theory was conceived to be both interested and active in the political discourse. Knowing that the question of *who* is to be sovereign and *how* this power was exercised were the most fundamental questions of social life, classical theorists, quite logically, could not conceive that any citizen would ignore the discussion by which the decision was made.

But it is abundantly clear that the voter of today does lack both high political interest and an urge to participate in the political discourse. The voting studies indicate that political discourse is limited, sparse, and desultory. Indeed, most voters make up their minds, and act ultimately on that decision, even before the campaigns begin. Family background, cultural milieu, all of the inchoate pressures of "socioeconomic status" seem subtly to work on the voter in a process which is neither rational nor accompanied by high interest. The conveyors of political information are massively ignored, except by small nuclei of partisans.

Political principles

The citizen of classical theory was supposed to vote in terms of a set of values or principles. The ultimate referent might range from a luminous hagiolatry, to an enthusiasm for revolutionary slogans, to a cold calculation of interest; but that the citizen might make his political decisions in an unprincipled manner, classical theory could not concede. More recently there has evolved a more realistic theory based on the assumption that the plurality of principles in a complex modern society was amalgamated into the principles of a political party.

The voting studies, however, do not allow even this last slight image of the principled citizen to remain. The voting studies seem agreed that "if this requirement [of principled voters] is pushed at all strongly it becomes an impossible demand on the democratic electorate." The political party is not regarded as a variegated repository where the conflicting principles of the electorate are merged and made compatible. Much more it is viewed as a traditional allegiance of one very low affect or another in a series of acts aimed at coming to adjustment with one's environment.

In summary, the voting studies etch a portrait of the contemporary voter as a person who votes with relatively high frequency, but on very low information, with very little interest, and with very low emotional involvement in the entire process. The act of voting seems divorced from any coherent set of principles. The original cause of the voter's attitude, the steps by which it is modified before coming to formal decision (what voting scholars call intervening variables), and the whole subtle process of change in political attitudes and institutions are, of course, not so clearly known.

But although the etiology of individual voter motivation and the over-all process of collective political change are not clear, the image of the contemporary voter is clear enough to give serious pause to political theory. For it is evident that the "citizen" of the theorists is really an ideal construction; more paradigm than reality.

Now as has been indicated above this changed version of the citizen does not necessarily destroy previous ethical theory nor does it damage theories of intention. But it does substantially alter some parts of political theory by supplying relatively firm answers for what were previously conjectures or mere statements of preference. The relevance for much of classical theory is so obvious that it need not be remarked. Theories of consent, majoritarianism, the role of elites, the nature of individual and collective will, and theories of social contract are areas which would need radical revision if the findings of the voting studies on the nature of political man and political participation are accurate.

The relevance for contemporary political problems is even more striking. One wonders, for example, if in recent attempts to involve "the public" more directly in international relations, the involvement is either possible or desirable. Given the demonstrated low interest in domestic politics and the even lower interest in foreign affairs one wonders how this is to be accomplished. If the only manner in which their heightened interest and affect could be achieved is through the adoption of a form of "total politics," the fact would have to be faced that a corollary of high political interest might be a sharp rise in ideology with a parallel rise in tensions and rigidity. Can popular participation mean anything less than "intrusion of the masses" into politics? And if it can, what are the educational and motivational means which must be developed? And how will these means be controlled and to what end? . . .

CONCORD AND THE VOTING STUDIES

The authors of *Voting* cite an excellent quotation from Judge Learned Hand that, without using the word, focuses upon the problem of concord in a diverse modern society. Hand, after commenting that the act of voting "is one of the most unimportant acts of my life," remarks that if he were to acquaint himself with the facts on which his vote ought really to depend he could only bring a "fatuous conclusion to a fatuous undertaking." He then goes on to say, however, that the system, for all its difficulties and uncertainties, "abuse it as you will, it gives a bloodless measure of social forces—bloodless, have you thought of that?—a means of continuity, a principle of stability, a relief from the paralyzing terror of revolution."

Hand states, however puckishly, a paradox. It seems *not* to be true that the chaos of democratic government, the irresponsibility of political parties, the blatant appeal to interest, and the confused political warfare could actually result in public concord. But this *is* what happens. Whatever the qualities of the individual voter, whatever the defects of political parties, whatever the shortcomings of the democratic process, it has, at least in the United States and Britain, resulted in a remarkable degree of concord.

The problem of concord is, of course, most central for political theory. Theories of cyclical development, notions of social contract, problems of individual and social will, the basis for tyrannicide—indeed, almost every problem of political theory comes to bear upon one problem: How *is* concord achieved and what can *make* it legitimate?

The voting studies under consideration, I shall argue, supply a partial answer to the problem of concord, but leave very basic problems of etiology unanswered. Before turning to this matter, however, it is necessary to dispose of a theory of concord which it has frequently been alleged that the pollsters, survey experts, and voting scholars advocate. This is the notion that concord is achieved by allowing public opinion to be expressed in public policy. Or, more crudely and explicitly, the argument that simple majority opinion should find a quick and ready response in political policy.

Whatever may be said by other polling, survey, and voting experts, the authors of the three volumes discussed advance no such theory. Only by committing some form of the fallacy of *petito principii* could they be conceived as supporting a crude form of majoritarianism. In all three cases they seem fully aware that the mood or opinion of the whole society is far from being the equivalent of desirable political policy.

However, the three studies do seem in agreement in suggesting that concord, at least in two modern democratic states, flows from simple disinterest in politics. *Voting* states directly that the very low affect of most voters, their lack of ideological commitment, and the low faith in the efficacy of politics make political concord relatively easy to achieve. One is instantly reminded of Bagehot's statement that the true strength of the government of England is the stupidity of the population and his thesis that the very boredom of the citizens and the mediocrity of the statesmen makes for a "rut of freedom." This hard conclusion, needless to say, none of the voting studies are prepared to make.

The reluctance of the voting studies to pursue the more pessimistic aspects of their data is, I think, altogether regrettable. For some time there has been a recognition by political theorists that the irrational impulses of individuals were a substantial element in politics. The findings of psychoanalysis and psychiatry, because they emphasize so strongly the individual, have answered few of the questions which would be helpful to students of politics. At the same time they have made a consideration of irrationality in politics incumbent upon political theorists. By explicating the more pessimistic and melancholy of their findings, the voting scholars might do much to reconstruct both political theory and politics.

There is, for example, no reason why a theory of concord could not be based on the assumption of passivity and low information on the part of most of the voters. Acceptance of such a state of affairs might, for example, allow us to explore more energetically the nature of elites in modern society. Samuel Stouffer has suggested that among elites there is a remarkable unanimity of view: leaders tend to be more alike in viewpoint than do their followers. It is conceivable that a liberal theory of concord might be quite consistent with a theory of political elites. A necessary prerequisite, however, would be the willingness of behavioral scientists to explore, and present, all of the possible evidence on the matter. At the present time, however, the voting studies seem directed at supporting existing theories, even when the strain of fitting data into conventional and optimistic theory is very great.

I have suggested that the voting studies, as they stand, might be incorporated in a theory of concord based on the notion of low citizen interest and information. One hesitates, however, because of an implicit warning within the studies and because of explicit statements by their critics. The voting studies make it quite clear that in terms of the etiology—the true causation of political partisanship and of political attitudes—they are at a loss. The authors of the studies still find the basis of concord as "deep, silent and obscure" as did Calhoun. *The Voter Decides,* for example, suggests that membership in large regional, ethnic, and social groups "determines" one's voting preferences. The authors are as aware as their critics that this is a descriptive statement having little to do with causation. *Why* Catholics vote more heavily Democratic or farmers more heavily Republican is still unknown. *Voting* draws the focus more sharply and states that, in Elmira at least, "it is the socioeconomic classes, on the one hand, and the religious and ethnic groups, on the other, that serve as the social carrier of political traditions." Apparently the voter is caught in an intricate and invisible web of religion, desire for security within status, social aspiration, economic class, and family background. But *how* these elements work on him, *why* one argument is persuasive at one time and ineffective at another, the *way* these attitudes are transmitted is still unknown. Until these elements are isolated and explicated it is impossible to conscientiously draw up a theory of concord based on contemporary empirical data from the voting studies. That the voting studies raise doubts about classical theories of concord is beyond question. That they supply the material for a sure new theory of concord is in great doubt.

CIVILITY
AND THE VOTING STUDIES

I have indicated above that the voting studies do not technically lend support to a theory of political pluralism. I have also indicated that the studies are either moot on the question of concord or give only partial answers. There are, however, a number of contemporary theories of politics to which the studies, in part or whole, give considerable support. I have selected one of these to indicate how reconstruction of theory might take place and also how this process might be instructive to the voting scholar in terms of his future research.

One such theory is the notion of "civility" advanced by Walter Lippmann. Lippmann's theory of civility is complex and ultimately is based on a theory of natural law which is not relevant to our discussion here. However, Lippmann's effort is directed at isolating the proper qualities of citizenship and leadership and the relations between the two. His exploration is classical in the most literal sense of the word. However, when Lippmann advances empirical evidence for his theory of civility there is a remarkable parallel between his evidence and that of the voting studies.

Lippmann in response to the question "What are the true boundaries of the people's power?" answers: "The answer cannot be simple. But for a rough beginning let us say that the people are able to give and to withhold their consent to being governed—their consent to what the government asks of them, proposes to them, and has done in the conduct of their affairs. They can elect the government. They can remove it. They can approve or disapprove its performance. But they cannot administer the government. They cannot themselves perform. They cannot normally initiate and propose the necessary legislation. A mass cannot govern."

Lippman goes on to argue that a proper balance between skills and interests and capabilities, in short, civility, has been disturbed by the gradual domination of Jacobin ideas. By this he means the notion that any person is competent in government, that everyone possesses equal talents, and that politics is the means by which the sentiment working up from the masses comes to political expression. The result has been that the masses have either intruded into public policy or been invited to. In either case the result was catastrophic. By arguing the *individual* was possessed of political competence (as differentiated from general political judgment) and by emphasizing the individual above the needs of the collectivity, the Jacobin revolution has resulted in a theory of politics which is wholly incompatible with reality.

This, admittedly, is a conservative and pessimistic point of view. But when we turn to the voting studies we find considerable empirical justification for the argument. All three of the studies under consideration indicate a remarkably low degree of political information. The Jacksonian notion of sound political judgment "trickling up" from the citizenry is, in our time and situation, obviously feckless.

The authors of *Voting* are, in the end, very close to Lippmann when they suggest that classical democratic theory by concentrating upon individual qualities of citizenship lost sight of the over-all demands of the political system. "That is the paradox," they say. "*Individual voters* today seem unable to satisfy the requirements for a democratic system of government outlined by political theorists. But the *system of government* does meet certain requirements for a going political organization. The individual members may not meet all the standards, but the whole nevertheless survives and grows." . . .

46.   The Election of 1964

Louis Harris and Newsweek

The various influences on the vote are resolved differently in each election. The following articles describe the outcome in 1964. The first is opinion analyst Louis Harris' prediction on election eve of the group breakdown of the vote. The actual

vote differed only insignificantly. The second is a more general description of the results, as published in Newsweek *and based on the elaborate system of Vote Profile Analysis.*

* * *

HARRIS CALLS THE ELECTION— BY SEX, PLACE, RACE, RELIGION

Voters believe that in making their choice for a President they are carefully weighing all the issues and the personalities of the candidates. Issues can prove decisive, as Communism, corruption, and Korea worked for Eisenhower in 1952. In the final days of this 1964 campaign, the issues appear to be peace vs. morality and security risks.

But voters also cast their ballots according to patterns. In this election, the odds are 10 to 1 that a Negro will vote Democratic and 2 to 1 that a resident of Orange County, south of Los Angeles, will vote Republican.

Some cross-pressures work to lock in a vote, and make it virtually impossible for a voter to kick over the traces. Other voters are under severe cross-pressures right up to the time of the voting itself. Among those with sharp inner conflict in this election are professional and executive people who have been life-long Republicans, but who feel that foreign policy would be safer in the hands of Lyndon Johnson; also wool-hat Democrats in South Georgia, who stood fast for Kennedy despite the religious issue, but now are for Goldwater over segregation.

Following is an analysis of the dominant currents now running in seven of the major channels into which the electorate can be divided. All voters are affected by each of these. How the cross-pressures balance out, tempered by the issues and personalities, will determine the results on Nov. 3. The outlook:

From *Newsweek* (vol. 44, no. 18, November 2, 1964), pp. 28–29 and *Newsweek* (vol. 44, no. 19, November 9, 1964), pp. 28–29.

By region

East (32% of the electorate). JFK brought the East back to the Democrats. Mr. Johnson has increased the Democratic majority, particularly among minority groups. Best region for LBJ—by well over 60 percent.

Midwest (33%). In the traditional home of the U.S. conservative, Barry Goldwater is regarded by many as a radical. Humphrey is popular with the farmers, and the peace issue favors Mr. Johnson. His vote: over 60 percent.

South (18%). The Deep South is the only area where Goldwater is strong. The rest of the South is close. The Republicans are running on regional issues—segregation and states' rights. Democrats must appeal on national issues—peace and preparedness. Political face of region will never be the same. Goldwater leads by over 55 percent.

West (17%). Despite signs of late Goldwater gains, Mr. Johnson leads by over 55 percent.

By size of place

Cities (31%). Cities came back to the Democrats in 1960, and President Johnson is holding firm despite GOP efforts to split them on the issue of lawlessness in the streets. The cities go for LBJ by over 60 percent.

Suburbs (23%). The Democrats have cracked this traditional GOP base wide open. They have been helped mightily by moderate Republican defectors, also by the migration from the cities of Democrats. LBJ could break even here.

Towns (21%). The bitter anti-Catholic feeling of 1960 is not an issue this year. But peace is. President Johnson by more than 55 percent.

Rural (25%). This onetime GOP heartland seems to be going Democratic for the first time since 1948. Farmers like the Johnson-Humphrey "old shoe" appeal. Could be carried by the Democrats this time, but will be close.

By race

White (92%). One out of three white persons polled expresses some concern over race issue, but peace and prosperity have come to mean more. Prefer Democrats by just over 55 percent.

Negro (8%). Negroes are over 90 percent for LBJ; they were only 55 percent Democratic last time. The Negro vote in the South (where registrations are setting records) could provide LBJ with margin of victory in close Southern states.

By religion

Protestant (70%). Protestants have been traditionally GOP, were heavily anti-Kennedy in 1960. To have any chance at all, Goldwater would have to win a clear majority here. But they prefer LBJ by close to 55 percent.

Catholics (24%). Protestant Johnson will probably win more Catholic votes than JFK did four years ago. Goldwater's attempts to make an issue of the "soft on Communism" charge have had little effect so far. Peace issue runs strong. Miller, a Catholic, hasn't helped. LBJ: over 60 percent.

Jewish (6%). Traditionally Democratic, Jewish voters have been unimpressed by the fact that Goldwater's father was Jewish. They see him surrounded by right-wingers. For LBJ by well over 70 percent.

By ethnic groups

Irish (7%). The President's emphasis on the peace issue and his appeals for moderation have scored heavily. He should get a bigger vote than JFK in 1960. LBJ: over 55 percent.

Italian (5%). Long essentially Democratic, Italian voters showed some signs of defection in the off-year Congressional elections of 1962 (they felt left out on appointments, recognition), are somewhat upset by the race issue. Will go Democratic over 60 percent, but by less than in 1960.

Polish (3%). Some signs of concern over race tensions earlier this year. But still heavily for Johnson-Humphrey, though under JFK's 1960 record total. LBJ by over 60 percent.

German (12%). Normally a heavily Republican voting bloc, the Germans are impressed by LBJ's handling of peace and defense issues, have not responded to Eisenhower's endorsement of Goldwater. Went over 60 percent for Ike. Could go over 50 percent for LBJ.

Sex by age
Men (49%)

21–34 (15%). Senator Goldwater appeals to an enthusiastic minority of men in this age group. This group misses Kennedy but majority still are for Mr. Johnson, should give him an over-all edge of over 55 percent.

35–49 (16%). These men with growing families like LBJ's style and middle-of-the-road outlook. LBJ by over 60 percent.

50 and over (18%). This group could go Democratic for the first time since 1936. LBJ's personality and his role as a moderate both appeal, and may bring him a majority.

Women (51%)

21–34 (14%). LBJ appeals here on the peace issue; some slippage discernible since the Jenkins affair, but young women are still for Mr. Johnson by over 55 percent.

35–49 (17%). Fear of Goldwater on the nuclear issue has cost him dearly here. LBJ by over 60 percent.

50 and over (20%). Older women have solid Republican inclinations, normally go 3-to-2 GOP. Goldwater and war worried them at first, but Jenkins case could help give them to Barry. Look for an even split here.

By occupation

Professionals (11%). Heavily GOP in the past, but think Goldwater too radical on foreign policy. For first time in years, Democratic by over 50 percent.

Business executives (8%). Mr. Johnson has wooed ardently here, and with some effect. Majority still express some fear of Democrats' spending and Federal control. Will be down from normal 70 percent GOP. But still Goldwater by 55 percent.

Small businessmen (6%). One of the groups most favorable to Barry Goldwater as a rugged individualist and a champion in the fight against "big government." Some Democratic defection, but Goldwater by over 55 percent.

White collar (18%). The heart of the old Eisenhower majority. Torn between worries over Goldwater on peace issue, and cost of living under Democrats. Backlash has eased. For Mr. Johnson by over 55 percent.

Labor (15%). Traditionally Democratic, but some wavering during Ike's administrations. LBJ holding firm but not gaining over solid JFK majorities in 1960. Over 60 percent for Mr. Johnson.

Skilled labor (17%). Upset early in campaign over civil-rights issue, but since calmed somewhat by efficient union activity on prosperity issue; fear of Goldwater on social security. LBJ by over 60 percent.

Farmers (5%). Disenchanted with Democratic farm program in North, unhappy about civil rights in South. Goldwater scared them on peace issue. Kennedy lost heavily in '60. But LBJ, helped by Humphrey, can squeak through here.

Retired (14%). Traditional Republican vote, went 2 to 1 for Nixon last time. Goldwater scoring some late gains here. But Mr. Johnson's "old shoe" style popular. Close, but LBJ could just win this vote.

* * *

VPA: THE MAKING OF AN AVALANCHE—1964

History would mark 1964 as the year Vermont went Democratic, the Deep South turned Republican—and a landslide named Lyndon upset all the delicately balanced equations of American Presidential politics.

It was the year of the computer, and political analysts were better equipped than ever to take the seismographic measure of even the slightest tremors of change in the U.S. electorate. But this time the tremblors were earthquake-sized. It took no finely attuned needle to record the dimension of President Johnson's precedent-smashing victory. By any gauge—and in virtually every sector of the body politic—it was a full-scale avalanche.

The President fashioned his victory out of a politics of consensus—a ratification of the domestic and foreign policies of a generation and a massive repudiation of Barry Goldwater's pledge to reverse that course.

CBS's Vote Profile Analysis (VPA)—a computerized measuring system operated with IBM and Louis Harris & Associates and based on a microcosmic set of precincts in each state—reduced the task of analysis from months to minutes. It yielded these findings:

The much-discussed "white backlash" against the revolutionary thrust of the American Negro—a sine qua non in the Goldwaterite strategy—simply failed to materialize. But the "frontlash" did; Republicans in startling numbers—up to 50 percent in some areas—defected to LBJ.

In every region—even in the divided South—the President won by landslide margins averaging thirteen percentage points ahead of John F. Kennedy's run in 1960. He swept the peace-conscious East 69–31, the prosperity-minded Midwest 64.5–35.5, the preparedness-conscious West 64–36. In Dixie, Goldwater's states-righteous "Southern Strategy" swept the band of five segregationist states from Louisiana to South Carolina. Yet LBJ took eight states—and, by 52–48, the popular vote as well.

Mr. Johnson swept the demographic board, too. Barry Goldwater held him to a 57–43 conquest of small-town America. But Johnson carried the cities nearly 3 to 1 and harvested the farms, 53–47. And the frontlash brought the normally Republican suburbs under LBJ's big tent by 59 percent—asserting, in the process, an independent streak deep enough to give the GOP pause in its future calculations.

Every significant racial, religious, and ethnic group went most of the way with LBJ. Running without the religious issue that hurt Mr. Kennedy, Mr. Johnson carried the WASP vote—the white Anglo-Saxon Protestants—by an indicated 54–46 majority. But he ran even better among Catholics than the first Catholic President, with 72 percent to Mr. Kennedy's 63. And the Negro vote—bigger and solider than ever before—deserted the party of Lincoln for the party of Lyndon en masse by a staggering 96 percent.

The phenomenal sweep cut across income lines as well. Mr. Johnson was the nearly unanimous, 19-to-1 choice of low-income voters and a solid, 2-to-1 favorite in the middle-income brackets. But this time, even half the fat cats who had purred so long and so lovingly for the GOP joined the frontlash—and the Democrats —to the tune of 49 percent for LBJ, a switch of thirteen points from 1960.

Most of the issues seemed to work for Mr. Johnson. But, in the year when Barry Goldwater promised a "choice" instead of an echo, the single, over-riding issue was peace—and the choice seemed to reduce itself for most voters to the proven hand of LBJ on one side and the suspect trigger-finger of Barry Goldwater on the other. John Kennedy had successfully begun the task of remaking the Democratic image from the party of war to the party of peace. Lyndon Johnson inherited that new look, and, in a year in office and two months on the hustings, cemented it.

Potent magic

The peace issue scored heavily among Catholics, who had defected from the Democrats in 1936 and 1940 and started back only under the allure of a Catholic candidate four years ago. It was the over-riding concern of the Farm Belt—even in areas where Administration farm programs are unpopular. And it was the most potent magic of all in the East, with its traditional orientation to events abroad. There, Mr. Johnson picked up some of his finest plums. A Democrat carried New Hampshire for the first time since 1944, Maine for the first time since 1912, Vermont—by an eye-popping 67 percent—for the first time in history. The President swept New York, upstate and down; he took not only the nation's biggest city but its usually Republican suburbs as well. Rhode Island went for Mr. Johnson 4 to 1—the President's biggest percentage victory in any state in the union. And the District of Columbia, voting for the first time since 1800, topped that with a staggering 84.1.

The Arizona senator, by contrast, had based his hopes from the beginning in San Francisco to the end in Phoenix on a beguilingly simple equation not unlike Harry Truman's winning hand in 1948. His apostles quoted the arithmetic persuasively: a majority of the South, plus the usually dependable West, plus a handful of pivotal, industrial states where a conservative "silent vote"—and the white backlash—offered untapped reservoirs of strength.

They were wrong on all counts.

To make the gains it did in the South, the Goldwater GOP had to present itself as a regional, states' rights party. That worked in the wool-hat belt—the deep-dyed Democratic country areas where segregation is the dominant—and often, indeed, the only—issue. As good as his word, he was the first Republican to carry Mississippi, Alabama, or South Carolina since Reconstruction—and the first ever to take Georgia. But those four states, plus Louisiana, were the only trophies of the Southern Strategy. They had been rebellious and ripe for plucking since J. Strom Thurmond's Dixiecrat revolt of 1948 collared all but Georgia. In the process of winning them, Goldwater lost the very Southern states that Dwight Eisenhower had coaxed into the Republican column in 1952 and 1956: the upper and border South and Florida.

Crucial vote

And, by his open courtship of the segregationist South, he forfeited whatever claim the GOP had on the Negro vote. Everywhere, North and South, Negroes registered in record numbers and voted with record solidarity for the nation's first Southern President since Andrew Johnson. The Negro vote was a crucial element in Mr. Johnson's Southern majority; it was the swing vote that tipped Virginia back to the Democrats for the first time since 1948. In the North it was all but unanimous: 95.9 percent in Pennsylvania, 94 percent in New York, 97 percent in Illinois, 99 percent in Ohio. In the South, it completed the swing from the party that claimed Emancipation as its birthright. In Kentucky, Negroes voted 61.9 percent for Richard Nixon in 1960—and more than 96 percent for Lyndon Johnson in 1964. In one all-Negro settlement in Mississippi with 257 registered voters, the winner was Mr. Johnson —257 to 0.

The Midwest and West, too, fell before Mr. Johnson like wheat before a scythe. In the normally Republican Midwest, prosperity was Lyndon Johnson's hole card; voters, according to a Louis Harris poll, rated him a 2-to-1 best bet to keep the nation's economy sound. Moreover, Midwest Republicans simply distrusted Goldwater's credentials as a conservative; Mr. Johnson swept Bob Taft's Ohio by 63 percent and wrought the first Democratic victory in Indiana, Kansas, Nebraska, and the

Dakotas since FDR's in 1936. Even in the Western seedbed of right-wing activity—the crescent curving wide out of Wyoming into Southern California—Mr. Johnson turned back a late Goldwater surge on the corruption issue to win by margins ranging from 55 percent in Wyoming to 57 percent in Oklahoma.

Backlash

The backlash—the most tantalizing of unknowns in the GOP formulation—simply evaporated. In no major city of the North or West was there a decisive defection over civil rights—not even in the Mittel-Europan workingmen's sections of Milwaukee and Gary, Ind., that had contributed so heavily to segregationist Alabama Gov. George Wallace's winless victories in last spring's Presidential primaries. In a few cities, there were some defections among Polish-Americans. But they only diminished Democratic majorities from JFK's king-size 4-to-1 sweep of the Polish-American vote in Baltimore and Pennsylvania to LBJ's merely princely 3-to-1 this year. New York City, Chicago, Maryland's Eastern Shore—all racial pressure points during the past summer—all voted Democratic in even larger numbers than usual.

And if there was a silent vote, it was all but lost in the deafening stampede of the GOP defectors moved principally by the issues of peace, defense, and nuclear control. The "frontlash" delivered usually Republican Indianapolis to LBJ, 54–46. The President slipped through to victories in Illinois' most stolidly Republican areas, in the Cook County suburbs and downstate, to cement a 70 percent machine-made landslide in Mayor Dick Daley's Chicago. Philadelphia's suburbs and the Pennsylvania Dutch country—solid for Nixon in 1960—were solid for LBJ this time around. So was granite-Republican Vermont, where Mr. Johnson captured up to half the GOP vote in some areas. And Goldwater's last, best hope among the big, pivotal states—California—went aglimmer when Mr. Johnson swept to 2-to-1 victories even in San Diego and Orange County, where Nixon had piled up better than 60 percent.

The Johnson victory, indeed, was rivaled in Democratic history only by FDR's 46-state avalanche in 1936. But its components more closely approached the 1956 landslide for that last great voice of the American consensus, Dwight Eisenhower.

Mainstream

The fiber of Roosevelt's majorities was the Solid South and the new urban majority created when the focus of U.S. population moved from the town to the city between the 1928 and 1932 elections. Ike's appeal, by contrast was directed to the centrist mainstream of the American electorate—an appeal that worked on both sides of the city limits and either side of the Mason-Dixon Line. And so was LBJ's.

Barry Goldwater had tried to wrench that mainstream to the right: he had reopened the debate over welfare capitalism that FDR had foreclosed in 1932 and called the question the bipartisan foreign policy that had guided the nation since World War II. But, in Lyndon Baines Johnson, he was up against a man who had mastered the uses of the American consensus so skillfully that he needed only to call. Mr. Johnson isolated the right, formed a coalition ranging from nostalgic New Deal liberals to stand-pat conservatives. It mattered little if the coalition was more against than for. This week, the consensus answered at the nation's polls—solidly and plainly. It was all the way for LBJ.

THE MEANING OF ELECTIONS

47. Presidential Election Methods and Urban–Ethnic Interests

Allan P. Sindler

The significance of elections is partially conditioned by the electoral method employed. Different procedures favor different groups and promote interpretations of the vote favorable to their interests. In discussing proposed reforms of the Electoral College, Allan Sindler, Professor of Government at Cornell University, analyzes the effect of these reforms on the party system and on various interests. He seeks to demonstrate the antiurban character of most proposed changes.

* * *

This paper attempts to evaluate American presidential election methods by criteria including, but extending well beyond, the commonly used ones of vote equality, reduction in the distortion of the popular vote, and minimization of the chances of electing a minority President. The conclusion reached is that retention of the current procedure is preferable to any of the major suggested reforms that has some chance of being adopted as a constitutional amendment. In support of that conclusion, a justification for inflated urban influence is offered and some perspectives for the understanding of ethnic politics are suggested.

EVALUATING PRESIDENTIAL ELECTION METHODS

The importance of the Presidency to the character and operation of the over-all governmental and party system needs no belaboring. The mode of presidential election constitutes one of the important determinants of the nature of the office. It therefore follows, and the point merits emphasis because too many popular criticisms of the electoral college have overlooked it, that any analysis of the current method or of proposed reforms must take very much into account the broader consequences of the election procedure for the political system. In pursuing such an approach, we shall probably find wider agreement on what the probable effects of one or another election device are than on any ultimate evaluation of the relative worth of the respective alternatives. The latter disagreement derives basically from the variety of important criteria relevant to the problem, and from the fact that different observers attach different weight to each criterion.

Debate over presidential election methods is refreshing in that much of it may proceed from a contemporary rather than an eighteenth-century perspective. By this we mean simply that because the electoral college device has never operated in the manner intended by the Framers, considerably less attention may be given on this problem, compared to many others, to the question of the intent of the Framers. The thoroughness and rapidity with which the operation of the electoral college was altered should be a familiar enough story to permit treatment of it here in summary terms.

The functioning of the electoral college method, as originally envisioned, depended too much on the absence of political factionalism. When partisanship made its clear and enduring appearance—and the evidences of it were apparent throughout President Washington's administrations—fundamental changes in the actual operation of the electoral college necessarily followed, even though most of the form remained intact. The electors abandoned, in effect, the discretionary powers granted to them by the Constitution and became the controlled spokesmen for the authority designating them, whether that was the state legislature or the electorate. In a matter of several decades, because the states were coerced into adopting a uniform state-unit (or general ticket) system by the dynamics of that device, there remained little significance to the exclusive power granted each state to determine for itself the manner in which it would distribute its electoral vote. The expectations inferable from the arrangements for contingent House selection of the President, involving state equality, also proved illusory within a relatively short time. Aided generally by the structuring force of partisanship, and particularly by the arithmetical consequences of the state-unit ("winner take all") system, the actions of the electoral college itself regularly produced Presidents instead of merely supplying the top contenders from whose ranks the House would designate the victor. A similar turnabout occurred when the neatness of the Framers' plan in regard to the Vice Presidency—to award that post to the losing major presidential candidate rather than to contest directly for it—was rudely shattered by the partisan-inspired necessity for electors to distinguish sharply between candidates for the two different offices. This deviation from intent led to formal alteration of the Constitution by means of the twelfth amendment in 1804. Finally, the broad politicization of the electoral college procedure modified its indirect character, though it still remained and remains importantly different from direct popular election. . . .

THE CURRENT ELECTORAL COLLEGE PROCEDURE

Once an indirect election procedure distorts, as it must, the popular vote, the possibility exists that the verdict of the popular vote may be overturned. In our day of intense commitment to *vox populi*, it is obviously insufficient to rejoin that the Framers planned it that way. To facilitate a direct examination of that possibility, inspection of the data on presidential elections from 1872–1960 in Table One should be of use.

It will be seen that the polarization of the total vote between the two candidates is much greater in the electoral vote than in the popular vote. Of the total of forty-six candidate races covered, thirty-eight of them fell within a forty-sixty percent division of the total popular vote, but only thirteen of them fell within a forty-sixty percent division of the total electoral vote. Note further that on all but one of the thirteen times a candidate secured less than forty-five percent of the popular vote he got less than forty percent of the electoral vote; and in all of the eight elections in which a candidate gained more than fifty-five percent of the popular vote, he won more than sixty percent of the electoral vote. At least at the extremes, then, the direction of exaggeration by the electoral vote is consistent with the direction of the popular vote. If it be granted that it is beneficial to the nation for an incoming President to have the appearance of greater support than that which he actually obtained, then the tendency of the electoral college procedure to exaggerate the magnitude of the winner's victory can be viewed as an advantage of the present system.

Table one also suggests that the problem of "minority Presidents" relates to situations of a close division of the popular vote when both candidates approach but neither achieves a majority of the popular vote. Of the seven instances of a candidate garnering from fifty to 54.9 percent of the popular vote, in only one—the disputed election of 1876—did he fail to secure a majority of the electoral vote. In sharp

TABLE I   Relationship of Popular Vote Proportion to Electoral Vote Proportion, Democratic and Republican Presidential Candidates, 1872–1960

Proportion of Total Popular Vote	PROPORTION OF TOTAL ELECTORAL VOTE						Total
	Losers			Winners			
	39.9% or Less	40.1–44.9%	45.0–49.9%	50.0–54.9%	55.0–59.9%	60% or More	
39.9% or less	6	—	—	—	—	—	6
40.1–44.9%	6	—	—	—	—	1	7
45.0–49.9%	5	3	2	3	4	1	18
50.0–54.9%	—	—	1	—	—	6	7
55.0–59.9%	—	—	—	—	—	6	6
60% or more	—	—	—	—	—	2	2
TOTAL	17	3	3	3	4	16	46

contrast, the electoral vote proportions of candidates having forty-five to 49.9 percent of the popular vote are distributed across the board, almost equally divided between losers (10) and winners (8). In the latter category, then, judging from the data, the possibility of electoral vote repudiation of the popular verdict appears greatest.

That possibility has not become an actuality with any frequency in American political history, the only clear-cut instance being that of 1888. In that election, Cleveland led Harrison by about 100,000 votes (48.7 to 47.8 percent of the total popular vote), but secured only 41.9 percent of the electoral vote. It may be argued, of course, that even a single such occurrence constitutes damaging evidence against the current method. It must be stressed in response, however, that *any* indirect election scheme could as easily produce a minority President when the popular vote balance between the candidates is as close as that of 1888—or as that of 1960. Judged by this more realistic standard, the record of performance of the electoral college device gives little comfort to those who advocate its replacement by some other form of indirect election.

On the clearly positive side, the electoral college's distortion of the popular vote contributes mightily, in conjunction with other factors, to freezing out serious (power-seeking) third parties in national politics. (Some refinements of this point will be offered in a later section.) The requirement of an absolute majority of electoral votes, without provision for a runoff election, tends away from multipartyism, while the state-unit system tends to produce the requisite electoral vote majority for one or the other of the major parties. The strong support given by the current device to the maintenance of a national two-party system satisfies a criterion of critical importance to many, including the writer.

The biases of the present method that sustain two-partyism also so condition the conduct of presidential campaigns and, through that means, so shape the larger governmental and party system as to directly involve all the remaining criteria noted earlier. The presidential election strategy imposed on the major parties recognizes and acts on the inequality of voter influence stemming from the operation of the state-unit procedure. The political rule of thumb that emerges may be simply put as follows: states safe for either party merit relatively less attention from both parties; attention must be concentrated on those states in which the election outcome is uncertain and, within that category, on those states in which large blocs of electoral votes are at stake. The latter group, that of key unsafe states, includes most of the populous, urbanized, ethnicized and industrialized states in the nation. Voters and interests in those states, therefore, are able to wield political influence disproportionate to their numbers, especially if the groups involved maintain self-consciousness and high cohesion, *e.g.*, certain ethnic and labor groups.

The pressures generated by the current election procedure thus provide at least a partial explanation for such diverse conditions as the declining influence of the Democratic South within the national Democratic Party, the increasing attention paid by both parties to the aspirations of the Negro, the Republican tendency to choose a presidential nominee markedly more "liberal" than the policy outlook characteristic of that party's congressional wing, and the overrecruitment of twentieth-century presidential candidates from the states of New York and Ohio. And many of the policy differences between President and Congress, regardless of party labels, may be traced in good part to the more-urban constituency and outlook of the former and the more-rural electorates and attitudes of the latter. . . .

We shall analyze these two reforms with an eye to determining whether either remedies defects of the current method without sacrificing the latter's advantages and without creating new disadvantages of an equally or more serious nature.

PROPORTIONATE DIVISION OF THE ELECTORAL VOTE

The core of this reform is to substitute for the state-unit allocation of all electoral votes to one candidate a system of proportionate division of the electoral vote by which each presidential candidate will get the same proportion of the state's electoral vote as he does of the state's popular vote. The present formula for determining the number of electoral votes to be assigned to each state remains unchanged. The proportion of the total electoral vote required for victory has been set, in various versions of the proposal, at a plurality, forty percent, or fifty percent. (Although some of the effects of the proposal differ depending on which figure is adopted, the present analysis will not turn on that problem.) Over the years the major legislative sponsors of the measure have been Representative Ed Gossett (D., Texas) and Senators Henry Cabot Lodge (R., Mass.), Estes Kefauver (D., Tenn.) and Price Daniel (D., Texas).

The advantages of this scheme over the current method may be readily gauged. By making the electoral vote reflect, rather than suppress, the intrastate division of the popular vote, the proposal would sharply reduce, though not eliminate, inequality of voter power. The distortion of the popular vote based on the electoral weight assigned each state and on the irrelevance of turnout rates would remain, though the impact of the latter would be minimized because of the incentives inherent in the proposal to enlarged turnout in all states. Since a vote gained anywhere would become an increment of electoral vote strength, the major parties would move away from disproportionate attention to the populous states and would campaign broadly and vigorously in every state. On a national basis, the electoral vote proportions of the major-party candidates would tend to come within a few percentage points of their popular vote proportions. Under conditions of a close division of the popular vote, then, a minority President would still be possible. If the popular vote balance were not close, however, in theory the proportionate method would be considerably less likely to produce a minority President than the current system. (Recall, however, that the latter eventuality has not as yet occurred under those conditions.)

However, the probable impact of the reform on the maintenance of the national two-party system is adverse, and that criterion is of sufficient importance to the writer to require the judgment that the reform, on balance, should be rejected. . . .

The assertion is that the proportionate plan, in the light of contemporary political alignments of the voters, would tend to produce a trend to predominant one-party-ism in presidential politics, namely, facilitating Democratic control of the White House by means which would reflect and contribute to the heightened influence of the southern faction of the Democratic Party. . . .

In recent decades, the eleven southern states of the Confederacy have been allocated a little under one-quarter of the total electoral votes (about 127 of 531). During the four Roosevelt administrations, the South watched its influence decline in the presidential wing of the Democratic Party even as it continued to cast its regional vote solidly for Roosevelt—and the two patterns were much related, for reasons set forth in the earlier analysis of the current method. Even assuming, though, that the South had rebelled and had cast all its electoral votes for his Republican rivals, Roosevelt would nonetheless have won every one of his elections. The state-unit system, in brief, permitted the Democratic Party to free itself from any great dependency on the South

because the party could get its electoral majority by slimmer margins of popular strength in many non-southern states. The same pattern, of necessity, would have to underlie Republican presidential victories, at least prior to recent elections.

It seems evident that the South's political influence would be enhanced under the proportionate plan, the extent of the increased influence depending on one's estimate of the two-party division of the electoral vote in the South under conditions encouraging maximum turnout of registered voters. Suppose, for example, that the South's electoral vote were to divide seventy-five to fifty-two in favor of the Democrats, giving the latter a net gain of twenty-three electoral votes from the region. Those twenty-three electoral votes could not easily be offset in the rest of the nation, by either the Republicans or the non-southern Democrats, because of the small net electoral vote gain to either party derived from slim margins of popular victory in the urban-industrialized states. A lead of twenty-three electoral votes in the non-South would represent a popular vote lead of several millions. If the estimate made is realistic, then the Democratic Party would gain significant competitive advantage for control of the Presidency, an advantage that could be counteracted effectively by the Republicans only if their candidate was able to secure that margin vote lead in the non-South portion of the nation. This important Democratic edge in presidential elections, in turn, would bear the price tag of a considerable dependency on the continued support of its southern wing, a dependency that would inflate southern influence over the content of public policy.

Is the estimate realistic? No demonstration is possible for this estimate, or for any other. To this writer, it does seem more rather than less probable that the South, under the proportionate plan, would contribute an important number of electoral votes to the Democrats. A significant portion of the notable upsurge of presidential Republicanism in the South in recent elections, for example, stems from popular disaffection with the national Democratic Party. If the southern point of view were to receive more attention within Democratic councils, then presumably most of those protesting voters would happily return to the Democratic fold. Moreover, important as the presidential election method is to the larger political process, it would be rather extreme to suggest that the current method has distorted what otherwise would be a closely-competitive two-partyism into the situation of Democratic dominance as we have known it. Surely the pronounced and durable past attachment of the region to the Democratic Party has roots deeper and more complex than merely the pressures generated by the mode of presidential election. The election method, on the other hand, does appear to be a critical factor in the extent to which the southern commitment to the Democratic Party becomes the determining element in the outcome of presidential elections.

It is conceivable, if northern Democrats found it impossible to accommodate the South while continuing to try to appeal to metropolitan interests, that the Republican Party might become the beneficiary of southern support. Either way it developed, effective two-party competition in presidential politics would be hampered and the South's influence would rise. It should be remembered that the proportionate plan enhances the political influence of "safer" states and decreases that of closely-divided states. States sharing pronounced sectional interests, like those of the South, would be given every incentive to maximize their power by *not* developing effective two-party presidential politics. In the light of these considerations, the predictions of advocates of the proportionate plan that the South will achieve durable two-partyism seem to be based more on hope than reason, and the former provides a poor base to justify fundamental alteration of the mode of presidential election.

DISTRICT DIVISION OF THE ELECTORAL VOTE

In place of the state-unit system, this reform would establish a district-unit system. Congressional districts would serve also as electoral districts, each of which would be assigned one vote, to be cast in favor of the presidential candidate with the highest popular vote in the district. In addition, each state would cast two electoral votes on the basis of the state-unit procedure. The formula for assigning electoral votes to the states remains unchanged. To win, a presidential candidate has to secure an absolute majority of electoral votes. The legislative sponsors of this reform have included Senators Karl Mundt (R., S.D.) and Everett Dirksen (R., Ill.), and Representative Frederic Coudert, Jr. (R., N.Y.).

The strongest argument against adoption of this reform lies in the fact that the exact nature of most of its important consequences depends too much on the particulars of the districting pattern of each state. American states have no developed tradition of equity in the apportionment of seats or in the drawing of district boundary lines for either the state or national legislature. The reform under discussion, by vastly increasing the stakes involved in districting, could not help but persuade the controlling partisans of the necessity to rig the political boundaries in their party's favor. Any "reform" permitting the projection of these inequitable practices directly into the presidential arena should be repudiated out of hand. . . .

To say that the district plan defies definitive analysis of its consequences is not to say that some suspicions about the probable directions of its effects are not in order. The bias of the current method is clearly known, and the district proposal would eliminate the main source of that bias, the state-unit system. The legislative sponsors of the reform are conservative in policy complexion. And several of the respective backers of the proportionate plan and the district plan are on record as indicating that, if their plan failed of adoption, they would support the other plan. In its intent, then, the district plan suffers from no ambiguity: its aim is to distribute political influence in a manner quite different from that which obtains under the current system. The exact details of which non-urban interests gain what share of increased influence become quite secondary to that central aim, as indicated by the contingent pledges of mutual support by the backers of the two reform proposals here examined. The identification of common anti-urban motivations underlying these reforms provides an appropriate context for the concluding section of the analysis.

THE ANTI-URBAN POLITICS OF ELECTORAL COLLEGE REFORM

It should be clear, if not on *a priori* grounds then on the basis of the analysis presented, that presidential election methods are neither neutral nor identical in their consequences for the distribution of political influence. The truth of that observation is insufficiently realized by those civic-minded citizens whose advocacy of the need for electoral college reform derives primarily from a sense of outrage at the arithmetical distortions of the current system and the biases of voter inequality that result. From such an essentially superficial view, either or both the proportionate and district plans appear more preferable to follow. More tough-minded political observers and participants, however, are keenly aware that the replacement of the state-unit system results, not in the elimination of bias, but in the substitution of one kind of bias for another. The broader directions of the consequences of enacting either of the two reform proposals are anti-urban,

anti-ethnic, and anti-labor, in the sense of reducing the political influence of those interests. And many of those favoring adoption of a different indirect election scheme than the present method are motivated consciously to realize those ends.

The determination of the precise beneficiaries in the redistribution of political influence that would occur is not so certain a matter as the identification of the anti-urban effects. The analysis here undertaken suggests that, under the proportionate plan, southern political power would increase and most probably would constitute a critical element in the election outcome. Whichever party the South gave disproportionate support to—and it would doubtless be the Democrats in the beginning—would gain a significant enough edge over its rival to depress the chances of maintaining the turnover rate in party control of the Presidency at a level consistent with effective two-partyism. Under the district plan, it is less clear whether rural Republicans or rural Democrats would get the lion's share of the power wrested from metropolitan groups.

Party and factional congressional alignments on the proposals support the analytic themes and inferences here drawn. In 1950, when the House defeated the proportionate plan, most of the support for the measure came from southern Democrats. In 1956, the Senate sponsors of the two reform proposals combined forces and offered a constitutional amendment that, among other things, permitted a state to choose between the proportionate plan and the district plan for each election. Although such a hybrid proposal lacked most of whatever merit either reform would have if taken alone, it nearly secured the two-thirds vote needed for passage. For present purposes, we need note only that southern and rural-state senators provided the bulk of the votes for the measure.

Deviation from the alignments indicated requires a word of additional explanation.

Some liberal legislators, such as Senators Lodge and Kefauver, believe that the proportionate plan would revitalize southern two-party competition to the extent that both major parties could effectively compete in the region and, therefore, in the nation. Their motivation, as they would doubtless see it, is not anti-urban but pro-equity. Some Republican conservative legislators supporting one or both reform proposals, on the other hand, may have thought through the policy consequences more carefully than the party consequences. They probably have assumed that whatever reduces the political power of metropolitan areas must also result in a reduction of the power of the Democratic Party. To many in this group, of course, it would not be a very bitter pill to swallow if it turned out that conservative southern Democrats were the prime gainers.

It appears, then, that any indirect election device not closely approximating direct popular election is productive of strong biases favoring some segments of the population and disadvantaging other segments. The question of "reform" in this area, as a consequence, should not be understood as a nonpartisan matter of "fairness versus inequity," but as a profoundly political problem: Whose interests should the necessarily biased procedures favor?

To take a position on that problem in terms other than the rhetoric of partisans, one must move away from a restricted focus on presidential election methods to encompass the larger political system. Whose interests are unduly served by the election procedures for the state legislatures, the Senate, the House? Should the Presidency also be brought into the orbit of that exaggerated rural influence? Or should not urban-ethnic-labor influence, by the doctrine of a checks and balances of interests, be granted one important area of countervailing power?

To invoke a standard of offsetting one inequity by another may be disturbing or offensive to some, but a realistic analysis of presidential election methods leaves little choice in the matter. After all, many of those most outspoken on the immorality of the current system are conspicuously silent when it comes to extending their principles to the arena of election methods for state and national legislatures. It should be understood that the basis for judgment here is a contingent one which would call for quite different conclusions if the condition of excessive rural influence were corrected. But not even those who, like the writer, are highly pleased with the Supreme Court's recent decision in *Baker v. Carr* would hold that the time to draw those different conclusions had arrived. . . .

48.   A Classification of Presidential Elections

Angus Campbell,
Philip E. Converse,
Warren E. Miller,
and Donald E. Stokes

Each election affects the relative strength of the two major parties. Four political scientists at the University of Michigan here classify presidential contests into three categories: "maintaining," "deviating," and "realigning." Recent national elections could be usefully analyzed by means of this classification. Did the elections of 1960 and 1964 simply "maintain" the Democratic party majority or did they result in a more basic party "realignment"?

* * *

When we look to other campaigns beyond [those of 1952 and 1956], we find a

From Angus Campbell, Philip E. Converse, Warren E. Miller, and Donald E. Stokes, *The American Voter* (New York: John Wiley and Sons, 1960), pp. 531–538.

long succession of presidential contests resembling each other closely in the institutional framework within which they are conducted, but differing substantially from year to year as the new candidates, the contemporary issues, and the minority parties that spring to life have given them individuality. As we have just seen, it is possible to describe the disordered confusion of acts and events that make up an election in terms of the basic partisan attitudes that we have conceived as directly underlying the individual voting act. And a good deal of the meaning of an election for future years can be indicated by comparing the force of these attitudes with the electorate's long-term partisan loyalties. We propose now to reach beyond these recent elections and apply our theory of political motivation more broadly, using it to develop a more generalized system of classification of presidential elections.

We propose to classify American presidential elections into three basic types, which we may call maintaining, deviating, and realigning.[1] A *maintaining* election is one in which the pattern of partisan attachments prevailing in the preceding period persists and is the primary influence on forces governing the vote. In this sense many, if not most, presidential elections during the past hundred years have been maintaining elections. If we assume that during the period immediately following the Civil War the majority of the electorate were Republican in their partisan sympathies and that this majority declined to something near an even balance during the 1876–1892 period and was revitalized in 1896, we may conclude that the numerous Republican victories down through the 1920's fall largely in this category.

[1] The reader will recognize that this classification is an extension of V. O. Key's theory of critical elections. See V. O. Key, Jr., "A Theory of Critical Elections," *Journal of Politics, 17* (February 1955), 3–18. See also V. O. Key, Jr., "Secular Realignment and the Party System," *Journal of Politics, 21* (May 1959), 198–210.

Among more recent elections we would describe the contest of 1948 as a maintaining election. The events surrounding the campaign of that year seemed signally devoid of circumstances that could generate forces running counter to existing partisan loyalties. In 1948 the total popular vote was 48.4 million, the lowest turnout in relation to the size of the total adult population since 1928. No compelling political issue stirred intense reaction throughout the electorate. Although the Taft-Hartley Act and the elimination of certain wartime economic controls were offensive to some groups of voters, the nation was prosperous, employment was high, and the threat of economic stress was slight. Similarly, international issues had receded in the mind of a public that appeared to concern itself with world affairs only under the greatest compulsion. The attempt of the short-lived Progressive Party to arouse public interest in issues of foreign policy proved a failure. It was, in other words, an election in which no overriding issue intruded to deflect the electorate from voting with its standing partisan allegiances.

Neither was it an election in which significant numbers of voters were activated by the personalities or accomplishments of the presidential candidates. Neither President Truman nor Governor Dewey stirred the enthusiasm of the general electorate. On the contrary, they were both criticized for presumed inadequacies and were undoubtedly seen in highly partisan terms. The Democratic victory in 1948 is sometimes referred to as a personal triumph for Mr. Truman, but the evidence does not support this interpretation. A presidential nominee who runs behind his party in the election returns, as Truman did in well over half the states in which there was a Democratic candidate for Governor or Senator, can hardly be said to be leading his party to victory. In the election to which we refer, Truman and Dewey both drew their support primarily from the most highly committed followers of their parties. Neither was able to swing the independent vote in any significant way, attract any sizable number of defectors from the opposition party, or stimulate any important fraction of the in-and-out vote to go to the polls in his behalf. These are the marks of strong candidate appeal, and they were not present in the 1948 election.

It is likely, then, that in 1948 the electorate responded to current elements of politics very much in terms of its existing partisan loyalties. Apparently very little of the political landscape attracted strong feeling in that year. But what feeling there was seemed to be governed largely by antecedent attachments to one of the two major parties. On election day the Democrats turned out to support Truman and the Republicans to support Dewey. Neither party marshalled its forces at full strength. But Mr. Truman was fortunate in representing a party whose followers considerably outnumbered the opposition, and the electoral decision maintained his party in power.

In a *deviating* election the basic division of partisan loyalties is not seriously disturbed, but the attitude forces on the vote are such as to bring about the defeat of the majority party. After the personalities or events that deflected these forces from what we would expect on the basis of party have disappeared from the scene, the political balance returns to a level that more closely reflects the underlying division of partisan attachments. A deviating election is thus a temporary reversal that occurs during a period when one or the other party holds a clear advantage in the long-term preferences of the electorate.

In the previous pages we have described characteristics of the Eisenhower victory of 1952 that establish this election as a deviating one. The election of Woodrow Wilson in 1916 suggests itself as an additional example. There seems little doubt that during the period of the Wilson elections the electorate was predominantly Republican.

Wilson attained the White House in 1912 with a minority (42 percent) of the total vote, as Roosevelt and Taft split the Republican Party; his incumbency and the public emotion aroused by the shadow of the First World War apparently provided the additional votes he needed in 1916 to reach the narrow plurality that he achieved over his Republican opponent. According to Key, the Democratic gains of 1916 were due principally to "a short-term desertion of the Republican Party by classes of British origin and orientation."[2] The temporary character of the Democratic victory began to become apparent in the 1918 elections when the Republican Party won control of the Congress. In 1920 and the two elections following, the minority status of the Democratic Party was again convincingly demonstrated.

The definition we have given of a deviating election implies that in such an election more people than usual will cross party lines in casting their votes. As a result, the events of a deviating election can easily suggest that traditional party loyalties have become less important. To be sure, they have —in an immediate sense. But if our view of the motivational basis of voting is correct, a deviating election should not be taken as evidence of a secular decline in the importance of party identification. . . . We have examined the profound impact of party allegiance even in elections in which a great many people voted against their traditional loyalties. What is more, the interrelations of education, political involvement, and strength of partisanship suggest that as the electorate becomes more sophisticated and involved psychologically in politics, it may well become more, rather than less, fixed in its partisan commitments. In any event, demonstrating a lasting decline in the role of party identification needs more evidence than that which one or two deviating elections can supply.

[2] V. O. Key Jr., "A Theory of Critical Elections," *op. cit.*, 11.

Key has pointed out that there is a third type of election, characterized by the appearance of "a more or less durable realignment" of party loyalties. In such a *realigning* election, popular feeling associated with politics is sufficiently intense that the basic partisan commitments of a portion of the electorate change. Such shifts are infrequent. As Key observes, every election has the effect of creating lasting party loyalties in some individual voters, but it is "not often that the number so affected is so great as to create a sharp realignment."

We have said that changes in long-term party allegiances tend to be associated with great national crises. The emergence of the Republican Party and its subsequent domination of national politics were the direct outgrowth of the great debate over slavery and the ultimate issue of the Civil War. The election of 1896, following the panic of 1893, is regarded by Key as a "critical" election since "the Democratic defeat was so demoralizing and so thorough that the party made little headway in regrouping its forces until 1916." It may be argued that the Democratic Party did not in fact hold the loyalties of a clear majority of the electorate at the time of the Cleveland elections, but the election statistics make it appear that whatever hold it did have on the voters was greatly weakened after 1893.

The most dramatic reversal of party alignments in this century was associated with the Great Depression of the 1930's. The economic disaster that befell the nation during the Hoover Administration so discredited the Republican Party that it fell from its impressive majorities of the 1920's to a series of defeats, which in 1936 reached overwhelming dimensions. These defeats were more than temporary departures from a continuing division of underlying party strength. There is little doubt that large numbers of voters, especially among the younger age groups and those social and economic classes hardest hit by the Depression, were converted to the Democratic Party during this period. The program of welfare legislation of the New Deal and the extraordinary personality of its major exponent, Franklin D. Roosevelt, brought about a profound realignment of party strength, which has endured in large part up to the present time.

Key has pointed out that the shift toward the Democratic Party that occurred in the early 1930's was anticipated in the New England area in the 1928 election. It is difficult to determine whether the changes in these successive election years were actually part of the same movement. Since the shifts in New England were highly correlated with the proportions of Catholic voters in the communities studied, it would not be unreasonable to attribute them to the presence of Governor Alfred E. Smith at the head of the Democratic ticket in 1928. Had the depression not intervened, the New England vote might have returned to its pre-1928 levels in the 1932 election. It may be recalled, however, that the Smith candidacy had not only a religious aspect but a class quality as well. The resemblance of the class contrast between Smith and Hoover in 1928 and that between Truman and Dewey in 1948 is more than casual. It may well be that New England voters, having moved into the Democratic ranks in 1928 for reasons having to do with both religious and economic considerations, found it easy to remain there in 1932 when economic questions became compellingly important.

The ambiguity of the relation between the Hoover-Smith contest of 1928 and the Roosevelt elections of the 1930's, at least in New England, emphasizes the importance of having adequate measures of the attitude forces on the vote and of the distribution of party identification if we are to interpret the character of an election. This ambiguity also cautions us against too easily associating with a single election a major realignment of party strength. In order to describe with confidence the movement of part of the electorate from the Republican to the Democratic Party a generation ago, we would need to know when it was that these people formed a stable emotional attachment to the Democratic Party. If we had this information we might well find that an attachment of this kind appeared in some of the changers as early as 1928, whereas it appeared in others only in the late 1930's or early 1940's, after they had voted Democratic several times. It is worth noting that the Democratic harvest of votes continued through the mid-thirties. Although Roosevelt's margin of victory in 1932 was large (59 percent of the two-party vote), it was not until 1936 that the Democratic wave reached its peak. The long-entrenched Republican sympathies of the electorate may not have given way easily in the early years of the Depression. Had not Roosevelt and his New Deal won the confidence of many of these people during his first term—or even his second—there might well have been a return to earlier party lines similar to that which occurred in 1920. From this point of view we might speak not of a realigning *election* but of a realigning *electoral era*.

What is more, it is clear that the changes of such an era arise not alone from changes in the party loyalties of those who are past the age of socialization to politics. It comes as well from the relative advantage of the party that dominates the era in recruiting new identifiers from among those who are first developing their political values. The past histories of persons we have interviewed in the 1950's indicate that the New Deal-Fair Deal era produced a lasting change in party strength primarily by attracting to the Democratic Party most of the age cohort entering the electorate during the 1930's and 1940's.

One other aspect of change has been evident in most periods of lasting displacements of party strength. We have said that the distinguishing characteristic of a realigning era is a shift in the distribution of party identification. By this we mean that a *net* shift occurs, benefiting one party rather than the other. But it is clear that a net shift in the party balance does not imply that individual changes have been in one direction only. Such a shift may result from partially compensating changes of party loyalties in several population groups.[3] For example, one party may gain strength overall from a greater polarization of politics along class lines. We know that this is part of what happened in the 1930's, as the Depression and New Deal prompted working-class people to identify more closely with the Democratic Party and middle-class people with the Republican Party. Which party gains more from a reshuffling of this sort depends on which class grouping is the larger and how strongly each grouping moves toward complete homogeneity of opinion. Lasting changes in the party balance may also accompany political realignments along regional lines. This was what happened in the elections after the Civil War. And, as Key has made clear, the realignment accompanying the election of 1896 moved the industrial East toward the Republican Party and the West toward the Democrats, giving our presidential politics a regional cast that persisted through subsequent elections. If the Republicans gained from this dual sectional movement, it was largely because the East was by far the more populous region.

We do not mean to say that changes in the political loyalties of groups are an indispensable part of long-term displacements of party strength. We may think of factors, such as a protracted foreign war, which would benefit one party or the other in virtually all groups. Yet there are two reasons why a change in the group basis of politics is likely to presage a lasting shift in the party balance. First, changes in the political loyalties of groups tend to be associated

[3] Indeed, the concept of realignment as it is used by Key includes the idea of change in the group basis of party strength.

with issues that persist through time. We may suppose, for example, that issues which sharpen class differences will prove to be more durable than the impact of a magnetic political figure who has drawn strength to his party from a great many groups. Second, changes in party loyalty occurring on a group basis tend to be reinforced by group opinion processes. Attitudes rooted in social groups are likely to be more stable than are attitudes that are denied the status of group norms.

In view of all that we have said, how are we to characterize the two elections for which we have adequate survey data? The Eisenhower elections were clearly not maintaining elections. Neither were they realigning elections in the sense of a profound shift of the nation's party identifications having occurred in this period. Yet the question might well be raised of whether they were not the early elections of a realigning electoral era. We believe they were not, for reasons that a brief review of our findings may serve to make clear.

The most immediately relevant information that we can draw out of these studies is the fact that in both 1952 and 1956 the number of people who called themselves Democrats outnumbered those who identified themselves as Republicans, and this ratio showed no tendency to move in the Republican direction between the two years. What is more, the Republican Party did not recruit a heavy majority of young voters who were coming into the electorate, although these years did see the Democratic proportion of new voters reduced to something like half.

A second important item is the evidence that for the most part those Democrats and Independents who voted for Eisenhower at the time of his two elections preferred the man but not the party. This is dramatically demonstrated by the high proportion of ticket-splitting reported by these people. Three out of five in 1952 and three out of four in 1956 were not willing to support the Republican slate even though they

voted for its presidential candidate. It is especially significant that this separation of the candidate from his party was greater in the second Eisenhower election than in the first. If we compare 1952 to 1932 it seems probable that the potential for shift created by the Democratic victory in 1932 was realized in 1936, whereas whatever readiness for shift was present in the electorate in 1952 seems to have largely faded out by 1956.

That the Republican Party did not prepare the ground in the Eisenhower years for a basic shift of party loyalties is attested by the congressional vote in 1954 and 1956. Without Eisenhower's name at the top of their ticket in 1954 the Republicans could not hold either house of Congress. And even with Eisenhower again heading the ticket in 1956 the Republican congressional candidates ran several percentage points *further* behind their pace setter than they had in 1952, and in doing so they once again lost both houses of Congress. There is evidence from our 1956 survey that Eisenhower's coattails were not without influence and that without them the Republican candidates for Congress would have fared even more poorly than they did.

We may observe, finally, that political change in the Eisenhower years was not accompanied by a marked realignment of the loyalties of groups within the electorate. The factors in these years that deflected the vote from what we would have expected on the basis of party identification alone, acted quite generally across the electorate and were all of a relatively brief duration. The Far Eastern War, which had influenced popular opinion so powerfully in 1952, was settled within a year of Eisenhower's first victory. What corruption there was in the prior Democratic Administration ended perforce when the party was turned out of power. And, above all, the Eisenhower personality could not continue to be a prime influence on the behavior of the electorate with the coming of new candidates.

These considerations lead us to the conclusion that the Eisenhower elections did not presage a critical realignment of partisan attachments. They did not seriously threaten the prevailing Democratic majority, and the factors that made them possible seem not to have been of a long-term character. One may ask how long a party can hope to hold the White House if it does not have a majority of the party-identified electorate. There would not appear to be any certain answer to this question. The unfolding of national and international events and the appearance of new political figures to take the place of the old hold the potential for unforeseeable political consequences. We should expect, however, that the circumstances that keep a minority in power would tend over time to increase the proportion of the electorate whose loyalty it commanded. If this increase does not occur, the minority party cannot hope to continue its tenure in office over a very extended period.

49.   A Theory of Critical Elections

V. O. Key, Jr.

The stability of voter allegiances and of party relationships is periodically upset by elections that recast the entire two-party system. Focusing on the New England vote, V. O. Key, Jr., late Professor of Government at Harvard University, examined such "critical elections" in 1896 and 1928. In each case, the election marked the end of one era of party dominance and the onset of a new majority coalition. This article has provided the intellectual stimulus for much recent research on party and electoral history. It also illustrates the analytical uses of community voting statistics.

Perhaps the basic differentiating characteristic of democratic orders consists in the expression of effective choice by the mass of the people in elections.[1] The electorate occupies, at least in the mystique of such orders, the position of the principal organ of governance; it acts through elections. An election itself is a formal act of collective decision that occurs in a stream of connected antecedent and subsequent behavior. Among democratic orders elections, so broadly defined, differ enormously in their nature, their meaning, and their consequences. Even within a single nation the reality of election differs greatly from time to time. A systematic comparative approach, with a focus on variations in the nature of elections would doubtless be fruitful in advancing understanding of the democratic governing process. In behavior antecedent to voting, elections differ in the proportions of the electorate psychologically involved, in the intensity of attitudes associated with campaign cleavages, in the nature of expectations about the consequences of the voting, in the impact of objective events relevant to individual political choice, in individual sense of effective connection with community decision, and in other ways. These and other antecedent variations affect the act of voting itself as well as subsequent behavior. An understanding of elections and, in turn, of the democratic process as a whole must rest partially on broad differentiations of the complexes of behavior that we call elections.[2]

[1] For most of the detailed compilations of data underlying this discussion I am indebted to Stanley D. Hopper. Contributory analyses were also made by Hugh D. Price.
[2] Elections need not be equated to revolutions to appreciate the suggestive value in speculation about the nature of elections of the categorization of revolutions. See Carl J. Friedrich, *Constitutional Government and Democracy: Theory and Practice in Europe and America* (Boston: Ginn and Company, rev. ed., 1950), pp. 145–155.

From the *Journal of Politics*, vol. 17, no. 1 (February 1955), pp. 3–18.

While this is not the occasion to develop a comprehensive typology of elections, the foregoing remarks provide an orientation for an attempt to formulate a concept of one type of election—based on American experience—which might be built into a more general theory of elections. Even the most fleeting inspection of American elections suggests the existence of a category of elections in which voters are, at least from impressionistic evidence, unusually deeply concerned, in which the extent of electoral involvement is relatively quite high, and in which the decisive results of the voting reveal a sharp alteration of the pre-existing cleavage within the electorate. Moreover, and perhaps this is the truly differentiating characteristic of this sort of election, the realignment made manifest in the voting in such elections seems to persist for several succeeding elections. All these characteristics cumulate to the conception of an election type in which the depth and intensity of electoral involvement are high, in which more or less profound readjustments occur in the relations of power within the community, and in which new and durable electoral groupings are formed.[3] These comments suppose, of course, the existence of other types of complexes of behavior centering about formal elections, the systematic isolation and identification of which, fortunately, are not essential for the present discussion.

I

The presidential election of 1928 in the New England states provides a specific case of the type of critical election that has been described in general terms. In that year

Alfred E. Smith, the Democratic Presidential candidate, made gains in all the New England states. The rise in Democratic strength was especially notable in Massachusetts and Rhode Island. When one probes below the surface of the gross election figures it becomes apparent that a sharp and durable realignment also occurred within the electorate, a fact reflective of the activation by the Democratic candidate of low-income, Catholic, urban voters of recent immigrant stock.[4] In New England, at least, the Roosevelt revolution of 1932 was in large measure an Al Smith revolution of 1928, a characterization less applicable to the remainder of the country.

The intensity and extent of electoral concern before the voting of 1928 can only be surmised, but the durability of the realignment formed at the election can be determined by simple analyses of election statistics. An illustration of the new division thrust through the electorate by the campaign of 1928 is provided by the graphs in Figure A, which show the Democratic per-

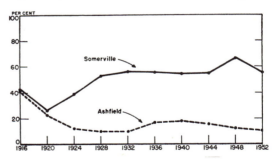

Fig. A Democratic percentages of major-party presidential vote, Somerville and Ashfield, Massachusetts, 1916–1952.

centages of the presidential vote from 1916 through 1952 for the city of Somerville and the town of Ashfield in Massachusetts. Somerville, adjacent to Boston, had a population in 1930 of 104,000 of which 28 per cent was foreign born and 41 per cent was

[3] These notions have been put forward in fragmentary form elsewhere: V. O. Key, Jr., "The Future of the Democratic Party," *The Virginia Quarterly Review*, 28 (Spring, 1952), 161–175, where the argument is stated unencumbered by supporting data; Key, *A Primer of Statistics for Political Scientists* (New York: Thomas Y. Crowell Company, 1954), pp. 53–55, an analysis of an illustrative case.

[4] The campaign and its effects are described by Samuel Lubell, *The Future of American Politics* (New York: Harper & Brothers, 1952), pp. 34–41.

of foreign-born or mixed parentage. Roman Catholics constituted a large proportion of its relatively low-income population. Ashfield, a farming community in western Massachusetts with a 1930 population of 860, was predominately native born (8.6 per cent foreign born), chiefly rural-farm (66 per cent), and principally Protestant.

The impressiveness of the differential impact of the election of 1928 on Somerville and Ashfield may be read from the graphs in Figure A. From 1920 the Democratic percentage in Somerville ascended steeply while the Democrats in Ashfield, few in 1920, became even less numerous in 1928. Inspection of the graphs also suggests that the great reshuffling of voters that occurred in 1928 was perhaps the final and decisive stage in a process that had been under way for some time. That antecedent process involved a relatively heavy support in 1924 for La Follette in those towns in which Smith was subsequently to find special favor. Hence, in Figure A, as in all the other charts, the 1924 figure is the percentage of the total accounted for by the votes of both the Democratic and Progressive candidates rather than the Democratic percentage of the two-party vote. This usage conveys a minimum impression of the size of the 1924–1928 Democratic gain but probably depicts the nature of the 1920–1928 trend.

For present purposes, the voting behavior of the two communities shown in Figure A after 1928 is of central relevance. The differences established between them in 1928 persisted even through 1952, although the two series fluctuated slightly in response to the particular influences of individual campaigns. The nature of the process of maintenance of the cleavage is, of course, not manifest from these data. Conceivably the impress of the events of 1928 on individual attitudes and loyalties formed partisan attachments of lasting nature. Yet it is doubtful that the new crystallization of 1928 projected itself through a quarter of a century solely from the momentum given

it by such factors. More probably subsequent events operated to re-enforce and to maintain the 1928 cleavage. Whatever the mechanism of its maintenance, the durability of the realignment is impressive.

Somerville and Ashfield may be regarded more or less as samples of major population groups within the electorate of Massachusetts. Since no sample survey data are available for 1928, about the only analysis feasible is inspection of election returns for geographic units contrasting in their population composition. Lest it be supposed, however, that the good citizens of Somerville and Ashfield were aberrants simply unlike the remainder of the people of the Commonwealth, examination of a large number of towns and cities is in order. In the interest of both compression and comprehensibility, a mass of data is telescoped into Figure B. The graphs in that figure compare over the period 1916–1952 the voting behavior of the 29 Massachusetts towns and cities having the sharpest Democratic increases, 1920–1928, with that of the 30 towns and cities having the most marked Democratic loss, 1920–1928.[5] In other words, the figure averages out a great many Ashfields and Somervilles. The data of Figure B confirm the expectation that the pattern exhibited by the pair of voting units in Figure A represented only a single case of a much more general phenomenon. Yet by virtue of the coverage of the data in the figure, one gains a stronger impression of the difference in the character of the elec-

[5] The measure of Democratic gain was the difference between the Democratic percentages of the town vote in 1920 and 1928. Something might be said for the use of the percentage increase from one election to another as a measure of change. Thus, a town 10 per cent Democratic in 1920 and 15 per cent Democratic in 1928 would have had, with a constant total vote, a Democratic percentage increase of 50. This sort of measure obviously has its peculiarities and conceivably its uses. It was rejected on the ground that the method of percentage differences gave a roughly comparable figure from town to town in that it represented the net proportion of the voting population affected by the trend under observation.

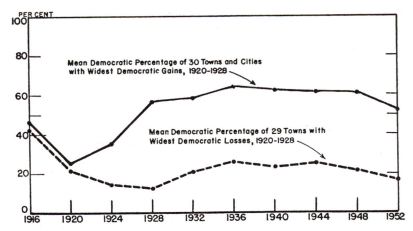

Fig. B Persistence of electoral cleavage of 1928 in Massachusetts: mean Democratic percentage of presidential vote in towns with sharpest Democratic gains, 1920–1928, and in towns of widest Democratic losses, 1920–1928.

tion of 1928 and the other elections recorded there. The cleavage confirmed by the 1928 returns persisted. At subsequent elections the voters shifted to and fro within the outlines of the broad division fixed in 1928.

Examination of the characteristics of the two groups of cities and towns of Figure B —those with the most marked Democratic gains, 1920–1928, and those with the widest movement in the opposite direction—reveals the expected sorts of differences. Urban, industrial, foreign-born, Catholic areas made up the bulk of the first group of towns, although an occasional rural Catholic community increased its Democratic vote markedly. The towns with a contrary movement tended to be rural, Protestant, native-born. The new Democratic vote correlated quite closely with a 1930 vote on state enforcement of the national prohibition law. . . .

The Massachusetts material has served both to explain the method of analysis and to present the case of a single state. Examinations of the election of 1928 in other New England states indicates that in each a pattern prevailed similar to that of Massachusetts.[6] The total effect of the realign-

[6] Not only was the pattern in terms of the behavior of towns with greatest Democratic gains and

ment differed, of course, from state to state. In Massachusetts and Rhode Island the number of people affected by the upheaval of 1928 was sufficient to form a new majority coalition. In Maine, New Hampshire, and Vermont the same sort of reshuffling of electors occurred, but the proportions affected were not sufficient to overturn the Republican combination, although the basis was laid in Maine and New Hampshire for later limited Democratic successes. To underpin these remarks the materials on Connecticut, Maine, New Hampshire, and Rhode Island are presented in Figure C. The data on Vermont, excluded for lack of space, form a pattern similar to that emerging from the analysis of the other states.

In the interpretation of all these 1928 analyses certain limitations of the technique need to be kept in mind. The data and the technique most clearly reveal a shift

widest Democratic losses similar: it is evident, too, that the same sorts of population groups were affected. In Connecticut the towns with the broadest Democratic gains 1920–1928 had a mean foreign-born population percentage of 23.8 and a mean rural-farm percentage of 14.9. In contrast, the towns showing the sharpest Democratic losses had a mean foreign-born population percentage of 15.0 and a mean rural-farm population percentage of 45.5.

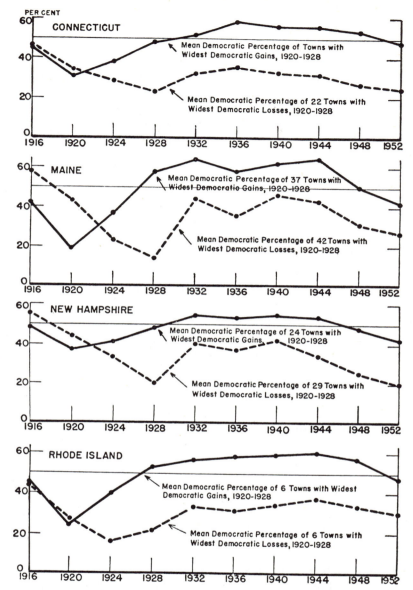

Fig. C Realignment of 1928 in Connecticut, Maine, New Hampshire, and Rhode Island.

when voters of different areas move in opposite directions. From 1928 to 1936 apparently a good deal of Democratic growth occurred in virtually all geographic units, a shift not shown up sharply by the technique. Hence, the discussion may fail adequately to indicate the place of 1928 as the crucial stage in a process of electoral change that began before and concluded after that year.

II

One of the difficulties with an ideal type is that no single actual case fits exactly its specifications. Moreover, in any system of categorization the greater the number of differentiating criteria for classes, the more nearly one tends to create a separate class for each instance. If taxonomic systems are to be of analytical utility, they must almost inevitably group together instances that are unlike at least in peripheral characteristics irrelevant to the purpose of the system. All of which serves to warn that an election is about to be classified as critical even though in some respects the behavior involved differed from that of the 1928 polling.

Central to our concept of critical elections is a realignment within the electorate both sharp and durable. With respect to these basic criteria the election of 1896 falls within the same category as that of 1928, although it differed in other respects. The persistence of the new division of 1896 was perhaps not so notable as that of 1928; yet the Democratic defeat was so demoralizing and so thorough that the party could make little headway in regrouping its forces until 1916.[7] Perhaps the significant feature of the 1896 contest was that, at least in New England, it did not form a new division in which partisan lines became more nearly congruent with lines separating classes, religions, or other such social groups. Instead, the Republican succeeded in drawing new support, in about the same degree, from all sorts of economic and social classes. The result was an electoral coalition formidable in its mass but which required both good fortune and skill in political management for its maintenance, giving its latent internal contradictions.

If the 1896 election is described in our terms as a complex of behavior preceding and following the formal voting, an account of the action must include the panic of 1893. Bank failures, railroad receiverships, unemployment, strikes, Democratic championship of deflation and of the gold standard, and related matters created the setting for a Democratic setback in 1894. Only one of the eight New England Democratic Representatives survived the elections of 1894. The two 1892 Democratic governnors fell by the wayside and in all the states the Democratic share of the gubernatorial vote fell sharply in 1894. The luckless William Jennings Bryan and the free-silver heresy perhaps did not contribute as much as is generally supposed to the 1892-1896 decline in New England Democratic strength; New England Democrats moved in large numbers over to the Republican ranks in 1894.

The character of the 1892–1896 electoral shift is suggested by the data of Figure D, which presents an analysis of Connecticut and New Hampshire made by the technique used earlier in examining the election of 1928. The graphs make plain that in these states (and the other New England states show the same pattern) the rout of 1896 produced a basic realignment that persisted at least until 1916.[8] The graphs in Figure D also make equally plain that the 1892–1896 realignment differed radically from that of 1928 in certain respects. In 1896 the net movement in all sorts of geographic units was toward the Republicans; towns differed not in the direction of their movement but only in the extent. Moreover, the persistence of the realignment of 1896 was about the same in those towns with the least Democratic loss from 1892 to 1896 as it was in those with the most marked decline in Democratic strength. Hence, the graphs differ from those on 1928 which took the form of opening scissors. Instead, the 1896 realignment appears as a parallel movement of both groups to a lower plateau of Democratic strength.

If the election of 1896 had had a notable differential impact on geographically segregated social groups, the graphs in Figure D of towns at the extremes of the greatest and least 1892–96 change would have taken the

[7] The data generate the impression that the 1896 alignment persisted in its basic form until 1928, with the Democratic gains of 1916 being principally a short-term desertion of the Republican Party by classes of British origin and orientation.

[8] In the graphs in Figure D the 1912 figure is the Democratic percentage of the three-party vote which is used to provide a measure of the Democratic proportions of the electorate roughly comparable with that used for the other years in the series.

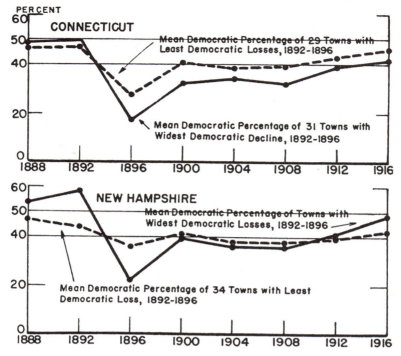

Fig. D Realignment of 1896 in Connecticut and New Hampshire.

form of opening scissors as they did in 1928. While the election of 1896 is often pictured as a last-ditch fight between the haves and the have-nots, that understanding of the contest was, at least in New England, evidently restricted to planes of leadership and oratory. It did not extend to the voting actions of the electorate. These observations merit some buttressing, although the inference emerges clearly enough from Figure D.

Unfortunately the census authorities have ignored the opportunity to advance demographic inquiry by publishing data of consequence about New England towns. Not much information is available on the characteristics of the populations of these small geographic areas. Nevertheless, size of total population alone is a fair separator of towns according to politically significant characteristics. Classification of towns according to that criterion groups them roughly according to industrialization and probably generally also according to religion and national origin. Hence, with size

of population of towns and cities as a base, Table 1 contrasts the elections of 1896 and 1928 for different types of towns. Observe from the table that the mean shift between 1892 and 1896 was about the same for varying size groups of towns. Contrast this lack of association between size and political movement with the radically different 1920–28 pattern which also appears in the table.

Table 1 makes clear that in 1896 the industrial cities, in their aggregate vote at least, moved toward the Republicans in about the same degree as did the rural farming communities. Some of the misinterpretations of the election of 1896 flow from a focus on that election in isolation rather than in comparison with the preceding election. In 1896, even in New England cities, the Democrats tended to be strongest in the poor, working-class, immigrant sections. Yet the same relation had existed, in a sharper form, in 1892. In 1896 the Republicans gained in the working-class wards,

TABLE 1   Contrasts between Elections of 1896 and 1928 in Massachusetts: Shifts in Democratic Strength, 1892–1896 and 1920–1928, in Relation to Population Size of Towns

Population Size Group[a]	Mean Democratic Percentage		Mean Change 1892–96	Mean Democratic Percentage		Change Mean 1920–28
	1892	1896		1920	1928	
1–999	34.0	14.7	−19.3	16.5	18.6	+2.1[b]
2000–2999	38.8	18.3	−20.5	21.0	33.1	+12.1
10000–14999	46.7	26.9	−19.8	25.8	43.7	+17.9
50000+	47.7	30.1	−17.6	29.5	55.7	+26.2

[a] The 1892–1896 towns are grouped according to 1900 population; the 1920–28 towns, according to the 1930 census. The composition of the size groups is, therefore, not the same for the two periods. It is of some interest that the identical towns included in the 1892–96 groupings had about the same group means in Democratic percentage in 1920 as in 1896. The 1920 means for the 1892–96 groups, as composed in 1900, were, in the order given in the table, 15.9; 20.2; 31.2; 31.3. The similarity of these means to those for 1896 would give comfort to supporters of the position that the 1896 cleavage persisted until 1928.

[b] It might be expected from Figure B that this figure would be negative. Although towns tend to be separated into groups with different political characteristics when classified according to size, the category of quite small towns is by no means homogeneous. A suggestion of the variety included among the 78 towns underlying this figure is provided by their division into those over and those less than 40 per cent wet in a 1930 referendum on a measure to repeal the act for state enforcement of the Volstead Act. The towns under 40 per cent wet had a mean change of −1.2 points in Democratic strength from 1920 to 1928. Those over 40 per cent wet had a mean change of +6.2.

just as they did in the silk-stocking wards, over their 1892 vote. They were able to place the blame for unemployment upon the Democrats and to propagate successfully the doctrine that the Republican Party was the party of prosperity and the "full dinner pail." On the whole, the effect apparently was to reduce the degree of coincidence of class affiliation and partisan inclination.[9] Nor was the election of 1896,

in New England at least, a matter of heightened tension between city and country. Both city and country voters shifted in the same direction.[10] Neither urban employers nor industrial workers could generate much

[9] While the Boston ward votes of 1892 and 1896 cannot be compared directly because of boundary changes, an indirect check on the comments in the text is feasible. In 1892 the coefficient of correlation between the percentage of males 21 and over foreign-born in each ward and the Democratic percentage of the ward vote +0.88, with $Y_c = 16.28 + .931X$. In 1896 the coefficient of correlation between the ward percentages of registered voters foreign-born (*Boston City Documents*, 1897, v. I, Doc. 9) and the Democratic percentage of the ward vote was +0.82 with $Y_c = -9.0 + 1.428X$. In 1892 the mean Democratic percentage of the wards was 58.2; in 1896, 38.1. In both years Democratic strength varied from ward to ward directly with foreign-born population proportions (which may be regarded also as an index of economic status) but in all sorts of areas, rich and poor, the Repub-

licans apparently had a net gain of approximately 20 percentage points in 1896 over 1892.

[10] William Diamond has discussed urban-rural tension in his "Urban and Rural Voting in 1896," *The American Historical Review*, XLVI (January, 1941), 281–305. His measures of tension rest on a comparison of the Bryan percentages of the vote in cities of over 45,000 and in the remainder of each state. In his analysis New England emerges as an area of relatively high urban-rural tension. To the extent that urban-rural tension played a part in Massachusetts in 1896 it was evidently no more salient than it had been in 1892; Democratic candidates did relatively better in the cities than in the country at both elections. Between 1892 and 1896 Democratic strength declined in both rural and urban populations and to about the same extent. Rice's index of likeness between groups (which is the complement of the differences between divisions in percentages) computed for Diamond's urban and rural groups in the 1892 presidential voting in Massachusetts is 91.6; for 1896, 88.6. In other words, the point of party division of urban and rural populations did not differ greatly between the two groups in either election. Apart

enthusiasm for inflation and free trade; rather they joined in common cause. Instead of a sharpening of class cleavages within New England the voting apparently reflected more a sectional antagonism and anxiety, shared by all classes, expressed in opposition to the dangers supposed to be threatening from the West.[11]

Other contrasts between the patterns of electoral behavior of 1896 and 1928 could be cited[12] but in terms of sharpness and

durability of realignment both elections were of roughly the same type, at least in New England. In these respects they seem to differ from most other elections over a period of a half century, although it may well be that each round at the ballot boxes involves realignment within the electorate similar in kind but radically different in extent.

III

The discussion points toward the analytical utility of a system for the differentiation of elections. A concept of critical elections has been developed to cover a type of election in which there occurs a sharp and durable electoral realignment between parties, although the techniques employed do not yield any information of consequences about the mechanisms for the maintenance of a new alignment, once it is formed. Obviously any sort of system for the gross characterization of elections presents difficulties in application. The actual election rarely presents in pure form a case fitting completely any particular concept. Especially in a large and diverse electorate single polling may encompass radically varying types of behavior among different categories of voters;[13] yet a dominant characteristic often makes itself apparent. Despite such difficulties, the attempt to move toward a better understanding of elections in the terms here employed could provide a means for better integrating the study of electoral behavior with the analysis of political systems. In truth, a considerable pro-

---

from these quantitative resemblances there may well have been qualitative differences in urban-rural antagonisms in the two elections.

[11] An analysis of states such as that used in dealing with towns in the preparation of Figure B and similar charts shows something of the sectional coloration of the 1896 voting. Outside the South, eight states moved more than 12 percentage points (in differences in Republican proportions of the total vote) toward the Republicans from 1892 to 1896. These states with the most marked Republican gains included the New England states, New Jersey, and Wisconsin. States with the widest Republican losses were Colorado, Idaho, Montana, Nevada. The mean percentages of these two groups, when graphed, have a suggestion of the opening scissors form. The mean percentages for the two groups were:

	1892	1896	1900	1904	1908
Gaining Republican	52	67	61	63	61
Declining Republican	38	18	42	58	45

[12] The 1896 voting evidently involved a great deal of crossing of party lines by Democrats while it seems probable that in 1928 the Democratic gain came in considerable measure from the attraction of new voters into the active electorate. In 1896 electoral participation nationally was at a high level, in the neighborhood of 80 per cent of the total potential vote. From 1892 to 1896 in New England the total presidential vote increased only 3 per cent, while the Republican vote grew by 35.8 per cent and the Democratic vote declined by 37.7 per cent. Such figures point toward a large scale conversion of Democrats to the Republican cause. From 1896 to 1924 the proportions of the potential national electorate voting in Presidential elections underwent a secular decline to around 49 per cent, a movement by no means attributable entirely to the expansion of the suffrage but probably more fundamentally reflective of a contraction of national attention on matters political. In any case, by 1928 the population included large numbers of persons eligible for political activation. In 1928, the total New England presidential vote grew by 34.6 per cent over 1924, an unusually high rate of growth between elections, while the Republican vote was increasing by only 13 per cent and the Democratic by 135 per cent, a disparity accounted for in part in Democratic de-

fections to La Follette in 1924. The absolute Democratic gain was of the general order of magnitude of the gain in the total vote. A substantial proportion of the new Democratic vote probably came from accretions to the active electorate. A reexamination of elections with an eye to the bearing on the results of sharp increases in the electorate, either sectionally or within other subdivisions, might produce significant reinterpretations of episodes in the American party battle.

[13] For example, the 1928 election in the South, in contrast with New England, involved large but short-lived accretions to the Republican ranks.

portion of the study of electoral behavior has only a tenuous relation to politics.

The sorts of questions here raised, when applied sufficiently broadly on a comparative basis and carried far enough, could lead to a consideration of basic problems of the nature of democratic orders. A question occurs, for example, about the character of the consequences for the political system of the temporal frequency of critical elections.[14] What are the consequences for public administration, for the legislative process, for the operation of the economy of frequent serious upheavals within the electorate? What are the correlates of that pattern of behavior? And, for those disposed to raise such questions, what underlying changes might alter the situation? Or, when viewed from the contrary position, what consequences flow from an electorate which is disposed, in effect, to remain largely quiescent over considerable periods? Does a state of moving equilibrium reflect a pervasive satisfaction with the course of public policy? An indifference about matters political? In any case, what are the consequences for the public order? Further, what are the consequences when an electorate builds up habits and attachments, or faces situations, that make it impossible for it to render a decisive and clear-cut popular verdict that promises not to be upset by caprice at the next round of polling? What are the consequences of a situation that creates recurring, evenly balanced conflict over long periods? On the other hand, what characteristics of an electorate or what conditions permit sharp and decisive changes in the power structure from time to time? Such directions of speculation are suggested by a single criterion for the differentiation of elections. Further development of an electoral typology would probably point to useful speculation in a variety of directions.

[14] See the related discussion by Alexis de Tocqueville, *Democracy in America* (New York: Alfred A. Knopf, 1945), Vol. 1, pp. 205–206.

50.   Electoral Myth and Reality: The 1964 Election

*Aage R. Clausen,
Philip E. Converse,
and Warren E. Miller*

To the political scientist, a national election provides an opportunity to gather new empirical data. In 1964, the United States was presented not only with its quadriennial choice of leadership, but also with an opportunity to test established theories of political behavior. Propositions based on academic survey research were matched against contrary beliefs of the conservative movement. In this article, the overwhelming election results are analyzed as a verification of the academic theories. The authors, of the University of Michigan, suggest, however, that there is more validity to the conservatives' beliefs in regard to specialized groups in the electorate.

* * *

On Election Day, 1964, the aspirations of Senator Barry Goldwater and the conservative wing of the Republican Party were buried under an avalanche of votes cast for incumbent President Lyndon Johnson. The margin of victory, approaching 16 million votes, was unprecedented. Historical comparisons with other presidential landslides are left somewhat indeterminate by the intrusion of third parties. However, it is safe to observe that Johnson's 61.3 percent of the two-party popular vote put him in the same general range as the striking victories of Franklin Delano Roosevelt in 1936, Harding in 1920, and Theodore Roosevelt in 1904.

Before the fact, the election was also expected to be the most intensely ideologi-

From the *American Political Science Review*, vol. 59, no. 2 (June 1965), pp. 321–336.

cal campaign since 1936, in no small measure because of Goldwater's reputation as a "pure" conservative. After the fact, doubts existed as to whether this expectation had been fulfilled. Goldwater supporters, in particular, expressed disappointment that President Johnson had refused to join battle on any of the fundamental ideological alternatives that were motivating the Goldwater camp. However, as we shall see, the mass public had some sense that "important differences" between the two major parties were heightened in 1964 compared with parallel data from either 1960 or, as is more impressive, the relatively tense election of 1952.[1] And certainly no one questioned the importance of ideological differences in the factional dispute that split the Republican Party along liberal-conservative lines with an enduring bitterness unmatched in decades.

Indeed, these three prime elements of the 1964 election—faction, ideology and the contest for votes—became intertwined after the manner of a classic script. That is, the "outer" ideological wing of a party captures its nomination, leaving a vacuum toward the center of gravity of national opinion. This vacuum is gleefully filled by the opposing party without any loss of votes from its own side of the spectrum. The outcome, logically and inexorably, is a landslide at the polls.[2]

With a script so clearly written in advance, the outsider would naturally ask why any party controlled by rational strategists should choose a course likely to lead to such massive repudiation in its name. The answers to this question in the 1964 case are not particularly obscure, although they can be made at numerous levels. One

answer, of course, is that Republican Party strategists were themselves in deep disagreement as to just what script was relevant: many recognized the classic script and predicted the eventual outcome, with all of its attendant losses for other Republican candidates, in deadly accuracy.

For the factional dispute within Republican ranks involved not only an ideological clash, but also major differences in the perception of that political reality which becomes important in winning votes and elections. The Goldwater faction was told by its Republican adversaries, as the conservative wing had been told for years, that a Goldwater could not conceivably defeat a Democratic President, and would instead greatly damage the party ticket at all levels. The Goldwater group countered that a victory for their man was entirely plausible despite the danger signals of the spring polls and the normal difficulties of challenging an incumbent. It is not clear how sincere or widespread this confidence was: some statements sounded as though the Goldwater candidacy had little chance of winning but would at least provide a forum for the conservative philosophy, along with control of the Republican Party. But even in their more pessimistic moments, the Goldwater people would argue that while victory might be difficult, they certainly saw no reason to believe that Goldwater would do worse than any other Republican challenger, or encounter the electoral disaster the liberals were predicting.

Similarly, at the San Francisco nominating convention, his opponents vehemently charged that Goldwater was a "minority candidate," even among Republicans in this country. In another direct clash of perceptions, Senator Goldwater is said to have remarked to a group of Midwestern delegates, "What the minority [the convention liberals] can't get through their heads is that this is a true representation of the Republican Party."[3]

[1] The collection of data from a national sample of the electorate around the 1964 election was made possible by a grant to the Survey Research Center of the University of Michigan from the Carnegie Corporation of New York, which had also supported the 1952 election study.

[2] The most fertile elaboration of this classic script is of course contained in Anthony Downs, *An Economic Theory of Democracy* (New York, 1957).

[3] *The New York Times*, July 19, 1964.

In this article we wish to examine the relationship between such conflicting perceptions and what is known of the relevant reality in the context of the 1964 election. Our information comes primarily from sample survey studies of the mass public that formed the electorate in 1964, and whose reactions represent one level of political reality about which so many conflicting opinions and predictions were made. While the most important aspect of that reality was unveiled by the election outcome, there remained some of the customary latitude of interpretation as to its full significance. And with respect to the interplay between the stratagems of party elites on one hand and the grass-roots American voters on the other, the chronology of the 1964 election does indeed provide a fascinating composite of sheer myth, genuine but discrepant reality worlds, and self-fulfilling prophecies.

I. THE MYTH OF THE STAY-AT-HOME REPUBLICANS

The first theory of electoral reality on our agenda may be rapidly disposed of, for it lies more simply and unequivocally in the realm of myth than any of the others we shall treat. It should not be overlooked, however, both because of its historical persistence and because of its enshrinement in the battle cry of 1964 Goldwater supporters: "A choice, not an echo!"

In the quadrennial competition between liberal and conservative wings of the Republican Party for the presidential nomination throughout the 1940s and 1950s, the conservatives were consistently bested. One of the prime contentions of the liberals was that all of the entries of the conservative wing were so distant from the "middle-of-the-road" that they had no hope of attracting the independent votes necessary for victory over the Democrats. At an ideological level, the conservative wing coined the epithet "me-tooism" to ridicule the liberals for their refusal to reject Democratic innovations of the New and Fair Deal eras root and branch. The liberals, it was charged, were slowly selling out the fundamental principles on which earlier days of G.O.P. ascendancy had been based.

This accusation of ideological "flabbiness" was not, however, compelling of itself without some further comment on the problem of winning votes. As a consequence, a theory became widely current among conservative Republicans that G.O.P. difficulties in maintaining much contact with the White House were in fact directly tied to the "me-tooist" flavor of its presidential candidates. Republicans running for that office tended to lose not because there was any lack of potential Republican votes (as the superficial observer might have thought), but because many of the "real" Republicans were sufficiently offended by "me-tooism" that they simply didn't bother to vote at all. Nominate a true Republican rather than a Tweedledee, the theory went, and enough of these stay-at-homes would return to the polls to put him into the White House.

As such theories go, this contention was remarkably verifiable. That is, the critic need not argue that few Republicans were disappointed by the nominees of their party, for disappointment in itself is irrelevant for argument. The question is simply whether or not Republicans, however disappointed, did continue to turn out and vote even for "me-tooist" candidates through this period—a matter much easier to ascertain. Nor is there any point in arguing that there were *never* any stray Republicans who in the last analysis vented their frustrations by refusing to go to the polls. Undoubtedly there were. But the theory hinges less on the question as to whether such people existed, than on the contention that they existed in significant numbers: not merely several hundred or several thousand or even a few hundred thousand, but in the millions needed to overcome the persistent Democratic majorities.

Such a pool of potential voters would be large enough to be discriminated reliably in most sample surveys. And we know of no reputable sample surveys at any time in this period that gave any shred of reason to believe that this significant pool of stay-at-home Republicans existed. Indeed, such findings as were relevant pointed massively in the opposite direction. From 1944 on, for example, one can contrast turnout rates between Democrats and Republicans of comparable strengths of identification. And over election after election featuring "me-tooist" Republican nominees, one finds that turnout rates are consistently higher —and often much higher—on the Republican side. Indeed, each time we isolate that polar minority who not only have an intense commitment to the Republican Party, but whose commitment is of a highly sensitive ideological sort, turnout typically reaches proportions staggering for the American system: 96 percent, 98 percent— levels almost implausible in view of registration difficulties, travel, sickness and other accidents which can keep the most devoted American from the polls upon occasion. More impressive still, we find that in 1952 those Republicans who reported during the campaign that they would have preferred the "conservative" Taft over the "liberal" Eisenhower—exactly those Republicans to whom the theory refers—actually turned out at much *higher* rates to vote for Eisenhower in the November election (94 percent) than did the set of Republicans who indicated satisfaction with Eisenhower's nomination (84 percent).[4]

These brief observations do not begin to exhaust the evidence none of which lends any support whatever to the theory of a silent pool of frustrated conservative Republicans. Hence it is scarcely surprising that the Goldwater cause in 1964 was not buoyed up by some sudden surge of new support at the polls which other strategists had overlooked; for the hitherto silent people expected to provide such a surge existed principally in the imaginations of conservative strategists who in time of adversity needed desperately to believe that they were there. It is less of a wonder that this theory was generated, particularly before sample survey data took on much scope or stature in the 1940s, than that it persisted with greater or lesser vigor into the 1960s in the face of repetitive contradictory evidence readily available to any proponents with an edge of interest as to what the facts actually were.

II. THE MINORITY CANDIDATE OF A MINORITY PARTY

On the eve of the Republican nominating convention, an irate Goldwater supporter wrote to the Paris edition of the *Herald Tribune,* upbraiding it for the doubts it had expressed as to the extent of Goldwater sentiment beyond the convention delegates themselves, and pointing out that a massive groundswell of support had built up for Goldwater throughout the country "west of Madison Avenue."

The charge of the liberal wing of the G.O.P. that Goldwater not only was unattractive to Democrats and Independents but was not even the majority preference of Republicans was a particularly severe

[4] This datum is not as absurd as it might appear if the reader has failed to grasp the import of the preceding text. That is, in 1952 it was the most intense and ideologically "pure" Republicans who tended to prefer Taft to Eisenhower, much as 12 years later their counterparts chose Goldwater over the other Republican alternatives. It was the less ideologically committed (either by persuasion or by lack of ideological sensitivity) who were more satisfied with the Eisenhower candidature. The erstwhile Taft supporters did not perversely turn out at higher rates because they were disappointed in the convention choice, but because their striking commitment to Republicanism compelled them to more ardent support of its candidate whatever his ideological position.

allegation in view of the constraints under which the Republican Party has been obliged to operate in recent years. It has been the consensus of observers for quite some time that the Republican Party is a minority party in the affections of the American public. Our relevant data collections at frequent intervals since 1952 have left little question in our minds both as to the minority status of the Republicans, and as to the stability of that status during this epoch. For most of this time, our estimates would suggest that in terms of underlying loyalties, the Democrats could expect to receive, all other things equal, something in the neighborhood of 54 percent of the national popular vote; and if any change has been occurring in this figure in the past 15 years, it is that this Democratic majority is slowly increasing.[5] In practical terms, this means that a Democratic candidate need not have much attraction for grass-roots Republicans: he can win easily if he can carry the votes of a reasonable share of independents, and has general appeal for Democrats. A Republican candidate, on the other hand, can only win at the national level by drawing nearly monolithic support from Republicans, attracting the votes of a lion's share of independents, and inducing unusual defection among the less committed Democratic identifiers as well. The latter was the Eisenhower formula, and one which Nixon had nearly succeeded in following in 1960. More generally the liberal wing of the Republican Party had sought candidates with this kind of broad appeal throughout this period. In this light, the question of Goldwater's popularity was serious: for if a minority party nominates a figure enjoying only minority support within his own party, it is an obvious invitation to disaster.

In the spring and early summer of 1964, the opinion polls lent much weight to the contention that Goldwater enjoyed no broad support even among Republicans. The Goldwater supporters tended to counter this kind of evidence either (1) by ignoring the polls; or (2) by questioning the validity of the polls (some Goldwater placards were to read "Gallup didn't count us!"); or (3) by questioning the immutability of the early poll readings. Of these reactions, certainly the last-mentioned was entirely appropriate. That is, in the very early stages of a push toward the presidency, even a person who has been something of a "national" figure as Senator or major Governor for a considerable period may not be recognized by very large portions of the public. Until he has received much more intense national exposure in the limelight of presidential primaries and the nominating convention, "straw polls" as to his popularity can be highly misleading and unstable, particularly if the polling pits such a candidate against other figures with more longstanding national prominence and "household" names.[6]

However, survey data gathered over the course of 1964 can be put together with "hard" data from the presidential primaries to provide an illuminating picture of Goldwater's general popularity and, in particular, the reactions of grass-roots Republicans to him. In January, 1964, before the beginning of the spring primaries, we asked a national sample of the electorate:

Many people are wondering who will run for President on the Republican side this fall. . . . If you had to make a choice, which Republican leader do you think would be best for our country in 1964?

Who would be your second choice?

Are there any of the leading Republicans that you think would make very bad candidates?

Table I summarizes the responses to this sequence of questions. The open-ended na-

---

[5] See "The Concept of a 'Normal Vote,'" ch. 1 in A. Campbell, P. Converse, W. Miller and D. Stokes, *Elections and the Political Order* (New York, 1965).

[6] In our estimation, some challengers of this description have been prematurely discouraged from competition by poll results which might well have changed radically with greater exposure.

TABLE I   Preferences for the Republican Presidential Nomination among Selected Segments of the Electorate, January, 1964

	Percent Mentions[a]	Segments of the Electorate		
		Score across Total Electorate[b]	*Score within "Minimal Majority": All Independents and Republicans*[b]	*Score among All Republicans*[b]
	(%)			
Nixon	42	+25	+32	+37
Lodge	10	+11	+13	+13
Romney	11	+ 9	+11	+10
Rockefeller	49	+19	+10	+ 1
Scranton	11	+ 7	+ 6	+ 5
Goldwater	54	− 8	− 5	+ 9

[a] The percentage entered represents the proportion of individuals in the total sample mentioning the Republican leader indicated, either as one of two best or one of two very bad candidates.

[b] Each mention of a leader as the "best" candidate received a score of +2. Each mention as second best received a score of +1. The first-mentioned "bad" candidate received a score of −2. Any negative second mentions were scored −1. The entries in the table represent the net balance of positive or negative scores for the leader, expressed as a proportion of the maximum possible score an individual would have received had he been awarded all of the "best" choices given by the indicated segment of the electorate.

ture of the questions meant that individuals only rated those Republicans whom they were aware of at the time, and thought of as plausible candidates. The table excludes a thin scattering of other mentions. Since the scoring used reflects both the breadth and the intensity of support, a Republican receiving relatively few mentions could not achieve any very high score. Thus, for example, another possible scoring could have shown Henry Cabot Lodge vastly outdistancing all other aspirants, as his references were almost unanimously positive, whereas the other Republicans suffered numerous descriptions as "very bad candidates." However, at this time he was not commonly regarded as an aspirant for the nomination and the scoring deliberately puts this warm but limited positive feeling toward him in perspective.[7]

[7] Lodge's strong grass-roots popularity was one of the untold stories of the 1960 election, when he ran for vice-president. Well-known for his televised

The table speaks for itself as to Goldwater's attractiveness as a candidate. Clearly Goldwater's problem was not that he was still too little known: he received mentions from a wider proportion of the electorate than any of his competitors. But for much of the electorate he was an object of antagonism even in January, 1964. And among grass-roots Republicans, where his strength was concentrated, he remained fourth in a field of six.

The sequence of Republican primary elections in the succeeding months tended, with some local variation, to fit the lines

confrontations with the Russian delegation in the United Nations, he was far and away the most widely recognized and warmly regarded first-time vice-presidential candidate in the elections we have studied. Given the tarnish which seems to accompany second efforts at the presidency in American elections and which would undoubtedly have hurt Nixon, it may well be that Lodge, had he been acceptable to the Republican Party leadership, could have pushed Lyndon Johnson to a closer race than any other of the Republican hopefuls.

suggested by these January reactions. The table presages the startling Lodge write-in victory over both Goldwater and Rockefeller among New Hampshire Republicans in March, as well as his numerous subsequent strong showings. It contains ample warning as well of the amazingly poor Goldwater record in the primaries throughout the spring, including the scattered victories in such seemingly congenial states as conservative Nebraska, where by standing alone on the ticket he managed to win about half of the votes cast over a flood of Nixon and Lodge write-ins. It even renders intelligible the crucial Goldwater victory in California, where write-ins were not permitted, where the sole opponent was Rockefeller, and where Democrats had a hotly fought primary of their own. Indeed, there is room to wonder whether any presidential aspirant has ever contested so many primaries with as disastrous a showing, and still captured the nomination of his party's convention.

No evidence from polls of the period, moreover, suggests that Goldwater's popularity showed any sudden increase, even among Republicans, in the short interval between the final primary and the San Francisco convention. In interviewing our sample of the national electorate in September and October, we asked respondents to recall their reactions to the decisions of the Republican convention, including the identity of the candidates they had preferred at the time the convention began, as well as their gratification, indifference or disappointment at the outcome. While these responses suffer the inevitable frailties of any retrospective accounts that go back over an evolving situation, the social and political lines of support and antagonism for the various major contestants in July as reported during the campaign bear so close a resemblance to the lines of support visible in the January, 1964 data, as to make it unlikely that they are badly distorted by selective recollection, *post hoc* rationalization, and the like.

It is most instructive, perhaps, to set these popular reactions to the 1964 Republican convention against a fairly comparable set of data collected in 1952 after the conservative wing had lost its bid to nominate Senator Taft for the presidency against the liberal wing's offering of General Eisenhower, for the bitterness engendered in the 1952 struggle came closer to matching that of 1964 than either of the intervening conventions. Our question in 1952 asked respondents irrespective of partisan allegiance whether they would have preferred to have seen any other candidate nominated in either of the major-party conventions held in Chicago. Thus Republican identifiers could focus their remarks on the Democratic convention in a way that the 1964 question did not permit. However, partisans tended to comment primarily on the outcomes of their own party's nominating conventions.

Among Republican identifiers in the fall of 1952, about one in five recalled having felt a preference for Taft at the time of the convention. Another eight percent had preferred some third candidate. The vast majority of the remaining 72 percent indicated that they had been indifferent to the choices at either convention, or expressed gratification in the selection of Eisenhower as the Republican candidate. Some other Republicans responded that they would have preferred a candidate other than Stevenson from the Democratic convention. Presumably, however, these citizens were satisfied with the Republican convention, and it seems reasonable to conclude that a maximum of some 30 percent of all Republicans in 1952 had ground to recall any disappointment over their party's nomination.

The picture from 1964 is remarkably similar in one respect, and drastically different in another. Among Republican identifiers in this latter year, slightly less than 20 percent of all Republicans recalled having preferred Goldwater at the time of the convention. This figure is only one percent less than the proportion of Taft supporters among Republicans in 1952. What was different, of course, was that in 1952 Taft lost the nomination on the first ballot, whereas in 1964 Goldwater won it handily on the first ballot. Although in our 1964 data a large segment (30 percent) of Republican identifiers indicated that they had held no preference for a specific candidate at convention time, very nearly half of all of our Republicans did recall some preference other than Goldwater. Thus these grass-roots Republicans with non-Goldwater choices outnumbered the Goldwater supporters within Republican ranks by a margin of better than two and one-half to one. A clear majority (60 percent) of those with other preferences, when asked "Were you particularly unhappy that Goldwater got the nomination, or did you think that he was nearly as good as your man?," expressed their lingering unhappiness about the outcome.

In sum, then, it is hard to turn up any bit of evidence to challenge the conclusion that Goldwater was, in rather startling degree, a minority candidate within a minority party. If his camp actually believed that the San Francisco delegates represented a true cross-section of grass-roots Republican sentiment, then they had grossly misunderstood the situation. There was, however, at least one extenuating circumstance: the support among Republican citizens for other candidates than Goldwater was split badly among the four or five other leading candidates. Thus while any of several pairs of other candidates had grass-roots party support at convention time which would have outnumbered the Goldwater faction quite readily, the fact remains that the 20 percent Goldwater support represented a plurality for any single candidate.

However this may be, disappointment at the convention outcome in 1964 had radically different consequences in November than the comparable disappointments among Republicans in 1952. As we have seen above, the former Taft supporters in that year turned out at the polls in near-

perfect proportions and cast a very faithful Republican vote for Eisenhower. In 1964, however, the widespread defections among Republicans necessary to account for the Johnson landslide tended to follow rather closely the lines of lingering discontent with the nomination.

These recollections of San Francisco varied according to the different camps in which rank-and-file Republicans had located themselves at the time. So, for example, about three Lodge supporters in four reported they were unhappy with the Goldwater nomination; for Rockefeller supporters, the figure was closer to two in three. Slightly over half of the Nixon supporters, however, indicated that they thought Goldwater was "nearly as good" as their man, Nixon. With minor departures, similar patterns marked the ultimate defections to Johnson among these varying Republicans. Since Nixon supporters were, like Goldwater's, more frequently "strong" Republicans than the adherents of some of the other camps, lower defection rates here were only to be expected. However, defections to Johnson among Republicans who had preferred Nixon at convention time remained about double what could be expected from past norms for Republicans of this particular mixture of strengths of identification. Over three times as many Republicans for Lodge and Scranton defected to Johnson as parallel "normal" expectations would suggest, and—perhaps surprisingly defections among Republicans who expressed no pre-convention favorite at all were in this range as well. Most extreme were the Rockefeller and Romney supporters, with defection rates at the polls exceeding expectation by a factor of greater than four.[8]

These differences across the several non-Goldwater camps are intriguing, in part

[8] While these rates may sound mountainous, it should be remembered that the expected defection rates for most of these groups are rather low—in the vicinity of 10 percent. Nonetheless, 40 percent of the Rockefeller Republicans in our sample voted for Johnson.

because they appear related to reactions of the various G.O.P. leaders to the Goldwater candidacy. That is, of the set of major Republicans under discussion, Nixon took greatest pains to maintain relations with the Goldwater group before the convention, and undertook to help unify the party behind him after the nomination. Therefore it seems fitting that dismay at the nomination was least in his camp, and defections relatively limited. Neither Rockefeller nor Romney made any major show of reconciliation after the nomination, and subsequently went to some lengths to dissociate themselves from the Goldwater aspects of the Republican campaign.

Yet if it were true that nothing more than a "follow-the-leader" response is needed to account for these variations in defection rates among Republicans, the data would cast a somewhat different light on the question of conflicting perceptions between liberal and conservative wings of Goldwater's voting strength. For in such a case the Senator's problem would have been less one of gross overestimates of his strength, than of self-fulfilling prophecy on the part of the disgruntled liberal leaders. In other words, they first refused to support Goldwater on grounds that he could not win enough votes, and then proceeded to withhold in large quantities the votes of their "followers" to assure exactly this outcome.

No airtight way is available to determine whether or not Republican defections at the presidential level might have been reduced significantly had Rockefeller or some of the other liberals effected a more genuine reconciliation with Goldwater to unite the party for the campaign. Nevertheless, if we were to compare the issue positions and ideological persuasions of 1964 Nixon Republicans with those of Rockefeller or Romney Republicans and find no substantial differences, we might be tempted to judge that differences in leader behavior did play some independent role in mini-

mizing or maximizing Republican defections in November. Preliminary analyses suggest rather clearly, however, that substantial ideological differences did exist across the range of Republican factions. Republicans enthusiastic about Goldwater showed a rather unique (or "extreme") pattern of ideological positions. Nixon supporters, while unmistakably different, looked more nearly like the Goldwater people than the adherents of any of the other camps. Next in order moving away from the Goldwater position were the Scranton and Lodge followers, and the Rockefeller and Romney adherents show slightly more liberal positions still. Ideological differences, therefore, plainly existed between grass-roots supporters of the various factions, and these differences were indeed correlated with defections from a Goldwater vote. This does not exclude the possibility that the defections might have been lessened by a genuine "unity" move on the part of more liberal Republican leaders. It indicates nevertheless that the desertions were rooted not only in leader-follower behavior, but in a more personal sense of ideological distance between many rank-and-file Republicans and the Goldwater faction—a distance that would have produced increased defections quite apart from examples set by the leadership.

However this may be, it was a significant feature of the election that the customary post-convention reconciliation between party factions was in the 1964 Republican case lack-lustre at best, and at many levels simply non-existent. Many of the liberals wished to avoid the Goldwater platform. At the same time, Goldwater seemed to do less than most candidates in making it easy for the dissident brethren to return to the fold. Among several possible reasons, one may have been that in the blueprint laid out by Goldwater strategists for a November victory, the support of most of these leaders did not appear to be critical.

III. CAMPAIGN STRATEGY:
THE SOUTH
AS REPUBLICAN TARGET

The strategy of the Goldwater camp for a November victory was both simple and relatively selective. Goldwater felt, to begin with, that he could hold on to essentially the same states that Nixon had won in 1960. This meant a clean sweep of the populous states of the Pacific Coast, most of the Mountain and Plains states, and a scattering east of the Mississippi. To reap the additional electoral votes for victory, Goldwater believed that the way lay open, under proper circumstances, for the Republican Party to make further major inroads in the once solidly Democratic South. The plan implied that Goldwater could largely afford to write off the populous industrial states of the Northeast and some, if not all, of the Midwest—a matter which greatly reduced the importance of the dissident liberal Republican bloc. And it represented a dramatic departure from any past Republican strategy in making of the South a fulcrum for victory.

Such a strategy was not only unusual but, against the long sweep of American electoral history, it might even be thought of as implausible. Yet it was no hastily devised scheme. For years Goldwater had participated in the Congressional coalition between conservative Republicans and Southern Democrats. The same drive for ideological neatness that led him to call for the reorganization of American politics into "Conservative" and "Liberal" parties impressed upon him the grotesque incongruity of a Democratic South. The South had no reason to be a Democratic bastion; by all of its affinities and traditions, it should long since have become Republican. Part of the problem lay with the national Republican Party, which, in the control of the Northeastern bloc, had failed to present national-level candidates making clear that

Republicanism was the natural home of the Southern voter. This had been a frustrating fact since Goldwater's entry into national politics—a period during which political observers had frequently predicted an imminent partisan realignment of the South; but gains in the region, while very obvious, had remained rather modest. In discussions of Republican difficulty in recapturing majority status in the land, Goldwater had opined that the Party had to learn to "go hunting in the pond where the ducks are" —the South. As bitterness began to mount in that region toward the civil rights pressures of the Kennedy Administration, the time seemed more ripe than ever for the presentation of a purely conservative Republican candidate who could appeal to the Southern ethos in a most direct way, thereby breaking the Democratic hold on the region in one dramatic and decisive stroke.

This long-planned strategy had suffered two temporary but alarming setbacks. The assassination of President Kennedy suddenly placed a Southerner in the White House, and removed from power the most feared personal symbols of federal intrusion. The continuation of the Kennedy beginnings by the Johnson Administration, however—particularly in the 1964 Civil Rights bill—helped to reset the stage. So did the increased signs of Negro unrest, and the new element of "white backlash" in the North as well as the South that seemed apparent in the spring primaries. The capping touch was Goldwater's vote against the Civil Rights bill. This vote, to be sure, represented no condoning of segregationism *per se,* but rather a blow for states' rights against the encroachment of the federal government. Nevertheless, white supremacists in the South had so long paraded under the states' rights banner as to leave little room for fear lest the Goldwater gesture go unappreciated. The liberal wing of the Republican Party, having worked for years to prevent the Democrats from "gaining position" on the civil rights issue, was further horrified as it envisioned the G.O.P. suddenly transformed into "the party of the white man" at just the moment when the Negro vote was becoming effectively mobilized.

The second setback threatened when Governor Wallace of Alabama decided to enter the presidential race as a states' rights candidate. This was especially alarming for Wallace would have competed for exactly the same votes that Goldwater had been wooing toward the Republican column. However, Wallace's subsequent withdrawal left the field open again for the original victory blueprint, and the implementation began in force. Mid-campaign accounts of the Goldwater organizational efforts spoke of a high-powered, modernistic campaign apparatus in the South stocked with volunteer labor in numbers that would have been unbelievable for the earlier Eisenhower and Nixon campaigns. While this machine had been humming efficiently from the start, the Goldwater organization in the West was described as effective but less advanced; in the Midwest it was chaotic, and in the Northeast next to non-existent. At few if any points in recent political history have so many campaign resources—in both issue positions taken and organizational efforts made—been devoted to the cultivation of a single region. The first discordant note came when, during the campaign and apparently as the result of new poll data, Goldwater remarked to reporters that he was not as strong in the South as everybody seemed to think.

After the votes were counted, what was the success of this strategy? The verdict must come in two halves. From one point of view, the strategy was a brilliant success, and it left its imprint on the geographical voting returns with greater strength than any other of what we have called "short-term forces" in the 1964 election. One crude way of separating these immediate or new effects from those better attributable to long-term standing loyalties is to create a different kind of electoral map, entering state by state or region by region the departure of a particular presidential vote in a more Republican or more Democratic direction than the normal voting of the area involved. A map so constructed for 1964, with pro-Goldwater deviations regarded as "high ground" and pro-Johnson deviations as "low," would show one primary "tilt" or gradient across the nation. The very lowest ground would appear in the northern reaches of New England, and the gradient would move upward with fair regularity all the way west to the Pacific Coast. The same gradient would appear, but much more sharply tilted still, as one moved southward to the Gulf of Mexico. In other words, Goldwater's regional emphases were indeed profoundly reflected in the vote.

As soon as one leaves the relative question of the regional and the geographic, however, the strategy was a dismal failure. For while the whole continent tilted in the expected direction, the strong Democratic tide nationally left virtually all of the country submerged under what from a Goldwater point of view was "sea level"—the 50-50 mark in popular votes. In terms of electoral votes, Goldwater was stranded on a few islands which remained above the tide on the outer Southern and Southwestern fringe of the continent. These islands represented stunning "firsts" or dramatic historic reversals in states like Georgia, Alabama, Mississippi and South Carolina. But their historic interest did not bring Goldwater any closer to the presidency.

Indeed, while Goldwater scored sharp Republican gains through the "Black Belt" of the deepest South, his assault on the South as a whole produced rather pathetic results. All observers agree, for example, that the South has been drifting away from its old status as a one-party Democratic bastion for at least two decades, if not for five or more. Hence Goldwater could have hoped to profit from four years more of this drift than Nixon, and a decade more than Eisenhower. Secondly, all observers are equally agreed that not only in the Black Belt but well north into the Border States of the South, civil rights was the prime political issue, and there is no doubt where the mass white population stood on the matter. Our data from the late 1950s and the early 1960s have consistently made clear that the potential of this issue for dramatic partisan realignment in the South had been muffled because of lack of clarity in the eyes of the mass population, prior to 1964, that either of the two major national parties offered much hope to the Southern white. It was exactly this ambiguity that Goldwater set out to remove by providing a clear party differentiation on civil rights at the national level. Putting these two ingredients together, the actual 1960 election results from the South as a whole might seem astonishing. For Goldwater actually did less well in the region than either Nixon in 1960 or Eisenhower in 1952 and 1956. One has to return at least to 1948 to find a comparably poor showing for a Republican presidential candidate; and there are reasonable treatments of the 1948 Thurmond vote which would send one back to 1944 for a parallel. Given the fact that Goldwater wooed the South so straightforwardly, and injected the new and potent ingredient of clear party differentiation on civil rights into the 1964 picture, this retrogression of Republican popular voting strength for a presidential candidate back to levels of the 1940s may seem quite incomprehensible.

A possible explanation, although one that we can summarily reject, would be that the clear party differentiation on civil (or "states' ") rights which Goldwater tried to communicate failed to come across to the mass voters.[9] Perhaps to the dismay of the

liberal wing of the Republicans, however, the communication was near-perfect. In our 1960 election study, a measure of association between the two parties and the policy extremes of the civil rights controversy showed values of .02 and .05 (the Democrats only very slightly associated with a pro-civil rights position) on two different civil rights policy items.[10] In 1964, the perceived association in the same terms on the same two items had risen to values of .54 and .50. The change in *volunteered* identifications of the two parties with the issue, among the much smaller subset of people so concerned that they brought the matter up themselves, showed even more dramatic change. In 1960 these civil rights-concerned people had tended to associate Kennedy somewhat with a pro-civil rights position, and Nixon with more of a "go-slow" approach (an association of .30). For Johnson and Goldwater in 1964, the association had mounted to .84, approaching consensus. The same volunteered materials include images of the parties, as well as of the candidates, and it is a matter of some interest to know in what measure Goldwater's 1964 position "rubbed off" on the Republican Party as a whole. In 1960, the civil rights association appeared to lie more clearly with the Kennedy-Nixon pairing (.30) than with any differences between the two parties, for these volunteered references to the parties showed only an association of .08. The comparable figure for the two parties

---

[9] We have examined this possibility in some seriousness simply because often in the past we have found public perceptions of party differences on major issues totally confused and muddy. Even on issues where the politically sophisticated see marked party differences, general public inattention and the ambiguities which politicians exploit to blur the edges of their positions combine to produce either lack of recogniton of differences, or very conflicting impressions of what those differences are at any given point. See Campbell *et al.*, *The American Voter* (New York, 1960), pp. 179ff.

[10] The statistic is such that if all citizens in the sample agreed that the Democrats represented one side of the issue and the Republicans the other, the figure would be 1.00 (perfect association). A figure of .00 represents the case of no aggregate association whatever.

in 1964 was .86. In short, we cannot explain why Goldwater produced a retrogression of Republican presidential voting strength in the South by suggesting that his key civil rights position failed to get across.

The Southern vote for Goldwater becomes intelligible if we add three elements to the consideration. First, while civil rights lent an important new pro-Goldwater force to the situation, various strong short-term forces which had pushed the Southern electorate in a pro-Republican direction in 1952, 1956 and 1960 were no longer present. We have argued elsewhere that the popular vote for Eisenhower and Nixon in the South was a very misleading index of the degree of solid Republican advance there.[11] While our data do show the Republican Party inching forward in the affections of mass Southern voters, the pace has been slow; the South remains a preponderantly Democratic region. In 1952 and 1956, the Southern presidential vote swung far to the Republican side of normal for the region, just as it did in all other parts of the United States. In 1960, with the Eisenhower appeal gone, most other regions moved back toward the Democrats as we expected. This return toward normal was almost invisible in the South, since a new and offsetting short-term force—Kennedy's Catholicism—had arisen which was peculiarly repugnant to the Southern population with its concentration (Louisiana excepted) of devout and fundamentalist Protestants.[12] Thus if any other of the Republican aspirants had run in 1964, we might have expected a delayed return toward a much more normally Democratic vote in the South. From this point of view,

the injection of a new civil rights differentiation by Goldwater did not occur in a void, but was something of a replacement for other forces which had kept the Southern vote extended in a remarkably pro-Republican direction for three consecutive presidential elections.

Once we take this into account, the Republican retrogression is less perplexing, although intuitively we would expect civil rights to have an impact on the Southern voter more potent than either Eisenhower's appeal or fear of a Catholic president. It is here that the second and third considerations enter. While Goldwater's civil rights position drew Southern whites toward the Republicans, Negroes both South and North moved monolithically toward the Democrats. Although Southern Negro voting was still limited by registration difficulties, it increased over 1960 and was almost unanimously Democratic for the first time.[13] If this sudden new increment of Negro votes could be removed from the Southern totals, the Goldwater vote proportion would undoubtedly appear to be a slight progression, rather than a retrogression, over the Eisenhower and Nixon votes.

Finally, it must be recognized that civil rights, while the primary issue in the South, was not the only one. Beyond civil rights, Southerners reacted negatively to the Goldwater positions much as their fellow citizens elsewhere. Many Southern white respondents said in effect: "Goldwater is right on the black man, and that is very important. But he is so wrong on everything else I can't bring myself to vote for him." From this point of view, the civil rights issue did indeed have a powerful impact in the South: without it, the 1964 Goldwater vote probably would not only have slipped to

[11] Philip E. Converse, "A Major Political Realignment in the South?" in Allan P. Sindler, ed., *Change in the Contemporary South* (Durham, N. C., Duke University Press, 1963).

[12] These religious effects were described in Converse *et al.*, "Stability and Change in 1960: a Reinstating Election," this REVIEW [*The American Political Science Review*] Vol. 55 (June, 1961), pp. 269–80.

[13] In our data, expressions of party loyalty from the South which had been slowly losing Democratic strength throughout the 1950s show a sudden rebound in 1964. However, all of the rebound can be traced to Southern Negroes; the downward trend among Southern whites continued and at about the same pace.

normal Republican levels, but would have veered as elsewhere to the pro-Democratic side. The more general ideological appeal to what Goldwater saw as Southern "conservatism" aside from the Negro question, did not have major impact.

Much the same comments hold for the failure of "white backlash" to develop in the way many expected outside the South. Our data show that civil rights feeling did not lack impact elsewhere. But for many non-Southern whites who resented the advance of the Negro cause and the summer of discontent, the election involved other important issues as well; and Goldwater's positions on them struck such voters very negatively. Thus "white backlash" feelings were translated into Goldwater votes by Democrats only where fear of the Negro was so intense as to blot out virtually all other considerations. Voters fitting this description existed in fair number and geographic concentration in the deepest latitudes of the South. Elsewhere, they were thinly scattered.

IV. THE ELECTION "POST-MORTEM"

Up to this point we have referred only vaguely to the many negative reactions Goldwater occasioned in all sectors of the country, which tended to dim out isolated attractions he did present. The Goldwater "image" was indeed phenomenally unfavorable. We have measured such images in the past, among other ways, by tallying the simple number of favorable and unfavorable references made by respondents to broad questions inviting them to say what they like and dislike about each of the candidates. Typically, American voters have tended on balance to speak favorably, even about candidates they were about to send down to defeat. The least favorable image we have seen—in Adlai Stevenson's second try in 1956—involved only about 52 percent of all responses that were favor-

able. Less than 35 percent of the Goldwater references were favorable.

Just after the election, Goldwater observed that "more than 25 million people" voted "not necessarily for me, but for a philosophy that I represent. . . ." At another time, in assessing the magnitude of his defeat, he chastised himself for having been a personally ineffective spokesman for that philosophy. This seemed particularly odd against the descriptions of Goldwater before his nomination, in which even opponents concurred that at long last the right wing had found an articulate spokesman with a magnetic personality.

The candidate references we collect are a mixture of observations concerning the personality and leadership qualities of the individuals themselves as well as reactions to policy positions they represent in the public eye. Ideally, we could take this image material and split it cleanly into references to personal attributes as opposed to policy positions, in order to judge the accuracy of the proposition that what the public repudiated was the spokesman, and not the philosophy. Practically speaking, such divisions present many difficult coding decisions.[14]

Nevertheless, we have sifted Johnson and Goldwater references into categories more or less purely reflecting "policy" as opposed to "personality" significance. Among the most pure policy references, Johnson's were favorable by an 80–20 margin, visibly ahead of the 69–31 balance of his total image. Mentions of Goldwater policies ran less

[14] Take, for example, the charge hung on Goldwater by Democrats and some Republicans that he was "impulsive." This allegation reverberated in the public and came to make up one of our largest single categories of negative references to Goldwater. "Impulsiveness" is a personality trait that on one hand might have been less plausible for some other right-wing leader. Yet the charge took roots and began to flourish with respect to a cluster of policies that Goldwater shared with other Republican leaders of similar persuasions. It seems quite arbitrary to decide that it is exclusively either the person or the policy which is "impulsive."

than 30–70 favorable, thereby trailing the rest of his image slightly. In general, the farther one moves from pure policy to pure personality, Johnson's advantage declines. His "wheeler-dealer" style and the aura of conflicts-of-interest which dogged him during the campaign came through to dilute his attractiveness. Against this backdrop, Goldwater's personal "integrity" and "sincerity" drew praise. Throughout, the data suggest that Johnson was carried along to an image nearly as positive as Eisenhower's best, less by his personal characteristics than by the policies with which he was associated (many of them identified by respondents as continuations from the Kennedy Administration). For Goldwater, if anything, the reverse was true.

Aside from civil rights and a faint flutter of approval brought by Goldwater's latter-day stand against immorality, none of his major positions was attractive to voters outside the most hard-core Republican ranks. In general, the mass of public opinion has been quite unsympathetic to traditional Republican thinking in areas of social welfare and other domestic problems for several decades. A major Goldwater theme involved attacks against the increasingly heavy hand of "big government," yet this struck little in the way of a responsive chord. Most Americans in the more numerous occupational strata do not appear to feel the governmental presence (save for local civil rights situations) in any oppressive or day-to-day manner, and as a consequence simply have no reactions to the area which have any motivational significance. Among those more aware of the practices and potentials of federal government, a slight majority feels that if anything, governmental services and protections are inadequate rather than overdone. Thus for better or for worse, such contentions on Goldwater's part had little popular resonance.

Goldwater's failure to make much capital of domestic policy was not uncharacteristic of a Republican presidential candidate. What was new for a Republican, however, was his performance in the area of foreign policy. In a degree often overlooked, the 1950s were a period during which, from the point of view of many Americans inattentive to the finer lines of politics and reacting to the parties in terms of gross associations and moods, something of an uneasy equilibrium prevailed between the two major parties. Much more often than not, for these Americans the Democratic Party was the party of prosperity and good times, but also the party more likely to blunder into war. The Republican Party, conversely, was more skilled in maintaining peace, but brought with it depression and hard times.

The foreign policies proposed by Goldwater and refracted through the press and other commentators, shifted this image more dramatically than one might have thought possible (Table II). Setting aside the large mass of voters who throughout the period did not see any particular differ-

TABLE II   Perceptions as to the Party Most Likely to Keep the United States Out of War in the Ensuing Four Years

	1956	1960	1964
	(%)	(%)	(%)
Democrats would handle better	7	15	38
No party difference	45	46	46
Republicans would handle better	40	29	12
Don't know, not ascertained	8	10	4
	100	100	100

ences between the parties in foreign policy capability, the balance of expectations in the area favored the Republicans by better than a 5–1 margin in 1956. This margin deteriorated somewhat in the late stages of the Eisenhower Administration, but remained at an imposing 2–1 edge. During the Goldwater campaign it reversed itself to a 3–1 margin favoring the Democrats.

Thus to the many ways of describing the public's repudiation of the Goldwater candidacy, another may be added: between a party of prosperity and peace, as against a party of depression and war, there is little room for hesitation.

V. LEVELS OF PUBLIC OPINION AND THE BASES FOR MISPERCEPTION

From at least one point of view, it is less interesting that Goldwater lost the 1964 election than that he thought he had a chance to win. What most of our descriptions of the election year have had in common is a sort of chronic miscalculation of electoral reality: miscalculations of standing strength, of new strength that might be won, and of what appeals were necessary to win that new strength. Since "electoral reality" is at many points a nest of uncertainties, and since we are told that in the face of uncertainty personal needs are likely to color perceptions the more strongly, there is little surprising in the fact that Goldwater overestimated his strength and drawing power. But as these misperceptions of Goldwater and his aides went grossly beyond what many observers felt were the margins of uncertainty, they deserve closer comment.

Rather than write off these perceptions as figments of imagination, let us suppose that to persist in the way many electoral misperceptions of the right wing have persisted, there must be some sustaining reality bases; and let us ask instead what such bases might be. For "public opinion" is a protean thing, and we shall discover that there are perfectly sound ways of measuring public opinion during the 1964 campaign which, instead of illustrating Johnson's towering lead in the opinion polls, would actually have shown Goldwater enjoying a slight margin.

As is well known, public opinion was spoken of and roughly gauged long before

the operations of public opinion polling were developed. What was gauged was opinion from a variety of kinds of sources: informal reactions to events among ancillary elites around the centers of government; the writings of intellectuals and newspaper editors; representations from leaders of interest groups, and the like. While it was apparent that this conglomerate of opinion came disproportionately from relatively elite and informed sources and hence need not have coincided with what the "real public" thought, beyond mass elections themselves there were (and *are,* for those who totally distrust the polls) few further ways of understanding what the public below an elite level was thinking. One of those few ways of "digging down" into the real population was letters of opinion: letters sent from unassuming constituents to public officials, "letters to the editor" composed by non-professional writers reacting to daily events and even, in no few cases, to the opinions of the editor himself. This was one level of public opinion that seemed to be generated below the elite level and that, for the observer interested in opinion beyond the localisms of municipal government, could be monitored regularly on a wide geographic base.[15]

In our 1964 interview schedule we spent some time investigating the behavior of our respondents with respect to the writing of politically relevant letters. We ascertained first whether or not they had ever written such a letter either to any kind of public official, or to the editor of a newspaper or magazine. Then, among the minority who could recall ever writing such a letter, we went on to ask about the fre-

[15] Undoubtedly, for such an observer, letters were not weighted equally in his impressions as to how opinion stood: some were more cogent than others, some were more distressed, and so on. But as a rough first approximation, one can imagine that what registered as "public opinion" on a particular issue in the mind of such an observer was closely related to the simple frequency of letters pro and con.

quency of such activity—whether any of the letters had been written in the past four years, and if so, roughly how many such letters the respondent would estimate he had written to each of the two types of targets over that recent period.

Many aspects of these data remain intriguing despite their general predictability. Thus, for example, the materials demonstrate handsomely that the large bulk of letters to public officials or the printed media come from a tiny fraction of the population, which tends to write very repetitively. Thus, in the data summarized in Figure 1, we find that only about 15 percent of the adult population reports ever having written a letter to a public official, and of the total stream of such letters from the grass roots, two-thirds are composed by about 3 percent of the population. Where letters to newspapers or magazines are concerned, the constituency is even more restrictive still: only about 3 percent of the population recalls ever having written such a letter, and two-thirds of such letters are turned out by not more than half of one percent of the population.[16] Needless to say, there is fair overlap between those who write to the printed media and those writing to public officials, so that the observer monitoring both lines of communication would tend to count the same people twice.

Furthermore, as these few people write more and more letters over time, they are counted again and again, and this of course is the phenomenon that interests us. What we have done is to reconstruct our data on various preferences relevant to the 1964 election *not* by a raw head-count, which is what a mass election measures, but rather with each individual's preference on an

item weighted by the number of letters that he has reported writing to either target in the four preceding years. This provides a basis, within reasonable limits, for a fair replication of the different kind of "public opinion" as it might be assessed by a hypothetical observer.[17]

Figure 2 contrasts "public opinion" in the head-count sense, with that form of public opinion as measured by letter-writing. We suggest that this figure may usher us into the reality world on which many of Goldwater's assessments and stratagems were based. This is not to say that Goldwater had no other bases from which to calculate public opinion. He had, among other things, public opinion as measured by the polls, and he did not entirely discredit this information. Yet as we have noted there was evidence that poll data perplexed him, not simply because they customarily brought bad news, but also because they failed to square with all of his other intuitive impressions as to what the public was thinking. In the measure that these impressions came from a variety of sources not very different from the letter-writers among the public (*i.e.*, from party activists, from campaign personnel and from informal associations), it is not hard to believe that they may have been displaced from the head-count of public opinion in much the same ways.

If we accept letter-writing for the moment then as a relevant indicator of public opinion, we see a rather marvelous change

16 Data on letters to the news media are not presented graphically, in part because the inequality is so complete that there is little one can discriminate in the figure. The Gini index of concentration for the newspaper and magazine letters is .99. See H. Alker and B. Russett, "On Measuring Inequality," *Behavioral Science,* Vol. 9, No. 3 (July, 1964), pp. 207–18.

17 We wish to stress that it remains a crude approximation, in part because we do not know, letter by letter, what political opinions the respondent was expressing. Conceivably in many cases they lay outside the range of our items. But the exercise is worth completing in part because it is likely that our hypothetical observer generalizes beyond the specific content of letters ("if ultra-conservative opinion on issue *x* is running about 30 percent, then it is likely that ultra-conservative opinion on issue *y* would run about the same level if something made that issue salient"); and in part because the systematic lines of displacement of "letter opinion" from "public opinion" in the mass electoral sense are undoubtedly valid in their general direction, whatever the details.

in the state of political affairs. In Figure 2(a), instead of trailing Johnson sadly in the anonymous crowd in mid-campaign, Goldwater holds a visible lead. Moving back to the time of the San Francisco convention (b), Goldwater is no longer the candidate of a small minority among Republicans and Independents, but rather is the toast of an absolute majority, even counting "no preferences" against him. In (c), we discover that not only is a vast majority of the public interested in the problem of the growing strength of the federal government,[18] but those upset by this growing strength outnumber their opponents by a ratio approaching 3 to 1! In Figure 2(d), the displacement of "letter opinion" from public opinion is much less, in part because the item wording brought a relatively consensual response. However, it is clear that Goldwater's "hard" inclinations in foreign policy are somewhat overrepresented as well in the letter-writing public.

In some ways, Figure 2(e) contains more grist than any of the others, however. First, the very form of the distributions of ideological preference differs rather dramatically. Where "public opinion" is concerned, nearly half the population falls in the "zero" category, making no affective distinction whatever between conservatives

18 The wordings of the issue items involved in Figure 2(c) and (d) were as follows:

(For 2c) "Some people are afraid the government in Washington is getting too powerful for the good of the country and the individual person. Others feel that the government in Washington has not gotten too strong for the good of the country. . . . What is your feeling?"
(For 2d) "Some people think our government should sit down and talk to the leaders of the Communist countries and try to settle our differences, while others think we should refuse to have anything to do with them. . . . What do you think?"

Figure 2(e) is based on a set of questions that asked people to indicate their affective reactions toward a variety of groups, including "conservatives" and "liberals." The scores for the figure are based on the difference in reaction to the two stimuli.

and liberals.[19] In addition, the clustering around this zero-point is very tight: over three-quarters of the population is located within one category of the zero-point. The distribution of "letter opinion," however, is quite different. The central mode of indifference or ignorance shrinks dramatically, and voices from more extreme positions on the continuum gain in strength. Other analyses show that virtually all letter-writers rank very high on measures we have used of ideological sensitivity. Hence those who remain toward the middle of the continuum in the right half of Figure 2(e) are not there through indifference or ignorance: they understand the ideological alternatives and place themselves toward the middle of the road with forethought. And, as the bimodal shape of the distribution suggests, political discourse becomes most notably a dialogue between very mild liberals and ultra-conservatives.

It is to the world of letter opinion or one like it that the Goldwater campaign, in its original design, was addressed. At least until its late stages, it assumed an electorate with near-total ideological comprehension and sensitivity. The appeal to the Southern conservative tradition in any abstract vein was indeed joyfully received in the South, and created great ferment among a part of the Southern population. Except as this theme became concretized in day-to-day problems with Negroes, however, the part of the population affected was tiny, even though in the letter-writing and related senses it was so visible as to appear to be "most of the South," politically speaking.

19 It is likely that this contingent is roughly coterminous with that 40–50 percent of the American electorate which we have described elsewhere as having no impression as to what such terms as "conservative" and "liberal" mean. See Philip E. Converse, "The Nature of Belief Systems in Mass Publics," in David E. Apter, ed., *Ideology and Discontent* (New York, 1964), pp. 206–61. The data presented there were gathered in 1960. In the 1964 study we collected the same data on recognition of ideological terms, thinking that perhaps the nature of the Goldwater campaign might render these terms and meanings more salient to a wider public. The data show that it did not.

Similarly, the distribution of the population in this world of letter opinion helped maintain persistent overestimations of strength. Empirically speaking, the center of Goldwater support lay roughly in the third bar of the figure on the conservative side. It weakened rapidly with any further steps toward the center, and was relatively solid in the outer two bars of the graph. If one looks at "letter opinion" with this zone in mind, it would appear that the base of standing Goldwater support was very substantial. Goldwater hoped to firm up the support on his side of the center sufficiently to create a majority, and in this figure it would have taken only a modest extension of influence to achieve this. In the world of public opinion relevant for mass elections, however, the distribution of actual and potential support was radically different. Rather than starting from a solid base of support on the conservative wing, the initial springboard was scarcely populated at all. To win a majority, a much deeper penetration into the center would have been required.

In the measure that we have delineated in Figure 2(e), the kind of political environment familiar to many practicing politicians, we can also better understand the first of our puzzles, the myth of the stay-at-home Republicans. For ultra-conservatives who found a wide measure of social support and resonance for their views in the world of public opinion which they understood, it must indeed have been perplexing that uniquely at election time, and uniquely in vote totals, this vigorous support had a habit of evaporating. How could one interpret this gross discrepancy between what one heard and read about public sentiments and what happened at the polls? The easiest explanation was that strong conservatives in large numbers simply refused to go to the polls, however vigorously they would express themselves otherwise. And as soon as a useful reason was worked out as to why this willful non-voting should occur, a theory was born. It persisted in

part because it was a handy tactical weapon; but it persisted in some part as well because the discrepant realities which helped to catalyze the theory also persisted. For its proponents, the election of 1964 was a sobering reality test.

VI. CONCLUSIONS

It should be apparent that the phenomena we have examined in this paper have a significance that stretches considerably beyond the 1964 election, or questions of the credibility of public opinion polls, or the playing of games with the epistemologies of practicing politicians, fascinating though each of these subjects may be.

But the more important implications flow from the reflection that while these opinion worlds may be discrepant from one another in many regards, and it behooves us not to confuse them, it is not a simple matter of fact vs. fantasy: both worlds are real, and have real effects on the political process. Save for the obvious fact that the reality of "one man, one vote," governs the mass election with greater or lesser modification, while other public-opinion realities like the letter-writing world tend to hold sway otherwise, we know all too little empirically about the counterpoint between the two in actual political systems, and the normative significance of motivation-weighted votes is largely unexamined.

However this may be, if the reality of one of these worlds was manifest on Election Day, 1964, then the reality of the other was equally apparent in the San Francisco convention. For it is obvious that the intense levels of political motivation which underlie the letter-writing of the ultra-conservative wing are part and parcel of the ingredients which led to a Republican convention delegation so markedly discrepant from either the rank-and-file of the Party or its customary leadership. What had been lacking around the country in bodies was made up for in dedication; but the outcome of the convention was in no sense the less real for it. And from this juxtaposition of two worlds, the oddities of the 1964 election grew.

51. Elections and Public Opinion

V. O. Key, Jr.

The effect of elections on public policy has been confused by traditional beliefs in the character of the vote as a "mandate" for specific programs. V. O. Key, Jr., late Professor of Government at Harvard University, demonstrated the difficulties in any such theory of mass control of government. Nevertheless, he argues, there is meaningful popular control. Elections serve as judgments of leaders and as indicators of the general concerns of the voters.

* * *

Elections are basic means by which the people of a democracy bend government to their wishes. In both their symbolism and their reality free elections distinguish democratic regimes. They occupy a prominent place in the political faith of democratic orders. The morale of a democracy depends in part on the maintenance of the belief that elections really serve as instruments of popular government, that they are not rituals calculated only to generate the illusion of deference to mass opinion. Since American parties attract the loyalties of persons with considerable similarity of policy views, it might be supposed that elections would merely record the numbers who identify with the major parties. Although the sense of party identification introduces a degree of stability into voting

behavior, the looseness of party attachments also assures that at each polling a sector of the electorate considers the alternatives anew. Elections are not occasions at which solid partisan phalanxes march to the polls; they are opportunities for decision, and politicians are not without anxiety as they await their outcome.

The travails of democracies in the past half-century have tarnished the image of elections as an instrument of popular decision. Abortive installations of democratic practices in nations scattered over the world have contributed to this disenchantment, though the moral may be that democratic procedures are workable only under some circumstances and then only by people habituated to their requirements. Yet even American publicists seem to share the global disillusionment with electoral decision. The ancient distrust of democracy gains reinforcement from the indiscriminate projection to mass electoral behavior of the findings of psychology that men's behavior contains an element of irrationality. Dissemination of these views makes it easy for many people to believe that the highbinders of Madison Avenue can humbug the American people in an election. Among some intellectuals doubts about the vitality of the electoral process may flow from sociological interpretations of electoral behavior as but the conditioned by-product of social status, occupational position, or some other deterministic relation. Of the relevance of these factors for electoral behavior there can be no doubt, but of their controlling influence in the political system there must be serious reservation. The American electorate sooner or later belies all predictions built on deterministic assumptions.

Obviously one cannot maintain that public opinion is projected through elections with a crystalline clarity to animate gov-

From *Public Opinion and American Democracy*, by V. O. Key, Jr., pp. 458–460, 472–480, with footnote omissions. © Copyright 1961 by V. O. Key, Jr. Reprinted by permission of Alfred A. Knopf, Inc.

ernments to actions in accord with patterns it prescribes in precise detail. If such were the reality, governments would be hamstrung. Nevertheless, by elections the people make great decisions, which may have a heavy substantive policy content. Elections probably serve better as instruments for popular decision on broad and great issues; the details and the trivia may be beyond popular control, a fact that at times may lead to a defeat of the majority preferences in the minutiae of administration. The popular decision has components in addition to those of substantive policy. Elections cannot be regarded solely as a conduit for the transmission of policy preferences to government. They also express other judgments and preferences—such as those about candidates and about past performance of government—as well as policy desires. In short, elections matter, and they serve in the political system as a basic connection between public opinion and government. The problem is to indicate how this linkage occurs and on what kinds of questions it seems most clearly controlling.

VOTING
AND SUBSTANTIVE ISSUES

The despair that leads some analysts to dismiss elections as of no avail in the expression of public opinion comes in part from the simple-minded model against which they test actual elections. That model assumes that elections ought in some way to separate people into two groups: a majority consisting of persons in agreement on a series of propositions to the execution of which their candidate was committed and the majority made up of persons on the other side of the same issues to which position their candidate had committed himself. So stark a model is so remote from reality that its uses are limited in speculation about the place of elections in the political process. Its assumption that

the world of opinion is one of blacks and whites does not accord with the existence of gradations of opinion. Nor does the model take into account variations in intensity of opinion from question to question. In it the relative salience of issues for people finds no recognition. Nor does it make allowance for the fact that on many specific questions mass opinion may be uninformed, though most people may have broad sentiments or preferences that may be regarded as logically, if not always practically, controlling of subsidiary issues. Moreover, the model assumes that public opinion is to be regarded as acting prospectively when, in fact, its most forceful expressions may be retrospective judgments about policy and performance.

As has been demonstrated, the citizen's identification with party tends to produce a tie consistent with his policy preferences. To some extent this results from the matching of conscious policy preferences with policy positions taken with some clarity by the parties. To some extent it consists in policy through agency as the citizen perceives his party to be dedicated to the interests of persons like himself. When election day rolls around, though, the citizen may not vote in accord with his party identification. His party attachment is somewhat like his church membership; he regards it as no binding commitment to attend Sunday services. The looseness of their party attachments permits many Americans to bring their voting closer into line with the concerns salient to them at the moment of the election than it would be if undeviating partisan loyalty prevailed. As the voters respond to the changing realities, a fairly impressive correlation prevails between the vote and policy preferences on the salient issues. Moreover, voting decisions inconsistent with party identification often result from policy preferences. The act of voting is by no means devoid of policy content and intent. . . .

ELECTIONS
AS COLLECTIVE DECISIONS

If elections express a public opinion, it should be possible to assign meaning to them as they are examined in the context of the circumstances of the moment at which they occur. Scholars habitually shy away from the task of translating the indistinct mutterings of the people's voice as it projects itself through the ballot boxes and the voting machines, but politicians must as a matter of course attribute a decisional content to elections. While their readings of the verdict of the people may on occasion be erroneous, they have a quality of authority. Scholars, too, should by the findings of electoral research be able to make appraisals of the meaning of the grand decisions by the electorate. In a minor referendum—as, for example, a vote on a proposal for the issuance of building bonds by a school district—the expression of public opinion is direct and unmistakable in its meaning, but interpretation of the meaning of great national electoral contests presents a problem of far greater complexity. Granted that these grand electoral decisions have a meaning whose clarity differs from election to election, the problem remains of appraising particular elections or types of elections in their total context to divine the nature of the collective purpose expressed in the balloting. Such an attempt assumes that, despite the variety of motives and preferences that guide individual voters, their individual actions can be summed into a broad decision of one or more major components of some clarity, at least in some elections.

Disapprobation. Perhaps the public can express itself with greatest clarity when it speaks in disapprobation of the past policy or performance of an administration, though the collective decision may not specify with minuteness the elements of policy or performance of which it disapproves and cannot indicate with precision the lines of policy that should be pursued, save that changes should be made. The presidential election of 1932 could be regarded as one in which the collective decision was one of disapproval of past performance. Although from the vantage point of hindsight, many elements of the New Deal may be read into Roosevelt's campaign speeches and into his earlier record as Governor of New York, the dominant element of the collective decision consisted in a rejection of the broad policies of the Hoover Administration rather than a mandate for future action. About the only clear prospective instruction contained in the electoral verdict was a mandate for the repeal of the Prohibition Amendment, and that action itself constituted to a degree a judgment of past experience.

Another election in which a major component of the decision consisted in the disapproval of past performance was that of 1952. From data presented earlier, the conclusion is inescapable that the election marked no majority rejection of the major trends of domestic policy under the New Deal and the Fair Deal, although Eisenhower had the support of those bitterly opposed to intervention in the economy. The major content of the decision related rather to the performance of the Truman Administration in the field of foreign policy. That interpretation is supported by the relationships between party identification and vote that appear in Table 1. The question of whether "it was our government's fault that China went Communist" or whether there was "nothing that we could do to stop it" separated out with some clarity those who deserted the Democratic party to vote for Eisenhower. Of those strong Democrats who thought that it was our government's fault that China went communist, only 69 percent voted Democratic. Of those who thought that there was nothing "we could do to stop

TABLE 1   **Presidential Vote in Relation to Party Identification and to Opinion on United States Responsibility for Communist Capture of Control of China**[a]

Party Identification	Opinion on China Policy		
	Our Fault	*Don't Know*	*Nothing U.S. Could Do*
Strong D	69%	84%	89%
Weak D	40	66	67
Independent	28	20	45
Weak R	3	6	8
Strong R	1	0	1

[a] Entries are Democratic percentages of reported presidential vote for the groups in each cell in 1952. The question was: "Some people feel that it was our government's fault that China went Communist, others say there was nothing that we could do to stop it. How do you feel about this?"
DATA SOURCE: *Survey Research Center, University of Michigan, 1952.*

it," 89 percent voted Democratic. Similar contrasts appear at other levels of party identification. This is not to say that the election turned on the China issue alone. Rather, the probabilities are that this question tapped a broad dimension of dissatisfaction with the conduct of foreign affairs that found expression in the vote. And that dissatisfaction was compounded by an unhappiness about the conduct of domestic affairs as well.

Confirmation and ratification. If public opinion expresses itself with relative clarity in retrospective disapproval of performance or policy, it may also express itself in the same manner in confirmation or ratification of past policy or performance. Only infrequently is a new program or a new course of action advocated with such force and the attention it receives so widespread that the polling may be regarded as advance approval of a proposed course of action. Those governments that regard elections as clear mandates for new policy actions probably often mirror the beliefs of the political elite rather than reflect an understanding of the vote widely shared in the population.

The congressional election of 1934 and the presidential election of 1936 are probably the elections in recent American history that could most certainly be regarded as mass approvals of newly instituted public policies. The actions taken from 1933 to the election of 1936 constituted a program of unusual range and novelty in American domestic policy. Subjected to frontal challenge by the minority, that program undoubtedly won broad popular ratification in the increased Democratic congressional majorities of 1934 and in the overwhelming vote by which Roosevelt was re-elected in 1936.

At a different level the election of 1956 could be regarded as a mass confirmation or approval of the performance of the Eisenhower Administration perhaps principally in the field of foreign affairs. The motivation of the vote contained a generous component of a political admiration for Eisenhower as a person; it contained practically no motivation of approbation for his innovations in domestic policy—which were, of course, negligible. Probably the approval of past performance in the foreign field, as well as expectations about the future, were captured by the responses to the question: "Now looking ahead, do you think the problem of keeping out of war would be handled better in the next four years by the Republicans or by the Democrats, or about the same by both?" Comments in the replies to this inquiry were heavily loaded with professions of confidence in Eisenhower based on his military and diplomatic experience and with expressions of approbation for his success in "keeping us out of war." And the position on this question, as may be seen from Table 2, was closely associated with the vote. Those Democrats who thought the problem of "keeping out of war" would be better handled by the Republicans deserted their candidate with far greater frequency than did those Democrats who had confidence with the peace-

TABLE 2   Presidential Vote in Relation to Party Identification and to Opinion about Party Capabilities in Handling "Problem of Keeping Out of War"[a]

Party Identification	Better by Democrats	Same by Both	Better by Republicans
Strong D	87%	90%	47%
Weak D	96[b]	71	24
Independent	[c]	42	11
Weak R	[c]	14	2
Strong R	[d]	0	[e]

[a] Entries are percentages of those in each cell reporting a Democratic presidential vote. The question was: "Now looking ahead, do you think the problem of keeping out of war would be handled better in the next four years by the Republicans, or by the Democrats, or about the same by both?"
[b] This percentage rests on only 24 cases.
[c] Too few cases to percentage.
[d] No case fell in this cell.
[e] Less than one-half of 1 per cent.
DATA SOURCE: *Survey Research Center, University of Michigan, 1956.*

maintaining capacity of their own party. The consideration was not an issue of policy; the Democrats had not advocated war. Although expressed as an expectation about the future, it reflected fundamentally a broad approval of past performance.

Rejection.   As has been said, one source of difficulty in discerning the import of the popular decision in an election has been the supposition that elections do, or ought to, involve a choice between new and alternative policies for the future. American public policy rarely develops in this manner. Its evolution is more commonly by gradual stages. Policy breaks with the past, when they occur, more generally come about without precise prospective mandate; popular action takes place mainly in retrospect rather than in prospect.

Something can be said, however, for the existence of a type of election in which the electorate rejects a proposed panacea. By so doing, it may or may not give positive approval to the alternative. A clear-cut instance of an election of this type is that of 1896. William Jennings Bryan took control of the Democratic party from the conservative Cleveland forces and crusaded in advocacy of the free coinage of silver as a cure for the ills that beset the country. Here was a positive proposal, certainly widely known if not always understood in its details, to depart from the prevailing monetary policy. If we had for 1896 data of the kind that have been available for recent elections, we could speak with more confidence about what was in the minds of people as they rejected Bryan for McKinley. But the electors clearly rejected the radical alternative offered by Bryan, and it is not implausible to suppose that doubt and anxiety about free silver had more to do with their actions than did a powerful attraction to the gold standard.

Frustration of policy-motivated decision. The structure of the American electoral system is such that certain types of policy-motivated decisions are frustrated or cannot be made by election. Or the more correct interpretation may be that certain types of combinations of opinions encounter obstruction as they percolate through almost any electoral system. When two or more issues divide an electorate along different planes, if a majority on one of the issues prevails, the majority on the other may be defeated. . . . . In recent decades those who cherished both isolationist and liberal views have suffered some inconvenience in adapting themselves to the alternatives offered by the American party system. Similarly, those who embraced both internationalist and conservative opinions had some uncertainty about how their opinions might best be translated into electoral preference. On lesser issues such conflict is commonplace.

In the American system several routes are open for the avoidance of the political dead-ends created by the existence of noncongruent majorities on a series of issues. Some of these ways around the problem are individual; others are institutional. The individual often places a higher value on his position on this issue than on another; or one issue may be more salient than the other. This permits him as he votes to bring his candidate preference into line with his dominant policy preference. Berelson, Lazarsfeld, and McPhee suggest that the unity of the supporters of a candidate may consist, not in their agreement on a series of issues, but in their opposition to one or another of the policy positions of the candidate they reject. "One Republican," they conclude from their Elmira study, "may be most concerned with foreign policy, and on that subject he is against the Democrats. Another Republican may be most concerned with domestic economics, and on that subject he is against the Democrats."[1] Unity may thus exist along a common denominator of dis-

agreement with the opposition on a series of issues, but this is unity for election day only. Someone is bound to find himself in the majority on election day and in a minority on policies of interest to him the next day. Nevertheless, individuals may accommodate themselves to the situation to some extent by emphasizing in their actions those considerations most important to them.

Institutional structures also enable, or even require, governments to take into account the circumstance of the simultaneous existence of noncongruent majorities. The looseness of the party system, especially in its nominating practices, permits the election of Senators and Representatives with unorthodox combinations of policy outlook. Thus, the isolationist-liberal combination of opinion can find its spokesmen through the representative system. Witness the career of the late Senator William Langer, of North Dakota. A New Dealer with most pronounced convictions on domestic matters and a man markedly lacking in zeal for one-worldism, he probably reflected relatively well the mixed policy pattern of his constituency. Such adjustments through the representative system are commonplace.

In a more notable fashion, the system of separated powers on occasion, perhaps accidentally, permits governmental adaptation to the requirements of noncongruent majorities. The most striking case, or at least the one on which the data are most complete, is that of the election of 1952 and its consequences. A foreign policy majority supported Eisenhower in his promise to do something other than that which Truman had been doing. That majority, though, was not also, as some dedicated Republicans believed, committed to a rollback in domestic-welfare policy. The two noncongruent majorities, as a result of the congressional elections of 1954, found their voice through different organs of government. The President spoke for one majority; Congress, with its Democratic

[1] Berelson, *et al.: Voting* (Chicago: University of Chicago Press; 1954), p. 206.

complexion, was beholden to the other majority.

When noncongruent majorities exist, the meaning of the outcome of an election may be obscure; the election may, in fact, settle only one of the great issues. There are also other types of questions that are not apt to be settled in any clear fashion by elections. Those are questions on which the popular opinion distribution is of the type we earlier denominated as "concentrated"— that is, questions about which comparatively few persons have an opinion one way or another. In the excitement of the presidential campaign these matters are overshadowed by more important questions, and few persons would regard their vote as an expression of opinion on them. Such questions are not likely to be settled by elections unless they are definitely related to some major ideological position of the winner or governed by the group interests associated with the winner.

Acceptability of election results. It is plain that elections involve broad decisions on policy questions, although estimation of precisely what those determinations are requires a degree of artistry. A more important feature of elections, whatever else they decide, is their production of acceptable decisions on the succession to power in the state. At the leadership levels that quality of elections manifests itself when the losers surrender the seals of authority to the winners of the popular majority. The development of norms, expectations, and restraints that enable those with authority to surrender it in response to popular decision is a rare phenomenon among the rulers of men; they usually fear that they may suffer personal discomfort if they transfer the apparatus of state power to their enemies. Nevertheless, in a few regimes those who occupy office have learned how to accomplish the peaceable transfer of authority. Or perhaps they have learned how to conduct themselves in office so that they will not be shot by the outs who win an election.

Within the mass of the people, too, some sort of reconciliation to the defeat of one's candidate evidently occurs. Though the opposition winner may not be embraced with enthusiasm, many people accomplish a psychological adjustment to the loss of an election. That adjustment may take the form of concluding that the stakes of the election were not after all so important as they were thought to be in the heat of the campaign. . . . Before the election in 1952 a national sample was asked whether it thought that it would "make a good deal of difference to the country whether the Democrats or the Republicans win the election." About three fourths of the strong Democrats and strong Republicans opined that important differences, big differences, or at least some difference was at stake. After the election a substantial proportion of the strong Democrats made their peace with the situation by adopting the view that the Eisenhower victory would make no difference, only minor differences, or perhaps no difference at all.

This phenomenon of reconciliation to defeat has been noted in many surveys.[2] It also manifests itself in other ways. In postelection surveys that inquire about the vote, an overreport of the vote for the winner ordinarily occurs. Some people do not wish to admit that they were on the losing side and, ex post facto, change their vote, so to speak. The odds are that some of the acceptance of election outcomes may be attributable to a sportsmanship whose efficacy may be most marked among people with the least knowledge and awareness of the stakes of the political game. Then, too, after an election other persons may come around to the view that, though their man lost, the result was the "best thing" for the country.

[2] See, for example, Arthur Kornhauser *et al.: When Labor Votes* (New York: University Books; 1956), pp. 135, 161.

VI. RESULTS AND PROSPECTS

Donald G. Herzberg

It is clearly apparent as attention is turned to the future of the American political system that American politics is fast changing. It is also evident that the rate of this change, rapid as it has been since the election of Franklin D. Roosevelt in 1932, may be even more rapid in the remaining decades of the twentieth century.

The changes that will take place in the American political system in the future stem from many sources. It is possible in this essay to examine only some of the more significant ones.

First in its impact on the political system is the rise of the Negro vote in America—the Negro vote in the South and, equally important, in the North. The Civil Rights Act of 1964 and the Voting Rights Act of 1965 mean that increasing numbers of Negroes will be registered in the South. The U.S. Civil Rights Commission estimates that there are almost three million potential Negro voters in the Deep South. Until the enactment of the Voting Rights Law, only a small number of these Negroes were registered to vote. That the South, for the first time, was unable to muster a filibuster against the Voting Rights Bill or stop the Civil Rights Bill in the House is ample proof that the congressional delegations from the South are well aware of the implications of Negro voting power. Indeed, the filibuster against the Civil Rights Act may well have been the death rattle of politics as it has been practiced in the South since Reconstruction.

Whether the rise of the Negro vote will stimulate the parties to produce a genuine two-party system in the South remains to be seen. It depends to a large extent on the ability and the willingness of the leadership of the southern parties to look to the future. If they are willing to sacrifice their present position for long-term gains, then there is hope for a genuine two-party system. But in 1964 the Republican parties in the South were not willing to make such a sacrifice, as is indicated by the fact that the five Southern states carried by Senator Goldwater in 1964 were the five states with the lowest percentage of Negro voters. The Republicans made no effort to court Negro voting strength. The Democratic parties of the South are also challenged to welcome to their ranks the significant numbers of Negro voters. They cannot assume on the basis of their past performances that the newly liberated Negro voter is automatically a Democrat. How the parties respond to the Negro voter will affect the future political complexion of the South. There is room for optimism concerning the effect of the Negro voter on Southern politics, however. The Negro voter may be regarded as a part, albeit a tragically late part, of the immigration wave to the United

States. A study of the history of this movement indicates that after a period of initial hostility toward the immigrant, the political parties accepted him with sympathy and made use of his talents. Indeed, if America is a great melting pot, then the two parties have been the spoons stirring the pot.

It is not only the South that will feel the impact of the increasing number of Negro voters. In many Northern cities as well, large numbers of Negroes are not registered to vote. One example is shown by the registration figures of Essex County, New Jersey, the county which includes within its borders Newark, the largest city in the state. In 1960 in Newark, only 55 percent of persons over twenty-one voted, whereas in the suburbs of Verona and Millburn, 82 and 86 percent, respectively, of persons over twenty-one voted. The education and income medians for Newark fall far below those for the suburbs, but far more significant is the city's percentage of nonwhites. In Newark, Negroes comprise 34.4 percent of the population, whereas in Verona and Millburn these figures are 2.6 and 1.1 percent, respectively. The most predominantly Negro wards in Newark represent the smallest voter participation. The same situation applies in Atlantic City and Trenton, New Jersey, and what is true of these cities is true throughout the North.

A variety of factors contribute to low Negro registration. The lack of education among Negroes, with its accompanying apathy, and the hostility toward Negroes of established political leaders who fear a threat to their power positions are perhaps the main reasons. But the signs of the future point to a change. Among changes that will affect Negro voting registration are the growing sophistication of Negro leaders, the impact of the Education Act of 1965, reapportionment, and the national registration drives of the political parties and the labor unions. There is also the political fact of life that the more the members of a minority group register, the easier it is to get others of the same group to register. The response of the political parties to the challenge of accepting large numbers of Negroes into the body politic will be an exciting aspect of American politics.

The population explosion, too, is certain to affect American politics. Anyone reading this book in his college years who lives his three-score and ten will see 100 million and more American citizens vote in national elections. This is likely to happen fairly soon. In 1964 over 69 million Americans voted, representing some 61 percent of the estimated eligible voters. It should be noted that this figure is almost a 3 percent drop from the record 63.8 percent of the eligible voters, 68 million of them, that voted in the 1960 election. Population experts note that millions of Americans are on the threshold of the voting age. A look at school and college enrollments confirms this fact. The basic question to be asked as we watch this growing army of adult citizens is whether we can gear our political process to cope with the numbers involved. To do so will require a vast overhauling of our electoral system and major revisions in our state election laws. For the most part state election laws are archaic. Rooted in the nineteenth century, they are inadequate to deal with a society rapidly on its way to the twenty-first century. For example, these laws have not generally been responsive to the mobile nature of our society. In the year before the 1964 election, based on Bureau of the Census' mobility figures, it is estimated that some 23 million adult Americans changed residences. In some cases the move was to a different part of town or to another part of the same county. In other cases the move was to a different county within the same state or to another state. But at least 21 million Americans lost their voting privileges for some period of time, and 15 million of them were not able, because of residency laws, to regain their vote in time for the November election.

Another example of old-fashioned electoral procedures is the early cut-off date that many states have for registration. In New Jersey, the election law decrees that no one may register to vote in the forty-day period before any election—primary or general, municipal or state-wide. California halts registration fifty-four days before an election. The purpose of these cut-off dates is valid. Election officials need time to prepare the voting lists so that they will be ready for election day use, but given today's modern methods of record keeping, there is little reason for the period to be as long as these are.

Outmoded electoral procedures are also reflected in voting hours. As more and more balloting is done on voting machines there is less and less reason for not keeping the polls open until later at night. Yet Illinois, for example, closes the polls at 6 P.M., barely allowing time for a person to get to the polls if he must vote after work. Indeed, as millions more people vote, it will be necessary to extend voting hours to accommodate them.

There are signs of progress in the electoral reform field. In 1963, President Kennedy appointed a bipartisan Presidential Commission on Registration and Voting Participation. This commission, reporting to President Johnson in December 1963, made specific recommendations in the form of standards for state action. It also recommended that the states themselves take the initiative in electoral reform. By the time the Commission legally expired in March 1964, over half the states had set up commissions of one kind or another to examine their election laws.

The declining importance of the state governorship as a training ground for national leadership will soon bring in its wake significant changes in American politics. Textbooks in American government are fond of stating that, by and large, presidential and vice-presidential candidates come from among the state governors. These texts point out that traditionally the states have served as schools for our national leaders. This situation was true until 1960; in that year all four top candidates were United States senators or former senators. None had ever had any experience as the governor of a state. Indeed, with the exception of Senator Lodge's United Nations experience, none of them had had training in an executive branch of any government. The election of 1964 continued this trend. President Johnson chose a senator for his running mate and Senator Goldwater selected a congressman. True, at the Republican National Convention, Governors Romney and Scranton were dark horses, but their bids failed. Governors will continue to make bids for national office and on occasion they will be successful in gaining nomination; but the heyday of the governor is over. There was widespread unseating of incumbent governors running for re-election in the 1960, 1962, and 1964 elections, a fact that dramatizes the difficult situation confronting governors all over the country. In the same elections there were widespread changes in party control over the governorships. In 1960, for example, out of twenty-seven gubernatorial races, only eight incumbents were re-elected, and there were nineteen freshman governors. Of these governorships won by freshmen, six switched from Democratic to Republican control, seven switched from Republican control, and the six remaining stayed in the control of the party that had previously held the office. This shift occurred at a time when there was relatively little upheaval in congressional elections. In 1960 out of thirty-four Senate races, only one incumbent who sought re-election was defeated. In the House of Representatives, the shift was only slightly greater. The Republicans made a gain of twenty-two seats. Considering the high-water mark achieved by the Democrats in the 1958 congressional elections, this was a relatively small gain.

In 1962 seventeen incumbent governors out of thirty-five were re-elected. There were eighteen freshmen governors, and six of the seats went from Democratic to Republican control, six from Republican to Democratic control, and the six remaining stayed in the control of the party that had previously held the office. In 1964, out of twenty-five races, twelve incumbents were re-elected and thirteen freshmen were elected. Of the latter, three offices went from Democratic to Republican control and two offices went from Republican to Democratic control. The remaining freshmen offices stayed in the control of the party that had previously held the office.

There are many reasons for this overturn and they vary from state to state. One common theme, however, runs throughout. There is not a state in the Union that does not face severe financial difficulties. Across the country the demands for increased services—more highways, more spending for state institutions and agencies, more aid for local and higher education—have put an increasing burden on the already drained state resources and on the state governors who have the responsibility for finding the ways to meet their states' increasing obligations. It is the state governor who has to call for higher and new taxes. Furthermore, while the governor has to call for new taxes, he is less and less able to be inventive and imaginative. The growth of the federal government along with the rise in federal grants-in-aid to states, make the governor more an administrative caretaker than a leader.

Another factor in the decline of the power and position of the office of governor is the assumption by the United States of the leadership of the free world, increasing importance of foreign policy, and the basic question of war or peace, survival or destruction, as the dominant political issues of our time. It is obviously difficult for a man sitting in a state capitol to have much influence on these issues or to relate them to the problems of his state.

There is little evidence that the governor's lot in American politics is going to improve. Text books on American government will have to be amended to indicate that state houses now are likely to be the burying ground of political ambition and that the path to national prominence and office is through the United States Senate or other national public service.

Other changing factors of our political institutions need to be mentioned. One of these is the reapportionment of state and city legislatures that is presently taking place. The redressing of the imbalance between rural and urban representation will have a large impact on our political parties. Of particular importance will be the role of the suburbs as they gain in strength in the state legislative bodies. The challenge to the political parties to remake state legislatures and to restore them to their traditional position as a coordinate branch of government is great. In the twentieth century the trend in state power has been a shift toward executive control over the legislature. This development has occurred despite the overall decline on a national scale in prestige of the governorship. The reason is not difficult to understand. The governor, a full-time official, commands a full-time and generally efficient bureaucracy. State legislators, however, are only part-time public servants, and for the most part they command little or no staff. They have been ill prepared to gather information or to prepare enough of the necessary legislative proposals. Therefore, the executive has tended to step this gap. There are signs now, however, that this situation may be altered to a degree. Many able state legislators and many civic organizations recognize that our system of government demands that the legislative branch be bolstered so that it can assert its share of power. It remains to be seen if reapportionment will help in this matter.

Another factor relates to the increasing nationalization of our politics. Many of our congressional districts are microcosms of the nation. A midwestern congressman representing a heretofore rural district finds that his district is becoming more and more suburbanized and industrialized. He finds, for example, that he and a congressman from the state of Washington have more problems in common than differences. This trend is apparently growing. The question is what effect will it have on the two major parties. Will it bring them together in major issues or will the differences between them be made more pronounced?

Many political scientists have been seeking the answer to this and other questions that affect our political system. In this chapter many ideas for the reform of American politics within the framework of its present structure are presented in detail. Many of these reforms deserve serious consideration. Especially to be noted are the reforms suggested by Dean Bailey (59). He proposes that the parties should make a massive effort to increase second party activity in all congressional districts and states and to develop machinery for obtaining a roster of likely candidates. Bailey does propose stronger party policy committees in Congress, frequent party caucuses, and joint hearings and reports by both houses of Congress. In addition, he makes a number of other proposals that are not organizational in character but are designed to foster political activity on the part of a greater number of citizens. Bailey's proposals, in general, do deal with national organizational aspects of party activity in the electoral process, and with the reorganization of the parties under legislative conditions. A combination of electoral and legislative organizational changes would best serve our end, Bailey points out.

The suggestions put forth by the American Political Science Association Committee on Political Parties in its 1950 report[1] were based on a strongly stated desire for a party system that would be democratic, responsible, and effective. This system was envisioned only within the framework of the two-party system. The concept of one strong opposition party was a key recommendation.

---

[1] See "Toward a More Responsible Two-Party System, A Report of the Committee on Political Parties: American Political Science Association," *The American Political Science Review*, vol. 44, no. 3, part 2 (supplement), September 1950. This report marked the start of continuing discussions on reform and change in the structure and nature of the political parties in the United States. The report is not reprinted in this book, but several of the articles contained in this chapter are based on the report, and the student is urged to become familiar with its proposals beyond the brief outline given here.

To these ends, the Committee proposed specific organizational changes within the framework of the present party structure rather than any kind of nationalization of parties.

Several proposals concerned national conventions and party headquarters. It was recommended that there be a permanent headquarters and staff, that national conventions be held biennially, and that national committee membership be decided at national conventions. It was pointed out that the composition of national committees should reflect the actual strength of the party within the area represented. The biennial meeting would undoubtedly be of benefit to the "out" party, but its usefulness to a President and Congress in office is highly questionable. The proposal on representative membership might prove an incentive to local groups in one-party and weak-party areas to increase their control in order to have a larger role at the national level. This proposal might well be adopted by both parties. It would be particularly useful for the Republicans, who should, perhaps, take a long look at the areas in which they have succeeded and the types of Republicans that they have been able to elect. On this basis, they could judge the candidates and issues that most benefit them at the polls. A permanent staff and headquarters would be beneficial to both parties.

A proposed party council of fifty members to administer the party, draft platforms, and recommend congressional candidates would probably be unworkable because such a council would not represent at large party opinion.

The proposal that platforms be based on general principles that represent the permanent, long-range philosophy of the party as well as the less important issues of the day is endorsed by most political scientists. The most significant aspect of this recommendation is that the platform be binding. Areas of disagreement arise in considering the extent to which any platform should be binding upon all candidates. A general rule of thumb should probably be that all congressional and senatorial candidates reflect the national image of the party record and platform. Candidates who take advantage of running on a party ticket owe allegiance to their party's platform. The authority to discipline members of a party should probably rest with the elected members of the party rather than with national, state, or local party arms. Most recently, an example of this type of discipline occurred when two Democratic members of the House who had bolted the party to support Goldwater were disciplined by their party mates in the House. Discipline among elected members is preferable to rigidity in the preprimary selection of candidates.

Proposed congressional reforms that would include the formation of leadership committees, more frequent caucuses with binding decisions, a new and more equitable system of assignment and rotation of committees and chairmanships, amendment of cloture rules, a lessening of power of the Rules Committee, and provision of a minority staff for all committees are all important, and in spite of the overlapping of several of the proposals with those made later by Bailey, all should be given serious consideration as to the effect they could have on party organization.

Adoption of many of these reforms would tighten party organization and legislative responsibility in Congress. It is in the legislative arena (and to a lesser degree in the election process) that party organization has failed to be as responsible as we would wish. Our parties have served us well in the winning of power; it is in the process of wielding power that they have failed us. Internal congressional reform would go a long way toward creating a more responsible party system.

Among other proposals made by the Committee, the elimination of blanket primaries and cross-filing should be adopted, and the suggestions for direct presidential primaries and the direct election of delegates to the national conventions should probably be discarded. It is sounder practice for the bona fide party members to make such decisions. Permanent registration, the expanded use of the absentee ballot, and the use of the short ballot are reforms that all groups endorse but few enact. The proposal to lengthen the term of members of the house to four years would not accomplish as much as might be accomplished by a twelve-term limitation on service. The Committee raised the question of federal financing and rejected it in favor of more private financing. Several criticisms of the proposals of the American Political Science Association have been included in the selections that follow. Perhaps the selections will reflect the viewpoint of one who is firmly committed to the two-party system and to the belief that the essential value of our political parties is their flexibility; as Arthur Schlesinger has said, "Experimentation and opportunism rather than pre-conceived theories have been the animating spirit of American progress."

PARTY IN GOVERNMENT

52.   Constituency Influence in Congress

Warren E. Miller and Donald E. Stokes

In view of the fact that much of the evidence for constituency control of the House of Representatives rests on inference, the authors, who teach at the University of Michigan, have interviewed incumbent congressmen, nonincumbent opponents, and a sample of constituents of each of 116 sample unit districts. The interviews were correlated with roll-call votes and the social and political character of the particular district represented. The scope of influence considered for the analysis was limited to issues falling within three policy domains: the social welfare field, support for U.S.

involvement in foreign affairs, and approval of federal action to protect the civil rights of Negroes.

The evidence shows that a representative's roll-call behavior is strongly influenced by his own policy views and by his perception of the views of his constituents. However, congressmen generally have imperfect information about the issue preferences of their constituency and the constituency, in turn, has little knowledge of the stands taken by its representative on these issues.

* * *

Substantial constituency influence over the lower house of Congress is commonly thought to be both a normative principle and a factual truth of American government. From their draft constitution we may

From the *American Political Science Review*, vol. 57, no. 1 (March 1963), pp. 45–56.

assume the Founding Fathers expected it, and many political scientists feel, regretfully, that the Framers' wish has come all too true.[1] Nevertheless, much of the evidence of constituency control rests on inference. The fact that our House of Representatives, especially by comparison with the House of Commons, has irregular party voting does not of itself indicate that Congressmen deviate from party in response to local pressure. And even more, the fact that many Congressmen *feel* pressure from home does not of itself establish that the local constituency is performing any of the acts that a reasonable definition of control would imply.

I. CONSTITUENCY CONTROL IN THE NORMATIVE THEORY OF REPRESENTATION

Control by the local constituency is at one pole of *both* the great normative controversies about representation that have arisen in modern times. It is generally recognized that constituency control is opposite to the conception of representation associated with Edmund Burke. Burke wanted the representative to serve the constituency's *interest* but not its *will,* and the extent to which the representative should be compelled by electoral sanctions to follow the "mandate" of his constituents has been at the heart of the ensuing controversy as it has continued for a century and a half.[2]

Constituency control also is opposite to the conception of government by responsible national parties. This is widely seen, yet the point is rarely connected with normative discussions of representation. Indeed, it is remarkable how little attention has been given to the model of representation implicit in the doctrine of a "responsible two-party system." When the subject of representation is broached among political scientists the classical argument between Burke and his opponents is likely to come at once to mind. So great is Burke's influence that the antithesis he proposed still provides the categories of thought used in contemporary treatments of representation despite the fact that many students of politics today would advocate a relationship between representative and constituency that fits *neither* position of the mandate-independence controversy.

The conception of representation implicit in the doctrine of responsible parties shares the idea of popular control with the instructed-delegate model. Both are versions of popular sovereignty. But "the people" of the responsible two-party system are conceived in terms of a national rather than a local constituency. Candidates for legislative office appeal to the electorate in terms of a *national* party program and leadership, to which, if elected, they will be committed. Expressions of policy preference by the local district are reduced to endorsements of one or another of these programs, and the local district retains only the arithmetical significance that whichever party can rally to its pro-

[1] To be sure, the work of the Federal Convention has been supplemented in two critical respects. The first of these is the practice, virtually universal since the mid-19th Century, of choosing Representatives from single-member districts of limited geographic area. The second is the practice, which has also become virtually universal in our own century, of selecting party nominees for the House by direct primary election.

[2] In the language of Eulau, Wahlke, *et al.,* we speak here of the "style," not the "focus," of representation. See their "The Role of the Representative: Some Empirical Observations on the Theory of Edmund Burke," this REVIEW [*American Political Science Review*], Vol. 53 (September, 1959), pp.

742–756. An excellent review of the mandate-independence controversy is given by Hanna Fenichel Pitkin, "The Theory of Representation" (unpublished doctoral dissertation, University of California, Berkeley, 1961). For other contemporary discussions of representation, see Alfred de Grazia, *Public and Republic* (New York, 1951), and John A. Fairlie, "The Nature of Political Representation," this REVIEW [*American Political Science Review*], Vol. 34 (April–June, 1940), pp. 236–248, 456–466.

gram the greater number of supporters in the district will control its legislative seat.

No one tradition of representation has entirely dominated American practice. Elements of the Burkean, instructed-delegate, and responsible party models can all be found in our political life. Yet if the American system has elements of all three, a good deal depends on how they are combined. Especially critical is the question whether different models of representation apply to different public issues. Is the saliency of legislative action to the public so different in quality and degree on different issues that the legislator is subject to very different constraints from his constituency? Does the legislator have a single generalized mode of response to his constituency that is rooted in a normative belief about the representative's role or does the same legislator respond to his constituency differently on different issues? More evidence is needed on matters so fundamental to our system.

AN EMPIRICAL STUDY
OF REPRESENTATION

To extend what we know of representation in the American Congress the Survey Research Center of The University of Michigan interviewed the incumbent Congressman his non-incumbent opponent (if any), and a sample of constituents in each of 116 congressional districts, which were themselves a probability sample of all districts.[3] These interviews, conducted imme-

[3] The sampling aspects of this research were complicated by the fact that the study of representation was a rider midway on a four-year panel study of the electorate whose primary sampling units were not congressional districts (although there is no technical reason why they could not have been if the needs of the representation analysis had been foreseen when the design of the sample was fixed two years before). As a result, the districts in our sample had unequal probabilities of selection and unequal weights in the analysis, making the sample somewhat less efficient than an equal-probability sample of equivalent size.

It will be apparent in the discussion that follows

that we have estimated characteristics of whole constituencies from our samples of constituents living in particular districts. In view of the fact that a sample of less than two thousand constituents has been divided among 116 districts, the reader may wonder about the reliability of these estimates. After considerable investigation we have concluded that their sampling error is not so severe a problem for the analysis as we had thought it would be. Several comments may indicate why it is not.

To begin with, the weighting of our sample of districts has increased the reliability of the constituency estimates. The correct theoretical weight to be assigned each district in the analysis is the inverse of the probability of the district's selection, and it can be shown that this weight is approximately proportional to the number of interviews taken in the district. The result of this is that the greatest weight is assigned the districts with the largest number of interviews and, hence, the most reliable constituency estimates. Indeed, these weights increase by half again the (weighted) mean number of interviews taken per district. To put the matter another way: the introduction of differential weights trades some of our sample of congressional districts for more reliable constituency estimates.

How much of a problem the unreliability of these estimates is depends very much on the analytic uses to which the estimates are put. If our goal were case analyses of particular districts, the constituency samples would have to be much larger. Indeed, for most case analyses we would want several hundred interviews per district (at a cost, over 116 districts, of several small nuclear reactors). However, most of the findings reported here are based not on single districts but on many or all of the districts in our sample. For analyses of this sort the number of interviews per district can be much smaller.

Our investigation of the effect of the sampling variance of the constituency estimates is quite reassuring. When statistics computed from our constituency samples are compared with corresponding parameter values for the constituencies, the agreement of the two sets of figures is quite close. For example, when the proportions voting Democratic in the 116 constituencies in 1958, as computed from our sample data, are compared with the actual proportions voting Democratic, as recorded in official election statistics, a product moment correlation of 0.93 is obtained, and this figure is the more impressive since this test throws away non-voters, almost one-half of our total sample. We interpret the Pearsonian correlation as an appropriate measure of agreement in this case, since the associated regression equations are almost exactly the identity function. The alternative intraclass correlation coefficient has almost as high a value.

Although we believe that this analysis provides a textbook illustration of how misleading intuitive ideas (including our own) about the effects of sampling error can be, these figures ought not to diately after the congressional election of 1958, explored a wide range of attitudes and perceptions held by the individuals who play the reciprocal roles of the representative relation in national government. The distinguishing feature of this research is, of course, that it sought direct information from both constituent and legislator (actual and aspiring). To this fund of comparative interview data has been added information about the roll call votes of our sample of Congressmen and the political and social characteristics of the districts they represent.

Many students of politics with excellent reason, have been sensitive to possible ties between representative and constituent that have little to do with issues of public policy. For example, ethnic identifications may cement a legislator in the affections of his district, whatever (within limits) his stands on issues. And many Congressmen keep their tenure of office secure by skillful provision of district benefits ranging from free literature to major federal projects. In the full study of which this analysis is part we have explored several bases of constituency support that have little to do with policy issues. Nevertheless, the question how the representative should make up his mind on legislative issues is what the classical arguments over representation are all about, and we have given a central place to a comparison of the policy preferences of constituents and Representatives and to a causal analysis of the relation between the two.

In view of the electorate's scanty information about government it was not at all clear in advance that such a comparison could be made. Some of the more buoyant advocates of popular sovereignty have regarded the citizens as a kind of kibitzer who looks over the shoulder of his representative at the legislative game. Kibitzer and player may disagree as to which card should be played, but they were at least thought to share a common understanding of what the alternatives are.

No one familiar with the findings of research on mass electorates could accept this view of the citizen. Far from looking over the shoulder of their Congressmen at the legislative game, most Americans are almost totally uninformed about legislative issues in Washington. At best the average citizen may be said to have some general ideas about how the country should be run, which he is able to use in responding to particular questions about what the government ought to do. For example, survey studies have shown that most people have a general (though differing) conception of how far government should go to achieve social and economic welfare objectives and that these convictions fix their response to various particular questions about actions government might take.[4]

What makes it possible to compare the policy preferences of constituents and Representatives despite the public's low awareness of legislative affairs is the fact that Congressmen themselves respond to many issues in terms of fairly broad evaluative dimensions. Undoubtedly policy alternatives are judged in the executive agencies and the specialized committees of the Congress by criteria that are relatively complex and specific to the polices at issue. But a good deal of evidence goes to show that when proposals come before the House as a whole they are judged on the basis of

---

be too beguiling. It is clear that how close such a correlation is to 1.0 for any given variable will depend on the ratio of the between-district variance to the total variance. When this ratio is as high as it is for Republican and Democratic voting, the effect of the unreliability of our constituency estimates is fairly trivial. Although the content of the study is quite different, this sampling problem has much in common with the problem of attenuation of correlation as it has been treated in psychological testing. See, for example, J. P. Guilford, *Fundamental Statistics in Psychology and Education* (New York, 1956), pp. 475–478.

4 See Angus Campbell, Philip E. Converse, Warren E. Miller, and Donald E. Stokes, *The American Voter* (New York, 1960), pp. 194–209.

more general evaluative dimensions.[5] For example, most Congressmen, too, seem to have a general conception of how far government should go in the area of domestic social and economic welfare, and these general positions apparently orient their roll call votes on a number of particular social welfare issues.

It follows that such a broad evaluative dimension can be used to compare the policy preferences of constituents and Representatives despite the low state of the public's information about politics. In this study three such dimensions have been drawn from our voter interviews and from congressional interviews and roll call records. As suggested above, one of these has to do with approval of government action in the social welfare field, the primary domestic issue of the New Deal-Fair Deal (and New Frontier) eras. A second dimension has to do with support for American involvement in foreign affairs, a latter-day version of the isolationist-internationalist continuum. A third dimension has to do

with approval of federal action to protect the civil rights of Negroes.[6]

Because our research focused on these three dimensions, our analysis of constituency influence is limited to these areas of policy. No point has been more energetically or usefully made by those who have sought to clarify the concepts of power and influence than the necessity of specifying the acts *with respect to which* one actor has power or influence or control over another.[7] Therefore, the scope or range of influence for our analysis is the collection of legislative issues falling within our three policy domains. We are not able to say how much control the local constituency may or may not have over *all* actions of its Representative, and there may well be pork-barrel issues or other matters of peculiar relevance to the district on which the relation of Congressman to constituency is quite distinctive. However, few observers of contemporary politics would regard the issues of government provision of social and economic welfare, of American involve-

[5] This conclusion, fully supported by our own work for later Congresses, is one of the main findings to be drawn from the work of Duncan MacRae on roll call voting in the House of Representatives. See his *Dimensions of Congressional Voting: A Statistical Study of the House of Representatives in the Eighty-First Congress* (Berkeley and Los Angeles: University of California Press, 1958). For additional evidence of the existence of scale dimensions in legislative behavior, see N. L. Gage and Ben Shimberg, "Measuring Senatorial Progressivism," *Journal of Abnormal and Social Psychology,* Vol. 44 (January 1949), pp. 112–117; George M. Belknap, "A Study of Senatorial Voting by Scale Analysis" (unpublished doctoral dissertation, University of Chicago, 1951), and "A Method for Analyzing Legislative Behavior," *Midwest Journal of Political Science,* Vol. 2 (1958), pp. 377–402; two other articles by MacRae, "The Role of the State Legislator in Massachusetts," *American Sociological Review,* Vol. 19 (April 1954), pp. 185–194, and "Roll Call Votes and Leadership," *Public Opinion Quarterly,* Vol. 20 (1956), pp. 543–588; Charles D. Farris, "A Method of Determining Ideological Groups in Congress," *Journal of Politics,* Vol. 20 (1958), pp. 308–338; and Leroy N. Rieselbach, "Quantitative Techniques for Studying Voting Behavior in the U. N. General Assembly," *International Organization,* Vol. 14 (1960), pp. 291–306.

[6] The content of the three issue domains may be suggested by some of the roll call and interview items used. In the area of social welfare these included the issues of public housing, public power, aid to education, and government's role in maintaining full employment. In the area of foreign involvement the items included the issues of foreign economic aid, military aid, sending troops abroad, and aid to neutrals. In the area of civil rights the items included the issues of school desegregation, fair employment, and the protection of Negro voting rights.

[7] Because this point has been so widely discussed it has inevitably attracted a variety of terms. Dahl denotes the acts of *a* whose performance *A* is able to influence as the *scope* of *A's* power. See Robert A. Dahl, "The Concept of Power," *Behavioral Science,* Vol. 2 (July 1957), pp. 201–215. This usage is similar to that of Harold D. Lasswell and Abraham Kaplan, *Power and Society* (New Haven: Yale University Press, 1950), pp. 71–73. Dorwin Cartwright, however, denotes the behavioral or psychological changes in *P* which *O* is able to induce as the *range* of *O's* power: "A Field Theoretical Conception of Power," *Studies in Social Power* (Ann Arbor: Research Center for Group Dynamics, Institute for Social Research, The University of Michigan, 1959), pp. 183–220.

ment in world affairs, and of federal action in behalf of the Negro as constituting a trivial range of action. Indeed, these domains together include most of the great issues that have come before Congress in recent years.

In each policy domain we have used the procedures of cumulative scaling, as developed by Louis Guttman and others, to order our samples of Congressmen, of opposing candidates, and of voters. In each domain Congressmen were ranked once according to their roll call votes in the House and again according to the attitudes they revealed in our confidential interviews. These two orderings are by no means identical, nor are the discrepancies due simply to uncertainties of measurement.[8] Opposing candidates also were ranked in each policy domain according to the attitudes they revealed in our interviews. The nationwide sample of constituents was ordered in each domain, and by averaging the attitude scores of all constituents living in the same districts, whole constituencies were ranked on each dimension so that the views of Congressmen could be compared with those of their constituencies.[9] Finally,

by considering only the constituents in each district who share some characteristic (voting for the incumbent, say) we were able to order these fractions of districts so that the opinions of Congressmen could be compared with those, for example, of the dominant electoral elements of their districts.

In each policy domain, crossing the rankings of Congressmen and their constituencies gives an empirical measure of the extent of policy agreement between legislator and district.[10] In the period of our research

---

[8] That the Representative's roll call votes can diverge from his true opinion is borne out by a number of findings of the study (some of which are reported here) as to the conditions under which agreement between the Congressman's roll call position and his private attitude will be high or low. However, a direct confirmation that these two sets of measurements are not simply getting at the same thing is given by differences in attitude-roll call agreement according to the Congressman's sense of how well his roll call votes have expressed his real views. In the domain of foreign involvement, for example, the correlation of our attitudinal and roll call measurements was .75 among Representatives who said that their roll call votes had expressed their real views fairly well. But this correlation was only .04 among those who said that their roll call votes had expressed their views poorly. In the other policy domains, too, attitude-roll call agreement is higher among Congressmen who are well satisfied with their roll call votes than it is among Congressmen who are not.

[9] During the analysis we have formed constituency scores out of the scores of constituents living

in the same district by several devices other than calculating average constituent scores. In particular, in view of the ordinal character of our scales we have frequently used the *median* constituent score as a central value for the constituency as a whole. However, the ordering of constituencies differs very little according to which of several reasonable alternatives for obtaining constituency scores is chosen. As a result, we have preferred mean scores for the greater number of ranks they give.

[10] The meaning of this procedure can be suggested by two percentage tables standing for hypothetical extreme cases, the first that of full agreement, the second that of no agreement whatever. For convenience, these illustrative tables categorize both Congressmen and their districts in terms of only three degrees of favor and assume for both a nearly uniform distribution across the three categories. The terms "pro," "neutral," and "con" indicate a relative rather than an absolute opinion. In Case I, full agreement, all districts relatively favorable to social welfare action have Congressmen who are so too, etc.; whereas in Case II, or that of no agreement, the ordering of constituents is independent in a statistical sense of the ranking of Congressmen: knowing the policy orientation of a district gives no clue at all to the orientation of its Congressman. Of course, it is possible for the orders of legislators and districts to be *inversely* related, and this possibility is of some importance, as indicated below, when the policy position of non-incumbent candidates as well as incumbents is taken into account. To summarize the degree of congruence between legislators and voters, a measure of correlations is introduced. Although we have used a variety of measures of association in our analysis, the values reported in this article all refer to product moment correlation coefficients. For our hypothetical Case I a measure of correlation would have the value 1.0; for Case II, the value 0.0. When it is applied to actual data this convenient indicator is likely to have a value somewhere in between. The question is where.

this procedure reveals very different degrees of policy congruence across the three issue domains. On questions of social and economic welfare there is considerable agreement between Representative and district, expressed by a correlation of approximately 0.3. This coefficient is, of course, very much less than the limiting value of 1.0, indicating that a number of Congressmen are, relatively speaking, more or less "liberal" than their districts. However, on the question of foreign involvement there is no discernible agreement between legislator and district whatever. Indeed, as if to emphasize the point, the coefficient expressing this relation is slightly negative (-0.09), although not significantly so in a statistical sense. It is in the domain of civil rights that the rankings of Congressmen and constituencies most nearly agree. When we took our measurements in the late 1950s the correlation of congressional roll call behavior with constituency opinion on questions affecting the Negro was nearly 0.6.

The description of policy agreement that these three simple correlations give can be a starting-point for a wide range of analyses. For example, the significance of party competition in the district for policy representation can be explored by comparing

the agreement between district and Congressman with the agreement between the district and the Congressman's non-incumbent opponent. Alternatively, the significance of choosing Representatives from single-member districts by popular majority can be explored by comparing the agreement between the Congressman and his own supporters with the agreement between the Congressman and the supporters of his opponent. Taking *both* party competition and majority rule into account magnifies rather spectacularly some of the coefficients reported here. This is most true in the domain of social welfare, where attitudes both of candidates and of voters are most polarized along party lines. Whereas the correlation between the constituency majority and congressional roll call votes is nearly $+0.4$ on social welfare policy, the correlation of the district majority with the non-incumbent candidate is -0.4. This difference, amounting to almost 0.8, between these two coefficients is an indicator of what the dominant electoral element of the constituency gets on the average by choosing the Congressman it has and excluding his opponent from office.[11]

These three coefficients are also the starting-point for a causal analysis of the relation of constituency to representative, the main problem of this paper. At least on social welfare and Negro rights a measurable degree of congruence is found between district and legislator. Is this agreement due to constituency influence in Congress, or is it to be attributed to other causes? If this question is to have a satisfactory answer the conditions that are necessary and

Case I: Full Policy Agreement

Constituencies

Congressmen	Pro	Neutral	Con	
Pro	33	0	0	33
Neutral	0	34	0	34
Con	0	0	33	33
	33	34	33	100%

Correlation = 1.0

Case II: No Policy Agreement

Constituencies

Congressmen	Pro	Neutral	Con	
Pro	11	11	11	33
Neutral	11	12	11	34
Con	11	11	11	33
	33	34	33	100%

Correlation = 0.0

[11] A word of caution is in order, lest we compare things that are not strictly comparable. For obvious reasons, most non-incumbent candidates have no roll call record, and we have had to measure their policy agreement with the district entirely in terms of the attitudes they have revealed in interviews. However, the difference of coefficients given here is almost as great when the policy agreement between the incumbent Congressman and his district is also measured in terms of the attitudes conveyed in confidential interviews.

sufficient to assure constituency control must be stated and compared with the available empirical evidence.

THE CONDITIONS
OF CONSTITUENCY INFLUENCE

Broadly speaking, the constituency can control the policy actions of the Representative in two alternative ways. The first of these is for the district to choose a Representative who so shares its views that in following his own convictions he does his constituents' will. In this case district opinion and the Congressman's actions are connected through the Representative's own policy attitudes. The second means of constituency control is for the Congressman to follow his (at least tolerably accurate) perceptions of district attitude in order to win re-election. In this case constituency opinion and the Congressman's actions are connected through his perception of what the district wants.[12]

[12] A third type of connection, excluded here, might obtain between district and Congressman if the Representative accedes to what he thinks the district wants because he believes that to be what a representative *ought* to do, whether or not it is necessary for re-election. We leave this type of connection out of our account here because we conceive an influence relation as one in which control is not voluntarily accepted or rejected by someone subject to it. Of course, this possible connection between district and Representative is not any the less interesting because it falls outside our definition of influence or control, and we have given a good deal of attention to it in the broader study of which this analysis is part.

These two paths of constituency control are presented schematically in Figure 1. As the figure suggests, each path has two steps, one connecting the constituency's attitude with an "intervening" attitude or perception, the other connecting this attitude or perception with the Representative's roll call behavior. Out of respect for the processes by which the human actor achieves cognitive congruence we have also drawn arrows between the two intervening factors, since the Congressman probably tends to see his district as having the same opinion as his own and also tends, over time, to bring his own opinion into line with the district's. The inclusion of these arrows calls attention to two other possible influence paths, each consisting of *three* steps, although these additional paths will turn out to be of relatively slight importance empirically.

Neither of the main influence paths of Figure 1 will connect the final roll call vote to the constituency's views if either of its steps is blocked. From this, two necessary conditions of constituency influence can be stated: *first,* the Representative's votes in the House must agree substantially with his own policy views or his perceptions of the district's views, and not be determined entirely by other influences to which the Congressman is exposed; and, *second,* the attitudes or perceptions governing the Representative's acts must correspond, at least imperfectly, to the district's actual opinions. It would be difficult to describe the

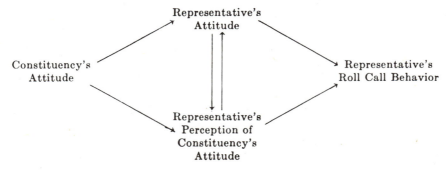

Fig. 1 Connections between a constituency's attitude and its Representative's roll call behavior.

relation of constituency to Representative as one of control unless these conditions are met.[13]

Yet these two requirements are not sufficient to assure control. A *third* condition must also be satisfied: the constituency must in some measure take the policy views of candidates into account in choosing a Representative. If it does not, agreement between district and Congressman may arise for reasons that cannot rationally be brought within the idea of control. For example, such agreement may simply reflect the fact that a Representative drawn from a given area is likely, by pure statistical probability, to share its dominant values, without his acceptance or rejection of these ever having been a matter of consequence to his electors.

EVIDENCE OF CONTROL: CONGRESSIONAL ATTITUDES AND PERCEPTIONS

How well are these conditions met in the relation of American Congressmen to their constituents? There is little question that the first is substantially satisfied; the evidence of our research indicates that members of the House do in fact vote both their own policy views and their perceptions of their constituents' views, at least on issues of social welfare, foreign involvement, and civil rights. If these two intervening factors are used to predict roll call votes, the prediction is quite successful. Their multiple correlation with roll call position is 0.7 for social welfare, 0.6 for foreign involvement, and 0.9 for civil rights; the last figure is especially persuasive. What is more, both the Congressman's own convictions and his

perceptions of district opinion make a distinct contribution to his roll call behavior. In each of the three domains the prediction of roll call votes is surer if it is made from both factors rather than from either alone.

Lest the strong influence that the Congressman's views and his perception of district views have on roll call behavior appear somehow foreordained—and, consequently, this finding seem a trivial one—it is worth taking a sidewise glance at the potency of possible other forces on the Representative's vote. In the area of foreign policy, for example, a number of Congressmen are disposed to follow the administration's advice, whatever they or their districts think. For those who are, the multiple correlation of roll call behavior with the Representative's own foreign policy views and his perception of district views is a mere 0.2. Other findings could be cited to support the point that the influence of the Congressman's own preferences and those he attributes to the district is extremely variable. Yet in the House as a whole over the three policy domains the influence of these forces is quite strong.

The connections of congressional attitudes and perceptions with actual constituency opinion are weaker. If policy agreement between district and Representative is moderate and variable across the policy domains, as it is, this is to be explained much more in terms of the second condition of constituency control than the first. The Representative's attitudes and perceptions most nearly match true opinion in his district on the issues of Negro rights. Reflecting the charged and polarized nature of this area, the correlation of actual district opinion with perceived opinion is greater than 0.6, and the correlation of district attitude with the Representative's own attitude is nearly 0.4, as shown by Table I. But the comparable correlations for foreign involvement are much smaller —indeed almost negligible. And the coefficients for social welfare are also smaller,

TABLE I   **Correlations of Constituency Attitudes**

Policy Domain	Correlation of Constituency Attitude with	
	Representative's Perception of Constituency Attitude	*Representative's Own Attitude*
Social welfare	.17	.21
Foreign involvement	.19	.06
Civil rights	.63	.39

although a detailed presentation of findings in this area would show that the Representative's perceptions and attitudes are more strongly associated with the attitude of his electoral *majority* than they are with the attitudes of the constituency as a whole.

Knowing this much about the various paths that may lead, directly or indirectly, from constituency attitude to roll call vote, we can assess their relative importance. Since the alternative influence chains have links of unequal strength, the full chains will not in general be equally strong, and these differences are of great importance in the relation of Representative to constituency. For the domain of civil rights Figure 2 assembles all the intercorrelations of the

variables of our system. As the figure shows, the root correlation of constituency attitude with roll call behavior in this domain is 0.57. How much of this policy congruence can be accounted for by the influence path involving the Representative's attitude? And how much by the path involving his perception of constituency opinion? When the intercorrelations of the system are interpreted in the light of what we assume its causal structure to be, it is influence passing through the Congressman's perception of the district's views that is found to be preeminently important.[14] Un-

14 We have done this by a variance-component technique similar to several others proposed for dealing with problems of this type. See especially Herbert A. Simon, "Spurious Correlation: A Causal Interpretation," *Journal of the American Statistical Association,* Vol. 49 (1954), pp., 467–479; Hubert M. Blalock, Jr., "The Relative Importance of Variables," *American Sociological Review,* Vol. 26 (1961), pp. 866–874; and the almost forgotten work of Sewall Wright, "Correlation and Causation," *Journal of Agricultural Research,* Vol. 20 (1920), pp. 557–585. Under this technique a "path coefficient" (to use Wright's terminology, although not his theory) is assigned to each of the causal arrows by solving a set of equations involving the correlations of the variables of the model. The weight assigned to a full path is then the product of its several path coefficients, and this product may be interpreted as the proportion of the variance of the dependent variable (roll call behavior, here) that is explained by a given path.

Civil rights: intercorrelations

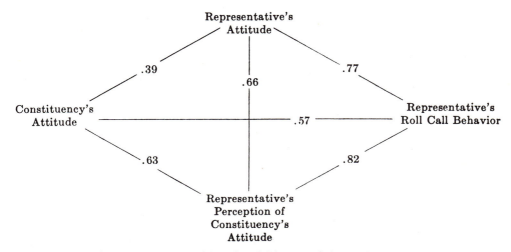

Fig. 2   Intercorrelations of variables pertaining to Civil Rights.

A special problem arises because influence may flow in either direction between the Congressman's attitude and his perception of district attitude (as noted above, the Representative may tend both to perceive his constituency's view selectively, as consistent with his own, and to change his own view to be consistent with the perceived constituency view). Hence, we have not a single causal model but a whole family of models, varying according to the relative importance of influence from attitude to perception and from perception to attitude. Our solution to this problem has been to calculate influence coefficients for the two extreme models in order to see how much our results could vary according to which model is chosen from our family of models. Since the systems of equations in this analysis are linear it can be shown that the coefficients we seek have their maximum and minimum values under one or the other of the limiting models. Therefore, computing any given coefficient for each of these limiting cases defines an interval in which the true value of the coefficient must lie. In fact these intervals turn out to be fairly small; our findings as to the relative importance of alternative influence paths would change little according to which model is selected.

The two limiting models with their associated systems of equations and the formulas for computing the relative importance of the three possible influence paths under each model are given below.

der the least favorable assumption as to its importance, this path is found to account for more than twice as much of the variance of roll call behavior as the paths involving the Representative's own attitude.[15] However, when this same procedure is applied to our social welfare data, the results suggest that the direct connection of constituency and roll call through the Congressman's own attitude is the most important of the alternative paths.[16] The reversal of the relative importance of the two paths as we move from civil rights to social welfare is one of the most striking findings of this analysis.

EVIDENCE OF CONTROL: ELECTORAL BEHAVIOR

Of the three conditions of constituency influence, the requirement that the electorate take account of the policy positions

[15] By "least favorable" we mean the assumption that influence goes only from the Congressman's attitude to his perception of district attitude (Model I) and not the other way round. Under this assumption, the proportions of the variance of roll call behavior accounted for by the three alternative paths, expressed as proportions of the part of the variance of roll call votes that is explained by district attitude, are these:

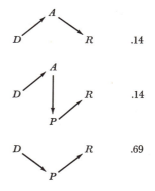

Model I: $A \rightarrow P$ Model II: $P \rightarrow A$

$r^2AR = d + ce$ $r^2AR = d'$
$r^2PR = e$ $r^2PR = e' + c'd'$
$r^2DA = a$ $r^2DA = a' + b'c'$
$r^2DP = b + ac$ $r^2DP = b'$
$r^2AP = c$ $r^2AP = c'$

$R = ad$ $R = a'd'$

$R = ace$ $R = b'c'd'$

$R = be$ $R = b'e'$

Inverting the assumed direction of influence between the Congressman's own attitude and district attitude (Model II) eliminates altogether the effect that the Representative's attitude can have had on his votes, independently of his perception of district attitude.

[16] Under both Models I and II the proportion of the variance of roll call voting explained by the

of the candidates is the hardest to match with empirical evidence. Indeed, given the limited information the average voter carries to the polls, the public might be thought incompetent to perform any task of appraisal. Of constituents living in congressional districts where there was a contest between a Republican and a Democrat in 1958, less than one in five said they had read or heard something about both candidates, and well over half conceded they had read or heard nothing about either. And these proportions are not much better when they are based only on the part of the sample, not much more than half, that reported voting for Congress in 1958. The extent of awareness of the candidates among voters is indicated in Table 2. As the table shows, even of the portion of the public that was sufficiently interested to vote, almost half had read or heard nothing about either candidate.

TABLE II **Awareness of Congressional Candidates among Voters, 1958**

		Read or Heard Something about Incumbent [a]		
		Yes	*No*	
Read or heard something about Non-incumbent	Yes	24	5	29
	No	25	46	71
		49	51	100%

[a] In order to include all districts where the House seat was contested in 1958 this table retains ten constituencies in which the incumbent Congressman did not seek re-election. Candidates of the retiring incumbent's party in these districts are treated here as if they were incumbents. Were these figures to be calculated only for constituencies in which an incumbent sought re-election, no entry in this four-fold table would differ from that given by more than two per cent.

Just how low a hurdle our respondents had to clear in saying they had read or heard something about a candidate is indicated by detailed qualitative analysis of the information constituents *were* able to associate with congressional candidates. Except in rare cases, what the voters "knew" was confined to diffuse evaluative judgments about the candidate: "he's a good man," "he understands the problems," and so forth. Of detailed information about policy stands not more than a chemical trace was found. Among the comments about the candidates given in response to an extended series of free-answer questions, less than two per cent had to do with stands in our three policy domains; indeed, only about three comments in every hundred had to do with legislative issues of *any* description.[17]

This evidence that the behavior of the electorate is largely unaffected by knowledge of the policy positions of the candidates is complemented by evidence about the forces that do shape the voters' choices among congressional candidates. The primary basis of voting in American congressional elections is identification with party. In 1958 only one vote in twenty was cast by persons without any sort of party loyalty. And among those who did have a party identification, only one in ten voted against their party. As a result, something like 84 per cent of the vote that year was cast by party identifiers voting their usual party line. What is more, traditional party voting is seldom connected with current legislative issues. As the party loyalists in a nationwide sample of voters told us what they liked and disliked about the parties in 1958, only a small fraction of the comments (about 15 per cent) dealt with current issues of public policy.[18]

[17] What is more, the electorate's awareness of Congress as a whole appears quite limited. A majority of the public was unable to say in 1958 which of the two parties had controlled the Congress during the preceding two years. Some people were confused by the coexistence of a Republican President and a Democratic Congress. But for most people this was simply an elementary fact about congressional affairs to which they were not privy.

[18] For a more extended analysis of forces on the congressional vote, see Donald E. Stokes and

influence path involving the Representative's own attitude is twice as great as the proportion explained by influence passing through his perception of district attitude.

Yet the idea of reward or punishment at the polls for legislative stands is familiar to members of Congress, who feel that they and their records are quite visible to their constituents. Of our sample of Congressmen who were opposed for re-election in 1958, more than four-fifths said the outcome in their districts had been strongly influenced by the electorate's response to their records and personal standing. Indeed, this belief is clear enough to present a notable contradiction: Congressmen feel that their individual legislative actions may have considerable impact on the electorate, yet some simple facts about the Representative's salience to his constituents imply that this could hardly be true.

In some measure this contradiction is to be explained by the tendency of Congressmen to overestimate their visibility to the local public, a tendency that reflects the difficulties of the Representative in forming a correct judgment of constituent opinion. The communication most Congressmen have with their districts inevitably puts them in touch with organized groups and with individuals who are relatively well informed about politics. The Representative knows his constituents mostly from dealing with people who *do* write letters, who *will* attend meetings, who *have* an interest in his legislative stands. As a result, his sample of contacts with a constituency of several hundred thousand people is heavily biased: even the contacts he apparently makes at random are likely to be with people who grossly overrepresent the degree of political information and interest in the constituency as a whole.

But the contradiction is also to be explained by several aspects of the Representative's electoral situation that are of great importance to the question of constituency influence. The first of these is implicit in what has already been said. Because of the

Warren E. Miller, "Party Government and the Saliency of Congress," *Public Opinion Quarterly*, Vol. 26 (Winter 1962), pp. 531–546.

pervasive effects of party loyalties, no candidate for Congress starts from scratch in putting together an electoral majority. The Congressman is a dealer in increments and margins. He starts with a stratum of hardened party voters, and if the stratum is broad enough he can have a measurable influence on his chance of survival simply by attracting a small additional element of the electorate—or by not losing a larger one. Therefore, his record may have a very real bearing on his electoral success or failure without most of his constituents ever knowing what that record is.

Second, the relation of Congressman to voter is not a simple bilateral one but is complicated by the presence of all manner of intermediaries: the local party, economic interests, the news media, racial and nationality organizations, and so forth. Such is the lore of American politics, as it is known to any political scientist. Very often the Representative reaches the mass public through these mediating agencies, and the information about himself and his record may be considerably transformed as it diffuses out to the electorate in two or more stages. As a result, the public—or parts of it—may get simple positive or negative cues about the Congressman which were provoked by his legislative actions but which no longer have a recognizable issue content.

Third, for most Congressmen most of the time the electorate's sanctions are potential rather than actual. Particularly the Representative from a safe district may feel his proper legislative strategy is to avoid giving opponents in his own party or outside of it material they can use against him. As the Congressman pursues this strategy he may write a legislative record that never becomes very well known to his constituents; if it doesn't win votes, neither will it lose any. This is clearly the situation of most southern Congressmen in dealing with the issue of Negro rights. By voting correctly on this issue they are unlikely to increase their visibility to constituents.

Nevertheless, the fact of constituency influence, backed by potential sanctions at the polls, is real enough.

That these potential sanctions are all too real is best illustrated in the election of 1958 by the reprisal against Representative Brooks Hays in Arkansas' Fifth District.[19] Although the perception of Congressman Hays as too moderate on civil rights resulted more from his service as intermediary between the White House and Governor Faubus in the Little Rock school crisis than from his record in the House, the victory of Dale Alford as a write-in candidate was a striking reminder of what can happen to a Congressman who gives his foes a powerful issue to use against him. The extraordinary involvement of the public in this race can be seen by comparing how well the candidates were known in this constituency with the awareness of the candidates shown by Table II above for the country as a whole. As Table III indicates, not a single voter in our sample of Arkansas' Fifth District was unaware of either candidate.[20] What is more, these interviews show that Hays was regarded both by his supporters and his opponents as more moderate than Alford on civil rights and that this perception brought his defeat. In some measure, what happened in Little Rock in 1958 can happen anywhere, and our Congressmen ought not to be entirely disbelieved in what they say about their impact at the polls. Indeed, they may be under genuine pressure from the voters even while they are the forgotten men of national elections.[21]

CONCLUSION

Therefore, although the conditions of constituency influence are not equally satisfied, they are met well enough to give the local constituency a measure of control over the actions of its Representatives. Best satisfied is the requirement about motivational influences on the Congressman: our evidence shows that the Representative's roll call behavior is strongly influenced by his own policy preferences and by his perception of preferences held by the constituency. However, the conditions of influence that presuppose effective communication between Congressman and district are much less well met. The Representative

TABLE III Awareness of Congressional Candidates among Voters in Arkansas Fifth District, 1958

		Read or Heard Something about Hays		
		Yes	No	
Read or heard something about Alford	Yes	100	0	100
	No	0	0	0
		100	0	100%

[19] For an account of this episode see Corinne Silverman, "The Little Rock Story," Inter-University Case Program series, reprinted in Edwin A. Bock and Alan K. Campbell, eds., *Case Studies in American Government* (Englewood Cliffs, 1962), pp. 1–46.

[20] The sample of this constituency was limited to twenty-three persons of whom thirteen voted. However, despite the small number of cases the probability that the difference in awareness between this constituency and the country generally as the result only of sampling variations is much less than one in a thousand.

[21] In view of the potential nature of the constituency's sanctions, it is relevant to characterize its influence over the Representative in terms of several distinctions drawn by recent theorists of power, especially the difference between actual and potential power, between influence and coercive power, and between influence and purposive control. Observing these distinctions, we might say that the constituency's influence is *actual* and not merely *potential* since it is the sanction behavior rather than the conforming behavior that is infrequent (Dahl). That is, the Congressman is influenced by his calculus of potential sanctions, following the "rule of anticipated reactions" (Friedrich), however oblivious of his behavior the constituency ordinarily may be. We might also say that the constituency has *power* since its influence depends partly on sanctions (Lasswell and Kaplan), although it rarely exercises *control* since its influence is rarely conscious or intended (Cartwright). In the discussion above we have of course used the terms "influence" and "control" interchangeably.

has very imperfect information about the issue preferences of his constituency, and the constituency's awareness of the policy stands of the Representative ordinarily is slight.

The findings of this analysis heavily underscore the fact that no single tradition of representation fully accords with the realities of American legislative politics. The American system *is* a mixture, to which the Burkean, instructed-delegate, and responsible-party models all can be said to have contributed elements. Moreover, variations in the representative relation are most likely to occur as we move from one policy domain to another. No single, generalized configuration of attitudes and perceptions links Representative with constituency but rather several distinct patterns, and which of them is invoked depends very much on the issue involved.

The issue domain in which the relation of Congressman to constituency most nearly conforms to the instructed-delegate model is that of civil rights. This conclusion is supported by the importance of the influence-path passing through the Representative's perception of district opinion, although even in this domain the sense in which the constituency may be said to take the position of the candidate into account in reaching its electoral judgment should be carefully qualified.

The representative relation conforms most closely to the responsible-party model in the domain of social welfare. In this issue area, the arena of partisan conflict for a generation, the party symbol helps both constituency and Representative in the difficult process of communication between them. On the one hand, because Republican and Democratic voters tend to differ in what they would have government do, the Representative has some guide to district opinion simply by looking at the partisan division of the vote. On the other hand,

because the two parties tend to recruit candidates who differ on the social welfare role of government, the constituency can infer the candidates' position with more than random accuracy from their party affiliation, even though what the constituency has learned directly about these stands is almost nothing. How faithful the representation of social welfare views is to the responsible-party model should not be exaggerated. Even in this policy domain, American practice departs widely from an ideal conception of party government.[22] But in this domain, more than any other, political conflict has become a conflict of national parties in which constituency and Representative are known to each other primarily by their party association.

It would be too pat to say that the domain of foreign involvement conforms to the third model of representation, the conception promoted by Edmund Burke. Clearly it does in the sense that the Congressman looks elsewhere than to his district in making up his mind on foreign issues. However, the reliance he puts on the President and the Administration suggests that the calculation of where the public interest lies is often passed to the Executive on matters of foreign policy. Ironically, legislative initiative in foreign affairs has fallen victim to the very difficulties of gathering and appraising information that led Burke to argue that Parliament rather than the public ought to hold the power of decision. The background information and predictive skills that Burke thought the people lacked are held primarily by the modern Executive. As a result, the present role of the legislature in foreign affairs bears some resemblance to the role that Burke had in mind for the elitist, highly restricted *electorate* of his own day.

[22] The factors in American electoral behavior that encourage such a departure are discussed in Stokes and Miller, *loc. cit.*

53. Democratic Party Leadership in the Senate

Ralph K. Huitt

Ralph Huitt, who worked for Senator Lyndon Johnson, has described the operations of the principal elective officer of the Democratic party in the Senate as the role was filled by Lyndon Johnson. It is Huitt's premise that reform proposals for model party leadership have been ignored by the Senate because such proposals have tended to do much violence to the political context within which members operate. Huitt describes the informal and highly personal means by which Johnson ran the majority leadership position. His conclusions are that the successful Senate leader—as suggested by Johnson's performance—is the man who can and does help individual senators to maximize their effectiveness in playing their personal roles in the Senate and who structures roles and alternatives so that a maximum number of senators can join in support of the proffered solution to the problem.

* * *

Party leadership in Congress has been one focal point for the sustained attack on the structure and performance of the American party system that has gone on for a decade and a half. Academic critics and members of Congress, individually and in committees, supplemented by a wide array of interested citizens and groups, have laid out blueprints for institutional reorganization. While there is some variety in their prescriptions, it is not hard to construct a composite model of party leadership in legislation on which there has been a fairly wide consensus among the reformers.[1]

[1] Some representative selections from the voluminous literature are: *Organization of Congress,*

The fount of party policy would be a reformed national convention, meeting biennially at the least. The obligation of the majority party in Congress, spurred by the president if he were of the same party, would be to carry out the platform put together by the convention. For this purpose frequent party conferences would be held in each house to consider specific measures. Some would be for the purpose of discussion and education, but on important party measures the members could be bound by a conference vote and penalized in committee assignments and other party perquisites for disregarding the will of the conference. Party strategy, legislative scheduling, and continuous leadership would be entrusted to a policy committee made up, in most schemes, of the elective officers of the house and the chairmen of the standing committees. Some have suggested a joint policy committee, made up of the policy committees of the respective houses, which might then meet with the president as a kind of legislative cabinet. The committee chairmen would not be exclusively, and perhaps not at all, the products of seniority. Power to override or disregard seniority, regularly or in exceptional cases, has been suggested for the conference, the policy committee, or the principal elective

Hearings, Joint Committee on the Organization of Congress, 79th Cong., 1st sess., pursuant to H. Con. Res. 18 (1945), pp. 28, 77–78, 334, 801, 805, 822–823, 846, 851, 872, 931; *Legislative Reorganization Act of 1946,* Hearings, Senate Committee on Expenditures in the Executive Departments, 80th Cong., 2d sess. (1948), pp. 38–39, 66, 118–119, 210–211; *Organization and Operation of Congress, ibid.,* 82d Cong., 1st sess. (1951), pp. 276–278, 287–290, 460; Committee on Congress, American Pol. Sci. Assn., *The Reorganization of Congress* (Wash., D. C., 1945), pp. 53–54; *Toward A More Responsible Two-Party System,* Report of the Committee on Political Parties, Amer. Pol. Sci. Assn., 1950, pp. 50–65; R. Heller, *Strengthening the Congress* (Wash., D. C., 1945), pp. 6–9; George B. Galloway, *Congress at the Crossroads* (New York, 1946), esp. ch. 4; Estes Kefauver and Jack Levin, *A Twentieth Century Congress* (New York, 1947), pp. 96–142.

From the *American Political Science Review,* vol. 55, no. 2 (June 1961), pp. 333–344 with footnote omissions.

officer of each house. Individual chairmen would be expected to push the program of the conference and policy committee through their respective committees, that being the principal justification for their membership on the policy committee.

The same kind of organization would obtain in the minority party, though of course it would not bear the same responsibility for legislative program and scheduling.

Despite the frequency with which this model (with some variations) has been sponsored by informed and respected persons, precious little of it has made any headway in Congress. Policy committees have been created, it is true, first by both parties in the Senate and later by the Republicans in the House of Representatives. But they are not composed of committee chairmen nor do they perform the functions hopefully suggested for them. Beyond that Congress has not gone. The reason can not be simply congressional hostility to change; other reforms proposed at the same time (notably professional staffs for committees and individual senators, and a reduction in number and simplification of jurisdiction of committees) have been successfully carried out.

A basic premise of this paper is that the reformers' model has failed to attract support in Congress because it does too much violence to the political context in which members operate—that is, to the relationships of the members with the constituencies which they serve and must please, and to the internal power systems of the respective houses. An attempt will be made briefly to establish this point. A second premise is that the preoccupation with reform has obscured the fact that we have no really adequate model of party leadership as it exists in Congress, and that none can be constructed because we lack simple descriptions of many of the basic working parts of the present system. The major portion of the paper will be devoted there-

fore to an attempt to describe some of the operations of the principal elective officer of the Democratic Party in the Senate, the floor leader, especially in the eight-year period that Lyndon B. Johnson of Texas occupied that position. The description will be based primarily on personal observation and on interviews with men who have served as Democratic leader or worked on his staff, and secondarily on the small store of scholarly and journalistic material available. The description is only a partial one. Leadership in the Senate is highly personal and exceedingly complex. People who know a great deal about it are prevented from describing it by the heavy work loads they bear and the restrictions of confidentiality. The justification for a study with obvious limitations is the importance of the subject and the possibility that it will stimulate others to add to it.

It should be understood that the paper makes no value judgments about the actual operations of Senate Leadership nor the many proposals for change.

THE POLITICAL CONTEXT

One of the most durable notions in commentaries on American politics holds that the national convention is the supreme organ of the party and so the platform it draws up ought to have strong moral claims on the leadership to Congress. The advocates of party responsibility (who support the proposition) are too sophisticated, to be sure, to defend the convention out of hand as it now exists. It should be made smaller and more representative, they say, and its sessions should be longer so that more deliberation may occur.

The prognosis for these reforms, it must be said, is poor; the dominating influence of television runs in the other direction. Conventions get larger and noisier and their sessions shorter, and largely successful efforts are made to prevent them from deliberating at all. But what no amount of reform can change is the central fact that the convention's main business is to nominate a presidential candidate who has a chance to win; and a presidential candidate, like a man running for Congress, has a constituency to think about. It is fashionable to say that a member of Congress has a local constituency, the president a national one, but both statements, while technically true, are only partially correct in a political sense. Either man is free to be as national in his concerns as he pleases so long as he does not neglect the overriding importance of the people who can elect or defeat him. In the president's case these are primarily the voters in populous two-party states of the industrial North, and especially (because of the unit rule in the electoral college) the minority blocs within them which may swing a close state, and perhaps a close election.

The member of Congress recognizes the convention for what it is, a device of the presidential party, and the deliberations of the platform committee for what *they* are, a forum in which the party determines the maximum program which can be stated without shattering the party. The platform is a useful instrument for gauging the extent to which one wing of the party can go in meeting its constituent problems without alienating irrevocably another wing of the party which has opposing constituency interests; indeed, it is the only party device which provides quite this test. But not all party members can support all parts of such an instrument with equal fervor. The attitude of the member of Congress toward the platform is precisely the same as that of the president: he uses it, condemns it, or ignores it as it suits him in dealing with *his* constituency. This suggests then one of the insuperable (at present) obstacles to powerful central party leadership in Congress: the member's relationship to his constituency is direct and paramount. The constituency has a virtually unqualified power to hire and fire. If the member

pleases it, no party leader can fatally hurt him; if he does not, no national party organ can save him.

Arguments for responsible party government fall before the lessons of life. The most powerful effort to advance party responsibility in this century was made not by political scientists but by Franklin Roosevelt when he tried to purge intransigent Democrats in 1938. Every politician in the country knows how that came out—just as he knows that the prestige of national party leadership was not enough to save Senate Democratic leaders Scott Lucas and Ernest McFarland, nor Republican Policy Committee Chairman Homer Ferguson, nor Senate Foreign Relations Committee Chairmen Tom Connally and Walter George. He knows that the efforts of popular presidents to help favorite candidates have been generally unsuccessful and that, on the other hand, senators like the senior LaFollette (one of five chosen from its history by the Senate for special honor), Borah, Langer, Byrd and many others have made careers of party dissidence. He knows how much his own success has turned on his knowledge of constituency interests and prompt service to them. When constituents demand that he follow national party leadership the member responds quickly; in the early months of Franklin Roosevelt's regime many congressmen boasted that they voted "down-the-line" with his program. That kind of regularity would be permanent if voters wanted it. In the long haul they neither want nor respect it, and members of Congress act accordingly.

This is not to say that the member's identification with a national party is meaningless to him. Far from it. His attachment is intensely practical and probably deeply sentimental. Without its label he would have almost no chance to win. Party victory enhances his chances and adds to the sweetness of triumph the solid perquisites of the majority. Within the legislative body he depends on it for services and for almost indispensable cues for voting on a wide range of technical issues. But the legislative party, as David Truman has put it, "is mediate and supplementary rather than immediate and inclusive in function." It is important, but not crucial.

The second immovable object in the way of legislative party leadership is the system of specialized standing committees. The establishment of standing committees with preemptive jurisdiction over categories of legislation is more than a division of legislative labor, it is an allocation of political power. The committee chairmen, especially when they are clothed with the immunity of a seniority rule, are chieftains to be bargained with, not lieutenants to be commanded. A party leadership of formal power, as distinguished from one of persuasion and accommodation, is incompatible with specialized committees.

The direct relationship of representative to constituent, and the specialized committee, are not the only hindrances to central party leadership, but they are formidable. It is significant that the politicians who operate the two great representative systems which are most often compared, the British and the American, are acutely aware of these basic elements in their respective power structures. British governments have rigorously suppressed everything likely to enable the individual member to build up independent support—residence requirements, private bills, services to constituents, personal expertise. And they have made their parliamentary committees small editions of the House of Commons, few in number, large in size, and unspecialized (except for Scottish business). The Americans have done just the opposite. The persons least enthusiastic about a policy committee made up of committee chairmen probably were the committee chairmen themselves, who had no wish to trade sovereignty for a vote in council. Moreover, some standing committees of Congress have

with good logic resisted dividing into subcommittees, which inevitably stake out their own claims to preemptive power.

THE FLOOR LEADER'S JOB

The elective party officer in the Senate upon whom, more than any other, falls the burden of central leadership is the floor leader. Needless to say, it is not the same job at all times. Much depends upon the leader's objective situation *vis-à-vis* the White House and upon his subjective view of his relationship to the presidency.

One situation is that of a majority leader with a popular and aggressive president of the same party in the White House who makes strong demands on Congress. Good examples would be John Worth Kern in Woodrow Wilson's administration, and Joseph T. Robinson in that of Franklin D. Roosevelt. The support of that kind of president gives the leader great leverage with his colleagues so that he can accomplish much, but his power (however personally skillful he may be) is essentially derivative. The president may push him into unwelcome adventures, perhaps without consultation or even warning.

A second situation, perhaps the most difficult of all, is that of a majority leader with a president who is legislatively aggressive without being able to muster adequate popular support for his program. This was the position of Senators Scott Lucas and Ernest McFarland with President Truman. Lucas especially was in sore straits. Truman regarded his remarkable reelection victory as a mandate, particularly for the civil rights pledges he had made. Lucas shared Truman's goals and believed it was his job to advance them, but he was not so optimistic about what could be done. Taking from the president's long list of legislative demands a few upon which Democratic senators might unite, he hoped to make a legislative record before hopelessly splitting the legislative party over civil rights. Nevertheless he loyally put the civil rights legislation first, with the results he had predicted.

Other situations carry their own problems. The least difficult relationship perhaps is that of the majority leader with a president of his party who is not legislatively aggressive, the relationship enjoyed by Senators Taft and Knowland with Eisenhower. Not unlike it perhaps was the situation of majority leader Johnson, who had to carry the programming responsibilities of the majority without a Democratic president.

The leadership of the congressional minority, with the opposition's man in the White House, offers opportunity as well as problems. It is a good position from which to rally the troops; the initiative rests with the opponent, but there is no compulsion for the minority to take party stands on divisive issues. The leader of a minority with a president of his party would seem to have the worst arrangement possible. His relationships with the White House and his senatorial colleagues deserve close study.

The job of the majority leader obviously will be affected by his notion of his responsibilities toward a president of his party. William S. White contends that the Senate expects that a floor leader of a party occupying the presidency "will not so much represent the President as the Senate itself," and that the image of him as the president's man is a popular heresy born of the days of Roosevelt's enormous prestige. David B. Truman argues that "the fundamental complexity and subtlety of the role lie in the fact that the elective leaders are, and probably must be, both the President's leaders and the party's leaders." They may both be right, without affecting the proposition that the perception of the leader's role may vary considerably with the incumbent.

Alben Barkley, for instance, regarded himself as responsible for Roosevelt's program, but he resigned his leadership when the president sharply criticized and vetoed a tax bill passed by Congress. Congress considers revenue legislation to be peculiarly within its own domain and the veto was bitterly resented. Barkley was promptly reelected unanimously by his colleagues and the president made amends as gracefully as he could. Senator Lucas shared Barkley's general view. He believed that if a leader could not agree with his president 80 percent of the time, the leader should resign. In constant touch with the White House over a direct telephone, Lucas put Truman's program ahead of his own health and his political career. His successor, Ernest McFarland, had no direct telephone and wanted none. His relations with Truman were good, but he liked the long mile between the Hill and the White House; it was not too far for the Senate's ambassador to travel. His general view seems to have been shared by two other leaders very unlike him and each other, Senators Knowland and Taft.

Lyndon Johnson, as majority leader, did not work with a Democratic President, and it would be presumptuous to speculate about hypothetical relationships. But he *did* work with a Republican President for six years, and this relationship is illuminating. Johnson regarded the presidency as the one office in the American system which can give national leadership. He scoffed at the notion that his own initiative, in the absence of presidential leadership of Congress, made him a kind of "prime minister." His own description of his activity was that "we prod him [Eisenhower] into doing everything we can get him to do, and when he does something good we give him a 21-gun salute." He consistently refused to turn the Democrats in the Senate loose to attack Eisenhower at will, believing that no president can be cut down without hurting the presidency itself—with the American people the losers. Johnson worked with Eisenhower with dispassionate professionalism, supporting or differing with him as he believed he should.

Needless to say, Johnson was very far from regarding the Senate as a rubber stamp for any president, or even as a body which waits to deliberate upon what he sees fit to initiate. It is doubtful that any leader was ever more consciously proud of the Senate as an institution, nor more determined to preserve and expand the unique and independent role which the Constitution and its history have made for it.

THE LEADERSHIP
OF SENATOR JOHNSON

Lyndon B. Johnson was Democratic leader in the Senate from 1953 through 1960. With Robinson and Barkley, he is one of only three men in recent times to hold the position for an extended period, and he was by general agreement the most skillful and successful in the memory of living observers. What accounts for his success? How did he perceive his job? What powers had he and what strategems and tactics did he employ?

Philosophy and approach. Johnson was a legislative pragmatist. He believed it possible to do anything that was worth the effort and the price, and so considered every problem from the standpoint of what was necessary to achieve the desired objective, and whether the objective was worth the cost. He learned early and never forgot the basic skill of the politician, the ability to divide any number by two and add one. But to find a ground on which a majority could stand, he did not regard as "compromise." "I always seek the best and do the possible," he said. "I have one yardstick that I try to measure things by: Is this in the national interest? Is this what I believe is best for my country? And if it is we outline it to these fellows of various

complexions . . .", Democrats as different as Byrd and Morse, Republicans as far apart as Case and Dworshak. Johnson respected these differences: "The thing you must understand is that no man comes to the Senate on a platform of doing what is wrong. They will come determined to do what is right. The difficulty is finding an area of agreement . . ." To do that, "first you must have a purpose and an objective and the vision to try to outline what the national interest requires, what the national need is. Then you lay that on the table, and are as reasonably patient and as effective as you can be, from a persuasive standpoint."

This is the way to "do the possible" and pass bills—the pragmatist's test of legislative achievement. More than that, he wanted the bills to become laws. Johnson consistently declined to pass strings of bills he knew Eisenhower would veto. "What do you want," he demanded, "houses [or farm legislation etc.] or a housing issue?"

Johnson's emphasis on persuasion was crucial. He said the "only real power available to the leader is the power of persuasion. There is no patronage; no power to discipline; no authority to fire Senators like a President can fire his members of Cabinet."

His formal powers certainly were not impressive; as Truman says, the majority leader must build his influence "upon a combination of fragments of power." The office of Democratic leader, it is true, combines all the most important elective positions—Chairman of the Conference, of the Steering Committee, of the Policy Committee. (The Republicans fill these positions with four different men.) Each position adds something to his influence and to the professional staff he controls. The Steering Committee handles committee transfers and assignment of new members, and Johnson's voice as chairman was highly influential, to say the least. One of his most successful political acts was his decision in 1953 to put all Democratic senators, even new ones, on at least one important committee. As Chairman of the Policy Committee he had substantial control over legislative scheduling (in close collaboration with the minority leader), which gave him not only the power to help and hinder but an unequalled knowledge of legislation on the calendar and who wanted what and why. A tactical power of importance was what Johnson called the "power of recognition"—the right of the majority leader to be recognized first when he wanted the floor. He exploited this right with great skill to initiate a legislative fight when and on the terms he wanted.

The "power of persuasion" may be abetted by some favors Johnson was in a position to perform. He could help a senator move his pet legislation, not only in the Senate but, through his friendship with Speaker Rayburn and other crucially influential leaders, in the House as well. The senator, it should be added, did well to observe a "rule of prudence" and not ask for too much. Because there were always members who would help him on legislation of little interest to themselves, Johnson could muster a respectable vote for a senator's bill or amendment that was bound to lose—a substantial boon to a man who wants his constituents to take him seriously. Johnson had largesse to bestow in the form of assignments to special committees, assistance in getting appropriations for subcommittees, and appointments as representatives of the Senate to participate in international meetings. Because intelligence flowed in to him and he was the center of the legislative party's communication network (in a system which lacks formal, continuous communication among the specialized committees which do the work), a cooperative member could be enormously better informed through the leader's resources than his own. A master of parliamentary technique, Johnson could tell a senator how to do what he wished

or untangle the Senate from a procedural snarl, instructing senators what motions to make and bringing them and the chair in on cue.

Nevertheless persuasion was, in Johnson's case, overwhelmingly a matter of personal influence. By all accounts, Johnson was the most personal among recent leaders in his approach. For years it was said that he talked to every Democratic senator every day. Persuasion ranged from the awesome pyrotechnics known as "Treatment A" to the apparently casual but always purposeful exchange as he roamed the floor and the cloakroom. He learned what a man wanted and would take, and he asked for help. He did not hesitate to "cross the aisle"; Republican votes saved him more than once, sometimes to the surprise and chagrin of *their* leadership. Although he had, as Stewart Alsop said, "a real talent for friendship, and that talent is the final weapon in Johnson's huge armory," some of his colleagues undoubtedly found his overpowering personality somewhat trying to live with. Johnson sometimes approached those senators he was not "easy" with through the Democratic Whip, Senator Mike Mansfield, or the Secretary to the Majority, Robert G. Baker. Always the goal was the same: the combination that would yield one more than half the votes. Because he so often found it, because he spurned the hopeless fight, he was able to fashion a myth of invincibility which was itself mightily persuasive: when he moved, it was taken for granted that "Lyndon's got the votes."

Johnson always actively cultivated a close working relationship with the Republican leader, except for rare and calculated clashes. This served to broaden his leadership to include the whole body, adding to his control over it and his ability to obtain the magic majority. This relationship moreover made "the leadership" more nearly invulnerable to incipient rebellion. It also satisfied the Senate's historic sense of its role as the conservator of minority rights, and greatly improved the temper of the proceedings.

Strategy and tactics of influence. Although it is not likely that he ever quite used these terms, Lyndon Johnson's legislative strategy frequently reflected an acute awareness that senators must play many different and often conflicting roles, and that one task of leadership is to structure a situation so that a member can select a role which will allow him to stand with the party.

One evidence of this awareness was the care with which he tried to keep his own roles straight. As a senator from Texas, for instance, he had to give the oil and gas industry the same kind of support that other senators give the principal industries in their states. Before he became leader, he did not hesitate, as a Texas senator, to lead the attack on Leland Olds' reappointment to the Federal Power Commission. In the submerged oil lands controversy of 1953, on the other hand, Johnson voted as a Texas senator but stayed carefully in the background, leaving spokesmanship for the states' rights position to his Texas colleague, Price Daniel, and to Florida's Senator Holland. As a consequence, northern Democrats were able to make an issue of Republican support of the bill and of President Eisenhower's signing it. Likewise, when the annual attempt was made to reduce the depletion allowance granted in the tax code to producers of oil and gas, Johnson carefully stayed out of the floor debate. The so-called natural gas bill (to forbid the Federal Power Commission to regulate the sales by independent producers of natural gas to interstate pipe line companies), which comes up periodically, caused more trouble. Johnson could leave its sponsorship to other oil state senators until he came to announce a legislative program at the beginning of a session. Failure then to include the natural gas bill

simply could not have been explained away in Texas. Again, when liberal Democrats staged a filibuster against the Dixon-Yates contract in 1954, Johnson stood aloof for two weeks while the issue was made, then stepped in as leader to end the filibuster when the point of diminishing returns was reached. The timing was well calculated. Majority support for anti-monopoly and rural electrification provisions in the Atomic Energy Act had been achieved by the filibuster and they were promptly voted when it ended.

Even more important as a leadership technique was the manipulation of the role perceptions of other senators. This was an important part of Johnson's major effort as minority leader to reunite his then bitterly divided legislative party. He exploited every opportunity to get his colleagues to think, not as northerners or southerners, liberals or conservatives, but as Democrats. A homely illustration is suggestive. In 1954 when some Republican orators came close to accusing Democrats of disloyalty, many southern Democrats tended to shrug it off as attacks on Harry Truman and northern liberals. But each time Johnson talked to a southern colleague he produced a freshly typed copy of some of the statements about Democrats made by Republican wavers of the "bloody shirt" after the Civil War. The parallel was striking and the lesson plain.

A better illustration perhaps was furnished by the appointment in the same year of one Albert Beeson to the National Labor Relations Board. The Democratic minority on the Labor and Public Welfare Committee was strongly opposed to Beeson, whom organized labor accused of anti-labor bias, because they said his failure to sever his relations completely with a California corporate employer constituted a conflict of interests. This left conservative Democrats unmoved; they recalled many years when the NLRB had been frankly stacked in favor of labor. The Senate vote on Beeson seemed sure to provide yet another occasion for a sharp division between northern and southern Democrats.

Then a careful reading of the committee testimony showed that Beeson's statements had shifted from one hearing to another. Immediately Johnson saw the way: Beeson should be opposed not for conflict of interest, but for flouting the dignity of the Senate. The key man he perceived to be Senator Walter George: as a conservative southerner, he was almost sure to support Beeson; but as a *senator,* proud of the Senate and sensitive about its dignity, he would vote against a man he believed guilty of misrepresentations to its committee. Either way, he would take most southerners with him.

The Democratic Policy Committee decided to rally Democrats against Beeson, not on conflict of interest but for false statements to its committee. The minority report was written that way. Speeches were written for Democrats, stressing the theme that the Senate's dignity had been flouted. Lister Hill, a southern Democrat, dominated the presentation. A Republican senator detected the shift in emphasis; had the conflict-of-interest objection been dropped? The Democrats assured him it had not, but said no more about it. The strategy called for delay over the weekend, to rally more votes, but when Johnson knew George was convinced the speeches were cancelled and a vote taken. Beeson was confirmed, but the Democratic minority had stood solidly together on the kind of issue which usually divided them. The Beeson incident, multiplied many times in their two years in the minority, taught the Democrats once more the habit of voting together.

The concentration on Senator George illustrates two other tenets of Johnson's strategy of leadership. One is that in most situations a single man holds the "key" to it. The problem is to know how to turn the key. A second is that a highly esteemed senator may be used as an "umbrella" on a controversial issue, for other senators who feel they can safely vote with him. Thus a southern senator could feel secure in the explanation that he voted "just like Mr. George."

Both were strikingly demonstrated in the enactment of two bitterly controversial labor bills in 1958. The first came in April when Senator Kennedy's Labor and Public Welfare subcommittee reported a welfare and pensions plans disclosure bill. The principal hazard to the bill was the prospect that far-reaching amendments to the Taft-Hartley Act might be piled on it, killing any chance it had to pass the House —a threat which materialized when minority leader Knowland announced his intention to do just that. But the move was anticipated. For three days the Senate stalled while Johnson conferred almost continuously with Kennedy, Lister Hill (chairman of the full committee) and John McClellan. Senator McClellan was the "key" to the situation. His Select Committee on Improper Activities in the Labor or Management Field had issued an interim report in March urging many of the amendments which Knowland intended to offer. An agreement was reached: Hill and Kennedy pledged that they would offer a labor reform bill by June 10, and McClellan promised to vote against his own amendments until they had received proper committee consideration. The Senate thereupon was thrown into 12-hour daily sessions until the bill was passed. Fourteen amendments (six by Knowland) were beaten down, 12 by roll-call votes. Only one Democrat voted against his party consistently, and only two others voted against it even once. Only one amendment (prohibiting convicted felons from serving in the administration of pension and welfare funds) was adopted.

When the general labor reform bill was reported promptly on June 10, it too had the united support of Johnson, Hill, Kennedy and McClellan. Consequently, only one relatively insignificant amendment (continuing Taft-Hartley's non-communist oath for labor leaders and extending it to employers) and adopted over the opposition of the bill's sponsors, while 20 amendments were defeated. Once again most Democrats stood firmly together. Senator McClellan furnished the "umbrella" for conservative Democrats; when he publicly and repeatedly urged support for the bill as "the best that can be passed in this Congress," he made it safe and respectable for them to vote for it.

Parenthetically, these bills also illustrated Johnson's strategy of alternately riding with loose reins while the Senate handled miscellaneous business and rested from its exertions, then keeping it in early and late on a major bill. The long, driving sessions undoubtedly reduced the Senate's notorious tendency to waste time.

There was a place in the Johnson scheme of things for floor debate. It furnished a forum for senators who love to talk; it registered positions and who held them; it kept the Senate in session while the serious business of legislation was going on somewhere else. Johnson knew how to make skillful use of the versatile Democratic "bench." But what emerged from Johnson's own statements and from examples of his work was the view that good legislation is not the product of oratory and debate but of negotiation and discussion, designed not to make issues but to find common ground that equal, independent and dissimilar men could occupy.

A small-scale model of a typical operation was the amendment of the Fair Labor Standards Act in 1955. Labor and liberals wanted to increase the number of workers covered and to raise the minimum wage from 75 cents to $1.25 an hour. Eisenhower supported a 90-cent minimum wage. Southern Democrats would go no higher than that and opposed any increase in coverage. Johnson found the formula: $1 an hour

with no additional coverage. Both sides were warned that amendments might be dangerous to it. The issue was settled with less than an hour of debate. This procedure, with all factors intensified, explains how two civil rights bills were got through the Senate.

OTHER AGENCIES OF PARTY LEADERSHIP

The roles appropriate to other agencies of party leadership—the Conference (or Caucus), the Policy Committee, the Steering Committee (committee on committees), and standing committee chairmen—have been the subject of recurring controversy within Congress as well as outside it, as they probably will continue to be. No attempt will be made to settle it here. Instead we shall show how Democratic leaders generally and Senator Johnson in particular made use of these agencies, and then consider some criticisms and suggestions made recently by Democratic senators.

The party conference theoretically is the supreme organ of the legislative party, as the national convention is of the national party. Actually, its influence on policy has waxed and waned. Democrats historically have been more willing than Republicans to be bound by its decisions. Beginning in 1903, the Senate Democratic Conference could bind its members by a two-thirds vote, though there were occasional individual rebels. Conference discipline reached its peak in Woodrow Wilson's administration. It was so effective (or oppressive) that Nebraska Senator Gilbert M. Hitchcock introduced, during the 1915 ship-purchase bill debate, a resolution requiring senators "to vote in accordance with their own convictions and judgments"; and open rebellion broke out against it after World War I. An even more stringent rule binding Democrats to support an Executive measure on a majority vote in conference was adopted at the beginning of the New

Deal era, but a member was excused if he had conscientious objections to a bill or if it ran counter to pledges made to his constituents.

The principal function of the Democratic Conference in recent years had been the selection of party leaders at the beginning of a Congress. Senator Johnson also used it at the beginning of a session to present his own "State of the Union" speech on the legislative program. (Developments in the second session of the 86th Congress will be discussed later.) His frank opinion was that "not much" can be accomplished in conference. Issues which really divide the legislative party cannot be settled that way; indeed, differences are exacerbated and new rifts may be opened. For example, in 1954 (his second year as minority leader) Johnson responded to criticism of the infrequency of conferences by calling one. Two issues were carefully selected for discussion because the legislative party seemed to be united on them, the contested election of Senator Dennis Chavez and the question of tying together the Alaska and Hawaii statehood bills. The party united happily behind Chavez and agreed on the statehood issue, but a member's speech on the latter almost upset the concord. Party members frequently stand together for different reasons, but talking about those reasons may only open old wounds and drive them apart. Floor debate may do the same, but it is not so likely, since many members are usually absent and arguments are not made directly to each other.

More than any other party agency, the Policy Committee has become what the floor leaders have chosen to make it. Senator Barkley—Democratic leader in 1947, when the policy committees were established in an appropriation for the legislative branch—determined the method of selection. To sit with three *ex-officio* members (Leader, Whip, Secretary to the Conference), he chose six members on the basis of geography, deliberately omitting the older party leaders (at the cost of some resentment) and committee chairmen. He knew that men of established power would be hard to control. He wanted younger men, more pliable, willing to work hard to make reputations, who should be easier for him to work with. His method of selection prevailed—though in time, because succeeding leaders only filled vacancies, Policy Committee members gained in personal power and some became committee chairmen. Some leaders have thought privately that members should resign when they assume chairmanships, but this is not the practice. But the dominant consideration in filling vacancies still is the one Barkley established: the new member should be a man the leader *wants* on the committee. Senator Lucas left a seat vacant two years rather than take a man he did not really prefer to have. McFarland, too, in honoring geographical and ideological considerations, nevertheless chose men he considered friends. Senator Johnson tended to appoint older men with established positions of leadership. But in the 86th Congress he added the members of the Legislative Review Committee to the Policy Committee meetings which gave wider geographical representation and assured that there would always be three freshman senators present. Like Barkley's inclusion of the Whip and Secretary to the Conference, this practice is likely to become custom.

Their use of the Policy Committee has varied with the leaders. Barkley set out to have weekly meetings but seldom did; his leadership was personal, intuitive, and informal. Both Lucas and McFarland held weekly meetings. Lucas used it to select bills for Senate consideration, make the legislative schedule, and help plan floor strategy. Vice President Barkley was invited to attend the meetings which he often did, and after committee discussion to add his comments. Discussion led to general agreement; no votes were taken and no decision was considered binding on the party. Mc-Farland considered the Policy Committee a kind of "cabinet." He too cleared the legislative program with the committee, but he used it primarily for discussion, to give him a sense of what was possible.

When Senator Johnson chose new members of the Policy Committee he tried to balance considerations of geography, seniority, ideology, and influence in the Senate. He wanted men he could work with, but each also should represent a power group in the legislative party. They were men he would have to deal with if there had been no Policy Committee though in that event he probably would have chosen to work with them individually rather than as a group. A Policy Committee meeting therefore was like a conference of chieftains. Each man had independent power; each unofficially represented a group. He brought more than intelligence on Senate attitudes; he brought influence also, since other votes were almost sure to go with his. The Policy Committee was far from being "the Johnson organization" in the Senate, although some of its members sometimes helped with tactical operations.

The meetings were for discussions, to thrash out ideas on an issue. Few votes were taken, and the minutes were brief and confidential. The Policy Committee made few decisions or announcements, although a statement sometimes was issued through the Committee to suggest broad party support. Thus the Policy Committee's declaration that the McCarthy censure vote was not a party issue probably was more effective than a statement by the leader alone. But Policy Committee decisions committed no one, not even the members of the committee themselves.

Johnson's employment of the Conference and the Policy Committee was criticized by some Democratic senators in the 86th Congress, with the result that more frequent conferences were held in the second ses-

sion. The first public criticism came from Senator William Proxmire of Wisconsin in three Senate speeches in the Spring of 1959. Proxmire called for "regular caucuses with specific agendas proposing consideration of our legislative program," a strengthened Policy Committee which would "find and express the party position on vital over-all issues," and closer adherence to the party platform. He was supported in whole or in part, by Senators Clark, Morse, McNamara, and Douglas.

A motion was made at the first conference of the second session (January 7, 1960) to hold conferences every two weeks or whenever 15 Democrats requested it, but this was withdrawn when Johnson reiterated his willingness to call a conference on any Democratic senator's request. Five days later, at a second conference, Senator Gore's motion that the Policy Committee be made into "an organization for evolving a coherent party policy on legislation," with its membership increased to 15 and selected by the Conference, was defeated 51–12. A motion to confirm Johnson's power to fill vacancies on the Democratic Steering Committee was adopted 51–11. After that, several conferences were held. Senator Gore has said that one of them "paid off in Democratic unity in the passage of the first aid-to-education bill in 11 years" on February 4 by a 51–34 vote after only two full days of debate. Another conference on February 15 discussed the report of the Joint Economic Committee and the Administration's proposal to remove the ceiling on federal bond interest rates.

Without a systematic survey of Democratic senatorial reaction to the conferences, it is safe to say only that sentiment has been mixed. Much can be and is said in favor of more frequent conferences. They provide a good way for members to learn about broad problems beyond the scope of their committee work. Younger members may find it easier to talk there than on the floor of the Senate, and may prefer an institutionalized procedure for expressing their views to the leader and learning his plans. Perhaps the strongest argument is simply that it seems like a better, more democratic way to run a party.

The critics of the conference say that so long as members are not bound it is futile and this is quickly reflected in the attitudes of senators toward it. Those not in favor of the policy under discussion tend to stay away; their votes have to be corralled in the traditional manner, through individual conferences with the leader. More senior members may not come because their opinions can be made effective where decisions are actually made. Other members avoid them simply because of business more pressing than a non-binding caucus. Furthermore, no real division of sentiment is likely to be reflected in candid discussion in a party conference. Aside from the danger of intensifying differences, there is the likelihood that views stated in confidence will be "leaked," probably in distorted form, to the press. The result of all these factors, say the critics, is a rather academic discussion, poorly attended, which was not requested in 1960 by any member after the middle of February.

From the lively senatorial discussion of party leadership three pertinent points might be emphasized. One is that the proponents of change do not want increased party discipline. As Senator Proxmire put it: "I will follow the dictates of my conscience against the decision of a caucus as readily as a decision of any leader, if I believe my course to be right and theirs wrong." The goal is discussion, not decision. The problem of putting together a majority remains. A second is that the Policy Committee could be changed in size, composition and method of membership selection without increasing its influence. This seems to be the history of the Republican Policy Committee. There is not tradi-

tion of leadership in the Policy Committee. Its influence depends upon the use the leadership makes of it. A third is that Johnson did not believe (and his view apparently was shared by most Democratic senators) that either the Conference or the Policy Committee was a proper agency to make policy. That function belongs to the standing committees. Johnson has said that if members want to influence policy "the first place to make it is in committees of which they are members . . . If they cannot get a majority vote there, how do they expect me to get a majority vote out here?"

Johnson's acceptance of the standing committees as the primary source of legislative policy did not deny to their chairmen the benefits of his friendly persuasion. What they had in committee, what they could get out and when ("Give me a bill!"), what could pass the Senate—these were the topics of repeated personal conferences.

One of the most important and least generally appreciated arms of party leadership was the group of people Stewart Alsop called "the biggest, the most efficient, the most ruthlessly overworked and the most loyal personal staff in the history of the Senate," most of whom had been with Johnson for many years. Lucas and McFarland tried to keep staff members assigned to them for the party separate from their state offices. Johnson used the best man for the job, whether it was state or party. Because he took ideas from anyone and used those he liked, Johnson got a steady flow of them from his staff. They had much to do with his ability generally to move first with the best information.

CONCLUSION

Suggestions for change in the leadership structure of the Senate seem to fall into two classes. The first class, which has had strong academic sponsorship, has sought to strengthen central leadership through conference and policy committee, looking toward the party responsibility of the British for their model. These suggestions have failed because they do not fit the character of the American representative system, with its direct responsibility of representative to constituent, nor the internal power system of Congress, with its specialized committees presided over by senior officers. They have sought to impose party coherence through organizational devices, and to take power from those who have it and assign it to those who do not. The second class of suggestions has aimed not at a more disciplined party but at additional leverage for a minority group within the legislative party. These have so far had small success because their sponsors *are* a minority.

What should be fully exploited by academic writers on the Senate is the insight which can be gained from studies of strong leadership which *has* emerged there from time to time. Whether it is exercised by a formal leader or some other person, it reveals much about the structure of the Senate as a social system precisely because it is indigenous to the Senate.

Systematic analysis of Lyndon Johnson's tenure as Democratic leader should be especially rewarding. As a majority leader without the leverage furnished by a president of his party, he had to make the best use of purely senatorial tools of influence. In this he succeeded to the point that he could manage the enactment of two laws on the most devisive domestic issue of our time. This brief description of some aspects of his leadership suggests that the successful senatorial leader is one who (1) can and does help individual senators to maximize their effectiveness in playing their personal roles in the Senate, and (2) structures roles and alternatives so that a maximum number of senators can join in support of the proffered solution of an issue.

54. The Republican-Dixiecrat Coalition

Frank Thompson, Jr.

Congressman Frank Thompson of New Jersey delivered this speech on the floor of the House of Representatives in January 1960. In it he gave a detailed account of Republican-Dixiecrat cooperation in the period from 1937 to the date of delivery. Although liberal legislation has recently been passed in the House of Representatives, the underlying conservative coalition, as described by Thompson, has not yet ceased to exist and remains as a potential force in the future.

* * *

[MR. THOMPSON:] The gentleman from Missouri seems to have some doubt in his mind about the existence of a coalition between Republicans and some southern Democrats here in the House.

Based on last year's analysis, the average House Republican voted with the coalition 82 percent of the time on these coalition rollcall votes. Republicans and Southern Democrats hold 264 seats in the House, 45 more than a constitutional majority needed to pass or defeat any bill.

The operation of the coalition is a matter of record and has been most successful on legislation such as education, social welfare, public housing, immigration, taxes, labor, antitrust, civil rights, public works, and resource development.

Mr. Speaker, I include at this point in the RECORD a research paper on this subject which reviews the history of the Republican-southern Democratic coalition in the House from 1937 to 1959:

From the *Congressional Record*, 86th Congress, 2d session (1960), vol. 106, pp. 1441–1442.

The Republican-Southern Democratic co-alition, or conservative coalition, as it is sometimes called, has exerted vast influence over the outcome of various types of legislation since its loose formation 22 years ago.

The 1st session of the 86th Congress saw a tightening of the coalition's voting alliance under the leadership of Minority Leader Halleck and Judge Smith, chairman of the House Rules Committee.

The scope and effectiveness of the coalition as described in this study is limited to legislation reaching the House floor, where its impact can be measured by analysis of rollcall votes. Of course, much of the important work of the coalition takes place in standing committees, and particularly in the House Rules Committee, where many measures are pigeonholed or watered down before a rule is granted. These aspects of coalition activity are not subject to the same type of precise analysis.

The purpose of this study is to analyze the party lineup in the 86th Congress and to briefly review the history of the Republican-Southern Democratic coalition since its beginnings in 1937 so that its operation in the present Congress may be placed in proper perspective.

THE 86TH CONGRESS—
BASIC ARITHMETIC

An understanding of the role of the coalition in the 86th Congress must begin with an analysis of the real party alignment in the House. On paper it would appear that the Democratic majority in the House is the largest since New Deal days—280 Democrats, 152 Republicans. The party lineups are:

Southern Democrats	104
Border Democrats	24
Northern and western Democrats	152
Republicans	152
TOTAL	432[a]

[a] Excludes vacancies (Illinois, Ohio, New York, Pennsylvania).

But on the basis of three key rollcall votes in the first session on which the conservative coalition achieved its maximum

strength (Thomas amendment—housing bill financing; H.R. 3—States rights issue; Landrum-Griffin substitute—labor bill), the approximate real party alignment is:

Coalition	
Southern Democrats	80
Border Democrats	9
Northern and western Democrats	6
Republicans	130
TOTAL	225
Liberals	
Southern Democrats	20
Border Democrats	15
Northern and western Democrats	143
Republicans	18
TOTAL	196

Absentees and vacancies, 16.

THE CONSERVATIVE COALITION:
1959

A Congressional Quarterly study of Republican-Southern Democrats voting alignments during the first session of the 86th Congress shows that a majority of both groups opposed a majority of northern and western Democrats on 11 of the 87 House rollcall votes. The coalition won on 10 of the 11, or 91 percent. By comparison, the coalition won on 64 percent of the showdown votes in 1958 and 81 percent in the 1957 session.

A separate Congressional Quarterly study also reveals that southerners split with the rest of the House Democrats on 23 percent of all rollcalls during the 1959 session. They included votes on such issues as housing, civil rights, taxes, labor legislation, States rights (H.R. 3), farm price supports, surplus disposal policies, and Hawaiian statehood.

During the 1959 session, southern Democrats cast 82 percent of their votes with the Republicans and against the majority of their own party on these coalition rollcalls. The 12 southern Democratic committee chairmen cast 86.5 percent of their votes with the Republicans on these coalition rollcalls, only 10 percent with the majority of their own party.

On these same votes, 79 percent of the northern and western Democratic votes were cast with the party majority. Republicans cast 88 percent of their votes with southerners on these key rollcalls, only 9 per cent with northern and western Democrats.

Coalition voting frequency would have been even greater if the House Rules Committee had permitted such measures as the area redevelopment bill, the civil rights bill, and Federal aid school bill to reach the House floor.

THE COALITION GERMINATES: 1937

Beginnings of the Republican-Southern Democratic coalition in Congress can be traced back to 1937, the 1st session of the 75th Congress.

Franklin Roosevelt had just won his landslide reelection victory over Alf Landon and Democrats controlled the House by a 333 to 89 margin. Major New Deal reform measures were already on the statute books and the overwhelming Democratic victory in 1936 had provided a clear mandate for the Roosevelt administration to continue its New Deal reform and economic recovery programs.

But there were rumblings of discontent among powerful conservative forces in the Nation. The Supreme Court had already ruled several New Deal programs unconstitutional. Southerners were smarting over the repeal of the two-thirds nominating rule at the 1936 Democratic Convention, which denied them their traditional veto power over presidential choices. Resentment against the White House efforts to pack the Supreme Court began to grow in Congress.

On the national scene, organized labor was beginning to assert itself as an economic force, aided by enactment of the Wagner and Walsh-Healy Acts. Sitdown strikes became a new economic weapon in the hands of unions. Organizational strikes were being conducted in the basic industries. However, the Liberty League was strongly resisting these inroads and confidently expected the Supreme Court to rule the Wagner Act unconstitutional in a test case.

When the Court upheld the act in April 1937, it became clear to many conservatives in the industrial North and the low-wage farm areas of the South that only by forging a bipartisan conservative alliance in Congress could they hope to stem the tide of new dealism, with its growing emphasis on the needs of city dwellers, minority groups, workers, small farmers, and other underprivileged segments of the population.

This was the year that conservatives succeeded in seizing control of the House Rules Committee. They were able to change its role from that of a traffic cop in scheduling measures reported by standing committees for floor action, subject to majority leadership decisions, to that of a policy-making body—dictating to all Members which bills it deemed worthy of being considered on the House floor.

During the 1937 session, almost 10 per cent of all House rollcalls showed Republicans and a majority of southern Democrats voting against a majority of Democrats from the rest of the country. Democrats divided sharply on such votes as those to authorize an investigation of sitdown strikes, on antilynching legislation, alien relief, and immigration measures. The coalition also succeeded in blocking consideration of the fair labor standards bill for the remainder of the session. However, a concerted drive by the administration resulted in passage of the bill in the second session, after it was pried out of the Rules Committee by a discharge petition.

EARLY COALITION VICTORIES

During the 1st session of the 76th Congress, the coalition won two important victories—forcing an investigation of the NLRB because of alleged "prolabor" rulings and in passing the Hatch Act to prohibit political activity by Federal employees. Cleavages between northern and southern Democrats widened on such issues as housing, civil rights, labor legislation, immigration bills, relief measures, and regulation of business.

THE COALITION
DURING WORLD WAR II

Although the outbreak of World War II in Europe curtailed the New Deal domestic programs, the influence of the conservative coalition continued to grow. By 1941, coalition voting frequently had increased to more than 13 percent of all House rollcalls.

During the war years, the coalition succeeded in passing the Smith anti-strike bill, a States' rights and armed services' voting bill, established the Un-American Activities Committee as a permanent House committee, and watered down the price control program and the excess profits tax measures.

By 1945, coalition voting alinements took place on 16 percent of all House rollcalls, as a combination of Rules Committee power, seniority, and attrition among northern Democrats in off-year elections helped conservatives strengthen their grip on the legislative machinery of the House.

THE COALITION
IN POSTWAR YEARS

In the immediate postwar period of the 79th Congress the coalition used its power to pass the Case strike-control bill, to exclude farm labor from NLRB jurisdiction, to turn over the U.S. Employment Service to the States, and to take the first steps toward gutting the price control program. This latter action soon resulted in a wave of speculation, profiteering, and inflation, costing the American public billions of dollars in lost purchasing power.

After the election of the Republican 80th Congress in 1946, the coalition achieved its greatest numerical strength. It succeeded in passing the Taft-Hartley Act and in overriding President Truman's veto of the measure. It reduced coverage under the Social Security Act, overrode Truman's veto of the "rich man's" tax reduction bill, and further weakened price and rent controls.

The hand of the coalition was also seen in blocking such measures as an effective public housing program, Federal aid to education, civil rights, an increase in the minimum wage, an adequate farm program, and other legislation which President Truman proposed to the 80th Congress. His 1948 "whistle stop" campaign against the "special interests" which dominated the 80th Congress won him his upset victory over [Thomas] Dewey and formed the basic planks of his Fair Deal program.

THE COALITION
VERSUS THE FAIR DEAL

The Republican-Southern Democratic coalition in the 81st Congress was a major force in blocking enactment of important segments of the Truman legislative program and in watering down others. A majority of Republicans and southern Democrats voted together against administration proposals on about 30 percent of all substantive rollcalls in the House.

The high frequency of coalition voting is at least partially explained by the change in House rules on the opening day of the session. The House Rules Committee was stripped of its power to pigeonhole bills reported by standing committees by adoption of the 21-day rule, which permitted committee chairmen to call up bills reported by [their committees] if they were not acted upon by the Rules Committee within a 21-day period. This meant that many of the controversial administration bills reached the floor for debate and vote which otherwise would have been held up in the Rules Committee.

Among the measures brought to the floor under the new 21-day rule were Hawaiian and Alaskan statehood bills, a rivers and harbors bill, the National Science Foundation bill, an antipoll tax bill, a VA hospital bill, and a joint resolution providing for U.S. participation in international organizations. In addition, the threat of using the new rule forced a reluctant Rules Committee to act on minimum wage, social security, and public housing legislation, all of which were subsequently enacted into law.

The conservative coalition did succeed in defeating an attempt to repeal the Taft-Hartley Act, in rejecting the Brannan farm plan; in permitting "local option" decontrol of rents; in defeating the National Minerals Act; in watering down the minimum wage bill; in passing the natural gas and basing point bills (both vetoed); in reducing foreign aid funds and funds for public housing; in rejecting controls over commodity speculation, and in watering down an FEPC bill.

A coalition attempt to repeal the 21-day rule early in the 2d session of the 81st Congress failed. However, the new rule was repealed by the coalition on the opening day of the 82d Congress. Since that time, the Rules Committee has tightened its hold over the legislative machinery of the House.

THE COALITION
DURING THE EISENHOWER YEARS

During the Eisenhower administration, the coalition has continued to play a dominant role. It has won a number of impor-

tant victories, including those in which it turned over offshore oil resources to a few coastal States, reduced funds for the soil conservation program, blocked liberalization of the unemployment compensation system, watered down several public housing bills, passed the natural gas bill, defeated school construction legislation, watered down a minimum wage bill increasing the extent of coverage, blocked an investigation of administration fiscal and monetary policies, defeated the Kennedy-Ives labor reform bill, blocked consideration of the community facility loan program.

The coalition has also appeared on such issues as antitrust legislation, water pollution control measures, civil rights, natural resource development, public works, foreign aid, H.E.W. appropriation measures, and legislation affecting the District of Columbia.

SUMMARY

Over the years since 1937, the Republican-Southern Democratic voting coalition has operated with varying degrees of effectiveness, being most successful on legislation dealing with education, social welfare, labor, regulation of business, public works and resource development, civil rights, immigration, taxes and other economic issues, and those where States' rights have been involved.

It is in these areas that the major differences between the Republican and Democratic parties are to be found. These are also the types of issues [that were] of such vital concern to Northern and Western Democrats in the 1960 campaign.

Scholars and political writers have attempted to explain the basis for the Republican-Southern Democratic coalition in these broad areas of legislation. Many factors have been mentioned, including the high degree of party discipline among Republicans and the correspondingly low degree of party unity, loyalty, and responsibility to the party platform among congressional Democrats from the South.

Other factors often mentioned are the procedural roadblocks in the House legislative machinery, controlled by coalition leaders; the seniority system which assures conservatives of the chairmanships of a majority of the committees and subcommittees; the one-party system in most Southern States; the lack of communication and unity of purpose among Northern and Western Democrats; the antiquated apportionment formulas in many States, which give rural areas disproportionate representation in State legislatures and in Congress; and the basic need for a realinement of the American political party system.

PARTY REFORM AND THE FUTURE

55. Toward a More Responsible Two-Party System: A Commentary

Austin Ranney

Austin Ranney, of the Department of Political Science at the University of Wisconsin, raises questions concerning the "Report of the Committee on Political Parties" of the American Political Science Association. He questions the concept of intraparty democracy and the failure of the Committee to give a meaningful definition of the significance and extent of membership in political parties. The Committee also failed, in his view, to examine the type of discipline that would be necessary to produce the kind of party and program loyalty it envisioned. Ranney discusses the causes of the decentralized nature of American political parties and the influence of the separation of powers in keeping a disciplined and majority-type party government from having developed.

* * *

Every American concerned with the future of democratic government in the United States owes a considerable debt to Professor Schattschneider and the American Political Science Association's Committee on Political Parties. Their *Report,* ostensibly concerned with bringing about "fuller public appreciation of a basic weakness in the American two-party system,"[1] in fact addresses itself to two of the most pressing questions confronting us: How can we in America establish a governmental system capable of performing effectively the Herculean tasks thrust upon it by the demanding times in which we live? And how can we make sure that such a government will at the same time be thoroughly responsible to the people? The members of the Committee appear to consider both questions to be of equal importance. The goal, they feel, must be a government which is both effective *and* democratic. And if their *Report* does nothing more than precipitate a general and serious discussion of these urgent questions, the Committee will have more than justified its existence.

The *Report* deserves the serious attention of a far wider audience than one exclusively of specialists in political parties for it takes the position that a responsible party system is the only possible institu-

[1] "Toward a More Responsible Two-Party System," *American Political Science Review,* Vol. 44, Supplement (Sept., 1950), p. v. This document will subsequently be cited simply as *Report.*

From the *American Political Science Review,* vol. 45, no. 2 (June 1951), pp. 488–499, with footnote omissions.

tional mechanism for providing us with effective and democratic government. Its explication of that position, its analysis of why and in what respects American parties are at present incapable of doing the job, and its prescription of remedies for their deficiencies—all these merit the most careful consideration of the political theorist and the general student of American government, as well as of the specialist in parties.

It is precisely because of agreement with the members of the Committee upon the importance of the questions raised, and because of gratitude to them for their attempt to answer these questions, that the writer feels it necessary to point out why their analysis of the problem is inadequate in certain respects. For purposes of brevity, this commentary will be confined to the two sections of the *Report* which most seriously weaken its total argument: (1) its explication of the notion of "intraparty democracy"; and (2) its analysis of why American parties are as they are and what must therefore be done in order to improve them.

I. THE IDEA OF "INTRAPARTY DEMOCRACY"

One of the ideas stressed most diligently in the *Report* is that there must be, along with the "external responsibility" of the parties to the electorate at large, also "internal responsibility," or "the responsibility of party leaders to the party membership, as enforced in primaries, caucuses and conventions." "Intraparty democracy," it is further explained, means three things: (1) "the internal processes of the parties must be democratic," (2) "the party members must have an opportunity to participate in intraparty business," and (3) "the leaders must be accountable to the party." And not only is this "internal responsibility" as important a goal as the "external responsibility" of the parties themselves to the

voters, but, the *Report* adds, the former will, by promoting closer relations between the leaders and the rank and file and by enlarging the areas of agreement within the parties, also tend to *promote* the latter.

Two questions about such a conception of "intraparty democracy" immediately suggest themselves: (1) What persons should be considered "party members" whose right to participate in intraparty business should be guaranteed and to whom party leaders should be accountable? And (2) how may this "accountability" be institutionalized and made effective? The *Report* has a great deal to say about the first question, but, so far as the writer can tell, no clear and unequivocal answer emerges. The Committee comments initially:

> The vagueness of formal leadership that prevails at the top has its counterpart in the vagueness of formal membership at the bottom. *No understandings or rules or criteria exist with respect to membership in a party.* . . . It is obviously difficult, if not impossible, to secure anything like harmony of policy and action within political parties so loosely organized as this.

Under our present direct primary laws, the only "rule" or "criterion" of party membership is the voter's assertion that he is a "member" of the party in which he desires to register, and, in a few states, also his promise to vote for the party's candidates. Many observers believe the introduction into these laws of more precise and demanding qualifications to be indispensable to the achievement of a more useful and meaningful standard of party membership. The Committee apparently does not agree, for the only reforms in the primary laws it recommends are the general adoption of the closed primary and the prohibition of such practices as cross-filing in California and the blanket primary in Washington.

The *Report,* in fact, does not expressly deal with the question of what would (if we could achieve it) constitute a more useful conception of party membership, except to suggest that such a conception would include a more general agreement (though by no means complete unanimity) on matters of public policy. The Committee proposes to solve the problem by a series of measures designed to encourage increased "grass-roots" discussion of party policies and candidates by the rank and file; for, we are told, more discussion will produce greater party unity, and "with increased unity within the party it is likely that party membership will be given a more explicit basis." The Committee apparently hopes that the party "members" will talk themselves into such a degree of agreement that it will be unnecessary to face the difficult and unpleasant problem of whether a "member," who after full discussion with his fellow "members" is still not willing to go along with the policies and candidates the party majority has settled on, continues to have the "right" to participate in its deliberations.

The original question thus remains unanswered. We have not been told *who* has a right to be considered a party member. Yet this consideration is fundamental to the committee's notion of "intraparty democracy"; for, if the members are to have the "right" of holding party leaders to account "in primaries, caucuses and conventions," we must first know just who will be permitted to exercise this "right." Will the party leaders, for example, be "responsible" to all those persons who register as party members and vote in the closed primaries? Or will they be "responsible" to all those persons who vote for the party ticket?

The Committee does not clearly state its adherence to either of these concepts of party membership; but its discussion, in another part of the *Report,* of the "unrepresentativeness" of the National Conventions strongly suggests an inclination toward the ticket-voter conception. As evidence of that "unrepresentativeness," the *Report* cites the fact that the "rank and file" strength of both parties is not truly represented in the National Conventions because the number of delegates each State sends to them is based, not upon the number of voters for the party in the State, but upon the number of presidential electors it has, modified only by a certain number of additional delegates at large. To clinch the argument the *Report* quotes figures showing the great variations from delegation to delegation in each party convention in the number of party voters per delegate. This argument clearly rests upon the premise that party conventions *should* represent those who vote for the party's ticket. And, if this argument about the National Conventions indicates its real position on the matter, the Committee apparently believes that anyone who votes for a party's national ticket, must be regarded as a "member" of that party, one who must be "represented" in its decision-making bodies if "intraparty democracy" is to exist.

If this is indeed what the Committee means by "membership" in a party, "intraparty democracy" seems very far away, however much discussion may go on among such "members." As Professor E. E. Schattschneider has previously argued, such individuals can be called party "members" by courtesy only, for they assume no real obligation to the party, and the party in turn has no control over them. This is not true, he points out, of the relationship between any other organization and its members. In actuality, such "members" can hardly hope to exert any more effective control of the party leaders than rooters for the New York Yankees can exert over the operations of the team—and for the same reason. If we operate in terms of such a conception of party membership, in other words, it seems very likely that Michels' familiar "iron law of oligarchy" will obtain: the control of the parties will remain in the hands of those who assume some real obligation to them, and "intraparty democracy"—so far as the ticket-voting "members" are concerned—will remain only a slogan.

The reader cannot be certain, however, just what the Committee regards as the requirements and obligations (if any) of party membership and how those requirements and obligations should be enforced. The *Report's* lack of clarity on this point notably affects its answer to the question of how the accountability of the leaders to the "members" is to be made effective. The "machinery of intraparty democracy" which it proposed consists of a biennial National Convention "broadly and directly representative of the rank and file of the party," and the encouragement of the discussion of issues and the suggestion of policies to the proposed Party Council by local party groups that meet frequently.

But the only specific item of machinery suggested whereby the rank and file can hold the leaders *responsible* is the closed primary; and there is little evidence to suggest that, where it is employed, this institution has greatly increased "intraparty democracy" as the Committee seems to visualize it.

Perhaps the primary cause of the obscurity of the Committee's argument on this whole point is its failure to make clear just what it means by "democracy" in this context. In its preliminary argument for the desirability of more responsible parties as a way of achieving a greater degree of democracy in the United States, the Committee (although the point is not made explicit) seems to regard "democracy" in the community at large as necessarily consisting in the popular choice between alternate ruling-groups, not as popular *participation* in its day-to-day processes. Yet its idea of "democracy" inside the parties seems to include participation as well as control. Whatever it means, one may ask, with Professor Schattschneider, if it is possible for twenty-seven million Democrats to "participate" in the close supervision of the affairs of the Democratic party any more effectively than 150 million Americans can "participate" in the close supervision of their government. "Will it be necessary," he further asks, "to develop parties within the parties in order to simplify and define the alternatives for the members?"

Finally, it is difficult to see how the Committee's notion of "intraparty democracy" is calculated to promote the achievement of its other goal, the "external" responsibility of the parties to the whole community. The *Report* argues that "intraparty democracy" will promote party responsibility by increasing the unity of the members of each party behind their respective programs, but the Committee does not seem to recognize the possibilities for promoting factionalism in the parties by trying to make them into something other than purely private associations. Professor Schattschneider, for one, has argued that we can hope for more genuinely responsible parties in the United States only when their essentially *private* nature is recognized:

> Will the parties be less responsive to the needs of the voters if their private character is generally recognized? Probably not. The parties do not need laws to make them sensitive to the wishes of the voters any more than we need laws compelling merchants to please their customers. The sovereignty of the voter consists in his freedom of choice just as the sovereignty of the consumer in the economic system consists in his freedom to trade in a competitive market. That is enough; little can be added to it by inventing an imaginary membership in a fictitious party association. Democracy is not to be found *in* the parties but *between* the parties.[2]

Perhaps the Committee has a reply to this argument; but the *Report* does not provide it. Until we know what that reply is, we must receive the assertion that "internal responsibility" will promote "external responsibility" with considerable reservation.

[2] E. E. Schattschneider, *Party Government* (New York, 1942), p. 60 (emphasis in original).

II. WHY ARE AMERICAN PARTIES AS THEY ARE?

A considerable portion of the *Report* is devoted to the suggestion of a number of reforms for American parties, all intended to make them more responsible. The Committee apparently regards the primary function of its *Report* to be that of showing the politicians and the people some practical ways and means of obtaining these goals. The validity of its program of reform, however, depends upon its answer to the logically prior question of *why* American parties at present display what the Committee regards as their unsatisfactory characteristics—for does not the soundness of any therapeutic regimen depend upon the accuracy of the diagnosis upon which it is based?

Most present-day students of the American party system believe that the primary determinant of its nature is the fact that it must operate within a constitutional system that sets up too many and too effective barriers to the development of unified and responsible parties. The *Report* begins its explanation as though it too were going to follow the orthodox course. "Party institutions and their operations," we are told, "cannot be divorced from the general conditions that govern the nature of the party system." The paragraphs that follow, however, do not suggest what general *conditions* "govern" the nature of American parties; instead the Committee lists certain *characteristics* of the parties which it considers undesirable: generally, localism, the absence of any effective central leadership, and the ambiguity of membership; more specifically, the inadequacy of the national party organs and platforms, the absence of "intraparty democracy," and the failure of the parties to carry on party research. Thus we are told a great deal, here and elsewhere, about the respects in which American parties are unsatisfactory, but nowhere in the *Report* is there an explicit statement of the reasons for their deficiencies.

An explanation of the unsatisfactory nature of American parties, however, is strongly implied in the Committee's position upon the *kind* of reforms needed to achieve responsible parties. They begin by rejecting any wholesale constitutional change, such as, for example, the adoption of a cabinet system. Such a system, they argue, presupposes the existence of strong parties but does not always produce them; and if we should achieve strong parties in the United States, cabinet government would be unnecessary. So the indicated program of reform is one that concentrates solely on changing the parties; when they are made more responsible, the Committee feels, the constitutional system will not seriously retard the achievement of truly effective and democratic government—

> it is easy to overestimate . . . the rigidity of the existing constitutional arrangements in the United States. Certainly the roles of the President and Congress are defined by the Constitution in terms that leave both free to cooperate and to rely on the concept of party responsibility. . . . It is logical first to find out what can be done under present conditions to invigorate the parties before accepting the conclusion that *action has to begin with changing a constitutional system that did not contemplate the growing need for party responsibility when it was set up.*

The *Report,* then, clearly rejects the notion that the nature of American parties is basically determined by our constitutional system. It agrees with Professor Schattschneider that

> The greatest difficulties in the way of the development of party government in the United States have been intellectual, not legal . . . [and that] . . . once a respectable section of the public understands the issue [*sic*], ways of promoting party government through the Constitution can be found.[3]

[3] *Op. cit.* pp. 209–210.

As the Committee puts it, "The character of this publication is explained by the conviction of its authors that the weakness of the American two-party system can be overcome as soon as a substantial part of the electorate wants it overcome." And the electorate, they feel, *will* want the party system made stronger as soon as they fully *understand* that more responsible parties, as the Committee defines them, will produce the more effective and more democratic government which they so strongly desire.

The Committee's position on the fundamental questions of what barriers now exist against the achievement of responsible party government in the United States and how the Committees may contribute to their removal may therefore be reduced to these propositions: (1) Americans want effective and democratic government; (2) a responsible two-party system will, despite the Constitution, produce such a government; (3) the present weakness of our parties is basically a result of the fact that the people do not understand that a more responsible party system will produce the kind of government they want; (4) therefore, the way to remedy the present unsatisfactory situation is to educate the people to the possibilities of a responsible two-party system, and to start reforming the parties themselves without attempting the difficult and probably unnecessary task of formally amending the Constitution. Of the many specific reforms the *Report* proceeds to suggest, all but three are concerned solely with party matters and would require no change in the formal constitutional system.

The Committee's whole position upon the question of why American parties are as they are—and consequently its whole program for reforming them—rests upon the validity of propositions (1) and (3) above. It is therefore necessary at this point to examine those propositions more critically than the Committee has done in its *Report*. Two questions that arise in this

regard are: How long have American parties displayed what the Committee regards as their unsatisfactory characteristics? And does there seem to be any significant tendency for them to change in those respects? The *Report* gives somewhat ambivalent answers to both questions. There have been great changes in American society over the past fifty years, we are told, and the party system has reflected those changes—although it is not made clear in just what respects the party system has changed. "Despite these tendencies toward change, however," the *Report* continues, "*formal party organization in its main features is still substantially what it was before the Civil War*. . . . The result is that the parties are now probably the most archaic institutions in the United States."

But is it only *organizationally* that the parties have remained the same? Have they changed greatly with respect to what the Committee considers to be their basic deficiencies: decentralization and localism, fragmentation of leadership, ambiguity of membership, inability to hold their lines on matters of public policy, etc.? The evidence strongly suggests that in these respects they have *not* changed significantly. It is illuminating, in this connection, to examine the writings on parties produced by leading American scholars of the past seventy-five years. Such political scientists as Woodrow Wilson, Henry Jones Ford, A. Lawrence Lowell, Jesse Macy, M. I. Ostrogorski, Herbert Croly and J. Allen Smith described the American party system of 1875–1915 in almost exactly the same terms that the Committee employs to describe the parties of 1950. And the first statistical evidence of the weakness of party lines in Congress and the state legislatures was provided by the famous and still relevant study of party-voting which Lowell made in 1902.

If the nature of American parties has remained largely the same, it next becomes necessary to understand *why* this is so. Although the Committee does not enlighten us on this point, it might be argued that American parties have remained decentralized and irresponsible because the people have not, until very recently, been told of the desirability of a more responsible system. Yet an examination of the literature on parties produced fifty years ago will soon show the inaccuracy of such an argument. Some of the most prominent writers of the time, notably Wilson, Lowell, Ford, and Frank J. Goodnow, presented a case for a more responsible American two-party system that was at least as convincing as any made today. It received, moreover, a very wide hearing. The inescapable fact is that the people and the politicians have been exposed to the doctrine of responsible party government (and to its criticism of American parties) for at least sixty-five years, but that the essential nature of our party system has remained the same. However one may deplore that system, he must concede that it has displayed, if nothing else, a very impressive ability to survive. The Committee's inarticulate premise that it has survived because the people have not "understood" that responsible parties will give them the kind of government they want, would be more convincing if, having made it articulate, they had adduced some evidence to support it. The assumption that of course the people don't understand, because if they did they would demand responsible parties, is hardly borne out by the presently available evidence.

Fifty-odd years ago, A. Lawrence Lowell suggested another explanation of the resistance of American parties to change which the authors of the *Report* might well ponder. His thesis was that American parties are the way they are because they are entirely appropriate to the kind of government the American people want. He developed it thus: Unified, disciplined and responsible parties are appropriate *only* to a government which seeks to locate *full* public power in the hand of popular majorities.

England is the leading example of such a government, and the English people have quite properly established a cabinet system in order to enable responsible parties and majority rule to flourish; for "if the object of government is to divide the people into two political parties, and to give rapid and unlimited effect to the opinions of the majority, no better political system has ever, perhaps, been suggested. . . ." A responsible party system, in short, is indispensable to a system of "unlimited" majority rule. To any other system it is quite inappropriate.

In the United States, Lowell continued, the people want majority rule only up to a point and within very definite limits:

> It is here considered of the first importance to protect the individual, to prevent the majority from oppressing the minority, and, except within certain definite limits, to give effect to the wishes of the people only after such solemn formalities have been compiled with as to make it clear that popular feeling is not caused by temporary excitement, but is the result of a mature and lasting opinion.[4]

Americans, that is to say, want *both* majority rule *and* minority rights; but they feel that the former must never be allowed to abridge the latter, and that the latter should constitute a fundamental limitation upon the former. Furthermore, Americans believe that there must be far more effective restraints upon the majority than are imposed simply by trusting them to behave with self-restraint. It was to institutionalize just this set of ideas about government, Lowell explained, that the Founding Fathers wrote the kind of Constitution they did—a Constitution planned to make it as difficult as possible for any bare popular majority (or any party or "faction" representing such a majority) to command the *whole* power of the government. Thus the framers divided the power of the national government among three different agencies,

---

[4] A. Lawrence Lowell, *Essays on Government* (Boston, 1897), p. 22.

no one of which has full power. They made each of these agencies independent of the others by having it derive its power from a different source and acquire its personnel by a different mode of selection. And they provided that the enormously important power of making the final decision upon the limits of the powers of the various agencies and of the government as a whole be given to the body furthest removed from control by bare popular majorities—the courts of law. The Founding Fathers did *not* create this elaborate and complex structure for the reason which the *Report* suggests, i.e., because they "did not contemplate the growing need for party responsibility when [the Constitution] was set up." They did it because they wanted to make sure that no unified and disciplined majority "faction" would ever be able to trample upon the rights of minorities; and the only sure way to prevent such a situation seemed to be to give any substantial minority the power to protect itself by vetoing any act of any majority it sees fit to veto.

But where does the American party system fit into such a scheme of government? American parties *as they exist,* said Lowell, are not only appropriate to it, but they are of considerable help in making it work. For one thing, he pointed out, our decentralized and irresponsible parties make it difficult for strong-willed and self-conscious popular majorities even to form. The American party leader thus does not seek to rally a strong popular majority around a concrete and consistent program of public policy; instead

> he usually attempts, on the contrary, to conciliate all classes and delights in such language as "a tariff for revenue only, so adjusted as to protect American industries"; an expression intended to win the votes of free-traders without offending the the protectionists. He is a member of an army of office-seekers, whose warfare is not directed against private rights, or the interests of particular classes, or even against what might be considered crying abuses,

but is waged chiefly with a rival army of office-seekers. . . . The result is, that party agitation in America does not in general involve any threat against the property or rights of private persons, and that those statutes which may be classed as socialistic rarely find a place in party programmes, and are not carried by party votes. *This state of things is not an accident. It is the natural consequence of the political system of the United States.*[5]

Elsewhere Lowell showed how American parties distort the expression of what majority opinions do exist, and how their responsibility and weak party lines keep even distorted majority opinions from being translated into governmental action. They are, he argued, but one more aspect, albeit it an important one, of a *total* system of anti-majoritarian government, sustained by the conviction of the American people that "unlimited" popular majorities are a constant and dangerous threat to minority rights, the security of which is the primary desideratum of good government. To compare the American party system unfavorably with a model system based upon British party practices is therefore pointless, he added; for British parties are an integral part of a governmental system aimed at quite different goals than those the American system seeks to realize. So long as Americans continue to refuse to place minority rights at the mercy of bare popular majorities, Lowell concluded, the American system of government, *including* its present system of irresponsible parties, is not likely to change.

It is by no means necessary to accept Lowell's analysis in its entirety to realize that he raised a number of questions which, whether the Committee recognizes it or not, lie at the heart of the problems with which it deals. What is the nature of democratic government? And do the American people really want such a government? Only *after* we have answered these ques-

[5] *Ibid.,* pp. 107–108.

tions can we decide what kind of party system is appropriate for the United States.

Perhaps the most-valuable contribution of Lowell's discussion is his clear presentation of the necessity of a *choice* between majority rule and minority rights, and his reminder that the doctrine of responsible party government makes sense only in a context where the former has been chosen. His analysis serves to show us that, unless we are willing to leave it to the good will and sense of self-restraint of bare popular majorities, the protection of minority rights necessarily involves giving some agency *external to* such majorities and *not responsible to* them the power to veto any act of a majority which it disapproves. We must, if "minority rights" in that sense is our choice, enable the minorities both to determine the boundaries of their rights *and* to have the final say as to whether any given act of a majority transgresses those boundaries. We must furthermore recognize that the power to veto is the power to *rule,* however we may wish to soften that harsh fact verbally; for the power to veto is the power to select the status quo from among the many alternative policies a government might, in any given situation, pursue. We must, in short, decide whether democracy to us means majority rule *or* minority rights. We cannot have both, for the latter in essence means minority *rule.*

In the writer's opinion, the issues involved in the majority rule *vs.* minority rights controversy are not, and have not been, as clearly seen and faced by the American people as Lowell seems to have believed; and the people therefore cannot be said to have made the clear choice of minority "rights" that he attributed to them. Probably the prevailing attitude in the United States is that we want *both* majority rule *and* inviolable minority rights, and that neither deserves any priority over the other.

Certainly the Committee makes no clear choice, as its reluctance to make a clear statement about the position of dissident minorities within "responsible" parties shows. In the *Report's* discussion of "intra-party democracy" and the proper nature and sources of party discipline, the whole emphasis is upon the "generally [*sic*] binding" nature of party platforms and caucus decisions; and for the most part their explanation of the proper nature of party discipline consists of showing how fine it would be if all party members would argue themselves into agreement on program and candidates so that there would *be* few dissidents. Their proposals for creating party "unity" are thus designed to build it up, not by any system of forcing members of party minorities to choose (as they must, for example, in England) between going along with the decisions of the party majority or getting out of the party, but by a series of "positive measures" for discussion, by which the Committee apparently hopes that all factions in the party will argue themselves into agreement and that the problem of the relative rights of majorities and minorities seldom need arise. The *Report* never tells us, however, how a "democratically organized" party should handle a situation in which the party majority has decided to do something with which a party minority cannot "conscientiously" agree.

Whatever the Committee believes democracy requires, it seems clear that only when the American people have clearly faced the necessity of choosing between majority rule and minority veto-power will we be able to tell whether Lowell's judgment of their preference for the latter is valid. And only then will we be able to predict the popular reception likely to be accorded the doctrine of responsible party government in the United States.

The authors of the *Report,* however, apparently feel that it is both possible and necessary to "sell" the people on the desirability of a "more responsible" party system without dealing with such "theoretical" matters as majority rule and minority rights and such "impractical" questions as that of constitutional revision. They must be reminded, in this connection, that their conception of a responsible party system is a *model* (not something which actually exists in this country), and a *democratic* model. It is founded upon the conviction that only *parties,* not individuals, can effectively be held responsible by the electorate for the manner in which the government is carried on. It is therefore necessary, if genuinely responsible parties are to exist, for the party which wins a *majority* of the popular votes to secure thereby the *full* power of the government. If the majority party does not exercise full power, it can hardly be held fully responsible for whatever the government does or fails to do; for is it not an axiom of contemporary political science that responsibility depends upon the possession of power? Yet a people which is not "sold" upon the idea of majority rule can hardly be "sold" a way of making majority rule effective. And a people which believes that unrestrained popular majorities cannot be trusted to rule wisely and well, is likely to continue to consider such majority-restraining traits of its party system as "independence" desirable attributes of statesmanship. A majoritarian party system, as Lowell so ably pointed out, is not likely to flourish in an anti-majoritarian governmental system. And what is much more pertinent, a majoritarian party system is not likely to be acclaimed by a people which is not sure that majority-rule democracy is what it wants.

In short, if the Committee really wishes to see genuinely effective *and* democratic government achieved in the United States, it must, however "impractical" it may seem, work for popular acceptance of the *whole* package of majority-rule democracy; it is highly impractical to plead just for a responsible party system, which after all is just one part of the total democratic package—and one which logically comes rather late in the argument. No matter how much the President and Congress may wish to "cooperate," a responsible party system can hardly flourish in a constitutional system where it is possible for a small bloc of Senators to filibuster to death any part of the winning party's program, where it is impossible, because of the staggered calendar of elections, to replace the *entire* government at any one election, and where, most important of all, a Supreme Court selected for life and largely beyond the reach of any popular majority can, for all practical purposes, declare any of the majority party's leading measures null and void.

The problem we face is not one of deciding whether the constitutional system or the parties should be changed "first." The point is that the same popular beliefs about government which sustain our present anti-majoritarian constitutional system will continue to sustain (as they have for a very long time) our anti-majoritarian party system. Only when the American people have fully accepted the doctrine of majority-rule democracy can the doctrine of responsible party government expect to receive the popular acclaim which, whether in Lowell's time or our own, it has so far been denied.

56. American Myths about British Parties

David E. Butler

David Butler, who teaches at Neufield College, Oxford, has pointed up the fallacy of regarding the British party system as the perfect model of the majority-type party government. It is his contention that the internal discipline of the British parties, upon investigation, appears to exist far more in form than in substance.

From *The Virginia Quarterly Review,* vol. 31, no. 1 (Winter 1955), pp. 46–56.

I

Among British writers on British government there is a strain of complacency which would be hard to match even among the more chauvinistic American students of American government. Although there can be found British scholars who have indulged in stern self-criticism—Ramsay Muir and Harold Laski are the most outstanding —there are none who have looked across the Atlantic for examples of how government might be improved. In the United States, on the other hand, there has always been a school of critics which has seen in the British system of government a remedy for the weaknesses which to some seem all too obvious on the American scene. Woodrow Wilson and William Yandell Elliott are perhaps the best known of this school while E. E. Schattschneider and Thomas Finletter are the most recent.

Despairing at the roadblocks placed in the way of strong and efficient government —constitutionally by the separation of powers and the federal system, and politically by party confusion and party indiscipline—they have looked enviously to British arrangements and asked whether some at least of that apparently simple orderliness could not be imported. The idealised picture offered in British treatises is faithfully accepted; British executive authority rests fully in the hands of a Cabinet drawn from, and loyally supported by, the party which has a majority in the House of Commons; untroubled by any traditional struggle between the legislative and executive branches, secure in its own unified authority, the Cabinet carries out the programme on which the majority party won the last election; the Cabinet has complete power to act in the national interest, yet it is saved from the dangers of tyranny by the internal democracy of the party from which it is drawn, by the miraculous device of the Parliamentary Question, by the British sense of fair play, and, most important of all, by the fear of the voters at the next general election. Such is the idyllic system, the example which has tempted some Americans to ask whether parts of it at least might not be copied. Would it not be possible to effect some fusion of the legislative and executive branches to reduce the wasteful and wearisome friction which is so customary between White House and Capitol Hill? Would it not be possible to develop a disciplined and responsible two-party system?

Even if the British system possessed all the virtues attributed to it, and even if the American people were willing to indulge in constitutional experimentation, it seems very doubtful whether any successful transplantation could be achieved. But, in any event, the excellencies of the British system are misunderstood; the party system is especially misunderstood.

In 1950 a group of eminent American political scientists produced a report entitled "Towards a more responsible two-party system," which in effect pleaded for the development of parties democratically organised and differentiated in ideology; there could be no doubt that the British system was in the minds of many of the authors. It is the purpose of this article to show that the British parties are in fact much less differentiated and much less democratic than is often supposed, and that it is a good thing that this should be so.

II

There is a very deep-rooted assumption that Britain has two clearcut parties standing for clearly opposed philosophies of government. Since the eighteenth century and even more since the passage of the Great Reform Bill in 1832, the opposing parties have been seen as the stand-patters and the reformers, once the Tories and the Whigs, then the Conservatives and the Liberals, and now the Conservatives and the Labourites. When the socialist and working-class Labour party replaced the more moderate and middle-class Liberals as the standard-bearer of progress the contrast became all the sharper. In the 1930's it was perhaps to be seen at its peak. On the one side stood the Conservatives, ready to maintain or cautiously to improve upon the status quo—the capitalist economic system and the established social order. On the other side stood the Labour party, committed to a drastic programme for the nationalisation of industry, the redistribution of wealth, and the transformation of many of the existing institutions of government. The two parties were well-disciplined and could be trusted to support their leaders in implementing these policies. At a British general election the voter knew what faced him; the programme he voted for stood a good chance of being enacted if his party won. He had perhaps to choose the lesser of two evils, to select between misguided prescriptions for the nation's ills—but his choice was at least clear. The conscientious American citizen seeking, for example, to choose between a left-wing Republican and a right-wing Democrat or to estimate what chance rival Presidential candidates would have of getting their respective programmes through Congress, could envy the sharp distinctions which confronted the British voter. It is, of course, probable that if the Labour Party had in fact attained power in the 1930's its performance would have seemed decidedly less drastic than its mildly revolutionary promises. Nonetheless, the fact remains that twenty years ago there was thought to be, and to a large extent there was, a sharp cleavage between the parties. The public picture of government always lags behind reality. Too many people—and too many textbooks—still see the British party struggle in the terms of the 1930's. But it has changed profoundly.

The main revolution took place during the war; events began to effect a compro-

mise between the parties. Full employment and much increased wage-rates went far to abolish extreme poverty while penal taxation went far to abolish extreme wealth. The Conservatives accepted as inevitable these equalising consequences of the war. They went further; partly as a concession to their Labour partners in the coalition government, and partly as an expression of the reformist zeal which, at the climax of the war, swept over so many Western European countries, they accepted the principle of the Welfare State. Americans often forget that the characteristic institutions of the Welfare State in Britain, the National Health Service and the comprehensive system of social insurance originated not from the postwar Socialist government but from the wartime coalition which was based on an overwhelming Conservative majority. By the end of the war the social grievances which had seemed to call for radical political action were on the way to being remedied—with the consent and approval of the Conservatives. At the same time the Labour leaders, with the chastening experience of five years in office, had learnt to operate and respect the British governmental machine. They no longer believed that it would be necessary to reconstruct the machine before they could carry their programme into action; and their programme had, with the march of events and the modification of their own ideas, come to seem less radical.

This does not mean that the election of 1945 was not fought about real issues or that there was nothing to choose between the parties at that time; but in the fields of social and foreign policy they were far less divided than in the 1930's. The really big issue at stake in 1945, if personalities are ignored, was the nationalisation of industry. In its manifesto the Labour party promised to take into public ownership the production of coal, domestic gas, electricity, and of iron and steel, as well as the main branches of public transport. The Labour victory in the election was followed in the next five years by the complete fulfillment of these pledges, in the face of determined Conservative opposition. There has been no other question in postwar British politics on which the parties have been so unequivocally opposed. That is not to say that there were not many other issues on which there were major clashes during the life of the Labour government or that, nationalisation apart, British politics would have been little different if the Conservatives had won in 1945. Unquestionably, the Labour government was in general more lavish with the taxpayers' money, more ready to control the detailed working of the national economy, and more hasty in yielding up sovereignty in India and the Colonial Empire than a Conservative government would have been. But since 1945 the parties have never clashed fundamentally on the principle of establishing the Welfare State and the levelling rates of taxation therein involved or on the basic issues of foreign and colonial policy. The general continuity in policy between the Labour government which left office in 1951 and the Conservative government which has ruled since then clearly underlines the narrowness of the gap between the parties.

In the last few years, moreover, the issue of nationalisation, the one real policy issue at stake in 1945, has receded from the political scene. The Conservatives on coming into power reversed the nationalisation of the Iron and Steel Industry—which had not proceeded very far—and they turned back to private ownership a large section of the Road Haulage Industry. The Labour party has promised that it will, at least in part, renationalise these two industries when it returns to power; this it was perhaps bound to say, if only to justify its past action. But the Labour party, it should be noted, has no definite plans to nationalise any other specific industry—except the largely municipalised one of

water supply. In the several hundred resolutions sent in to the 1954 Labour party conference, only one explicitly asked for further drastic measures of nationalisation. The truth is that British public opinion has come to feel that nationalisation is neither a panacea nor a disaster. In none of the industries to which it has been applied has it failed spectacularly, but in none has it brought the full benefits for which its sponsors hoped. With the tacit consent of the Labour party, it has receded from the centre of the political scene.

What, then, divides the parties today? If one judged them by their extremists—particularly the Labour Party—one would find an unbridgeable gulf between wholehearted and sometimes almost fellow-travelling Socialists and high and dry orthodox Conservatives. But if one judges the parties by the words of their responsible leaders and, still more, by their performance in office, one finds that the gap is remarkably small. There will always be differences on day-to-day issues, the differences between the "ins" and the "outs," between those who circumscribed by the hard facts of the situation, have to face the responsibility of action, and those who are living up to the traditional maxim of British politics, "The duty of the opposition is to oppose." There will always be differences between a Conservative party whose leadership is overwhelmingly recruited from the prosperous classes and a Labour party drawn from most sections of the community but primarily dependent upon the goodwill of the Trade Unions and the working class. The instinctive reactions of Conservative and Labour politicians differ appreciably. Nonetheless, their politics remain astonishingly similar.

During the summer of 1954, Labour Members of Parliament have been rejoicing in Mr. Eden's performance and, in private at least, proclaiming that no Labour Foreign Secretary would have been so courageous in standing up against American policy. On the domestic scene a new word, "Butskellism," has been added to the political vocabulary by an article in The Economist entitled "Mr. Butskell's Dilemma," which explored the economic problems faced and the solutions likely to be found, by a British Chancellor of the Exchequer, be he the Conservative R. A. Butler or the Socialist Hugh Gaitskell. Most people in Britain would be surprised at the suggestion that there are no clear differences between the policies of the parties. But if one looks at realities and not at words, it is hard to see what they are. It seems reasonable to argue that the fate of Britain ten years hence will be far less affected by whether the Conservatives or the Labour Party win the next election, than the fate of the United States will be affected by the decision it will have to take in 1956 between a Republican and a Democrat. The choice may seem more confused in the United States, but it is more far-reaching. The parties in Britain may be distinct from each other, but they are not very different from each other.

III

More people have fallen into the trap of seeing the parties as clearly opposed rivals than into the trap of taking the parties' internal democratic machinery at its face value. Nonetheless, anyone who has escorted American political scientists to the British party conferences is forced to recognise a widespread confusion about the extent to which the British parties are, while democratic in form, oligarchic in fact. Facilities for the rank and file to participate in the decision-making process undoubtedly exist, but in practice they scarcely circumscribe the authority of the party leaders. American observers who go to local party meetings in Britain or to the annual conferences of the parties are usually much impressed by the serious purpose of the gathering, by the articulate and informed speeches of the men in the street who attend, by the devotion to questions of policy or principle to the exclusion of issues of personality, and by the absence of the jamboree atmosphere which sometimes characterises American political gatherings. The British example provokes speculation whether such earnestness could not be introduced into American parties, whether they too could not become educational and policy-formulating clubs instead of arenas for fights over patronage and the choice of candidates. To suggest this is to misconstrue first the nature of British parties and secondly the practical limits of the democratic process. It is a complete illusion to suppose, as some have done, that party democracy on the British model provides a workable substitute for direct democracy. The impracticability of Athenian democracy, of every citizen sharing in every decision, has long been realised; but, so runs the argument, even today it is still open to any citizen to join a party, to propose a resolution in the local branch, and, if it wins support there, to have it put forward at the annual conference of the party; if the conference approves, it becomes an item in the national policy of the party, a policy that will be enacted when the party is next returned to power; anyone who wants to can take his share in choosing his candidate for parliament, in shaping his party's programme, and in restraining or encouraging, in effect in selecting, its leaders. This is the idealised theory. What is the reality? How much say do the rank and file of the British parties actually have in the selection of their party's policy or its leaders?

It is proper to begin an examination of the extent of democracy in British parties by examining how many take any active share in it. At the 1951 election approximately fourteen million people voted for each of the major parties. But only three million people are even nominally subscribing members of the Conservative party and, despite the fact that five million Trade Unionists are formally affiliated to the Labour party, barely a million people have taken the trouble to join the party as individuals. Even party members, however, are for the most part totally passive. In very few constituencies do as much as ten percent of them in either party play any active role. Even at an election only a few hundred thousand contribute any effort beyond going themselves to vote and, in between elections, when party policies are being hammered out, the number who participate in serious discussions can be at most fifty thousand; it is probably much less.

Do these few party zealots in the constituencies by their debates on national issues have much influence on the conduct of their leaders? It would seem not. In the Conservative party very much less policy discussion goes on than in the Labour party. The vast majority of Conservative Constituency Associations are characterised by loyalty to their leaders, by an unintellectual conviction that their leaders know best. The Conservative Annual Conference has virtually never made a decision of any importance. It is for all practical purposes a carefully managed pep-rally, a chance for the party workers and the party leaders to get together. It is true that should the leaders violently offend the susceptibilities of their followers, the machinery of revolt does exist. But it has long been idle, for the leaders of the Conservative party know their business. Within enormously broad limits they are free to shape the party's policy as seems best to them. They have to worry a lot about what the voters will think of them at the next election, but very little about what their party rank-and-file demand of them from day to day.

Is it the same with the Labour party? Its protagonists boast much about its democratic structure and its intellectual vitality. It is true that the constituency parties are constantly passing resolutions, asking their leaders for a change in policy. Of late years there has been a great deal in the newspapers about the struggle between the left and right wings of the party, between the Bevanites and the rest. But the dominant right wing of the party have been able to carry on in control, untroubled by the fact that a large majority of the active rank-and-file in the constituencies are Bevanites. The Bevanites are outnumbered by at least four to one both among the Labour Members of Parliament and on the National Executive Committee of the party, and nothing in the foreseeable future seems likely to change this situation. The Bevanites may struggle to get resolutions for a more pacific foreign policy or a more revolutionary domestic policy passed by the Annual Conference of the Labour Party. But apart from the fact that the "block vote" of the Trade Unions is mainly right wing and can usually be trusted to defeat radical resolutions from the constituencies, such resolutions can also be lost or rendered meaningless by manipulating the complicated parliamentary procedure of a Labour Party Conference. Even if the Conference were to pass a resolution involving a change of policy, the National Executive would still have the right to decide when —if ever—and how the resolution should be implemented. People write of Mr. Bevan's "bid for power" and speak as though he had a serious chance of securing the leadership of the Labour Party in the near future. They forget that the Leader of the Labour Party is elected by the Labour Members of Parliament and that it is scarcely conceivable that he would ever command a majority among the present group of M.P.'s. The mortality of M.P.'s is low and the turnover is slow. It is a singular fact that, although many right-wing Labour M.P.'s represent constituencies in which the local Labour Party is Bevanite, there is not a single case where an M.P.'s views have or seem likely to cost him renomination. Even where vacancies have occurred, Bevanite local parties have far from always chosen a Bevanite. The local parties have the power to choose whom they will; but, in the case of incumbents, a natural loyalty to good and conscientious representatives and, in the case of vacancies, a desire to get the most appealing of the available candidates have prevented any drastic change in the proportion of Bevanite M.P.'s or candidates. Until the local Labour Parties start rigourously applying political tests, the present leadership of the Labour Party is secure.

All that has been said does not mean that there are not real and important struggles over policy going on throughout the Labour Party. But it would seem that, all things considered, the leaders of the Labour Party are as secure in power and have almost as free a hand in policy-making as their Conservative opposite numbers.

Those in America who envy the internal democracy of the British parties and imagine that the rank-and-file have a substantial share in settling party programmes, might well pause to examine whether in practice American party policies are not more effectively influenced by popular pressure than are British. Upon investigation the internal democracy of British parties appears to exist far more in form than in substance.

IV

To minimize the difference between, and the democracy within, the British parties is not to dispraise them. The British should be thankful that their parties have such similar policies and such untrammelled oligarchies.

The existence of deep divisions between the two parties which are alternately to be entrusted with full control of the machinery of state is not to be applauded. Lord Balfour achieved the classic summary of the situation when he wrote, "Our whole political machinery presupposes a people so fundamentally at one that they can safely afford to bicker." The party differences being as small as they are, the course of British politics is likely to be an even one in the years to come; elections will not bring the risk of drastic and dislocating reversals in national policy. They will provide an opportunity for the voters to judge the performance of the governing party, to decide whether a change of men is desirable, to choose between different variants of basically similar policies; they will not open the way to drastic or irreversible decisions which might divide and endanger the nation.

The placing of excessive power in the hands of the militant rank-and-file of political parties would be equally to be deplored. This would be to place the destinies of the country at the mercy of a small, and not always very wise, minority of the people. If the determination of party policy were indeed to be left to the zealots in the constituencies, the gap between the parties would be widened to an extent unsuited to the smooth running of national affairs and repugnant to the more moderate, if more apathetic, bulk of British citizens. It is well that the party leaders, relatively immune from the danger of revolt by their active supporters, should be free to determine party policy, subject to the sure and certain checks of having to defend their views and actions in Parliament and, still more, of having in due course to present themselves for judgment before the British electorate.

Much may be wrong with American parties but those who have looked to the British system for remedies have surely erred in their analysis of its excellencies.

57. Southern Politics and the Negro

Paul Duke

This article, written by NBC correspondent Paul Duke, discusses the effect of Negro registration and voting in the South in the 1964 presidential election. The author notes particularly the fact that Negro votes provided Johnson with his margins of victory in Virginia, Florida, Tennessee, and Arkansas. Formerly a congressional reporter for the Wall Street Journal, *Duke cites those areas in the South where Negro votes are at last starting to outweigh those of segregationist whites. He discusses the potential party realignment of the future South, noting the irony that the Negro was the issue that created the one-party South and that it will be the issue that eventually destroys it.*

* * *

A few days after November third, two Negro leaders and a prominent member of Senator Harry F. Byrd's Democratic organization conferred quietly for two hours at a Richmond hotel over the future role of Negroes in Virginia politics. The Negro spokesmen emphasized that from now on they expect to share in the rewards of patronage and to be included in policy-making councils. The message and its supporting statistic—the 140,000 Negro votes that enabled President Johnson to carry Virginia by 76,704 votes—were not lost on the representative of Senator Byrd, whose most immediate concern is shoring up his defenses against an anticipated Republican assault on the governorship next year.

The meeting was a sign of the new times in the South. With the emergence of the Negro vote as a powerful force in parts of the old Confederacy, venerable political customs are tottering. Racism is not about to disappear, but clearly it can no longer serve as the principal support of the political structure throughout the South. Moreover, the growing Negro electorate seems certain to accelerate a reshuffling of Southern alliances along the lines prevailing elsewhere in the nation, the Republican Party becoming the major voice of conservatism and the Democratic Party representing moderation and even liberalism. The ultimate consequence promises to be a truly competitive two-party system.

WINNERS AND LOSERS

The most impressive evidence that this metamorphosis is already well advanced may be found in some rather striking statistics from the November 3 election. Not only did Negro votes provide President Johnson with his margins of victory in Virginia, Florida, Tennessee, and Arkansas, but exceptionally large Negro turnouts helped swell the outcome to landslide proportions in North Carolina and Texas.

Moreover, five states carried by Barry Goldwater were those with the lowest percentage of Negro registrants, where rural segregationist influences remain strongest, and where Democratic leaders deserted the national ticket in greatest numbers. While thousands of woolhat Democrats were shattering tradition to back a Republican for the first time in these states, other rural areas were giving Johnson more support than anticipated. The President swept all fifty-one counties in eastern North Carolina, carried all but four of the twenty-one Arkansas delta counties, and took fifty-nine of the sixty-two flatland counties in northern and eastern Texas. In San Jacinto County, Texas, where Negro voters outnumber whites, Johnson got 1,680 votes to Goldwater's 343.

From *The Reporter*, vol. 31, no. 11 (December 17, 1964), pp. 18–19+, by permission of the author and The Reporter Magazine Company.

The signs of change were also manifest in Congressional contests. While Republicans captured five House seats in Alabama, one in Georgia, and one in Mississippi on the strength of the so-called civil-rights backlash, all Democratic incumbents were re-elected in the states Johnson carried. And while seven segregationist Democrats were defeated, the nine Southern Democratic members of Congress who voted for the Civil Rights Act were all re-elected, most of them without serious difficulty.

The Negro vote has naturally had its greatest impact in large cities where there are no bars to enfranchisement. It clearly made the difference in the victories of moderate Democratic Representatives Hale Boggs of New Orleans and Charles Weltner of Atlanta. It turned what would have been cliffhanging contests into runaway triumphs for James A. MacKay, the newly elected moderate Democratic congressman from Atlanta's suburbs, and liberal Representative Richard Fulton of Nashville. Furthermore, the outpouring of Negroes voting for Johnson helped pull through some conservative Democrats not noted for their espousal of civil rights but who nonetheless backed the national ticket. Without Negro backing, Representatives Harold Cooley and Ralph Scott would have gone down in North Carolina. Cooley, chairman of the House Agriculture Committee and a veteran of thirty years in Congress, managed to eke out a 4,988-vote victory over his Republican opponent, James Gardner, with the help of a significant amount of Negro support, including a 3,727,321 rout in six Raleigh precincts.

Another remarkable illustration of the way Negro votes are beginning to outweigh those of segregationist whites was provided by the House contest in Tennessee's Ninth District. The district embraces Memphis, long regarded as a kind of spiritual font of the Old South. But the city has changed a good deal since the days when residents of the large Negro quarter could be herded to the polls by Boss Ed Crump to do his bidding. Memphis Negroes now constitute a generally sophisticated voting bloc of ninety-three thousand—more than three times the Negro registrants in all of Mississippi. Although custom decreed that candidates chant the customary paeans to the past, the liberal Democrat George Grider defied tradition during the Democratic primary last August when he ran against Representative Clifford Davis, a product of the old Crump machine. Grider unhesitatingly proclaimed his belief in equal rights for all, implying that he would have voted for the civil-rights bill, while Davis boasted of his vote against it. With overwhelming Negro support, Grider upset Davis.

It seemed likely that Grider would lose in the general election, however, and the first returns showed him getting only one out of three votes cast by whites and even trailing his Republican rival, Robert B. James, in low-income Democratic wards. But ninety minutes after the polls closed, returns from Negro wards began coming in and put Grider in front. He led 3,370 to 27 in one ward, for example. The Negro turnout provided about sixty-five thousand, or fifty-nine percent, of the 109,705 votes Grider ran up in defeating James.

Other results would seem to indicate a diminishing concern about the civil-rights issue among many white voters. The 568,005 votes received by Democratic Representative Ross Bass of Tennessee in winning election to the remaining two years of the late Senator Estes Kefauver's term was negligibly less than the 570,542 total of Democratic Senator Albert Gore. Bass voted for the civil-rights bill; Gore did not. In Texas, Democrat Ralph Yarborough, who had also supported the measure, easily won another Senate term by a 324,-079-vote margin, well above the approximately 225,000 Negro votes that went to him. Yarborough's Republican opponent,

George Bush, tried hard to capitalize on the civil-rights vote early in the campaign, but eased up in his criticism when polls showed that the issue wasn't winning him appreciable support. The two Republican House members from Texas, Bruce Alger and Ed Foreman, both vigorous foes of the civil-rights bill, were also defeated.

A PLACE TO GO

The importance of this ferment can hardly be underrated in a region where the race issue has been standard campaign fare for more than a century. The Richmond hotel meeting was an indication that even a conservative oligarchy that did not hesitate to use racism to solidify its power ten years ago is at least cognizant of change and might even alter its course considerably in order to stay in power. It is significant that the Byrd organization's prospective candidate for governor, Lieutenant Governor Mills Godwin, a formulator of the discredited massive-resistance policies, has recently taken a notable turn toward racial accommodation.

Even where the race issue is still hot, there is a greater recognition of Negro power. It was no idle gesture of friendliness that led Senator Herman Talmadge of Georgia to give his private telephone number to a Negro state senator, Leroy Johnson of Atlanta. The Democratic disasters in Georgia, South Carolina, Alabama, and Louisiana already have emboldened loyalists to challenge the conservative apostates, and steps to increase Negro registration figure prominently in their plans. In Alabama, where the Republican tide inundated even incumbent county judges and constables, some moderates are boldly talking of toppling Governor George Wallace from his throne. "The Democratic Party will be reorganized from top to bottom," asserted outgoing Representative Carl Elliott. "The problem has been to hold both the progressive wing

and the ultraconservative wing under the same tent. Now the birth of the Republican Party in Alabama has given the ultraconservatives a place to go."

The new Republicanism of conservative Democrats in the South coincides with the tendency of Negro voters to settle down in the Democratic Party. From Reconstruction to New Deal days, most Southern Negroes were Republicans. As late as the 1950's Negroes controlled party affairs in some parts of Dixie, and the 1956 Mississippi delegation to the Republican national convention was biracial. Even though whites began taking command in the Eisenhower years, Negroes continued to vote Republican in sizable numbers, especially in the cities. A majority of Atlanta Negroes who voted in 1960 voted for Nixon. At a Republican conference in Atlanta in 1961, G.O.P. officials went out of their way to contrast the attendance of Negro delegates with a recently held white-only testimonial dinner for Senator Richard B. Russell.

But all this changed dramatically with the ascendancy of Goldwaterism. In many areas of the Deep South, G.O.P. units took on the trappings of Sons of the Confederacy chapters. Not only were Negroes systematically excluded from party affairs, but the watered-down civil-rights plank adopted at the San Francisco convention in July was interpreted as an open bid for segregationist votes in preference to Negro votes. Reporters traveling with Goldwater recall vividly a speech at the Knoxville airport in which the candidate spoke beneath a huge Confederate flag.

To say that this trend cost the party dear is to labor the obvious; but it is worth noting that Virginia, Florida, and Tennessee —all hit by the Negro avalanche—had gone Republican in every Presidential election since 1948. Consider the history of Memphis Ward 35, which gave 36 percent of its votes to Stevenson in 1956, 67 percent to Kennedy, and 99.4 percent to Johnson.

Many Democrats have concluded that the Goldwater candidacy has guaranteed that the vast majority of the Negro electorate will stay Democratic for a long time to come. "The Republicans had done well in keeping the Lincoln image alive in the South," according to one Democratic leader, "but to the Negro, Goldwater shot Lincoln in the head as surely as John Wilkes Booth."

While Southern Republicanism takes on overtones of white supremacy, Southern Democrats have increasingly moved to cultivate Negro voters. Except in Mississippi, Alabama, and Louisiana, Negroes now serve on many local Democratic committees and on some state executive groups. In a few places Negro office seekers have been nominated to run on the regular party ticket, and all the Negroes elected to city councils and legislatures in recent years have invariably been Democrats. Perhaps most remarkable of all, Negro and white straw-hatted "Johnson girls" whooped it up side by side at major campaign rallies in many Southern cities.

The Democratic national convention's directive against discrimination in conducting party business—with the threat of expulsion from the 1968 convention—is an added incentive that should help lower racial barriers in the political affairs of the Deep South. A number of Negro leaders who led nonpartisan voter-registration drives and are well known in the Negro communities have now been given field jobs with the Democratic National Committee. And in January, the committee will hold a meeting of Southern Negro leaders in Washington to make plans for a new registration drive and to draw Negro leadership even more firmly into the party.

Of 5.2 million Negroes of voting age in the eleven Southern states, approximately 2.2 million are registered and about 1.6 million voted on November 3—roughly double the number who cast ballots in 1960. By 1968, registrants will probably total more than three million, which would represent about twenty percent of the Southern electorate. "What this year's election did was to prove to the Negro janitor and the Negro maid that they have power at the polling booth," one Southern Negro leader remarked. "I predict that Negroes will become more politically conscious in the South than in the North. It's like Jackie Robinson hitting the big leagues and giving every kid on a back alley the ambition to get there, too."

"THE PORK BARREL EVERY TIME"

The main result of the Negro's new power is likely to be a transformation of the free-for-all nature of Southern politics into the kind of pyramidal organizational structure that prevails in the North. For the most part, the South has lacked a real party system with a clearly defined chain of command. Instead politics has revolved around various factions, courthouse cliques, and dynasties of the Byrd, Talmadge, and Long type. As Georgia's newly elected Representative MacKay put it: "We haven't had a one-party South; we've had a no-party South. There's been the machinery of a two-party system but not the foundation for one."

With the region less bound to tradition and personalities, it follows that economic interests will become far more significant in deciding elections. Thus, in the rural sections carried by Johnson in Texas, Arkansas, and North Carolina, the threat to abolish farm subsidies proved more persuasive than the threat to a segregationist way of life. A Yarborough aide, analyzing the senator's strong showing in the segregationist belt, remarked: "These people are social reactionaries and economic liberals. When faced with a choice, they'll take the pork barrel every time."

Ultimately, then, the South's voting habits will not be distinguishable from those of the rest of the country, with a Democratic Party primarily for lower-income groups and a Republican Party primarily for the well-to-do.

There are signs, however, that the Republicans may inherit the North-South Democratic split over civil rights along with a number of conservative Democrats. It was, after all, the Republicans who fought over civil rights at their convention, and it is the G.O.P. that has seven new segregationist congressmen, one of whom, Georgia's Howard Callaway, has already proclaimed the repeal of the Civil Rights Act as his No. 1 objective. It was hardly a coincidence, either, that Goldwater's successes, with the exception of Georgia, were in those states that supported the 1948 States' Rights candidacy of Strom Thurmond. Or that in Georgia the Republican nominee's support was drawn principally from the same racially sensitive counties carried by the demagogical Marvin Griffin in his abortive attempt to recapture the governorship in 1962. The inescapable conclusion, as Harry Golden noted, is that many Southerners viewed the Goldwater candidacy as a last chance "for putting the Negro back in back of the bus and resegregating the schools, restaurants, motels, parks and movie houses."

Whether such motivation can provide the foundation for an enduring political party is doubtful at best. If, as Herman Talmadge has suggested, the Goldwater movement consisted principally of "mad Democrats," many of those who played hooky may be back in school before long. Already there are signs that some Goldwater zealots will not stay put if a liberal Republican is nominated for President four years hence. As a Sumter County, Georgia, G.O.P. leader told Arlen J. Large of the *Wall Street Journal:* "If the Republican Party deserts us in the next four years, we'll jump the fence to something else."

Such remarks greatly disturb those Southern Republicans who want to dissociate themselves from Goldwaterism, believing that the party can ill afford either a personality cult or a futile fight to retain segregation. It was for this reason that a group of Upper South moderates dispatched a hurried message to the seven new congressmen urging them to remove racism from their political vocabulary. Robert R. Snodgrass, Republican national committeeman for Georgia until his ouster by a Goldwater faction early this year, was more blunt. "The Republican Party of Georgia cannot afford—and it must not be led by—hatemongers like the Ku Kluxers, the John Birchites, the cast-offs and has-beens of the Democratic Party," he said at a luncheon of the Atlanta Rotary Club.

Snodgrass and other moderate Republican leaders like Virginia's Robert Corber and Tennessee's Howard Baker, Jr., believe the G.O.P. must discard ante-bellum racial attitudes. Instead, they argue, the party's future should be linked to the rapid urbanization and industrialization now taking place in the region, holding onto the rising middle-class elite that is attracted to the Republicans on grounds of fiscal conservatism. Nixon, it must be remembered, carried thirty of the forty-seven major Southern cities. With the prosperous urbanites, small-town merchants, and traditional Republican pockets in the Appalachian highlands and other rural areas, the party could have the nucleus for steady growth. Within this framework of non-racial conservatism, the modern strategists are convinced that their party must find a place for Negroes as well.

But it is likely that most Southern Democrats will adjust to the changed complexion that Negro voters have given "their" party. It is more apt to be the oncoming generation of conservative Southerners that will ignore tradition and make the alignment with Northern conservatives in the Republican Party. Here there is irony indeed. For the Negro was the issue that created the one-party South, and he will be the issue that eventually destroys it.

58.   The Changing Political Parties

Paul T. David

In this article Paul T. David, Professor of Political Science at the University of Virginia, considers whether competition both between the parties and within the parties is increasing. The implications of competition in the organization of party leaderships, the requirements of party finance, and the development of nationalizing tendencies in congressional politics are reviewed here.

* * *

CHANGES LATENT IN THE PARTY SYSTEM

Viewed retrospectively, the eight years of the Eisenhower administration were something of an interregnum in the evolution of the political parties. Some innovative changes occurred that seemed of moderate importance at the time, but mostly it was a period of catching up. The Republicans shook off their out-party reluctance to embrace programs that had long since had the support of overwhelming majorities of the American people. To some extent, at least, they abandoned what Julius Turner and Ivan Hinderaker have identified as the "self-destructive tendencies in the minority major party."[1] The Democrats, out of power in the White House for the first time in twenty years, discovered that even in defeat

could retain most of their New Deal and Fair Deal party followings, and they made some progress in dealing with the problems of how to operate when in the opposition.

But during six of the eight Eisenhower years, the Democrats held ostensible majorities in both houses of Congress while out of power in the administration. The period was one of almost unprecedented ambiguity in regard to partisan responsibility for the conduct of the government. Neither party could develop much of a sense of direction, and there was no strong impulse to deal firmly with the party institutions.

With the advent of the Kennedy administration, the situation changed. . . . This may be an eight-year period in which considerations of party responsibility will be given a renewed emphasis.

It is the general purpose of this essay to note some of the more important kinds of change existing and latent within the parties, and to explore their potential consequences.

Specifically, the objectives are as follows:

First, to discuss whether the American political parties are becoming more competitive with each other, and whether there is a rising level of competitive tension within the party system.

Second, to comment briefly on the relationships between competition, cohesion, and centralization in the party system, and to suggest some of the implications of these relationships.

Third, to consider the consequences of party competition for the organization of party leadership, the requirements of party finance, and the development of nationalizing tendencies in congressional politics.

[1] Julius Turner, "Responsible Parties: A Dissent from the Floor," *American Political Science Re-* view, XLV, March 1951, at pp. 151–52; Ivan Hinderaker, *Party Politics* (New York: Holt, Rinehart & Winston, Inc., 1956), pp. 634–36. The quoted phrase is Hinderaker's.

Marian D. Irish, *Continuing Crisis in American Politics*, © 1963, pp. 47–57, 61–65. Reprinted by permission of Prentice-Hall, Inc., Englewood Cliffs, N.J.

A MORE COMPETITIVE
PARTY SYSTEM?

In a review of contemporary politics in 1961, it was my conclusion that "the party system as a whole now occupies what is probably the most highly competitive position it has ever reached in national politics."[2] This conclusion was based on such factors as the following:

the scale, scope, and nature of the national campaign of 1960;

the number of states in which the election was fought hard to a close outcome in presidential, congressional, and state elections;

the speed with which the professionals and the party organizations in each party turned to preparations for the 1962 campaigns;

the number of close votes in Congress on major items in the President's legislative program;

the evident disposition of the administration to sharpen issues in Congress in preparation for future election campaigns;

the aggressive character of the leadership that has come to the top in each of the national parties.

These signs, however, may be more persuasive than probative; and the future remains uncertain. We would like to know whether the 1960 elections were merely the highest point of a competitive tension that will recede until 1964 or 1968; and also whether the long-term drift toward a more competitive situation that has been evident for a generation will continue, despite the fluctuations that may be related to the circumstances of particular election years.

On the short-term side, there were indications early in 1962 that the Republican Party might do poorly in the 1962 elec-

tions, contrary to the historical experience in which the party out of power has usually gained seats in Congress in midterm elections.[3] The Republican Party also has been engaged in an unusual amount of soul-searching over its internal problems; but the kind of ferment that is in process suggests that the Party will eventually recover strongly even if its competitive fortunes become worse before they become better.[4]

The longer-term aspect of the problem of interparty competition is obviously the more important for students of the party system; and an opinion that projects past trends into the future needs to be supported by some long-term interpretation of party history. Such a view could begin by noting the political events of 1896, when a Republican sweep elected William McKinley president.

The election of 1896 is generally credited with a restructuring of political affiliations that endured for more than a generation. The South became the solidly Democratic South. It is all too often forgotten that twenty northern states became so solidly Republican that they could reasonably have been called the "solid North." The period was the high point of a sectional political

---

[2] Paul T. David *et al., The Presidential Election and Transition 1960–61* (Washington, D. C.: The Brookings Institution, 1961), p. 339.

[3] The most specific evidence came from the Gallup Poll, which from April 1961 to March 1962 was reporting that voter preferences for the Democratic party were at a level indicating Democratic gains in the 1962 elections. In March 1962, the apparent split in the two-party vote for Congress was placed at Democratic, 61 per cent; Republican, 39. George Gallup, "GOP Lag in Congress Races Indicated," *Washington Post and Times Herald*, Mar. 25, 1962.

On February 24, 1962, Republican Chairman Miller told a closed meeting of Republicans that "continued stress" on adverse public opinion polls would "undermine the enthusiasm of the rank-and-file," and that the party should not "succumb to the psychological warfare of the Democrats." *Congressional Quarterly Weekly Report*, XX, Mar. 2, 1962, p. 361.

[4] Robert C. Albright, "Republicans Fretting Over Future of Party," *Washington Post and Times Herald*, Mar. 4, 1962; "Self-Analysis by GOP Brings Gleams of Hope," *ibid.*, Mar. 5, 1962.

alignment, and the low point in the effectiveness of the competitive relationship between the Democratic and Republican parties, both nationally and in most states.

These relationships were changed by the realignments that occurred in 1928, 1932, and 1936. The Democratic Party replaced the Republican as the party with a majority following; and whereas the former Republican majority had been sectional, the Democratic majority was national. By 1940, the Republican Party had begun to recover, but a new cleavage line had been established between the parties. Though the South was still solid and still Democratic, in most of the nation, and especially in the central urban and industrial areas from Massachusetts to California, the parties were again competitive in state-wide

elections. The cleavage line within the electorate, moreover, essentially followed social and economic divisions in the states where the parties were competitive.[5]

The broad effect of these changes is apparent in the election returns when they are arranged to show the relative amounts of one-party voting by states, taking first the period from 1896 to 1927 and second the period from 1928 to 1956. This has been done in a tabulation of the voting in presidential and gubernatorial elections, giving each state its percentage weight in the electoral college as follows:

In presidential voting, as these figures show, most of the states were solidly for one party or the other in the earlier period, while in the recent period, the solidly Republican states had almost disappeared and

Categories of States[a]	Period of 1896 to 1927		Period of 1928 to 1956	
	President	*Governor*[b]	*President*	*Governor*
One-party Republican	50.0%	35.1%	1.5%	7.5%
Two-party leaning Republican	10.7	10.5	23.1	18.4
Two-party uncertain	10.3	16.4	23.4	33.0
One-party leaning Democratic	4.9	12.3	40.2	14.0
One-party Democratic	24.1	25.7	11.8	27.1
	100.0	100.0	100.0	100.0

a States were classified in the one-party category when the party concerned was victorious in 80 per cent or more of the elections during the period; as leaning to one party when the party was victorious in 60 to 79.9 per cent of the elections; and as uncertain when neither party won more than 60 per cent of the time. These tabulations were originally made by Richard C. Bain for a paper by Paul T. David, "Intensity of Inter-Party Competition and the Problem of Party Realignment," presented at the annual meeting of the American Political Science Association, September 1957.
b Based on the period 1901–1927.

there had been major inroads in the solidly Democratic states, coupled with a great increase in the number of states leaning toward the Democratic Party. In gubernatorial elections, the shifts were somewhat different. The shrinkage in Republican areas was reflected mainly in an increase in the competitive areas; and the solid South was still solid in electing Democratic governors.

In recent years, the partisan attachments of the electorate have been remarkably stable in most parts of the country.

Throughout the Eisenhower period, apparently about 60 per cent of the voters continued to consider themselves Democrats. In a "normal" election, however, it has been computed that the Democratic share would be no more than 54 per cent, because many Democrats are habitual non-voters. This relatively narrow Democratic

5 For a fuller statement, see Paul T. David, Ralph M. Goldman, and Richard C. Bain, *The Politics of National Party Conventions* (Washington, D. C.: The Brookings Institution, 1960), chap. 3; paperback ed., chap. 2.

vote, moreover, consists of a lopsided majority in the South, and a 49 per cent *minority* outside the South.[6]

It would be easier to predict that the two national parties will continue to become more competitive if some increase could be predicted in the Republican Party's share in the southern vote. On this, the Party's shortage of effective candidates is one of its most serious problems. As recently as 1960, it offered no candidate for Congress in 62 of the 106 congressional districts in the eleven one-time Confederate states. But in the more than forty districts where it offered candidates, it polled 26.5 per cent of the vote in 1948, 27.4 in 1952, 38.0 in 1956, and 37.8 in 1960. In recent years, seven of these districts sent Republican members to Congress. The Republican vote in many of the other districts is high enough to fall within striking range of a majority whenever the Party is again in a favorable position nationally in a presidential election.

Republican prospects in the South—and the prospects for a two-party system in the southern region—were substantially improved by the Supreme Court's decision of March 26, 1962, in the Tennessee reapportionment case, *Baker v Carr*. The new Republicans of the South have been concentrated in the most under-represented urban and suburban areas. If given fair representation, they seem certain to expand their beachheads in southern state legislatures and in Congress. Attractive candidates developed through these opportunities could in turn do much to expand the Party's following throughout the South. On the other hand, liberal Democrats of the southern cities, also under-represented in

previous districting arrangements, will be able to increase their weight in southern Democratic Party affairs. Where this happens on a sufficient scale, conservative southern Democrats may find their inclination to shift to the Republican Party somewhat increased.

By a coincidence that is not entirely accidental, the effects of the Tennessee case are coming at the same time that major efforts to increase Negro registration and voting in the South are reaching fruition. If the increased Negro vote materializes, the new Negro voters may help to maintain Democratic Party majorities in presidential elections, while engaging in split-ticket voting locally on the basis of the characteristics of the candidates locally available. Obviously these are complex processes, but they seem more likely to increase competition between the parties in the end than to reduce it; and in time they will certainly change the nature of the Democratic Party in the South and in Congress.[7]

In other parts of the country, substantial revisions of the political map are also in prospect as a result of the redistricting activity impelled by judicial action. The rapidly growing suburban areas and smaller cities will be the major beneficiaries. The Republican Party will lose representation in some northern rural areas, but may achieve offsetting gains in big city suburbs. More important, however, opportunities for new political leadership may emerge in both parties from the new political units where population growth and economic activity are greatest.

In most of the states, neither party can any longer anticipate a permanent monopoly in the statewide elections for governor, for senator, and for President. In these states, the long-term outlook continues to point toward a rising level of competitive tension. The readjustments resulting from

[6] Philip E. Converse, Angus Campbell, Warren E. Miller, Donald E. Stokes, "Stability and Change in 1960: A Reinstating Election," *American Political Science Review*, LV, June 1961, pp. 269–80; Donald E. Stokes, "1960 and the Problem of Deviating Elections," paper presented at annual meeting of the American Political Science Association, September 1961.

[7] Louis E. Lomax, "The Kennedy's Move in on Dixie," *Harper's*, May 1962, pp. 27–33.

Baker v Carr and from other contemporary changes are likely to enhance the tension rather than to lessen it.

COMPETITION, COHESION, AND CENTRALIZATION

Politicians of both parties are undoubtedly like many businessmen in their preference for monopolistic situations in which benefits accrue with a minimum of risk and uncertainty. Situations of this kind have been so common that the normal thinking of party strategists seem often to run in terms of how to develop or maintain a monopoly, rather than in terms of how to be competitive if it is necessary to compete.

The logic of competitive success is different from the logic of monopolistic success. Monopolistic success usually turns on the exploitation of some built-in strategic advantage. Competitive success requires continuous attention to such factors as effective leadership, adequate campaign resources, and attractive programs and candidates.

We can suppose, therefore, that if the competitive tension within the party system continues to rise during the years ahead, there will be a growing disposition to deal with the institutional problems that affect party leadership, campaign finance, the development of party programs, and the selection of party candidates. Conversely, if the tension sags and there is some kind of return to a less competitive party system, then the prospects for any form of innovative change in dealing with these problems would be poor.

The basic competition in politics today, however, is not between the Republican and Democratic Parties as such, but rather between the Republican Party and the majority wing of the Democratic Party, with a third force of southern Democrats who sometimes vote with one party sometimes with the other, while generally also pursuing some special objectives of their own. The one-party Democrats will continue to be a confusing influence in Congress and elsewhere as long as they survive, but they are not likely to reduce materially the pressures of competition between the major parties in the states outside the South and in the nation as a whole.

If this is true, the theoretical relationships among competition, cohesion, and centralization in the party system may become increasingly important. Cohesion within the competing elements is a normal product of competition in any competitive system. Cohesion need not extend to a complete identity of points of view or objectives. What it does extend to generally is a program of cooperative action on whatever is deemed most essential for success in the competitive struggle. In the party system, those elements of each party that carry the burden of competition with the other party tend to become increasingly cohesive. This applies not only in the case of campaign efforts, but also to the party task of governing when the party is in power—to the extent that party success in the activities of governing is deemed essential for party success in the next electoral competition.[8]

Centralization is in turn a product of the cohesion that is induced by competition. For success in the competition, the executive functions of centralized communication, policy leadership, and strategical decision all take on an obvious importance. Under conditions of competition and cohesion, there is not much objection to a centralization of such executive functions and there may be a strong desire to achieve it. In such cases, centralization is not so much imposed from above, as supported from below. This is especially the case when institutions of majority rule make possible a choice among alternative sources of leadership; in this case, the chosen leadership can be instructed to maintain disci-

8 Relationships between competition and cohesion have been noted by many analysts, but see particularly Robert T. Golembiewski, "A Taxonomic Approach to State Political Party Strength, *Western Political Quarterly*, XI, September 1958, pp. 494–513.

pline and apply such sanctions as may be feasible in dealing with dissident minorities who are found to be trading with the enemy.

There are many areas of American politics in which we might conduct a search for the centralizing tendencies of party competition, examine their nature, and consider their effects. Within the limited scope of this essay, the search will be devoted to areas previously suggested: party leadership, party finance, and some aspects of congressional politics.

LEADERSHIP PROBLEMS:
INS VERSUS OUTS

Within the last century, the President has been gaining stature in his own party. The solid base of the President's power is found in his position as the nation's leader in a dangerous world. Often he must rise above party; but most students hold that it is not safe to rise too far—a capable President must continuously make certain that his partisan troops are still with him.

The evolution of the President's role as party leader has not been traced in adequate detail. Most scholars have given more attention to his role as leader of the legislature. Under modern conditions Congress cannot function effectively unless the President provides the legislative agenda. Even the Republican Party now accepts this; during the Eisenhower administration, many Republicans also came to feel rather strongly that when the President is functioning as legislative leader, he must also act visibly as the leader of his party if the basis is to be laid for partisan success in the congressional elections that are always just around the corner.

The President's connection with the party machinery and party functioning involves a series of problems on which there has been much controversy. It is also an area in which change in the norms of our political culture has come late and probably remains incomplete. Presidents had

been renominated in national party conventions for a century before an incumbent President appeared in person to accept renomination, as Franklin Roosevelt did in 1936. It is generally accepted that the President may name the chairman of his national party committee, but this is not a responsibility of great antiquity. Presidential involvements in campaigns and elections have developed intermittently through a trial-and-error process, with every innovative precedent under attack, but generally with some net increment of presidential influence when the dust had settled.

The President's combined role as party leader and legislative leader took on new importance on at least one occasion, however, with a minimum of fanfare. This was the meeting held at the White House on Monday morning, November 15, 1937; those present included President Roosevelt, Vice President Garner, Speaker Bankhead, Senate Majority Leader Barkley, and House Majority Leader Rayburn. This was not the first time this group had met, but it was the first time that they met with an intention to meet once a week, with a fixed membership constituted on an *ex officio* basis. This was the beginning of the regular weekly congressional leadership meetings at the White House—meetings that have continued through the successive administrations of Presidents Roosevelt, Truman, Eisenhower, and Kennedy. If those present had been formally designated "The Legislative Cabinet," and if the meetings had been initiated by an Act of Congress, they would have attracted immediate attention as a major innovation in American constitutional practice. As it was, even the White House press corps remained unaware for some years that the leadership meetings were different from the many other meetings at the White House that continued to involve members of Congress.

There is still much less than a full realization among political scientists that the American government now contains a collegial body, constituted on a partisan basis at the highest political level, that regularly concerns itself with the forward program of the party in power, with special reference to those program elements involving legislation, appropriations, and congressional action. Political scientists as eminent as Edward S. Corwin and Charles S. Hyneman, apparently unaware of what already existed, continued to advocate the creation of a presidential legislative council in books published long after 1937.[9] The true importance of the leadership meetings was probably first noticed by the Committee on Political Parties in its report entitled *Toward a More Responsible Two-Party System*, published in 1950.[10]

Out-party difficulties in developing a leadership that can compete for public attention have long been obvious, but only under the competitive pressures of recent years has there been any strong impulse to do something about it. Two leading precedents were provided by the Democrats while out of power between 1953 and 1961. One was Adlai Stevenson's demonstration

of the potentialities inherent in the out-party titular leadership under modern conditions; his performance as Party spokesman and chief campaigner was especially noteworthy during the midterm campaign of 1954. The second precedent was the creation of the Democratic Advisory Council as an instrument of collective leadership for the presidential wing of the out-party between 1956 and 1960. Although the Council was boycotted by the congressional leaders, it provided an influential voice for majority elements in the Party. It also regularly brought together most of those who were most concerned over the succession in the Party nomination in 1960. By the end of 1959, all the Party's leading contenders for the presidential nomination of 1960 except Senate Majority Leader Lyndon Johnson had accepted membership on the Council.[11]

Both precedents just mentioned were actively debated in the Republican Party as it went through its leadership crisis on leaving office in 1961. For a brief interval, it appeared that former Vice President Nixon would accept major responsibilities as the Party's new titular leader. Instead, he seems to have abandoned the role, apparently having concluded that he would be committed to a hopeless race in 1964 if he functioned actively in the titular leadership in the meantime.

Discussions of alternative patterns of collective leadership resulted in agreement that the Party's congressional leaders and the national Party chairman would hold weekly meetings (while Congress is in session), after which the leaders make their views public through a television show— the so-called Ev and Charlie show.[12] Later, plans for an "All-Republican Conference" were developed, and six senators and six representatives were designated to draft a

---

[9] Edward S. Corwin, *The President, Office and Powers 1781–1957*, 4th rev. ed. (New York: New York University Press, 1957), pp. 297–305; Charles S. Hyneman, *Bureaucracy in a Democracy* (New York: Harper & Row, 1950), pp. 571–579. Corwin in 1957 was still repeating the proposal of his first edition in 1940; in the 1957 edition, he refers to the leadership meetings of the Eisenhower administration, but the description is less than fully accurate and makes no reference to the prior practice of the Roosevelt and Truman administrations.

[10] David, Goldman, and Bain, *op. cit.*, pp. 67–68. It has since been discovered that the origin and continuity of the meetings can be documented for the initial years from the appointment books in the Roosevelt Library at Hyde Park.

Because of a considerable strain in the relationships between President Roosevelt and Vice President Garner between 1937 and 1940, the meetings began experimentally and with no certainty that they could be continued indefinitely. The problem was resolved in part by the fact that Garner absented himself from Washington for long periods; but when in Washington, he continued to attend as long as he was Vice President. The meetings seem to have been suggested initially by Mr. Rayburn, and were an attempt to improve procedures for consultation after the difficulties engendered by the Supreme Court proposal of 1937.

[11] On the long-term evolution of out-party leadership, see David, Goldman, and Bain, *op. cit.*, chap. 5; paperback ed., chap. 4.

[12] Thruston B. Morton, "Leadership Problems in the Opposition Party," in David *et al.*, chap. 11; see also pp. 327–328, 333–334.

statement of Republican principles, with staff service provided by the Republican National Committee.[13]

In all these efforts, the prize at stake is the opportunity to influence the development of the party image. The symbolism of program intentions can provide clues to whether the party is being merely defensive, or whether it is indeed actively developing alternatives to the programs advocated by the party in power. For much of this, the real payoff is the party's voting record in Congress. This is always likely to be more conservative than the party's next candidate for President might desire. Yet if leadership structures are devised in which the presidential wing of the out-party can be more effective, some influence may be exerted on the party's congressional leaders and on the party's legislative record.

NATIONALIZING TENDENCIES IN CONGRESSIONAL POLITICS

For some years, Professor E. E. Schattschneider has been saying in his various writings that Congress is increasingly involved in politics. He means, of course, an increasing involvement in the important varieties of politics: the politics of national issues, of nationally oriented interest groups, of the national parties, and of national campaigns and elections.

The evidence of increasing congressional involvement in presidential and vice-presidential nominations is especially clear. Senators have been gaining in strength as vice-presidential nominees and as potential presidential nominees; the successful nomination of Senator John F. Kennedy brings this progression to a realization. For about thirty years, congressional leaders have been dominant in both parties most of the time as the presiding officers at the national party conventions. This is a complete reversal of the nineteenth century practice under which convention leadership was almost completely divorced from congressional leadership.[14]

For a century, there has been a slow increase in the proportion of senators who attend the party conventions as delegates; 64 of them did so in 1960.[15] The patterns associated with this long-term tendency are highly revealing. Even in the late nineteenth century, when a state had one senator of each party—a prima facie case of active party competition—*both* senators were usually present at their respective party conventions as delegates. Conversely, in the states represented by two Republican senators, the integration between state and national politics has been so weak that the senators from these states still usually refrain from active participation in the conventions. The one-party Democratic states occupy an intermediate position in this form of political behavior: the senators from these states have usually attended the Democratic national conventions in recent years, presumably to defend sectional interests.

Members of the House of Representatives, less nationally oriented and less capable of securing prestige recognition from their state party organizations, have not served as convention delegates proportionately as often as senators. But even here there has been marked change; the number of members of the House of Representatives who served in convention delegations (as delegates or alternates) is as follows since 1948:[16]

Year	Democrat	Republican
1948	32	20
1952	56	18
1956	80	39
1960	136	32

In view of the long-term data from the conventions, we can suppose that there may

[13] *Congressional Quarterly Weekly Report,* XX, Mar. 2, 1962, p. 361.

[14] David, Goldman, and Bain, *op. cit.,* Table 4.1 and pp. 64–69.

[15] For the historical statistics, see *ibid.,* Table 14.5, p. 345. The 1960 data were provided by Thomas N. Schroth, Executive Editor of Congressional Quarterly Service.

[16] *Ibid.,* Table 14.7, p. 347, and Mr. Schroth.

have been a similar long-term increase in the numbers of senators and representatives who have worked in national party campaigns outside the limits of their own states and districts. The data to test this tendency have never been accumulated, although possibly they could be secured from the archives of party speakers' bureaus or from newspaper files.

Campaigning by the candidates for President and Vice President has clearly become more national in scope, reaching the limits of the 50-state type of campaign in 1960. There is a general impression that the ticket-leaders are involved with the local candidates in more states than formerly as they progress from state to state. This is to be expected as more states become competitive, and the various candidates become more dependent on each other for marginal increments of strength in appealing to the voters.

The changing patterns of midterm campaigning are even more striking and suggest marked change in the relationships of national party leaders to the congressional campaigns. For years, Woodrow Wilson was criticized for even his mild intervention in the 1918 campaign—an intervention that took the form of a brief press statement in which he expressed a hope for congressional majorities of his own party. But as the Roosevelt and Truman years wore on, there seemed to be increasing activity by the national party leaders in the midterm campaigns.

When President Eisenhower faced the issue for the first time, in 1954, his first inclination was one of withdrawal, following the doctrine of those who had criticized Woodrow Wilson. But after Adlai Stevenson had announced his intention to campaign actively from July to November, 1954, pressures from within the Republican Party brought President Eisenhower to a much more active performance than he had previously contemplated; Vice President Nixon was assigned the duty of cam-

paigning in as many of the critical states as possible.

In 1962 President Kennedy kicked off the midterm campaign on January 20 at a $100-a-plate fund-raising dinner in Washington. Six thousand Democrats were present, including most Democratic members of Congress. He said:

> What we are attempting to do tonight is to lay the groundwork for the Congressional campaigns of 1962, and we realize, I think, all the Members of the House and Senate, that history is not with us, that in this century only in 1934, during the periods of the great pre-eminence of the Democratic Party, did the Party in power ever win seats, let alone hold its own. But we believe in 1962 that the Democratic Party, both at home and abroad, is best fitted to lead this country—and therefore we start tonight on the campaigns of 1962.[17]

Later it was indicated that the President would undertake on-the-spot campaigning to assist members of his party in some instances, and that Vice President Lyndon Johnson would be available for active campaigning in at least a dozen states.[18]

The dinner at which President Kennedy spoke was a sign of the new centralization of party fund-raising for congressional cam-

---

[17] From the White House press release as subsequently issued. This was the occasion on which, in a high-spirited moment, the President produced a remarkable parody of portions of his Inaugural address:

> . . . we observe tonight not a celebration of freedom but a victory of party, for we have sworn to pay off the same party debt our forebears ran up nearly a year and three months ago. Our deficit will not be paid off in the next hundred days, nor will it be paid off in the first one thousand days, nor in the life of this administration. Nor, perhaps even in our lifetime on this planet, but let us begin—remembering that generosity is not a sign of weakness and that Ambassadors are always subject to Senate confirmation—for if the Democratic party cannot be helped by the many who are poor, it cannot be saved by the few who are rich. So let us begin.

[18] Jack Bell, "Johnson to Campaign in Dozen Key States," *Washington Post and Times Herald*, March 13, 1962.

paigns. For some years, the Republican National Finance Committee has been in charge of fund-raising for the Party's congressional campaign committees as well as for the National Committee. The Democrats came to this pattern in the spring of 1961 and seem likely to maintain it.

In the entire range of party affairs, centralization may come last and most slowly in the nomination of party candidates for Congress. Even here, however, one of the most respected students of the party system has suggested that "National party leaders in quest of a point of leverage to strengthen their party might well give thought to spending a few hundred thousand dollars a year in drumming up and supporting able House and Senate candidates for seats held by the oppositon."[19] Others have suggested that the Republican National Committee needs paid staff workers in every critical congressional district, presumably to perform functions somewhat similar to those of the British constituency agents who are paid from national party funds.[20] So far, however, the national Party authorities seem mainly to have contented themselves with urging the local Party groups to work actively on candidate recruitment, so the Party may secure the kind of candidates for Congress that will enable it to compete more effectively.

The manner in which Richard Nixon was initially recruited to run for Congress in 1946 by a local group of Republican businessmen is well known. The activities of similar groups locally based but nationally oriented are probably becoming more important in the congressional nominating processes of both parties. Apparently they are a natural result of the club movement spreading in suburban politics.[21] They also

[19] V. O. Key, Jr., *Politics, Parties, and Pressure Groups,* 4th ed. (New York: Thomas Y. Crowell Co., 1958), p. 497.

[20] Roscoe Drummond, "Memo to GOP," *Washington Post and Times Herald,* July 3, 1961.

[21] Stephen A. Mitchell, *Elm Street Politics* (New York: Oceana Publications, Inc., 1959).

seem to be a natural result of the increasingly effective interventions of organized labor and of organized business in their position efforts to compete with each other.

FROM THE TRADITIONAL TO THE RATIONAL

In view of the data so far reviewed, the party system of this country may well be moving in some greater degree than formerly from the traditional to the rational. This is a process going on throughout the world in the underdeveloped countries. Most countries seem to be politically underdeveloped, and there are times when it is possible to suspect that even the United States belongs in this category.

In a rational world, political philosophers might suppose that political life would be primarily concerned with a politics of issues. That, at least, was the supposition of the Committee on Political Parties in its report of 1950, *Toward a More Responsible Two-Party System.* In the years since that report was published, the system seems to have moved at least slightly in the direction favored by the Committee; and the prospects for a further movement in that direction now seem moderately favorable. If this is indeed the case, the workings of the competitive impulse in politics can be given most of the credit. Minority major parties that seriously seek to become competitive within the two-party system have found it expedient in state after state to develop a strong interest in issues—an interest that is practical and strategic, rather than doctrinaire, but one that nonetheless assist in the education of voter opinion, and that may eventually produce a marked increase in voter turnout—especially in those states where turnout has traditionally been low.

It has been assumed much too often in the one-party states and localities that it is necessary to join the dominant party in order to be politically effective. This may have been true thirty or forty years ago, but it does not seem to be true any longer. The situation has changed to the point where many of the greatest political opportunities of the future are probably now available in minority party situations where the smaller of the two major parties is still greatly outnumbered.[22] The exploitation of these opportunities will require an eye for issues and a willingness to open them up for public debate. The process can be assisted by help from the central party headquarters when the central staffs are sufficiently vigorous and alert, but often it has proceeded even more fully on the strength of local impulses. The game of competitive politics can be initiated at any level, and it is a game in which any number can play. Fortunately it is a game in which all who participate can obtain some reward, and in which it is to the nation's interest for many to be engaged.

59.   The Condition of Our National Political Parties

Stephen K. Bailey

Stephen Bailey, Dean of the Maxwell School, Syracuse University, proposes modest changes in the national party system. He points out that the changes were—and are—possible as a result of "great secular shifts in our social and economic life which are undermining traditional citadels of political power." His nine political reforms are (1) mass-based, long-range financing; (2) expanding two-party competition in all

[22] On the special problems of the Republican party in northern cities where the party organization is moribund or worse, see Robert L. Johnson, "We've Got to Wake Up in the Big Cities," *U.S. News & World Report,* April 23, 1962, pp. 68–70.

Congressional districts and states; (3) creation of advisory councils and staffs for national committees; (4) provision of headquarters and social facilities for national committees in Washington; (5) four-year terms for the House, eight-year terms for the Senate and presidency; (6) policy committees in Congress and frequent caucuses and joint hearings; (7) a new formula by which to compute seniority; (8) repeal of the 22d amendment; and (9) machinery for keeping a roster of people for executive posts in government.

* * *

THE PARTIES AND RESPONSIBLE POWER

The American government today suffers from three weaknesses:

1. its difficulty in generating sustained political power;
2. its difficulty in developing a flow of imaginative, informed, consistent, and power-related responses to pressing national and world issues;
3. its difficulty in making policy truly accountable to a national popular majority.

These are serious defects, not only because they interfere with wise and coherent governing in these dangerous days, but because they undermine the faith of the citizen in the reality or even the possibility of responsible representative government.

The temptation to blame all this on the President, the 22d Amendment, the split election of 1956, or the present Democratic majorities in Congress is easy—and perhaps partly justified. But the defects are not new. Occasionally, in the past, they have been masked by brilliant presidential leadership in times of crisis or by the virtuosity

From Stephen K. Bailey, *The Condition of Our National Political Parties* (Santa Barbara: The Fund for the Republic, 1959), by permission of the Center for the Study of Democratic Institutions.

of congressional leaders in times of presidential ineptitude. But the underlying defects have not disappeared. Nor, in spite of the hopes of a few recent writers, are they going to be overcome by countervailing pressure groups or by the expertness, decency, and continuity in office of civilian and military career officials, important as these factors are in the conduct of free and effective government.

V. O. Key sounds not a hopeful but an ominous note when he writes: "Representative bodies, the institutional embodiment of democratic ideology, have by the compelling force of events lost both power and prestige. Their role in the initiation of public policy has been diminished by losses to pressure groups and administrative agencies; their authority to decide many issues has, of necessity, been delegated to the administrative services. They have been driven towards a role of futile and uninformed criticism, at its worst motivated either by partisan or picayune considerations."

Even if we assume that the work of modern government is so technical and complex that enormous discretion must be lodged in the hands of experts, their capacity to act steadily in the public interest depends upon the effectiveness of the very institutions whose influence is threatened by the expert mind. This dilemma will continue until we recognize that our representative institutions invite disuse and denigration because their structure is inadequate to perform the functions required of them. It is increasingly obvious that there are innovative, integrative, and perhaps sacrificial tasks ahead for which our government is not institutionally equipped.

IS LEADERSHIP THE BASIC ISSUE?

To say that we need a new kind of political leadership may be true, but it begs the question. Where and how does political leadership arise in the United States? Who selects presidential and congressional candidates? How can the process of selection be improved? How can leadership be sustained? How can first-class political executives be found to run our great public departments? Why is their present tenure so ephemeral? By what means can presidential and congressional purposes be brought into a working relationship? And why cannot leadership be held more fully accountable to the desires of popular majorities?

All of these questions are related to the structural handicaps under which the American government now operates. At first glance, the problem seems to be constitutional—and in part it is. But the only two structural faults of the Constitution which really get in the way of responsible power in the national government are the 22d Amendment, which limits the President to two terms, and the provisions for staggered elections. The only two constitutional reforms that this paper will suggest are the repeal of the 22d Amendment and changes in the term of Members of the House from two to four years and of United States Senators from six to eight years (half the Senate coming up every four years at the same time as the presidential elections). The real problem is *political*. If our *political* institutions can be modernized by certain changes in statutory law and in political party rules, the old problems associated with separation of powers, checks and balances, and federalism would, it seems probable, largely disappear.

The root of the weakness is that while the two national parties for years have genuinely competed for the Presidency they have not made a similar effort in the election of United States Senators and Members of the House of Representatives. Nor have they been of sufficient help to the President and the Congress in providing candidates of high quality for the grand patronage of departmental and agency direction. So long as we lack strong national parties operating as catalysts in the Congress, the executive branch, and the national government as a whole, and between the national government and state and local governments, power will continue to be dangerously diffused or, perhaps what is worse, will whip-saw between diffusion and presidential dictatorship.

THE NATURAL PARTY DISTINCTIONS

Contrary to the view of many writers, the parties do not need to be strongly ideological or even strongly programmatic—that is, beholden to comprehensive and distinct sets of policies—in order to accomplish the kind of re-alignment of the party system that would stabilize the national power and help to make it responsible. There are vast areas of overlap in the rather vague programmatic shadows that our two great parties cast over the nation—and this is as it should be if consensus is to continue in the making of public policy and in the administration of foreign policy.

But the centers of gravity of the two parties are quite distinct. The Democratic party basically is a party of innovation, with a "pro-government" bias. The Republican party is an essentially "consolidating" party with a limited-government bias. The distinction has become blurred in the last two generations, largely because of the extreme economic and social conservatism of one-party areas in the South—a conservatism which has been reflected in the Congress through its seniority rules and some other carefully contrived rules and myths. But now, the peculiar condition which has smudged party images for so long is on its way out. The economic base of the solid South has shifted monumentally in the past fifteen years; one-party areas across the land are on the wane; the northern migration of the Negro is having vast political consequences.

Political reform does not include making the parties any more ideological than they are now. It does include making them competitive across the nation, allowing them to appeal to the natural ideological divisions within the population and within us as individuals. The stumbling block in this task is that neither party has a sufficiently unified structure to enable it to dramatize its program around its ideology; neither has the power, even if it had the right structure, to carry out the program; neither has sufficiently clear and unambiguous lines of political accountability running to the voters.

THE RESULTS OF PARTY DIFFUSION

The structural limitations of the parties have grave consequences. First, they virtually insure a government by fits-and-starts. Some historians claim that the United States was wise in having rejected the League of Nations; but few would claim that the *process* by which the League was rejected was a rational way of arriving at a major foreign policy decision. In more recent times presidential requests for an adequate United States Information Agency budget have been listened to one year and ignored the next by the House Appropriations Committee. As a result, cultural officers abroad have had to spend much of their time hiring and firing—inflating and deflating programs like an accordion. This has made us look ridiculous as a nation, and has also made it extremely difficult for a coherent information program to develop as a vital element in our foreign policy. The same has been true of foreign economic aid.

Spasms in domestic policy have been equally obvious and equally unsettling. The executive department and the Congress have been unable to agree on any coordinated methods of applying the kind of devices needed to stabilize the economy and promote the goals of the Employment Act of 1946. Similar fits and starts have been noticeable in defense policy, atomic energy policy, welfare policy, and conservation policy. They have been quite as apparent when the Presidency and both Houses of Congress have been in one party as when the control of the government has been divided.

The second consequence of the structural limitations of the parties has been the lack of rationality and consistency in the substance of much public policy. In Paul Appleby's phrase, in this day and age someone or something has to "make a mesh of things." In a world in which, for example, the indiscriminate dumping of rice on the world market in order to ease a temporary glut in Louisiana could cost us the friendship of Burma, there are huge dangers in having unlinked centers of power making their own policy for the nation. And yet, parochial groups in the Congress (often in league with sections of the executive branch and with outside pressure groups) still carry an inordinate amount of power.

The third consequence of the absence of coherent party machinery truly responsive to popular majorities is that congressional compromise tends to fall with considerable regularity on the side of minority rather than majority interests. Committee chairmen from "safe," and often sparsely populated, one-party states and districts; the minority-weighted bipartisan rules committee; and the myths, rules, and influence structure which enable congressional leaders to ignore demands for greater majority representation in policy decisions—all these combine to inflate the power of minority interests at the expense of the national popular majority. The pages of the *Congressional Record* or the *Congressional Quarterly Almanac* in any year since the war offer substantiating evidence. The bills and policies introduced or supported by Senators and Congressmen from the areas of greatest popular concentration in America have almost without exception been substantially watered down according to the predilections and petitions of powerful minority interests in and out of the Congress.

This is government by tollgate. It leads directly to consequence four: the increasing danger of public cynicism and apathy toward the Congress, partly because its power is too diffuse or too subtle to comprehend; partly because when the power *is* clearly identifiable it seems to work more consistently for minorities than for the majority.

The last and by no means the least important consequence stemming from the absence of a unified party structure is that desperately needed criticism of both domestic and foreign policy is dissipated and discouraged. There is no effective vehicle for responsible opposition criticism of programs; there is no machinery for anticipating the implications of social changes and their effects on policy. With the help of a huge and in part brilliant staff, Members of Congress may fill the air and the *Congressional Record* with daring solutions to our dilemmas. But without some sort of party sanction, these ideas are worth little more than an inch or two in *The New York Times*.

In sum, the absence of effective party machinery in each House, and in the government generally, means that policy is frequently developed by an infinitely intricate system of barter and legerdemain.

Some defenders of America's traditional disorder have discounted the dangers to policy-making of these intermittencies and irresponsibilities. They argue that our survival suggests that presidential leadership and a congressional desire to cooperate during periods of crisis can save us in the future as they have in the past; that the thermidor between crises allows the divergences in our society to have their day without being subject to the tyranny of a transient numerical majority; and that the accepted American tradition of government by extraordinary or concurrent majorities has not stopped innovation or social criticism, it has only slowed change, and in the process has insured a healthy unity behind public policy.

In relation to the past, these may be strong arguments. But are they addressed to a world of big bureaucracies, sustained cold wars, and chronic international and domestic crises? Are there any longer identifiable periods between crises? As long as the frontier was open and the spirit of laissez faire encouraged political parties to be barriers against government action, anarchy in program and uncontrolled shifts in power within the national government were of little consequence. For many years the parties were anti-governmental vehicles, so to speak, minimizing public policy and fencing off large sections of the population and of the domain for private exploitation and private dreams. But we are now in a very different world. As E. E. Schatt-schneider has pointed out:

"The revolution in communications, the dissolution of nationality blocs, the impact of the labor movement, urbanization, the revolution in public policy, the expansion of the practising electorate in recent years, and the new world position of the United States are only a few of the influences likely to give impetus to political reorganization in the present generation. It is obvious that the *purposes* of political organization are not what they once were. There was a time when it might have been said that the purpose of the party system, or large parts of it, was *obstruction*. In an era of perpetual crisis, political organization is reasonably certain to reflect the anxieties that now dominate all public life."

THE PROPHETS

For three quarters of a century America has heard warnings from a variety of distinguished political prophets about its governmental weaknesses. Whether their solution has been constitutional revision or political revision, they have all agreed about the limitations of our governing instruments. Starting with Woodrow Wilson, Henry Jones Ford, and A. Lawrence Lowell, and continuing through William MacDonald, William Y. Elliott, E. E. Schatt-schneider, Henry Hazlitt, Thomas K. Finletter, James M. Burns, and Paul T. David, criticism has been directed at a single issue: the difficulties of achieving sustained and responsible political power adequate to contemporary necessities.

All seem to accept one proposition: such power can be achieved through a greater synthesis of presidential and congressional purposes. Some say the synthesis is impossible without broad constitutional revisions along the lines of the British parliamentary system, including provision for the executive dissolution of the legislature in case of loggerheads and provision for concurrent terms for President and Congress. Others believe that the catalytic effect of a reformed party system, together with certain changes in congressional organization and procedure, will make drastic constitutional reform as unnecessary as they believe it to be improbable.

Two statements—one from Woodrow Wilson and one from Thomas K. Finletter —sum up seventy-five years of prophetic writing on this subject. In the 1880's, Wilson wrote:

The Constitution is not honored by blind worship. The more open-eyed we become, as a nation, to its defects, and the prompter we grow in applying with the unhesitating courage of conviction all thoroughly-tested or well-considered expedients necessary to make self-government among us a straightforward thing of simple method, single, unstinted power, and clear responsibility, the nearer will we approach to the sound sense and practical genius of the great and honorable statesmen of 1787.

Two generations later, Thomas Finletter wrote:

The question thus is whether means, that is the procedures of our government, are adequate in relation to its objectives, or its ends. The usual pattern has been long periods of negative government interlarded with short periods of strong action . . . The irregular flow of power endangers representative government in the United States . . . You cannot have a government capable of handling the most difficult problems that peacetime democracy has ever faced with the two main parts of it at each other's throats . . . A government of fits and starts is no longer good enough for our purposes.

In 1950, a Committee on Political Parties of the American Political Science Association brought out a report which was in the direct line of this earlier prophetic writing. Called "Towards a More Responsible Two-Party System," the APSA report discounted the possibility of drastic constitutional change, but put forward a series of suggestions for political reform designed to create a party system capable of enabling the national government to cope effectively and responsibly with the great national and international issues of the twentieth century.

Nearly a decade has elapsed since the publication of the Committee's report. Nothing has happened in that time to suggest that the basic issues raised have dwindled in significance. The report itself has been subject to academic debate. Some of its recommendations have been misunderstood or misinterpreted by its critics; other recommendations and assumptions have been justly criticized.

What is increasingly apparent is that the authors of the report were closer than its critics to the spirit and necessities of the age. And inexorable forces, only dimly observable when the report was being written, are now clearly at work preparing the soil for a crop of politics far different from what we have known in the past century.

It is time for a stringent look at the national politics we have had, the kind of national politics we want, and the reasons for believing that our traditional party system, like a vast glacier, may now have reached the edge of the sea.

THE PARTIES TODAY: A MYSTIC MAZE

The closer ones gets to our two great national parties, the more difficult it is to find them. If you contend that they exist in their quadrennial national conventions, you must be prepared to answer where they are between conventions. If you identify them with the national committee offices in Washington, or one of them with the White House, you will hear immediate disclaimers from the party leaders on Capitol Hill. If a temporary marriage should be negotiated between the party in Congress and the party's executive wing, the great cellular blocks of the party at the state and local levels might well ask embarrassing questions about the true locus of party power.

Perhaps the shortest route through the maze of national party structure begins with the presidential nominating conventions. These are the formal governing bodies of the parties, the selectors of national candidates and issues for the quadrennial elections. They are composed of delegates chosen in a variety of ways and responsible to a wide variety of power groups within the states and beyond the states; Governors, machine leaders, Senators, Members of Congress, pressure groups, individual presidential candidates and their followers, the incumbent President, and so on.

But national conventions generally last less than a week. In order to provide continuity and necessary machinery in the long years between conventions, both parties elect national committees to serve for four years from the adjournment of the conventions. Actually, each state delegation proposes the two national committeemen (one is a woman) who are "elected" by the convention.

The long history of the parties shows that it would be a mistake to suggest that the national committees have been at the power apex of their parties. "Although the party organization can be regarded as . . . capped by the national committee, it may be more accurately described as a system of layers of organization. Each successive layer —county or city, state, national—has an independent concern about elections in its geographical jurisdiction. Yet each higher level of organization, to accomplish its ends, must obtain the collaboration of the lower layer or layers of organization. That collaboration comes about, to the extent that it does come about, through a sense of common cause rather than the exercise of command."

But even this does not tell the whole story. In the case of election campaigns for the Senate and the House, for example, there is no one layer of the party organization clearly responsible for these campaigns. The groups that come closest are the respective party campaign committees in each House, but their power lies merely in the intermittent services and limited financial help they are able to offer; there is no hierarchical power or consistent influence here.

The formal organization of the parties can be described, if at all, then, as a series of pyramids with a common base in the shifting sands of active party membership, and generally with no clear locus of power in or out of the government.

As Professor Key has pointed out, there are a number of reasons why the party system has had more *pluribus* than *unum*: "Both unity and disunity within the national organization have their roots in the diverse social, economic, and political interests in the party following. Yet another foundation of deconcentration of party leadership is the federal form of government. State and local party organizations are built up around the patronage of state and local government; and these organiza-

tions, particularly in cities and states dominated by one party, have a continuous life regardless of whether the party is in or out of power nationally. State and local patronage makes the local machine financially independent of the national headquarters and contributes to a spirit of independence. Federalism in our formal governmental machinery includes a national element independent of the states, but in our party organization the independent national element is missing. Party structure is more confederative than federal in nature. The state and local machines, built on state patronage, are allied with or paralleled by machines built around the patronage controlled by Senators and Representatives; and owing to the method of dispensation of this patronage, the resultant machines are almost as independent of central control as are the purely local organizations. Federalism in government tends to encourage confederation in the party's government."

This state of affairs might excite no special interest if it were not that confederation in the government of the parties has had a substantial effect on the conduct of the federal government. This effect can best be highlighted, perhaps, by trying to answer a deceptively simple question: On matters of national policy, what individual or group speaks with authority for each of the national parties?

Who speaks for the party?

Obviously, this question cannot be handled without first asking such prior questions as "where" and "when." When we speak of the national party, are we speaking of the in-party? The out-party?[1] The party in the Senate? The party in the House? The

[1] "In-party" will be used to refer to the party which controls the Presidency regardless of whether it controls the Congress or either House thereof. "Out-party" is used throughout to refer to the party that does not control the White House, whether or not it controls either House or both Houses of Congress.

party as represented by its national committee? The party in quadrennial convention? All of these? Only some of these? And at what point in time?

Let us start with a presidential election year and a national convention. "Conventions," as Richard Rovere has written, ". . . are exercises in definition." The choice for the Presidency personifies the majority decision of the national convention, and in this respect the winning nominee speaks with special authority as a symbol of what the party stands for at that moment. The image may be particularly clear when an incumbent is renominated, since he usually has had a commanding influence over the drafting of the party platform. In any case, what the candidate decides to emphasize from (or outside of) the platform creates a more powerful image of party policy than the platform itself. From the moment of nomination until election, the presidential candidate is usually the undisputed voice of the party. This does not mean that the voice will necessarily be clear, but no other is likely to be clearer.

There is a circumstance, however, in which even this last generalization needs qualification. Special problems arise when an incumbent President and a new presidential nominee are of the same party. In 1952, for example, with Adlai Stevenson as the Democratic nominee but with Harry S. Truman still in the White House, a series of delicate issues developed over campaign strategy, organization, and policy. President Truman wanted Stevenson to retain Frank McKinney as chairman of the Democratic National Committee. Stevenson, however, exercised his influence to see to it that the Committee selected Stephen Mitchell. Once appointed, Mitchell set up office, as expected, in the Democratic National Committee headquarters in Washington. But Stevenson was still Governor of Illinois. His personal campaign had to be run from Springfield, Illinois. The question immediately arose, was Wilson Wyatt, as Stevenson's personal campaign manager, to give orders to Stephen Mitchell, the chairman of the National Committee? Chaos could have resulted if the answer to this had been no. Then, because of deteriorating relations between Springfield and the White House, Stephen Mitchell took pains to stress that President Truman was still the head of the party, that the Springfield headquarters was to be considered the Springfield office of the Democratic National Committee, and that one of the Committee's channels of authority would still run to the White House.

This resolution of a complex issue was verbal and political, but hardly organizational—and the National Committee found itself the center of a tug of war between the White House and Springfield. It was not until after the election that President Truman called Adlai Stevenson "the head of the nation's Democrats."

The President as party spokesman

Apart from the kind of conventions and campaigns that may create unusual ambiguities of the sort just mentioned, the recognized spokesman for a national party controlling the Presidency (the in-party) is the President himself. Not only does the magnificent singularity of the office give the incumbent an unparalleled vehicle for the construction of party programs and philosophy; he is also the accepted party leader.

"The President," as Clinton Rossiter has written, "dictates the selection of the national chairman and other top party officials, reminds his partisans in Congress that their legislative record must be bright if victory is to crown their joint efforts, delivers 'fight talks' to the endless procession of professionals who call upon him, and, through the careful distribution of the loaves and fishes of federal patronage, keeps the party a going concern. The loaves and fishes are not so plentiful as they were in the days of Jackson and Lincoln, but he is still a wholesale distributor of 'jobs for the boys.' "

The extent to which a President can create the image of a reasonably united party, depends, of course, on his capacity to make his own policy pronouncements dominant in the party. This is not always automatic, especially if the President is successfully blocked by powerful leaders of his own party in the Congress or is running out the last two years of his last term. But, even then, the power of his voice generally reduces the voices of self- or group-appointed party spokesmen to a subordinate level.

The problem of the "out-party"

If the in-party has problems in creating a clear party image, the task is many times more difficult for the out-party. No real answer has yet been found to the question of who speaks for the party when it does not control the White House, or when no presidential campaign is in progress. Over the years, some of the major contenders for the job of out-party spokesman have been congressional leaders, national committee chairmen, national committee executive committees, ex-Presidents, defeated presidential candidates, *ad hoc* groups established by the national committees, congressional policy committees, congressional campaign committees, and, most recently, a permanent advisory council to a national committee.

The contention that the leaders of the out-party in Congress have the responsibility and the right to speak for their party has been staunchly defended by those leaders. But, in the years since World War II, intramural struggles between national committee chairmen and spokesmen on the one hand, and congressional leaders and staff on the other, have been staples in out-party politics, regardless of which party was "out." And even when the congressional leaders have reluctantly shared with national committees the job of constructing

party policies for campaign purposes, there has been a tendency to insist, as Senate Republican leaders did in 1950, that the products should be limited to "a restatement of the aims and purposes of the Republican members of Congress." As *The New York Times* commented on this occasion, Republican Senate leaders "do not feel that the National Committee properly is a policy-making body, and, in off-year non-presidential elections, the party members in Congress have to make their own issues without outside interference."

Obvious problems arise in having the congressional leaders speak for the out-party. Congress itself is bifurcated, and its power, as we have said, tends to gravitate into the hands of men who are not necessarily responsive to the party majorities. On occasion, the minority or majority leader in the Senate, or the Speaker or minority leader of the House, may claim to speak for his own party. But whether anybody inside or outside the Congress believes that the voice of the party has been heard in the land depends either upon coincidence with already accepted party formulations or upon the personal prestige and political virtuosity of these congressional spokesmen. Congress is not over being what Woodrow Wilson once called a "disintegrate ministry"; but even when the ministry is not disintegrate, it is rarely representative of either party's national popular majority. Even party leaders in the Congress chosen in caucuses of their own party are captives, willing or unwilling, of the feudal barons who immediately surround them. There are no party policy or steering committees in the House worthy of the name, and those in the Senate lack power and representativeness.

The result is that there are a large number of Democratic and Republican party members who may have no effective voice in the Congress (to say nothing of the White House) but who still feel that they should have a hand in determining their party's national policies. The national committee tends to represent the interests of members of the out-party who feel un- or under-represented in the Congress. In addition, it may be said that the out-party's national committee is the official representative of the party's *executive wing*.

The internal squabbles in both parties frequently look like constitutional fireworks—sparks set off by "separation of powers" and "checks and balances." But without further explanation, these principles are shallow and misleading. The real issue is that the government, in a generation of prolific services and equally prolific regulation, has become a vast arena in which group interests and personalities struggle for power without sufficient reference to questions of the long-range public interest. These groups and personalities use the pressure points and divergent party roles and constituencies of the President, the bureaucracy, the national committees, and the two Houses of Congress as instruments of access and finagle. This produces a politics of "boodle" and accommodation, but not a politics of responsible power and clear national purpose.

The Democratic Advisory Council

The absence of any fully accepted out-party national spokesman has led each party sporadically over the years to try to fill the vacuum. More than a generation ago, the Republicans established an Advisory Committee on Policies and Platform to help focus ideas and power prior to the 1920 convention. The Committee performed its function and died. Similar groups have been formed from time to time.

Perhaps the most noteworthy out-party voice in recent years has been the Democratic Advisory Council of the Democratic National Committee. Established by a resolution of the Executive Committee of the Democratic National Committee on November 27, 1956, the Council exists to provide "a collective voice for the Democratic

Party, representing on a year-round basis the millions of Democrats who may or may not be represented in either House of the Congress." The official congressional leaders of the party have refused membership on the Council, but many of the party's national figures (e.g., Adlai Stevenson, Harry Truman, Herbert Lehman, Senator Hubert Humphrey, Governor G. Mennen Williams) belong, as do the members of the Executive Committee of the Democratic National Committee. The Council is helped in its deliberations by advisory committees of distinguished party intellectuals on such matters as foreign policy, domestic economic policy, labor policy, urban problems, science and technology, and party organization.

With their help, the Council has issued a series of statements on major issues facing the nation and the Congress. These pronouncements have not been accepted as party doctrine by the Democratic leaders in the Congress, but they have hardly been in a position to ignore them, if for no other reason than that each statement has had front-page treatment and editorial comment from leading newspapers.

The Democratic Advisory Council is a significant development, to which we shall return. At the moment, it is sufficient to note that although it has given the out-party a firmer voice and a clearer public philosophy than was available before, it has no effective power base in the party, it is not the only voice and image the out-party has, and the party portrait it paints can easily be distorted or obscured by the record of the party in the Congress.

Party finance and party coherence

The problem of the out-party in developing a recognizable philosophy and coherent political program is further complicated by the disorganized state of its finances. Actually, the in-party is also haunted by the same spectre. Money-raising for national and congressional campaigns is such a jungle, and so choked with the vines of subterfuge to get around the Hatch Act and other unrealistic laws, that efforts to develop coherent national party organizations are seriously impeded.

It is an axiom of congressional campaigning, for example, that little direct financial help can be expected either from Washington (campaign committees on Capitol Hill or the national committees) or from state committees. There are, of course, exceptions but these are sufficiently rare to prove the rule. Since the party as party (no matter how defined) has not been a sure source of financial help to the man campaigning for a seat in the Senate or House, what obligation does he owe to it, or to programs endorsed by it?

And there is a further complication. Some support for congressional candidates may come in the form of what Senator Benton used to call "emotional money"—money given by friends and admirers, with no strings attached. But much of it comes from constituent interests, or powerful national interests, expecting, if not favors, at least sympathetic understanding and ready access. It makes little difference if the President or an advisory council to a national committee comes out with a strong plea for more liberal foreign economic policies in the interests of national security and world economic development so long as powerfully placed Representatives or Senators are beholden financially to narrow anti-foreign aid and trade interests in their constituencies.

Attempts by the national committees to raise money for "the party" have gone largely into the staggering costs of presidential campaigns, past or present. And even when, as in the case of the Republican National Finance Committee, a consolidated drive has been carried out for the benefit of the campaign committees of Congress as well as for the national committee, no attempt has been made to develop any national party criteria for allocating the funds. Actually, none of the four congressional campaign committees purports to take any interest whatsoever in a congressional candidate's policy stand or his identification with a party majority. They are interested in electing "Republicans" period, or "Democrats" period.

It is true that both national committees have given increasingly large campaign contributions to congressional candidates in the form of services and advice. But these services have frequently caused frictions and jealousies between the national committees and the campaign committees of the Congress. As one careful student of the "Hill" campaign committees has noted, "In a large measure, the continued existence and importance of the senatorial and congressional campaign committees symbolize the desire of congressional leaders to protect their interests when they believe these interests to be counter to the ambitions of the national party organization." The linear mile that separates Capitol Hill from the White House also separates the campaign committees of Congress from the national committees of the two parties.

It is probable that the first national committee to develop a mass financial base sufficient to allow a spillover from presidential to legislative campaigns will have made the most important political break-through of the century. But this is still in the future, and will involve legal revision as well as monetary success.

These, then, are our national parties: unified for presidential contests, otherwise divided in power and lacking in definition; sporadically financed through various channels, subterfuges, and individual candidacies; peculiarly confused as out-parties; weak vehicles for executive-legislative co-operation as in-parties. They have performed valued services of reconciliation and compromise in our history—services which should not be underestimated. But the problem today is how to transcend these services in order to provide the government with sustained and responsible national power. How should our national party system be modified in order to make the parties effective instruments of our national purposes and needs?

NINE POLITICAL REFORMS

One reason why it is safe to suggest that the national party system must be strengthened in order to bring sustained power in our government is that the safe-guards of the Constitution will continue to discourage any force that becomes so unified as to threaten our freedom. The American people hold firm to the sanctity of the Constitution. It is inconceivable that they would countenance a wholesale revision of the Constitution in the foreseeable future. No model of a new or improved party system that rests on substantial constitutional change is realistic.

In suggesting new directions for our national party system, therefore, the British parliamentary model is ruled out. But it is not ruled out simply because its wholesale adoption here is unthinkable. It is ruled out because it has shortcomings which do not warrant emulation. The relative independence of the legislature in the American system of government is, within limits, a powerful asset. At its best, it assures continuing social criticism and review of the bureaucracy without which big government might easily become lethargic and unresponsive or officious and dangerous.

What we are after is a national two-party system that will continue to have room for diversity and compromise but will nevertheless bring about more coherent and responsible programming by the executive and legislative branches and more coherent and responsible criticism of policy and administration. We are after a system that will make parties compete vigorously to find the right answers; that will organize political power at the national level so that it is adequate to carry out those answers;

and that will make this power ultimately accountable to popular majorities.

This neither presumes nor suggests ideological or highly disciplined parties, although it does presume differences in the ideological propensities of each party and also presumes that party members who vote consistently against their own party's majority will not be favored with positions of party power inside or outside the Congress.

Various changes in state primary laws, in methods of choosing national convention delegates and national committee members, and in grass-roots political organization could have a profound influence on national party behavior. But, in my opinion, changes of this sort will come about rapidly only if prior attention is given to the following political reforms (some of which are already under way):

One. To create mass-based, long-range, and (in part) tax-supported national party financing—not only to underwrite and extend present functions but to increase national committee services and financial aid to congressional campaign committees and to individual candidates running in primary as well as general elections;

Two. To expand two-party competition into all congressional districts and states;

Three. To create, by formal action of the two national conventions, permanent advisory councils and staffs to both national committees;

Four. To provide social and office facilities for each national party along the Mall, between the White House and Capitol Hill, to serve as symbolic and practical links between the executive and legislative branches of government, as well as between the party and its membership across the country;

Five. To provide, by constitutional amendment, for the simultaneous election every four years of the President, the House of Representatives, and half the members of the United States Senate—all Senators to serve for eight years;

Six. To establish or strengthen party policy committees in the House and Senate to guide congressional business; hold reasonably frequent party caucuses; nominate members for committee assignments, who would then be elected in the caucuses; and receive, hold joint hearings, and report on all general presidential messages;

Seven. To find a mathematical formula for computing congressional seniority which will give added weight to those legislators who come from competitive two-party districts and states;

Eight. To repeal the 22nd Amendment;

Nine. To develop machinery for keeping an active roster of talented people for the important executive posts in the national government.

1. Broadly-based financing

Nothing comes closer to the heart of party reform than financial reorganization. As already noted, candidates for Congress, incumbent or new, receive little or no financial aid either from their national committees or from their campaign committees on Capitol Hill. If the normal concerns of a Congressman with his constituency are reenforced by heavy campaign contributions from local interests, and if there are no direct countervailing pressures or inducements from the national party, it should not be surprising that the Congressman fails to give due weight to the national interest. On the other hand, if the national party were able to help finance even a small proportion of a Congressman's campaign, and thus reduce his dependency on local money, he might feel freer to weigh short-term local against long-term national interests or, more accurately, to weigh the special interests against the common interests within his own constituency.

Important as it is to continue the Advertising Council-American Heritage Foundation campaign for mass financial support of our major parties, the experience of the 1958 campaign indicates that the state and local party organizations benefited from the national advertising far more than the national committees. The money that was collected locally rarely found its way to Washington.

The Democratic National Committee, however, has had significant success with direct-mail solicitation and with the selling of party membership cards and a monthly magazine, the *Democratic Digest*. The success of this direct-mail solicitation suggests that at least for sustaining operations the parties should depend heavily upon small gifts solicited by mail or by nationally sponsored party dinners.

To insure an increasingly responsible role for the national committees over national party finances, the Hatch Act provisions dealing with spending limitations for national campaigns should be repealed or realistically adjusted to meet the realities of political life. Furthermore, federal income-tax credits or exemptions should be allowed for individual contributions to the *national* organizations or candidates up to a certain amount.

The postage franking privilege and a block of network television time, radio time, and newspaper advertising space should be given to each national committee before each national election, to be financed by congressional appropriations and rigidly audited by the General Accounting Office.

2. Two-party competition

One of the most compelling reasons for the national committees to have more money is that greater riches may encourage more vigorous competition between the parties in all states and congressional districts in the country. Everything we know about one-party areas indicates that they tend to reflect minority interests and, through unopposed re-elections, produce Members of Congress who are pushed purely by seniority into positions of high and unrepresentative power.

"The variations in the degree to which the parties are competitive within their respective states condition in a major way the policy inclinations of Senators," V. O. Key writes. "Those from one-party states may be untouched by the great tides of national politics. On the other hand, Senators from close states may live under the strongest compulsion to collaborate among themselves in the promotion of the cause of their party nationally."

The more quickly the national party organizations succeed in stimulating opposition in districts and states where there is none, or in narrowing the margin of the dominant party's victory, the better chance there is of relating the Congress more closely to the interests of the national majority. The interests of a majority in one part of the nation are now more and more similar to the interests of majorities in all other parts of the nation, and the stimulation of political competition in all sections cannot help increasing the power of the national majority in the government as a whole. Furthermore, real party rivalries should tend to increase informed social criticism and encourage greater citizen interest and participation, including financial participation.

The process can be speeded if the national committees are enabled to work with the congressional campaign committees on the Hill in supplementing the services of the state and local organizations to congressional campaigns and in providing regional representatives to help unify the several campaigns in a multi-state region like New England or the Middle West. There are extremely delicate problems involved in having representatives of the national committees insinuate themselves in this way into matters traditionally considered to be the prerogatives of the local organizations. But local party leaders are often unequipped to recruit and develop the type of people needed to understand and execute national programs. The help

of national party representatives in this area could be of enormous long-range significance. And if the state committees can be encouraged to establish full-time party staffs in their state capitals, the job of the national committees and their regional representatives would be correspondingly easier.

As the national committees become stronger financially and organizationally, their prestige will also grow to the point where they could have a much more positive influence on the choice of congressional nominees. Until that time, their interests, and those of the country, would seem to be best served by a thoroughgoing drive to strengthen two-party competition in all parts of the country. It is obvious that the most intractable one-party areas are in the South. The voting rights of Negroes and low-income whites should increase as a result of the Civil Rights Bill of 1957. But the solution to the most obvious indignities undergone by the disenfranchised is to speed the extension of two-party competition. This can be done not only by active organizing on the part of the Republican Party but by extending the influence of the *national* Democratic Party in registration and voting drives below the Mason-Dixon line.

3. Advisory councils

At its best, an advisory council to an out-party's national committee can be a loyal opposition in the manner of the British shadow cabinet. The council obviously has less meaning for the in-party; although, even here, it is possible that a small group of discerning party members detached from direct governmental operations might bring fresh insights to the President. On the organizational level the in-party would profit by some such device to link the professional politician, as represented by the executive committee of the national committee, more closely to the policy functions of the President and the party in the Congress.

For both the out-party and the in-party an advisory council, unhampered by day-to-day governing, should be able to anticipate at least some of the kaleidoscope problems that arise almost daily in political affairs and provide more careful analyses of them than the over-burdened government official has time to do. Both parties could certainly use continuing intellectual labor directed towards the drafting of platforms for the conventions. Both parties could profit from systematically tapping the minds and talents of their most intelligent members outside the government bureaucracy.

Although the advisory councils should explicitly represent the executive wing of their parties, they should include in their membership, at least as non-voting observers, the congressional party leaders or their designates.

The Democratic Advisory Council has already shown what can be done to give greater substance to the Democratic image. It has not yet demonstrated its full power to stimulate robust social criticism and widespread public debate on issues of national consequence. But there is no reason why it or its Republican counterpart, if formed, cannot eventually accomplish these ends. If this should come about in tandem with the development of more responsible party power in the Congress, we will have taken giant strides towards a desired goal: harnessing creative thinking to judicious action.

The two national conventions, as the ultimate governing bodies of the national parties, should formally sanction the establishment of advisory councils as permanent policy arms of the two national committees.

4. Party clubs

The idea of having a "Democratic Club" and a "Republican Club" in Washington to house the national committees and congressional campaign staffs and to serve as a social headquarters for the parties has been considered off and on for many years

by both parties. Actually, *ad hoc* party clubs presently exist in Washington—but only for social purposes. If these clubs were given greater dignity and larger facilities for housing disparate party staffs, they would unquestionably promote more co-ordinated and efficient party efforts, not by hierarchy but by propinquity. Membership might be based on campaign contribution and include social and dining privileges for visiting party members as well as for Members of Congress and executive department officials. Dues would help to finance general party activities. The clubs would stand as reminders that important as it is to preserve open channels for third-party movements in America a sense of national community and forceful and responsible national action are functions of a competitive *two*-party system.

5. Congressional terms

The constitutional provisions for staggered elections are a significant cause of the pullings and haulings in our national government. It is equally clear that a two-year term for the House is too short to turn a freshman member into an effective legislator or to avoid the harassing and expensive responsibilities of perpetual campaigning. The last election and the next election are often an indistinguishable blur. Furthermore, if a truly competitive two-party system should develop across the nation, there will be more frequent alternation of victorious candidates between the parties, thus shortening the tenure of any one Congressman.

A four-year term for the House, if it coincides with the presidential term, should have a number of important effects. Under normal conditions, it would insure the same political complexion for the House as the President's. It would reduce the continuous campaign and constituency pressures which a two-year term almost inevitably fosters. It would give Congressmen sufficient time to learn their trade and to make a substantial contribution to public life.

Also, if an eight-year term were provided for members of the Senate (half of them coming up for election every four years at the same time as the Presidency), the likelihood that the President would have a working majority in both Houses would be overwhelming. At the same time, the conservative utility of overlapping terms would be maintained with only a slight modification in the constitutional wish for continuity.

Enhancing the possibility of one-party control of the government would enhance the possibility of substantial governmental power and would unmistakably fix responsibility for governmental policy.

6. Party policy committees in the Congress

The Legislative Branch Appropriation Act of 1946 established party policy committees in the Senate after the House of Representatives had rejected the idea in the Legislative Reorganization bill of that same year. The Democrats in the Senate have placed their majority leader in charge of their policy committee. Lyndon Johnson's power comes in large part from his own personal ability; but it seems certain that his leadership has been strengthened by his policy committee role. His power would more truly reflect the interests of the majority of his party in the Senate if the representative character of the policy committee were broadened and more caucuses were held. The Republican policy committee in the Senate is far more representative than its Democratic counterpart; what it needs is to be tied more closely to the operations of the Republican floor leader who is a member of the policy committee, but not its chairman.

With these changes, the example set by the Senate should be followed by the House of Representatives. Adequately staffed party policy committees should be elected in both Houses by caucus. In the House of Representatives, the Speaker should chair his party's committee; the minority leader should chair the minority party's committee. The majority policy committee should assume the functions of the House Rules Committee. Both policy committees should act as the committee on committees for their party, and should perform policy and steering functions presently scattered or moribund.

In order to bring greater cohesion to the handling of major presidential recommendations, the four policy committees should meet jointly for two weeks in late January and early February each year to conduct general hearings on the President's State of the Union message. The hearings should be widely covered by press, radio, and television; the leaders in the administration and in the out-party should be heard; and majority and minority reports should be issued for the general guidance of legislators and of the general public. These reports would demonstrate the differences in program between the parties and also the areas of national agreement.

These changes in the basic units of party power in the Congress are designed to make power more visible and more responsive to party majorities in each House than now obtains. But if they are to be effective they must be accompanied by the following reform.

7. Seniority

The principle of seniority has always been defended in the Congress on the ground that it is the only system for elevation to positions of power that has the virtue of being automatic. Congress, it is argued, is already so charged with tension and conflict that additional struggles for power would be dangerous to the underlying agreement upon which compromise and unity rest.

There is enough weight to this argument to suggest that if responsible majority rule can be achieved without destroying the impersonal attributes of the seniority system, the system should be kept. However, there seems to be no reason why a simple mathematical formula cannot be devised to give added seniority credit to legislators who come from competitive two-party districts and states. For example, a Member might receive two points for every *general* election in which his opponent received more than 20 per cent of the vote. Seniority would still rule, automatically, but power would tend to shift toward those Congressmen who come from districts in which vigorous two-party competition searches out the majority interest.

8. 22nd Amendment

The 22nd Amendment places a two-term limit on American Presidents. Its effect is to weaken the political power and influence of the President in his second term, particularly in his last two years. At a time when foreign policy and national defense hold apocalyptic potentialities, it is madness to retain in our Constitution an Amendment which *guarantees* fitful national power.

9. Executive talent

The strength and responsiveness of the national government depend upon many factors, but one of the most basic requirements is a core of able political executives to direct the sprawling departments and agencies of the government. Present recruiting for these men is a hit-or-miss affair carried on at the departmental, presidential, congressional, and national party level.

No greater service could be performed by the national party committees, especially by their regional representatives, than to compile a continuing roster of good people in and out of the party organization for these strategic jobs. Selecting the right men, of course, would have to be done ultimately by the President in a full understanding of state and congressional party interests.

But the job is too important not to be undertaken systematically, and the national committees are the ones to do it.

THE TRADITIONAL CONFLICTS

The contention that a political shift is inevitable in this country and that changes, such as those advocated above, in the traditional national party arrangements are now possible rests on a theory of politics supported by empirical evidence.

The theory, borrowed intact from Professor E. E. Schattschneider, is that politics is basically concerned with the expression and resolution of conflict. The relevant corollary of the theory is that if the nature of social conflict changes, either political institutions must adjust in order to reflect the new social impulses or society suffers the penalities which inertia and impairment of function exact. In a democratic society, the atmosphere is conducive to adjustment.

The parties historically have performed a variety of very valuable functions in American society. They have been functions of accommodation, compromise, and the peaceful transmission of power. Only rarely have the parties been concerned with insuring coherence of program or responsible power in the carrying out of program. Their lack of interest in national policies backed by national political power can be largely explained by the nature of the social conflicts with which they have had to deal. These traditional conflicts merit brief examination before we pass on to the contention of this paper that the character of the conflicts is changing and that the party system must change with it.

New and old settlers

One of the perennial conflicts in American history has been that between new and old settlers. Fear of the stranger is as old as and as far-flung as the earth. In this country the struggle was sometimes muted, sometimes intensified, but always present. Cries to stop immigration pre-date the Constitution. In the hundred years from 1820 to 1920, over thirty-five million Europeans came to the United States. Emma Lazarus' moving words inscribed on the base of the Statue of Liberty have not been a mockery, but it would be idle to pretend that the wave upon wave of newcomers did not cause frictions and controversies and, at times, bitter battles. We know it still. A quarter of a million people still enter the United States annually under our immigration quotas; and of course Puerto Ricans, the center of various current tensions in New York City, are not under the quota at all.

Historically, as one generation became settled and adjusted, it tended to look hostilely at new arrivals, particularly if the newcomers were from a different part of the old world, spoke a different language, or had a different religion. In the fourteen years before World War I, immigration rose to a peak of a million a year. In contrast to the nineteenth century immigration, the largest part of this million came from southern and eastern Europe: Italy, Poland, Russia, Hungary, Greece. Their attempts to find a life for themselves, especially in the urban areas of the East and Middle West; the resistances they met; the fears they created and suffered; the help local politicians gave them in exchange for their votes—all this has been and, although greatly modified by now, still is the stuff of American politics. Each group in turn has pursued the American dream; each in turn has found the upward ladder wobbly, and at times sticky. Part of the glory of our traditional party system has been that when other ladders were removed the political ladder was almost always open. But many crowded on the ladder at once; and as some of those below overtook those on the higher rungs, conflict was inevitable.

Sections and classes

If the new and the old have warred, so have sections and classes. In the early days it was the frontier farmer against the commercial and financial interests of the seaboard. How much of our history has been devoted to this struggle! The alignments that it formed were the most influential causes of our two-party system. Hamilton and Jefferson, Federalists and Republicans, found their focus in this sectional struggle.

As the continent expanded, other regional economic interests developed to complicate the conflict: commodity interests—tobacco, cotton, wheat, corn, sheep, minerals, fish, cattle, fruit, dairy products, oil, and an infinite variety of regional manufacturing interests. Some wanted high tariffs, some wanted low; some wanted federal aid, some wanted no federal interference of any kind. For years these regional interests were dominant forces in American politics.

For a brief period during the Jacksonian era, the Whig party forged an uneasy upper-class national alliance which attempted to bind regional interests into a national party. But the localized economic and social pressures were too strong, and the Whigs disintegrated in 1852. It was the parochialism of the economic and social interests of the South before the Civil War that made the irrepressible conflict irrepressible. After the war, a relatively nationwide two-party system came into being, but, as regional pressures erupted, the system became increasingly unstable. By 1896 the "solid Democratic South" had become a fixed political reality, and it was more than matched by a "solid Republican North" which effectively dominated American politics, except in the Wilsonian period, for a generation.

The remnants of these and other regional struggles are still with us, especially in the Congress, but they have been complicated—sometimes modified, sometimes egregiously promoted—by far-ranging class conflicts between rich and poor, debtor and creditor, capital and labor, small farmers and big farmers. On a few occasions, these class collisions have got beyond the control of existing political machinery. But this has been rare. In the words of David Potter we have been a "people of plenty," and for much of our history the frontier has provided a real as well as a psychological safety-valve. What it could not provide, democratic politics by and large has provided: a redress of intolerable economic grievances.

The Negro issue

In one form or another the Negro problem has always been with us. Like some vast geologic fault it has rendered the land unstable and created deep moral fissures. It was an issue in colonial days; it had to be compromised in the drafting of our Constitution. It was the emotional core of the Civil War. In the cruel and stupid days of reconstruction, the social and political inversions imposed by northern occupation terrified both whites and Negroes and left raw scars of fear, hatred, and anti-Republicanism.

The Negro issue has occupied a central place in the development of the national party organizations and in the formation of political alliances. Because the issue seemed until recently a "southern" problem, the Democratic party as the more national of the two parties had to live a precarious existence astride a two-headed donkey. It survived by promising the Presidency to the North and the Congress to the South. The Republican party, on the other hand, as a party operating effectively only in the North, was able to strike a bargain with southern Democrats which linked white supremacy and business supremacy in the policy labyrinths of the Congress. The bargain clouded the image of each party and put largely irresponsible power over policy in the hands of a southern Democratic-northern Republican coalition, buttressed by seniority and hallowed by carefully designed rules. None of this would have happened if the parties had not had to juggle the Negro issue. It has

been the single most useful device of the economic conservatives to keep the political parties from becoming coherent instruments of majority rule.

Personal ambitions

Like every country, America has known the conflicts of clashing personal ambitions. Politics is, among other things, a study of power and the powerful, of influence and the influential. Issues are often a cover for the struggle of personalities for deference and status. Politics is unintelligible without an understanding of the raw strivings of people for recognition. The struggles between ambitious politicians have left ineradicable marks on the history of the national parties.

THE CHANGES IN THE CONFLICTS

The national parties have become what they are because of these historical conflicts which they have had to settle, hide, or gloss over. In some cases they have been the master brokers between rich and poor, country and city, butter and oleo, capital and labor, Italian and Irish, new and old. At other times, they have hidden certain conflicts in order to satisfy powerful economic interests which have stood to gain by exploiting conflict locally and disguising it nationally. Each party has been caught in the dilemma, on the one hand, of trying to forge an image of harmony in the interests of the majority in order to win the Presidency, and, on the other hand, of being unable to eradicate the very different kind of image which generations of conservative log-rolls and bipartisan "inner-clubism" in the Congress have created in the public eye.

But what happens when the conditions of conflict change? For they are changing, and rapidly, in the United States.

The social changes

Take the struggle between the old and the new. We used to be able to tell the difference between old and new settlers by their accent, or dress, or occupational level. But we are fuller of hundred-per cent Americans every day and are rapidly reaching the time when nationality politics will be as anachronistic as the trolley car. Samuel Lubell has set the beginning of the end of this traditional conflict in the late Thirties, with the coming of age of those whose parents and grandparents had arrived in the great immigration surge at the turn of this century. With the acceptance of the stranger as a person has come acceptance of his ways and his beliefs. A Jew is Governor of Connecticut; a Catholic is almost certain to be on the national ticket of at least one of our two national parties in 1960. Matters which once split us and made us fearful are now absorbed almost without question as our population becomes increasingly homogenized.

Or take sectional and class conflict. The heart has been cut out of sectionalism by vast changes in technology and communications which have dispersed industry and revolutionized agriculture. Where are the one-crop "Cotton Ed" Smiths of a few years back? The fact is that there are precious few one-crop areas left in America. And even where there are, as in some of the great agricultural regions of the Great Plains, technology is bringing a revolution of another kind. In the last five years almost four million people have left the farm. The forecast for reapportionment of congressional seats after the 1960 census suggests a dramatic decrease in rural representation in the United States Congress, and this trend will continue as the rise in population throws more and more people into metropolitan areas.

The movement in urban politics tends to be toward class rather than regional politics. But even class politics has changed. It is no longer a kind of rabble vs. gentry rivalry. Rather, among other things, it is national industry against highly bureaucratized and well-paid national labor. Senator

Barry Goldwater of Arizona is not a regional figure. In the congressional elections of 1958, national giants contended in that sparsely populated desert state, and for national stakes.

What bothers the auto worker in Detroit bothers the auto worker in Los Angeles. What worries the businessman in Chicago worries his competitor in Boston. With transcontinental jet planes, the political or labor or industrial leader whose home is in San Francisco is almost more accessible to his counterpart in New York than is a train traveler from Boston; and, in any case, distance has been obliterated by electricity, electronics, and the direct-dial telephone.

And what is happening to the Negro issue? It, too, is becoming nationalized. Today there are more Negroes in New York than in New Orleans; more in Detroit than in Birmingham, Alabama; more in Pittsburgh than in Little Rock; more in Los Angeles than in Richmond; more in Chicago than in Atlanta. The Negroes' locust-like migration to northern metropolitan centers may have brought new problems to city governments, but it has aroused a critical competition between the two major parties in the North and West to capture the Negro vote. In heavily populated, evenly divided states, a bloc shift of a few votes can mean thirty or forty electoral college votes for a presidential candidate.

Perhaps more than any one other factor, the northern migration of the Negro is working tremendous transformations in our political life. The South no longer can exercise a veto in either presidential convention. Some diehards may walk out in 1960, but the result will only be that they will risk losing what waning power they have in the Congress. For, in more than sixty congressional districts in the North and West, the Negro holds the political balance of power if he decides to bloc-vote; and in the South his political power is likely to increase steadily despite the present tensions.

As for the clash of personal political ambitions in the United States, they are being completely submerged by the international and domestic concerns of the American public. War and peace, inflation and depression, are both personal and universal issues; tariffs, taxes, foreign aid, military spending, federal reserve policies, and hosts of other national policies affect local economic activities across the land. Politicians who wish to become statesmen must be able to talk intelligently about issues that concern people in *all* constituencies. The extraordinary social and economic changes now going on are absorbing and transcending the old conflicts of personal ambitions.

The party changes

The shifts in the nature of the conflicts are reflected in the changes that are already taking place in our party system:

1. The number of one-party states and one-party congressional districts is dramatically declining.

   In less than twenty years, the number of one-party delegations in Congress (in which the two Senators and all members of the House from a single state are of one party) has dropped more than 50 per cent—from twenty-four in 1942 to eleven in 1958.

   The number of southern congressional districts which had contested elections increased from forty-eight to sixty in the brief period from 1952 to 1956. In the same period of time, the total Republican vote in the South for members of the House rose from 1,872,000 in 1952 to 2,371,000 in 1956.

2. The permanent staffs of the national party committees and the variety of committee functions have grown greatly during the past decade. Until World War II both national committees were served by skeletal staffs, except for the few months before national presidential elections. Today both of them maintain year-round staffs of between seventy-five and a hundred people. In election years this number doubles or triples. The annual budget of each committee amounts to almost a million dollars—a figure which skyrockets during election years.

3. Both national committees are doing everything within their power to spread their financial base. The evolution has been from fat-cats and expensive fund-raising banquets to mass appeals and direct-mail solicitation.

4. Almost unnoticed, a revolution has occurred in the "nationalization" of off-year senatorial and congressional campaigns. As recently as 1938, the press and the public criticized President Roosevelt for campaigning in an off-year election. But in 1954, when both the President and the titular leader of the Democrats actively campaigned in their parties' congressional elections, both the newspapers and the voters seemed to accept the fact that it was perfectly all right for the executive wings of the parties to interest themselves actively in the outcome of the legislative contests. In 1958, both national committees sent out representatives to help develop party strength in various regions and to give services to local campaigns. The campaign committees on Capitol Hill also provided services to these campaigns as a matter of course and, in spite of occasional frictions, worked in closer cooperation with the national committees than in any previous off-year election in history.

5. Since 1937, the Presidents have met regularly with party leaders in the Congress on matters of legislative priority and strategy. This has elevated the prestige and power of these men, particularly on matters of foreign policy and national defense. The passage of the Legislative Reorganization Act of 1946 further rec-

ognized the need for party leadership in the Congress, and succeeded to some degree in institutionalizing the leadership function in the Senate which established party policy committees with paid staffs.

6. The creation of the Democratic Advisory Council and the recent appearance of an embryonic Republican counterpart show a new concern in both parties for clarifying the party image. There is little doubt that, eventually, pronouncements of these "executive wings" of the parties will be more effective than similar attempts by congressional leaders or individual party spokesmen excepting the President.

The conclusion

This far from exhaustive list of the responses of our political system to nationalizing forces represents only the beginnings of adaptation and adjustment. Our basic political institutions, and their relationships to each other and to the public, are in a state of flux. If we want a political system designed to give full play to America's political energies and to hold them within bounds set by a popular majority, we are obligated to modify the system still further.

The reforms outlined in these pages will not obviate America's continuing need for personal force and political virtuosity in the office of the Presidency and in top positions in the Congress. Nor will these or any other party reforms dispel the terrifying military, diplomatic, and social problems of our age. But they will help the parties toward stronger leadership in a more responsible framework than has been traditional. To paraphrase Emerson, they can help us to perceive the terror of life and to man ourselves to face it. In this apocalyptic age, can we ask for greater service from our political parties? We must not ask for less.

60. The Strength of Our Political System

Allan Nevins

Written shortly before the election campaign in which President Truman defeated Thomas Dewey, Nevins' article is equally applicable today. Pointing out that our Constitution was so drawn that it could as easily have given way to one-party class control, Nevins underlines the importance of the instant emergence of a two-party system. Nevins restates that the strength of the party system is its function of limiting and compromising issues and differences, thus making for national stability.

* * *

The pageantry of the Republican and Democratic conventions is over. Now comes the discipline, the semi-military marshaling of forces and the hard campaign work. It is all distinctively American, and in most respects it is all comparatively new. Though political parties are as old as our Government, the tremendous mechanism of national, state and local party organizations, pivoted upon local, state and national conventions, dates only from the second administration of Andrew Jackson. We have little over a hundred years of history to illustrate the function of fully developed parties in general and the two-party system in particular.

Have they a healthy function? Some of the principal leaders of Washington's era (a theoretical era, given to abstract speculation upon government) thought not. They held that parties simply bred factions and discord. Virtuous citizens of the new republic should adjure them, and return to the fine Roman spirit later hymned in

From The New York *Times Magazine* (July 18, 1948), pp. 5+. © 1948 by The New York Times Company. Reprinted by permission.

Macaulay's Lays: "Then none was for a party, then all were for the state." The unanimous election of Washington as first President seemed to vindicate this ideal. But realities, described by Jefferson in a trenchant passage, sheared through this utopian theorizing. Parties were essential to express political aims, to educate the people, to carry on government, and to criticize the Government. In short, wrote Jefferson, parties were vital to liberty:

"In every free and deliberating society, there must, from the nature of man, be opposite parties, and violent dissensions and discords; and one of these, for the most part, must prevail over the other for a longer or shorter time. Perhaps this party division is necessary to induce each other to watch and to relate to the people at large the proceedings of the other."

Probably few Americans realize just how important the instant emergence of parties in the United States was, and how inevitable it was that the division between Federalists and Republicans should follow the two-party model of Great Britain. Our Constitution was so drawn that it might as readily have been given an anti-democratic as a democratic cast; it might long have been the instrument of one-party class control. The electoral college as first devised, was anti-democratic. The Senate, chosen by the state legislatures (in which property seemed at first supreme) was anti-democratic. The Federalists who, with Washington as nonpartisan head, came into executive power, and who showed a remarkable genius for efficient administration, were anti-democratic. The question whether the Constitution might be given a permanently anti-democratic character had to be settled within ten or fifteen years.

Inevitably, the dominance of the men who wished to see the national Government powerful, well-centralized, and anti-democratic called into existence a counter-

party who wished the Government kept weak, uncentralized, and democratic. Washington in the selection of his first Cabinet recognized two parties. On the national and aristocratic side he chose Hamilton for the Treasury and Henry Knox for War; on the democratic side he selected Jefferson for the State Department and Edmund Randolph for Attorney General. The divergence of opinion in Cabinet meetings was paralleled by an even more passionate divergence in the nation at large. Within a few years the two parties were formally reorganized, and every American knew that their struggle would decide the course of constitutional development. Federalist and Republican fought to put Government within their particular molds just as Whig and Tory fought to shape the unwritten British Constitution.

Here was a difference in principle. The dominant purpose of the Federalist party was to place such a construction on the letter of the Constitution as to broaden the powers of the Federal Government and restrict those of the states. The essential purpose of the Jeffersonian party was to interpret the Constitution in such wise as to limit the national and foster the local power. Two rival ideologies were in frontal collision. In France of the period this meant battles and guillotines. In America, however, from the very beginning three factors operated to lessen the violence of the party clash.

What were they? First, principle itself was interpreted with a saving grace of reservations and modifications, and was subject to sudden changes dictated by expediency. Thus Jefferson, once in power, actually made more far-reaching use of the central Government as in the Louisiana Purchase and the embargo, than John Adams had done, while that good Democrat, Andrew Jackson, proved the sternest nationalist in our history. Second, both parties took up all manner of subsidiary issues, ranging from tariffs and internal improvements to foreign policy; and as they did so, both appealed to a wide variety of constantly fluctuating groups. Third, each party had such a healthy respect for public sentiment that, following the old Anglo-Saxon rule of compromise (undoubtedly the most vital single element in our Government), the majority abstained from abusing its authority, and the minority yielded to the majority on the tacit understanding that no abuse would be practiced.

For a variety of reasons, from Hamilton to Truman the two-party system has perpetuated itself. For one, in a populous democracy the costs of maintaining a party on a national scale, quadrennium after quadrennium, are so great that splinter parties cannot meet them. Also, most great leaders rise to influence within the two main parties. But, above all, the two-party system suits the genius of the people. They want a responsible authority, on which they can count for stability; they want it closely watched by a strong opposition; they want to use its power, but to do so in the spirit of compromise, with a due regard for minority rights.

Is such a party system democratic? "A party," William H. Seward once remarked, "is in one sense a joint stock association, in which those who contribute most direct the action and management of the concern." Accepting this definition, we can see why great parties sometimes fall under an undemocratic control.

Just before the Civil War the Democratic party, as Seward complained, was dominated by a comparatively restricted body of slaveholders who contributed more money, determination and brains to its direction than any other group. After the Civil War the Republican party fell, for a long period, under the domination of big business. But party machinery (through the direct primary, better publicity, restric-

tion of campaign gifts and so on) has been improved to permit of broader controls. If much still remains to be done, as James Reston has pointed out, it *can* be done. And the very heterogeneity of our parties makes for democracy.

If any lesson is written in our history, it is that an undemocratically controlled party sooner or later pays a heavy penalty. Elements of revolt gather within its ranks. Reform groups rise up against the slavery oligarchy, or the Tammany-Bourbon alliance, or the special privilege corporations, or whatever other group has become dominant. They join the opposition party, in such a tremendous accession of "independent" strength as that which in 1884 elected Cleveland over Blaine, for example; or they stage a revolt within their own party, like Bryan's revolt against the Tammany-Ryan combination in 1912; or they organize a third party, as the Progressives did. In one way or another, they strike a decisive blow for a more democratic management of party affairs.

So little is the American system understood that some people are constantly asking: "Why don't the parties stand for hard and fast principles? Why is it so difficult to tell Republican aims from Democratic aims? Why are they so much alike?" Bryce wrote about 1880 that the abiding object of the Democratic party was still to oppose a unitary and much-interfering Government in Washington; but under Woodrow Wilson and Franklin D. Roosevelt the traditional party role on this head seemed reversed.

And so little is the system appreciated that some critics continually repeat the question: "Why can't we have a Conservative party and a Liberal party? Why can't we have parties on economic lines?"

Such statements ignore the cardinal utility of our two great parties. They are an amalgam, not a solvent; their fundamental value in the United States is in pulling together an immensely varied mass of social groups, economic constituencies, racial stocks, and local and sectional interests for the purpose of governing by consent.

The greatest disaster that ever befell the nation in the past resulted from a temporary division of parties along sectional lines. The worst disaster that could possibly happen to it in the near future would be a division along economic and class lines. We have the utmost reason for rejoicing, not for regret, that the Republican and Democratic parties are so much alike that the scepter can pass from one to the other without perceptible shock.

It is of the first importance that each party represent a fair cross-section of the nation, with rich and poor, farmers and city clerks, Catholics, Jews and Protestants, old stock and immigrant stock. Our wide diffusion of property prevents any division between rich and poor. But if we did have a Conservative party of the propertied and a Radical party of the unpropertied we might at last be within sight of the day when the losers in an election would begin throwing up barricades in the streets.

Our type of two-party system has its manifest disadvantages and defects. Obviously, two big, loose, heterogeneous parties are always exposed to schism. Obviously, too, such mammoth parties, making constant compromises within their own ranks, must be guilty of a good deal of time-serving, trimming and hypocrisy. We have seen the spectacle of one Republican Administration after another uttering bright platitudes about Negro equality while courting the "lily whites" in the South. We have seen the Franklin D. Roosevelt Administration preaching noble political ideals while accepting the partnership of Boss Hague and Boss Crump. The alliance of low-tariff Iowa farmers and high-tariff Pennsylvania ironmasters under the Republican aegis, and the alliance of Tammany Hall with Alabama agrarians under the Democratic banner, have not made for political honesty of the austerest type.

At a grace crisis in the Civil War, just after the defeat of Fredericksburg, Lincoln kept the disharmonious Republican party together by obtaining written resignations from Secretary Seward, pet of the conservatives, and Secretary Chase, pet of the radicals; not to be used, but to be balanced against each other. It was an effective stroke, but it did not illustrate the highest kind of political forthrightness.

Nevertheless, the benefits of the existing system far outweigh its drawbacks. We, like the British, and for basically the same reason, find a multi-party system almost unthinkable. Our whole tradition is built on government by a strong and responsible majority, which will wield power effectively but will at the same time respect minority rights. The spectable of irresponsibility, confusion and intolerance presented by some Continental European nations of multitudinous parties may be exciting, and some of their parties may suggest an intellectual rigor unknown in our politics; but the practical results do not commend themselves to us.

We feel the safer in trusting to two major parties because, unlike the British, we have surrounded minority rights with an elaborate system of checks and balances. We feel the safer because even our strongest Presidents—Jackson, Lincoln, Wilson, the two Roosevelts—have never, despite much short-lived partisan talk to the contrary, shown any really dictatorial tendencies.

Nor are we willing to give up the vast benefits we reap from the fact that the two great parties are ponderous cross-sections of our varied society, representing every element. Third parties have never been that. They have usually been parties of one idea—abolitionism, prohibition, populism—and hence one group. In a nation so large and so variegated in resources and climate, so widely differentiated in economic and social interests, so complex in its stocks and faiths, it is essential that our parties promote unity. In a population which does now and then grow hotly emotional over changing issues, a party organization built on principles of cohesion and compromise is obviously invaluable.

The fundamental character of our political organism has changed astonishingly little between the days of Hamilton and Jefferson, and the days of Truman and Dewey. To that fact we may ascribe much of our national stability.

INDEX

Numbers in parentheses refer to article number.